*STOP GROPING FOR WORDS—
AND REACH FOR THIS BOOK!*

You may sense that it's not what you say but how you say it that's turning off your audience.

You may feel your writing lacks the spark that makes a reader's eye light up.

You yourself may be getting a little bored with using the same old words to convey a message that should be fresh and urgent.

If any of the above seems familiar, then you owe it to yourself to become familiar with—

A DICTIONARY OF SYNONYMS AND ANTONYMS

New Enlarged Edition

by Joseph Devlin

author of *How to Speak and Write Correctly* and *Development of the English Language*

edited and enlarged by
JEROME FRIED

Look for these outstanding reference
books at your local bookstore:

Webster's New World Dictionary of
The American Language

A Dictionary of Synonyms and
Antonyms

A New Guide to Better Writing

Webster's Red Seal Crossword
Dictionary

Webster's New World Thesaurus

Available from
WARNER BOOKS

A DICTIONARY OF SYNONYMS AND ANTONYMS

with 5000 WORDS
MOST OFTEN MISPRONOUNCED

by Joseph Devlin

author of *How to Speak and Write Correctly,
Development of the English Language,
Syntax and Analysis, English Idioms,* etc.

edited and enlarged by Jerome Fried

WARNER BOOKS

A Warner Communications Company

PREFACE

This volume needs few words to introduce it, as its object is apparent to the most casual reader. It was written to help those who use it in finding the exact words they need to express their written and spoken thoughts, with a minimum expenditure of time and effort, and a maximum reward in efficiency and accuracy.

It is designed primarily for busy people, those business men and women who are, of necessity, always in a hurry, who have both to think and act quickly to maintain their ground in fields of keen competition and rivalry, yet it will also be of service to those more deliberate readers, the students, writers, and public speakers who have, ordinarily, more time to hunt out the elusive *mot juste* to give body to their thoughts.

Everyone at some time finds himself groping futilely for a word to describe exactly the idea he wishes to convey; it may be a word to be used as a substitute for another in order to give variety of expression, or it may be one that, although familiar, eludes him at the moment so that he has to pause and ponder and lose time in trying to recall the one word that will suit. It is at such moments that the wise man will reach for this volume, and find immediately the word he wants. The simple arrangement and presentation of the synonyms and antonyms that he finds here put thousands of words literally at his fingertips.

All key words are arranged in alphabetic sequence, as the words in a dictionary, with their synonyms and antonyms following them *en bloc*. We can imagine, for example, a busy sales manager preparing a talk for his salesmen, and wishing to impress them with the fact that there is an *urgent* need for increased sales. However, he does not wish to repeat the word *urgent* so often that it loses its effectiveness. He solves his problem by turning to this volume, looking up the key word *urgent* and selecting the synonyms that will best stir his men to action. The salesmen will probably learn that the need for increased sales is *pressing, necessary, imperative, important, essential* and *vital,* and be duly impressed by the message.

The selection of the correct synonym to suit his purpose

has been left to the reader. There has been no attempt to arrange the synonyms in this book in categories or groups according to subject matter, through content, and other shades of meaning, since it is felt that these methods serve to confuse the reader who wishes a book for quick reference. Neither has space been given to the discussion of minute distinctions between similar words, as, in the author's opinion, such minutiae are for students of the language, teachers, and etymologists, rather than for the general reader. Dr. H. W. Fowler, the English lexicographer and authority on the English language, well observes: "Synonym books in which differences are analyzed, engrossing as they may have been to the active party, the analyst, offer to the passive party, the reader, nothing but boredom . . . everyone must, for the most part, be his own analyst."

In this volume everyone who consults its pages is allowed to be his own analyst. The natural selection will be by eye and ear, for almost everyone has a sense of words, developed by reading and listening to others, which merely needs jogging into alertness. For those readers who have no word sense, a golden rule is hereby set forth; *never use a word the meaning of which is not perfectly clear* to you. Consult the dictionary if you are uncertain, or discard the word for a simpler one that is familiar. The first course is the wiser, for by looking into the dictionary and finding the meaning, the structure of a good vocabulary is being laid. Word by word the foundation is built up, until the reader has developed a style of speech and writing that is colorful, varied and effective.

This book of synonyms and antonyms does not usurp the function of the dictionary, nor does it take the place of the dictionary on the reference shelf. However, it will prove a companion to it, and useful guide to everyone who wishes to speak or write vigorous, clear English.

JOSEPH DEVLIN

New York City

WORD FORMATION

ROOTS AND DERIVATIVES

Like all other things words had a beginning. Almost every word in the English language can be traced back to its beginning or origin, to the source from whence it came. The beginning, origin or source of a word is called its *root*. The root is the fundamental or primary element, the part from which the word springs, as the stem from the root of a tree.

Words may be divided into two classes, *primitives* and *derivatives*. Primitives are words that cannot be reduced to simpler forms, in fact they are root words. Derivatives are words formed by modifying the root or primitive word in some way, as by the addition of a prefix or suffix, either of which may be called an affix. A prefix is a word, or part of a word, as a syllable or letter, placed *before* the main body of a word to modify its meaning. A suffix is part of a word, a particle, placed after the root of a word to modify its meaning. The *stem* is the part of the word upon which inflections are based.

A large number of prefixes, especially of Latin and Greek origin, are used in the formation of English words. The following is a partial list of the principal ones:—

LATIN PREFIXES

a-, ab-, abs-, *from, away from*

ad-, *to:* becomes **ac-, af-, ag-, al-, an-, ap-, ar-, as-, at-,** to assimilate with the first consonant of the root word, for the sake of euphony

am-, amb-, ambi-, *about, around*

ante-, *before*

bi-, bis-, *twice*

com-, *with together:* also **co-, col-, con-, cor-,** for euphony

contra-, *against:* also **contro-, counter-**

de-, *down*

dis-, *apart, asunder*

ex-, *out of, from, off:* also **e-, ef-**

extra-, *beyond*

in-, *in, into:* also **em-, en-, il-, im-, ir-**

in-, *not:* also **ig-, il-, im-, ir-**

inter-, *between, within:* also **intro-**
male-, *bad, ill:* also **mal-**
non-, *not*
ob-, *against, in the way of:* also **oc-, of-, op-**
per-, *through:* also **par-, pel-**
post-, *after*
præ-, pre-, *before*
præter-, preter-, *beyond, past*
pro-, *before, in front of, forward, for, in behalf of*
re-, *back, again:* also **red-**
retro-, *backward*
se-, *aside, apart:* also **sed-**
semi-, *half*
sub-, *under:* also **suc-, sud-, suf-, sug-, sum-, sup-, sur-, sus-**
super-, *above, over*
trans-, *beyond, through, across*
ultra-, *beyond*
un-, uni-, *one*
vice-, *in the place of*

GREEK PREFIXES

a-, an-, *not, without*
amphi-, *on both sides*
ana-, *back, again, up*
anti-, *opposite, against*
ap-, apo-, *from, away from:* also **aph-**
arch-, archi-, *chief*
auto-, *self*
cat-, cata-, *down:* also **cath-**
dia-, *through*
di-, dis-, *twice*
dys-, *ill*
ec-, *out of:* also **ex-**
en-, *in:* also **el-, em-**
endo-, *in*
ep-, epi-, *upon*
eu-, *well:* also **ev-**
hemi-, *half*
hyp-, hypo-, *under*
hyper-, *over, above*
met-, meta-, *after, over*
mon-, mono-, *alone, one, single*

ortho-, *right*
pan-, *all*
par-, para-, *beside*
peri-, *round, around*
pro-, *before*
pros-, *towards*
proto-, *first*
sy-, syn-, *with, along with:* also **syl-**

Suffixes abound in English; there are so many that to list all would be impossible in this book; they comprise noun, adjective, verb and adverb suffixes. The principal noun suffixes are:—

Latin Suffixes

-age, used chiefly in forming abstract nouns.
-al, used in forming action words
-ant, denoting an agent or doer
-ary, denoting *a thing belonging to*
-ate, denoting an *office or function*
-cle, -cule, denoting *diminution*
-ess, denoting *the feminine of*
-et, -ette, denoting *diminution*
-ice, -ise, denoting *quality, condition, act*
-ine, denoting *feminine:* also in forming abstract nouns
-ion, -tion, -sion, in forming abstract nouns
-ment, *instrument of, act*
-mony, *instrument or means of*
-on, -oon, denoting *increase* or *augmentation*
-ory, *place where*
-tude, in forming nouns from Latin adjectives
-ty, *quality, state, condition*
-ure, *action, result of*

Greek Suffixes

-ic, *pertaining to*
-isk, denoting *diminution*
-ism, *act, state, condition:* also in forming abstract nouns
-ist, *a doer, one who does, who practices or professes*
-sis, -sy, *state, condition, action*
-y, used in forming abstract nouns

The root, of course, is the most important part of the word, for not only is it the source but in it is also implied the meaning. In its early period the English language had enough roots of its own on which to base all the words required. For quite a long time, to wit, from the Anglo-Saxon Invasion of England down to the Norman Conquest, English depended upon the native roots to furnish what words were necessary to carry on social and commercial intercourse. Many words derived from these roots of the Anglo-Saxon period constitute a large part of the language as it is today. The Normans brought over a lot of words—Norman-French—much of which was derived from the Latin and a little from the Greek, so the English began using the words of the Normans as ready-made and to hand, instead of continuing to build new words on native roots, and as time went on more words were taken from other languages. English has put Latin and Greek under heavy tribute to help supply words to serve its purposes and augment its vocabulary.

As just stated, we have many words of pure Anglo-Saxon origin, words which sprang from native roots and which owe nothing whatever to other languages.

In the following list are given some of the old English roots and a few of the words we still retain which were based upon them:—

OLD ENGLISH ROOTS AND DERIVATIVES

akr, a *field,* acre, acorn
bacon, to *bake,* baker, batch
beatan, to *strike,* beat, batter, battle
beran, to *bear,* bairn, burden, breed
bindan, to *bind,* bundle, bondage, band
blowan, to *blossom,* blow, bloom
brecan, to *break,* brake, breach, brittle
breowan, to *brew,* brewer, broth, bread
bugan, to *bend,* bow, bough, elbow
byrnan, to *burn,* burn, brown, brand
ceapian, to *buy,* cheap, chop, chap
ceowan, to *chew,* chew, cud, cheek
cleovan, to *cleave,* cleft, clover
cnawan, to *know,* know, knowledge
cwic, *alive,* quick, quicksilver
daelan, to *divide,* deal, dole, dale
deman, to *judge,* deem, doom, kingdom
doan, to *act,* do, deed

dragan, to *draw,* drag, draft, drain
drifan, to *push,* drive, drift
drincan, to *soak,* drink, drench
dripan, to *drip,* dribble, droop, drop
faran, to *go,* fare, ferry, ford
fengan, to *catch,* fang, finger
fleotan, to *float,* float, fleet, flotsam
foda, *food,* fodder, forage, father
freon, to *love,* friend, friendship
galan, to *sing,* gale, nightingale, yell
grafan, to *cut,* grave, carve, groove
gripan, to *seize,* grab, grasp, grope
gyrdan, to *surround,* girdle, garden, yard
haelan, to *heal,* hale, holy, health
hebban, to *raise,* heavy, heave, heaven
hlaf, *bread,* loaf, lord, lady (one who kneads dough)
liegan, to *live,* lie, lair, outlay
magan, *to be able,* main, mighty, may
mona, *moon,* month, moonshine
nasu, *nose,* nasal, nozzle, nostril
pennan, *to shut up,* pound, impound
pic, *point,* peak, pike, picket
sceapan, to *form,* shape, ship, landscape
sceotan, to *throw,* shut, shot, shoot
sceran, to *cut,* shear, share, shirt
schufan, to *push,* shove, shovel, scuffle
settan, to *set,* seat, settle, saddle
slagan, to *strike,* slay, slaughter, sledge
slipan, to *slip,* slipper, sleeve, slop
snican, to *crawl,* snail, snake, sneak
stearc, *stiff,* strong, strength, strangle
stede, *place,* instead, steady, homestead
stigan, to *climb,* stair, stirrup, sty
styran, to *direct,* steer, steerage, stern
swerian, to *declare,* swear, forswear, answer
tæcan, to *teach,* teach, taught, token
tellan, to *account,* teller, tale, talk
techan, to *draw,* tow, tug
thæc, *roof,* thatch, deck
tredan, to *walk,* tread, trade, tradesman
truwa, *good faith,* true, truth, troth
wefan, to *weave,* weaver, woof, web
war, *defense,* war, wary, guard

witan, to *know,* wit, witness, wisdom
wræstan, to *wrest,* wrest, wrestle, wrist

A large percentage of English words come from the Latin and Greek. Most of the modern words, especially technological and scientific terms, that have been incorporated into English have been compounded directly from these two languages. The following is a list of a number of the Latin roots, with some of the words in common use that have been derived from them:—

LATIN ROOTS AND DERIVATIVES

acer, sharp, acrid, acrimony, vinegar
ædes, a *building,* edifice, edify
ager, a *field,* agriculture, agrarian
ago, *I act,* action, agent, agitate
alo, *I nourish,* aliment, alimentary
alter, *another,* alternate, alteration
altus, *high,* altitude, exalt
amo, *I love,* amorous, amiable
anima, *breath, life,* animal, animate
animus, *mind,* unanimous, magnanimity
annus, a *year,* annual, anniversary, biennial
antiquus, *ancient,* antique, antiquity
appello, *I call,* appeal, appellation
aqua, *water,* aquatic, aqueduct, aquarium
arbor, a *tree,* arboreal, arborage, arboriculture
arcus, a *bow,* arcade, archer
ars, *art,* artist, artisan, artifice
audio, *I hear,* audible, audience, auditory
augeo, *I increase,* auction, augment
barba, a *beard,* barb, barber
bellum, *war,* bellicose, belligerent
bis, *twice,* bisect, biscuit
brevis, *short,* brevity, abbreviate
cado, *I fall,* accident, decadence
canis, a *dog,* canine
cano, *I sing,* canticle, chant
cavus, a *hollow,* cave, cavity, excavate
cedo, *I go, yield,* cede, accede, precede
cito, *I call, summon,* cite, recite, citation
civis, a *citizen,* civil, civilian, civic
clamo, *I cry out,* exclaim, exclamation, proclamation

clarus, *clear,* clarify, clarion, declare
claudo, *I shut,* exclude, seclusion
clino, *I bend,* incline, decline
cœlum, *heaven,* celestial
colo, *I tell,* cultivate, culture
cor, the *heart,* cordial, courage
corona, a *crown,* coronet, coronation
credo, *I believe,* creed, credible, incredulous
cresco, *I grow,* increase, decrease, crescent
crux, a *cross,* crucify, crucifix, cruciform
culpa, a *fault,* culprit, culpable
cura, *care,* curate, accurate
decem, *ten,* decimal, decimate, December
dens, a *tooth,* dental, dentist, indent
dexter, *right-handed,* dexterity, dexterous
dico, *I say,* dictation, verdict, diction
dies, a *day,* diurnal, diary
dignus, *worthy,* dignity, indignity, dignify
doceo, *I teach,* docile, doctrine
domus, a *house,* domicile, domestic
duco, *I lead,* induct, educate, ductile
durus, *hard, lasting,* durable, duration, endure
ego, *I,* egotist, egoist, egoism
emo, *I buy,* redeem, exemption, preëmption
erro, *I wander,* errant, error, aberration
esse, *to be,* essence, essential
facilis, *easy,* facile, facilitate, facility
fames, *hunger,* famine, famish
felix, *happy,* felicity, felicitous
femina, a *woman,* feminine, effeminate
fido, *I trust,* confide, fidelity, confident
finis, the *end,* finite, infinite, finish
fluo, *I flow,* flux, fluid, fluent
folium, a *leaf,* foliage, portfolio
fortis, *strong,* fortify, fortress, fortitude
frango, *I break,* fragile, fraction
frater, a *brother,* fraternal, fraternity, friar
frons, the *forehead,* front, frontal, frontier
fumus, *smoke,* fumigate, fumigation
fundus, the *bottom,* foundation, founder, profound
gelu, *frost,* gelid, congeal, gelatin
gens, a *race, people,* gentile, generation, gender
gradus, a *step,* grade, gradient, degrade

gravis, *heavy,* grave, gravity, grieve
grex, a *flock, herd,* aggregate, congregate, gregarious
habeo, *I have,* habit, habitual, inhabit
hæreo, *I stick,* adhere, cohere, cohesion
halo, *I breathe,* inhale, exhale
homo, a *man,* homage, human, homicide
hostis, an *enemy,* hostile, hostility
humus, *earth, soil,* humble, exhume
ignis, *fire,* ignite, ignition, igneous
impero, *I command,* empire, imperial, imperative
insula, an *island,* insular, peninsula
ira, *anger,* irate, ire
judex, a *judge,* judicial, judiciary
jungo, *I join,* juncture, junction
jus, *right,* justice, jurisdiction
lapis, a *stone,* lapidary, dilapidated
laus, *praise,* laudation, laudable
lavo, *I wash,* lave, lavatory
laxus, *loose,* lax, laxity, relax
lego, *I gather, read,* collect, lecture, legible
lego, *I send,* legate, delegate
lex, a *law,* legal, legitimate
liber, *free,* liberty, liberate, liberal
liber, a *book,* library, librarian
libra, a *balance,* librate, equilibrium
lignum, *wood,* ligneous, lignite, lignify
ligo, *I bind,* ligament, liable, religion
litera, a *letter,* literal, literary, literature
locus, a *place,* local, location, allocate
loquor, *I speak,* elocution, eloquent, loquacious
lumen, *light,* luminary, luminous, illuminate
luna, the *moon,* lunacy, lunatic, lunar
luo, *I wash,* ablution, dilute
lux, *light,* lucid, lucidity, elucidate
macula, *spot, stain,* immaculate, maculate
magnus, *great,* magnify, magnitude, magnificent
malus, *bad, evil,* malevolent, malady
manus, the *hand,* manual, manufacture, manuscript
mare, the *sea,* marine, maritime, mariner
Mars, *God of War,* martial, Martian
medius, *the middle,* median, medium, intermediate
memor, *mindful,* memory, memorial
mens, the *mind,* mental, mentality

mergo, *I dip,* emerge, immersion

miles, a *soldier,* military, militant, militia

miror, *I admire,* miracle, admirable

mitto, *I send,* commit, remit, mission

moneo, *I warn,* monitor, monition

mons, a *mountain,* ultramontane, promontory

mors, *death,* mortal, immortal, mortify

moveo, *I move,* motion, motive, motor

multus, *many,* multitude, multiply

munus, a *gift,* munificent, remunerate

murus, a *wall,* immure, mural

muto, *I change,* mutable, transmute

narro, *I relate,* narration, narrative

nascor, *to be born,* nascent, natal, native

navis, a *ship,* navy, naval, navigation

nihil, *nothing,* annihilate, nihilist

noceo, *I injure,* noxious, innocent, innocuous

nomen, a *name,* nominal, nomination, cognomen

norma, a *rule,* normal, abnormal, enormous

novus, *new,* novel, renovate, novice

nox, *night,* nocturnal, equinox

nudus, *naked,* nude, denude

nuntio, *I declare,* announce, denounce

octo, *eight,* octave, octagon, October

oculus, the *eye,* ocular, oculist

odi, *I hate,* odium, odious

omnis, *all,* omnipotent, omniscience, omnibus

onus, a *burden,* onerous, exonerate

opus, *work,* operation, cooperate

orno, *I adorn,* adorn, ornament

oro, *I speak,* orator, oration

ovum, an *egg,* ovate, oval

pando, *I spread,* expand, expanse, compass

pareo, *I appear,* apparent, appearance, apparition

paro, *I prepare,* preparation, repair

pars, a *part,* partial, partition, partner

paseo, *I feed,* pastor, pasture, repast

patior, *I suffer,* patient, passion, passive

pax, *peace,* pacific, pacify

pecco, *I sin,* peccable, peccant

pecunia, *money,* pecuniary, impecunious

pello, *I drive,* compel, repel, impulsive

pendeo, *I hang,* pendant, suspend, suspense

pleo, *I fill,* complete, complement, supplement
poena, *punishment,* penal, penalty, penance
pons, a *bridge,* transpontine, pontiff, pontifical
porto, *I carry,* export, report, deportment
primus, *first,* primary, primitive, primrose
probo, *I prove,* probable, approve, improve
proprius, *one's own,* proper, property, appropriate
pungo, *I prick,* puncture, pungent, expunge
puto, *I reckon,* compute, count
quaero, *I ask,* query, inquire, require
quartus, *fourth,* quart, quarter, quartet
radix, a *root,* radical, eradicate
rapio, *I seize,* rapine, rapture
rego, *I rule,* regent, regular, rector
rex, *a king,* regal, royal
rideo, *I laugh,* ridicule, deride, risible
rodo, *I gnaw,* rodent, corrode
rogo, *I ask,* interrogation, derogatory
rota, a *wheel,* rotary, rotate, around
rumpo, *I break,* rupture, disruption, eruption
rus, the *country,* rustic, rusticate
sacer, *sacred,* sacrament, sacrilege, sacristan
sanctus, *holy,* sanctify, sanctuary, saint
sanguis, *blood,* sanguinary, sanguineous
sanus, *sound,* sane, insane, sanity
sapio, *I taste,* sapid, insipid
scio, *I know,* science, omniscience
scribo, *I write,* scribe, scribble, scripture
senex, *old,* senior, senile, senator
sentio, *I feel,* sense, sentiment, sensual
septem, *seven,* septennial, September
sequor, *I follow,* sequel, sequence, consequence
servio, *I serve,* servant, service, sergeant
signum, a *sign,* signal, significant, designate
socius, a *companion,* social, socialist, society
sol, the *sun,* parasol, solar, solstice
specio, *I see,* inspect, circumspect, spectator
spero, *I hope,* desperate, despair
spiro, *I breathe,* aspire, inspire, conspire
struo, *I build,* structure, construct, construe
suadeo, *I advise,* persuade, dissuade
sumo, *I take,* assume, consume, assumption
tango, *I touch,* contact, tangible, contagious

tempus, *time,* temporal, contemporary
teneo, *I hold,* tenet, tenant, tendril
terminus, *boundary,* terminal, terminate, term
terra, the *earth,* terrestrial, subterranean
terreo, *I frighten,* terrible, terrify, terror
timeo, *I fear,* timid, timidity, timorous
traho, *I draw,* tract, traction, contraction
tumeo, *I swell,* tumor, tumid, tumult
umbra, *a shadow,* umbrella, umbrage
unus, *one,* unit, unite, union
urbs, *a city,* urban, urbane, suburban
valeo, *I am strong,* valiant, valid, invalid
venio, *I come,* convene, venture, advent
verbum, *a word,* verbal, verbiage, proverb
verto, *I turn,* convert, divert, versatile
verus, *true,* verity, verify, veracious
vestis, a *garment,* vestment, vesture, invest
video, *I see,* vision, visit, evident
vinco, *I conquer,* victor, victory, convince
vivo, *I live,* vivid, survive, revive
voco, *I call,* vocal, vocation, revoke
volo, *I will,* volition, voluntary, benevolence
vox, *the voice,* vocal, vocalist
vulgus, *common,* vulgar, vulgate, divulge
vulnus, *a wound,* vulnerable, invulnerable

English has built largely on the old Greek roots and still continues to utilize them as foundations upon which to construct new terms. Many, indeed most, of the words recently coined to meet the demands of scientific progress for expression in English have been based on the tongue words used in ancient Hellas more than two thousand years ago. In the following table are some words, now standard in English, which were derived from the old-time Greek roots:—

GREEK ROOTS AND DERIVATIVES

aer, the *air,* aeroplane, aeronaut, aerostat
agon, *a contest,* agony, antagonist
allos, *another,* allopathy, allegory
angelos, *messenger,* angel, evangelist
anthos, a *flower,* anthology, anthologist
anthropos, a *man,* philanthropy, misanthropy

arche, *rule* or *beginning,* archbishop, monarch, archaic
aristos, *best,* aristocracy, aristocrat
aster, astron, a *star,* astronomy, astrology, asteroid
atmos, *vapor,* atmosphere, atmology
autos, *self,* autocrat, autograph, automobile
ballo, *I throw,* symbol, hyperbole
bapto, *I dip,* baptise, baptism, baptistry
biblos, biblion, a *book,* Bible, bibliography, bibliomania
bios, *life,* biology, biography, amphibious
cheir, the *hand,* chiropodist, chirography, chirurgeon
chromos, *time,* chronicle, chronology, chronic
daklulos, a *finger,* dactyl, dactylography
deka, *ten,* decade, decalogue, decagon
demos, the *people,* democrat, demagogue, epidemic
dendron, a *tree,* rhododendron, dendrology
doxa, *opinion,* doxology, dogma, orthodox
dunamis, *power,* dynamite, dynamics
eidos, *form,* kaleidoscope, spheroid
eikon, an *image,* icon, iconoclast
electron, *amber,* electric, electricity, electrotype
ergon, a *work,* energy, chirurgeon (surgeon, archaic)
eu, *well,* euphony, evangel, eucharist
gamos, *marriage,* polygamy, bigamy, monogamy
gaster, the *stomach,* gastric, gastronomy
ge, the *earth,* geography, geology, geometry
glossa, the *tongue,* glottis, glossary
gramma, a *letter,* monogram, diagram, grammar
grapho, *I write,* biography, telegraph
gyne, a *woman,* gynecology, misogyny
haima, *blood,* hemorrhage, hemorrhoid
helios, the *sun,* heliography, heliotrope
hepta, *seven,* heptarchy, heptagon, heptachord
hieros, *sacred,* hieroglyphic, hierophant, hierarchy
hippos, a *horse,* hippopotamus, hippodrome, hippology
hodos, a *way,* method, exodus, period
homos, the *same,* homogenous, homologous, homeopathy
hydor, *water,* hydraulics, hydrogen, hydrophobia
ichthus, a *fish,* ichthyology, ichthyophagy, ichthyoid
isos, *equal,* isotherm, isosceles, isocracy
kakos, *bad, evil,* cacophony, cacogenic, cacodemon
kardia, the *heart,* cardiac, cardialgia, carditis
kosmos, the *world, order,* cosmology, cosmogony, cosmopolitan

krino, *I judge,* critic, criterion, hypocrite
kyklos, *circle, ring,* cycle, cyclopedia, cyclone
kyon, a *dog,* cynic, cynical, cynicism
lithos, a *stone,* lithograph, monolith, aerolite
logos, *word, discourse,* monologue, dialogue, trilogy
methon, a *measure,* diameter, barometer, thermometer
mikros, *small,* microscope, microphone, microcosm
misos, *hatred,* misogyny, misanthrope
monos, *alone,* monologue, monosyllable
morphe, *shape,* amorphous, metamorphosis
mythos, a *fable,* myth, mythical, mythology
naus, a *ship,* nautical, navigation, argonaut
nekros, *dead,* a *dead body,* necropolis, necrology,
     necromancy
neos, *new,* neophyte, neology, neologism
neuron, a *nerve,* neuritis, neuralgia, neuropath
nomos, a *law,* Deuteronomy, autonomy, astronomy
nosos, *disease,* nosology, nosologist, nosography
oide, a *song,* ode, prosody, palinode
oikos, a *house,* economy, ecology, ecologist
onoma, onyma, a *name,* synonym, patronymic, anonymous
orthos, *right,* orthodox, orthography, orthoëpy
pais, a *child,* pedagogue, pediatrics
pan, *all,* pandemic, panoply, panorama
pathos, *feeling,* pathetic, sympathy, apathy
pente, *five,* pentagon, pentameter, pentarchy
petra, a *rock,* petrify, petrography, Peter
phaino, *I show,* phantom, phenomenon, fancy
philos, *loving, fond of,* philosophy, philology, philanthropy
phobos, *fear, dread,* hydrophobia, claustrophobia
phone, *sound,* microphone, telephone, phonetic
phos, *light,* phosphorescent, photography, photometer
physis, *nature,* physiology, physiography, physician
poieo, *I make,* poem, poet, pharmacopoeia
polis, a *city,* politics, police, metropolis
polys, *many, much,* polyandry, polygamy, polygon
pous, a *foot,* chiropodist, pediatrist, antipodes
potamos, a *river,* hippopotamus, transpotamian
protos, *first,* prototype, protoplasm, protocol
pseudes, *false,* pseudonym, pseudepigrapha
psyche, *soul, mind,* psychology, psychiatry, psychoanalysis
pyr, *fire,* pyrotechnics, pyrology, pyromaniac
rheo, *I flow,* rhetoric, pyorrhea, catarrh

skopeo, *I see,* microscope, telescope, fluoroscope
sophia, *wisdom,* sophist, philosophy, theosophy
sphaira, a *sphere,* hemisphere, planisphere
stello, *I send,* apostle, epistle, epistolary
stratos, an *army,* stratagem, strategy, strategist
strepho, *I turn,* apostrophe, catastrophe
techne, *art,* skill, craft, technical, technician
tele, *afar, distant, end,* telegraph, telescope, telelectric
theos, *God,* theist, atheist, theocracy
therme, *heat,* thermometer, thermal, isothermal
topos, a *place,* topical, toponym, topography
treis, *three,* tripod, trinity, triangle
trepo, *I turn,* heliotrope, tropic, tropism
typos, *mark, impression,* type, stereotype, linotype
zoon, *an animal,* zoology, zootomy, epizoötic

All roots may be traced back to an Aryan origin. The
English language is a member of the Indo-European family
of languages and as such is of Aryan origin. It sprang from
an Aryan source, consequently, almost every word in
English, no matter from what source derived, comes from
an Aryan root. The original roots are not numerous.
Hindu grammarians have traced the whole of Sanskrit to
about two thousand roots, of which only about eight
hundred can be found in literature. On these eight hundred
primary elements rests the whole structure of the Indic
languages. Says Dr. Max Muller, "Their stock in trade is
no more than about eight hundred roots. I should say it
is considerably less, because as languages grow a number
of scarce and isolated words are dropped and their places
are supplied by new derivatives or new metaphorical ex-
pressions."

The learned Professor Skeat in his great work, "Etym-
ological Dictionary," gives a list of a little less than five
hundred, to be exact, only four hundred and sixty-one
principal roots occurring in English.

SYNONYMS
AND
ANTONYMS

ABANDON

abandon—*Syn.* desert, leave, forsake, quit, relinquish, give up, let go, surrender, resign, repudiate, cast off, discontinue, retract, vacate, abjure, forswear, withdraw from, abdicate. *Ant.* cherish, keep, maintain, uphold, support, advocate, favor, adopt, occupy, vindicate, prosecute, defend, assert, retain.

abandoned—*Syn.* forsaken, deserted, shunned, left, discontinued, given up, relinquished, forsworn, repudiated, surrendered, vacated. *Ant.*—cherished, maintained, upheld, defended, retained, favored, supported, adopted.

abandoned—*Syn.* lost, despised, scorned, cast off, wicked, reprobate, degraded, immoral, impure, dissolute, unchaste, lewd, sinful. *Ant.* chaste, pure, moral, innocent, virtuous, unsullied, unstained, virgin, holy.

abase—*Syn.* disgrace, debase, lower, cast down, mock, despise, disconcert, confound, expose, confuse, shame. *Ant.* uplift, respect, praise, cherish, honor, exalt, elevate, dignify, extol, glorify.

abasement—*Syn.* shame, dishonor, disrepute, scandal, debasement, degradation, humiliation, servility. *Ant.* honor, credit, repute, renown, respect, regard, esteem, fame, righteousness, integrity.

abash—*Syn.* discourage, disconcert, discompose, confuse, bewilder, shame, confound, mock, embarrass, humble, humiliate, dishearten, mortify. *Ant.* encourage, embolden, hearten, praise, uphold, cheer, buoy, rally, inspirit, stimulate.

abate—*Syn.* lower, lessen, moderate, mitigate, decrease, diminish, reduce, restrain, assuage, alleviate, allay. *Ant.* enlarge, extend, increase, magnify, amplify, aggravate, foment, enhance, intensify, prolong.

abatement—*Syn.* reduction, decrease, lessening, subsidence, diminution, mitigation, moderation.

ABIDE

Ant. increase, increment, augmentation, enlargement.

abbreviate—*Syn.* shorten, curtail, lessen, abridge, condense, contract, reduce. *Ant.* lengthen, enlarge, increase, expand, extend, distend, swell, inflate.

abbreviation—*Syn.* abridgment, contraction, abstraction, shortening, curtailment. *Ant.* enlargement, expansion, extension, increase, augmentation.

abdicate—*Syn.* resign, give up, abandon, forsake, renounce, quit, relinquish, forego. *Ant.* claim, defend, hold, maintain, retain, remain, assert, challenge, defy.

abdomen, *n.*—*Syn.* belly, stomach, middle, paunch, corporation, guts.

aberration, *n.*—*Syn.* deviation, irregularity, variation, divergence, wandering; insanity, eccentricity, peculiarity, anomaly.

abet—*Syn.* aid, assist, help, encourage, incite, stimulate, instigate, promote, uphold, embolden, support. *Ant.* discourage, impede, obstruct, frustrate, hinder, baffle, counteract, dissuade, resist, confound, deter.

abettor—*Syn.* assistant, helper, accomplice, accessory, instigator, promoter, coöperator, companion, associate. *Ant.* opponent, antagonist, resister, adversary.

abeyance—*Syn.* suspension, inaction, dormancy, indecision, reservation, expectancy, adjournment. *Ant.* operation, enforcement, renewal, exercise, revival, action, resuscitation.

abhor—*Syn.* hate, loathe, detest, despise, shun, abominate, dislike, scorn. *Ant.* love, cherish, esteem, like, desire, enjoy, admire, approve, relish.

abhorrent, *adj.*—*Syn.* hateful, odious, detestable, shocking, offensive, repulsive, loathsome, repellent.

abide—*Syn.* live, stay, sojourn, inhabit, dwell, reside, tarry, stop, lodge, continue, wait, remain.

Ant. go, move, depart, migrate, proceed.

abide—*Syn.* bide, bear, endure, tolerate. *Ant.* shun, resist, reject, despise.

ability—*Syn.* capacity, capability, qualification, ability, skill, understanding, aptitude, faculty, expertness, efficiency, attainment, accomplishment, talent, knowledge. *Ant.* incompetency, ignorance, weakness, dulness, stupidity, inability, limitation, incomprehension.

abject—*Syn.* despicable, worthless, servile, base, low, mean, vile, grovelling, contemptible, pitiful, absurd, ignoble, inferior. *Ant.* noble, exalted, proud, magnificent, imposing, excellent, worthy, praiseworthy, commendable, lofty, aristocratic.

abjure—*Syn.* forswear, recant, recall, retract, disclaim, revoke, renounce, repudiate, abrogate, disown, dismiss, deny. *Ant.* maintain, approve, confirm, certify, sanction, ratify, assent, justify, praise, laud, recommend, commend.

able—*Syn.* robust, stalwart, powerful, vigorous, qualified, capable, efficient, strong, clever, fitted, competent, effective, skilful. *Ant.* weak, delicate, infirm, feeble, ineffective, useless, powerless, feckless, inefficacious, inefficient, remiss, stupid, useless.

ablution—*Syn.* bath, bathing, cleansing, washing, lavation, laving, purification. *Ant.* defiling, defilement, soil, soiling, taint, tainting, polluting, pollution, befouling, besmearing, contaminating, contamination, smirching, besmirching.

abode—*Syn.* dwelling, residence, habitation, house, home, quarters, lodging, domicile, hearth, hearthstone, fireside.

abolish—*Syn.* disestablish, nullify, abrogate, annul, revoke, destroy, annihilate, invalidate, extinguish, quash, cancel, vitiate, demolish, exterminate. *Ant.* continue, confirm, establish, promote, reinstate, institute, legalize, restore,

set up, support, revive, repair, enact, sustain, uphold, ratify, sanction, strengthen, enforce.

abominable—*Syn.* odious, hateful, detestable, execrable, disgusting, horrible, repugnant, revolting, vile, infamous, loathsome, fetid, stinking, foul, nauseating, nauseous. *Ant.* lovable, likable, enjoyable, pleasant, sweet, alluring, pleasing, captivating, appealing.

abomination—*Syn.* disgust, nuisance, pest, plague, horror, evil, corruption, abhorrence, offense, annoyance, curse, aversion, execration, detestation, iniquity, hatred, shame, wickedness, villainy, anathema. *Ant.* cleanliness, purity, beauty, loveliness, affection, gratification, satisfaction, delight, blessing, joy, benefit, treat, entertainment, happiness.

abortive—*Syn.* vain, ineffective, ineffectual, useless, futile, fruitless, idle, inoperative, unproductive, worthless. *Ant.* effectual, efficient, efficacious, productive, fruitful, successful, satisfactory.

abound—*Syn.* teem, overflow, swarm, flow, flourish, swell, luxuriate, stream, prevail. *Ant.* want, lack, fail, be deficient in, be destitute of, need, be short of.

about—*Syn.* concerning, regarding, respecting, around, nearly, approximately. *Ant.* unlike, remote, afar, separated, distant.

abrasion, *n.*—*Syn.* attrition, rubbing, wearing, grinding, erosion, corrosion.

abridgment—*Syn.* outline, epitome, digest, synopsis, analysis, abstract, abbreviation, compendium, summary, precis. *Ant.* enlargement, extension, addition, expansion, increase.

abroad, *adv.*—*Syn.* away, out, outside, forth, overseas.

abrogate, *v.*— *Syn.* annul, cancel, nullify, negate, repeal, revoke, vacate, quash, abolish, void.

abrupt, *adj.*—*Syn.* sudden, precipitate, hasty, impetuous, quick, brusque, short, steep, sheer.

abscond—*Syn.* run off, run away, decamp, depart, retreat, flee, disappear, leave, bolt, hide, slip away, withdraw. *Ant.* remain, stay, abide, continue, tarry, stop, stand firm, endure.

absent—*Syn.* inattentive, abstracted, listless, dreamy, heedless, thoughtless, preoccupied, absorbed, oblivious. *Ant.* present, attentive, mindful, thoughtful, interested, receptive.

absolute—*Syn.* entire, complete, unconditional, unrestricted, unqualified, despotic, arbitrary, tyrannous, imperative, imperious, authoritative, exacting, positive, dogmatic, overbearing, arrogant, commanding, haughty, peremptory, lordly, unlimited, autocratic. *Ant.* mild, meek, gentle, lowly, humble, docile, submissive, yielding, compliant, contingent, complaisant, responsible, accountable, limited, lenient, tractable.

absolve—*Syn.* pardon, exonerate, forgive, overlook, release, clear, acquit, exempt, liberate, set free, discharge, exculpate. *Ant.* bind, charge, impeach, accuse, convict, compel, inculpate, condemn, obligate, blame, incriminate.

absorb—*Syn.* imbibe, consume, exhaust, engross, merge, engulf, swallow. *Ant.* disgorge, eject, vomit, exude, emit, dissipate, disperse, spew, belch.

abstinence—*Syn.* abstention, temperance, continence, moderation, frugality, self-denial, self-control, abstemiousness, abstaining, sobriety, self-restraint, fasting. *Ant.* excess, drunkenness, intoxication, greed, self-indulgence, intemperance, gluttony, sensuality, revelry, reveling, wantonness.

abstract—*Syn.* steal, appropriate, purloin, remove, divert, detach, eliminate, separate, withdraw, distract, discriminate, distinguish, take away. *Ant.* restore, unite, complete, add, fill up, increase, combine, strengthen, conjoin, repair, mend.

abstracted—*Syn.* absent-minded, heedless, careless, engrossed, listless, indifferent, inattentive, absorbed, negligent, oblivious, thoughtless, preoccupied. *Ant.* alert, thoughtful, wide-awake, ready, attentive, prompt, intent, observant.

abstruse, *adj.*—*Syn.* profound, recondite, difficult, abstract, esoteric, subtle, complicated, deep, obscure, mysterious.

absurd—*Syn.* stupid, senseless, silly, ridiculous, foolish, nonsensical, unreasonable, irrational, inconsistent, preposterous, ludicrous, ill-advised, chimerical, wild, crazy, false, erroneous, mistaken, infatuated, anomalous, monstrous, paradoxical, inconclusive. *Ant.* rational, reasonable, logical, wise, sound, solemn, sensible, true, undeniable, indubitable, incontestable, substantial, indisputable, infallible, unquestionable, incontrovertible, established, certain, sagacious, demonstrable, demonstrated.

abundant, *adj.*—*Syn.* plentiful, copious, ample, profuse, opulent, flowing, full, lavish.

abuse, *v.*— *Syn.* ill-use, ill-treat, damage, disparage, defame, violate, injure, harm, hurt, malign, traduce, slander, scandalize, revile, vilify, reproach, asperse, depreciate, maltreat, misuse, wrong, persecute, oppress, molest, victimize, aggrieve, prostitute, desecrate, ruin. *Ant.* praise, laud, applaud, extol, eulogize, shield, uphold, defend, favor, cherish, benefit, sustain, vindicate, protect, respect, conserve, preserve, approve, panegyrize, commend, flatter, honor.

abuse, *n.*—*Syn.* opprobrium, vituperation, ill-usage, contumely, scorn, ribaldry, scurrility, obloquy, reproach, ignominy, contempt, disgrace, dishonor, slander, humiliation, infamy, blame, censure, condemnation, denunciation, disapprobation, reproof, invective. *Ant.* praise, laudation, commendation, approbation, approval, sanction, respect, regard, encomium, plaudit, panegyric, acclamation, applause, adulation, flattery, compliment, syco-phancy.

abyss—*Syn.* depth, pit, gulf, chasm, void, avernus, hell. *Ant.* height, hill, eminence, elevation, summit, dome, canopy, empy-rean, heaven.

academic—*Syn.* learned, scholarly, lettered, literary, bookish, colle-giate, scholastic, pedantic, Pla-tonic. *Ant.* ignorant, illiterate, unlettered, uninstructed, un-taught, ordinary, simple, plain, practical, matter-of-fact.

accede—*Syn.* assent, consent, ac-quiesce, comply, concur, agree, coincide, approve. *Ant.* protest, dissent, deny, refuse, denounce, withhold, condemn.

accelerate—*Syn.* hurry, expedite, hasten, quicken, dispatch, push, forward, facilitate. *Ant.* retard, hinder, defer, postpone, obstruct, impede, block, resist, embarrass.

accentuate, *v.*—*Syn.* stress, ac-cent, mark, emphasize, under-line, affirm, exaggerate.

accept—*Syn.* receive, take, ac-quire, admit, get, gain, acknowl-edge, agree, assent, concur. *Ant.* refuse, discard, deny, disagree, dispute, renounce, decline, yield, reject.

acceptable—*Syn.* pleasing, wel-come, agreeable, pleasurable, gratifying, delightful, comfort-ing, fitting. *Ant.*—displeasing, unwelcome, disagreeable, annoy-ing, disturbing, unpleasant, re-pugnant, unfitting.

accessory—*Syn.* ally, assistant, partner, copartner, aide, helper, accomplice, abettor, henchman, follower, companion, colleague, associate, participator, retainer, confederate. *Ant.* opponent, en-emy, foe, betrayer, informer, spy, adversary, antagonist, rival, opposer, hinderer.

accident—*Syn.* casualty, mishap, hazard, happening, incident, chance, contingency, misadven-ture, adventure, disaster, hap, calamity, misfortune, hazard, possibility, fortuity. *Ant.* plan, purpose, law, fate, decree, pro-vision, ordinance, calculation,

certainty, intention, foreordina-tion, preparation, appointment, necessity.

acclaim, *v.*—*Syn.* cheer, applaud, extol, laud, honor, praise, glorify.

accommodate—*Syn.* serve, oblige, adapt, fit, suit, adjust, furnish, supply, reconcile, arrange, con-form, fashion, harmonize, at-tune, regulate, settle. *Ant.* im-pede, bar, unsuit, disbar, dis-oblige, disarrange, block, hinder, embarrass, obstruct, limit, pre-vent, stop, frustrate.

accompany, *v.*—*Syn.* attend, fol-low, escort, conduct, convoy.

accomplice—*Syn.* confederate, al-ly, helper, assistant, coworker, copartner, coöperator, associate, instigator, abettor, approver, in-citer, supporter, aid, aide, aider, sustainer. *Ant.* adversary, frus-trater, betrayer, opponent, ob-jector, destroyer, obstructor, op-poser, denouncer, enemy.

accomplish—*Syn.* perform, do, carry out, succeed, achieve, at-tain, effect, execute, consum-mate, perfect, complete, finish, manage, discharge, fulfil, realize. *Ant.* fail, undo, deter, frustrate, block, nullify, forsake, disap-point, give in, give up, relin-quish.

accomplishment—*Syn.* attainment, acquirement, fulfilment, qualifi-cation, performance, completion, desire, acquisition. *Ant.* defeat, failure, misadventure, frustra-tion, unfulfilment, hindrance, an-nulment, nullification.

accord, *v.*—*Syn.* admit, concede, grant, allow, acquiesce, give, permit, agree, harmonize, assent. *Ant.* refuse, deny, disagree, dis-pute, disallow, relinquish, dis-bar, contend, contest, question, challenge, controvert, antago-nize, oppose, argue.

accord, *n.*—*Syn.* agreement, har-mony, unison, acquiescence, rec-onciliation. *Ant.* disagreement, discord, denial, refusal, repudia-tion, denunciation, opposition.

accost—*Syn.* salute, greet, address, approach, assail, speak to, recognize. *Ant.* shun, avoid, ignore, scorn, evade, dodge, eschew.

account—*Syn.* narrative, description, recital, rehearsal, detail, relation, report, statement, explanation, moneys, bill, charge, reckoning.

accountable—*Syn.* answerable, responsible, amenable, liable, punishable, guilty, blameworthy, censurable. *Ant.* irresponsible, unreliable, untrustworthy, blameless, guiltless, innocent.

accounting, *n.*—*Syn.* reckoning, settlement, bill, computation, auditing.

accrue, *v.*—*Syn.* accumulate, grow, gather, increase, gain, result, derive.

accumulate—*Syn.* amass, collect, gather, bring together, pile up, hoard, assemble, heap, add to, aggregate. *Ant.* scatter, dissipate, disperse, divide, parcel, portion, spend, squander, waste.

accumulation—*Syn.* collection, mass, store, aggregation, concentration, congeries, heap, stock, bulk. *Ant.* dispersion, scattering, division, separation, dissipation, vanishment, disappearance.

accurate—*Syn.* correct, exact, precise, sure, trustworthy, right, minute, particular, authoritative, conclusive, just, certain, reliable, dependable. *Ant.* erroneous, doubtful, wrong, false, questionable, inaccurate, deceptive, misleading, mistaken, unjust, untruthful, erring, astray, faulty, unreliable, uncertain, vague.

accuse, *v.*—*Syn.* blame, charge, denounce, incriminate, censure, implicate, cite, indict, impeach.

accustom, *v.*—*Syn.* familiarize, inure, harden, acclimatize, addict, train, habituate, discipline.

ace, *n.*—*Syn.* one, iota, jot, particle, bit, scrap, trifle.

acerbity, *n.*—*Syn.* acidity, asperity, bitterness, sourness, surliness, severity, sullenness, acrimony, harshness, rancor, venom. *Ant.* mellowness, complaisance, mildness, amiability.

achieve—*Syn.* do, accomplish, fulfil, perform, execute, conquer, encompass, capture, act, effect, gain, win, wrest, get, enforce, administer, succeed. *Ant.* fail, fall down, neglect, ignore, retreat, forsake, give up, relinquish, let go, lose.

achievement—*Syn.* accomplishment, deed, exploit, feat, attainment, performance, act, action, execution, completion, fulfilment. *Ant.* failure, cessation, neglect, negligence, carelessness, loss, deprivation, defeat, injury, misfortune, forfeiture, prevention, waste.

acid, *adj.*—*Syn.* sour, stinging, acrid, sharp, pungent, tart, bitter. *Ant.* bland, sweet, smooth, mild.

acknowledge—*Syn.* admit, avow, own, confess, concede, allow, grant, recognize, accept, believe, profess, certify, endorse, subscribe, certify, uphold, declare. *Ant.* deny, decline, refuse, ignore, renounce, repudiate, disown, forswear, abandon, abjure.

acquaint—*Syn.* inform, tell, apprise, enlighten, notify, communicate, announce. *Ant.* deceive, delude, mislead, misrepresent, falsify, beguile.

acquaintance—*Syn.* friendship, familiarity, fellowship, companionship, intimacy, association, cognizance, knowledge, experience, friendliness, regard, esteem. *Ant.* unfamiliarity, ignorance, ignoring, inexperience, strangeness.

acquire, *v.*—*Syn.* get, obtain, procure, reap, reach, achieve, secure, collect, amass, gain, earn, attain, win, master.

acquit—*Syn.* pardon, forgive, free, clear, discharge, absolve, liberate, exculpate, release, exempt, exonerate, justify. *Ant.* convict, condemn, bind, hold, keep, defeat, convince, doom, sentence, reprove, reject, repudiate, blame, censure, denounce, disapprove, reprobate.

acrimony—*Syn.* acerbity, tartness, sharpness, harshness, bitterness, hatred, anger, irascibility, malevolence, acridity, poignancy, pungency, severity, malignity, asperity, virulence, causticity, moroseness, unkindness, sourness. *Ant.* amiability, gentleness, mildness, smoothness, suavity, sweetness, tenderness, kindness, courtesy, breeding, politeness, flattery, civility, blandness, unctuousness, complacency, obsequiousness.

act, *v.*—*Syn.* do, perform, make, play, enact, carry on, persist, operate, continue, effect, execute, transact, accomplish, enforce, administer, achieve, consummate, perpetrate, persevere. *Ant.* refrain, idle, hesitate, halt, stop, cease, give up, abstain, discontinue, hold back.

act, *n.*—*Syn.* action, deed, feat, work, operation, exercise, accomplishment, movement, motion, exploit, execution, proceeding, transaction, performance, achievement, consummation, exertion, effect. *Ant.* cessation, rest, suspension, idleness, inertia, stoppage, inaction, quiet, repose, immobility, inactivity, quiescence, indolence, passivity, sloth, sluggishness.

action—*Syn.* deed, achievement, feat, exploit, battle, engagement, accomplishment, instrumentality, agency, exercise, motion, operation, behavior, work, activity, exertion, movement, alertness, agility, business, performance, doing. *Ant.* inertia, inactivity, inaction, sluggishness, rest, repose, idleness, ennui, lassitude, passiveness.

active—*Syn.* alert, quick, sharp, sprightly, brisk, busy, spry, supple, lively, diligent, bustling, hustling, energetic, industrious, vigorous, wide-awake, mobile, expeditious, prompt, officious, restless, ready, nimble, agile. *Ant.* inactive, idle, indolent, slow, flat, dull, stupid, heavy, slothful, sluggish, inert, quiet, quiescent, lazy.

activity—*Syn.* exercise, business, action, motion, vigor, quickness, alertness, agility, readiness, nimbleness, sprightliness, liveliness,

speediness, swiftness, progress, progressiveness, celerity, rapidity. *Ant.* inactivity, idleness, sloth, laziness, dulness, stupidity, indolence, sluggishness, immobility, inertia.

actual—*Syn.* real, positive, genuine, certain, certified, confirmed, existent, factual, undoubted, sure, authentic, reliable. *Ant.* fictitious, false, doubtful, spurious, unreliable, counterfeit, assumed, mythical, legendary, feigned, pretended.

acumen—*Syn.* insight, keenness, penetration, sharpness, discernment, acuteness, shrewdness, sagacity, perspicacity, accuracy, intelligence, wisdom. *Ant.* dulness, obtuseness, stupidity, moroseness, bluntness, apathy, insensibility, stupefaction, stupor, sluggishness, slowness.

acute, *adj.*—*Syn.* sharp, keen, intense, penetrating, trenchant, shrewd, quick, smart, astute, pointed, poignant, critical. *Ant.* obtuse, dull, stupid, chronic.

adapt—*Syn.* suit, fit, conform, accommodate, model, remodel, arrange, harmonize, set, proportion, attune, regulate, settle, adjust. *Ant.* confuse, jumble, disarrange, misplace, misfit, disturb, displace, misapply, misjoin, discompose, derange, dismember, disorder, disjoint, dislocate, mix, mingle.

add—*Syn.* enlarge, increase, extend, augment, attach, append, amplify, annex, affix, adjoin. *Ant.* subtract, abstract, diminish, decrease, lessen, reduce, withdraw, deduct, dissever, remove.

addicted—*Syn.* attached, devoted, wedded, dedicated, accustomed, disposed, habituated, prone, given, predisposed, inclined. *Ant.* averse, unaccustomed, disinclined, indisposed, reluctant, inimical, opposed, contrary.

addition—*Syn.* increase, accession, appendage, adjunct, increment, annexation, additament. *Ant.* subtraction, abstraction, decrease, diminution, lessening, shrinkage, withdrawal, loss.

address, *v.*—*Syn.* speak to, greet, salute, hail, accost, approach, acclaim, apostrophize, court, woo. *Ant.* overlook, ignore, pass, shun, elude, cut, avoid, dodge.

address, *n.*—*Syn.* speech, discourse, appeal, oration, tact, skill, ability, dexterity, deportment, demeanor, politeness, manners, readiness, ingenuity, courtesy, adroitness, discretion. *Ant.* rudeness, ill-breeding, clumsiness, stupidity, boorishness, awkwardness, folly, fatuity, clownishness, unmannerliness.

adduce—*Syn.* cite, allege, advance, assign, quote, name, mention, urge, infer, declare, affirm, assert.

adept—*Syn.* master, seer, prophet, magician, wizard, soothsayer, diviner, scholar, savant. *Ant.* ignoramus, faker, fraud, pretender, dissembler, mountebank, charlatan, hypocrite.

adequate—*Syn.* adapted, suited, suitable, sufficient, satisfactory, enough, equal, fit, fitted, fitting, able, competent, commensurate, capable, qualified, ample. *Ant.* inadequate, unsuited, unsuitable, disqualified, unqualified, unfit, useless, insufficient, incompetent, inferior, poor, unequal, unsatisfactory, worthless.

adhere—*Syn.* stick, cling, unite, join, fasten, attach, cleave. *Ant.* separate, loose, loosen, divide, disunite, unfasten, disjoin.

adherent—*Syn.* follower, partisan, comrade, companion, backer, approver, aid, helper, assistant, ally, disciple, accomplice, abettor, supporter, accessory. *Ant.* opponent, opposer, hater, betrayer, vilifier, traducer, calumniator, adversary, traitor, renegade, deserter, antagonist, oppressor.

adhesion—*Syn.* adherence, attachment, connection, concurrence, assent, union, cohesion, stickiness, viscosity. *Ant.* separation, division, disunion, looseness, unattachment, disruption, disconnection, sunderance.

adhesive—*Syn.* sticky, glutinous, viscid, viscous, cohesive, gummy, tenacious, waxy, gelatinous. *Ant.* inadhesive, free, loose, separable, separated, apart, divisible, unattachable, oily, open.

adjacent—*Syn.* adjoining, near, beside, next, nigh, close, bordering, contiguous, coterminous, neighboring, abutting, attached, conterminous. *Ant.* distant, far, afar, far-away, away from, beyond, detached, disconnected, disjoined, remote, separate, apart.

adjourn—*Syn.* defer, postpone, prorogue, put off, procrastinate, delay, suspend, protract, stay, intermit, stop, interrupt, withhold. *Ant.* begin, continue, keep on, keep up, prolong, protract, support, persevere, urge, compel, impel, command, encourage, stimulate.

adjournment—*Syn.* postponement, discontinuance, prorogation, dissolution, consummation, respite. *Ant.* beginning, commencement, continuance, prolongation, continuity.

adjudge—*Syn.* assign, decide, sentence, decree, determine, settle, adjudicate, award, deem, relegate. *Ant.* defer, postpone, elude, dodge, shun, decline, refuse, withdraw, withhold.

adjunct—*Syn.* addition, appendage, appurtenance, help, complement, dependency, attribute, appendancy or appendency, auxiliary. *Ant.* subtraction, lessening, removal, sunderance, disjunction, separation.

adjuration—*Syn.* address, appeal, plea, charge, command, declaration, statement, oration.

adjure—*Syn.* charge, urge, beg, plead, beseech, implore, ask, command, entreat, appeal.

adjust—*Syn.* arrange, regulate, adapt, fit, settle, accommodate, organize, conform, classify, suit, prepare, straighten. *Ant.* disarrange, confuse, mix, mingle, unfit, unsuit, disorganize, scatter, disorder, derange, jumble, involve.

ad-lib, *adj.*—*Syn.* spontaneous, extempore, improvised, faked. *Ant.* rehearsed, deliberate.

administer—*Syn.* minister, dispense, distribute, execute, furnish, conduct, control, superintend, supply, afford, discharge, regulate, provide, mete out, manage, disburse. *Ant.* fail, neglect, refuse, restrain, deny, frustrate, oppose, nullify, forego, forswear.

admirable—*Syn.* worthy, attractive, striking, enticing, captivating, winsome, wonderful, surprising, good, excellent, astonishing, alluring, desirable, praiseworthy. *Ant.* repelling, repulsive, repugnant, detestable, unworthy, uninviting, hateful, loathsome, revolting, contemptible, despicable, disgusting, censurable.

admiration—*Syn.* wonder, appreciation, praise, deference, approbation, estimation, encomium, respect, regard, applause, approval, esteem, gratification, amazement, surprise, glorification. *Ant.* hate, hatred, detestation, disapproval, disregard, contempt, contumely, obloquy, dissatisfaction, distrust, denunciation, dislike, disgust, aversion, loathing, repugnance, antipathy, abhorrence.

admire—*Syn.* appreciate, approve, applaud, laud, praise, boost, extol, enjoy, honor, respect, esteem, love, venerate, adore, glorify, revere, wonder. *Ant.* condemn, contemn, hate, despise, censure, blame, ridicule, protest, detest, execrate, dishonor, scorn, abhor, vilify, abominate, dislike.

admissible—*Syn.* worthy, proper, right, suitable, confirmed, passable, permissible, fair, just, allowable, possible, probable, likely, agreeable, justifiable, justified, warranted, sanctioned, permitted, approved, attested. *Ant.* unworthy, wrong, unsuitable, unfair, unjust, unlikely, false, foreign, irrelevant, unlicensed, unwarrantable, unsuitable, inapplicable, absurd, ridiculous, inadmissible, illegitimate, unsafe.

admission—*Syn.* admittance, allowance, confession, acknowledgment, concession, access, approach, entrance, fee, charge, cost. *Ant.* denial, refusal, repudiation, disallowance, rejection, expulsion, repulsion.

admit—*Syn.* allow, permit, open for, suffer, acknowledge, avow, receive, welcome, assent, grant, concede, tell, confess, own. *Ant.* deny, refuse, shut, dismiss, dissent, dispute, repel, repulse, confute, reject.

admonish—*Syn.* warn, advise, counsel, reprove, disapprove, censure, forewarn, caution, rebuke, reprimand, dissuade, exhort. *Ant.* approve, laud, applaud, comment, praise, compliment, eulogize, flatter, acclaim, recommend, extol, puff (*colloq.*), boost (*colloq.*).

ado, *n.*—*Syn.* turmoil, bustle, commotion, stir, fuss, tumult, flurry, excitement.

adolescent, *adj.*—*Syn.* juvenile, youthful, teen-age, junior, pubescent.

adopt, *v.*—*Syn.* assume, appropriate, accept, embrace, espouse, approve, pass, choose.

adore—*Syn.* worship, venerate, glorify, honor, praise, extol, love. *Ant.* blaspheme, mock, despise, curse, condemn, hate, detest, abhor.

adorn—*Syn.* ornament, beautify, embellish, garnish, deck, bedeck, gild, decorate, illustrate. *Ant.* mar, spoil, deface, deform, disfigure, damage, tarnish.

adroit—*Syn.* slick, skilled, skilful, clever, proficient, dexterous, expert, artful, ready. *Ant.* unskilled, unskilful, awkward, dense, dull, stupid, uncouth.

adulterate—*Syn.* mix, alloy, debase, defile, corrupt, contaminate, vitiate, muddle, confuse. *Ant.* purify, clarify, clear, refine, improve, free, cleanse, filter, distil.

advance—*Syn.* go, move, proceed, progress, continue, improve, heighten, accelerate, promote, rise, increase, exalt, allege, adduce, assign. *Ant.* recede, turn, return, yield, back down, stop, stand, halt, hesitate, withdraw, retrograde, retrogress.

advancement—*Syn.* promotion, progress, progression, progressiveness, gain, knowledge, improvement, proficiency, preferment, enhancement, elevation, superiority, forwardness. *Ant.* retrogression, retrogradation, deterioration, decline, descent, downfall, return, reversion, retreat, recession, withdrawal, halt, stoppage, cessation, degeneration, regression.

advantage—*Syn.* benefit, profit, gain, help, assistance, emolument, good, interest, vantage, utility, expediency, superiority, victory, success. *Ant.* loss, drawback, hindrance, disadvantage, handicap, incumbrance, burden, obstacle, obstruction, barrier, restriction.

advantageous—*Syn.* beneficial, useful, profitable, gainful, helpful, assisting, favorable, good, expedient, friendly, propitious, amicable, convenient. *Ant.* hurtful, harmful, injurious, profitless, unfavorable, unpropitious, noxious, retarding, blocking, deleterious, detrimental, inimical.

adventure—*Syn.* incident, happening, event, occurrence, enterprise, undertaking, circumstance, affair, transaction, hazard, casualty, pursuit, risk, trial, experiment, engagement. *Ant.* seclusion, isolation, avoidance, stillness, passiveness, inaction, inertia, deadness, inertness, inactivity, latency, passivity, quiescence.

adversary—*Syn.* opponent, antagonist, opposer, disputant, competitor, rival. *Ant.* aid, helper, assistant, friend, co-worker, endorser, contributor, well-wisher, backer.

adverse—*Syn.* contrary, opposite, unfortunate, against, opposing, inimical, hostile, unlucky, un-

toward, conflicting, unfavorable, calamitous, antagonistic, incompatible, unpropitious. *Ant.* favorable, lucky, fortunate, good, agreeable, desirable, auspicious, benign, helpful, prosperous, sustaining, propitious, coöperative, contributory, aiding, supporting, advantageous, assisting.

adversity—*Syn.* misfortune, ill-luck, disaster, calamity, distress, misery, accident, opposition, antagonism. *Ant.* help, aid, assistance, encouragement, favor, fortune, coöperation, endorsement, approval.

advertisement, *n.*—*Syn.* notice, ad, announcement, proclamation, commercial.

advice—*Syn.* counsel, guidance, instruction, suggestion, directions, admonition, exhortation, opinion, charge, injunction, lesson, caution, warning. *Ant.* misdirection, misinformation, falsehood, betrayal, deception, misrepresentation, lie, lying, falsification, deceit, delusion, hoax.

advise—*Syn.* counsel, direct, inform, tell, apprise, acquaint, admonish, warn, instruct, suggest, show. *Ant.* lead astray, deceive, betray, pervert, dissemble, feign, pretend, delude, trick, cheat, take in, victimize, bamboozle, spoof (*slang*), hoodwink, gull, hoax, fool, humbug.

advocate, *v.*—*Syn.* support, recommend, champion, maintain, favor, promote, advance, forward, justify, plead, propound. *Ant.* attack, oppose, assail, impugn.

affable—*Syn.* easy, kindly, polite, courteous, gracious, mild, urbane, suave, complaisant, civil, pleasing, condescending, winning, inviting, benign, benignant. *Ant.* sour, grouchy, impolite, haughty, disdainful, arrogant, tyrannical, grumbling, surly, discontented, "blue," complaining, morose, dull.

affair, *n.*—*Syn.* incident, event, business, duty, concern, occasion, happening; liaison, amour.

affectation, *n.*—*Syn.* pretension,

artificiality, pose, mannerism, insincerity, air, pompousness, unnaturalness. *Ant.* artlessness, simplicity, naivete, naturalness.

affection—*Syn.* love, friendship, attachment, goodwill, friendliness, kindness, tenderness, fondness, solicitude. *Ant.* dislike, hatred, enmity, ill-will, unkindness, discouragement, aversion, animosity, antipathy.

affectionate—*Syn.* loving, caring, solicitous, devoted, tender, attached, fond, kind, ardent, warm, zealous. *Ant.* unkind, careless, neglectful, dour, sour, morose, fickle, harsh, cruel, cold, inimical, antagonistic.

affirm, *v.*—*Syn.* assert, state, aver, propose, depose, insist, declare, claim, swear, vow, say, warrant, maintain, assure.

affliction, *n.*—*Syn.* misfortune, trouble, distress, tribulation, sorrow, scourge, adversity, suffering, injury, woe, misery, disaster, wretchedness, anguish.

affluent, *adj.*—*Syn.* wealthy, abounding, rich, opulent, plenteous. *Ant.* destitute, penurious, impecunious, poor.

affray, *n.*—*Syn.* fight, battle, combat, fracas, conflict, controversy, contest, quarrel, struggle.

affront—*Syn.* insult, irritate, annoy, vex, taunt, provoke, exasperate, aggravate, tease, offend, displease, shame, reproach, mock, abash. *Ant.* placate, conciliate, gratify, please, appease, honor, soothe, satisfy, mollify, assuage.

afraid—*Syn.* timid, scared, frightened, alarmed, terrified, terrorstricken, cowardly, fearful, timorous, apprehensive, fainthearted, anxious. *Ant.* fearless, courageous, gallant, valiant, valorous, bold, brave, cool, confident, heroic, intrepid, undaunted, venturesome, undismayed, audacious, collected, calm, composed, confident, dauntless, reckless.

aged, *adj.*—*Syn.* old, senile, elderly, mellow, ripe; hoary, superannuated, antiquated, doddering, decrepit.

agent—*Syn.* operator, performer, actor, mover, promoter, doer, means, factor, consignee, functionary, deputy, representative, instrument. *Ant.* chief, principal, originator, inventor, master, employer, director, guide, supervisor, superintendent.

aggrandize—*Syn.* exalt, promote, enrich, augment, advance, elevate, dignify, ennoble, expand, magnify. *Ant.* humble, lower, reduce, shame, disgrace, dishonor, degrade, debase, enfeeble, impoverish, depress, abase.

agitate, *v.*—*Syn.* shake, move, perturb, provoke, excite, rouse, arouse, drive, impel, stir, convulse, trouble, actuate, disturb, annoy, bother, fluster.

agony, *n.*—*Syn.* pain, suffering, trial, affliction, torment, distress, torture, anguish, misery.

agree—*Syn.* comply, concur, approve, assent, accept, consent, admit, acquiesce, accede, coincide, combine, unite, accord, suit, match, join, harmonize. *Ant.* decline, refuse, demur, disagree, dissent, oppose, protest, differ, contend, dispute, contradict.

agreeable—*Syn.* pleasant, pleasing, charming, loving, enticing, inviting, willing, ready, acceptable, suitable, conformable, consistent. *Ant.* disagreeable, unpleasant, harsh, unsuitable, incongruous, offensive, odious, disgusting, hateful, repugnant, revolting, discordant, contentious.

aid, *v.*—*Syn.* help, advance, foster, encourage, abet, relieve, promote, assist, support, uphold, succor, advocate, second, back. *Ant.* hinder, impede, block, injure.

aim—*Syn.* goal, mark, object, aspiration, intention, endeavor, inclination, determination, purpose, tendency, design, end. *Ant.* aimlessness, oversight, neglect, heedlessness, thoughtlessness, negligence, avoidance, purposelessness, carelessness.

air—*Syn.* manner, look, appearance, style, mien, demeanor, carriage, behavior, port, way, sort, fashion, expression, bearing.

airy—*Syn.* light, lively, gay, joyous, sprightly, frolicsome, animated, ethereal, aerial, fairylike. *Ant.* heavy, dull, inert, ponderous, slow, sluggish, clumsy, wooden, stony.

alacrity—*Syn.* speed, swiftness, celerity, briskness, activity, eagerness, quickness, readiness, sprightliness, liveliness, agility, vivacity, animation, nimbleness, promptness, promptitude, alertness. *Ant.* apathy, laziness, indolence, indifference, slowness, reluctance, sluggishness, unwillingness, aversion, dulness, inertness, disinclination, stupidity, dislike, repugnance.

alarm—*Syn.* terror, fright, fear, dread, dismay, consternation, panic, affright, timidity, disquietude, apprehension, misgiving, solicitude. *Ant.* repose, quiet, quietness, security, assurance, confidence, calmness, peace.

alert—*Syn.* active, lively, nimble, ready, brisk, prompt, wide-awake, prepared, vigilant, watchful, sprightly, bustling, hustling. *Ant.* heavy, drowsy, dull, slow, sluggish, inactive, stupid, lethargic, weary.

alertness—*Syn.* quickness, promptitude, agility, vigilance, activity, watchfulness, readiness, sprightliness, alacrity. *Ant.* dulness, slowness, stupidity, heaviness, drowsiness, sluggishness, laziness.

alien, *adj.*—*Syn.* strange, opposed, foreign, distant, remote, hostile, contradictory, inappropriate, inapplicable, unlike, contrasted, conflicting, irrelevant, contrary, unconnected, extraneous, estranged. *Ant.* akin, alike, corresponding, appropriate, pertinent, relevant, proper, apropos, congenial, native, friendly.

alien, *n.*—*Syn.* foreigner, outlander, outsider, stranger. *Ant.* native, settler, citizen, fellow-countryman, denizen.

alike—*Syn.* same, like, resembling, akin, identical, kindred, analogous, homogeneous, similar,

equal, uniform, equivalent. *Ant.* unlike, dissimilar, distinct, heterogeneous, different, opposite, diverse.

alive—*Syn.* live, existent, animate, subsisting, breathing, active, vivacious, quick, lively, living, alert, existing, animated, brisk, agile. *Ant.* dead, lifeless, inanimate, deceased, defunct, spiritless, dispirited, dull, morose, stupid, drowsy, sluggish.

allay—*Syn.* soothe, quiet, pacify, tranquilize, mollify, calm, compose, still, appease, alleviate. *Ant.* agitate, excite, arouse, rouse, stir, fan, provoke, kindle.

allege—*Syn.* aver, state, cite, declare, affirm, advance, introduce, plead, asseverate, assert, adduce, say, produce, introduce, assign, claim, maintain, offer, quote. *Ant.* deny, conceal, dissent, object, negative, protest, repudiate, contradict, disagree.

allegiance—*Syn.* loyalty, submission, subjection, homage, devotion, fealty, obedience, faithfulness. *Ant.* dissatisfaction, disloyalty, sedition, treason, rebellion.

alleviate—*Syn.* mitigate, lessen, assuage, soften, moderate, abate, lighten, relieve, remove. *Ant.* increase, intensify, heighten, magnify, augment, aggravate, embitter.

alliance—*Syn.* union, fusion, federation, confederation, confederacy, coalition, partnership, league, compact. *Ant.* separation, secession, hostility, enmity, discord, disunion, war, rebellion, revolution, antagonism, schism, divorce.

allot—*Syn.* give, grant, distribute, divide, award, apportion, assign, destine, ordain, determine, design, arrange, dispose, allocate, collocate, parcel out, tabulate, catalogue, classify, set apart, dispense, administer, present, hand over, concede, yield. *Ant.* withhold, retain, keep, refuse, deny, reject, cast aside, disallow, confuse, shuffle, disorder, disarrange, preserve, conserve, save, guard, grasp, lay hold of, revoke, decline, negative, disapprove, resist, dissent.

allow—*Syn.* assent, authorize, accord, vouchsafe, empower, license, warrant, privilege, permit, let, grant, sanction, suffer, yield, consent, concede, admit, tolerate. *Ant.* deny, forbid, disallow, refuse, protest, disapprove, resist, reject, withstand.

alloy, *v.*—*Syn.* combine, amalgamate, mix, adulterate, debase, impair, lessen.

allure—*Syn.* lure, entice, coax, cajole, decoy, attract, draw, inveigle, captivate, win, tempt, seduce, invite, lead, wheedle, persuade. *Ant.* repel, warn, deter, damp, chill, threaten, dissuade, discourage, hinder, restrain, prevent.

alone, *adj.*—*Syn.* solitary, lonesome, single, unaccompanied, lonely, isolated, desolate, only, solo, sole, forlorn.

alter—*Syn.* change, transform, vary, modify, metamorphose, moderate, regulate, reduce, qualify, diversify, shift, veer, turn, twist, reconstruct. *Ant.* keep, retain, let stand, preserve, maintain, hold, persist, stay, refrain, sustain, continue.

altercation—*Syn.* controversy, contention, quarrel, wrangle, dispute, disturbance, fracas, brawl, row, broil, disputation, discussion, affray, dissension, scene, scuffle, strife, scrap, argument, debate, discord. *Ant.* union, harmony, peace, concord, agreement, unanimity, conformity, unity, concurrence, consonance, accordance.

alternative—*Syn.* option, preference, choice, resource, pick, election. *Ant.* necessity, compulsion, constraint, restraint, coercion, urgency, obligation.

amalgamation, *n.*—*Syn.* union, mixture, compound, blend, combination, merger, consolidation, mingling.

amass—*Syn.* heap, hoard, store, pile, gather, collect, accumulate, aggregate. *Ant.* disperse, disburse, scatter, spend, squander, dissipate, divide, waste.

amateur—*Syn.* tyro, novice, dilletante, dawdler, beginner, learner, neophyte. *Ant.* critic, connoisseur, professional, savant, scholar, philosopher, professor, pundit, pedagogue, teacher, doctor, scientist, master.

amazement—*Syn.* surprise, wonder, astonishment, bewilderment, admiration, awe, confusion, perplexity, perturbation. *Ant.* indifference, steadiness, stoicism, coolness, calmness, composure, self-possession, anticipation, expectation, preparation.

ambassador—*Syn.* minister, envoy, plenipotentiary, representative, diplomat, dignitary, negotiator.

ambiguous, *adj.*—*Syn.* unclear, uncertain, doubtful, equivocal, indistinct, vague, indefinite, obscure, indeterminate, cryptic, enigmatic. *Ant.* clear, lucid, definite, explicit.

ambition—*Syn.* aspiration, emulation, desire, striving, attempting, rivalry, competition, attainment, eagerness, earnestness. *Ant.* indifference, humility, placidity, non-fulfilment, carelessness, satisfaction, contentment, laziness.

amend—*Syn.* improve, better, correct, reform, rectify, mend, emend, advance, repair, purify, mitigate, ameliorate, meliorate, cleanse. *Ant.* harm, impair, spoil, mar, tarnish, corrupt, blemish, deteriorate, debase, injure, vitiate, aggravate, reduce, alloy, depress.

amiable—*Syn.* gentle, pleasing, good-natured, kindly, loving, affectionate, agreeable, winsome, pleasant, lovable, attractive, winning, sweet, engaging, charming, benignant, good-tempered. *Ant.* sour, dour, morose, testy, crusty, grouchy, troublesome, peevish, censorious, fault-finding, ill-tempered, sullen, surly, churlish, gruff, quarrelsome, ill-conditioned, pessimistic, gloomy, sad, reproachful, disagreeable, hateful, crabbed, acrimonious, unamiable, ill-humored, ill-natured, unlovely, dogged, irritable, irascible.

amplify—*Syn.* enlarge, increase, magnify, extend, develop, widen, expand, dilate, expatiate, augment, unfold, exaggerate. *Ant.* reduce, epitomize, summarize, curtail, abridge, amputate, condense, retrench, shorten, lessen, compress, contract.

amuse, *v.*—*Syn.* entertain, cheer, beguile, gladden, recreate, animate, please, divert, titillate, interest, engross.

ancestry, *n.*—*Syn.* lineage, parentage, family, line, descent, pedigree, race, stock, blood.

ancient, *adj.*—*Syn.* old, aged, antique, antiquated, archaic, dated, obsolete.

angel, *n.*—*Syn.* cherub, seraph, spirit, archangel. *Ant.* devil, demon, imp, fiend.

anger—*Syn.* ire, wrath, indignation, resentment, fury, rage, ebullition, scorn, displeasure, passion, excitement, violence, madness, turbulence, irritation, vexation, temper, peevishness, petulance, exasperation, impatience, animosity, offense, fretfulness. *Ant.* meekness, mildness, gentility, calmness, smoothness, good nature, jollity, frivolity, enjoyment, patience, forbearance, gentleness, placidity, self-consciousness, pleasantness, agreeability, love, gratitude, happiness, contentment, peace.

angle, *n.*—*Syn.* corner, bend, crotch, fork, viewpoint, aspect, slant, approach, position.

anguish, *n.*—*Syn.* distress, pain, affliction, sorrow, torment, woe, worry, misery, grief, suffering, anxiety, pang.

animal, *n.*—*Syn.* beast, creature; brute, savage.

animate, *v.*—*Syn.* enliven, inspire, quicken, vitalize, cheer, activate, encourage, vivify, rouse.

annihilate, *v.*—*Syn.* exterminate, eradicate, extinguish, extirpate, eliminate, annul, nullify, abolish, destroy, raze, obliterate, kill, efface, demolish, end.

announce—*Syn.* speak, tell, deliver, reveal, report, state, circulate, declare, give out, proclaim, say, publish, spread, notify, make known, blazon, advertise, promulgate, expound, propound, enunciate, communicate. *Ant.* hold, refrain, conceal, keep silent, hide, depress, repress, forbid, muzzle, suppress, restrain, quash, stifle, bottle up, withhold, reserve, smother.

annoy, *v.*—*Syn.* trouble, vex, irritate, plague, harass, irk, fret, pester, bother, molest, harry, badger.

answer, *v.*—*Syn.* reply, respond, retort, rejoin, rebut, confute.

antagonism, *n.*—*Syn.* antipathy, enmity, animosity, opposition, rancor, hostility, conflict, resistance, dissension, discord. *Ant.* harmony, accord, agreement, understanding.

antibiotic, *n.*—*Syn.* antibacterial, wonder drug, antitoxin, sulfa drug.

anticipation — *Syn.* expectancy, hope, foreboding, forecast, forethought, apprehension, foretaste, expectation, presentiment, prevision. *Ant.* fear, doubt, dread, despair, wonder, astonishment, amazement, sensation, surprise, stupefaction.

antipathy—*Syn.* hatred, hostility, bitterness, enmity, aversion, detestation, repugnance, abhorrence, repulsion, antagonism, opposition, disgust, dislike, revulsion, malevolence, ill-will. *Ant.* honor, admiration, love, respect, approval, approbation, esteem, estimation, commendation, appreciation, encomium, eulogy, reverence, veneration.

antique—*Syn.* ancient, quaint, curious, old-fashioned, superannuated, antiquated, time-worn, primitive, pristine, immemorial. *Ant.* new, modern, recent, stylish, up-to-date, fresh, modish, fashionable, current, conventional.

anxiety—*Syn.* anguish, care, concern, foreboding, worry, trouble, apprehension, disquiet, dread, solicitude, fretting, misgiving, fear, perplexity. *Ant.* ease, tranquillity, peace, contentment, calmness, carelessness, apathy, assurance, satisfaction, nonchalance, light-heartedness, indifference, coolness, unconcern.

apathy—*Syn.* carelessness, unconcern, indifference, passiveness, passivity, stoicism, composure, calmness, impassibility, lethargy, tranquillity, quietness, quietude, insensibility, immobility, unfeelingness, sluggishness, phlegm. *Ant.* care, emotion, passion, fury, frenzy, storm, disturbance, distress, feeling, sympathy, susceptibility, vehemence, violence, turbulence, sensitiveness, sensibility, alarm, agitation, anxiety, excitement, eagerness.

apology—*Syn.* excuse, plea, vindication, defense, justification, exculpation, acknowledgment, confession, evasion, subterfuge, entreaty, evasion, pretext, pretense, supplication. *Ant.* accusation, charge, censure, disapprobation, impeachment, indictment, arraignment, imputation, condemnation, offense, wrong, injury, insult, complaint.

apparel, *n.*—*Syn.* dress, clothing, clothes, attire, costume, garb, garments, outfit.

apparent—*Syn.* likely, probable, presumable, seeming, evident, obvious, clear, plain, visible, manifest. *Ant.* unlikely, improbable, doubtful, dubious, unimaginable, wavering, uncertain, fluctuating, equivocal, ambiguous, questionable.

appeal—*Syn.* call, request, invoke, plead, pray, ask, beg, beseech, entreat, supplicate, apply. *Ant.* deny, disclaim, disavow, refuse, abjure, recant, retract, renounce, revoke, recall, forswear.

appearance, *n.*—*Syn.* aspect, guise, semblance, features, shape, form, demeanor, presence, look, air, mien.

appendage—*Syn.* appendix, accessory, supplement, concomitant, addition, adjunct, appurtenance, extension, auxiliary, attachment, addendum, accompaniment. *Ant.*

total, whole, all, original, combination, entirety, bulk, mass, body.

appetite—*Syn.* craving, desire, liking, relish, longing, inclination, thirst, zest, proneness, proclivity, propensity, appetency, passion, lust, impulse, disposition. *Ant.* aversion, dislike, distaste, disrelish, antipathy, repulsion, revulsion, detestation, disgust, repugnance, indifference, hatred, loathing.

apportion, *v.*—*Syn.* allot, dispense, ration, share, allocate, mete, distribute, dole, assign.

approach, *v.*—*Syn.* near, accost, attempt; equal, approximate, arrive.

appropriate, *v.*—*Syn.* take, assume, arrogate, usurp, seize, set apart, assign. *Ant.* give, bestow, bequeath, set aside, return, abandon, reject, refuse.

appropriate, *adj.*—*Syn.* fitting, suitable, becoming, proper, meet, fit, apt, applicable, opportune. *Ant.* unfitting, unsuitable, unbecoming, improper, opposed, contrary, unsuited, unfitted.

approve, *v.*—*Syn.* endorse, confirm, commend, ratify, appreciate, esteem, sustain, compliment, praise, sanction, justify, validate, countenance.

approximation — *Syn.* approach, nearness, propinquity, neighborhood, similarity, resemblance, likeness, contiguity. *Ant.* remoteness, distance, difference, variation, unlikeness, diversity, change.

argue—*Syn.* dispute, debate, differ, discuss, reason, contest, battle, wrangle. *Ant.* ignore, overlook, scorn, despise, repudiate, reject, pass by.

arms, *n.*—*Syn.* weapons, matériel, armor, munitions, armament, array, ordnance, arsenal, hardware.

arraign—*Syn.* accuse, charge, impeach, prosecute, cite, censure, indict, summon. *Ant.* discharge, exonerate, free, overlook, pardon, release, excuse, condone, acquit, pardon.

arrange—*Syn*, adjust, assort, classify, group, range, set, sort, marshal, dispose, array, harmonize, compare. *Ant*. confuse, disorder, disperse, scatter, jumble, derange, disarrange, disturb.

arrive, *v.*—*Syn*. come, reach, attain, land, disembark, visit, appear, emerge.

art, *n.*—*Syn*. skill, science, profession, craft, artifice, cunning, dexterity, finesse.

artifice — *Syn*. ruse, stratagem, trick, wile, guile, maneuver, dodge, contrivance, machination, invention, imposture, device, art, craft, subterfuge, fraud, cunning, finesse, blind. *Ant*. innocence, candor, honesty, frankness, openness, ingenuousness, sincerity, truth, fairness, artlessness, guilelessness, simplicity.

artist, *n.*—*Syn*. adept, artificer, expert, virtuoso, craftsman, artisan, maker, author, creator, contriver.

ascend, *v.*—*Syn*. rise, advance, progress, scale, climb, mount, surmount, soar, leap, surge.

ascetic, *adj.*—*Syn*. austere, abstemious, stern, self-denying, rigid, anchoritic, puritanical. *Ant*. luxurious, voluptuous, dissolute, sensuous.

ask—*Syn*. crave, entreat, demand, exhort, solicit, supplicate, beg, beseech, request, appeal, apply for, petition, pray. *Ant*. refuse, reject, repudiate, deny, enforce, claim, insist, command, extort, appeal.

assemble, *v.*—*Syn*. collect, combine, gather, convoke, meet, unite, join, congregate, convene, compile, heap, muster, levy.

assent, *v.*—*Syn*. agree, concur, consent, allow, recognize, concede, ratify, acquiesce, accept, approve.

associate, *v.*—*Syn*. ally, combine, conjoin, link, unite, league, connect, attach, couple, affiliate, confederate. *Ant*. part, separate, sunder, sever, divide, disunite, disjoin, diverge, divorce, avoid, disconnect, estrange, dissociate.

associate, *n.*—*Syn*. companion,

comrade, pal (*slang*), buddy (*slang*), friend, helpmate, partner, auxiliary, chum (*colloq.*), colleague, mate, peer, fellow, consort, confederate, coadjutor, ally, accomplice. *Ant*. opponent, opposer, rival, stranger, antagonist, enemy, hinderer, blocker, foe, foeman, competitor.

association—*Syn*. society, lodge, club, combination, company, partnership, confederacy, confederation, corporation, union, fellowship, participation, fraternity, friendship, connection, conjunction, community, alliance, companionship. *Ant*. separation, disunion, disintegration, rupture, retirement, seclusion, division, isolation, loneliness, defection, solitude.

assurance—*Syn*. confidence, boldness, self-reliance, self-confidence, arrogance, effrontery, trust, assumption, presumption, impudence, assertion. *Ant*. doubt, distrust, dismay, fear, nervousness, trepidation, misgiving, timidity, hesitancy, confusion, shyness, bashfulness, consternation.

astute—*Syn*. clever, smart, intelligent, crafty, cunning, shrewd, sagacious, keen, artful, discerning, discriminating, clear-headed, clear-sighted, perspicacious, penetrative, penetrating, sharp, subtile, knowing, comprehensive. *Ant*. shallow, short-sighted, dull, dull-witted, obtuse, ignorant, stupid, asinine, non-comprehensive, imbecile, idiotic, undiscerning, unintelligent, stolid.

atomic, *adj.*—*Syn*. minute, infinitesimal, small, molecular, corpuscular.

atonement, *n.*—*Syn*. expiation, propitiation, apology, amends, appeasement, satisfaction, reparation, penitence, redemption.

attach—*Syn*. fasten, secure, stick, fix, unite, join, connect, conjoin, affix, annex, adjoin, add, append, combine, associate. *Ant*. sever, separate, disjoin, unconnect, detach, remove, disunite, disconnect, discard, alienate, divert, cut, rend, divert, dissociate, divorce.

attachment—*Syn.* love, friendship, devotion, esteem, respect, regard, estimation, affinity, affection, tenderness, union, adherence, inclination, adhesion. *Ant.* alienation, enmity, dislike, aversion, opposition, estrangement, repugnance, separation, animosity, antipathy, indifference, divorce, severance, distance.

attack, *v.*—*Syn.* assail, assault, encounter, beset, combat, besiege, beleaguer, storm, invade, charge, encroach, infringe, seize, violate. *Ant.* protect, defend, shelter, cover, support, uphold, sustain, resist, aid, befriend, shield, withstand.

attack, *n.*—*Syn.* invasion, assault, aggression, onset, onslaught, violence, intrusion, incursion, trespass, infringement, encroachment, inroad, charge. *Ant.* defense, repulsion, reprisal, resistance, submission, surrender, retreat, flight.

attain—*Syn.* get, gain, obtain, win, secure, grasp, achieve, procure, acquire, earn, compass, reach, accomplish, master. *Ant.* give up, let go, surrender, abandon, discard, forfeit, lose, miss, desist, desert, fail, cease.

attention, *n.*—*Syn.* application, heed, circumspection, observation, care, diligence, concentration, study, intentness, assiduity, notice.

attraction, *n.*—*Syn.* charm, affinity, allure, enticement, lure, pull, magnetism, invitation, fascination.

audacity—*Syn.* boldness, effrontery, hardihood, impudence, assumption, presumption, arrogance, pride, self-conceit, haughtiness, assurance, brazenness, vanity. *Ant.* meekness, mildness, humility, gentility, forbearance, yielding, modesty, self-abasement.

austere—*Syn.* rigid, rigorous, severe, stern, harsh, cruel, unrelenting, keen, sharp, strict, exacting, acrimonious. *Ant.* mild, meek, gentle, kind, suave, encouraging, bland, placid, soft, quiet, peaceful, soothing, indulgent.

authentic—*Syn.* true, real, veritable, genuine, reliable, accredited, trustworthy, certain, accepted, legitimate, authoritative, authorized, original, sure, received, current. *Ant.* spurious, false, fictitious, counterfeit, baseless, unauthorized, fabulous, disputed, exploded, apocryphal.

authority, *n.*—*Syn.* control, dominion, mastery, title, supremacy, power, command, sovereignty, jurisdiction, sway, right, rule, prestige.

auxiliary—*Syn.* helper, ally, aid, coadjutor, assistant, confederate, accessory, promoter, subordinate, mercenary, accomplice, associate, companion. *Ant.* opponent, opposer, hinderer, antagonist, adversary, competitor, rival, enemy, foe.

avaricious—*Syn.* miserly, parsimonious, niggardly, penurious, sordid, stingy, covetous, greedy, close, tight-fisted. *Ant.* generous, liberal, free, openhearted, prodigal, wasteful, spendthrift, bountiful, munificent.

average, *adj.*—*Syn.* mean, normal, medium, median, ordinary, moderate, mediocre, common, usual, standard. *Ant.* unusual, exceptional, extraordinary, outstanding.

aversion—*Syn.* antipathy, dislike, opposition, hatred, repugnance, disgust, detestation, abhorrence. *Ant.* love, affection, care, solicitude, fondness, attachment, kindness, tenderness.

aviation, *n.*—*Syn.* flying, aeronautics, flight; aircraft, airships, airplanes.

avoid, *v.*—*Syn.* shun, elude, escape, eschew, forbear, dodge, evade.

avow—*Syn.* own, acknowledge, profess, testify, admit, aver, declare, avouch, proclaim, witness, confess. *Ant.* disown, disclaim, repudiate, renounce, deny, contradict, ignore, dispute, censure, condemn.

awe—*Syn.* dread, fear, reverence, respect, veneration, solemnity, impressiveness. *Ant.* familiarity, intimacy, comradeship, fellowship, buoyancy, enthusiasm, calmness, coolness, steadiness, poise, equanimity.

awful—*Syn.* dread, dreadful, horrible, terrible, shocking, fearful, frightful, appalling, terrific, alarming, dire, direful, distressing, calamitous, august, grand, majestic, noble, imposing, stately. *Ant.* petty, cheap, paltry, insignificant, trifling, mean, despicable, miserable, beggarly, undignified, vulgar, inferior, low, lowly, base, humble, contemptible, commonplace.

awkward—*Syn.* ungainly, gawky, uncouth, slovenly, shuffling, clumsy, bungling, unskilful, unhandy, rough, maladroit. *Ant.* adroit, clever, dexterous, graceful, skilful, handy, apt, artful, expert.

axiom—*Syn.* maxim, proverb, aphorism, saw, byword, apothegm, adage, saying, dictum, motto, precept, rule, law. *Ant.* nonsense, absurdity, contradiction, paradox, sophism, foolishness, silliness, blunder, bull, ambiguity —moonshine, tommyrot, tomfoolery, buncombe, flapdoodle— all *slang* or *colloq.*

B

babble—*Syn.* twaddle, gabble, tattle, palaver, jabber, nonsense, absurdity, gossip, cackle, tattle, prattle, prate, chatter. *Ant.* sense, sensibility, earnestness, wit, wisdom, prudence, knowledge, learning, erudition, judgment, sagacity, understanding.

bad—*Syn.* wicked, evil, vile, wrong, corrupt, ill, base, abandoned, vicious, abominable, detestable, disgusting, spurious, false, rotten. *Ant.* good, upright, true, honest, just, sincere, beneficial, advantageous, profitable, virtuous, propitious, benevolent, serviceable, competent, worthy, right, valid, real, reputable.

baffle—*Syn.* confound, defeat, disconcert, cheat, outwit, foil, thwart, frustrate, counteract, balk, circumvent, elude. *Ant.* aid, abet, help, assist, support, succor, coöperate, befriend, relieve, second, incite, encourage, instigate.

balance, *n.*—*Syn.* equilibrium, symmetry, stability, harmony, poise, proportion.

balderdash, *n.*—*Syn.* nonsense, stuff, prating, drivel, twaddle, gibberish, bosh, bombast, froth, bull.

baleful, *adj.*—*Syn.* sinister, evil, noxious, malign, deadly, harmful, menacing, fiendish, poisonous, injurious.

banal, *adj.*—*Syn.* trite, flat, inane, vapid, fatuous, commonplace, ordinary, stale, stereotyped, hackneyed. *Ant.* fresh, original, new, exciting.

banish, *v.*—*Syn.* exile, proscribe, expatriate, expel, dismiss, oust, debar, ostracize.

barbarous—*Syn.* savage, barbaric, inhuman, uncivilized, atrocious, cruel, tyrannical, merciless, pitiless, brutal, untamed, barbarian, rude, uncouth. *Ant.* civilized, humane, cultured, refined, gentle, graceful, courteous, courtly, polite, urbane, nice, tender, delicate, merciful, sympathetic, benevolent.

barrier—*Syn.* bulwark, obstacle, rampart, breastwork, obstruction, parapet, restriction, hindrance, prohibition, bar, barricade, restraint, block, blockade. *Ant.* admittance, entrance, opening, passage, thoroughfare, road, way, transit.

base—*Syn.* vile, mean, corrupt, low, vulgar, contemptible, despicable, unworthy, dishonorable, ignoble, worthless, shameful, inferior, degraded. *Ant.* noble, high-minded, superior, exalted, majestic, grand, illustrious, magnanimous.

basic, *adj.*—*Syn.* fundamental, primary, principal, essential, indispensable, vital.

batter, *v.—Syn.* beat, smash, mar, belabor, dent, thrash, bruise, pummel, pound, disfigure, demolish, destroy.

battle—*Syn.* engagement, encounter, conflict, fight, combat, contest, action, skirmish, strife. *Ant.* peace, truce, suspension, cessation, concord, agreement, armistice, harmony, cessation.

battle-ax *n.—Syn.* virago, shrew, ball-and-chain, biddy, termagant, fishwife, vixen, witch. *Ant.* helpmate, helpmeet, better half.

bear—*Syn.* carry, convey, transport, support, sustain, suffer, endure, maintain, undergo, yield, produce. *Ant.* evade, dodge, shun, avoid, refuse, throw down, cast aside, be barren, be unproductive.

beastly—*Syn.* brutal, bestial, cruel, brutish, base, coarse, carnal, degraded, degrading, sensual, swinish, vile. *Ant.* noble, lofty, high, superior, pure, chaste, magnanimous, generous, illustrious, exalted.

beat—*Syn.* strike, batter, flog, castigate, pommel or pummel, spank, bruise, belabor, cudgel, crush, thrash, whip, chastise, punish, thump, trounce, drub, overcome, hit, smite, defeat, conquer. *Ant.* defend, protect, guard, safeguard, shield, side with, help, aid, assist, succor, submit, give in, fail, go under, give up, surrender, relinquish, cede, retreat.

beatnik, *n.—Syn.* hipster, cool cat. *Ant.* square.

beautiful—*Syn.* handsome, pretty, nice, fine, good-looking, lovely, elegant, fair, splendid, enticing, attractive, captivating, bonny, graceful. *Ant.* ugly, homely, offensive, repulsive, repugnant, revolting, depraved, disgusting, unattractive, unlovely, unpleasant, odious, horrid, grisly, hideous, deformed, frightful, grim, uncouth, clumsy, awkward, shocking, grotesque.

beauty, *n.—Syn.* fairness, comeliness, grace, elegance, loveliness, excellence, splendor, charm, handsomeness, pulchritude.

becoming—*Syn.* decent, proper, meet, fit, fitting, suitable, worthy, decorous, graceful, seemly, beseeming, befitting, comely, congruous, neat. *Ant.* unbecoming, unfitting, unseemly, displeasing, unpleasant, indecent, indecorous, unsuitable, ill-fitting, improper, awkward.

beg—*Syn.* beseech, implore, ask, supplicate, entreat, crave, solicit, pray, petition. *Ant.* give, bestow, grant, favor, cede, concede, benefit, reward, remunerate, assist, aid.

beginning—*Syn.* origin, source, rise, start, commencement, inception, opening, spring, fountain, outset, inauguration. *Ant.* end, finish, completion, goal, consummation, conclusion, outcome, result, termination, fulfilment, expiration, terminus.

behavior—*Syn.* deportment, manners, bearing, breeding, conduct, demeanor, action, life, bearing, attitude, management, tactics, policy, strategy.

bend, *v.—Syn.* deflect, mold, influence, flex, turn, contort, curve, twist, divert, crook.

beneficent—*Syn.* bountiful, generous, liberal, munificent, kind, charitable, benevolent. *Ant.* covetous, miserly, grasping, uncharitable, close-fisted, illiberal, greedy.

benefit—*Syn.* favor, advantage, kindness, civility, boon, service, utility, profit, blessing. *Ant.* injury, harm, hurt, drawback, hindrance, handicap, obstacle, disadvantage, disservice.

benevolence — *Syn.* beneficence, benignity, humanity, kindness, tenderness, almsgiving, bounty, charity, kindheartedness, goodwill, generosity, sympathy, liberality, kindliness, philanthropy, munificence, unselfishness, bounty. *Ant.* malevolence, ill-will, hatred, envy, malignity, selfishness, self-seeking, unkindness, niggardliness, illiberality, brutality, inhumanity, churlishness, stinginess, harshness, greediness, enmity, animosity, rancor, spite.

bigoted, *adj.*—*Syn.* intolerant, narrow-minded, hidebound, opinionated, blind, prejudiced, obstinate.

bind—*Syn.* fetter, chain, tie, fasten, hitch, secure, moor, shackle, restrict, restrain, tether. *Ant.* unbind, unloose, loose, untie, free, set free, unfasten, unchain.

binge, *n.*—*Syn.* spree, blow-out, caper, bat, bender, jag, ball, shindy.

blame—*Syn.* censure, condemn, reprove, reproach, upbraid, condemn, contemn, reprehend, accuse, carp, cavil. *Ant.* praise, thank, laud, boost, exalt, commend, applaud, magnify, glorify.

blank, *adj.*—*Syn.* void, bare, unfilled, vacant, barren, empty.

bleak—*Syn.* bare, chill, chilling, chilly, wild, unsheltered, dismal, gloomy, dreary, dull, waste, blank, cutting, cold, damp, windy, desolate, exposed, cheerless, stormy, monotonous. *Ant.* sunny, serene, cheerful, pleasant, comforting, genial, cheery, homelike, bright, balmy, warm, mild, appealing, sheltered.

blemish—*Syn.* flaw, fleck, spot, stain, mark, speck, defect, fault, imperfection, smirch, stigma, taint, dent, deformity, disfigurement, tarnish, defacement, daub, disgrace, dishonor, brand, blur, blot. *Ant.* ornament, adornment, embellishment, decoration, ornamentation, garnishment.

blind—*Syn.* sightless, unseeing, careless, stupid, heedless, dullwitted, obtuse, dense. *Ant.* sharp-eyed, cunning, farsighted, shrewd, penetrative, quick, keen, sharp, intelligent.

blithe, *adj.*—*Syn.* merry, jolly, cheerful, joyful, animated, gay, vivacious, glad, lighthearted, effervescent.

blooper, *n.*—*Syn.* error, blunder, bloomer, flub, bobble, boner, clinker.

blot—*Syn.* blacken, smudge, stain, smirch, darken, dirty, soil, foul, blotch, cancel, erase, efface, expunge, obliterate, delete, wipe out, destroy, annihilate. *Ant.* whiten, wash, cleanse, purify, restore, record, enter, inscribe, insert, retain, keep, note, set down, preserve.

blow—*Syn.* box, cuff, stroke, rap, knock, buffet, lash, stripe, thump, cut, hit, concussion, calamity, disaster, misfortune. *Ant.* caress, embrace, kiss, handshake, blandishment, wooing, clasp, smile, salute, hug, kindness, love.

bluff—*Syn.* gruff, rough, bold, brazen, impolite, inconsiderate, unmannerly, rude, discourteous, blustering, coarse, brusque, uncivil, outspoken, blunt, abrupt, open, frank, daring, hearty, free-and-easy. *Ant.* polite, refined, courteous, genial, kindly, bland, reserved, urbane, gracious, civil, suave, agreeable, pleasant, affable, conciliating, well-bred.

blunt, *adj.*—*Syn.* obtuse, bluff, rough, forthright, dull, harsh, direct, plain, stolid. *Ant.* subtle, tactful, suave, polite.

boast, *v.*—*Syn.* brag, exult, flourish, vaunt, bluster, crow.

body—*Syn.* frame, physique, trunk, system, corpse, remains, dust, cadaver, carcass, form, clay, organism, stem. *Ant.* soul, spirit, mind, shade, shadow, ghost, phantom, apparition, specter, phantasm.

body—*Syn.* mass, matter, substance, substantiality, lump, ponderousness, ponderosity, collection, collectiveness, assemblage, association, organization, corporation, whole, all, strength, denseness, density, ponderability, opacity. *Ant.* nothing, nothingness, unreality, insubstantiality, ethereality, ghostliness, phantasy, hallucination, concept, thought, immateriality, imponderability.

bold—*Syn.* brave, courageous, determined, fearless, intrepid, undaunted, daring, dauntless, valiant, manly, manful, confident, adventurous, venturesome, audacious, stout-hearted, strenuous, high-spirited, impudent, shameless, saucy, brazen, impertinent, pert, rude. *Ant.* timid, meek, gentle, backward, shy, reticent, silent, quiet, unobtrusive, retiring, cowardly, timorous, fearful, pusillanimous, mean, base, contemptible, despicable, low, groveling, sycophantic.

book, *n.—Syn.* volume, tome, work, publication, treatise.

booze, *n.—Syn.* liquor, whisky, spirits, drink, grog, alky, corn, soup, moonshine, bottle, creature, rum, brew, hooch, stuff, juice.

border—*Syn.* brim, brink, edge, margin, rim, verge, boundary, confine, frontier, limit, termination, extremity, end. *Ant.* center, interior, inside, territory, region.

bound, *v.—Syn.* circumscribe, limit, define, measure, confine, restrict, curb, restrain, check, coerce, impel, compel, leap, jump, spring, bounce, rebound, recoil, skip, dash. *Ant.* enlarge, widen, extend, liberate, free, set free, unbind, unchain, pause, halt, stop, stand, stand still, lie still, lie down, lie flat, stick fast.

bound, *adj.—Syn.* confined, held, tied, trussed, fettered, chained, restrained, obliged, compelled. *Ant.* free, loose, untied, unfettered, unchained, foot-loose, unrestricted, untrammeled, unbound.

boundary—*Syn.* limit, border, brink, confines, terminal, terminus, termination, margin, verge, marge, marches, enclosure, bourn, bourne, frontier, edge, line, barrier, landmark, circumference. *Ant.* inside, interior, center, middle, beginning, area, surface.

brainwash, *v.—Syn.* condition, persuade, convince, coerce, cow, terrorize, bulldoze.

brave—*Syn.* fearless, gallant, heroic, valiant, bold, chivalrous, undaunted, courageous, venturesome, adventurous, dauntless, unafraid, undismayed, dashing, daring, chivalric, doughty, intrepid, stout, stout-hearted, manly, manful, hardy, firm, plucky. *Ant.* cowardly, shrinking, skulking, timid, timorous, fearful, despicable, cringing, contemptible, mean, low, base, fainthearted, frightened, afraid, shy, diffident, backward, retiring.

brave, *v.—Syn.* face, confront, challenge, defy, dare, oppose, object, reject, scorn, command, demand. *Ant.* slink, run, flee, renounce, give up, acknowledge, hide, dodge, skip, get out, crave, beg, beseech, implore, cringe, crouch, grovel, whine, complain, bemoan.

bravery—*Syn.* courage, intrepidity, fearlessness, temerity, valor, venturesomeness, recklessness, daring, audacity, spunk, rashness, boldness, gallantry, heroism, prowess, resolution, fortitude, spirit, enterprise, hardihood, firmness, daring, manliness, dauntlessness, mettle, pluck. *Ant.* cowardice, pusillanimity, timidity, spinelessness, fear, trepidation, tremor, agitation, emotion, weakness, apprehension, misgiving, awe, dismay, consternation, alarm, dread.

brawl, *n.—Syn.* fight, fracas, wrangle, affray, altercation, scrap, row, tumult, rumpus.

break—*Syn.* crack, smash, shatter, split, burst, crush, shiver, sever, fracture, rend, rive, rupture, demolish, destroy, batter, tear, curb, subdue, violate, infringe, separate. *Ant.* mend, unite, join, bind, weld, solder, attach, fasten, secure, adhere, agree, combine, conjoin, couple, associate.

breeze—*Syn.* blast, gale, wind, storm, bluster, tempest, tornado, hurricane, typhoon, whirlwind, cyclone, agitation, disturbance, riot, rage. *Ant.* calm, stillness, quiet, tranquillity, placidity, peace, peacefulness, rest, repose.

bright—*Syn.* brilliant, flashing, scintillating, lustrous, shining, gleaming, glowing, glaring, luminous, radiant, illuminated, illumined, sunny, shiny, glittering, glossy, sparkling, shimmering, beaming, effulgent, dazzling, incandescent, burning, refulgent, twinkling, cheerful, cheering, cheery, glorious, glistening. *Ant.* dark, gloomy, threatening, cloudy, shady, obscure, dull, murky, swart, swarthy, dusky, dim, black, opaque, sable, shadowy, dismal, sombre, melancholy, clouded, depressing, depressive, dreary, doleful, horrid, horrible, dire, direful, dreadful, mysterious, indistinct, overcast, lustreless, faded, tarnished.

brilliant, *adj.*—*Syn.* bright, luminous, glowing, scintillating, splendid, effulgent, shining, radiant, glorious, dazzling.

brim—*Syn.* edge, verge, rim, lip, border, top, brink, margin, line, outline. *Ant.* center, interior, foot, base, side, circumference, bottom.

bring—*Syn.* carry, fetch, bear, convey, adduce, induce, produce, import, infect, cause, attract, draw, conduct, move, transmit, sustain, transfer, transport, support. *Ant.* leave, relinquish, pass up, refuse, give up, abandon, back out, drop, desist, forego, quit, cease, stop, eschew, hold back, avoid, shun.

brittle—*Syn.* fragile, weak, delicate, thin, frail, frangible, breakable, tenuous, slender. *Ant.* strong, tough, unbreakable, resistible, rotten, decaying, crumbling, thick, unbendable, wiry, endurable, enduring.

broad—*Syn.* wide, large, extensive, ample, open, clear, comprehensive, liberal, open-minded, liberal-minded, coarse, gross, lewd. *Ant.* narrow, short, circumscribed, contracted, curtailed, abbreviated, illiberal, narrow-minded, conservative, close, tight-fisted, miserly, near, covetous, envious.

broken—*Syn.* smashed, separated, parted, severed, disunited, uneven, rough, rocky, unsettled, unfulfilled, violated, ruined, subdued, tamed, reduced, poverty-stricken, wretched, humbled, crushed. *Ant.* smooth, easy, pleasant, joined, united, staid,

steady, fulfilled, untamed, wild, unsubdued, exalted, honored, flourishing, happy, contented.

brutish—*Syn.* brutal, coarse, beastly, bestial, savage, barbarous, swinish, cruel, tyrannical, repulsive, repugnant, revolting, carnal, lascivious, lewd, unspiritual, vile, depraved, animal, ignorant, imbruted, sensual, unintellectual, stolid, sottish, disgusting. *Ant.* kind, considerate, humane, gentle, mild, manly, noble, enlightened, exalted, refined, elevated, intellectual, intelligent, spiritual, soulful, chaste, clean, highminded.

build—*Syn.* erect, construct, put up, raise, frame, found, establish, make, manufacture. *Ant.* destroy, pull down, demolish, raze, dismantle, overturn, overthrow, ruin.

building, *n.*—*Syn.* structure, construction, edifice, house.

burn—*Syn.* set on fire, incinerate, consume, cremate, ignite, flash, brand, char, singe, kindle, scorch, cauterize, blaze. *Ant.* cool, smother, subdue, put out, extinguish, stifle, conquer, overcome.

business—*Syn.* occupation, calling, profession, duty, work, transaction, trade, barter, avocation, craft, concern, vocation, trading, commerce, pursuit, job, art, handicraft, affair, matter, employment. *Ant.* idleness, laziness, sloth, slothfulness, passiveness, passivity, inertia, inertness, inactivity, non-employment.

bustle—*Syn.* hustle, hurry, quickness, activity, action, haste, flurry, fuss, tumult, agitation, stir. *Ant.* slowness, inertia, inaction, inactivity, laziness, languor, sloth, slothfulness, sluggishness, indolence.

but—*Syn.* except, save, notwithstanding, still, yet, unless, though, provided, moreover, barely, besides, that, and, however, only, merely, nevertheless, just, further, furthermore.

butcher—*Syn.* kill, slay, murder, hack, destroy, maim, massacre, slaughter, mangle, tear, slice, mutilate. *Ant.* preserve, guard, safeguard, watch, tend, care for, nourish, nurture, heal, cure, restore, repair, mend, patch up, revive, reanimate.

buy—*Syn.* purchase, procure, acquire, obtain, secure, negotiate, bribe, influence, corrupt, pervert. *Ant.* sell, dispose (of), transfer, part (with), give, vend, market, retail.

byword—*Syn.* saying, proverb, maxim, apothegm, adage, saw, aphorism, precept, nickname, laughingstock, oddity, joke.

C

cabal—*Syn.* faction, gang, combine, combination, push, junto, confederacy, conspiracy, conclave, crew, party, intrigue, plot, artifice, design.

cabalistic, *adj.*—*Syn.* occult, recondite, secret, obscure, mystical, dark, esoteric.

cajole, *v.*—*Syn.* coax, inveigle, blandish, wheedle, lure, beguile.

calamity—*Syn.* disaster, misfortune, mischance, mishap, distress, misery, woe, adversity, affliction, trouble, sorrow, grief, sadness, tribulation, trial. *Ant.* benefit, benediction, blessing, comfort, happiness, joy, rejoicing, kindness, advantage, profit, boon, favor.

calculate—*Syn.* reckon, estimate, enumerate, rate, cast, consider, deem, number, account, count, compute, appraise, value, sum up.

call—*Syn.* shout, exclaim, bellow, bawl, scream, yell, vociferate, roar, clamor, cry (out), utter, shriek, ejaculate, invite, command, demand, speak, address, proclaim, convoke, summon, name, term, denominate, designate, assemble, rally, invoke. *Ant.* hush, hark, hearken, list, listen, refrain, suppress, restrain, stifle, smother, conceal, be still.

calling, *n.*—*Syn.* occupation, vocation, business, profession, trade, craft, art. *Ant.* hobby, pastime, avocation, amusement.

callous—*Syn.* unfeeling, indifferent, careless, insensible, unsusceptible, obdurate, hard, hardened, indurated. *Ant.* feeling, compassionate, tender, soft, merciful, indulgent, clement, gracious, pitying, sympathetic.

calm—*Syn.* cool, collected, quiet, reserved, unruffled, undisturbed, serene, self-possessed, tranquil, placid, dispassionate, gentle, mild, bland, composed, imperturbable, sedate, smooth, peaceful, balmy, pacific, still. *Ant.* rough, ruffled, boisterous, excited, agitated, inflamed, angry, passionate, raging, fierce, furious, roused, violent, stormy, wild, unbridled, turbulent, frenzied, heated, frantic, distracted, infuriate, mad, raving, outrageous, terror-stricken.

calumny—*Syn.* slander, defamation, libel, detraction, backbiting, lying, falsehood, aspersion, foulness, distortion, evil-mindedness, uncharitableness, scandal, scandal-mongering. *Ant.* charity, charitableness, praise, laudation, eulogy, encomium, commendation, recommendation, goodwill, friendliness, benevolence, kindness, sympathy.

cancel—*Syn.* quash, annul, abolish, rescind, remove, erase, expunge, repeal, nullify, abrogate, revoke, void, obliterate, vacate, wipe out, rub off. *Ant.* approve, uphold, sustain, maintain, record, enforce, enact, confirm, establish, reënact, continue, countenance, ratify, keep, endorse, sanction, perpetuate.

candid—*Syn.* truthful, impartial, sincere, frank, fair, unbiased, unprejudiced, honest, open, simple, ingenuous, artless, guileless, naïve, just, straightforward, aboveboard. *Ant.* intriguing, artful, sly, shrewd, tricky, wily, designing, insincere, deceitful, cunning, foxy, diplomatic, maneuvering, subtle, sharp, adroit, crafty, knowing, dissembling, false, hypocritical.

candidate, *n.—Syn.* applicant, nominee, aspirant, office-seeker.

candor—*Syn.* frankness, sincerity, truthfulness, fairness, openness, impartiality, ingenuousness. *Ant.* deception, falsehood, double-dealing, partiality, unfairness, deceit, artifice, trick, trickery, fraud, imposition, guile, stratagem, ruse, finesse.

canon, *n.—Syn.* rule, standard, ordinance, law, regulation, formulary, precept, criterion, schedule, list.

capable—*Syn.* able, competent, qualified, fitted, suitable, adequate, equal, efficient, skilful, susceptible, impressive. *Ant.* incompetent, unqualified, unable, unskilful, disqualified, inefficient, unsuitable, unfit, incapable.

capacity, *n.—Syn.* volume, size, expanse, magnitude, amplitude, content; faculty, aptness, genius, ability, gift, skill.

caper, *n.—Syn.* gambol, prank, bound, antic, cut-up, dido, romp.

caprice—*Syn.* freak, fancy, crotchet, vagary, whim, conceit, humor, inclination, emotion. *Ant.* steadiness, thoroughness, dependability, firmness, purpose, constancy, consistency.

capricious, *adj.—Syn.* fanciful, odd, changeable, crotchety, whimsical, freakish, fickle, wayward, idiosyncratic, vacillating. *Ant.* staid, steadfast, stanch, constant.

captain, *n.—Syn.* chief, leader, headman, head, master, skipper, commander, foreman.

captious—*Syn.* fretful, cross, peevish, petulant, splenetic, caviling, fault-finding, censorious, touchy, testy, irritable, critical, hypercritical, hypersensitive, cynical, carping. *Ant.* fair, considerate, appreciative, approving, encouraging, flattering, eulogistic, commendatory, complimentary, laudatory, good-natured, easy-going, thoughtful, reasonable.

captivate—*Syn.* enchant, charm, bewitch, enthral, fascinate, entrance, enslave, capture, subdue, overpower. *Ant.* hate, despise, loathe, disillusion, disgust, offend, displease.

captivity—*Syn.* confinement, bondage, servitude, slavery, enthralment, imprisonment, subjection. *Ant.* freedom, liberty, independence, liberality, license, unrestrictedness.

capture, *v.—Syn.* take, grasp, catch, seize, arrest, apprehend, trap, snare.

cardinal, *adj.—Syn.* principal, fundamental, leading, chief, capital, main, central, essential, vital, necessary. *Ant.* minor, lesser, negligible, insignificant.

care—*Syn.* concern, attention, heed, solicitude, anxiety, forethought, watchfulness, wariness, perplexity, precaution, prudence, oversight, caution, vigilance, trouble, worry, management, charge, bother, circumspection. *Ant.* carelessness, negligence, neglect, disregard, heedlessness, omission, oversight, slight, remissness, indifference, inattention.

career—*Syn.* life, progress, course, way, rush, pursuit, walk, line, experience, sphere, business, occupation, vocation, profession, calling. *Ant.* inactivity, idleness, torpor, inaction, inertia, sloth, stupor, ergophobia, indolence, otiosity, lethargy, oscitancy, sluggishness, statuvolence.

careful, *adj.—Syn.* cautious, attentive, meticulous, vigilant, watchful, wary, prudent, mindful, scrupulous.

careless—*Syn.* heedless, inattentive, negligent, thoughtless, unmindful, unconcerned, untidy, incautious, imprudent, improvident, unconsidered. *Ant.* careful, mindful, attentive, active, sharp, keen, ready, thoughtful, anxious, circumspect, prudent, cautious, concerned.

caress—*Syn.* pet, pamper, fondle, embrace, cuddle, court, flatter, kiss, salute, hug. *Ant.* spurn, neglect, forsake, abandon, buffet, beat, strike, lash, scourge, insult, provoke, irritate, exasperate, annoy, displease, aggravate, tease, vex, wound.

caricature—*Syn.* exaggeration, parody, travesty, extravaganza, imitation, copy, misrepresentation, burlesque, mimicry, farce, ridicule. *Ant.* truth, fact, reality, exactitude, exactness, accuracy, precision, naturalness.

carnage—*Syn.* slaughter, massacre, butchery, destruction, havoc, blood, bloodiness.

carnal, *adj.*—*Syn.* earthy, fleshly, lascivious, concupiscent, vulgar, sensual, lustful, animal, physical. *Ant.* spiritual, ethereal, chaste, intellectual.

carnival—*Syn.* festivity, feasting, carouse, carousal, revel, masquerade, merrymaking, jollification, rout.

carousal—*Syn.* revel, revelry, saturnalia, drinking-bout, orgy, wassail, spree, jollification, debauch, carnival. *Ant.* austerity, sobriety, privation, temperance, abstinence, fast, abstemiousness.

carping, *adj.*—*Syn.* caviling, hypercritical, faultfinding, captious, disparaging, pedantic.

carriage—*Syn.* walk, mien, pace, gait, manner, deportment, demeanor, behavior, bearing.

carry—*Syn.* transport, bear, convey, take, move, remove, transmit, bring, lift, sustain, support. *Ant.* throw off, throw down, cast off, cast aside, shake off, fall under, give up, let go.

cartel, *n.*—*Syn.* monopoly, syndicate, pool, trust, combination.

case, *n.*—*Syn.* instance, occurrence, contingency, situation, example, event, circumstance, subject, condition.

cast, *v.*—*Syn.* throw, pitch, shy, hurl, heave, fling, direct, propel, toss, chuck, sling.

caste—*Syn.* rank, class, race, blood, lineage, order, descent, ancestry.

casual, *adj.*—*Syn.* haphazard, contingent, fortuitous, careless, cursory, accidental, chance, heedless, random, negligent, inci-

dental. *Ant.* deliberate, planned, premeditated, formal.

cataclysm, *n.*—*Syn.* catastrophe, flood, upheaval, disaster, convulsion, calamity, misfortune.

catastrophe—*Syn.* calamity, misfortune, misadventure, disaster, mischance, mishap, misery, revolution, blow, visitation, affliction, denouement, cataclysm, reverse. *Ant.* blessing, benefit, benediction, favor, prosperity, comfort, success, privilege, boon, pleasure, happiness.

catch—*Syn.* grasp, clasp, capture, seize, snatch, take, grip, clutch, secure, apprehend, comprehend, entrap, ensnare, discover, overtake. *Ant.* lose, miss, give up, let go, fail, restore, release, cast aside, throw away.

category, *n.*—*Syn.* class, heading, concept, grade, group, division, rank, form, genus, order, denomination.

catharsis, *n.*—*Syn.* purification, purge, elimination, cleansing, lustration.

cause—*Syn.* agent, source, origin, spring, fountain, causation, antecedent, author, designer, originator, object, purpose, reason, inducement, incitement, condition, power, precedent, motive, occasion. *Ant.* effect, result, outcome, development, consequence, end, fruit, fruition, issue, product, outgrowth.

caution—*Syn.* care, heed, vigilance, prudence, watchfulness, circumspection, admonition, warning, forethought, reason, injunction, precept, advice, exhortation, provision (against), notice. *Ant.* neglect, negligence, heedlessness, imprudence, carelessness, thoughtlessness, remissness, rashness, indiscretion.

cautious—*Syn.* wary, watchful, circumspect, careful, prudent, attentive, discreet, thoughtful, calculating. *Ant.* incautious, impetuous, rash, headstrong, unthinking, hasty, heedless, unwary, regardless, unobserving, unobservant, inattentive, absentminded.

cavity—*Syn.* hollow, hole, cavern, ravine, depth, cave, depression, excavation, chasm, concavity, opening, orifice, crater, fissure, cleft, breach, slit, notch, tube, tunnel, burrow, bore, aperture, gap, indentation, perforation, dent, defile, dell, vale, valley, gorge, mine, shaft, hollowness. *Ant.* mound, hill, hillock, eminence, peak, knoll, height, prominence, projection, rising, elevation, protuberance, swelling, tumulus, heap, mountain, rampart, convexity.

cease—*Syn.* stop, quit, terminate, finish, end, conclude, refrain, desist, discontinue, withdraw, give over, intermit, pause, leave off. *Ant.* begin, start, commence, initiate, institute, inaugurate, originate, set on foot, set about, set going, enter upon, continue.

cede, *v.*—*Syn.* yield, relinquish, surrender, grant, accord, deliver, assign, transfer, convey.

celebrate—*Syn.* keep, observe, commemorate, solemnize, praise, extol, glorify, honor. *Ant.* forget, overlook, neglect, disregard, ignore, dishonor, violate, profane, contemn, despise.

celebration—*Syn.* commemoration, observance, glorification, jollification, merrymaking, festivity, gaiety, frolic, hilarity, joviality, merriment, mirth. *Ant.* sadness, solemnity, sorrow, grief, mourning, lamentation, wailing, bewailing, melancholy, depression.

celebrity—*Syn.* fame, honor, glory, renown, eminence, notoriety, notability, distinction, reputation, credit, rank, class. *Ant.* dishonor, discredit, obloquy, shame, scandal, ignominy, opprobrium, censure, disrespect, disgrace, blemish, infamy.

celerity, *n.*—*Syn.* speed, swiftness, alacrity, haste, quickness, rapidity.

celestial, *adj.*—*Syn.* heavenly, unearthly, empyrean, holy, divine, ethereal, angelic, supernal. *Ant.* hellish, infernal, mortal, earthly.

censorious—*Syn.* fault-finding, critical, hypercritical, captious, severe, carping, caviling, nagging, scolding, contemning, condemning, censuring. *Ant.* praising, lauding, laudatory, flattering, encouraging, endorsing, confirming, approving, sanctioning.

censure, *n.*—*Syn.* criticism, reproach, reprimand, blame, reprehension, contumely, invective, slur, accusation, rebuke, remonstrance, stricture, reproof, condemnation. *Ant.* praise, laudation, approval, commendation, recommendation, endorsement, approbation, sanction, confirmation, ratification.

censure, *v.*—*Syn.* criticize, judge, blame, reprove, reprimand, reprehend, reproach, upbraid, scold, denounce, condemn. *Ant.* praise, laud, approve, justify, commend, sanction, encourage, support, promote, admire, ratify, confirm.

center, *n.*—*Syn.* midpoint, focus, nucleus, heart, core, middle, hub, axis.

ceremony, *n.*—*Syn.* rite, ritual, form, solemnity, protocol, formality, observance.

certain—*Syn.* sure, unquestionable, indubitable, incontrovertible, indisputable, undeniable, unfailing, secure, reliable, infallible, real, true, genuine, undoubted. *Ant.* uncertain, unreliable, wavering, faltering, doubtful, dubious, equivocal, questionable, ambiguous, vague, obscure.

certify—*Syn.* declare, testify, assure, inform, demonstrate, attest, prove, avouch, vouch, aver, acknowledge, state, proclaim. *Ant.* deny, deprecate, repudiate, censure, disown, discredit, reject, negative, contradict, counteract.

cessation—*Syn.* intermission, rest, stop, pause, discontinuance, halt, armistice. *Ant.* continuance, prolongation, advancement, extension, persistence, perpetuation.

chagrin—*Syn.* vexation, mortification, shame, obloquy, humiliation, dismay, disappointment, confusion, discomposure, peevishness, fretfulness. *Ant.* delight, triumph, glorification, glory, rapture, exultation, rejoicing, gladness.

chain, *n.—Syn.* series, concatenation, succession, row, sequence, progression, string, course, set.

champion, *n.—Syn.* supporter, promoter, advocate, defender, upholder, partisan, protector, sustainer.

chance—*Syn.* fate, fortune, fortuity, hazard, risk, casualty, luck, random, accident, venture. *Ant.* design, certainty, intention, aim, purpose, plan, scheme, assurance, stability, fixedness.

change, *n.—Syn.* alteration, mutation, variation, variety, innovation, novelty, transformation, transmutation, transmogrification, modification, transition, vicissitude, deviation, revolution, reverse, regeneration, renewal, conversion. *Ant.* firmness, fixedness, permanency, constancy, steadiness, steadfastness, stableness, stability, changelessness, unchangeableness, certainty, duration, durableness, durability, lastingness.

change, *v.—Syn.* barter, exchange, substitute, vary, alter, turn, veer, shift, diversify, innovate, transmute, transmogrify, modify, transfigure, metamorphose, convert, commute, transform. *Ant.* hold, keep, stay, remain, retain, continue, persevere, advance, proceed, last, wait, tarry, abide, bide, persist, dwell.

changeable—*Syn.* fickle, inconstant, mutable, variable, uncertain, unstable, unsteady, wavering, whimsical, irresolute, vacillating, capricious, fitful, volatile, fluctuating, doubtful, unsettled. *Ant.* steady, stable, immovable, permanent, constant, continuing, fixed, firm, uniform, consistent, regular, undeviating, durable, abiding, lasting, irremovable, changeless.

chaos, *n.—Syn.* confusion, disorder, snarl, shambles, disorganiza-

tion. *Ant.* harmony, order, system, method.

character—*Syn.* personality, disposition, reputation, constitution, temper, temperament, nature, spirit, genius, repute, estimation, record, standing, species, symbol, mark, letter, type.

characteristic—*Syn.* personality, peculiarity, singularity, diagnosis, distinction, individuality, manners, bearing, attitude, specialty, idiosyncrasy, trait, mark, attribute, feature, property, quality, sign, trace, mark, indication, character.

charge, *v.—Syn.* accuse, indict, ascribe, score, tax, impute, blame, arraign, inculpate, condemn.

charity, *n.—Syn.* beneficence, philanthropy, benefaction, alms, giving, good will, altruism, generosity, bounty.

charlatan, *n.—Syn.* mountebank, impostor, quack, fraud, cheat, faker, humbug, pretender.

charm—*Syn.* captivate, enchant, enrapture, fascinate, attract, bewitch, allure, delight, please, control, move. *Ant.* frighten, terrify, repulse, repel, disgust, displease, offend, anger, provoke, rouse, irritate, inflame, enrage.

charming—*Syn.* entrancing, bewitching, captivating, fascinating, enchanting, enrapturing, delightful, winning, ravishing, irresistible, attractive, alluring, pleasing. *Ant.* disgusting, repellent, repugnant, revolting, hateful, horrid, horrible, forbidding, deterrent, awful, abominable, shocking, offensive, unpleasant, disagreeable, foul, loathsome, abhorrent, detestable.

chart, *n.—Syn.* map, project, plot, plan, design, graph.

chary, *adj.—Syn.* wary, careful, circumspect, cautious, prudent, hesitant, shy.

chase, *v.—Syn.* pursue, hound, seek, hunt, trail, track, tail, shadow.

chaste—*Syn.* pure, virtuous, modest, simple, innocent, incorrupt, immaculate, unstained, uncontaminated, undefiled, unaffected, uncorrupted, unsullied, unblemished, unspotted, guileless. *Ant.* unchaste, lewd, lascivious, libidinous, wanton, lustful, corrupt, defiled, sullied, licentious, dissolute, debauched, profligate, voluptuous, lecherous.

chasten—*Syn.* humble, humiliate, subdue, chastise, punish, castigate, correct, try, soften, purify, refine, afflict, discipline. (Note:—*Chasten* is applied only when the significance is moral or spiritual—"As many as I love, I rebuke and *chasten*." Rev. 3:19.) *Ant.* encourage, uplift, benefit, help, assist, embolden, incite, inspirit, animate, cheer, stimulate, urge, impel, promote, succor, comfort.

chastise—*Syn.* punish, reprove, chasten, correct, discipline, reprimand, reprehend, castigate, whip, afflict. *Ant.* See those under *chasten* above.

chastity—*Syn.* purity, continence, virtue, innocence, sinlessness, uprightness, integrity, cleanness, goodness, morality, chasteness. *Ant.* lewdness, lechery, fornication, adultery, licentiousness, lust, incest, uncleanness, unchastity.

cheap—*Syn.* inexpensive, inferior, common, low, low-priced, mean, worthless, petty, shabby, valueless, despicable, contemptible. *Ant.* dear, costly, valuable, expensive, priceless, worthy, precious, inestimable.

cheat, *v.*—*Syn.* deceive, gull, victimize, hoodwink, swindle, beguile, defraud, dupe, fool, cozen.

check—*Syn.* curb, bridle, repress, hinder, impede, counteract, restrain, moderate, inhibit, control, checkmate, obstruct, reduce, slacken, stay, stop. *Ant.* abet, aid, assist, help, encourage, expedite, accelerate, allow, urge (on), speed, quicken, loose, loosen, indulge, instigate, license, liberate, hurry, hasten.

cheer—*Syn.* conviviality, jollity, merriment, festivity, gaiety, mirth, hospitality, comfort, plenty, happiness, hope, animation, vivacity, buoyancy, airiness, liveliness, sprightliness, fun, frolic, hilarity. *Ant.* dulness or dullness, melancholy, gloom, sadness, depression, dejection, heaviness, seriousness, gravity.

cheerful—*Syn.* gay, merry, sprightly, buoyant, spirited, joyous, bonny, bright, lively, happy, joyful, gladsome, blithe, sunny, enlivening. *Ant.* dull, weary, stupid, dolorous, unhappy, sad, dejected, gloomy, melancholy, mournful, sorrowful, cast-down, heavy, heavy-hearted, morose.

cheerfulness—*Syn.* jollity, liveliness, sprightliness, gaiety, merriment, merriness, mirthfulness, vivacity, blithesomeness, gladness, happiness. *Ant.* dulness, care, anxiety, sorrow, trouble, discontent, melancholy, dejectedness, weariness, languor, heaviness, dreariness, gloom, gloominess, sadness, the blues.

cherish—*Syn.* indulge, nourish, nurse, nurture, foster, encourage, treasure, shelter, harbor, entertain, comfort, cheer, protect, value, cling to, hold dear. *Ant.* abandon, renounce, relinquish, desert, forsake, repudiate, give up, cast off, leave, denounce, scold, upbraid, nag, discourage.

chicanery, *n.*—*Syn.* double-dealing, duplicity, intrigue, fraud, deception, subterfuge, trickery, machination.

chide, *v.*—*Syn.* scold, rebuke, upbraid, reproach, reprove, censure, reprimand, admonish, berate.

chief—*Syn.* principal, leader, chieftain, head, ruler, king, captain, commander, prince, master, sachem, sagamore. *Ant.* subordinate, retainer, servant, minion, vassal, satellite, underling, follower, attendant, subaltern, adherent.

chief, *adj.*—*Syn.* supreme, principal, leading, prime, capital, cardinal, first, main, paramount, essential, predominant, pre-eminent.

childish—*Syn.* childlike, simple,

silly, foolish, infantile, infantine, absurd, ignorant, imbecile, paltry, petty, puerile, ridiculous, ludicrous. *Ant.* wise, witty, pertinent, apropos, opportune, seasonable, well-timed, timely, apposite, relevant, appropriate, proper, fitting, suitable.

chippy, *n.*—*Syn.* prostitute, whore, pick-up, bar girl, V-girl, B-girl, broad, bat, babe, chick, quail.

chiseler, *n.*—*Syn.* parasite, moocher, leech, beggar, toady, sponger, stooge, sycophant, schnorrer.

chivalrous—*Syn.* heroic, valiant, courageous, knightly, gallant, spirited, high-minded, brave, generous, valorous, intrepid, puissant. *Ant.* cowardly, fearful, terror-stricken, timid, timorous, afraid, base, mean, contemptible, petty, shy, faint-hearted, diffident, unmanly, frightened, alarmed, apprehensive, craven, pusillanimous.

choleric, *adj.*—*Syn.* angry, testy, splenetic, petulant, irascible, fiery, cross, cranky, wrathful. *Ant.* calm, placid, cool, nonchalant.

choose—*Syn.* pick, select, cull, prefer, elect, adopt, collect, separate, remove, arrange. *Ant.* discard, reject, refuse, dismiss, repudiate, · disclaim, decline, leave, cast away, cast out, throw aside.

chronic, *adj.*—*Syn.* persistent, settled, inveterate, confirmed, rooted, established, constant.

churl, *n.*—*Syn.* boor, rustic, clodhopper, bumpkin, curmudgeon, villain. *Ant.* gentleman, aristocrat, patrician.

circle, *n.*—*Syn.* coterie, clique, society, set, class, companions.

circumference, *n.*—*Syn.* perimeter, periphery, ambit, compass, bounds, boundary, girth, border.

circumlocution — *Syn.* prolixity, verbiage, redundance, redundancy, pleonasm, diffuseness, tautology, surplus, surplusage, verbosity, wordiness, periphrasis, tediousness. *Ant.* conciseness, plainness, terseness, condensation, compactness, compression,

directness, shortness, brevity, succinctness.

circumspect, *adj.*—*Syn.* careful, judicious, discreet, heedful, wary, vigilant, prudent, observant, cautious. *Ant.* audacious, bold, careless, foolhardy.

circumstance—*Syn.* fact, incident, occurrence, situation, accompaniment, event, item, detail, point, position, concomitant, particular.

circumvent, *v.*—*Syn.* thwart, balk, foil, check, prevent, frustrate, outwit, forestall.

cite—*Syn.* call, name, summon, quote, mention, adduce, arraign, convoke, invite, notify, warn. *Ant.* hush, ignore, neglect, disregard, pass by, be silent.

civil, *adj.*—*Syn.* polite, courteous, refined, gracious, urbane, affable, mannerly, suave, debonair, gallant. *Ant.* rude, churlish, boorish, ill-mannered.

claim, *v.*—*Syn.* maintain, contend, assert, allege, affirm, advance, demand, require, ask, exact.

clandestine, *adj.*—*Syn.* secret, furtive, covert, hidden, private, concealed, stealthy, surreptitious. *Ant.* open, forthright, clear, aboveboard.

clash, *v.*—*Syn.* conflict, differ, collide, quarrel, disagree, contend, dispute.

class—*Syn.* degree, order, rank, standing, grade, caste, coterie, clique, set, circle, clan, genus, division, category, kind, group, association, club, company.

clean—*Syn.* pure, unmixed, unadulterated, purified, cleansed, spotless, stainless, untarnished. *Ant.* dirty, filthy, adulterated, impure, mixed, foul, defiled, besmirched, tarnished, spotted, stained.

cleanse—*Syn.* clean, purify, disinfect, wash, scrub, rinse, wipe, sweep, dust, lave, mop, brush, sponge, scour, purge. *Ant.* soil, sully, defile, pollute, taint, stain, bespatter, besmirch, besmear, befoul, debase, corrupt, deprave, vitiate, contaminate, spoil.

clear—*Syn.* bright, vivid, lucid, sunny, pure, transparent, apparent, pellucid, limpid, translucent, perspicuous, plain, unmistakable, unequivocal, manifest, obvious, evident, free, guiltless, distinct, explicit, definite, straightforward. *Ant*. opaque, dark, obscure, shaded, shadowed, shadowy, muddy, dim, gloomy, mysterious, cloudy, ambiguous, unintelligible, vague, foggy, indistinct, turbid.

clever—*Syn*. able, skilful, expert, adroit, apt, dexterous, bright, capable, smart, talented, knowing, ingenious, sharp, intelligent, intellectual, keen, quick, quick-witted. *Ant*. dull, stupid, slow, thick-witted, thick-headed, perverse, idiotic, imbecile, bungling, clumsy, awkward, clownish, senseless, witless, foolish, ignorant.

climax, *n*.—*Syn*. culmination, apex, acme, summit, peak, vertex, zenith.

cling, *v*.—*Syn*. adhere, grasp, embrace, cleave, stick, persist.

clog, *v*.—*Syn*. jam, choke, stop, block, impede, encumber, obstruct, hamper, congest.

cloister—*Syn*. monastery, priory, convent, nunnery, abbey, seclusion, retirement, isolation, meditation, solitude.

close, *adj*.—*Syn*. near, intimate, adjoining, immediate, neighboring, adjacent, contiguous, attached.

clothes—*Syn*. raiment, clothing, garments, garb, vesture, dress, attire, array, apparel, habiliments, *tout ensemble*.

clumsy, *adj*.—*Syn*. awkward, cumbersome, maladroit, ponderous, heavy, unwieldy, bungling, incompetent, inept. *Ant*. dexterous, adroit, facile, clever.

coalition—*Syn*. combination, alliance, confederacy, conspiracy, league, union, treaty, compact. *Ant*. separation, disagreement, difference, contrariety, divergence, variation, contention, dispute, bickering.

coarse, *adj*.—*Syn*. rough, gross, indelicate, unrefined, vulgar, unpolished, crude, inelegant, harsh,

rude, bawdy, impure. *Ant*. delicate, fine, dainty, choice.

coax—*Syn*. wheedle, flatter, soothe, appeal, persuade, cajole, invite, inveigle, entice, fawn. *Ant*. scoff, scorn, gibe, jeer, sneer, deride, ridicule, mock, reproach, banter, taunt, tantalize, delude, fool, flout, insult.

cogent, *adj*.—*Syn*. convincing, powerful, potent, valid, forcible, urgent, effective, persuasive, strong.

cohesion, *n*.—*Syn*. consolidation, concretion, coagulation, cementing, conglomeration, coherence, integration.

cold—*Syn*. frigid, wintry, cool, frosty, bleak, chilly, shivering, shivery, indifferent, unconcerned, stoical, reserved, distant, unfeeling, forbidding, passionless, apathetic, spiritless, lifeless. *Ant*. warm, glowing, fiery, ardent, genial, hot, thermal, fervid, enthusiastic, zealous, eager, interested, animated, affectionate, excited, irascible.

collateral, *adj*.—*Syn*. subordinate, concurrent, secondary, related, dependent, allied.

colleague—*Syn*. partner, associate, collaborator, companion, coadjutor, ally, contributor, confederate. *Ant*. opponent, opposer, antagonist, foe, foeman, enemy, detractor, backbiter, calumniator.

collect—*Syn*. receive, obtain, get, gather, accumulate, assemble, amass, convoke, congregate, convene, muster, aggregate, summon, reap, gain. *Ant*. scatter, disperse, dissipate, strew, cast away, throw away, break up, divide, spread, disseminate, dispel, distribute, dispense, apportion, allot, partition, share, assign.

collision—*Syn*. impact, clash, contact, shock, encounter, meeting, concussion, clashing, conflict. *Ant*. concurrence, concord, agreement, harmony, conformity, amity, union, unison, unity, concert, coincidence.

color, *n*.—*Syn*. dye, stain, tint,

tinge, pigment, paint, hue, shade, tincture, kind, sort, variety, character, species.

color, v.—*Syn*. paint, tinge, tint, stain, dye, flush, blush, redden.

colossal, *adj*.—*Syn*. huge, immense, mammoth, vast, enormous, gigantic, tremendous, prodigious. *Ant*. tiny, wee, peewee, miniature.

combination—*Syn*. union, association, concurrence, alliance, league, confederacy, cabal, conspiracy, plot, party, faction. *Ant*. disunion, separation, division, severance, detachment, partition, sunderance, disjunction, dissolution.

come, v.—*Syn*. arrive, attain, reach, near, advance, proceed.

comely—*Syn*. handsome, pretty, seemly, pleasing, graceful, prepossessing, agreeable, beautiful, nice. *Ant*. ugly, repulsive, offensive, marred, scarred, plain, coarse, forbidding, unattractive, deterrent, disagreeable, uninviting, revolting, repellent.

comfort—*Syn*. consolation, solace, encouragement, support, help, aid, assistance, succor, alleviation, relief, assuagement, cheer, condolence. *Ant*. aggravation, annoyance, trouble, sorrow, grief, irritation, provocation, exasperation, exacerbation, harshness.

comfortable — *Syn*. cheerful, cheery, genial, pleasant, satisfied, satisfactory, contented, snug, well-off, well-to-do, warm, commodious, convenient, agreeable, cozy, sheltered, protected, cared (for). *Ant*. uncomfortable, miserable, unhappy, discontented, neglected, forsaken, abandoned, abject, forlorn, pitiable, wretched, disconsolate, sorrowful, dejected, melancholy, sad, cheerless, destitute, hopeless.

comic, *adj*.—*Syn*. funny, diverting, humorous, ludicrous, farcical, droll, amusing, witty. *Ant*. tragic, pathetic, solemn, sober.

command—*Syn*. injunction, order, precept, sway, mandate, control, power, authority, requisition,

charge, behest. *Ant*. countermand, revocation, contradiction, opposition, recall, reversal.

commence, v.—*Syn*. begin, initiate, start, inaugurate, found, institute, establish, introduce, cause, originate.

commend, v.—*Syn*. praise, recommend, laud, extol, cite, approve.

comment, n.—*Syn*. remark, observation, note, explanation, interpretation, exposition, gloss.

commerce, n.—*Syn*. trade, business, industry, intercourse, traffic.

commit—*Syn*. trust, entrust, confide, relegate, delegate, promise, assign, consign, intrust, do, enact, perpetrate, act, transact, perform, discharge. *Ant*. desist, stop, cease, wait, keep from, be inactive, stand still, rest, idle, loaf.

commodious—*Syn*. suitable, comfortable, fit, appropriate, useful, advantageous, expedient, roomy, convenient, accommodating. *Ant*. unsuitable, uncomfortable, unfavorable, inconvenient, disadvantageous, cramped, confined, narrow.

commodity—*Syn*. goods, articles, merchandise, wares, stock, materials, possessions, property, chattels, assets, belongings, thing, things.

common—*Syn*. ordinary, habitual, customary, usual, frequent, low, mean, vulgar, depraved, lewd. *Ant*. rare, unusual, scarce, peculiar, infrequent, superior, valuable, refined, cultured, uncommon, extraordinary, virtuous, high, high-minded, excellent, noble, aristocratic.

commotion—*Syn*. excitement, agitation, perturbation, tumult, turmoil, disturbance, emotion. *Ant*. calm, calmness, quietness, peace, tranquillity, placidity, stillness, rest, repose.

communicate—*Syn*. write, convey, impart, promulgate, announce, tell, state, publish, divulge, disclose, reveal, enlighten, make known. *Ant*. conceal, suppress, withhold, keep back, screen, cloak, cover, bottle up, reserve, hold one's tongue.

communion—*Syn.* fellowship, intercourse, agreement, concord, converse, union, brotherhood, harmony, friendship, association, relationship, bond, accordance. *Ant.* separation, division, antagonism, enmity, disunion, discord, disagreement, contention, variance.

compact, *adj.*—*Syn.* dense, snug, thick, solid, close, pressed, packed, condensed, concentrated. *Ant.* loose, diffuse, slack, thin.

companion—*Syn.* associate, friend, pal, buddy, comrade, consort, mate, fellow, follower. *Ant.* stranger, antagonist, enemy, opponent, alien, foreigner, outsider.

company—*Syn.* assembly, assemblage, party, partnership, meeting, throng, gathering, congregation, convention, multitude, band, conclave, conference, crowd, collection, concourse, convocation, group, host. *Ant.* loneliness, retirement, seclusion, solitude, privacy, dispersion, diffusion, dissemination, distribution.

compare, *v.*—*Syn.* contrast, test, balance, liken, match.

compassion—*Syn.* sympathy, pity, clemency, kindness, commiseration, tenderness, fellow-feeling. *Ant.* cruelty, severity, hatred, malignity, injustice, persecution, tyranny.

compel—*Syn.* force, enforce, coerce, necessitate, oblige, constrain, drive, make, influence. *Ant.* balk, bar, hamper, thwart, resist, retard, prevent, baffle, impede, interrupt, obstruct, block, check, stay, stop, frustrate, counteract, embarrass, deter, delay, clog, postpone, prolong, oppose, encumber, defer, foil.

compensation — *Syn.* remuneration, recompense, indemnity, satisfaction, requital, amends, reciprocity, set-off, reward, return, emolument, advantage, profit, benefit, gain. *Ant.* loss, deprivation, forfeiture, confiscation, sequestration, amercement, damage, penalty, fine.

competent, *adj.*—*Syn.* able, capable, proficient, efficient, sufficient, adequate.

complacent, *adj.*—*Syn.* contented, satisfied, smug, assured, conceited, stuffy.

complain—*Syn.* lament, murmur, regret, repine, remonstrate, growl, grumble, grunt, croak, grieve, bemoan, bewail, deplore. *Ant.* praise, laud, eulogize, commend, approve, sanction, applaud, recommend, confirm, authorize, allow, countenance, be glad.

complete, *adj.*—*Syn.* full, replete, entire, total, whole, plenary, perfect. *Ant.* incomplete, lacking, missing, defective, deficient, short, wanting, imperfect, unfinished.

complete, *v.*—*Syn.* execute, consummate, accomplish, terminate, finish, conclude, end, effect, realize, achieve. *Ant.* leave, halt, cease, forsake, abandon, neglect, ignore, forget, withdraw, give up.

complex—*Syn.* involved, entangled, abstruse, obscure, complicated, intricate, confused, composite, tangled, mixed, mingled, heterogeneous, conglomerate, manifold, multiform, compound, twisted. *Ant.* easy, simple, plain, clear, obvious, direct, unraveled, uniform, homogeneous, evident, manageable, manifest, indisputable, palpable, apparent, incontrovertible, discernible.

compliment—*Syn.* congratulate, flatter, felicitate, laud, praise, sanction, endorse, confirm, please, gratify, soothe, adulate. *Ant.* disparage, contemn, reflect (upon), minimize, lessen, lower, criticize, censure, blame, decry, denounce, stigmatize, reprehend, reproach, upbraid.

comply—*Syn.* accede, conform, submit, yield, concur, agree, assent, coincide, approve, acquiesce, consent. *Ant.* refuse, reject, repel, rebuff, decline, deny, disavow, disclaim, spurn, repudiate.

compose—*Syn.* form, make, fashion, formulate, write, arrange, construct, constitute, draw up, allay, smooth, soften, pacify, quiet, comfort. *Ant.* break, scatter, unmake, destroy, ruin, annul, disarrange, disperse, agitate, anger, rouse, taunt, tempt, excite, arouse, annoy, disturb, discompose.

compound, *adj.*—*Syn.* complex, mixed, combined, composite, complicated, heterogeneous, conglomerate. *Ant.* simple, elemental, unmixed, uncompounded, pure, plain, absolute, single.

comprehend—*Syn.* comprise, include, embrace, grasp, understand, perceive, encompass, contain, involve, apprehend, conceive, discern, grasp, embody, imagine. *Ant.* exclude, misunderstand, mistake, misapprehend, err, blunder, misinterpret, misconceive, miscalculate, trip, stumble.

comprise—*Syn.* comprehend, contain, embrace, include, imply, involve, inclose, encircle. *Ant.* lack, want, fail, fall short, exclude, except, reject, shut out.

compromise—*Syn.* adjustment, arrangement, settlement, conciliation, arbitration, agreement, concession, composition, compound, accommodation. *Ant.* disagreement, altercation, strife, dispute, disputation, quarrel, dissension, wrangle, wrangling, discussion, controversy, contention, contest, battle, war.

compulsion—*Syn.* constraint, restraint, force, coercion, obligation, urgency, necessity, violence. *Ant.* freedom, liberty, freewill, independence, license, supplication, entreaty, petition, craving, solicitation, appeal.

conceal—*Syn.* hide, secrete, screen, cover, bury, disguise, mask, dissemble, protect, seal, camouflage. *Ant.* uncover, open, lay bare, reveal, expose, strip, show, disclose, discover, unveil, divulge, impart, betray.

concede—*Syn.* assent, yield, permit, grant, allow, acquiesce, suffer, surrender, admit, acknowledge, own. *Ant.* deny, refuse, disallow, dissent, disagree, differ, dispute, turn down, contradict, repudiate, protest, reject.

conceit, *n.*—*Syn.* egotism, egoism, vanity, self-esteem, pride. *Ant.* humility, modesty, meekness, diffidence.

concise, *adj.*—*Syn.* compact, short, terse, crisp, pithy, pointed, brief, succinct, laconic, sententious, condensed. *Ant.* diffuse, redundant, repetitive, wordy.

conclusion—*Syn.* determination, inference, result, end, consequence, deduction, decision, disposal, resolution, opinion. *Ant.* preface, beginning, prelude, preamble, introduction, origin, genesis, start, commencement.

concrete, *adj.*—*Syn.* tangible, solid, particular, firm, specific, real, material, definite. *Ant.* abstract, ideal, immaterial, intangible.

concur—*Syn.* agree, join, unite, approve, endorse, certify, combine, meet, conjoin, approve, coincide. *Ant.* disagree, differ, dispute, argue, disapprove, dissent, object, oppose, reject.

condemn—*Syn.* convict, doom, denounce, censure, blame, reprove, reprobate, sentence. *Ant.* approve, praise, justify, exonerate, laud, applaud, absolve, pardon, acquit, free, release, discharge, forgive, clear, set free.

condign—*Syn.* adequate, deserved, suitable, meet, justifiable, justified, just, fit, appropriate, exemplary, merited, rigorous, severe. *Ant.* undeserved, unsuitable, inadequate, inappropriate, unjustified, unjust, gentle, mild, lenient, trivial, petty, moderate, scant, scanty, slight, trifling.

condone, *v.*—*Syn.* forgive, remit, absolve, overlook, disregard, pardon, excuse.

conduct, *v.*—*Syn.* direct, guide, lead, govern, regulate, manage, behave, act. *Ant.* desert, abandon, forsake, resign, refuse, leave, quit, relinquish, forswear, abjure, discontinue, retire (from), renounce, forego.

conduct, *n.—Syn.* behavior, deportment, demeanor, management, guidance, regulation, manners, air, bearing, attitude, government.

confederate, *n.—Syn.* ally, accomplice, partner, associate, accessory, colleague, supporter.

confess—*Syn.* concede, disclose, acknowledge, admit, allow, certify, endorse, recognize, grant, accept, own, avow. *Ant.* dissemble, dissimulate, mask, hide, screen, conceal, cover, cloak, deny, repudiate, disavow, disguise, secrete, veil, disown.

confident, *adj.—Syn.* sure, sanguine, positive, dauntless, assured, bold, certain. *Ant.* dubious, despondent, uncertain, apprehensive.

confirm—*Syn.* prove, establish, settle, sanction, corroborate, approve, attest, ratify, assure, sustain, uphold, support, affirm, substantiate, strengthen. *Ant.* upset, annul, cancel, void, abrogate, overthrow, shatter, destroy, weaken, shake, unsettle, contradict, oppose.

conflict—*Syn.* combat, contest, contention, struggle, duel, battle, fight, engagement. *Ant.* peace, tranquillity, calm, calmness, repose, quiet, quietness, harmony, concord.

confusion, *n.—Syn.* disarrangement, disorder, jumble, turmoil, muddle, snarl, clutter, chaos.

confute—*Syn.* disprove, refute, confound, defeat, confuse, baffle, dismay. *Ant.* prove, attest, verify, endorse, affirm, confirm, demonstrate, manifest.

conjecture, *n.—Syn.* guess, theory, inference, presumption, speculation, assumption, hypothesis, supposition, fancy, conception.

conjoin—*Syn.* join, connect, unite, attach, affix, combine, associate, connect, adjoin, concatenate. *Ant.* sever, dissever, remove, detach, disconnect, separate, disjoin, disunite, discard.

conquer—*Syn.* subdue, overcome, crush, defeat, overthrow, overpower, overmatch, overmaster, master, subjugate, vanquish, rout, worst, down, humble, discomfit, quell, checkmate, reduce, surmount. *Ant.* yield, succumb, surrender, forfeit, retreat, lose, fail, flee, fly, cede, capitulate, retire, give up, give way.

conscious—*Syn.* aware, sensible, cognizant, informed, sure, certain, apprised, assured, felt, known, advised. *Ant.* insensible, unconscious, unaware, ignorant, cold, impassive, indifferent, unfeeling, senseless, dead.

consent, *n.—Syn.* assent, compliance, acquiescence, accord, confirmation, ratification, approval, indorsement, affirmation, concordance, concession, agreement. *Ant.* dissent, dissension, refusal, noncompliance, protest, protestation, contradiction, nonconformity, diversity, difference, disagreement, discordance, denial, demur, objection.

consent, *v.—Syn.* accede, agree, assent, comply, yield, allow, permit, approve, acquiesce, concur. *Ant.* refuse, deny, disagree, disapprove, withhold, withdraw, dissent, disallow, differ, bar, stop, prevent, demur, object.

consequence—*Syn.* effect, result, outgrowth, end, issue, consequent, upshot, sequel, outcome, event. *Ant.* cause, origin, beginning, preparation, spring, wellspring, source, commencement, rise, inception, genesis, start, fountain, nucleus.

consider—*Syn.* ponder, examine, contemplate, regard, reflect, deliberate. *Ant.* dismiss, ignore, pass, neglect, reject, discard, abandon, leave.

considerate—*Syn.* kind, charitable, thoughtful, prudent, cautious, unselfish, serious, meditative. *Ant.* unkind, uncharitable, unfeeling, harsh, mean, contemptible, severe, tyrannical, overbearing, selfish, haughty, scornful, repressive, imperious.

consideration—*Syn.* attention, kindness, friendliness, reflection, forethought, motive, prudence, heed, watchfulness, care, caution. *Ant.* disregard, neglect, thoughtlessness, negligence, carelessness, heedlessness, default, remissness, omission, failure.

consistent—*Syn.* consonant, according, equable, uniform, regular, undeviating, same. *Ant.* inconsistent, varying, incongruous, incompatible, incoherent, unstable, unsuitable, disagreeing.

console—*Syn.* comfort, ease, sympathize (with), encourage, cheer, gladden, enliven, refresh, support, inspirit, feel (for), rouse, arouse, inspire, exhilarate, invigorate, freshen. *Ant.* depress, sadden, grieve, trouble, wound, disturb, annoy, scold, censure, blame, condemn, lower, dispirit, discourage, dishearten, cast down.

consolidate—*Syn.* unite, combine, compact, harden, thicken, condense, compress, render solid. *Ant.* sever, disjoin, separate, disunite, dissever, part, divide, sunder.

conspicuous—*Syn.* open, visible, plain, outstanding, eminent, famous, distinguished, celebrated, noted, illustrious, prominent, commanding, well-known. *Ant.* hidden, concealed, unseen, secret, mysterious, covered, obscure, humble, unknown.

constancy—*Syn.* fixedness, stability, firmness, steadiness, steadfastness, permanence, resolution, sameness, faithfulness, reliability. *Ant.* inconstancy, fickleness, variability, changeableness, variance, fluctuation, vacillation, mutability, instability, wavering, unsteadiness, volatility, capriciousness.

consternation—*Syn.* dismay, alarm, terror, horror, panic, fear, wonder, surprise, astonishment, amazement. *Ant.* tranquillity, peace, peacefulness, quiet, quietness, calm, repose, stillness, rest, quietude.

constrain—*Syn.* necessitate, compel, force, prevent, oblige, urge, drive, restrain, press, repress. *Ant.* ask, request, beg, beseech, implore, coax, flatter, cajole, plead, supplicate.

construct—*Syn.* make, erect, build, form, compose, fabricate, invent, create, produce. *Ant.* demolish, destroy, break, burst, overthrow, dismantle, raze, annihilate, ruin.

consume—*Syn.* absorb, waste, destroy, exhaust, expend, dissipate, squander, lavish, spend, ingulf, imbibe, suck up, drink in, swallow. *Ant.* hoard, accumulate, heap (up), collect, gather, store, treasure, amass.

contaminate—*Syn.* corrupt, pollute, infect, taint, tarnish, stain, blacken, deprave, vitiate, debase, spoil, defile, poison. *Ant.* improve, better, ameliorate, meliorate, enhance, freshen, brighten, ennoble, elevate, dignify, exalt, heal, cure.

contemn—*Syn.* despise, scorn, mock, ridicule, disdain, spurn, slight, neglect, abandon, reject, underrate, overlook, decry, disparage, censure. *Ant.* praise, laud, approve, succor, assist, aid, help, befriend, support, applaud.

contemplate—*Syn.* consider, study, ponder, muse, meditate (on), intend, design, plan, purpose. *Ant.* disregard, discard, reject, neglect, slight, disdain, scorn.

contempt—*Syn.* disdain, scorn, derision, mockery, contumely, neglect, disregard, disrespect, slight, slur. *Ant.* regard, respect, affection, love, admiration, praise, applause, estimation, approval, endorsement, sanction.

contemptible—*Syn.* abject, vile, despicable, base, mean, cowardly, worthless, depraved, degraded, pitiful, scurrile, scurrilous, valueless, degenerate. *Ant.* good, worthy, brave, courageous, respectable, decent, honorable, admired, loved, gracious, pleasing, obliging, philanthropic, charitable.

contend—*Syn.* compete, contest, battle, fight, wage, dispute, strive, struggle, combat, cope, oppose, vie, grapple, strain, antagonize. *Ant.* abandon, cede, give up, cease, stop, halt, leave, desert, desist, discontinue, quit.

contention—*Syn.* contest, struggle, controversy, quarrel, conflict, feud, animosity, bitterness, hard-feeling, enmity, variance, competition, disagreement, discord, litigation. *Ant.* love, affection, regard, good-will, benevolence, friendliness, friendship, amity, respect, consideration, kindness, sympathy.

contest, *v.*—*Syn.* dispute, debate, object, oppose, tackle, argue, contend, fight, battle, defend, struggle, strain, wrangle, altercate, question, probe, strive. *Ant.* be still, rest, stop, cease, abandon, retire, forsake, give up, resign, relinquish.

contest, *n.*—*Syn.* conflict, battle, engagement, altercation, controversy, fray, dispute, feud, broil, argument, competition. *Ant.* peace, quiet, quietness, tranquility, calm, repose, stillness, rest.

continual—*Syn.* constant, continuous, perpetual, incessant, uninterrupted, unceasing, unvarying, invariable, regular, unbroken, proceeding, advancing, ceaseless, unremitting. *Ant.* intermittent, uncertain, broken, interrupted, unprogressive, checked, clogged, stopped, finished, concluded.

continuance—*Syn.* continuation, duration, existence, extension, production. *Ant.* stoppage, arrest, hindrance, impediment, obstruction, end, finish.

continue—*Syn.* persist, persevere, proceed, advance, keep going, go on. *Ant.* stop, halt, cease, desist, end, complete, finish.

contract, *v.*—*Syn.* abbreviate, shorten, abridge, epitomize, narrow, lessen, condense, reduce, confine, incur, assume, covenant. *Ant.* enlarge, expand, lengthen, dilate, extend, spread, stretch, increase, protract, amplify.

contract, *n.*—*Syn.* covenant, agreement, compact, stipulation, promise, engagement, obligation, guarantee, pledge, liability, cartel, bargain, pact.

contradict—*Syn.* oppose, gainsay, deny, resist, impugn, correct, rectify, recall, recant, retreat, deny,

demur, disavow, disclaim, disown, refuse, resist, contravene, check, combat, obstruct, denounce. *Ant.* agree, acquiesce, indorse, confirm, approve, sign, seal, vouch, verify, sanction, accept, guarantee, O. K.

contrary—*Syn.* unlike, opposite, dissimilar, opposed, conflicting, antagonistic, contradictory, heterogeneous. *Ant.* like, similar, agreeing, suitable, harmonious, correspondent, concordant, homogeneous, resembling, alike.

contrast, *n.*—*Syn.* difference, opposite, contrariety, divergence, antithesis, contradiction, incongruity, incompatibility, disparity, variation, variance, dissimilarity, diversity. *Ant.* agreement, similarity, likeness, uniformity, sameness, conformity, homogeneity, homogeneousness, unity, identity, equality, facsimile.

contrast, *v.*—*Syn.* differentiate, compare, oppose, discriminate, distinguish. *Ant.* coincide, agree, concur, accord, be identical, be equal.

contravene—*Syn.* oppose, contradict, interpose, nullify, annul, thwart, defeat, void, obstruct, hinder. *Ant.* agree, coincide, concur, harmonize, consent, assent, indorse, approve, aid, help, assist.

contribute—*Syn.* add, give, share, coöperate, assist, supply, help, aid, furnish, befriend, favor, benefit. *Ant.* ignore, neglect, shun, harm, injure, denounce, relinquish, counteract, discountenance, disfavor, check, withhold, disapprove, oppose.

contrivance—*Syn.* appliance, mechanism, invention, device, design, ruse, trick, artifice.

contrive—*Syn.* invent, make, form, arrange, plan, frame, design, plot, scheme, devise, project, execute, carry out. *Ant.* destroy, ruin, wreck, waste, abolish, disrupt, overthrow, topple, tumble, smash, demolish, shatter.

control, *v.*—*Syn.* restrain, hold, rule, govern, direct, guide, check, repress, hinder, prevent, coerce.

Ant. let go, abandon, give up, resign, relinquish, retire, renounce, leave, quit, forsake.

control, *n.—Syn.* check, restraint, ascendancy, dominion, influence, regulation. *Ant.* inutility, futility, weakness, powerlessness, abandonment, relinquishment, helplessness.

controversy—*Syn.* argument, discussion, debate, dispute, quarrel, bickering, wrangling. *Ant.* peace, quietness, forbearance, restraint, patience.

contumacious—*Syn.* obstinate, obdurate, stubborn, wilful, self-opinionated, selfish, perverse, unyielding, intractable, stiff, inflexible, headstrong, refractory, heady, pig-headed. *Ant.* gentle, placid, mild, meek, forbearing, susceptible, tractable, docile, manageable, governable, obedient, impressible, sensitive, tender, affectionate.

contumacy—*Syn.* stubbornness, pigheadedness, obstinacy, doggedness, sullenness, moroseness, surliness, pertinacity, perverseness, inflexibility. *Ant.* docility, readiness, willingness, tractability, tractableness, compliance, acquiescence, assent, consent, obedience, submission.

convene, *v.—Syn.* meet, muster, collect, congregate, gather, assemble.

convenient—*Syn.* fit, ready, handy, suitable, adapted, available, fitted, suited, commodious, opportune, suited. *Ant.* unsuitable, unsuited, inopportune, out-of-the-way, unavailable, ineffectual, inconvenient.

conventional—*Syn.* customary, usual, formal, ordinary, stipulated, prevalent, social. *Ant.* unconventional, extraordinary, informal, foreign, strange, irregular, unusual.

conversation—*Syn.* talk, speech, discourse, communication, communion, intercourse, conference, chat, colloquy, parley, dialogue, converse, confabulation.

convert, *n.—Syn.* proselyte, neophyte, disciple. *Ant.* pervert,

apostate, renegade.

convert, *v.—Syn.* turn (from), change, metamorphose, transform, transmogrify, resolve, transmute, transfigure, modify. *Ant.* let be, fix, endure, maintain, remain, retain, persist, keep, hold.

convey—*Syn.* carry, move, shift, transfer, transport, transmit, remove, sell, change, give, bear. *Ant.* hold, keep, retain, preserve, possess, cling to, effect, accomplish, inform.

convivial, *adj.—Syn.* festive, hospitable, gay, cordial, jolly, merry, sociable, jovial. *Ant.* dismal, solemn, staid, severe.

convoke—*Syn.* convene, assemble, muster, summon, gather, call, collect. *Ant.* dismiss, prorogue, dissolve, discharge, adjourn, disband, disperse, scatter, separate.

cook-out, *n.—Syn.* barbecue, picnic, grill, wienie-roast, patio party, rotiss.

cool—*Syn.* frigid, frosty, wintry, shivery, fresh, gelid, calm, indifferent, unfeeling, apathetic, distant, irresponsive, cold. *Ant.* hot, burning, warm, glowing, torrid, sultry, sunny, responsive, kind, kindly, feeling, warmhearted.

cool, *adj.—Syn.* hip, beat, on the beam; satisfying, stimulating; in the groove; aloof, indifferent, disdainful. *Ant.* square.

cooperate—*Syn.* aid, assist, help, plan, plot, work together, perform, relieve, befriend, succor, support, second, approve, indorse, forward, promote, encourage. *Ant.* hinder, obstruct, encumber, handicap, retard, delay, impede, disturb, annoy, prevent.

cordial, *adj.—Syn.* hearty, sincere, kindly, earnest, pleasant, warm, genial, gracious, friendly. *Ant.* cool, unfriendly, hostile, indifferent.

corny, *adj.—Syn.* trite, banal, unsophisticated, square; old-fashioned; sentimental. *Ant.* cool.

corpulent—*Syn.* fat, fleshy, beefy, obese, stout, bloated, swollen, ponderous, plethoric. *Ant.* thin, lean, emaciated, consumptive, delicate, feeble, weak, enervated, debilitated.

correct—*Syn.* chastise, beat, punish, castigate, reform, improve, amend, rectify. *Ant.* coddle, pet, pamper, indulge, cherish, soften, effeminate, spoil.

corroborate—*Syn.* strengthen, confirm, certify, indorse, approve, sanction, back, support, assure, affirm. *Ant.* reject, deny, contradict, disclaim, oppose, disavow, disallow, disprove, refute.

corrupt, *adj.*—*Syn.* base, low, mean, contemptible, debased, lewd, impure, infected, putrid, rotten, tainted, vitiated, unsound. *Ant.* clean, pure, wholesome, sound, noble, magnanimous, pure-minded, exalted, high, decent, honorable.

corrupt, *v.*—*Syn.* debase, pervert, vitiate, falsify, degrade, infect, taint, contaminate, demean, tarnish, stain, defile, pollute, spoil. *Ant.* ennoble, elevate, improve, better, raise, dignify, exalt, purify, cleanse, refine, chasten.

corruption—*Syn.* pus, putridity, rottenness, putrefaction, decay, baseness, meanness, depravity, degradation, infamy, sinfulness, vice, wickedness, criminality, guilt, guiltiness. *Ant.* cleanness, purity, wholesomeness, virtue, chastity, uprightness, sinlessness, innocence, integrity, soundness, morality.

counsel, *n.*—*Syn.* advice, suggestion, recommendation, warning, instruction, admonition, guidance, exhortation.

counsel, *v.*—*Syn.* advise, admonish, inform, apprise, acquaint, suggest, recommend, warn, instruct, guide.

count, *v.*—*Syn.* number, calculate, score, compute, enumerate, figure, total, reckon, estimate.

courage—*Syn.* bravery, valor, boldness, intrepidity, fearlessness, firmness, fortitude, enterprise, hardihood, heroism, gallantry, mettle, pluck, determination, dauntlessness. *Ant.*

fear, cowardice, dastardliness, poltroonery, timidity, pusillanimity, weakness, diffidence, faintheartedness.

courteous—*Syn.* polite, suave, bland, obliging, mannerly, civil, urbane, affable, agreeable, condescending, conciliating, attentive. *Ant.* impolite, discourteous, rude, rough, unmannerly, pompous, tyrannical, overbearing, dictatorial, uncivil.

covert, *adj.*—*Syn.* hidden, clandestine, surreptitious, furtive, secret, sly, underhand, concealed, disguised, privy, dissembled. *Ant.* overt, open, candid, frank.

covetousness—*Syn.* avarice, cupidity, avariciousness, greediness, eagerness, miserliness, penuriousness. *Ant.* beneficence, liberality, benevolence, munificence.

cowardice—*Syn.* see *antonyms* for **courage.** *Ant.* see *synonyms* for **courage.**

cranky, *adj.*—*Syn.* testy, touchy, cross, choleric, irritable, perverse, petulant. *Ant.* calm, amiable, placid, good-natured.

credible, *adj.*—*Syn.* believable, reliable, plausible, trustworthy, probable, reasonable.

crime—*Syn.* transgression, sin, misdemeanor, vice, outrage, wickedness, immorality, sinfulness, misdeed, infringement, depravity, badness. *Ant.* virtue, goodness, benevolence, benignity, innocence, uprightness, honor.

criminal—*Syn.* vile, vicious, wicked, sinful, immoral, abominable, iniquitous, unlawful, wrong, illegal, felonious, culpable, blamable, flagitious, nefarious, guilty, delinquent. *Ant.* upright, honest, honorable, moral, good, unspotted, unstained, innocent, undefiled, faultless, immaculate, stainless, virtuous, sinless, innocuous, pure, blameless, legal, lawful, right, just, meritorious.

criterion—*Syn.* test, standard, rule, measure, proof, touchstone, fact, law, principle, opinion. *Ant.* guess, conjecture, possibility, fancy, supposition, probability, imagination, chance.

crooked—*Syn.* bent, curved, oblique, curving, incurvating, winding, wry, bowed, deformed, perverse, deceitful, lawbreaking, criminal. *Ant.* straight, right, upright, unbent, direct, regular, law-abiding, honest, respectable, right-living, moral.

cruel—*Syn.* barbarous, brutal, inhuman, savage, ferocious, merciless, pitiless, tyrannical, inexorable. *Ant.* kind, considerate, feeling, gentle, merciful, prudent, thoughtful, unselfish, charitable.

culture—*Syn.* education, learning, scholarship, manners, refinement, knowledge, breeding, experience, cultivation, propagation. *Ant.* ignorance, boorishness, stupidity, denseness, stolidity, vulgarity, pretension, illiteracy, unenlightenment.

curious, *adj.*—*Syn.* inquisitive, nosy, examining, prying, inquiring, meddling.

cursory—*Syn.* hasty, superficial, slight, desultory, careless. *Ant.* thorough, thoroughgoing, complete, perfect.

custom—*Syn.* fashion, habit, manner, practice, habitude, usage, wont. *Ant.* irregularity, deviation, divergence, departure, difference.

D

daffy, *adj.*—*Syn.* crazy, insane, balmy, wacky, dippy, goofy, nutty, batty, dizzy, dopey.

daily—*Syn.* diurnal, occurring every day, issued every day. *Ant.* nightly, nocturnal, occurring every night, done by night.

dainty—*Syn.* nice, delicate, particular, choice, sweet, fine, refined, pure, elegant, exquisite, rare, soft, tender, pleasing, squeamish. *Ant.* sour, bitter, tasteless, unpleasant, disgusting, repellent, revolting, inferior, coarse, harsh, acid.

dally, *v.*—*Syn.* trifle, idle, coquet, dawdle, prolong, toy, linger, delay, caress, flirt, fondle.

dam, *v.*—*Syn.* block, stop, impede, obstruct, clog, choke, suppress, bar, hinder, hamper.

damage—*Syn.* harm, injury, detriment, loss, evil, hurt, disadvantage, wrong, misfortune, bane, bruise, wound, spoil, spoliation. *Ant.* benefit, advantage, emolument, reward, recompense, award, boon, profit, favor, blessing.

damn—*Syn.* curse, reprobate, condemn, punish, execrate, anathematize, denounce, ban, banish. *Ant.* bless, cherish, praise, exalt, elevate, laud, benefit, favor, promote, magnify, glorify.

danger—*Syn.* peril, jeopardy, hazard, risk, exposure, venture, insecurity, chance, menace. *Ant.* safety, security, preservation, care, carefulness, sureness, certainty, confidence.

dangerous—*Syn.* risky, unsafe, insecure, perilous, hazardous, treacherous, precarious, uncertain, menacing, threatening. *Ant.* safe, secure, sure, protected, trustworthy, firm, safeguarded, harmless, innocuous.

dank, *adj.*—*Syn.* moist, soggy, wet, damp, soaked, humid, sodden.

daring—*Syn.* bold, brave, adventurous, courageous, fearless, intrepid, stout, stout-hearted, audacious, impudent, intrusive, obtrusive. *Ant.* modest, retiring, bashful, shy, timid, diffident, afraid, cowardly, chicken-hearted.

dark—*Syn.* obscure, dim, dismal, opaque, gloomy, murky, shadowy, shady, somber, swarthy, swart, black, sable, dusky, mysterious, sinister. *Ant.* light, clear, vivid, bright, transparent, plain, visible, lucid, manifest, apparent, evident, distinct, luminous, shining, radiant, dazzling, gleaming, illumined, brilliant, crystalline.

daunt—*Syn.* intimidate, discourage, dishearten, frighten, scare, dismay, terrify, cow, appal. *Ant.* encourage, assist, aid, help, succor, embolden, inspirit, instigate, stimulate, animate, incite, urge, impel, forward, promote, comfort, advance.

dawdle, v.—*Syn.* idle, dally, delay, loiter, fiddle, procrastinate, trifle, play, lag. *Ant.* hurry, hasten, speed, rally.

dazzle, v.—*Syn.* confound, daze, astonish, blind, overpower, impress, surprise, bewilder, amaze, astound, confuse.

dead—*Syn.* deceased, defunct, lifeless, inanimate, extinct, nonexistent, gone, departed. *Ant.* alive, live, living, existent, existing, being, continuing, subsisting, enduring, animate.

deadly—*Syn.* fatal, mortal, destructive, destructful, harmful, injurious, noxious, poisonous, enervating, weakening, debilitating. *Ant.* invigorating, stimulating, health-giving, wholesome, energizing, preservative, animating, strengthening.

deal, n.—*Syn.* agreement, affair, transaction, concern, racket, conspiracy.

deal, v.—*Syn.* distribute, allot, give, divide, bestow, apportion, share, mete.

dear—*Syn.* costly, expensive, valuable, scarce, high-priced, precious, beloved, cherished. *Ant.* cheap, inexpensive, low-priced, common, worthless, valueless, unimportant, despised.

death—*Syn.* decease, demise, dissolution, extinction, departure, release, separation. *Ant.* life, existence, being, entity, duration.

debase, v.—*Syn.* degrade, impair, humble, corrupt, dishonor, taint, adulterate, shame, abase, contaminate, disgrace, vitiate, pervert. *Ant.* elevate, enhance, lift, improve.

debauch, v.—*Syn.* corrupt, debase, deprave, pervert, vitiate, defile, pollute, seduce, contaminate.

debonair, adj.—*Syn.* buoyant, jaunty, gracious, lively, bright, sprightly, gay, chipper, urbane, elegant. *Ant.* awkward, clumsy, stolid, maladroit.

debt, n.—*Syn.* liability, charge, obligation, arrears, debit.

decay—*Syn.* decline, consumption, collapse, downfall, decadence, degeneracy, putrefaction, putridity, putrescence, decomposition, corruption, rot, rottenness. *Ant.* growth, germination, gemmation, birth, development, vigor, strength, health, healthiness, force, vigorousness, animation, robustness.

deceit—*Syn.* deception, duplicity, fraud, trickery, hypocrisy, doubledealing, cunning, guile, sham, beguilement, treachery, imposition, delusion, imposture, artifice, stratagem. *Ant.* truth, truthfulness, honor, honesty, uprightness, squareness, fair-dealing, openness.

deceive—*Syn.* delude, impose (upon), overreach, gull, dupe, cheat, outwit, mislead, trick, humbug, circumvent, defraud, bamboozle, betray, beguile, entrap, ensnare. *Ant.* advise, counsel, aid, assist, help, succor, assure, be truthful, be frank, be candid, be straightforward, be artless, be open.

decent, adj.—*Syn.* decorous, modest, chaste, seemly, befitting, proper, demure, pure, becoming, appropriate. *Ant.* ribald, gross, lewd, obscene.

deception—*Syn.* double-dealing, equivocation, lie, lying, falsehood, prevarication, fabrication, trickery, duplicity, delusion, cunning, craft, deceit, deceitfulness, dissimulation, imposition, fraud, finesse, guile, untruth. *Ant.* candor, honesty, square-dealing, squareness, sincerity, veracity, openness, simplicity, guilelessness, frankness.

decide—*Syn.* determine, settle, adjudicate, terminate, resolve, fix, arrange, regulate. *Ant.* put off, delay, hesitate, wait, defer, postpone, protract, procrastinate.

decipher—*Syn.* read, spell, interpret, solve, translate, reveal, unravel, expound, explain, construe, unfold, elucidate. *Ant.* misinterpret, muddle, mix, misconstrue, confuse, snare, tangle, pervert, falsify, distort, twist.

decision—*Syn.* determination, conclusion, resolution, result, outcome, disposal, opinion, issue, consequence. *Ant.* vacillation, procrastination, delay, postponement, deferment, prolongation, indetermination, indefiniteness, indecision.

declamation—*Syn.* oratory, elocution, harangue, effusion, debate, enunciation, recitation.

declaration—*Syn.* avowal, statement, profession, manifestation, affirmation, utterance, presentation.

decline, v.—*Syn.* deteriorate, lessen, ebb, decay, fail, depreciate, decrease, wane, degenerate, diminish, dwindle.

decompose, v.—*Syn.* rot, crumble, disintegrate, disperse, decay, putrefy.

decorum, n.—*Syn.* seemliness, form, propriety, sedateness, etiquette, decency, dignity. *Ant.* license, impropriety, indecency.

decoy, v.—*Syn.* lure, tempt, inveigle, beguile, entice, mislead, entrap.

decrease—*Syn.* abate, lessen, diminish, wane, decline, retrench, curtail, reduce, narrow, minimize. *Ant.* increase, enlarge, add, swell, extend, dilate, grow, develop, widen, expand.

decree, v.—*Syn.* decide, direct, prescribe, order, ordain, enjoin, determine, dictate, command, sentence, judge, adjust, settle.

decree, n.—*Syn.* law, edict, judgment, order, ordinance, pronouncement, promulgation, pronunciamento.

decry, v.—*Syn.* disparage, derogate, depreciate, condemn, criticize, discredit, belittle, censure. *Ant.* praise, extol, exalt, magnify.

dedicate—*Syn.* devote, consecrate, offer, set apart, apportion, hallow, sanctify, appropriate, inscribe, bless, enshrine, upraise, ascribe.

deduce, v.—*Syn.* infer, reason, deem, derive, judge, gather, reckon, conclude, believe.

deed—*Syn.* act, action, commission, achievement, accomplishment, exploit, feat, performance.

deem—*Syn.* judge, estimate, consider, think, imagine, suppose, conceive.

deep—*Syn.* down far, profound, beneath, below, low, low-down, submerged, subterranean, subaqueous, abstruse, learned, designing, scheming, experienced, artful, contriving, insidious, penetrating. *Ant.* shallow, superficial, ignorant, inexperienced, unintellectual, unintelligent, flighty, frivolous, unbalanced.

deface—*Syn.* disfigure, deform, blemish, mar, mark, injure, spoil, erase, obliterate, impair. *Ant.* beautify, bedeck, adorn, decorate, embellish, deck, grace, ornament, make attractive.

defame—*Syn.* calumniate, asperse, besmirch, accuse, charge, slander, traduce, detract, vilify, misrepresent, backbite, malign, debase, degrade, harm, scandalize. *Ant.* praise, laud, exalt, extol, eulogize, boost, applaud, commend, indorse, approve, magnify, glorify.

default—*Syn.* lapse, failure, forfeit, absence, omission, want, offense, neglect, defect, defection, blame, censure, delinquency, shortcoming, incompleteness. *Ant.* perfection, advantage, completeness, carefulness, accuracy, vigilance, watchfulness, observance.

defeat, n.—*Syn.* nonsuccess, failure, frustration, downfall, repulse, rebuff, overthrow, subjugation, discomfiture, beating, whipping, threshing, extermination, destruction. *Ant.* success, mastery, advantage, victory, conquest, triumph, walkover, ascendancy, attainment.

defeat, v.—*Syn.* overcome, vanquish, conquer, rout, beat, subdue, baffle, discomfit, frustrate, overthrow, disconcert, surmount, crush, drive off, annihilate. *Ant.* yield, submit, succumb, relinquish, accede, forego, resign, surrender, concede, give up.

defect—*Syn.* imperfection, flaw, fault, blemish, spot, stain, speck, drawback, deficiency, weakness, incompleteness, impediment. *Ant.* advantage, improvement, amendment, betterment, enhancement, beauty, perfection, completeness, faultlessness, goodness, excellence.

defend—*Syn.* guard, protect, justify, save, insure, shield, shelter, safeguard, safe-keep, secure, cover. *Ant.* desert, abandon, leave, forsake, quit, abdicate, resign, relinquish, renounce, vacate, give up.

defense—*Syn.* vindication, plea, excuse, apology, safeguard, bulwark, rampart, fortress, guard, shield, shelter, protection, justification, resistance. *Ant.* desertion, capitulation, surrender, flight, abandonment, betrayal, yielding.

defer—*Syn.* put off, delay, postpone, adjourn, prorogue, protract, prolong, procrastinate, retard, restrain, suspend, dissolve, break up. *Ant.* expedite, hasten, quicken, accelerate, stimulate, further, forward, advance, force, hurry, urge (on), despatch, act.

deficient—*Syn.* inadequate, incomplete, scanty, scarce, wanting, short, defective, imperfect. *Ant.* adequate, sufficient, enough, ample, full, satisfactory.

defile—*Syn.* pollute, corrupt, sully, soil, stain, taint, vitiate, infect, foul, befoul, contaminate, spoil, debauch, seduce. *Ant.* clean, cleanse, wash, disinfect, hallow, purify, sanctify, glorify.

define—*Syn.* fix, settle, determine, limit, describe, ascertain, explain, decide, elucidate, interpret, illustrate. *Ant.* mix, muddle, confuse, tangle, twist, distort, derange, disarrange.

definite—*Syn.* fixed, determinate, exact, bounded, limited, circumscribed, precise, certain,

positive. *Ant.* indefinite, uncertain, unknown, illimitable, unbounded, undefined, vague, indeterminate, unlimited, inexact, indistinct.

definition—*Syn.* explanation, exposition, meaning, significance, drift, elucidation, description, rendering, translation, comment, commentary, interpretation. *Ant.* nonsense, jargon, piffle (*slang*), rant, balderdash, bosh (*colloq.*), flapdoodle (*colloq.*), rigmarole, twaddle, fudge, poppycock (*U.S. colloq.*), absurdity.

deflect, *v.*—*Syn.* turn, swerve, avert, twist, deviate, divert, diverge.

deform, *v.*—*Syn.* distort, injure, contort, spoil, cripple, disfigure, mar, deface, impair.

deformed—*Syn.* malformed, crippled, disjointed, disfigured, distorted, misshapen, twisted, unsightly, unseemly, ill-favored, ugly, dwarfed. *Ant.* beautiful, handsome, shapely, graceful, symmetrical, well-formed, regular, well-built, comely.

defraud—*Syn.* cheat, dupe, swindle, deceive, rob, trick, cozen, impose (upon), delude, overreach, beguile, hoodwink, gull, fool, bamboozle, shuffle, prevaricate, inveigle, fleece, deprive. *Ant.* reward, award, recompense, give (to), subscribe (to), befriend, assist, help, support, contribute, remunerate, return, repay, requite.

defray—*Syn.* meet, liquidate, pay, discharge, satisfy, settle, clear, adjust. *Ant.* welch, decamp, repudiate, refuse, disavow, disown, abjure, deny, disclaim.

deft, *adj.*—*Syn.* adroit, nimble, adept, skillful, assured, dexterous, clever, agile, handy, expert. *Ant.* awkward, clumsy, inept, maladroit.

defy, *v.*—*Syn.* challenge, oppose, spurn, flout, disobey, slight, contemn, dare, brave.

degenerate, *v.*—*Syn.* deteriorate, decay, worsen, corrupt, decline, debauch, debase, sink.

degradation—*Syn.* baseness, meanness, disgrace, dishonor, abasement, debasement, degeneracy, dissipation, removal, dismissal. *Ant.* honor, elevation, exaltation, admiration, praise, reward, merit, ascendancy, superiority.

degree—*Syn.* grade, extent, measure, rank, station, order, quality, division, space, interval, step, distinction, honor, testimony, qualification.

dejection—*Syn.* depression, despondency, melancholy, gloom, sadness, heaviness, obscurity, darkness, pensiveness, the blues. *Ant.* joy, cheer, delight, merriment, merriness, merry-making, laughter, gaiety, frolic, hilarity, exhilaration, festiveness, mirthfulness.

delay, *v.*—*Syn.* defer, postpone, procrastinate, prolong, protract, retard, hesitate, halt, hinder. *Ant.* forward, advance, speed, haste, hurry, hasten, accelerate, expedite, despatch.

delectable, *adj.*—*Syn.* delightful, savory, pleasant, delicious, agreeable, palatable, luscious, gratifying, exquisite. *Ant.* offensive, repulsive, loathsome, nauseating.

delegate—*Syn.* representative, legate, proxy, deputy, substitute, envoy, commissioner, ambassador.

deliberate, *v.*—*Syn.* study, think, imagine, conceive, ponder, consider, weigh, estimate, reflect, meditate, consult, contemplate, confer, debate, examine, regard. *Ant.* put off, pass over, reject, discard, disclaim, repudiate, spurn, scorn, scoff.

deliberate, *adj.*—*Syn.* careful, cautious, intentional, purposed, thoughtful, considered, pondered, weighed, judged, reasoned, wary, cool, prudent, circumspect, slow. *Ant.* incautious, hasty, sudden, rash, unconsidered, unintentional, imprudent, careless, happy-go-lucky, chancy.

delicacy—*Syn.* niceness, daintiness, refinement, tact, modesty, softness, consideration, feeling; light-

ness, tenderness, weakness. *Ant.* indelicacy, boorishness, roughness, rudeness, grossness, coarseness, vulgarity, turbulence, churlishness, violence, fierceness, brutality, cruelty.

delicate—*Syn.* weak, sickly, feeble, dainty, fastidious, gentle, soft, fine, refined, slender, tender, nice, feeling, commiserate, compassionate. *Ant.* rough, rude, boisterous, boastful, coarse, vulgar, robust, cruel, savage, brutal, mean, contemptible, low, base, depraved.

delicious—*Syn.* sweet, palatable, pleasing, delightful, savory, gratifying, appetizing, tasteful, toothsome, exquisite, dainty, luscious. *Ant.* sour, bitter, unpalatable, distasteful, disagreeable, unsavory, nauseous, repulsive, acrid, loathsome.

delight—*Syn.* enjoyment, pleasure, happiness, transport, ecstasy, gladness, rapture, bliss, gratification, satisfaction, felicity, joy. *Ant.* sorrow, pain, distress, dismay, misery, sadness, gloom, despair, melancholy, disappointment, wretchedness.

delightful—*Syn.* agreeable, pleasing, pleasant, gratifying, satisfactory, joyful, joyous, glad, merry, inspiring, inspiriting, pleasurable, gladsome. *Ant.* sorrowful, sad, saddening, wearisome, wretched, mournful, painful, miserable, melancholy, hateful, horrible, disappointing, distressing, depressing.

delineate—*Syn.* depict, represent, describe, draw, design, paint, sketch, outline, picture, portray.

delirium—*Syn.* madness, mania, aberration, frenzy, lunacy, insanity, dementia, the jim-jams (*slang*), the heeby-jeebies (*slang*), hallucination. *Ant.* sanity, soundness, normality, regularity, steadiness, saneness, reason.

deliver—*Syn.* liberate, free, rescue, pronounce, utter, give, hand over, save, emancipate, release, discharge, surrender. *Ant.* hold, keep, retain, confine, restrain, imprison, immure, incarcerate, restrict, circumscribe, bind, limit.

delusion—*Syn.* phantasm, hallucination, illusion, fallacy, error, chimera, deception, phantom, apparition, ghost, specter. *Ant.* reality, actuality, certainty, fact, truth, verity, substance, substantiality, materiality.

demand—*Syn.* ask, request, solicit, seek, require, supplicate, want, beg, beseech, crave, implore. *Ant.* tender, present, offer, give, proffer, grant.

demeanor—*Syn.* air, bearing, behavior, manner, attitude, appearance, conduct.

demented, *adj.*—*Syn.* mad, insane, crazy, daft, maniacal, deranged, lunatic, irrational, frenzied. *Ant.* sane, rational, lucid, reasonable.

demolish—*Syn.* ruin, raze, destroy, overturn, overthrow, level, wreck, devastate, dismantle. *Ant.* build, upbuild, improve, mend, better, uphold, embellish, enrich, repair, restore, construct, create, make.

demon, *n.*—*Syn.* fiend, fury, devil, familiar, imp.

demonstrate—*Syn.* prove, show, exhibit, illustrate, evince, manifest, display, present, explain. *Ant.* hide, conceal, cover, disguise, dissemble, secrete, mask, screen, veil, cloak, puzzle, perplex, complicate, bewilder, confuse, confound, mystify.

demonstration—*Syn.* show, exhibition, explanation, evidence, proof, induction, deduction, inference, conclusion, consequence, certainty, manifestation, corroboration, verification, evidence. *Ant.* misrepresentation, falsification, distortion, concealment, mystery, mysticism, occultism, cabalism, confusion, mystification.

demoralize, *v.*—*Syn.* corrupt, discourage, disorganize, deprave, disconcert, confuse.

demur, *v.*—*Syn.* object, except, pause, waver, balk, hesitate, shy, scruple, vacillate, disapprove.

Ant. agree, accept, assent, consent.

demure, *adj.*—*Syn.* modest, sedate, decorous, coy, diffident, prudish, seemly, shy, sober. *Ant.* brazen, impudent, shameless, wanton.

denial—*Syn.* disavowal, renunciation, contradiction, dissent, rejection, abnegation. *Ant.* admission, acknowledgment, confession, avowal, declaration, profession, averment.

denote, *v.*—*Syn.* signify, mean, specify, imply, mark, intend, indicate, import, connote.

denounce—*Syn.* condemn, accuse, threaten, charge, blame, indict, arraign, impeach, scold, censure, reprimand, reprehend, reprove, reproach. *Ant.* praise, laud, commend, eulogize, applaud, extol, magnify, glorify.

dense, *adj.*—*Syn.* thick, solid, concentrated, compact, massive, close, compressed. *Ant.* thin, rare, scattered, scanty.

deny—*Syn.* contradict, disavow, disclaim, disown, oppose, refuse, reject, repudiate, renounce, abjure. *Ant.* acknowledge, confess, own, reveal, concede, avow, admit, attest, assent, accede, agree (to).

depart—*Syn.* leave, quit, decamp, retire, go, withdraw, vanish, vamose (*slang*), scram (*slang*), desert, deviate, vary, apostatize, die, decease. *Ant.* remain, stay, stand, linger, stop, wait, tarry, abide, dwell, continue, endure.

dependent, *adj.*—*Syn.* contingent, reliant, conditional, consequent, subject, collateral. *Ant.* absolute, unconditional, categorical, underived.

depict—*Syn.* delineate, portray, describe, draw, sketch, picture, paint, illustrate, represent.

deplete, *v.*—*Syn.* drain, debilitate, empty, exhaust, weaken, diminish, lessen. *Ant.* fill, augment, strengthen, enlarge.

deplore—*Syn.* bewail, bemoan, lament, mourn, grieve, complain, fret, sorrow, sigh (for), cry (for), regret. *Ant.* rejoice, delight, exult, joy, revel, triumph, cheer, glory.

deportment, n.—Syn. conduct, demeanor, manner, air, behavior, comportment, carriage, bearing, mien.

depravity—Syn. corruption, degeneracy, vitiation, contamination, pollution, deterioration, depravation, badness, wickedness, sinfulness, immorality. Ant. goodness, rectitude, honor, virtue, purity, nobleness, integrity, uprightness, justice, morality, probity, dignity, reputation, esteem, self-respect.

deprecate, v.—Syn. disapprove, regret, condemn, protest, deplore. Ant. approve, endorse, commend, applaud.

depreciate—Syn. undervalue, underrate, lower, decry, detract, traduce, disparage, contemn, despise, denounce. Ant. boost, raise, praise, recommend, commend, approve, eulogize, extol, exalt, laud, magnify.

depress—Syn. sink, lower, abase, degrade, deject, humble, dispirit, debase, humiliate, disgrace, mock, scorn, slur. Ant. upraise, praise, comfort, console, cheer, encourage, inspirit, embolden, animate, incite, spur, urge, stimulate, impel.

depression—Syn. oppression, misery, gloom, poverty, sorrow, unhappiness, abasement, humiliation, dejection, melancholy, abjectedness, mortification. Ant. joy, happiness, cheer, lightheartedness, contentment, satisfaction, comfort, gratification.

deprive—Syn. strip, bereave, despoil, take (from or away), rob, divest, hinder, debar, abridge, separate. Ant. give, add, confer, present, help, assist, restore, return, repay, replace, renew, refund, repair.

depute—Syn. appoint, commission, name, delegate, accredit, authorize, intrust, assign, constitute, empower. Ant. reject, eject, refuse, exclude, repudiate, bar, debar, pass over, shut out.

deranged, adj.—Syn. crazy, mad, insane, demented, unbalanced, disordered, disturbed, confused. Ant. sane, lucid, rational, reasonable.

deride—Syn. ridicule, mock, taunt, scoff, scorn, slur, gibe, banter, fool, trick, bamboozle (slang), humbug, delude, deceive, laugh (at), mimic, jeer, flout, insult. Ant. encourage, advise, guide, cheer, inspirit, stimulate, incite, animate, embolden, inspire, comfort.

derision—Syn. scorn, contempt, condemnation, mockery, ridicule, disdain, disrespect, disregard, slur, insult, contumely, slight. Ant. flattery, adulation, fawning, servility, submission, toadyism, sycophancy, obsequiousness, complaisance.

derivation—Syn. origin, source, beginning, cause, root, rise, fountain, foundation, nucleus, commencement, spring, primogeniture. Ant. end, result, resultant, consequence, issue, effect, outgrowth, outcome, inference, conclusion.

derive—Syn. deduce, infer, deduct, determine, conclude, acquire, obtain, procure, receive, get, inherit, draw from, produce from, proceed from, flow from, result from, accrue from, trace. Ant. misjudge, misreckon, misconjecture, deprive, divest, forfeit, lose, bereave, strip, take from.

descent—Syn. declivity, slope, slant, fall, degradation, abasement, debasement, extraction, origin, lineage, pedigree, ancestry, genesis, generation, invasion, incursion, assault, attack, decline, descension. Ant. ascent, climb, elevation, acclivity, eminence, rise, rising, mounting, ascension, upgrade, ramp, escalator, elevator, lift, grade, pitch.

describe—Syn. delineate, portray, explain, illustrate, depict, define, picture, relate, recount, narrate, represent, express. Ant. misrepresent, caricature, twist, distort, travesty, exaggerate, falsify, overstate, understate, lie, dissemble, deceive, misstate.

desecrate—*Syn.* profane, secularize, misuse, abuse, pollute, pervert, violate, defile, deprave, taint, debase. *Ant.* sanctify, purify, cleanse, clear, consecrate, hallow.

desert, *n.*—*Syn.* merit, worth, worthiness, excellence, due, emolument, reward, recompense, claim, right, compensation, payment, requital. *Ant.* punishment, penalty, fine, amercement, retribution, chastisement, castigation, infliction, condemnation. (Note—these *synonyms* and *antonyms* are interchangeable according to the sense in which the word is used—both signify what one deserves either as reward or punishment: the word is generally taken in *pl*).

desert, *v.*—*Syn.* forsake, abandon, leave, quit, abdicate. *Ant.* remain, stay, continue, wait, abide, dwell, tarry.

design—*Syn.* delineation, sketch, drawing, picture, object, contrivance, plan, project, intent, intention, aim, end, scheme, purpose, intention.

designate—*Syn.* name, specify, indicate, select, appoint, characterize, denominate.

desirable—*Syn.* good, acceptable, profitable, valuable, proper, judicious, beneficial, advisable, expedient, worthy. *Ant.* undesirable, baneful, hurtful, bad, malignant, evil, harmful, injurious, noxious, detrimental.

desire—*Ant.* longing, yearning, wish, craving, affection, appetency, aspiration, hankering, proclivity, propensity, coveting, inclination, concupiscence. *Ant.* repugnance, repulsion, hatred, hostility, opposition, dislike, disgust, aversion, antagonism, distaste, abhorrence, detestation.

desist—*Syn.* cease, stop, discontinue, drop, abstain, forbear, quit, relinquish. *Ant.* continue, persevere, endure, wait, hold, retain, sustain, remain, keep on, carry on.

desolate—*Syn.* abandoned, deserted, forsaken, bereaved, forgot-

ten, lonely, solitary, alone, forlorn, dreary, waste, uninhabited, wild, bare, bleak, dismal. *Ant.* pleasant, happy, genial, enticing, alluring, enchanting, lovely, enjoyable, inhabited.

desolation—*Syn.* ruin, bareness, barrenness, misery, wretchedness, unhappiness, loneliness, bleakness, havoc, devastation, gloom, waste, destitution. *Ant.* fertilization, fertility, productiveness, productivity, luxuriance, peace, pleasure, contentment, satisfaction, happiness, plenty, comfort, repose, gratification, solace, consolation.

despair—*Syn.* hopelessness, desperation, discouragement, despondency, dejection, depression. *Ant.* hope, courage, ambition, confidence, expectation, trust, faith, expectancy, encouragement, elation, assurance, anticipation, cheer.

despatch—*Syn.* send, transmit, speed, accelerate, hasten, expedite, conclude, perform, kill, slay, slaughter.

desperate—*Syn.* daring, wild, reckless, careless, bold, audacious, determined, rash, furious, despairing, hopeless, irretrievable. *Ant.* calm, cool, collected, peaceful, quiet, hopeful, confident, contented, satisfied.

despicable—*Syn.* low, mean, base, cowardly, lying, contemptible, abject, vile, worthless, depraved, sinful, pitiful, scurrile, scurrilous, contaminated, polluted, corrupt, vitiated, shameless. *Ant.* high, noble, exalted, high-minded, worthy, respectable, decent, virtuous, upright, honest, honorable, pure, exalted, praiseworthy.

despise—*Syn.* condemn, denounce, scorn, disdain, contemn, spurn, detest, deride, abhor, abominate, loathe. *Ant.* love, cherish, praise, exalt, extol, applaud, commend, recommend, admire, magnify, glorify.

despondent, *adj.*—*Syn.* forlorn, depressed, melancholy, low, despairing, sad, dejected, disheartened. *Ant.* buoyant, ebullient, elated, lighthearted.

destination, *n.—Syn.* objective, goal, port, bourne, terminus, end.

destiny—*Syn.* fate, decree, doom, end, lot, fortune, judgment, predetermination, predestination, condition, chance, portion, happening, finality, conclusion.

destitution—*Syn.* indigence, poverty, want, privation, distress, need, pauperism, penury. *Ant.* riches, wealth, luxury, plenty, plenteousness, abundance, supply, profusion, prosperity, affluence, opulence.

destroy—*Syn.* ruin, demolish, exterminate, consume, extirpate, raze, overthrow, devastate, kill, slay, slaughter, murder. *Ant.* construct, add, build, upbuild, restore, replace, embellish, adorn, ornament, upraise, renew, repair, refresh, revive, invigorate, reinvigorate, strengthen, resuscitate.

destruction—*Syn.* ruin, desolation, devastation, extirpation, waste, extinction, annihilation, eradication, extermination, demolition, subversion, downfall, abolition, abolishment, overthrow. *Ant.* restoration, replacement, renewal, reëstablishment, renovation, recovery, revival, reparation, restitution, redintegration, reinstatement.

destructive—*Syn.* detrimental, hurtful, harmful, noxious, poisonous, deleterious, injurious, baleful, baneful, subversive, ruinous, fatal, pernicious, noisome, mischievous, evil, deadly. *Ant.* beneficial, useful, profitable, advantageous, salutary, wholesome, helpful, good, serviceable, available, conducive.

desultory—*Syn.* cursory, rambling, wandering, discursive, loose, irregular, superficial, unsettled, erratic. *Ant.* steady, firm, regular, fixed, permanent, determined, stable, constant.

detach—*Syn.* separate, withdraw, disengage, disconnect, disunite, sever, part, disjoin. *Ant.* unite,

bind, join, connect, combine, conjoin, adhere, coalesce, merge, cohere, couple, concatenate, link, attach.

detail, *v.—Syn.* relate, report, narrate, particularize, tell, retail, spread, recite, describe, communicate. *Ant.* conceal, hide, keep silent, cover, screen, befog, withhold, evade, suppress, stifle, reserve, keep from, draw the veil.

detail, *n.—Syn.* minutia, particular, particularity, specification, item, part, article, portion, account, recital, description, narrative, narration, relation, paragraph.

detain—*Syn.* hold, keep, restrain, stop, stay, withhold, check, repress, hinder, curb, prevent, limit, bar, confine, coerce. *Ant.* free, let go, liberate, deliver, manumit, affranchise, disenthrall, ransom.

detect—*Syn.* expose, discover, find out, unmask, identify, catch, uncover, determine, disclose, ascertain, apprehend. *Ant.* miss, fail, omit, pass by, err, mistake, blunder, misapprehend.

deter—*Syn.* warn, stop, dissuade, terrify, frighten, scare, discourage, hinder, prevent, restrain. *Ant.* encourage, advise, foster, persuade, induce, cheer, animate, embolden, incite, promote, succor, support, influence, favor, countenance, inspirit, urge, impel, stimulate, instigate, comfort.

deteriorate—*Syn.* depreciate, lessen, degrade, debase, corrupt, degenerate, undervalue, lower, disparage, underrate, asperse, defame, knock (*colloq.*), deprecate, run down (*colloq.*), condemn, decry, detract. *Ant.* boost (*colloq.*), approve, endorse, acclaim, appreciate, praise, esteem, value, prize, appraise, commend, recommend.

determine—*Syn.* decide, ascertain, define, limit, fix, resolve, settle, conclude, find out.

determined—*Syn.* decided, firm, fixed, stable, immovable, unalterable, resolute, steady, obstinate, stubborn, unwavering. *Ant.* undecided, vacillating, wavering, fickle, uncertain, irresolute, unsteady, fluctuating, inconstant, unstable.

detest—*Syn.* hate, loathe, abhor, abominate, execrate, anathematize. *Ant.* like, prefer, love, admire, respect, appreciate, esteem, estimate, prize.

detract—*Syn.* defame, derogate, vilify, slander, calumniate, depreciate, deprecate, decry. *Ant.* boost (*colloq.*), laud, praise, commend, recommend, applaud, exalt, extol, magnify, glorify.

detraction—*Syn.* slander, defamation, calumny, backbiting, aspersion, depreciation, derogation. *Ant.* praise, adulation, flattery, admiration, respect, laudation, eulogy, plaudit, applause, encomium, commendation, recommendation, panegyric.

detriment—*Syn.* loss, harm, hurt, injury, bane, damage, deterioration, evil, disadvantage, impairment, wrong. *Ant.* advantage, gain, profit, emolument, interest, benefit, help, assistance, utility, vantage, favor.

devastate—*Syn.* ravage, sack, pillage, waste, ruin, demolish, desolate, wreck, sack, strip, spoil, despoil. *Ant.* enrich, beautify, furnish, replenish, restore, renew, build, upbuild, embellish, adorn, cultivate, refresh, benefit, preserve.

develop—*Syn.* uncover, unfold, disclose, enlarge, exhibit, disentangle, unravel, extend. *Ant.* curtail, shorten, abbreviate, conceal, hide, narrow, circumscribe, lessen, compress, confine.

deviate—*Syn.* deflect, digress, swerve, wander, stray, turn aside. *Ant.* keep on, keep to the right, go ahead, persevere, continue, stick to it (*colloq.*), stick it out (*colloq.*).

device—*Syn.* artifice, contrivance, machine, machination, invention, design, scheme, stratagem, emblem, motto, project.

devilish, *adj.*—*Syn.* fiendish, demonic, diabolical, infernal, hell-

ish, satanic, malignant, malevolent, wicked, barbarous. *Ant.* angelic, seraphic, heavenly, celestial.

devoid—*Syn.* void, wanting, destitute, unendowed, unprovided, empty, bare, lacking. *Ant.* full, complete, furnished, possessing, supplied, equipped, abundant, adequate, enough, sufficient, abounding (in or with).

devote—*Syn.* dedicate, destine, consign, assign, apportion, apply, appropriate, allot, set apart. *Ant.* waste, squander, misuse, misappropriate, misapply, pervert, desecrate, alienate, abuse.

devotion—*Syn.* consecration, devotedness, piety, zeal, ardor, earnestness, sincerity, devoutness, adherence, observance, intensity. *Ant.* apathy, carelessness, heedlessness, neglect, abandonment, indifference, unconcern, passiveness.

devour—*Syn.* consume, waste, destroy, gorge, raven, swallow (up), munch, chew, gulp, bolt, prey upon.

devout—*Syn.* holy, pious, religious, zealous, sincere, reverent, earnest, godly, righteous, devotional, moral. *Ant.* irreligious, irreverent, ungodly, unrighteous, sinful, profane, impious, wicked, blasphemous, unholy, unsanctified, worldly, godless, secular.

dexterity—*Syn.* art, ability, expertness, aptness, tact, facility, aptitude, adroitness, readiness, skill, cleverness, handiness. *Ant.* clumsiness, awkwardness, unskilfulness, blundering, stupidity, inaptitude, ineptitude, bungling, botching, obtuseness, stolidity, dulness.

dexterous—*Syn.* artful, skilful, clever, adroit, expert, active, keen, apt, quick, handy, ingenious, ready. *Ant.* slow, dull, clumsy, awkward, stolid, stupid, obtuse, unskilful, bungling, blundering, ungainly.

dictate—*Syn.* prompt, suggest, enjoin, order, command, direct, instruct, prescribe, deliver, tell, speak. *Ant.* beg, plead, ask, implore, beseech, solicit, entreat, petition, crave, supplicate, importune.

dictatorial—*Syn.* imperative, imperious, domineering, arbitrary, tyrannical, overbearing, arrogant, haughty, dogmatic, opinionated. *Ant.* submissive, modest, bashful, retiring, acquiescent, subservient, obsequious, passive, docile, yielding, reserved, unobtrusive, diffident.

diction—*Syn.* style, expression, wording, vocabulary, phrase, phraseology, verbiage, language.

die—*Syn.* expire, depart, cease, decease, perish, decay, fade, wither, decline, vanish, lose, recede, wane, sink, pass on, pass away. *Ant.* begin, live, move, continue, exist, endure, last, remain, survive, grow, flourish, luxuriate.

diet—*Syn.* food, fare, allowance, sustenance, victuals, nutriment, nourishment, support, subsistence, provisions, nutrition, aliment, meal, mess, dish, repast, breakfast, lunch, dinner, supper, entrée, regalement.

difference—*Syn.* separation, disagreement, dissent, discord, estrangement, variety, distinction, dissimilarity, dissimilitude, variation, variance, divergence, contention, dispute, disparity, inequality, unlikeness, discrimination, diversity, discrepancy. *Ant.* agreement, similarity, similitude, assent, consent, concurrence, accord, accordance, harmony, amity, concord, congruity, unison, union.

different—*Syn.* various, varying, manifold, diverse, unlike, separate, distinct, inharmonious, discordant. *Ant.* similar, like, alike, correspondent, resembling, concordant, harmonious, homogeneous, common, same.

difficult—*Syn.* hard, intricate, involved, perplexing, obscure, arduous, laborious, toilsome, troublesome, unmanageable, unyielding, rigid, puzzling, embarrassing, complex, complicated, confused, unaccommodating. *Ant.*

easy, facile, simple, yielding, complacent, light, lightsome, unconstrained, free, tranquil, calm, unconcerned, childish, smooth, plain, slight, trifling, trivial, pleasant.

difficulty—*Syn.* embroilment, quarrel, contention, argument, dispute, obstacle, obstruction, impediment, perplexity, trouble, annoyance, worry, fret, loss, embarrassment, discouragement, anxiety, complication, distress, stress, oppression, depression. *Ant.* ease, comfort, happiness, pleasure, contentment, satisfaction, independence, felicity, blessedness, bliss, enjoyment, gratification.

diffident, *adj.*—*Syn.* timid, shy, hesitant, reluctant, bashful, shrinking, modest. *Ant.* brash, brazen, bold, forward.

diffuse, *v.*—*Syn.* spread, expand, scatter, sow, extend, disperse, circulate, proclaim, publish, make known, pour out, permeate, disseminate. *Ant.* confine, narrow, limit, keep, control, circumscribe, restrict, prevent.

diffuse, *adj.*—*Syn.* discursive, prolix, diluted, wordy, copious, dispersed, scattered, protracted, tedious, tiresome, prolonged, wearisome. *Ant.* confined, limited, brief, restricted, circumscribed, short, shortened, abbreviated, lightsome, exhilarating, cheery.

dig, *v.*—*Syn.* understand, comprehend, appreciate, grasp, apprehend, discern.

digest, *v.*—*Syn.* transform, arrange, order, ponder, assimilate, absorb, consider, master.

dignify—*Syn.* exalt, elevate, prefer, honor, reverence, advance, promote, adorn, decorate, ennoble, proclaim, boost, extol, invest, aggrandize, magnify, glorify. *Ant.* degrade, shame, disgrace, stultify, condemn, contemn, despise, detract, slander, calumniate, blackball, ostracize, scorn, slur, insult, belittle, humble, humiliate, abase, debase, demean, lower, depose, expose, dishonor, disdain, spurn, ridicule, mock.

dignity, *n.—Syn.* decorum, propriety, nobility, grace, magnificence, decency, elegance, worth, majesty.

digression, *n.—Syn.* deviation, excursion, divagation, detour, divergence, departure, rambling, aberration.

dilate—*Syn.* stretch, widen, broaden, expand, swell, extend, enlarge, descant, expatiate, open, spread, comment, discuss, talk (about), speak (on), discourse (upon), debate, argue, dispute, sift, examine, ventilate, expound. *Ant.* shorten, contract, compress, epitomize, abridge, reduce, abstract, condense, summarize, limit, repress, lessen, circumscribe.

dilatory—*Syn.* tardy, procrastinating, behindhand, lagging, dawdling, slow, late, unwilling, reluctant. *Ant.* brisk, sharp, quick, active, keen, eager, willing, ready, fervent, zealous, enthusiastic, intense, fervid, vehement.

dilemma, *n.—Syn.* quandary, fix, pickle, difficulty, predicament, plight, perplexity.

diligence—*Syn.* care, assiduity, attention, keenness, earnestness, briskness, alertness, quickness, perseverance, industry, heed, carefulness, intent, intentness, intensity. *Ant.* sloth, laziness, carelessness, ennui, languor, dullness or dulness, lethargy, apathy, unconcern, indifference, impassiveness, indolence, disregard, sluggishness, slowness, inactivity.

dim, *adj.—Syn.* dull, obscure, blurred, clouded, indistinct, indefinite, mysterious, faint, opaque. *Ant.* clear, bright, brilliant, distinct.

diminish—*Syn.* lessen, reduce, contract, compress, curtail, retrench, decrease, abate, impair, minimize, lower, degrade, shorten, abridge, epitomize, cut off, abbreviate, prune, trim. *Ant.* increase, enlarge, magnify, widen, extend, expand, spread (out), lengthen, protract, prolong, swell,

amplify, diffuse, dilate.

din, *n.—Syn.* uproar, hubbub, noise, clatter, clamor, racket, ado, clangor, clash.

dingy, *adj.—Syn.* dirty, soiled, grimy, dim, dusky, discolored, faded. *Ant.* clean, spotless, immaculate, bright.

dip, *v.—Syn.* immerse, dive, duck, dunk, souse, plunge.

direct—*Syn.* conduct, lead, guide, dispose, order, contrive, manage, regulate, sway, adjust, govern, control, influence, train, show, demonstrate, explain, teach, inform, instruct, usher, point. *Ant.* deceive, delude, mislead, divert, cheat, beguile, misguide, diverge, lead astray.

direction—*Syn.* way, goal, course, aim, end, inclination, bearing, tendency, guidance, management, superintendence, oversight, government, control, order, command, instruction.

dirty—*Syn.* unclean, soiled, filthy, polluted, nasty, low, mean, depraved, degraded, lewd, lascivious, immoral, stained, spotted, base, contemptible, lying, cowardly, tarnished. *Ant.* clean, upright, decent, honest, honorable, pure, virtuous, unspotted, unstained, untarnished, noble, exalted, high, admirable.

disability—*Syn.* unfitness, incapacity, inability, weakness, decrepitude, incompetence, impotence, infirmity, feebleness, defect, powerlessness, inadequacy, disqualification, uselessness. *Ant.* fitness, capacity, qualification, suitableness, ability, power, powerfulness, efficacy, energy, capability, potentiality, force, might, mightiness, strength, effectiveness, adaptedness, adaptability.

disadvantage—*Syn.* loss, damage, detriment, injury, hurt, hindrance, prejudice, difficulty, harm, evil, stumbling block. *Ant.* advantage, gain, benefit, profit, emolument, help, aid, assistance, utility, interest, service, good luck, fortune, favor.

disagree—*Syn.* differ, dissent, vary, quarrel, dispute, contend, wrangle, combat, oppose, argue. *Ant.* agree, concur, consent, acquiesce, coincide, accept, accede, harmonize.

disappear, *v.*—*Syn.* vanish, dissolve, fade, depart, melt, evaporate, cease, vamoose, scram.

disappoint—*Syn.* thwart, frustrate, betray, baffle, defeat, foil, balk, delude, deceive. *Ant.* aid, assist, coöperate, succor, help, befriend, support, relieve.

disapproval, *n.*—*Syn.* depreciation, condemnation, blame, disapprobation, disparagement, censure, odium.

disaster—*Syn.* calamity, misfortune, mishap, mischance, misadventure, catastrophe, adversity, harm. *Ant.* fortune, advantage, privilege, benefit, blessing, welfare, prosperity, happiness.

discard, *v.*—*Syn.* eliminate, discharge, repudiate, dismiss, scrap, reject, divorce, shed, oust. *Ant.* adopt, embrace, retain, keep.

discern—*Syn.* perceive, observe, descry, recognize, behold, discriminate, separate, see, distinguish, understand, discover, look, know. *Ant.* overlook, neglect, slight, disregard, pass by, fail to see.

discharge, *v.*—*Syn.* dismiss, fire, unload, remove, shoot, project, perform, expel, emit, release, acquit, clear.

disciple, *n.*—*Syn.* pupil, follower, student, trainee, novice, satellite, supporter, votary, devotee, henchman.

discipline—*Syn.* order, method, regulation, training, rule, chastisement, instruction, drill, organization, systematic action. *Ant.* confusion, chaos, disorder, disturbance, disarrangement, derangement, irregularity, misrule, misgovernment, turbulence.

disclose—*Syn.* unfold, reveal, tell, utter, inform, uncover, unveil, discover, divulge, open.—*Ant.* hide, conceal, withhold, cover, veil, screen, cloak, mask, secrete, dissemble, disguise, palliate, deceive.

discompose—*Syn.* disturb, un-

settle, jar, annoy, disarrange, confuse. *Ant.* help, aid, assist, coöperate, mollify, calm, assuage, comfort, mitigate, ameliorate, moderate, soften.

discontent, *n.*—*Syn.* uneasiness, frustration, restlessness, dissatisfaction.

discord—*Syn.* confusion, disturbance, disagreement, discordance, dissension, contention, strife, clash, rupture, dissonance, variance, animosity, ill feeling. *Ant.* harmony, peace, concord, regulation, moderation, good will, agreement, agreeableness, coöperation, accordance, amity, congruity, unison, union.

discourse, *v.*—*Syn.* talk, confer, argue, lecture, debate, declaim, expatiate, discuss, converse.

discourteous, *adj.*—*Syn.* unmannerly, impolite, uncivil, forward, impudent, vulgar, rude, disrespectful. *Ant.* polite, civil, courteous, gallant.

discover—*Syn.* disclose, invent, expose, discern, detect, descry, ascertain, find, find out, contrive, reveal, make known. *Ant.* hide, mask, dissemble, secrete, conceal, screen, bury, disguise, cover, cloak, suppress, mask, veil, inter.

discreditable — *Syn.* disgraceful, shameful, disreputable, scandalous, slanderous, defamatory, libelous, opprobrious. *Ant.* creditable, praiseworthy, commendable, laudable, reputable, estimable, worthy.

discreet—*Syn.* cautious, thoughtful, prudent, wary, judicious, careful, wise, circumspect, watchful, attentive, serious, considerate. *Ant.* indiscreet, incautious, imprudent, reckless, foolish, disregardful, unwary, injudicious, rash, venturesome, hasty, foolhardy, precipitate, thoughtless, heedless, headlong, headstrong, incautious, adventurous, unguarded, unbalanced, regardless.

discrepancy—*Syn.* difference, variance, disagreement, contrariety, contrariness, inconsistency. *Ant.*

agreement, concordance, accordance, concurrence, harmony, fitness, union, unison, unity.

discretion—*Syn.* sagacity, wariness, thoughtfulness, caution, prudence, foresight, circumspection, carefulness. *Ant.* recklessness, imprudence, rashness, inconsiderateness, heedlessness, thoughtlessness.

discrimination — *Syn.* acuteness, perception, caution, prudence, forethought, foresight, care, heed, vigilance, discernment, circumspection, carefulness. *Ant.* foolhardiness, rashness, temerity, precipitancy, haste, recklessness, imprudence, carelessness, negligence, dulness or dullness.

discuss—*Syn.* argue, debate, dispute, controvert, comment, explain, contest, altercate, wrangle. *Ant.* ignore, reject, disregard, pass over.

disdain, *n.*—*Syn.* contempt, scorn, contumely, arrogance, scornfulness, superciliousness, pride, haughtiness, contemptuousness, insolence, reproach, reproachfulness, indignation. *Ant.* praise, laudation, encouragement, flattery, esteem, humility, humbleness, support, favor, countenance, incentive, incitement, commendation.

disdain, *v.*—*Syn.* scorn, detest, loathe, despise, reject, hate, spurn, ignore, abhor, abominate, dislike. *Ant.* approve, like, love, commend, praise, laud, glorify, eulogize, applaud, recommend.

disease—*Syn.* malady, sickness, ailment, disorder, complaint, illness, infirmity, unhealthiness, distemper, affection, unsoundness, indisposition. *Ant.* health, soundness, strength, vigor, virility, forcefulness, robustness, sturdiness.

disengage—*Syn.* loose, free, clear, disentangle, release, extricate, detach, withdraw, liberate, wean, separate, unravel, loosen, set free. *Ant.* bind, tie, tighten, entangle, ensnare, involve, fasten, attach, clench, unite.

disfigure, *v.*—*Syn.* mutilate, distort, blemish, mar, damage, deface, deform.

disgrace, *n.* — *Syn.* dishonor, shame, odium, reproach, disrepute, disfavor, ignominy, infamy, opprobrium, blemish, humiliation. *Ant.* honor, applause, praise, laudation, glorification, exaltation, elevation, dignity, respect, reputation, esteem, renown, self-respect.

disgrace, *v.*—*Syn.* debase, degrade, defame, abase, humiliate, dishonor, shame, disparage, seduce, ravish. *Ant.* honor, exalt, applaud, praise, glorify, extol, magnify, elevate, laud, ennoble.

disguise—*Syn.* change, mask, conceal, camouflage, dissemble, feign, hide, pretend, screen, cloak, cover, veil. *Ant.* open, bare, strip, uncover, unmask, unveil, dismantle, peel off, tear away.

disgust—*Syn.* loathing, abomination, abhorrence, dislike, distaste, aversion, hatred, repugnance, detestation, loathsomeness, resentment. *Ant.* liking, admiration, approval, reverence, approbation, sanction, commendation, praise, laudation, respect, favor, esteem.

disgusting—*Syn.* loathsome, abhorrent, detestable, sickening, repulsive, repugnant, forbidding, ungenial, unattractive, revolting, disagreeable, repellant. *Ant.* likable, lovable, inviting, pleasing, pleasurable, pleasant, genial, attractive, agreeable, acceptable, gratifying, enticing.

dishonest, *adj.*—*Syn.* deceitful, false, crooked, perfidious, fraudulent, untrue, lying, unscrupulous, cheating. *Ant.* upright, straightforward, scrupulous, honest.

dismal—*Syn.* gloomy, sad, melancholy, dreary, doleful, dire, direful, dreadful, dolorous, sorrowful, calamitous, unhappy, dark, unfortunate, horrid, horrible, depressing. *Ant.* joyful, joyous, glad, gladsome, pleasing, pleasant, exhilarating, delightful, gay, merry, inspiring, enlivening, cheerful, cheering.

dismay, *n.—Syn.* terror, dread, fear, fright, alarm, awe, horror, consternation, apprehension, misgiving, trepidation, anxiety. *Ant.* courage, assurance, intrepidity, boldness, unconcern, confidence, effrontery, presumption, temerity, venturesomeness.

dismay, *v.—Syn.* terrify, frighten, scare, daunt, cow, dishearten, depress, intimidate, abash, appal. *Ant.* aid, assist, encourage, help, praise, laud, approve, favor, incite, inspirit, support.

dismiss—*Syn.* discharge, discard, reject, refuse, decline, repudiate, repel, spurn, cast off, send off. *Ant.* retain, keep, hold, preserve, engage, secure, maintain, continue, carry on.

disobey, *v.—Syn.* defy, rebel, resist, ignore, violate, disregard, infringe.

disorder, *n.—Syn.* irregularity, disarrangement, confusion, tumult, bustle, disturbance, illness, sickness, indisposition, malady, distemper, disease. *Ant.* order, regularity, arrangement, neatness, conformity, regulation, method, system, health, vigor, robustness.

disorder, *v.—Syn.* disarrange, confuse, disturb, mix, discompose, derange, ruffle, shuffle, scatter. *Ant.* regulate, systematize, clear, clean up, adjust, conform, classify, arrange, settle, adapt.

disorderly—*Syn.* irregular, confused, tumultuous, intemperate, unruly, lawless, vicious, unrestrained. *Ant.* regular, neat, trim, calm, quiet, disciplined, orderly, temperate, modest, retiring, law-abiding.

disparage—*Syn.* belittle, lower, underestimate, depreciate, deprecate, decry, discredit, dishonor, underrate, undervalue. *Ant.* praise, eulogize, acclaim, approve, laud, applaud, commend, recommend, compliment, flatter, sanction, esteem.

dispel—*Syn.* scatter, disperse, dissipate, dismiss, spread, disseminate, strew, banish, drive away. *Ant.* collect, gather, assemble, accumulate, amass, increase, aggregate, garner, muster.

disperse, *v.—Syn.* scatter, sow, strew, dispel, disseminate, fade, diffuse, separate, spread, dissipate.

displace—*Syn.* misplace, disarrange, disturb, mislay, confuse, derange, unsettle, jumble, mix, remove, dislodge, crowd out. *Ant.* arrange, classify, order, assort, adjust, dispose, place, array, sort, group, put in place, put in order.

display, *n.—Syn.* show, exhibit, exhibition, layout, spread, exposition, showing, arrangement, ostentation, demonstration, pageant, spectacle, turnout (*colloq.*), flourish. *Ant.* concealment, unobtrusiveness, reserve, suppression, restraint, repression.

display, *v.—Syn.* show, arrange, spread, exhibit, expose, open, unfold, expand. *Ant.* hide, conceal, cover, secrete, cloak, camouflage, veil, disguise, mask, suppress.

displease—*Syn.* annoy, vex, disturb, tease, anger, provoke, pique, dissatisfy, disgust, offend, rile, irritate, exasperate, torment, taunt, harass, tantalize, plague, chagrin, mortify, bother, worry, trouble, pester, afflict, chafe, inflame, incense, enrage. *Ant.* please, placate, satisfy, mollify, tranquilize, quiet, allay, calm, pacify, soothe, appease, lull, compose, still, assuage, conciliate, propitiate, reconcile, delight, gratify, humor.

dispose—*Syn.* arrange, place, order, give, bestow, settle, regulate, adjust, classify, adapt, conform. *Ant.* disarrange, disorder, retain, keep, hold, displace, dislodge, disturb, secrete, hide, conceal, secure, cover, cloak, veil.

disposition, *n.—Syn.* nature, temperament, inclination, character, temper, tendency.

dispute—*Syn.* argument, debate, controversy, quarrel, disagreement, estrangement, discussion, contention, contest, conflict, feud, variance, dissension, discord. *Ant.* agreement, harmony, unison, unity, concurrence, covenant, compact, accordance, amity, congruence, congruity, concord.

disreputable, *adj.*—*Syn.* disgraceful, despicable, ignoble, shameful, unworthy, scandalous, shocking, low, base, vulgar, odious.

disrespectful, *adj.*—*Syn.* disparaging, discourteous, rude, irreverent, uncivil, contemptuous, derisive, impolite, impertinent.

dissatisfaction—*Syn.* discontent, discontentment, disappointment, uneasiness, displeasure, dislike, distaste, disapprobation, disapproval, constraint, discomfort. *Ant.* satisfaction, content, contentment, rest, repose, quiet, acquiescence, gratification, relief, atonement, recompense, compensation, amends.

dissemble—*Syn.* disguise, conceal, cloak, cover, veil, screen, hide, feign, falsify, pretend. *Ant.* uncover, unveil, open, expose, show, disclose, expound, explain, lay open.

dissent—*Syn.* disagree, differ, vary, except, contend, dispute, object, disclaim, condemn, oppose, censure, cancel, disapprove. *Ant.* agree, coincide, concur, join, approve, credit, sanction, indorse, commend, ratify, confirm, countenance, abet, authorize, allow, assent.

dissipate, *v.*—*Syn.* waste, spread, diffuse, scatter, lavish, squander, disperse. *Ant.* accumulate, concentrate, absorb, save.

dissolute—*Syn.* loose, licentious, evil, vicious, bad, abandoned, lewd, lascivious, profligate, wanton, dissipated, impure, depraved, unchaste, obscene, defiled. *Ant.* pure, virtuous, moral, good, untainted, unstained, chaste, virginal, uncon-

taminated, undefiled, immaculate, incorrupt.

dissolve, *v.*—*Syn.* melt, divide, disintegrate, disappear, separate, disorganize, fade, vanish, destroy, evaporate.

distant—*Syn.* remote, apart, far, afar, removed, separate, separated, indifferent, cool, cold, haughty, shy, faint, indirect, indistinct. *Ant.* near, adjacent, convenient, close, nigh, next, warm, affectionate, caring, friendly, solicitous, kind, sympathetic, helpful.

distasteful, *adj.*—*Syn.* repugnant, disgusting, obnoxious, loathsome, offensive, repellent, nauseating, unpalatable, repulsive. *Ant.* agreeable, pleasing, welcome, delectable.

distinct—*Syn.* clear, plain, obvious, well-marked, different, disjoined, disunited, separate. *Ant.* obscure, complicated, difficult, abstruse, intricate, complex, indistinct, mixed, involved.

distinction—*Syn.* eminence, superiority, elevation, rank, note, discrimination, discernment, office, division, difference, penetration, acuteness, acumen, clearness, judgment. *Ant.* inferiority, humbleness, humility, meekness, lowliness, abjectness, meanness, baseness, servility, sameness, indifference, mixture, amalgamation, combination.

distinguished—*Syn.* eminent, illustrious, conspicuous, famous, renowned, celebrated, well-known, prominent, noted, notorious, glorious, brilliant, noble. *Ant.* obscure, lowly, humble, meek, unknown, unpretentious, unassuming, unobtrusive, ordinary, unpretending, submissive, despised, scorned, disdained, spurned, contemned, despicable.

distort, *v.*—*Syn.* twist, deform, pervert, disfigure, contort, deface, impair, bend, falsify, misshape, misconstrue.

distract—*Syn.* perplex, bewilder, puzzle, disorder, derange, confuse, daze, dazzle, confound, mystify, embarrass, mislead, complicate, involve. *Ant.* assure, placate, mollify, please, assuage, mitigate, embolden, pacify, calm, reassure, soften, ameliorate, moderate, allay, conciliate.

distress—*Syn.* suffering, pain, agony, misery, grief, trouble, perplexity, misfortune, adversity, calamity, catastrophe, evil, misadventure, unhappiness, wretchedness, sorrow. *Ant.* pleasure, gratification, satisfaction, joy, gaiety, mirth, merriment, frolic, festivity, revelry, jollity, hilarity.

distribute—*Syn.* share, dispense, apportion, scatter, allot, deal, divide, dispose, allow, give away. *Ant.* hoard, retain, keep, collect, lay up, gather, draw together, preserve, secure, get, obtain, maintain.

distribution—*Syn.* allotment, dispensation, deal, division, dispersion, partition, arrangement, apportionment, classification, disposal. *Ant.* maintenance, preservation, hoard, store, storage, retention, retainment, reservation.

disturb—*Syn.* discompose, annoy, trouble, worry, vex, confuse, derange, agitate, arouse, rouse, disarrange, disorder, displace, disconcert, unbalance. *Ant.* pacify, quiet, calm, soothe, soften, mollify, placate, please, conciliate, appease, still, allay, assuage, compose, propitiate, reconcile, tranquilize.

disuse—*Syn.* discontinuance, abolition, desuetude, cessation, intermission, abolishment, abrogation, pause, rest, stop. *Ant.* use, continuance, continuation, continuity, repetition, prolongation, extension, usage, production.

dive, *n.*—*Syn.* joint, dump, hole, pad, jungle, flop, dig, hangout, nest, fleabag.

divergent, *adj.*—*Syn.* deviating, disagreeing, various, varying, variant, contrary, differing, diverse, separating, branching. *Ant.* convergent, parallel, similar, identical.

divest, *v.*—*Syn.* denude, unclothe, bare, deprive, uncover, peel, strip, undress. *Ant.* clothe, cover, invest, dress.

divide—*Syn.* part, separate, distribute, sever, sunder, disunite, disconnect, disjoin, detach, disengage, dissolve, set apart. *Ant.* join, unite, attach, connect, combine, append, add, annex, couple, associate, link, tie, fasten, bind.

divine, *n.*—*Syn.* parson, padre, clergyman, minister, priest, pastor, curé, curate, archbishop, bishop, reverend, ecclesiastic, prelate, sky pilot (*slang*), abbé, churchman. *Ant.* layman, laic, secularist, catechumen, parishioner, follower, disciple.

divine—*Syn.* holy, sacred, heavenly, godlike, consecrated, dedicated, devoted, venerable, sanctified, sanctimonious. *Ant.* evil, wicked, profane, blasphemous, satanic, devilish, diabolical, impious.

division—*Syn.* separation, detachment, partition, section, compartment, portion, difference, discord, disunion, share. *Ant.* union, unity, accord, agreement, indivisibility, singleness, uniformity, oneness, concord, conjunction.

divulge—*Syn.* tell, inform, describe, relate, disclose, impart, reveal, communicate, betray, discover, show, uncover, unveil, make known. *Ant.* secrete, cover, cloak, veil, hide, conceal, disguise, mask, dissemble, prevaricate, retain, keep silent.

do—*Syn.* execute, perform, accomplish, make, finish, transact, complete, achieve, effect, commit, fulfil, realize, transact, consummate, perpetrate, actualize, discharge, act, carry out, bring about. *Ant.* fail, neglect, shun, avoid, miss, spoil, miscarry, defeat, destroy, ruin, frustrate, baffle, mar, spoil, idle, tarry, hesitate, procrastinate, defer, put off.

docile—*Syn.* meek, mild, gentle, tractable, pliant, submissive, manageable, pliable, tame, compliant, yielding, teachable, amenable, obedient, soft, governable. *Ant.* stubborn, unyielding, resolute, determined, dogged, obstinate, wilful, self-willed, intractable, inflexible, firm, opinionated, pertinacious, sullen, morose, obdurate, tough, headstrong, refractory, contumacious, pigheaded.

doctrine—*Syn.* belief, dogma, precept, tenet, principle, teaching, proposition, opinion, theory, religion, creed, credence, faith, persuasion, conviction, cult. *Ant.* heresy, heterodoxy, schism, unbelief, error, falsehood, disbelief, infidelity, incredulity, skepticism.

dogged, *adj.*—*Syn.* determined, stubborn, tenacious, unyielding, pertinacious, obstinate, intractable, inflexible, persistent. *Ant.* irresolute, faltering, wavering, undecided.

dogmatic—*Syn.* positive, immovable, unchangeable, opinionated, dictatorial, overbearing, magisterial, self-opinionated, imperious, authoritative, doctrinal, systematic, arrogant, domineering. *Ant.* uncertain, wavering, doubtful, hesitating, skeptical, ambiguous, equivocal, dubious, questionable, precarious, unsettled, fluctuating, hesitant, vacillating, indecisive.

doleful—*Syn.* sad, sorrowful, sorry, dolorous, woebegone, rueful, dismal, piteous, woeful, cheerless, mournful, pathetic, pitiable, wretched, miserable, abject, disconsolate, forlorn. *Ant.* cheerful, jolly, joyous, sprightly, gay, mirthful, jovial, merry, lively, sportive, happy, sunny, buoyant, enlivening, blithe, bright, entertaining, amusing.

domestic, *adj.*—*Syn.* tame, domesticated, internal, household, home, native. *Ant.* wild, untamed, savage, foreign.

domesticated, *adj.*—*Syn.* tamed, broken, attached, naturalized, bred, trained.

domicile, *n.*—*Syn.* home, abode, residence, dwelling, digs, habitation, apartment.

dominant—*Syn.* controlling, predominant, commanding, imperious, aggressive, governing, ruling, prevailing, imperative, authoritative, lordly, despotic. *Ant.* humble, obscure, meek, lowly, unassuming, retiring, backward, bashful, modest, reserved, nonaggressive, reluctant.

domineering—*Syn.* haughty, arrogant, proud, tyrannical, despotic, overbearing, imperious, arbitrary, peremptory, tyrannous, oppressive, cruel. *Ant.* retiring, modest, self-effacing, self-denying, humble, gentle, mild, kind, soft, merciful, pitying, reserved, unobtrusive coy, shy, diffident, bashful, timid, shrinking, chary.

dominion—*Syn.* authority, jurisdiction, sway, control, government, territory, region, district, country. *Ant.* subjection, service, bondage, slavery, thraldom, subjugation, dependency.

donation—*Syn.* grant, gratuity, endowment, gift, benefit, benefaction, bequest, boon, bounty, charity, alms, present, provision, subscription.

done, *adj.*—*Syn.* ended, finished, executed, completed, achieved, solved, concluded, performed. *Ant.* incomplete, unfinished, raw, inchoate.

doom—*Syn.* sentence, verdict, judgment, fate, lot, destiny, decree, fortune, destination, finish, end.

double, *adj.*—*Syn.* dual, duplicate, twofold, coupled, bipartite, duplex, paired.

doubt, *n.*—*Syn.* distrust, disbelief, skepticism, unbelief, incredulity, suspicion, uncertainty, scruple, misgiving, perplexity, indecision, irresolution, suspense, hesitancy, hesitation, mistrust. *Ant.* faith, belief, confidence, fidelity, trust, credence, conviction, reliance, assurance, certainty, dependence, faithfulness, constancy.

doubt, *v.*—*Syn.* question, suspect, impugn, contradict, insinuate, mistrust, surmise, distrust, discredit, disbelieve, hesitate, scruple. *Ant.* believe, trust, credit, confide, approve, sanction, indorse, commend, support, promote, authorize, ratify.

D.P., n.—Syn. displaced person, refugee, outcast, expatriate, émigré.

draw—Syn. pull, haul, drag, attract, inhale, sketch, describe, move, bring, convey, lure, tow, tug, allure, induce, entice, trail. Ant. repel, repulse, alienate, estrange, rebuff, reject, leave, abandon.

dread—Syn. fear, horror, terror, alarm, dismay, awe, fright, panic, consternation, apprehension, trepidation, anxiety, timidity, misgiving, commotion, cowardice. Ant. boldness, bravery, courage, calmness, intrepidity, audacity, assurance, confidence, presumption, effrontery, heroism, valor, fearlessness, arrogance, haughtiness, hardihood, daring, quietness, quietude, repose, reposefulness, tranquillity, placidity.

dream—Syn. fantasy, illusion, imagination, vision, fancy, conceit, hallucination, romance, trance, reverie, chimera, deception, delusion, fallacy. Ant. certainty, fact, reality, substance, verity, realization, actuality, truth, existence, body, solidity, matter, materiality.

dress—Syn. clothes, attire, apparel, garments, costume, garb, livery, raiment, vesture, habit, uniform, vestments, robes, habiliments, array. Ant. nudity, nakedness, undress, exhibitionism, exposure, disarray, bareness, dishabille or deshabille.

drift—Syn. tendency, tenor, issue, course, effort, direction, end, purpose, design, meaning, object, objective, inference, scope, aim, intention, result, purport, motion. Ant. aimlessness, purposelessness, nullity, motionlessness, inactivity, inertness, inertia, laziness, sluggishness, passivity, passiveness.

drink, v.—Syn. imbibe, quaff, swallow, tipple, swig, swizzle, guzzle, absorb.

drive—Syn. impel, urge, direct, propel, compel, push, ride, repel, repulse, resist, coerce, thrust, actuate, incite, force, move, instigate, press, stimulate, encourage. Ant. check, stop, halt, hinder, discourage, retard, control, curb, restrain, repress, entice, allure, attract, induce, incline, lead, lure, tug, tow, drag, haul.

droll—Syn. laughable, comic, comical, funny, whimsical, amusing, queer, exciting, entertaining, diverting, pleasing, pleasurable, humorous, witty, jocose, jocular, merry, facetious, waggish, mirthful, ludicrous. Ant. dull, prosaic, heavy, serious, ponderous, weighty, monstrous, dreary, insipid, humdrum, tedious, wearisome, vapid, stupid, stolid, slow, sluggish, sleepy, tiresome, uninteresting, commonplace, irksome, prolix, prosy.

drone, n.—Syn. idler, loafer, bum, sponger, good-for-nothing, ne'er-do-well, sluggard. Ant. worker, enthusiast, eager beaver.

drop—Syn. drip, trickle, dribble, ooze, emanate, distil, percolate, fall, descend, droop, give up, relinquish, abandon, stop. Ant. empty, spill, flood, flow, overflow, squirt, spout, splash, sprinkle, pour, take up, continue, pursue.

drown—Syn. inundate, swamp, immerse, submerge, engulf, overwhelm, perish, plunge, deluge, sink, overflow. Ant. rescue, save, perserve, raise, haul out, buoy up, float, recover, deliver, extricate.

drug, n.—Syn. medicine, narcotic, pharmaceutical, simple, specific, physic, dope, biological.

drunk—Syn. intoxicated, inebriated, fuddled, full, soused (slang), soaked, (slang), spifflicated (slang), pickled (slang), half-seas-over (slang), boozy (slang), tipsy, drunken, exhilarated, sottish, overcome, maudlin, muddled. Ant. sober, steady, temperate, abstemious, abstaining, abstinent, moderate, exemplary, self-possessed, regular, calm, serious, solemn, sedate, ascetic, nonindulgent.

dry—*Syn.* arid, parched, lifeless, dull, tedious, uninteresting, meagre, juiceless, barren, dull, vapid, prosy, jejune, severe, hard, cynical, sneering, sarcastic. *Ant.* wet, moist, damp, soggy, boggy, soppy, soaky, soaked, soaking, oozing, oozy, watery, saturated, dripping, humid, muddy, soft, spongy.

dubious, *adj.*—*Syn.* doubtful, equivocal, unclear, hesitant, wavering, unreliable, unsettled, problematical, uncertain, suspicious, questionable, reluctant. *Ant.* certain, sure, cocksure, positive.

dud, *n.*—*Syn.* failure, flop, fizzle, bore, misfit, pain, drag, wallflower, turkey, washout.

dull—*Syn.* stupid, stolid, doltish, besotted, half-witted, insensate, obtuse, prosy, dry, lifeless, witless, senseless, heavy, insipid, vapid, gloomy, sad, dismal, commonplace. *Ant.* lively, sprightly, keen, quick, sharp, witty, humorous, brisk, gay, animated, spirited, vivacious, active, smart, brainy, intelligent.

dunce—*Syn.* simpleton, fool, ninny, nincompoop (*colloq.*), idiot, dolt, blockhead, dunderhead (*slang*), jolterhead (*colloq.*), numskull, booby, chowderhead (*dial.*), ass, mutt (*slang*), goose, babbler, bonehead, (*slang*), ignoramus. *Ant.* sage, philosopher, scholar, wit, humorist, genius, prodigy, teacher, preceptor, guide, leader, commander, chief.

dupe, *n.*—*Syn.* victim, gull, mark, chump, pigeon, cluck, touch, sucker, catspaw, butt.

duplicate—*Syn.* likeness, facsimile, copy, replica, imitation, transcript, reproduction, tracing, representation, portrait, similarity, similitude, resemblance. *Ant.* original, pattern, prototype, model, archetype, example, exemplar, precedent, standard.

durable—*Syn.* lasting, permanent, abiding, continuing, constant, changeless, enduring, remaining. *Ant.* passing, transitory, evanescent, vanishing, fleeting, impermanent, perishable, ephemeral, temporary, brief, short.

duty—*Syn.* office, function, responsibility, accountability, business, obligation, right, righteousness, part, province, calling, service, employment, integrity. *Ant.* irresponsibility, disloyalty, betrayal, faithlessness, falsehood, treachery, dishonesty, inconstancy, perfidiousness, unfaithfulness, deceit, untrustworthiness.

dwell—*Syn.* stay, inhabit, stop, abide, sojourn, linger, tarry, remain, continue, lodge, live, await, reside. *Ant.* move, remove, discontinue, renounce, abandon, give up, forsake, desert, leave, quit, relinquish.

dwelling, *n.*—*Syn.* home, abode, house, habitation, quarters, domicile, residence.

dwindle—*Syn.* pine, waste, diminish, decrease, lessen, narrow, shrink, decline, reduce, curtail, shorten, abridge. *Ant.* increase, grow, multiply, add, augment, enlarge, swell, heighten, dilate, expand, spread, widen, extend.

dye, *v.*—*Syn.* stain, imbue, color, infuse, tint, tinge.

E

eager—*Syn.* earnest, enthusiastic, anxious, keen, fervent, ardent, zealous, desirous, intent, impatient, vehement, longing, yearning, glowing, burning, intense, hot, importunate, impetuous, impassioned, forward. *Ant.* diffident, backward, retiring, bashful, apathetic, cool, frigid, heedless, calm, phlegmatic, uninterested, purposeless, slow, stolid, regardless, dispassionate, careless, indifferent, unconcerned, stony, unmindful, unmoved, neglected.

earn—*Syn.* gain, achieve, acquire,

obtain, win, merit, deserve, attain, compass, get, procure, realize, accomplish, consummate, effect, perform, win. *Ant.* lose, waste, idle, shirk, fail, miss, forfeit, loaf, dodge, spend, consume, exhaust, squander, dissipate.

earnest—*Syn.* ardent, serious, grave, solemn, sincere, eager, urgent, zealous, warm, importunate, fervent, weighty, sober, sedate, thoughtful, intense, determined, forceful, decided, firm, fixed, resolute, steady, obstinate, immovable. *Ant.* trifling, frivolous, light, unheeding, careless, heedless, inattentive, negligent, incautious, inconsiderate, thoughtless, unconcerned, unmindful, unsteady, capricious, regardless, slack, hesitant.

earthly, *adj.*—*Syn.* mundane, worldly, profane, temporal, material, base, sordid, carnal, earthy. *Ant.* spiritual, heavenly, immaterial, incorporeal.

earthy, *adj.*—*Syn.* material, sensual, coarse, earthly, gross.

ease, *n.*—*Syn.* comfort, rest, quietness, quietude, repose, tranquillity, restfulness, easiness, satisfaction, calmness, solace, consolation, expertness, facility, knack, readiness. *Ant.* worry, sorrow, grief, trouble, discomfort, annoyance, disquiet, irritation, unrest, harassment, turmoil, strife, vexation, chagrin, mortification, perplexity, difficulty, uneasiness, constraint.

ease, *v.*—*Syn.* alleviate, allay, mitigate, lighten, comfort, soothe, calm, soften, pacify, compress, assuage, appease, disburden, rid, abate, tranquillize, ameliorate, meliorate. *Ant.* worry, annoy, oppress, distress, harass, weary, tire, pain, grieve, afflict, perplex, puzzle, bewilder, confuse, distract, plague, tease, molest, bother, confound, mystify.

easy—*Syn.* light, comfortable, unrestrained, pleasant, facile, indulgent, gentle, smooth, unconcerned, manageable, flexible,

pliant. *Ant.* hard, difficult, puzzling, intricate, complex, involved, arduous, laborious, toilsome, troublesome, severe, oppressive, complicated, entangled, perplexed, obscure, onerous, trying, exhausting.

ebb, *v.*—*Syn.* recede, wane, dwindle, retire, lessen, sink, abate, decline, fall. *Ant.* flow, wax, increase, climb.

eccentric—*Syn.* odd, queer, strange, abnormal, wayward, particular, singular, anomalous, irregular, deviating, unusual, quaint, fantastic, droll, comical, whimsical, crochety, cranky, erratic. *Ant.* regular, normal, ordinary, plain, customary, orderly, methodical, formal, usual, natural, common, systematic, conventional, steady, firm, fixed, constant, uniform, equable, consistent, undeviating, well-regulated.

economical—*Syn.* saving, sparing, careful, frugal, thrifty, provident, niggardly, miserly, stingy, mean, parsimonious, avaricious, close, penurious, chary, watchful, circumspect. *Ant.* liberal, generous, wasteful, squandering, careless, bounteous, beneficent, free, munificent, improvident, thoughtless, lavish, prodigal.

ecstasy—*Syn.* joy, overjoy, delight, rapture, rejoicing, transport, merriment, bliss, exultation, triumph, revel, revelry, gratification, cheer, glorification, hilarity, emotion, glee, fun. *Ant.* worry, trouble, sorrow, blues (*colloq.*), blue devils (*colloq.*), doldrums, hypochondria, hypochondriasis, the dumps, despair, grief, misfortune, low spirits, pessimism, hopelessness, misery, pain, calamity, wretchedness, unhappiness.

eddy, *v.*—*Syn.* swirl, whirl, spin, reverse.

edge—*Syn.* border, brink, boundary, brim, margin, verge, side, rim, ring, periphery, circumference, sharpness, keenness. *Ant.* surface, flat, level, area, space, site, range, interior, extension, plain, plane, bluntness, thickness, dullness or dulness.

edict—*Syn.* decree, proclamation, order, command, law, manifesto, announcement, judgment, ordinance, public notice, mandate.

edifice, *n.*—*Syn.* building, structure, house.

education—*Syn.* schooling, tuition, training, culture, learning, study, cultivation, reading, information, instruction, teaching, discipline, knowledge, development, refinement, enlightenment, scholarship, wisdom. *Ant.* ignorance, illiteracy, obtuseness, stupidity, dullness or dulness, stolidity, doltishness, asininity, boorishness, stagnation, degradation, disgrace, shame, dishonor.

educe, *v.*—*Syn.* extract, elicit, draw, infer, evoke.

eerie, *adj.*—*Syn.* weird, strange, peculiar, grotesque, horrific, fantastic, odd, curious, uncanny.

efface—*Syn.* expunge, obliterate, erase, cancel, blot out, wipe out, annul, destroy. *Ant.* keep, retain, confirm, indorse, sanction, strengthen, approve, renew.

effect, *n.*—*Syn.* consequence, result, issue, event, execution, operation, meaning, reality, outcome, end, finish, consummation, inference, conclusion, decision, determination, deduction, completion. *Ant.* cause, beginning, origin, commencement, foundation, source, spring, wellspring, fount, fountain.

effect, *v.*—*Syn.* accomplish, achieve, realize, execute, operate, finish, conclude, do, perform, fulfill, consummate, bring about. *Ant.* fail, neglect, abandon, cease, disappoint, desert, omit, quit, leave, overlook, give up.

effective—*Syn.* efficient, serviceable, useful, operative, efficacious, adequate, productive, capable, competent, yielding, resultant. *Ant.* inoperative, inefficient, useless, inadequate, incapable, incompetent, barren, fruitless, nonproductive.

effeminate, *adj.*—*Syn.* womanly, womanish, feminine, unmanly, emasculate, soft, sissy, queer. *Ant.* manly, masculine, he-man, virile, robust.

effervescent, *adj.*—*Syn.* bubbling, volatile, gay, frothy, buoyant, hilarious, gleeful. *Ant.* flat, staid, sober, sedate.

efficiency—*Syn.* ability, capability, capableness, effectiveness, fitness, power, capacity, competency, qualification, suitableness, suitability, adaptedness, adaptability, adaptation, thoroughness, completeness. *Ant.* inability, incapacity, incompetency, inadequacy, defectiveness, weakness, impotence, unskifulness, deficiency, powerlessness, helplessness.

efficient—*Syn.* competent, fitting, fitted, suitable, suited, effectual, effective, efficacious, able, capable, adapted, adequate, qualified, skilful, clever, energetic. *Ant.* inefficient, inadequate, unsuitable, incapable, incompetent, unqualified, stupid, ignorant, unskilful, unfit, ineffectual, dull, unable, insufficient, weak, feeble, deficient.

effort, *n.*—*Syn.* exertion, application, endeavor, trouble, essay, strain, work, pains, attempt, energy.

effrontery—*Syn.* hardihood, impudence, boldness, audacity, insolence, assurance, brass (slang), shamelessness, immodesty, gall (slang), nerve (slang), cheek (slang), brazenness, presumption, daring, sauciness, courage, bravery, fearlessness. *Ant.* modesty, reluctance, humbleness, humility, backwardness, bashfulness, reserve, reservedness, confusion, shyness, timidity, unobtrusiveness, coyness, propriety, meekness, mildness, diffidence, sensitiveness.

egghead, *n.*—*Syn.* intellectual, brain, thinker, long-hair, liberal, pinko.

egotism—*Syn.* egoism, conceit, vanity, pride, assurance, self-confidence, self-consciousness, self-conceit, self-assertion, self-esteem, elation, presumption, arrogance, insolence, overconfidence, haughtiness, ostentation, boastfulness. *Ant.* humility, meekness, mildness, modesty, self-depreciation, humbleness, submissiveness, self-abasement, reserve, reservedness, diffidence, hesitation, shyness, coyness, restraint, backwardness, bashfulness, deference, self-distrust.

egotistic—*Syn.* egoistic, vain, vainglorious, boastful, conceited, inflated, bombastic, self-centered, showy, hifalutin, affected, high-flown, proud, ostentatious, pretentious, pompous. *Ant.* retiring, reserved, meek, modest, humble, unobtrusive, unostentatious, modest, diffident, bashful, shy, coy, timid, shrinking, timorous, fearful, lowly, submissive, unassuming, unpretending.

eject—*Syn.* banish, dismiss, discharge, expel, oust, dispossess, dislodge, remove, evict, exile, eradicate, cast out, discard. *Ant.* take in, accept, establish, confirm, place, sanction, fix, settle, approve, authorize, allow, countenance, appoint, abet.

elaborate, *adj.*—*Syn.* gaudy, showy, garnished, decorated, ostentatious, imposing, ornamented, embellished, polished, refined, beautified. *Ant.* plain, common, ordinary, general, usual, unrefined, normal, regular.

elaborate, *v.*—*Syn.* improve, refine, perfect, embellish, beautify, adorn, ornament, decorate, deck, bedeck. *Ant.* mar, deform, deface, blotch, botch, injure, disfigure, impair, diminish, lessen, spoil, despoil, destroy.

elastic, *adj.* — *Syn.* resilient, pliant, supple, limber, rubbery, springy, lithe, adaptable, flexible, extensible. *Ant.* rigid, stiff, inflexible, tense.

elated, *adj.*—*Syn.* animated, exultant, delighted, ecstatic, exalted, high-spirited, exhilarated, enraptured, enlivened, flushed.

Ant. depressed, downhearted, gloomy, low.

elation—*Syn.* enthusiasm, delight, rapture, exaltation, transport, ecstasy, joy, overjoy, bliss, charm, gratification, satisfaction. *Ant.* depression, gloom, sadness, misery, mortification, despair, abasement, dejection, humiliation, despondency, melancholy.

elect, *v.*—*Syn.* choose, opt, resolve, judge, take, select, call, prefer, settle, pick.

elegant—*Syn.* polished, refined, graceful, pleasing, well-formed, symmetrical, regular, polite, pleasant, agreeable, courteous, handsome. *Ant.* crude, awkward, uncouth, slovenly, repellent, repulsive, repugnant, obnoxious, rude, boorish, rough, coarse, unrefined, clownish, rustic, ungraceful, displeasing, disagreeable.

elementary—*Syn.* primary, rudimental, rudimentary, simple, easy, pure, unmixed, uncompounded, incomplex, undeveloped, plain, unaffected, not difficult. *Ant.* difficult, complex, complicated, mixed, involved, hard, troublesome, abstruse, composite, entangled, heterogeneous, confused, intricate.

elevate—*Syn.* raise, hoist, heighten, exalt, glorify, elate, promote, extol, magnify, dignify, honor, reverence, respect, revere, esteem. *Ant.* lower, deprecate, denounce, despise, humble, humiliate, mortify, shame, disgrace, condemn, contemn, slight, scorn, mock, traduce, disdain, spurn.

elicit, *v.*—*Syn.* evoke, wrest, extort, extract, draw, educe.

eliminate—*Syn.* expel, dislodge, banish, proscribe, oust, cancel, discharge, remove, take away, score out, eject, suppress, displace. *Ant.* replace, restore, keep, retain, maintain, hold, preserve, sanction, approve, accept, ratify.

eloquence—*Syn.* oratory, rhetoric, declamation, oration, expression, ability, style, diction, speech, voice, talent, address, harangue, appeal, fluency, wit, wittiness. *Ant.* dullness, stupidity, ignorance, silence, stuttering, stammering, asininity, sluggishness, clownishness, hesitancy, slowness.

elucidate—*Syn.* explain, illustrate, clear up, point out, interpret, expound, clarify, illuminate. *Ant.* obscure, darken, becloud, mix, confuse, disorder, jumble, distract, puzzle, embarrass.

elude—*Syn.* dodge, shun, avoid, escape, evade, baffle, parry, fence, frustrate, mock, equivocate, prevaricate, escape, eschew. *Ant.* seek, invite, court, solicit, ask, allure, attract, entice, decoy, seduce, draw, inveigle.

emanate, *v.*—*Syn.* issue, spring, emerge, proceed, stem, originate, flow, arise.

emancipate—*Syn.* free, liberate, deliver, release, lose, discharge, acquit, clear, enfranchise, remit, exempt, rescue, affranchise, manumit. *Ant.* suppress, imprison, hold, check, restrain, bind, curb, confine, prevent, hinder, shackle, immure, restrict, repress, coerce, limit, circumscribe, chain, enchain, enslave.

embarrass—*Syn.* perplex, entangle, distress, annoy, trouble, puzzle, disconcert, hamper, obstruct, confuse, involve, complicate, bewilder, distract, harass, vex, plague, worry, confound, tease, mystify, bother. *Ant.* please, mollify, help, assist, encourage, inspire, inspirit, cheer, exhilarate, incite, invigorate, urge, impel, stimulate, embolden, instigate, promote, advance, forward, gladden, spur, goad, enliven, animate, rouse, arouse.

embellish—*Syn.* adorn, decorate, deck, bedeck, beautify, ornament, illustrate, garnish. *Ant.* spoil, despoil, injure, impair,

mar, tarnish, destroy, obliterate, soil, deteriorate, disfigure, deface, botch, batter, wreck, ruin.

embezzle—*Syn.* steal, forge, pilfer, appropriate, misappropriate, purloin, peculate, misuse, plunder, rob, thieve, swindle, rifle, filch, cheat, defraud. *Ant.* reimburse, pay back, make good, return, recompense, satisfy, remunerate, defray, requite, reward, indemnify, compensate.

emblem—*Syn.* symbol, figure, image, token, sign, attribute, memento, type, representation, reminder, souvenir, keepsake, medal, miniature, character, device, motto, design.

embody, *v.*—*Syn.* incorporate, embrace, integrate, contain, comprehend, comprise, include.

embolden,—*Syn.* inspirit, animate, encourage, urge, impel, stimulate, instigate, cheer, nerve, strengthen, incite, rouse, arouse, press, push, force, importune, spur, invigorate, *Ant.* weaken, discourage, dishearten, depress, deject, unnerve, lower, abase, cast down, dispirit, humiliate, mock, ridicule, despise.

embrace—*Syn.* clasp, encircle, hug, comprehend, accept, contain, espouse, subscribe to, adopt, seize, take advantage of, cling to. *Ant.* neglect, ignore, miss, lose, shun, evade, scorn, despise, slight, contemn, weaken, waver, hesitate, shrink from.

emend, *v.*—*Syn.* correct, revise, improve, rectify, reform, repair. *Ant.* corrupt, debase, spoil.

emergency—*Syn.* crisis, strait, necessity, exigency, pressure, urgency, dilemma, puzzle, embarrassment, perplexity, state, difficulty, importunity, tension, distress, compulsion, obligation. *Ant.* commonness, commonplaceness, normalcy, normality, regularity, fixedness, stability, steadiness, routine, conventionality, smooth sailing, fair wind.

emigrate—*Syn.* migrate, leave,

quit, abandon, go away from, depart, move. *Ant.* remain, stay, abide, reside, dwell in.

eminent—*Syn.* distinguished, well-known, famous, prominent, noted, conspicuous, illustrious, renowned, celebrated, superior, supreme. *Ant.* obscure, unknown, humble, modest, diffident, lowly, unpretentious, retiring, despicable, contemptible, petty, paltry, insignificant.

emissary—*Syn.* agent, plotter, spy, scout, investigator, go-between, mediator, representative, deputy, factor, substitute, actor, commissioner, proxy, delegate, intermediary, envoy, legate, ambassador, messenger, diplomat, nuncio, plenipotentiary.

emit—*Syn.* exhale, discharge, vent, open, utter, report, publish, issue forth, give out, draw out, evaporate, express, issue. *Ant.* retain, keep in, stifle, withhold, suppress, repress, conceal, stop, smother, restrain, refrain.

emotion—*Syn.* perturbation, agitation, trepidation, tremor, commotion, excitement, disturbance, feeling, worry, discomposure, disquiet, uneasiness, tumult, turmoil, dread, fear, apprehension. *Ant.* quiet, quietness, quietude, rest, tranquillity, placidness, repose, restraint, calm, calmness, stillness, peace, peacefulness, harmony, concord, dispassion, apathy.

empathy, n.—*Syn.* understanding, appreciation, compassion, sensitivity.

emphatic—*Syn.* strong, determined, forceful, forcible, earnest, impressive, positive, important, energetic, consummate, solemn, effective, affecting, cogent, potent, powerful, irresistible. *Ant.* weak, vacillating, wavering, hesitating, uncertain, timid, timorous, diffident, faint-hearted, shy, fearful, sensitive, reserved, modest, shrinking, loath, averse, unwilling, reluctant, bashful.

employ—*Syn.* engage, hire, commission, use, occupy, devote, busy, procure, contract, retain, reserve. *Ant.* dismiss, discharge, reject, remove, banish, abandon, bounce (*colloq.*).

employment—*Syn.* work, business, vocation, avocation, engagement, employment, calling, occupation, trade, pursuit, craft, office, profession. *Ant.* idleness, unemployment, inactivity, sluggishness, sloth, languor, ennui, weariness, laziness.

empower—*Syn.* grant, authorize, permit, sanction, license, commission, delegate, warrant, depute, commit, intrust, appoint, confirm, approve, countenance, allow, ratify. *Ant.* see those for **employ** above.

empty—*Syn.* hollow, bare, unfilled, unfurnished, unoccupied, vacant, vacated, void, devoid, destitute, unsatisfactory, weak, silly, senseless, stupid, ignorant, hungry, fasting, barren, fruitless, meaningless, foolish. *Ant.* full, filled, replete, occupied, tenanted, inhabited, complete, entire, adequate, sufficient, sated, satisfied, copious, abundant, wise, thoughtful, brainy, far-seeing, smart, erudite, scholarly.

emulation—*Syn.* competition, rivalry, contention, controversy, jealousy, strife, contest, imitation, envy, antagonism, striving, earnestness, struggle, vanity, ambition. *Ant.* lethargy, sluggishness, carelessness, heedlessness, inactivity, negligence, apathy, unconcernedness, regardlessness.

enable, v.—*Syn.* empower, authorize, sanction, permit, allow, let.

enamour—*Syn.* please, entice, enthral, attract, charm, captivate, fascinate, enslave, bewitch, enchain, enchant, entrance, enrapture, ravish, transport, draw, allure. *Ant.* displease, disgust, repel, repulse, revolt, antagonize, offend, anger, provoke, vex, pique, dissatisfy.

enchant—*Syn.* charm, fascinate, bewitch, captivate, enthral, enrapture, ravish, attract, allure, entice. *Ant.* repel, disgust, revolt, offend, displease, anger, provoke, dissatisfy, disappoint.

enchantment—*Syn.* magic, spell, witchery, fascination, captivation, allurement, sorcery, necromancy, incantation. *Ant.* revulsion, repulsion, irritation, uneasiness, dread, fear, antagonism, antipathy, loathing, loathsomeness.

encomium—*Syn.* praise, laudation, glorification, eulogy, eulogium, panegyric, commendation. *Ant.* denunciation, condemnation, disapprobation, blame, censure, reprehension, reproval, reproach.

encompass—*Syn.* encircle, surround, gird, beset, inclose, include, environ, invest, hem in, envelop.

encounter—*Syn.* attack, conflict, combat, assault, onset, engagement, battle, action, meeting, assailment, invasion, inroad, charge, clash, collision, impact, concussion. *Ant.* peace, amity, agreement, concord, truce, conformity, harmony, union, concurrence.

encourage—*Syn.* countenance, sanction, support, foster, cherish, inspirit, embolden, animate, cheer, incite, urge, advise, stimulate, impel, instigate, enliven, exhilarate, inspire, comfort, approve, goad, spur. *Ant.* discourage, dispirit, dampen, depress, dishearten, deject, dissuade, deter, mock, deride, distract, confuse, sink, lower, abase, humble, humiliate, denounce.

encroach—*Syn.* infringe, trespass, invade, intrude, enter upon, transgress, infract, violate. *Ant.* shun, keep off, avoid, eschew, dodge, evade, elude, recede, withdraw, retire.

encumbrance—*Syn.* burden, hindrance, drawback, drag, clog, impediment, load, obstacle, difficulty. *Ant.* advantage, help, assistance, incentive, spur, goad, vantage, aid, succor, stimulus, stimulant.

end, *n.*—*Syn.* aim, object, purpose, result, conclusion, upshot, close, expiration, termination, extremity, sequel, terminal, limit, issue, consequence, decease, death. *Ant.* beginning, origin, commencement, start, rise, fountain, source, cause, spring, initiation, inception, opening, outset, inauguration, foundation.

end, *v.*—*Syn.* stop, finish, close, wind up, quit, terminate, break off, cease, desist, conclude, settle, leave, relinquish. *Ant.* begin, start, commence, originate, institute, inaugurate, enter upon, initiate, introduce, set out, set up, establish, found.

endanger—*Syn.* peril, imperil, expose, hazard, risk, jeopard, jeopardize, venture, chance. *Ant.* guard, safeguard, protect, watch, cover, hide, conceal, defend, secure.

endeavor—*Syn.* attempt, try, essay, strive, aim, exert, undertake, attack, contend, struggle, wrangle, contest, labor, work, purpose, aspire. *Ant.* idle, rest, cease, stop, quit, give up, shun, trifle, discard, ignore, laze (*colloq.*), put off, procrastinate, postpone, defer, delay.

endless, *adj.*—*Syn.* eternal, everlasting, incessant, perpetual, continuous, unlimited, interminable, uninterrupted, infinite, boundless, ceaseless, constant, imperishable. *Ant.* transient, transitory, passing, ephemeral.

endowment—*Syn.* benefit, benefaction, gift, provision, bequest, bounty, donation, gratuity, grant, capacity, attainment, qualification, natural gift, mentality, talent. *Ant.* loss, damage, detriment, injury, harm, drawback, confiscation, mulct, amercement.

endurance—*Syn.* sufferance, fortitude, submission, forbearance, resignation, patience, continuance, continuation, duration, tolerance, allowance, inconvenience, pain, misery, trial, tribulation, firmness, coolness, courage, perseverance, stamina, restraint, resistance. *Ant.* surrender, weakness, breakdown, faltering, succumbing, yielding, failing, despair, hopelessness, faintness, giving up.

endure—*Syn.* suffer, bear, tolerate, allow, permit, support, undergo, sustain, brook, abide, submit, feel, experience. *Ant.* faint, falter, resign, give up, give in, fail, fall, sink, succumb, yield, surrender, break, break down, droop, despair.

enemy—*Syn.* foe, rival, antagonist, adversary, opponent, attacker, detractor, backbiter, informer, calumniator, falsifier, competitor, slanderer, vilifier, defamer, traducer, asperser, defiler. *Ant.* friend, benefactor, helper, assistant, adviser, wellwisher, patron, encourager, inciter, backer, supporter, associate, companion, ally, chum (*colloq.*), buddy (*slang*), messmate, pal (*slang*), confidant, adherent, coadjutor, upholder, protector, guardian, abettor, accomplice, accessory.

energetic—*Syn.* industrious, effective, effectual, efficacious, forcible, powerful, vigorous, determined, strong, lusty, potent, adequate, mighty, cogent, active, diligent. *Ant.* weak, vacillating, unsteady, wavering, fluctuating, hesitant, puny, inadequate, inactive, lazy, idle, slow, sluggish, slothful, indolent, listless, spiritless, careless.

energy—*Syn.* strength, vim, vigor, pep (slang), activity, force, power, effectiveness, capacity, endurance, momentum, efficacy, capability, potentiality, powerfulness, robustness, toughness, lustiness, puissance, vehemency, potency, efficiency. *Ant.* weakness, uncertainty, vacillation, hesitancy, laziness, idleness, ennui, tiredness, weariness, apathy, negligence, inactivity, lassitude, languor, fatigue, heaviness, dullness, sluggishness, slothfulness, indolence, vapidness.

enervate—*Syn.* debilitate, weaken, enfeeble, impair, reduce, sap, paralyze, attenuate, injure, soften, daze, flabbergast (colloq.). *Ant.* strengthen, buoy up, invigorate, animate, energize, encourage, enthuse, inspirit, cheer, enliven, incite, exhilarate.

enforce—*Syn.* urge, compel, incite, exert, drive, strain, constrain, execute, exact, require, coerce, oblige, force, necessitate, press, impel. *Ant.* neglect, abandon, dodge, drop, omit, slight, overlook, disregard, dismiss, default, leave, quit, forego, renounce, give up.

engage—*Syn.* employ, busy, occupy, attract, invite, allure, enlist, entertain, engross, accept, hire, retain, reserve, attack, take part in, use, commission, appoint, delegate, authorize, depute, ordain, constitute, empower. *Ant.* dismiss, discharge, remove, reject, release, displace, oust, eject, put out, cancel, banish, discard, shun, expel, refuse, decline, dislodge, bounce (*slang*).

engagement, *n.*—*Syn.* betrothal, obligation, pledge, plighting, espousal, consenting.

engine, *n.*—*Syn.* machine, instrument, apparatus, device, contrivance.

engross—*Syn.* absorb, busy, engage, take up, forestall, monopolize, allure, fascinate, bewitch, enamour, attract, charm, influence, captivate. *Ant.* repel, disgust, shock, annoy, displease, weary, tire, offend, anger, vex, provoke, dissatisfy, pique, irk, pain, torment, afflict, distress, trouble.

engulf—*Syn.* absorb, swallow up, imbibe, submerge, drown, bury, entomb, overwhelm, sink, swamp, deluge, inundate, overflow, overcome, fill up.

enigmatic, *adj.*—*Syn.* puzzling, mysterious, vague, cryptic, perplexing, obscure, problematic, ambiguous. *Ant.* clear, plain, explicit, specific.

enjoin—*Syn.* order, ordain, appoint, prescribe, direct, admonish, instruct, advise, counsel, exhort, enforce, forbid, stop, halt, command, charge, require, debar, prevent, prohibit, preclude, inhibit, interdict, hinder, disallow.

enjoyment—*Syn.* pleasure, gratification, satisfaction, sensuality, indulgence, self-indulgence, voluptuousness, hedonism, delight, happiness, comfort, rapture, charm, joy, gladness, ecstasy, exultation, triumph. *Ant.* sorrow, sadness, woe, misery, grief, calamity, affliction, worry, strife, unhappiness, wretchedness, misfortune, suffering, sickness, sorrowfulness, mournfulness, melancholy, dissatisfaction, discomfort, uneasiness, care.

enlarge—*Syn.* increase, extend, augment, swell, broaden, widen, expand, dilate, magnify, grow, spread, add, lengthen, amplify, heighten, protuberate, distend. *Ant.* diminish, lessen, reduce, decrease, abate, lower, curtail, a b r i d g e, contract, epitomize, shorten, abbreviate, prune, condense, compress, boil down, impair.

enlighten—*Syn.* illumine, illuminate, instruct, divulge, inform, teach, tell, impart, educate, train, direct, enjoin, persuade, acquaint, apprise, disclose, notify, counsel, admonish, advise, inculcate, indoctrinate, communicate, reveal. *Ant.* befog, becloud, puzzle, confuse, delude, befool, lead astray, obscure, darken, dim, perplex, embarrass, nonplus, disconcert, confound, discompose, unsettle, disorder, derange, distract.

enlist—*Syn.* enter, register, enroll, incorporate, embody, interest, attract, employ, engage, hire, retain, reserve, procure, induce, obtain, get: *Ant.* dissuade, shun, avoid, discourage, prevent, restrain, hold back, check, deter,

dishearten, constrain.

enliven—*Syn.* cheer, vivify, quicken, stir up, animate, inspire, exhilarate, gladden, delight, gratify, please, rejoice, charm, satisfy, incite, encourage, comfort, enthuse, indulge, rouse, arouse, excite, stimulate, brighten, refresh. *Ant.* sadden, dull, dampen, stupefy, cloy, pall, dim, darken, tire, weary, bore, exhaust, jade, debilitate, fatigue, bother, pester, stultify, surfeit, harass, enervate.

enmity—*Syn.* hatred, malice, rancor, spite, animosity, malignity, acrimony, hostility, antagonism, malevolence, bitterness, ill-will, opposition, dislike, unfriendliness, antipathy, aversion, detestation, spitefulness, grudge, pique, abhorrence, repugnance, disgust. *Ant.* friendship, friendliness, kindness, kindliness, concord, amity, regard, agreement, sympathy, harmony, alliance, intimacy, affinity, attachment, fellowship, companionship, adherence, confidence, good-will, beneficence, benevolence, accordance, concurrence, concordance, conformity, esteem, comity, peace, brotherliness, love.

ennui, *n.*—*Syn.* boredom, listlessness, languor, tedium, surfeit. *Ant.* enthusiasm, ebullience, buoyancy, vigor.

enormous—*Syn.* gigantic, colossal, huge, vast, immense, prodigious, monstrous, amazing, extraordinary, marvelous, miraculous, astonishing, ponderous, great, mammoth, stupendous, w o n d e r f u l, wondrous. *Ant.* small, little, insignificant, microscopic, inconsiderable, light, trivial, petty, paltry, slight, trifling, dwarfish, imponderable, u n i m p o r t a n t, inconsequential, slender, diminutive, infinitesimal, minute, Lilliputian, delicate, attenuated, thin.

enough, *adj.*—*Syn.* sufficient, plenty, abundant, adequate, full, plenteous, copious, ample, complete. *Ant.* scarce, lacking, wanting, scant, deficient, bare, insufficient, inadequate.

enough, *n.*—*Syn.* plenty, sufficiency, abundance, plenitude, copiousness, plenteousness, plentifulness. *Ant.* scarcity, insufficiency, want, famine, deficiency, inadequacy, dearth, lack, scantiness.

enrage—*Syn.* anger, goad, tempt, infuriate, madden, exasperate, incense, inflame, agitate, irritate, provoke, chafe, nettle, excite, craze. *Ant.* soften, mollify, soothe, calm, pacify, appease, conciliate, reconcile, assuage, compose, mitigate, ameliorate, moderate.

enrapture—*Syn.* enchant, charm, allure, fascinate, bewitch, captivate, enthral, enthuse, entrance, ravish, delight, enamour, please. *Ant.* repel, repulse, disgust, shock, annoy, anger, agitate, irritate, weary, tire, displease, offend, vex, pique, provoke.

enroll—*Syn.* register, enlist, inscribe, subscribe, list, record, enter, fill out, sign, mark, affix. *Ant.* discard, reject, abrogate, repudiate, pass over, omit, neglect, protest, cancel, dismiss.

enter, *v.*—*Syn.* penetrate, intrude, insert, invade, begin, pierce, encroach.

enterprise—*Syn.* undertaking, venture, adventure, work, endeavor, energy, performance, scheme, risk, hazard, engagement, business, action, activity. *Ant.* idleness, inactivity, inaction, sloth, slothfulness, indolence, passiveness, ergophobia, unemployment.

entertain—*Syn.* amuse, cheer, please, interest, enliven, delight, divert, beguile, recreate, disport, gratify, occupy, charm, rouse, exhilarate, inspirit, enthuse. *Ant.* weary, tire, disgust, bore, annoy, distract, disquiet, disturb, sadden, vex, harass, distress, pain, afflict, grieve, perplex, trouble, dishearten.

entertainment—*Syn.* amusement, enjoyment, merriment, fun, pleasure, sport, cheer, delight, frolic, recreation, pastime, diversion, play, feast, banquet, picnic, dance, concert, merrymaking. *Ant.* gloom, sadness, misery, lassitude, woe, weariness, fatigue, ennui, listlessness, trouble, sorrow, misfortune, grief, drudgery, work, toil, labor, melancholy, depression.

enthusiasm—*Syn.* rapture, fervor, ardor, passion, transport, joy, joyousness, joyfulness, excitement, vehemence, feeling, emotion, zeal, warmth, eagerness, earnestness, exhilaration, frenzy, intensity, ecstasy, hilarity, mirth, merriment, gaiety. *Ant.* dulness or dullness, tiredness, weariness, ennui, melancholy, moroseness, coldness, indifference, lassitude, carelessness, apathy, lukewarmness, wariness, calmness, calculation, caution, timidity, lifelessness, deadness.

entrance—*Syn.* gate, door, doorway, entry, ingress, inlet, gateway, portal, opening, access, adit, approach, admission, admittance, access, accession, entree, introduction, penetration, passage, vestibule. *Ant.* egress, exit, departure, withdrawal, rejection, expulsion, exclusion, ejection, refusal, recall.

entrap—*Syn.* catch, ensnare, decoy, lure, inveigle, entice, involve, allure, seduce, deceive, attract, entangle, implicate, fool, beguile, mislead. *Ant.* warn, advise, admonish, counsel, guide, direct, befriend, aid, assist, help, free, release, clear, liberate, deliver, rescue.

entreat—*Syn.* beg, implore, supplicate, beseech, ask, importune, solicit, petition, request, pray, crave. *Ant.* demand, command, take, force, compel, snatch, rob, coerce, drive, impel.

entry, *n.*—*Syn.* inlet, door, entrance, access, gate, passage. *Ant.* exit, outlet, egress.

envious—*Syn.* jealous, suspicious, watchful, cautious, resentful, displeased, covetous, invidious, malignant, hateful, odious. *Ant.*

kind, kindly, kind-hearted, well-disposed, charitable, trustful, friendly, amicable, propitious, helpful, favorable, sympathetic, conciliatory, laudatory, laudative.

envoy, n.—Syn. ambassador, agent, plenipotentiary, commissioner, representative, nuncio, legate, messenger.

ephemeral—Syn. transient, evanescent, fleeting, fugitive, momentary, transitory, temporary, passing, brief, short, short-lived, vanishing. Ant. long, long-lived, lasting, enduring, durable, permanent, perpetual, eternal, endless, everlasting, immortal, interminable, infinite.

epicurean, adj.—Syn. sensual, luxurious, voluptuous, sybaritic, fastidious, particular. Ant. ascetic, puritanical, self-denying.

episode, n.—Syn. incident, occurrence, happening, event, circumstance, adventure.

epistle, n.—Syn. letter, missive, message, note, report, writing.

epithet—Syn. name, title, appellation, ascription, praenomen, agnomen, cognomen, eponym, patronymic, nickname, byword, sobriquet, denomination; any combination of adjective and noun, when the adjective denotes quality or characteristic, as a good man, a bad boy.

epitome—Syn. brief, abridgment, abstract, compend, compendium, summary, synopsis, précis, digest, abbreviation, contraction, condensation, curtailment, outline. Ant. enlargement, development, expansion, extension, distention, dilation, dilatation, increase, increasement, addition, augmentation, increment, accretion.

equable, adj.—Syn. even, calm, unvarying, equal, serene, constant, steady, unruffled, regular. Ant. variable, changeable, fitful, spasmodic.

equal—Syn. equable, even, like, alike, same, uniform, invariable, unvarying, fair, just, equitable, adequate. Ant. unequal, unfair, unjust, unlike, changeable, variable, varying, disproportionate, disproportioned, inadequate, illmatched.

equanimity, n.—Syn. composure, poise, evenness, self-control, serenity, balance, calmness.

equipment, n.—Syn. apparatus, gear, paraphernalia, array, matériel, outfit, furnishings.

equitable, adj.—Syn. impartial, fair, unprejudiced, objective, just, reasonable.

equivocal—Syn. ambiguous, uncertain, indefinite, indeterminate, puzzling, doubtful, dubious, perplexing, enigmatic, obscure, indistinct, suspicious, questionable, vague, involved, hazy, wavering, fluctuating. Ant. clear, plain, obvious, distinct, lucid, transparent, evident, open, manifest, apparent, visible, unclouded, discernible, unequivocal, certain, indubitable.

eradicate—Syn. extirpate, exterminate, root out, destroy, annihilate, pull up, uproot, abolish, disperse, extinguish, nullify, devastate, consume, kill, remove. Ant. plant, implant, embed, settle, fix, infix, establish, stabilize, institute, strengthen, fortify, secure, confirm.

erode, v.—Syn. corrode, eat, wear, destroy, rub, gnaw, abrade.

erotic, adj.—Syn. amorous, sexual, sensual, amatory, passionate, ardent, lustful, appetent, concupiscent. Ant. cold, frigid, passionless, spiritual.

erroneous—Syn. false, inaccurate, incorrect, inexact, wrong, mistaken, erring, deviating, faulty, blundering, lying, untruthful, fictitious, counterfeit, fabricated, fictional. Ant. right, correct, O.K. (okeh), truthful, factual, literal, exact, genuine, accurate, determinate, dependable, faultless, precise, straight, true, unerring.

error—Syn. blunder, mistake, fault, fallacy, mission, oversight, delusion, wrong, deviation, fall, slip, transgression, indiscretion. Ant. correctness, certainty, certitude, rightness, truth, exactness, exactitude, accuracy, precision, rectitude, faultlessness.

erudite, *adj.*—*Syn.* learned, scholarly, knowing, cultured, recondite, educated, bookish. *Ant.* unlettered, illiterate, doltish, uneducated.

escape, *v.*—*Syn.* flee, fly, evade, avoid, elude, decamp, abscond.

especially—*Syn.* chiefly, mainly, particularly, principally, specially, firstly, definitely, truly. *Ant.* generally, commonly, usually, indefinitely, loosely, ordinarily, normally.

espouse, *v.*—*Syn.* embrace, assume, adopt, marry, betroth. *Ant.* abandon, reject, abjure, forsake.

essay—*Syn.* dissertation, tract, treatise, attempt, effort, trial, endeavor, paper, composition, disquisition, thesis, article, editorial, comment.

essential, *adj.*—*Syn.* necessary, fundamental, substantive, vital, inherent, elemental, requisite, basic, intrinsic, characteristic. *Ant.* secondary, accessory, auxiliary, subsidiary.

establish—*Syn.* confirm, make good, build up, verify, found, endow, institute, confirm, ratify, authorize, set up, prove, fulfil, demonstrate, substantiate, fix, plant, carry out, settle, constitute, determine. *Ant.* overthrow, topple, ruin, destroy, raze, disestablish, do away with, tumble, defeat, wreck, pull down, confute, disprove, prove false, break up, unsettle.

esteem, *v.*—*Syn.* appreciate, respect, prize, value, revere, reverence, treasure, uphold, regard, reckon, deem, consider, account, think, rate, judge, admire. *Ant.* despise, condemn, contemn, slight, mock, ridicule, oppugn, attack, hate, scorn, spurn, disdain, repel, reject, repulse.

esteem, *n.*—*Syn.* regard, respect, appreciation, favor, reverence, admiration, approbation, veneration, approval; commendation, sanction, praise, honor, deference, estimation. *Ant.* contempt, disregard, disrespect, contumely, disapprobation, disdain, scorn, derision, mockery, slight, ridicule, insult, insolence, contemptuousness, reproach, abuse, antipathy, abhorrence, aversion, loathing, repugnance, dislike, hatred.

estimate—*Syn.* compute, rate, appraise, appreciate, esteem, prize, value, measure, calculate, count, number, reckon, weigh, think, reason.

estrangement—*Syn.* abstraction, alienation, removal, withdrawal, diversion, transference, disaffection, disagreement, difference. *Ant.* union, bond, affinity, closeness, comradeship, friendship, partnership, coalition, attraction, alliance, combination, coalescence.

eternal—*Syn.* everlasting, unending, perpetual, never-ending, endless, infinite, boundless, immortal, interminable, continual, timeless, imperishable, unceasing, incessant, ceaseless, constant, enduring, permanent, undying, eonian. *Ant.* finite, ending, temporary, transitory, short, ceasing, inconstant, changeable, mutable, fluctuating, variable, transient, brief, evanescent, ephemeral, fleeting, momentary.

ethical, *adj.*—*Syn.* moral, virtuous, righteous, good, honest. *Ant.* immoral, vicious, unbecoming, dishonest.

evade—*Syn.* equivocate, prevaricate, lie, dodge, duck (*colloq.*), shun, shuffle, avoid, elude, trick, baffle, quibble, shift, cavil, mystify, dissemble, cloak, cover, conceal, deceive, screen, veil, pretend, confuse. *Ant.* acknowledge, declare, testify, meet, face, confront, speak boldly, speak openly, make clear, explain, expound, elucidate, illustrate, prove, verify, confirm.

evaluate, *v.*—*Syn.* estimate, weigh,

appraise, value, assess, calculate, rate, judge.

even—*Syn.* level, plain, smooth, equal, uniform, flat, open, clear, regular, unbroken. *Ant.* uneven, rough, lumpy, jagged, ridged, rugged, broken, irregular, rugose, rugate, wrinkled, furrowed.

event—*Syn.* incident, fact, case, result, issue, outcome, consequence, circumstance, chance, contingency, possibility, episode, occurrence, fortune, sequel, accident, adventure, end, happening.

evict, *v.*—*Syn.* oust, expel, dispossess, deprive, eject, exclude, debar, discard.

evidence, *n.*—*Syn.* data, testimony, grounds, authority, indication, facts, premises.

evident—*Syn.* clear, plain, open, obvious, public, manifest, distinct, patent, transparent, perceptible, visible, discernible, conspicuous, unmistakable, tangible, glaring, indubitable, palpable, overt, apparent, distinguishable, indisputable, incontrovertible. *Ant.* obscure, hidden, concealed, puzzling, unknown, occult, invisible, unseen, dark, impenetrable, latent, impalpable, undiscovered, imperceptible, covert, secret, unimagined, unthought of, embarrasing, confusing, confused, intricate, perplexing, complex, involved.

evil—*Syn.* ill, harm, mischief, misfortune, sin, wickedness, depravity, corruption, crime, sinfulness, vice, immorality, badness, vileness, baseness, malignity, hatred, scandal, calamity, viciousness, wrong, pollution, contamination, depravation, lewdness, licentiousness, lasciviousness, wantonness, lustfulness, obscenity, profligacy. *Ant.* good, goodness, virtue, honor, uprightness, rectitude, decency, respect, reputation, nobleness, nobility, esteem, renown, honesty, integrity, chastity, justice, sinlessness, repute, fame, credit, esti-

mation, respectability, worth, merit, character.

evince, *v*—*Syn.* show, evidence, disclose, manifest, prove, indicate, exhibit, display, demonstrate. *Ant.* hide, conceal, suppress, repress.

evoke, *v.*—*Syn.* summon, rouse, educe, elicit, stimulate, excite, provoke, arouse, waken.

exact—*Syn.* right, correct, proper, true, reliable, punctual, particular, accurate, careful, methodical, precise, nice, definite, scrupulous, prompt, timely, suitable, appropriate, meet, adapted, fitting, specific, determinate. *Ant.* wrong, false, untrue, unreliable, inaccurate, careless, inappropriate, unfitting, inexact, indefinite, unsuitable, indeterminate, varying, variable, irregular, untimely, erroneous, fallacious, deceptive, incorrect.

exaggerate, *v.*—*Syn.* magnify, amplify, heighten, enlarge, overdo, stretch, expand. *Ant.* minimize, lessen, shrink, depreciate.

exalt—*Syn.* ennoble, dignify, raise, elevate, heighten, promote, extol, magnify, glorify, boost (colloq.), praise, commend, recommend, advance, honor, laud, applaud. *Ant.* degrade, denounce; condemn, contemn, despise, depose, accuse, charge, lower, impair, scorn, disdain, spurn, humble, humiliate.

examination—*Syn.* investigation, inquiry, search, research, scrutiny, inspection, inquisition, trial, test, assay.

example—*Syn.* model, pattern, sample, type, archetype, ideal, specimen, standard, warning, ensample, exemplar, exemplification, precedent, prototype, original, copy, mold, design, representation.

exasperate, *v.*—*Syn.* irritate, exacerbate, vex, anger, infuriate, enrage, provoke, chafe, nettle, annoy. *Ant.* mollify, placate, assuage, conciliate.

exceed—*Syn.* excel, outdo, overdo, overtax, exaggerate, surpass, transcend, outstrip, outvie, eclipse, rise above, pass over, go beyond. *Ant.* lag, dally, dawdle, slow up, fall short, loiter, linger, delay, saunter, tarry, be tardy, fall behind.

excellent, *adj.—Syn.* superior, admirable, estimable, surpassing, eminent, meritorious, valuable, prime. *Ant.* inferior, lesser, valueless, negligible.

exceptional—*Syn.* uncommon, extraordinary, rare, scarce, unusual, unique, singular, remarkable, unparalleled, incomparable, unprecedented, wonderful, marvelous. *Ant.* common, commonplace, ordinary, customary, usual, habitual, frequent, normal, expected, regular, general, accustomed, wonted.

excess—*Syn.* profusion, abundance, luxuriance, extravagance, waste, wastefulness, lavishness, redundance, redundancy, surplus, superfluity, superabundance, plenty, overplus, exorbitance, prodigality, dissipation, intemperance, drunkenness. *Ant.* lack, want, necessity, insufficiency, poverty, dearth, deficiency, need, scantiness, defect, destitution, failure, shortcoming, economy, frugality, inadequacy, hunger, pauperism, indigence, privation, distress.

exchange, *v.—Syn.* trade, swap, substitute, convert, transfer, barter.

excite—*Syn.* rouse, stir up, provoke, awaken, incite, arouse, irritate, agitate, inflame, kindle, anger, stimulate, induce, offend, chafe, incense, enrage, aggravate, exasperate, tease, annoy, worry, infuriate, madden, craze, goad, taunt, mock. *Ant.* allay, pacify, soothe, soften, lull, quiet, compose, check, repress, assuage, appease, abate, subdue, calm, alleviate, reconcile, conciliate, mollify, mitigate, ameliorate, palliate, tranquillize, propitiate, lessen, moderate, ease, comfort.

exclude, *v.—Syn.* prohibit, omit, debar, prevent, boycott, obviate, blackball, bar, ostracize, reject, except. *Ant.* admit, include, accept, welcome.

excoriate, *v.—Syn.* flay, abrade, chafe, skin, gall, upbraid, fret, lash, score.

excruciating, *adj.—Syn.* agonizing, racking, tormenting, rending, severe, intense, painful, acute, extreme.

excursion—*Syn.* jaunt, ramble, tour, trip, outing, expedition, journey, voyage, travel.

excuse, *n.—Syn.* apology, defense, vindication, pretext, extenuation, plea, explanation, alibi.

execrate, *v.—Syn.* curse, objurgate, condemn, imprecate, revile, reprehend, abhor, damn, berate. *Ant.* praise, commend, applaud.

execute—*Syn.* fulfil, perform, do, carry out, accomplish, effect, complete, achieve, consummate, enforce, administer, finish, realize, attain, gain, win, compass, reach, get, obtain. *Ant.* fail, fall short, omit, neglect, ignore, overlook, forget, miss, disregard, pretermit, slight, undo, leave, abandon, give up, relinquish, quit, forego, resign.

exempt, *adj.—Syn.* free, clear, liberated, privileged, excused, absolved, irresponsible, unamenable, excluded, released, freed, not liable, unrestrained, unbound, uncontrolled, untrammeled, unshackled, unchecked, unrestricted. *Ant.* liable, responsible, subject, accountable, obliged, bound, necessitated, answerable, amenable, coercible, constrained, restrained, checked, confined, shackled, trammeled, coerced, driven, compelled, commanded.

exempt, *v.—Syn.* free, liberate, pass by, pass over, release, discharge, excuse, exculpate, exonerate, dispense with, let off. *Ant.* hold, confine, keep, bind, oblige, obligate, compel, command, force, drive, coerce, enforce, constrain, necessitate, conscript, restrain, commandeer, press, insist upon.

exercise—*Syn.* practice, exertion, application, drill, training, employment, use, performance, act, action, activity, occupation, operation. *Ant.* inactivity, rest, relaxation, idleness, laziness, sloth, slothfulness, inaction, sluggishness, indolence, repose, cessation.

exhausted—*Syn.* tired, wearied, worn, spent, consumed, wasted, drained, empty, fatigued, jaded. *Ant.* fresh, keen, ready, strong, forceful, refreshed, invigorated, vigorous, powerful, lusty.

exhibit, *v.*—*Syn.* show, display, reveal, demonstrate, discover, manifest, offer, present, disclose, evince, flaunt.

exigency—*Syn.* emergency, necessity, distress, difficulty, crisis, strait, urgency. *Ant.* normalcy, normality, regularity, ordinariness, commonplaceness.

expand, *v.*—*Syn.* amplify, extend, spread, widen, magnify, augment, increase, stretch, dilate, enlarge, develop.

expect, *v.*—*Syn.* await, contemplate, hope, anticipate, foresee.

expedite, *v.*—*Syn.* forward, urge, accelerate, facilitate, advance, hasten, quicken. *Ant.* delay, obstruct, hinder, retard.

expedition, *n.*—*Syn.* trip, journey, excursion, voyage, cruise, campaign, quest, safari, trek.

expel, *v.*—*Syn.* discharge, evict, remove, eliminate, banish, eject, oust, proscribe, excrete.

expense—*Syn.* cost, price, expenditure, outlay, charge, payment, outgo, disbursement, value, worth, sum, amount, upkeep, loss. *Ant.* profit, profits, return, returns, receipt, receipts, proceeds, product, income, gain, acquisition, accession, increase, emolument, perquisites.

experiment—*Syn.* proof, trial, test, verification, attempt, examination, practice, exercise, endeavor, undertaking.

explain—*Syn.* interpret, elucidate, illustrate, expound, teach, manifest, translate, decipher, construe, unravel, unfold, solve. *Ant.* puzzle, perplex, complicate, tangle, confuse, involve, bewilder, confound, obscure, darken, cloud, befuddle, mystify.

explicit—*Syn.* express, definite, plain, positive, clear, intelligible, comprehensible, evident, certain, determinate, exact, precise, obvious, manifest, distinct. *Ant.* indefinite, doubtful, hazy, mixed, confused, unintelligible, puzzling, vague, uncertain, indeterminate, obscure, ambiguous, dubious, equivocal, involved.

expound, *v.*—*Syn.* express, explain, present, analyze, interpret, elucidate, state, construe.

express—*Syn.* declare, signify, utter, tell, set forth, communicate, designate, denote, represent, send, forward, despatch. *Ant.* keep silent, withhold, retain, hold back, check, repress, restrain.

extemporaneous—*Syn.* offhand, unpremeditated, improvised, extempore, extemporary, impromptu, unprepared, unstudied, informal, ready. *Ant.* elaborated, premeditated, studied, prepared, recited, read, written, contrived, designed, formed, provided, procured.

extend—*Syn.* reach, stretch, lengthen, enlarge, increase, protract, amplify, augment, add, expand, dilate, spread, elongate. *Ant.* contract, curtail, shorten, abbreviate, narrow, compress, decrease, abridge, epitomize, lessen, condense, reduce, cut down.

exterior, *n.*—*Syn.* outside, surface, skin, shell. *Ant.* interior, inside, innards.

exterminate—*Syn.* annihilate, destroy, banish, extirpate, expel, uproot, remove, overthrow, abolish, root out, wipe out, eradicate. *Ant.* preserve, protect, foster, cherish, nurture, keep, guard, secure, defend, save, maintain, plant, propagate, replenish, settle, develop, colonize, breed, beget, build up.

extract, *v.—Syn.* educe, extort, draw, obtain, derive, pull, eradicate, extirpate, elicit, remove, evoke.

extravagant—*Syn.* lavish, profuse, prodigal, wasteful, liberal, immoderate, destructive, excessive, inordinate, extreme. *Ant.* parsimonious, miserly, beggarly, niggardly, mean, avaricious, stingy, close, close-fisted, penurious.

extreme—*Syn.* last, final, terminal, ultimate, utmost, farthest, remote, intensive, immoderate, extravagant, outermost, far. *Ant.* moderate, medium, limited, calm, quiet, steady, ordinary, subdued, repressed, sober, dispassionate, near, nigh, adjacent.

extricate—*Syn.* free, deliver, liberate, unbind, unchain, disengage, disentangle, evolve, loose, release, unfasten, untie, let go, manumit, ransom, affranchise, rescue. *Ant.* tie, bind, chain, confine, imprison, incarcerate, immure, restrict, circumscribe, limit, restrain, retain, fetter, shackle.

exuberant, *adj.—Syn.* overflowing, profuse, energetic, lavish, rank, luxuriant, prolific, abundant, vigorous, wanton. *Ant.* sterile, austere, barren, depleted.

exult—*Syn.* rejoice, make merry, boast, crow, vaunt, vapor, swagger, brag, bluster, bully. *Ant.* wail, bewail, mourn, sorrow, grieve, deplore, lament, cry, weep, bemoan.

F

fable—*Syn.* apologue, romance, novel, tale, yarn, parable, allegory, myth, fabrication, invention, simile, story, fiction. *Ant.* reality, truth, fact, certainty, gospel, certitude, veracity, authenticity, orthodoxy.

fabric, *n.—Syn.* cloth, textile, dry goods, stuff, substance, material.

fabricate—*Syn.* make, construct, manufacture, frame, produce, build, form, compose, invent, devise, plan, put together, arrange, erect. *Ant.* tear down, ruin, destroy, wreck, raze, shatter, break, disarrange, derange, demolish, disintegrate, split, disrupt.

fabulous—*Syn.* legendary, mythical, feigned, fictitious, untrue, false, ridiculous, absurd, incredible, immense, wonderful, amazing, extraordinary. *Ant.* historical, proven, true, admitted, testified, warranted, guaranteed, known, credible, attested, ordinary, normal, simple, usual, general, common.

face, *n.—Syn.* visage, countenance, appearance, outside, front, surface, exterior, physiognomy, feature, boldness, confidence, effrontery, impudence, impertinence. *Ant.* interior, inside, back, rear, humility, bashfulness, backwardness, humbleness.

face, *v.—Syn.* meet, confront, oppose, resist, dare, venture, defy, brave, challenge. *Ant.* fear, shrink, slink, withdraw, retire, refuse, creep away, sneak, crouch, truckle, fawn.

facetious—*Syn.* jocular, jocose, funny, humorous, witty, merry, pleasant, sportive, sprightly, jesting, waggish, comical, droll, laughable. *Ant.* serious, solemn, morose, melancholy, sad, dull, dull-witted, stolid, phlegmatic, grave, formal, ceremonial, somber, gloomy, pensive, dejected.

facile—*Syn.* easy, ready, dexterous, skilful, quick, flexible, artful, clever, adroit, expert, apt, tactful, able, proficient, ingenious. *Ant.* hard, difficult, laborious, unskilful, clumsy, unhandy, awkward, slow, plodding, arduous, toilsome, wearisome, tedious.

facility—*Syn.* readiness, quickness, dexterity, ease, easiness, skilfulness, expertness, adroitness, cleverness, proficiency.

Ant. hardness, difficulty, slowness, ineptitude, unfitness, unsuitableness, clumsiness, awkwardness, unskilfulness, tardiness.

facsimile—*Syn.* copy, likeness, reproduction, picture, photograph, resemblance, similitude, similarity, imitation, transcript, pattern, model, prototype, archetype. *Ant.* difference, distinction, dissimilarity, diversity, divergence, variation, mutation, deviation, modification, change, opposite.

faction, *n.*—*Syn.* coterie, party, clique, combination, sect, set, cabal, division, circle.

factious, *adj.*—*Syn.* recalcitrant, dissident, seditious, rebellious, insubordinate, contentious. *Ant.* co-operative, helpful, united.

factitious, *adj.*—*Syn.* artificial, counterfeit, phony, bogus, spurious, synthetic, fabricated, sham, unnatural. *Ant.* genuine, authentic, bona fide, real.

factor—*Syn.* agent, steward, bailiff, representative, manager, deputy, substitute, delegate, proxy, commissioner, vicar, attorney, actor, doer.

faculty, *n.*—*Syn.* ability, aptitude, knack, skill, talent, gift, capacity, bent, function.

fail—*Syn.* fall short, miss, omit, decline, weaken, desert, disappoint, funk, back out, leave, miscarry, abandon, neglect, shrink from, drop, pass by, quit, forego, give up. *Ant.* win, capture, gain, make good, get, obtain, pass, discharge, deliver, merit, earn, attain, procure, reach, accomplish, finish.

faint—*Syn.* weak, timid, faltering, feeble, languid, powerless, worn, worn down, worn out, weary, wearied, listless, half-hearted, faint-hearted, fatigued, purposeless, irresolute, exhausted. *Ant.* brave, courageous, bold, dashing, unafraid, strong, resolute, daring, fearless, adventurous, intrepid, hazardous, fresh, hearty, vigorous, sturdy, energetic.

fair—*Syn.* clear, sunny, dry, pleasant, mild, open, frank, honest, impartial, candid, just, reasonable, moderate, honorable, decent, civil, beautiful, nice, equitable, upright. *Ant.* wet, cloudy, rainy, showery, dark, threatening, rough, tempestuous, stormy, unjust, dishonest, partial, double-dealing, unfair, unreasonable, dishonorable, unprepossessing, ugly, unfavorable, repellent.

fairy—*Syn.* sprite, elf, goblin, hobgoblin, spirit, apparition, ghost, witch, warlock, enchantress, specter, phantom, puck, fay, imp, demon, fiend, devil, genius, ogre, succubus, deva, ogress, ghoul, vampire, harpy, ouphe, jinnee, flibbertigibbet, pixy or pixie, oaf, bogie or bogey or bogy, afreet, siren.

faith—*Syn.* creed, belief, trust, confidence, assurance, credence, conviction, assent, tenets, credit, doctrine, trust, reliance, fidelity, opinion. *Ant.* unbelief, misgiving, infidelity, disbelief, suspicion, incredulity, rejection, distrust, skepticism, doubt, denial, faithlessness, dissent.

faithful—*Syn.* true, loyal, constant, attached, dependable, honest, straight, honorable, trustworthy, firm, incorruptible, trusty, sure, stanch, unwavering, devoted, unswerving. *Ant.* capricious, fickle, uncertain, unreliable, unfaithful, untrue, untrustworthy, false, faithless, wavering, perfidious, treacherous, irresolute, variable, changeable, unstable, inconstant, vacillating, whimsical, dishonest, dishonorable.

faithless—*Syn.* perfidious, treacherous, traitorous, deceitful, false, unfaithful, untrustworthy, unreliable, treasonable, untrue, tricky, fraudulent, insincere, deceptive. *Ant.* true, loyal, upright, honorable, sincere, dependable, trustworthy, reliable, friendly, frank, honest, magnanimous, generous, noble, helpful, just, fair, conscientious, faithful.

fake, *n.—Syn.* counterfeit, fraud, deception, fabrication, imposture, phony, falsification, imitation.

fall—*Syn.* sink, tumble, descend, topple, drop, totter, lower, settle, droop, decline, plunge, lessen, diminish, weaken. *Ant.* rise, ascend, surmount, climb, scale, tower, soar, improve, strengthen, make good, reach, attain, obtain.

fallacy—*Syn.* delusion, sophism, sophistry, illusion, phantasy, quibble, casuistry, quibbling, subterfuge, evasion, equivocation, misconception, error, mistake, misstatement, aberrance, aberrancy, perversion. *Ant.* truth, truism, sureness, fact, evidence, certainty, demonstration, axiom, soundness, proof, verity, surety, logic, argument, experience, experiment, verification, reality, realness.

false—*Syn.* untrue, lying, erroneous, fallacious, spurious, bogus, fabricated, sophistical, deceptive, counterfeit, sham, mock, incorrect, make-believe, pretended, shadowy, illusory, unreal, deceptive, misleading. *Ant.* true, correct, right, unassailable, established, known, confirmed, tested, genuine, pure, real, substantiated, honest, exact, straight, axiomatic, just, legitimate, admitted, sanctioned, actual, certain.

falter—*Syn.* hesitate, doubt, stammer, stutter, weaken, demur, waver, flinch, shrink, vacillate, sidestep, hobble, slip, fluctuate, scruple, pause, delay, stagger, reel. *Ant.* persevere, continue, persist, pursue, insist, demand, stay, endure, remain, maintain, contend, urge, press, incite, impel, compel, instigate, stimulate, encourage.

fame—*Syn.* celebrity, renown, reputation, credit, honor, report, rumor, notoriety, repute, distinction, eminence, glory, laurels, regard, character, esteem, estimation, elevation. *Ant.* infamy, discredit, dishonor, shame, ignominy, disrepute, contumely, contempt, abandonment, disgrace, oblivion, obscurity, humiliation, blemish, opprobrium.

familiar—*Syn.* intimate, free, unceremonious, affable, unconstrained, easy, unreserved, courteous, complaisant, accessible, benign, gracious, urbane, suave, approachable, unrestrained. *Ant.* reserved, restrained, unfamiliar, cold, distant, ceremonious, stiff, constrained, affected, formal, strange, arrogant, pretentious, assuming, presumptuous, haughty.

famous—*Syn.* well-known, celebrated, notorious, illustrious, eminent, noted, distinguised, renowned, conspicuous, brilliant, glorious, noble. *Ant.* obscure, unknown, humble, retired, hidden, infamous, degraded, debased, dishonorable, base, mean, vile, corrupt, ignominious, shameful, disgraced, dishonored, contemptible.

fanatical—*Syn.* bigoted, narrowminded, illiberal, prejudiced, domineering, credulous, superstitious, obstinate, unreasonable, stubborn, self-opinionated, biassed, unfair, partial. *Ant.* broad, broad-minded, liberal, just, impartial, unprejudiced, free-thinking, reasonable, rational, comfortable, tolerant, indulgent, forbearing, magnanimous, fair-minded.

fanaticism—*Syn.* bigotry, intolerance, prejudice, hatred, superstition, narrow-mindedness, injustice, obstinacy, illiberality, unreasonableness, bias, unfairness, partiality. *Ant.* liberalism, broad-mindedness, liberality, tolerance, nobleness, honesty, impartiality, catholicism, generousness, generosity, indulgence, free-thinking, indifference, latitudinarianism, cynicism.

fanciful—*Syn.* capricious, fantastic, fantastical, odd, queer, whimsical, freakish, crotchety, changeable, changing, fickle, fitful, unsteady, inconstant, chimerical, grotesque, imaginative, visionary, imaginary, unreal, dreamy, creative, romantic, fluctuating, variable, mutable, unstable, vacillating, ideal, erratic. *Ant.* steady, constant, serious, grave, earnest, sincere, firm, fixed, uniform, regular, undeviating, equable, steadfast, unchanging, resolute, determined, invariable, unalterable, accurate, sure, literal, sound, sensible, true, reasonable, calculable, calculated, real, ordinary, commonplace, solid, prosaic.

fancy—*Syn.* imagination, supposition, vagary, predilection, conception, conceit, caprice, mood, humor, whim, inclination, belief, idea, notion, image, freak. *Ant.* fact, reality, verity, truth, actuality, certainty, veracity, exactness, exactitude, accuracy, precision, definiteness, positiveness.

fantastic—*Syn.* fanciful, whimsical, capricious, odd, queer, vague, imaginary, peculiar, strange, wonderful, singular, quaint, uncommon, comical, eccentric, erratic, visionary, farfetched. *Ant.* common, commonplace, ordinary, customary, usual, trite, regular, normal, hackneyed, stale, conventional, serious, solemn, steady, fixed, constant, formal, ceremonious, precise.

fantasy—*Syn.* vision, image, imagination, ideality, unreality, concept, conception, thought, notion, idea, view, conceit, appearance, fancy, whim, vagary, freak. *Ant.* reality, actuality, existence, certainty, truth, substance, substantiality, materiality, corporeality, corporeity, leave, departure, parting.

far, *adj.*—*Syn.* distant, removed, remote, long. *Ant.* near, close, convenient, handy.

farcical, *adj.*—*Syn.* ludicrous, absurd, extravagant, ridiculous, droll, comic, funny.

farewell—*Syn.* adieu, good-by, dismissal, furlough, valediction, valedictory, leave, departure, parting.

far-out, *adj.*—*Syn.* cool, beat, hip, very, gone, modern, deep, intense, progressive, intellectual, absorbed, appreciative.

fascinate—*Syn.* charm, enchant, captivate, entrance, bewitch, beguile, enamour, enrapture, attract, draw, attach, please, allure, entice, invite, enslave, overpower, delight, ravish. *Ant.* repel, disgust, displease, weary, worry, fatigue, tire, exhaust, shock, agitate, anger, horrify, frighten, terrify, appall, scare, daunt.

fashion, *v.*—*Syn.* shape, make, design, create, plan, mold, form, contrive, fabricate, manufacture.

fast—*Syn.* quick, rapid, fleet, swift, expeditious, speedy, flying, accelerated, nimble, active, agile, alert, brisk, lively, wild, reckless, gay, dissipated, dissolute, abandoned. *Ant.* slow, sluggish, tardy, dilatory, slothful, inactive, heavy, dull, drowsy, clownish, dull-witted, settled, steady, plodding, solemn, quiet, virtuous, upright, model, exemplary, good, well-behaved.

fasten, *v.*—*Syn.* bind, affix, anchor, attach, tie, connect, link, secure, lock.

fastidious, *adj.*—*Syn.* delicate, particular, dainty, fussy, finicky, nice, meticulous, prissy, prudent, squeamish, choosy, critical. *Ant.* gross, boorish, uncritical, tasteless.

fat—*Syn.* fleshy, beefy, brawny, corpulent, unwieldy, portly, stout, obese, oleaginous, unctuous, swollen, bulky, rich, pursy, luxuriant, wealthy, well-to-do. *Ant.* lean, thin, attenuated, slender, *svelte,* lithe, sinewy, graceful, slim, slight, poor, impoverished, beggarly, indigent, penniless.

fatal—*Syn.* deadly, mortal, lethal, destructive, killing, murderous, causing death. *Ant.* enlivening, vivifying, healthy, healthful, invigorating, strengthening, wholesome, nourishing, vital, animating, salutary.

fate—*Syn.* destiny, doom, lot, fortune, luck, death, goal, end, finish, destination, chance, predetermination, consummation, fortune, or misfortune.

fatigue—*Syn.* weariness, lassitude, exhaustion, languor, enervation, debilitation, weakness, feebleness, faintness, dullness, heaviness, listlessness, tiredness, *ennui*. *Ant*. vigor, briskness, liveliness, keenness, alertness, vim, pep (*slang*), strength, force, forcefulness, energy, activity, spirit, sprightliness, animation, vivacity.

fault—*Syn.* blemish, flaw, imperfection, misdeed, detriment, failing, misdemeanor, delinquency, slip, defect, drawback, weakness, omission, foible, error. *Ant*. vantage, advantage, help, assistance, gain, benefit, utility, boon, good, favor, blessing.

favorable—*Syn.* advantageous, helpful, assisting, friendly, kind, kindly, propitious, conducive, useful, convenient, beneficial, salutary, fair. *Ant*. unfavorable, disadvantageous, hindering, hurtful, derogatory, harmful, unpropitious, injurious, detrimental, unprofitable, inconvenient, threatening.

fear—*Syn.* fright, affright, terror, horror, panic, consternation, dismay, dread, scare, trepidation, timidity, misgiving, tremor, alarm, awe, reverence, trembling, apprehension, disquietude, veneration, anxiety, solicitude. *Ant*. boldness, bravery, courage, endurance, heroism, resolution, endeavor, fortitude, valor, intrepidity, fearlessness, gallantry.

fearless—*Syn.* bold, brave, courageous, gallant, intrepid, undaunted, daring, spirited, valorous, hardy, dauntless, resolute, firm, heroic. *Ant*. timid, retiring, bashful, backward, cowardly, timorous, fearful, craven, pusillanimous, weak, shy, diffident, afraid, faint-hearted.

feasible, *adj.*—*Syn.* workable, practical, attainable, achievable, practicable, possible. *Ant*. unfeasible, fantastic, visionary, impractical.

feast—*Syn.* banquet, entertainment, festivity, festival, treat, repast, refreshment, carousal, wassail, merrymaking, jollification, barbecue, carouse, picnic. *Ant*. want, privation, famine, poverty, destitution, abstinence, fast, fasting, need, necessity, indigence, distress, hunger, penury, deficiency, scarcity, lack, dearth.

feat—*Syn.* act, effort, deed, performance, exertion, action, exploit, exercise, execution, movement, attainment, accomplishment, achievement, maneuvre, acquirement, acquisition. *Ant*. inaction, abstinence, idleness, stagnation, unemployment, quiescence, inactivity, loafing, passiveness, sloth, slothfulness, laziness.

fecund, *adj.*—*Syn.* fertile, productive, fruitful, yielding, prolific. *Ant*. sterile, barren, unfruitful, impotent.

fee, *n.*—*Syn.* payment, compensation, pay, emolument, wage, charge, cost, remuneration.

feeble—*Syn.* weak, puny, delicate, frail, debilitated, infirm, faint, forceless, enervated, weakened, languid, exhausted, decrepit, impaired, enfeebled. *Ant*. strong, vigorous, forceful, powerful, lusty, forcible, stout, robust, firm, hardy, solid, muscular, sound, hale, hearty.

feed, *v.*—*Syn.* nourish, foster, sustain, supply, maintain, fuel, provide, furnish, nurture. *Ant*. starve, deprive, strip.

feeling—*Syn.* sense, sensation, sensibility, susceptibility, emotion, passion, perception, excitement, consciousness, impression, sensitiveness, conviction, tenderness, opinion, sentiment. *Ant*. insensibility, apathy, immobility, stolidity, indifference, stupidity, unfeelingness, impassiveness, lethargy, stoicism, unconcern, unconsciousness, deadness.

feign, v.—Syn. pretend, affect, dissemble, falsify, simulate, counterfeit, mask, sham.

felicitate, v.—Syn. congratulate, compliment, greet.

felicity—Syn. bliss, rapture, ecstasy, happiness, joy, joyousness, comfort, blessedness, blissfulness, blessing, gladness, cheer, mirth, merriment, gaiety, delight, charm, pleasure, gratification, satisfaction, enjoyment, cheerfulness, blithesomeness, jollity, joviality, frolic, hilarity, festivity. Ant. unhappiness, misery, sadness, sorrow, dejection, melancholy, grief, woe, misfortune, distress, despondency, pain, loss, gloom, the blues, worry, torment, strife, calamity, wretchedness, depression, heaviness, dullness, despair.

felonious—Syn. malignant, malicious, depraved, evil, underhand, vile, despicable, villainous, traitorous, perfidious, virulent, heinous, malevolent, corrupt, harmful, hurtful, noxious, pernicious, injurious, baneful, baleful, wicked, perverse, base, vicious, destructive, wrong. Ant. good, noble, generous, praiseworthy, commendable, charitable, kind, ennobling, honorable, decent, laudable, exalted, magnanimous, helpful, remedial, beneficent, benevolent, benign, worthy, meritorious, estimable, advantageous.

feminine—Syn. womanish, womanly, female, effeminate, womanlike, soft, tender, delicate. Ant. masculine, mannish, manly, manlike, manful, male, virile, brave, strong, hardy.

ferocious—Syn. fierce, savage, wild, barbarous, untamed, fell, brutal, cruel, sanguinary, ravenous, vehement, violent, unrestrained, bloodthirsty, murderous, brutish, pitiless, merciless, unmerciful, fearsome,

frightful. Ant. mild, meek, gentle, tame, docile, tractable, tender, peaceful, quiet, modest, harmless, innocent, inoffensive, innoxious, innocuous, manageable, susceptible, yielding, soft, effeminate, affectionate, frail, delicate, pitiful, weak, feeble, tottering.

fertile—Syn. fruitful, prolific, plenteous, productive, yielding, producing, fecund, rich, luxuriant, generative, abundant, plentiful, ample, copious, exuberant. Ant. sterile, barren, unproductive, unyielding, empty, fruitless, waste, destitute, unprofitable, useless, valueless.

fervent, adj.—Syn. ardent, earnest, animated, passionate, glowing, fiery, hot, vehement, enthusiastic, eager, intense, zealous. Ant. cool, chilly, phlegmatic, impassive.

fetch, v.—Syn. bring, obtain, bear, take, procure, carry, yield, elicit.

fetid, adj.—Syn. noisome, foul, malodorous, mephitic, putrid, repulsive, stinking, rank. Ant. aromatic, fragrant, sweet-smelling, balmy.

fetters—Syn. gyves, manacles, shackles, chains, irons, bonds, handcuffs, imprisonment, duress, durance, bondage, slavery, custody. Ant. freedom, liberty, independence, unrestrictedness, immunity, exemption, privilege, unrestraint.

feud—Syn. quarrel, row, strife, animosity, bitterness, enmity, hostility, dissension, dispute, controversy, brawl, affray, broil, fray, riot, contention, fracas, contest, vendetta, antagonism, fuss, altercation, wrangle, bickering, argument, disagreement. Ant. peace, fraternity, brotherhood, brotherliness, friendliness, calm, repose, tranquillity, pacifism, pacification, order, harmony, concord, love, confidence, regard, esteem.

fever, n.—Syn. heat, ardor, fire, mania, frenzy, delirium, disease.

fickle—Syn. uncertain, unreliable,

vacillating, variable, varying, unstable, unsettled, fanciful, inconstant, mutable, fitful, changeable, changeful, wavering, spasmodic, irresolute, whimsical, capricious, unsteady, versatile, unfixed, restless, purposeless, hesitant, crotchety, shifting, wayward, volatile. *Ant.* steady, constant, settled, unchanging, unchangeable, resolute, determined, persevering, unshaken, fixed, firm, steadfast, loyal, dependable, unswerving, unvarying, definite, decided, obstinate, undeviating, regular, equable, unwavering, faithful, attached, stanch, incorruptible, immutable, changeless, stable, unalterable, sure, invariable.

fiction—*Syn.* invention, myth, fable, figment, creation, story, romance, novel, legend, fabrication, apologue, allegory, falsehood, untruth, imagination, fancy. *Ant.* history, fact, reality, truth, certainty, sureness, verity, literalness, truthfulness, genuineness, authenticity, actuality, happening, occurrence, incident, event, circumstance.

fictitious—*Syn.* false, untrue, counterfeit, spurious, feigned, imaginary, erroneous, fallacious, deceptive, fabricated, bogus, mendacious, sham, lying, fraudulent, untruthful, apocryphal, fanciful, unreal. *Ant.* true, proven, genuine, real, veritable, authentic, certain, reliable, official, recognized, authorized, trustworthy, factual, literal, exact, actual, certain, positive, accurate, unquestionable, unquestioned, precise, correct, confirmed, guaranteed.

fidelity—*Syn.* conscientiousness, trustworthiness, fealty, allegiance, constancy, integrity, faithfulness, devotion, attachment, loyalty, trueness, sincerity, obedience, steadfastness, resolution, stanchness, adherence, support, devotedness, zeal, ardor, earnestness. *Ant.* unfaithfulness, traitorousness, treachery, double-dealing, chicanery,

stratagem, trickery, faithlessness, perfidiousness, falseness, falsity, falsehood, lie, lying, prevarication, shuffling, quibbling, disloyalty, insincerity, vacillation, fluctuation, wavering, unsteadiness, inconstancy.

fidget, *v.*—*Syn.* fret, stew, toss, twitch, jitter, chafe.

fiendish, *adj.*—*Syn.* devilish, malignant, malicious, infernal, inhuman, diabolical, cruel, demoniac. *Ant.* angelic, benign, benevolent, kindly.

fierce—*Syn.* furious, ferocious, fiery, wild, violent, enraged, raging, impetuous, savage, uncultivated, untrained, passionate, angry, outrageous. *Ant.* mild, gentle, quiet, docile, soft, tame, peaceful, placid, meek, kind, patient, submissive, affectionate, harmless, tender, innocent, inoffensive, innoxious, innocuous, unoffending.

fiery—*Syn.* fierce, passionate, unrestrained, ardent, vehement, spirited, mettlesome, fervid, impassioned, impetuous, irascible, angry, choleric, violent, furious, burning, excited, intense, enthusiastic, animated, vivacious. *Ant.* dull, phlegmatic, sluggish, monotonous, subdued, moderate, humdrum, tedious, wearisome, tiresome, irksome, flat, uninteresting, slow, prosy, commonplace, prosaic, stupid, vapid.

fight, *v.*—*Syn.* battle, contest, brawl, dispute, contend, wrangle, struggle, quarrel, strive.

figure—*Syn.* allegory, emblem, metaphor, symbol, picture, type, design, representation, character, outline, shape, form, construction, appearance.

filch, *v.*—*Syn.* pilfer, steal, snatch, pinch, swipe, rob.

fill—*Syn.* pack, stuff, put in, pour, feed, distend, swell, make complete, satisfy, pervade, occupy, take up, cover, engage, use, dwell in. *Ant.* empty, exhaust, pour out, void, discharge, drain, dry, draw off, remove, expend, spend, waste, scatter, leave, vacate, move out.

filth—*Syn.* dirt, ordure, dung, feces, contamination, corruption, pollution, foulness, nastiness, filthiness, excrement, alvine discharge, pus, dregs, lees, sediment, putridity, putrescence, putrefaction, rottenness, impurity, defilement. *Ant.* cleanliness, purity, spotlessness, purification, cleanness, innocence, incorruptibility, incorruptibleness, incorruptness, stainlessness, honor, virtue, moral rectitude.

finagle, *v.*—*Syn.* scheme, contrive, plot, figure, calculate.

final, *adj.*—*Syn.* last, extreme, ending, terminal, decisive, ultimate, definitive.

find—*Syn.* meet, confront, ascertain, experience, detect, perceive, discover, furnish, supply, invent, recover, attain, observe, reach, arrive at, descry, espy, find out, discern, see, spy. *Ant.* lose, miss, fail, mislay, forfeit, neglect, omit, fall short, ruin, destroy, deprive of, block, thwart, prevent, overlook, forget, drop, abandon, forsake, give up.

fine, *adj.*—*Syn.* beautiful, attractive, showy, dainty, choice, rare, delicate, excellent, polished, refined, slender, minute, thin, suitable, keen, nice, admirable, exquisite, clarified, sharp, clear, small, comminuted, smooth, elegant, handsome, subtle, pure, sensitive, slight, tenuous, splendid, grand, imposing, gorgeous. *Ant.* coarse, clumsy, heavy, awkward, stout, thick, rude, blunt, rough, gross, indelicate, uncouth, immodest, vulgar, unrefined, brutal, brutish, beastly, bluff, impolite, indecorous, unbecoming, indecent, impudent, shameless, barbarous, uncivil, clownish, ignorant, churlish, rustic, insolent, illiterate, surly, impertinent, saucy, unpolished.

fine, *n.*—*Syn.* penalty, forfeiture, forfeit, confiscation, sequestration, amercement, damage, mulct, loss, punishment. *Ant.* reward, recompense, remunera-

tion, indemnity, satisfaction, reimbursement, compensation, amends, satisfaction, requital.

finish, *n.*—*Syn.* end, completion, termination, close, conclusion, terminus.

fire—*Syn.* blaze, conflagration, flame, burning, luminosity, light, illumination, fuel, sparks, glow, incandescence, warmth, heat, ardor, passion. *Ant.* cold, coldness, gelidity, gelidness, frigidity, chill, chilliness, shivering, frigidness, iciness, bleakness, wintriness, dullness, listlessness, apathy, deadness.

firm—*Syn.* solid, strong, enduring, fixed, steady, stanch, steadfast, unyielding, tenacious, unfaltering, resolute, rugged, sturdy, robust, stable, constant. *Ant.* weak, yielding, unsettled, loose, deficient, defective, wobbling, unfastened, untied, unconnected, slack, unstable, disjoined, disjointed.

fishy, *adj.*—*Syn.* suspicious, improbable, unlikely, absurd, specious, misleading.

fit—*Syn.* suitable, adapted, meet, becoming, appropriate, proper, expedient, apt, adequate, apposite, congruous, competent, conformable, suited, correspondent, seemly, befitting, calculated, contrived, decent, decorous, fitted, fitting, pertinent, prepared, qualified. *Ant.* unfit, unfitted, unfitting, unsuitable, unsuited, ungainly, unseemly, untimely, amiss, misfitted, misfitting, awkward, ill-timed, inadequate, miscontrived, improper, miscalculated, misapplied, ill-fitting, inappropriate, ill-fitted, ill-contrived, inexpedient.

fitful, *adj.*—*Syn.* spasmodic, capricious, flickering, intermittent, convulsive, variable, fickle, random, whimsical, desultory. *Ant.* steady, uniform, constant, even.

fix—*Syn.* determine, settle, establish, limit, place, prepare, adjust, fasten, bind, attach, locate, plant, secure, tie, apply, set, root, consolidate, decide. *Ant.*

change, unsettle, weaken, unlock, unbolt, loose, loosen, shake, disturb, unfix, unlatch, detach, disarrange, displace, free, set free.

flaccid—*Syn.* soft, flabby, weak, lax, hanging, limber, drooping, yielding, loose, pending. *Ant.* firm, solid, strong, resisting, sturdy, steady, close-knit, tenacious, tough, unyielding.

flag, *v.*—*Syn.* decline, pall, sag, sink, droop, fail, languish, lag.

flagrant, *adj.*—*Syn.* glaring, outrageous, wicked, atrocious, infamous, monstrous, gross, heinous, rank.

flame, *v.*—*Syn.* blaze, burn, light, flare, ignite.

flash, *v.*—*Syn.* sparkle, flare, burst, glance, twinkle, shimmer, glisten, scintillate, blaze.

flashy, *adj.*—*Syn.* garish, showy, flamboyant, pretentious, meretricious, gaudy, jazzy, ostentatious. *Ant.* sober, simple, neat, natural.

flat—*Syn.* dull, tasteless, insipid, unpleasing, heavy, depressed, dejected, spiritless, prostrate, fallen, horizontal, level, even, downright, absolute, positive, low. *Ant.* sharp, acrid, bubbling, effervescing, frothing, frothy, keen, spirited, lively, raised, elevated, rough, uneven, rugged, hilly, mountainous.

flatter—*Syn.* praise, laud, exalt, extol, cringe, fawn, crouch, grovel, truckle, wheedle, blarney, blandish, caress, cajole, soothe, soften, placate, gratify, humor, satisfy, please, coax, entice. *Ant.* condemn, denounce, mock, despise, scorn, ignore, spurn, detest, offend, anger, taunt, affront, displease, shock, annoy, ridicule, insult, abuse, shame, disgrace, scoff, gibe, jeer, sneer at, deride, tantalize, flout.

flaunt, *v.*—*Syn.* brandish, flourish, display, blazon, parade, flash, expose. *Ant.* hide, conceal, cloak, disguise.

flavor, *n.*—*Syn.* gusto, savor, aroma, taste, zest, relish, essence.

flawless, *adj.*—*Syn.* perfect, exact, unmarred, spotless, whole, impeccable, unblemished. *Ant.* imperfect, damaged, flawed, defective.

fleeting—*Syn.* transient, transitory, brief, ephemeral, evanescent, short, flitting, flying, fugitive, passing, temporary, vanishing, momentary. *Ant.* long, long-lived, enduring, lasting, constant, continual, daily, yearly, fixed, unchanging, permanent, unalterable, everlasting, eternal, endless, perpetual.

flexible—*Syn.* pliant, supple, pliable, yielding, limber, lithe, bending, ductile, docile, tractable, obsequious. *Ant.* stiff, unbending, inflexible, unyielding, rigid, resistant, stubborn, obstinate, constrained, austere, stern, rigorous, formal, ceremonious.

flicker, *v.*—*Syn.* waver, fluctuate, shimmer, quiver, glint, flare, gutter.

flimsy—*Syn.* gauzy, thin, transparent, trifling, poor, inane, puerile, slight, superficial, weak, shallow, unsubstantial, feeble. *Ant.* thick, solid, opaque, heavy, serious, strong, firm, substantial, sound, real, tough, unbreakable, stiff, tenacious, hard.

flinch, *v.*—*Syn.* shrink, wince, blench, cringe, recoil, falter, retreat.

fling, *v.*—*Syn.* throw, heave, cast, toss, chuck, pitch.

float, *v.*—*Syn.* drift, fly, hover, glide, sail, skim, wave.

flock—*Syn.* group, herd, litter, brood, drove, pack, hatch, swarm, set, bevy, covey, lot, collection, company, throng, gathering, congregation.

flourish—*Syn.* thrive, prosper, increase, grow, win, accumulate, triumph, lead, rise, overcome, conquer, enlarge, boast, vaunt, brag, brandish, wave, twirl, shake. *Ant.* decay, diminish, weaken, descend, fall, sink, decrease, lessen, decline, tumble, collapse, degenerate, deteriorate, fade, wither, starve, lose, pass, pass away.

flout, v.—*Syn.* scorn, disdain, insult, mock, jeer, spurn, contemn, despise, sneer. *Ant.* revere, respect, esteem, praise.

flow—*Syn.* stream, issue, progress, glide, course, career, run, float, move, pass, circulate. *Ant.* stop, stagnate, close up, check, retard, cease, obstruct, prevent, cork, bottle up.

fluctuate—*Syn.* vacillate, waver, hesitate, digress, oscillate, deflect, wander, wave, undulate, veer, vary, swerve, deviate, alter, change, rise and fall. *Ant.* stand fast, hold fast, stay, stick, abide, persist, remain, keep still, stop, cease, delay, postpone, decide.

fluent—*Syn.* flowing, liquid, moving, changing, changeable, voluble, ready, smooth, easy, glib, unembarrassed, apt, expert, copious, prepared. *Ant.* hesitant, hesitating, stuttering, stammering, slow, dull, prosy, unprepared, dilatory, heavy, firm, embarrassed, sluggish, still, motionless, inactive.

flurry, n. — *Syn.* disturbance, squall, bustle, hurry, agitation, commotion, hubbub, gust.

fly, v.—*Syn.* soar, hover, wing, float, rise, ascend, glide, skim.

foe—*Syn.* enemy, antagonist, adversary, opponent, attacker, combatant, hater, rival, competitor, backbiter, vilifier, defamer, traducer, slanderer. *Ant.* friend, well-wisher, helper, assistant, adviser, associate, companion, pal (*slang*), buddy (slang), familiar, ally, comrade, messmate, coadjutor, confidant, adherent.

foil, v.—*Syn.* balk, check, circumvent, defeat, thwart, disappoint, frustrate. *Ant.* abet, advance, further, assist.

folk—*Syn.* people, persons, individuals, family, group, crowd, gathering, congregation, race, nation, community, members, brotherhood, society, associa-

tion, league.

follow—*Syn.* pursue, chase, accompany, imitate, copy, succeed, ensue, practise, use, go after, observe, attend, chase, obey, heed, mimic, ape, mock. *Ant.* discard, reject, scorn, ignore, shun, pass over, disregard, avoid, elude, eschew, neglect, slight, abjure.

follower—*Syn.* retainer, henchman, attendant, servant, partisan, disciple, adherent, pursuer, successor, pupil, protegé. *Ant.* enemy, antagonist, adversary, contemner, scoffer, scorner, objector, rejecter, oppressor, persecutor.

folly—*Syn.* weakness, silliness, foolishness, absurdity, imbecility, imprudence, madness, misconduct, unwisdom, simplicity, brainlessness, shallowness, weakmindedness. *Ant.* wisdom, knowledge, sapience, prudence, forethought, understanding, discernment, judgment, craftiness, discrimination, cunning, cunningness, artfulness, shrewdness, astuteness, wiliness, subtlety, acuteness, cleverness, ingenuity.

fond—*Syn.* enamored, attached, affectionate, kind, loving, devoted, ardent, zealous, solicitous, anxious, concerned, sentimental. *Ant.* distant, cold, reserved, unattached, haughty, scornful, indifferent, shy, cool, restrained, apathetic, unconcerned, disinterested.

fondle, v.—*Syn.* caress, pet, toy, stroke, spoon, neck, cuddle, dally.

fondness—*Syn.* affection, attachment, kindness, love, concern, regard, desire, devotion, devotedness, ardor, zeal, liking, tenderness. *Ant.* aversion, hate, hatred, dislike, antipathy, repugnance, disgust, detestation, abhorrence, opposition, enmity, spite, spleen.

food—*Syn.* diet, nutrition, sustenance, nutriment, nourishment, provender, feed, victuals, viands, regimen, pabulum, fodder, forage, fare, diet, aliment.

fool, *n.*—*Syn.* dunce, simpleton, dolt, oaf, boob, blockhead, ninny, idiot, imbecile, nitwit, buffoon, clown.

foolhardy—*Syn.* rash, impetuous, precipitate, headlong, incautious, venturesome, reckless, careless, heedless, thoughtless, regardless. *Ant.* careful, cautious, prudent, thoughtful, heedful, watchful, provident, circumspect, attentive, wary, calculating, guarded, discreet.

foolish—*Syn.* simple, silly, irrational, brainless, imbecile, crazy, nonsensical, absurd, preposterous, ridiculous, witless, fatuous, insane, mad, daft, loony or luny (*dial.*), boneheaded, (*colloq.*) thickheaded. *Ant.* wise, astute, clear-sighted, keen, careful, cautious, thoughtful, prudent, judicious, sagacious, sensible, well-advised, discerning, circumspect, discreet, considerate, provident, frugal.

fop—*Syn.* coxcomb, dandy, dude, beau, jackanapes, puppy, idler, loafer, gigolo (*slang*), lounger, lounge-lizard (*slang*), trifler, humbug, pretender, impostor. *Ant.* gentleman, hero, scholar, philosopher, savant, seer, prophet, minister, priest, clergyman, divine.

forbear—*Syn.* abstain, refrain, pause, spare, desist, avoid, lay off, delay, stop, cease, bear, endure, suffer, stay. *Ant.* act, do, perform, accomplish, insist, persist, carry on, persevere, continue, pursue.

forbid—*Syn.* prohibit, debar, restrain, interdict, preclude, oppose, cancel, hinder, obstruct, bar, prevent, deny, deprive, exclude. *Ant.* sanction, encourage, commend, recommend, authorize, approve, countenance, order, command, abet, allow, permit, confirm.

force, *n.*—*Syn.* power, strength, energy, vigor, might, violence, army, navy, body, organization, armament, troops, battalion, company, regiment, division, number, aggregation. *Ant.* weakness, powerlessness, uselessness, feebleness, debility, frailty, impotence, inability, disability, incapacity, incapability, helplessness, incompetence, incompetency.

force, *v.*—*Syn.* coerce, compel, drive, make, impel, necessitate, constrain, oblige, urge, press, rush, push, move, actuate, instigate, incite. *Ant.* restrain, hinder, impede, block, obstruct, prevent, hold, stay, stop, check, arrest, repress, keep back, suppress, delay, retard, hamper, thwart.

forebode—*Syn.* augur, betoken, portend, foretell, prophesy, prognosticate, presage, divine, surmise, foreknow, foreshow, predict, soothsay, forewarn, foreshadow, vaticinate.

forecast, *n.*—*Syn.* premeditation, prognostication, prognosis, divination, forethought, foresight, prescience, foreknowledge, foretoken, prognosis, prediction, conjecture, prophecy, foretelling, foreseeing, prevision, vaticination, augury. *Ant.* retrospect, retrospection, reminiscence, recollection, memory, preterition, langsyne, looking back.

forecast, *v.*—*Syn.* predict, prophesy, foretell, divine, prognosticate, foreshadow, foreshow, soothsay, presage, vaticinate. *Ant.* recall, call up, call back, call to memory, remember, recollect, commemorate, think of the past, dwell on the past, look back.

foregoing—*Syn.* antecedent, preceding, anterior, prior, former, previous, preliminary, before, preparatory, introductory, precedent, antecedent. *Ant.* succeeding, following, subsequent, posterior, ensuing, consequent, after, afterward, behind, behindhand.

foreign—*Syn.* alien, strange, outside, extraneous, extrinsic, exotic, remote, far, distant, irrelevant, irregular, exterior, different, unaccustomed, unknown. *Ant.* native, indigenous, like, similar, familiar, original, aboriginal, known, regular, near, interior, accustomed.

forerunner—*Syn.* herald, harbinger, precursor, ancestor, predecessor, forefather, forebear, progenitor, proclaimer, pioneer, prognostic, sign, omen, warning. *Ant.* successor, descendant, offspring, follower, disciple, henchman, attendant, servant, dependent.

foresight—*Syn.* forethought, forecast, premeditation, prescience, foreknowledge, prognostication, prudence, prevision, carefulness, economy. *Ant.* ignorance, waste, wastefulness, carelessness, folly, foolishness, unwisdom, thoughtlessness.

forever, *adj.*—*Syn.* everlasting, continual, unending, ceaseless, unceasing, endless, eternal, enduring, immortal, undying, deathless, never-ending, perpetual. *Ant.* temporary, brief, short, transitory, evanescent, momentary, transient, temporal, short-lived, ephemeral, fleeting, fading, vanishing, perishable, cursory.

forever, *adv.*—*Syn.* perpetually, everlastingly, continually, endlessly, constantly, unceasingly, lastingly, unremittingly. *Ant.* temporarily, shortly, briefly, transitorily, fleetingly.

forge—*Syn.* falsify, counterfeit, fabricate, coin, invent, frame, feign, force, drive, impel, make, fashion, design, imitate, produce, copy, trump up, transcribe, duplicate, reproduce, trace.

forget, *v.*—*Syn.* ignore, lose, omit, overlook, slight, disremember. *Ant.* remember, recollect, recall, bethink.

forgive—*Syn.* pardon, remit, absolve, acquit, excuse, except, cancel, release, overlook, clear, exculpate, exonerate, free. *Ant.* withhold, retain, indict, accuse, charge, arraign, impeach, blame, discredit, censure.

forgo—*Syn.* quit, relinquish, waive, renounce, resign, leave, abandon, let go, give up, pass by. *Ant.* hold, keep, retain, preserve, act, fulfil, perform, accomplish, maintain, continue, carry on.

forlorn—*Syn.* abandoned, forsaken, forgotten, wretched, miserable, woebegone, friendless, alone, solitary, depressed, helpless, comfortless, deprived, bereft, destitute, deserted, abject, pitiable, lone, lonesome, desolate, lost, dejected, cast down, bereaved. *Ant.* glad, merry, cheerful, cheery, joyful, joyous, gay, sunny, serene, happy, gratified, delighted, pleased, satisfied, comfortable, animated, spirited, buoyant, exalted, exhilarated, lively, mirthful, sportive, sprightly, vivacious, blithe, hilarious.

form, *v.*—*Syn.* make, shape, mold, fashion, construct, devise, plan, design, contrive, produce, invent, arrange, frame, scheme, plot, compose, erect, build, put together, create. *Ant.* destroy, ruin, wreck, disarrange, scatter, pull down, tear down, demolish, overthrow, dismantle, devastate, raze, overturn, subvert, damage, upset, undo.

form, *n.*—*Syn.* shape, figure, appearance, plan, arrangement, structure, formation, outline, likeness, image, representation, mold, sketch, conformation, resemblance, rite, ritual, ceremony, observance, condition, state. *Ant.* shapelessness, irregularity, deformity, amorphism, amorphousness, derangement, disfigurement, defacement, mutilation, distortion, monstrosity.

formal—*Syn.* ceremonial, ceremonious, precise, exact, stiff, methodical, punctilious, orderly, pompous, systematic, official, ministerial, imposing, functional, solemn, impressive, decorous. *Ant.* informal, common, ordinary, usual, customary, normal, habitual, regular, conventional, general, accustomed, wonted.

former—*Syn.* antecedent, anterior, previous, preceding, foregoing, before, prior. *Ant.* latter, after, succeeding, following, subsequent, ensuing, consequent.

formidable—*Syn.* terrible, dangerous, impregnable, dreadful, invincible, tremendous, shocking, awe-inspiring, impressive, indomitable, redoubted, awful, fearful, appalling. *Ant.* harmless, helpless, feeble, weak, contemptible, despicable, powerless, paltry, puny, insignificant, petty, trivial.

forsake—*Syn.* abandon, desert, leave, quit, relinquish, fail, renounce, give up, forego, resign, abdicate, evacuate, abjure, disown, disclaim. *Ant.* remain, stick, stay, continue, persevere, stand by, succor, aid, assist, help, comfort, nurture, nourish, cherish, keep, hold, maintain, acknowledge, claim, cling to.

forsaken—*Syn.* abandoned, forlorn, deserted, desolate, lone, lonely, lonesome, neglected, ignored, relinquished, renounced, rejected, shunned. *Ant.* remembered, cared for, nurtured, nourished, cherished, befriended, aided, helped, assisted, encouraged.

fort, *n.*—*Syn.* stronghold, bulwark, fastness, citadel, fortress, fortification.

forthwith—*Syn.* immediately, instantly, directly, presently, right away, at once, right off, straightaway. *Ant.* anon, soon, by-and-by, shortly, never, not at all.

fortification—*Syn.* fort, fortress, breastwork, escarpment, dugout, defense, defenses, fastness, citadel, castle, works, trenches, stronghold, field-works, entrenchment, intrenchment, rifle-pit, parapet, protection.

fortitude—*Syn.* courage, endurance, heroism, resolution, strength, firmness, power, coolness, intrepidity, spunk, spirit, fearlessness, courageousness, boldness, bravery, patience, daring, enterprise, dauntlessness, valor, mettle, pluck, hardihood, heroism, gallantry, forbearance. *Ant.* weakness, cowardice, spirit-

lessness, fear, funk (*colloq.*), panic, timidity, shyness, pusillanimity, dastardliness, cravenness, poltroonery, cowardliness, timorousness, terror, fright, trepidation, consternation, awe, dismay, dread.

fortuitous, *adj.*—*Syn.* casual, random, incidental, adventitious, chance, accidental. *Ant.* planned, plotted, rehearsed, deliberate.

fortunate—*Syn.* lucky, happy, auspicious, prosperous, successful, contented, satisfied, fortuitous, favorable, flourishing, propitious, well-off, encouraging, advantageous, well-to-do. *Ant.* unfortunate, unlucky, discontented, dissatisfied, unhappy, miserable, wretched, ill-fated, sad, downcast, sorrowful, cheerless, heartbroken, oppressed, crushed, persecuted, despised, condemned.

fortune—*Syn.* chance, fate, luck, doom, destiny, goal, end, lot, judgment, determination, decree, property, possession, riches, wealth, inheritance.

forward, *v.*—*Syn.* promote, encourage, advance, foster, expedite, help, favor, aid. *Ant.* hinder, impede, discourage, frustrate.

foster—*Syn.* cherish, nurse, nurture, nourish, tend, harbor, indulge, gratify, pamper, favor, humor, please, coddle, cosset, fondle, comfort, care for. *Ant.* neglect, ignore, spurn, scorn, despise, contemn, disregard, slight, shun, overlook, omit, disdain, reject, cast off, leave, abandon.

foul—*Syn.* dirty, filthy, nasty, unclean, impure, defiled, tainted, polluted, obscene, offensive, disgusting, putrid, rotten, mephitic, corrupt, pestilential, contaminated, vitiated, soiled, tarnished, diseased, decayed, fetid, stinking, carious, putrescent, coarse, vulgar, indecent, noxious, unfair, dishonest. *Ant.* clean, sweet, pure, undefiled, cleansed, purified, spotless, untainted, untarnished, uncorrupted, unsullied, unblemished, guileless, innocent, virgin, fair, white, speckless, pleasing, gratifying, lovely, enticing, attractive, alluring, wholesome, unadulterated, becoming, good, honest, just, agreeable, inviting, compelling, sound, delightful, satisfying.

foundation—Syn. base, basis, ground, root, origin, substructure, substratum, bottom, groundwork, underpinning, foot, endowment, establishment, institution, footing, rudiments, layer, subsoil, understructure, support. Ant. top, superstructure, crown, apex, roof, dome, cupola, tower, spire, arch, canopy, cover, covering, summit, vertex, pinnacle, peak.

foxy—Syn. cunning, sly, tricky, experienced, crafty, knowing, shrewd, acute, astute, discerning, sagacious, sharp, penetrating, skilful, intelligent, artful, subtle, wily, designing, guileful, shifty, insidious, wary, careful. Ant. foolish, rash, impetuous, headstrong, heavy, dull, doltish, stupid, heedless, inexperienced, innocent, open, frank, boobyish, silly, dull-witted, careless, undiscerning, guileless, artless.

fraction, n.—Syn. part, section, division, piece, bit, segment, portion, fragment.

fractious—Syn. peevish, peeved, fretful, cross, captious, testy, petulant, splenetic, touchy, irritable, perverse, pettish, waspish, snappish, quick-tempered, passionate, quarrelsome, bickering, grouchy, irascible. Ant. mild, calm, even-tempered, patient, meek, forbearing, gentle, unruffled, enduring, submissive, resigned, peaceful, quiet, agreeable, uniform, docile, tranquil, placid, undisturbed, cool, dispassionate, self-possessed, composed, tractable.

fracture, n.—Syn. break, rift, split, rent, crack, breach.

fragile—Syn. brittle, frail, delicate, feeble, frangible, weak,

breakable, infirm. Ant. strong, lusty, robust, hardy, tough, thick, coarse, unbreakable, resistant, infrangible, wiry, sinewy, enduring.

fragments—Syn. pieces, scraps, leavings, chips, remains, remnants, residue, balance, remainder. Ant. whole, all, total, aggregate, entire, entirety, gross, completeness.

fragrant, adj.—Syn. aromatic, sweet-smelling, perfumed, redolent, spicy, scented. Ant. malodorous, noisome, stinking, mephitic.

frailty—Syn. weakness, debility, feebleness, languor, infirmity, failing, imperfection, foible, faintness, lassitude, puniness, inability. Ant. strength, vigor, verve, energy, might, power, robustness, health, ability, soundness, force, lustiness, puissance, potency.

frame—Syn. form, fashion, construct, make, fabricate, invent, mold, forge, coin, feign, plan, shape adjust, contrive. Ant. wreck, scatter, ruin, destroy, tumble, demolish, raze, pull down.

franchise—Syn. right, freedom, suffrage, liberty, privilege, vote, voice, choice. Ant. bondage, slavery, serfdom, deprivation, servitude, oppression.

frank—Syn. artless, candid, sincere, free, easy, familiar, open, ingenuous, plain, aboveboard, straightforward. Ant. secretive, deceptive, insincere, hypocritical, deceitful, dissembling, disingenuous, tricky, crafty, sly, cunning.

frantic—Syn. distracted, mad, furious, raging, raving, frenzied, violent, agitated, deranged, crazy, delirious, insane, rabid, angry. Ant. quiet, calm, peaceful, composed, subdued, meek, mild, docile, tractable, bland, easy, gentle, kind, cool, collected, self-possessed, dispassionate.

fraud—Syn. deceit, deception, duplicity, guile, imposition, cheat, artifice, imposture, chicanery,

swindle, swindling, treason, trick,
dishonesty, cheating, treachery.
Ant. honesty, integrity, truth,
good faith, fairness, justice,
frankness, probity, sincerity, rectitude, uprightness, equity, conscientiousness, right.

freak—*Syn.* vagary, whim, caprice, crotchet, humor, fancy,
whimsy, quirk, conceit, change,
fickleness, unsteadiness, inconstancy, abnormality, monstrosity, irregularity. *Ant.* purpose,
steadiness, resolution, firmness,
honesty, normalcy, conformity,
perfectness, regularity, resoluteness, constancy, steadfastness,
resolve.

free, *adj.*—*Syn.* liberal, generous,
bountiful, bounteous, munifi-
cent, frank, artless, candid,
open, familiar, independent, unconfined, loose, unreserved, unrestricted, exempt, clear, easy,
careless, unobstructed, ingenuous, unattached, unencumbered,
unconstrained, unrestrained,
gratuitous, ready, eager, charge-
less, costless. *Ant.* enslaved,
enchained, imprisoned, bound,
fettered, restrained, confined,
compelled, incarcerated, shut
up, locked in, barred, checked,
prevented, curbed, suppressed,
jailed, restricted, stingy, slavish,
artful, costly, dear, expensive,
high-priced, chargeable, choice,
precious, scarce, priceless, attached, encumbered, constrained, detained.

free, *v.*—*Syn.* liberate, discharge,
unfetter, unbind, release, set
free, deliver, rescue, exempt,
emancipate, manumit, enfranchise, affranchise, acquit, ransom, absolve, clear, loose, extricate, disentangle, pardon, exonerate, forgive. *Ant.* enslave,
bind, imprison, incarcerate, shut
in, inclose, confine, immure, restrain, restrict, bound, limit,
circumscribe, check, curb, prevent, repress, suppress, chain,
fetter, hold, entangle, jail, jug
(*slang*), hobble, deprive, tie,
tether, fasten, secure, shackle.

freedom—*Syn.* liberty, independ-

ence, frankness, openness, outspokenness, unrestrictedness, license, liberality, unrestraint,
franchise, exemption, privilege,
advantage, right, prerogative,
immunity, self-government,
boldness, infringement, forwardness, familiarity. *Ant.* slavery,
serfdom, imprisonment, incarceration, confinement, servitude, bondage, subjection, submission, submissiveness, subordination, dependence, deprivation, servility, slavishness, abasement, obsequiousness, drudgery,
captivity, restraint, restriction,
hindrance, coercion, limitation,
compulsion.

frenzy, *n.*—*Syn.* fury, rage, derangement, mania, transport,
agitation, madness, aberration,
delirium. *Ant.* delight, ecstasy,
rapture.

frequent—*Syn.* many, repeated,
numerous, recurrent, general,
continual, usual, common, recurring, regular. *Ant.* rare, unusual, uncommon, infrequent,
irregular.

frequently—*Syn.* often, regularly,
usually. *Ant.* rarely, seldom,
infrequently.

fresh, *adj.*—*Syn.* new, novel, modern, unused, natural, vigorous,
recent, young, vivid, green, raw,
sweet. *Ant.* stale, trite, hackneyed, shopworn.

fret—*Syn.* chafe, gall, gnaw, corrode, rub, disturb, agitate, anger, vex, annoy. *Ant.* soothe,
calm, comfort, soften, please,
placate, smooth, heal.

fretful—*Syn.* peevish, cross, captious, irritable, annoying, nagging. *Ant.* calm-tempered, kind,
soothing, comforting, easy-
going, cheerful, cheery.

friend—*Syn.* associate, companion, acquaintance, familiar, ally, chum (*colloq.*), messmate,
comrade, pal (*slang*), buddy
(*slang*), side-kick (*slang*),
mate, accomplice, adherent,
partner, coadjutor, assistant,
confidant. *Ant.* enemy, adversary, opponent, backbiter, calumniator, slanderer, vilifier,

foe, foeman, antagonist, competitor, rival, defamer, detractor.

friendly—*Syn.* kind, helpful, sympathetic, favorable, conciliatory, propitious, amicable, careful, well-disposed, neighborly, sociable, social, kindly, loving, attentive, affectionate, fond, brotherly, agreeable, genial, hearty, solicitous, affable, tender, complaisant, companionable, cordial, accessible. *Ant.* unkind, antagonistic, censorious, ill-disposed, envious, uncharitable, grouchy, fault-finding, nagging, opposing, combative, false, treacherous, deceptive, grudging, harmful, hurtful, pernicious, prejudicial, baneful, adverse, hostile, cool, frigid, cold, disaffected, grumbling, contentious, estranged, inimical, unfriendly, alienated, warlike, unkind, distant, reserved.

friendship—*Syn.* friendliness, devotion, companionship, favor, regard, good will, brotherhood, alliance, fraternity, love, kindness, affection, attachment, comity, consideration, esteem, amity, fellowship. *Ant.* hatred, malignity, detestation, hostility, rancor, animosity, spite, malice, dislike, antipathy, aversion, grudge, hate, revenge, ill will, repugnance, enmity, resentment, abhorrence, disgust, loathing, malevolence, anger, bitterness, antagonism, acrimony, dissension, dispute, quarrel, row, fracas, fray, brawl, broil, controversy, contest, contention, combat, fight.

frighten—*Syn.* scare, daunt, appall, intimidate, dismay, terrify, browbeat, affright, cow, alarm, shock, dishearten, abash, dispirit, discourage, deject, depress, horrify, astound. *Ant.* assure, encourage, buoy up, invigorate, strengthen, vitalize, animate, inspirit, inspire, incite, cheer, enliven, exhilarate, gladden, rouse, embolden, impel, stimulate, instigate, comfort, excite, urge, energize.

frightful—*Syn.* fearful, dreadful, dire, calamitous, shocking, terrible, awful, horrible, horrid, direful, astounding, terrific, appalling, ugly, detestable, disgusting, abominable, hideous, ghastly, grim, grisly, Gorgonian. *Ant.* pleasing, appealing, attractive, fascinating, captivating, alluring, charming, lovely, beautiful, handsome, agreeable, prepossessing, inviting, enticing, gratifying, delightful, admirable, lovable, amiable, entrancing, enchanting, bewitching.

frigid, *adj.*—*Syn.* cold, stiff, chilling, passionless, lifeless, frosty, dull, rigid, formal. *Ant.* warm, ardent, fervid, amorous.

frivolous—*Syn.* petty, trifling, trivial, slight, silly, unimportant, indecorous, childish, puerile, worthless, inconsequential, inconclusive, small, paltry, insignificant, nugatory, inconsiderable, futile, light, little, shallow, foolish, idle, vain. *Ant.* serious, earnest, important, wise, witty, grave, solemn, weighty, formal, ceremonial, thoughtful, sound, deep, momentous, far-reaching, significant, relevant, dignified, essential, pertinent, applicable.

frolic, *v.*—*Syn.* sport, gambol, romp, frisk, skylark, caper.

front, *n.*—*Syn.* anterior, van, forepart, face, façade.

frown, *v.*—*Syn.* scowl, sulk, glower, glare, lower. *Ant.* smile, beam, shine.

frugality—*Syn.* economy, carefulness, conservation, providence, husbandry, management, thrift, saving, savingness, parsimony, parsimoniousness, miserliness, scrimping, scrimption (*dial., Eng.*), niggardliness, stinginess, avarice, avariciousness, penuriousness, covetousness. *Ant.* waste, lavishness, destruction, prodigality, spending, extravagance, liberality, luxuriousness, indulgence, voluptuousness, expenditure, wastefulness, profuseness, excess, superfluity, gratification, squandering, revelry, riotousness, profligacy, licentiousness, disbursement, scattering, sensuality, overindulgence.

fruitful—*Syn.* fertile, prolific, productive, plentiful, plenteous, abundant, rich, luxuriant, fecund, generative, proliferous, yielding, copious, ample, bountiful, exuberant. *Ant.* barren, waste, unproductive, empty, fruitless, unprofitable, sterile, unyielding, bare, useless, impotent, ineffective, arid, exhausted, spent, depleted, drained, worn out.

fruitless—*Syn.* vain, resultless, idle, abortive, barren, exhausted, bootless, unavailing, useless, unprofitable, empty, worthless, unsatisfying, unsatisfactory, ineffectual, ineffective, inconsequential. *Ant.* productive, gainful, availing, yielding, generative, cogent, forcible, potent, convincing, conclusive, influential.

frustrate—*Syn.* defeat, foil, balk, disappoint, nullify, baffle, confound, disconcert, bar, thwart, stop, hinder, neutralize, mar, counteract, prevent. *Ant.* help, assist, accomplish, encourage, coöperate, succor, support, aid, befriend, forward, second, facilitate, abet, countenance, stimulate, instigate, incite, connive at.

fugitive, *n.*—*Syn.* runaway, deserter, outcast, vagabond, escapee, refugee, lammister.

fulfil—*Syn.* accomplish, effect, complete, perform, execute, do, achieve, consummate, end, finish, terminate, realize, effectuate, bring about, discharge, carry out, attain. *Ant.* fail, neglect, omit, disappoint, miss, quit, cease, leave off, give up, resign, stop, abandon, forsake, relinquish, renounce, withdraw, forego.

full, *adj.*—*Syn.* replete, complete, abounding, swollen, glutted, sated, whole, ample. *Ant.* empty, incomplete, void, starved.

fulsome—*Syn.* coarse, gross, sickening, offensive, rank, loathsome, nauseous, excessive, disgusting, abhorrent, displeasing, disgustful, odious, detestable. *Ant.* pleasing, pleasant, agreeable, suitable, acceptable, grateful, delightful, gratifying, satisfying, satisfactory, consoling, comforting, encouraging, soothing, cheery, cheerful.

fun, *n.*—*Syn.* merriment, amusement, frolic, diversion, gaiety, play, sport, pleasantry, entertainment, glee.

function, *v.*—*Syn.* work, perform, serve, do, act, operate.

fundamental, *adj.*—*Syn.* basic, essential, radical, principal, primary, intrinsic, chief. *Ant.* superficial, subordinate, secondary, auxiliary.

funny, *adj.*—*Syn.* comical, diverting, ludicrous, humorous, amusing, droll, absurd, bizarre, odd. *Ant.* serious, grave, sober, melancholy.

furious—*Syn.* violent, boisterous, vehement, angry, dashing, sweeping, rolling, impetuous, frantic, distracted, stormy, raging, fierce, mad, desperate, dangerous, wild, passionate, ferocious, savage, ravening, crazy, delirious, frenzied, insane, rabid, infuriated, fanatical, inflamed, excited, reckless, deranged, unbalanced, fuming. *Ant.* calm, cool, collected, quiet, peaceful, mild, meek, gentle, kind, pleased, gratified, satisfied, pacific, tranquil, smooth, unruffled, contented, composed, easy-going, placid, undisturbed, easy, dispassionate, self-possessed, bland, suave, affable, courteous, civil, complaisant, benign, gracious, urbane, polite, moderate, indulgent.

furnish, *v.*—*Syn.* provide, present, yield, give, equip, supply, fit, outfit, appoint.

furniture, *n.*—*Syn.* fittings, equipment, apparatus, movables, supplies.

furtive, *adj.*—*Syn.* stealthy, covert, evasive, secret, sly, clandestine, surreptitious. *Ant.* open, forth-right, brazen, aboveboard.

fury, *n.*—*Syn.* frenzy, vehemence, wrath, rage, turbulence, passion, ferocity, violence.

futile —*Syn.* trifling, trivial, frivolous, useless, vain, ineffective, ineffectual, inefficient, fruitless, unavailing, abortive, idle, empty, worthless, resultless, unsatisfying, bootless, valueless. *Ant.* effective, satisfactory, productive, efficient, fruitful, advantageous, profitable, yielding, lucrative, gainful, beneficial, useful, helpful, serviceable, conducive.

G

gab, *v.*—*Syn.* chatter, gossip, prate, jabber, palaver, babble, chat, talk.

gad, *v.*—*Syn.* rove, idle, stroll, roam, ramble, saunter, wander, meander, range.

gag, *n.*—*Syn.* joke, jest, wisecrack, wheeze, rib, yack, trick, quip, crack, laugh, witticism.

gain, *n.*—*Syn.* profit, emolument, advantage, benefit, winnings, earnings, interest, achievement, realization, increase, improvement. *Ant.* loss, disadvantage, deprivation, forfeiture, defeat, privation, detriment, damage, overthrow, ruin.

gain, *v.*—*Syn.* win, earn, acquire, obtain, attain, realize, reap, procure, reach, accomplish, get, compass, secure, effect, achieve, consummate. *Ant.* lose, miss, forfeit, spend, expend, waste, exhaust, squander, lavish, scatter, dissipate, disperse, destroy, mislay, dispense.

gall, *n.*—*Syn.* nerve, audacity, impudence, temerity, daring, impertinence, cheek, brazenness, effrontery.

gallant—*Syn.* brave, bold, courageous, gay, fine, showy, intrepid, heroic, fearless, courteous, chivalrous, valiant, splendid, valorous, puissant, undaunted, strong, mighty, for-cible, daring, noble, renowned, kingly, knightly, high-minded, civil, polite, attentive, affable, urbane, condescending, manful, stout-hearted, high-spirited, plucky, dauntless. *Ant.* cowardly, timid, timorous, fearful, effeminate, craven, soft, sneaking, poor-spirited, dastardly, base, mean, contemptible, faint-hearted, chicken-livered (*slang*), rude, discourteous, ill-bred, impolite, unpolished, rough, gruff, churlish, ungentlemanly, foulmouthed, vulgar, ungracious.

galling—*Syn.* irritating, vexing, vexatious, annoying, chafing, provoking, troublesome, teasing, distressing, worrying, tantalizing. *Ant.* soothing, soft, consoling, emollient, mollifying, assuaging, mitigating, softening, ameliorating, ameliorative, improving, allaying, appeasing, satisfying, comforting.

gamble, *v.*—*Syn.* bet, wager, speculate, play, stake, hazard, game, chance.

game, *n.*—*Syn.* play, pastime, diversion, sport, frolic, recreation, amusement, fun, merriment, entertainment, festivity, gambol, prank, lark, spree, gaiety, merrymaking. *Ant.* work, drudgery, slavery, toil, labor, laboriousness, misery, gloom, sadness, melancholy, sorrow, woe, grief, uneasiness, pain, hardship, depression.

game, *adj.*—*Syn.* brave, bold, daring, enduring, gallant, courageous, cocky, conceited, dauntless, fearless, unafraid, assured, spirited, devil-may-care (*slang*), reckless, plucky, nervy, vigorous, resolute, determined, unflinching, unshrinking, unyielding. *Ant.* cowardly, shrinking, slinking, unmanly, mean-spirited, craven, yellow (*slang*), mangy (*slang*), low, contemptible, base, timid, timorous, fearful, pusillanimous, dastard, dastardly, sneaking, womanish, scared, frightened, intimidated.

gamut, *n.*—*Syn.* scale, range, purview, extent, scope, register, compass.

gang—*Syn.* horde, band, troop, crew, crowd, tribe, clan, combination, company, society, association, brotherhood, fraternity, set, collection, gathering, group, clique, sect, body, organization, assemblage.

gangster, *n.*—*Syn.* mobster, ruffian, racketeer, thug, desperado, goon, boy, punk.

gap—*Syn.* breach, chasm, hollow, cavity, cleft, crevice, rift, chink, break, opening, passage, space, vacuity, crack, aperture, fissure, hole, rent, orifice. *Ant.* inclosure, fence, wall, rail, bolt, barrier, barricade, obstacle, defense, shield, guard, stoppage, obstruction, stricture, impediment.

garb, *n.*—*Syn.* dress, apparel, clothing, clothes, attire, habit, costume, raiment.

garish, *adj.*—*Syn.* showy, ostentatious, dazzling, tawdry, bright, gaudy, flashy, blatant, glaring. *Ant.* sober, modest, discreet, somber.

garnish—*Syn.* embellish, adorn, beautify, deck, decorate, furnish, supply, ornament, bedeck, grace, strew, array, add to, trim. *Ant.* spoil, deface, disfigure, impair, mar, botch, injure, destroy, raze, erase, obliterate, bungle, ruin, harm, deteriorate, hurt, damage.

garrulous—*Syn.* talkative, loquacious, chattering, verbose, prattling, prolix, wordy, blabbing, babbling, gibbering, bumptious, self-assertive. *Ant.* silent, reserved, quiet, still, taciturn, speechless, laconic, reticent, modest, shy, restrained, retiring, pithy, terse, brief, curt, moody, melancholy.

gather—*Syn.* collect, accumulate, amass, assemble, meet, aggregate, group, congregate, pick, cull, muster, convene, convoke, hoard, heap up, pile, mass, bring together, store, garner, summon, infer, deduce. *Ant.* disperse, scatter, strew, spread, dispel, dissipate, disseminate,

distribute, give away, apportion, allot, dispense, deal out, share, assign, diffuse, disband, adjourn, separate.

gauche, *adj.*—*Syn.* inept, awkward, uncouth, blundering, stiff, clumsy, unpolished, clownish. *Ant.* adroit, skillful, deft, dexterous.

gaudy—*Syn.* showy, flashy, tawdry, glittering, bespangled, adorned, ornamented, fine, gay, garish, meretricious, alluring, dazzling, glaring, brilliant, bright, gorgeous, sparkling, scintillating, shining, flashing, gay, glistening, glamorous, glossy. *Ant.* dull, somber, lustreless, solemn, heavy, ugly, clouded, tarnished, uninteresting, dark, gloomy, depressing, dismal, dusky, shaded, obscure, darkened, dim, colorless, faded, pale, etiolate, blanched, withered, rusty.

gaunt—*Syn.* emaciated, scraggy, skinny, lank, meager, attenuated, spare, lean, thin, slender, empty, hollow, bony, shriveled, shrunk, shrunken, atrophied, withered, hungry. *Ant.* fat, stout, obese, plethoric, robust, heavy, fleshy, plump, corpulent, gross, brawny, portly, unctuous, oleaginous, rich, well-fed, lusty, vigorous, hale, hearty, strong, well-developed.

gay—*Syn.* merry, lively, blithe, sprightly, sportive, hilarious, jovial, frolicsome, showy, cheery, cheerful, jolly, joyous, happy, bright, buoyant, gladsome, blithesome, vivacious, jocose, jocular, witty, humorous, waggish, comical, festive, entertaining. *Ant.* dull, listless, discouraged, grouchy, morose, sulky, dogged, sullen, solemn, serious, moody, melancholy, languid, spiritless, supine, sour, petulant, gloomy, splenetic, grim, cross, angry, depressed, crushed, harassed, dejected, low-spirited.

gaze, *v.*—*Syn.* stare, watch, gape, look, peer, observe.

general—*Syn.* common, universal,

comprehensive, inclusive, public, prevalent, usual, commonplace, customary, ordinary, normal, everyday, frequent, habitual, familiar, popular, unlimited, whole, extensive, all-embracing, indefinite, undefined, conventional, regular. *Ant.* particular, definite, limited, rare, circumscribed, infrequent, unusual, unknown, uncommon, exceptional, unwonted, remarkable, extraordinary, unique, singular, unequaled, unlike, individual, sole, only, alone, single, solitary.

generally—*Syn.* usually, chiefly, mainly, commonly, ordinarily, principally. *Ant.* particularly, rarely, seldom, infrequently, not often.

generate—*Syn.* form, make, beget, produce, bear, furnish, bring forth, bring about, yield, breed, engender, occasion, cause, effect, propagate, originate, procreate. *Ant.* destroy, demolish, abolish, extirpate, extinguish, obliterate, dissolve, annihilate, suppress, break down, break up, annul, overthrow, wreck, shatter, undo.

generation—*Syn.* formation, race, breed, stock, kind, reproduction, procreation, creation, progeny, caste, age, era, span, period. *Ant.* destruction, wreck, extinction, demolition, demolishment, abolition, extirpation, dissolution, obliteration, breakdown.

generic, *adj.*—*Syn.* typical, general, ideal, characteristic, common, representative, comprehensive. *Ant.* individual, particular, peculiar, special.

generous—*Syn.* beneficent, noble, honorable, bountiful, liberal, free, munificent, open-handed, open-hearted, free, free-handed, free-hearted, magnanimous, chivalrous, disinterested, unselfish. *Ant.* miserly, niggardly, close, closefisted, parsimonious, illiberal, sparing, stingy, penurious, beggarly, avaricious, mean, sordid, covetous, grasping, greedy,

rapacious, ignoble, petty.

genial—*Syn.* cordial, kind, warm, warm-hearted, pleasing, pleasant, cheering, merry, hearty, revivifying, restorative, mild, inspiring, affable, courteous, civil, complaisant, benign, urbane, gracious, polite, condescending, brotherly, fraternal, cheerful, blithe, jolly, convivial, congenial, sunny, buoyant, joyous, enlivening, lively, joyful, sprightly, animated, spirited. *Ant.* dour, dull, moody, dolesome, gloomy, sorrowful, dismal, doleful, sour, grouchy, morose, sulky, dogged, sullen, melancholy, peevish, petulant, grim, cross, stern, solemn, austere, crabbed, crusty, cranky, irritable, testy, surly, crotchety, perverse, eccentric, depressing, dispiriting, rough, rude, uncongenial, splenetic, fretful, pensive.

genius—*Syn.* talent, talents, intellect, skill, skilfulness, brains, adeptness, nature, character, gift, disposition, ability, capacity, endowment, aptitude, power, quality, characteristic, faculty, wisdom, gumption, long-headedness, astuteness, perspicacity, subtlety, judgment, grasp, sagacity, discernment, wit, acumen, understanding, penetration. *Ant.* idiocy, folly, silliness, incapacity, imbecility, moroseness, hebetude, stupidity, asininity, foolishness, absurdity, brainlessness, stolidity, incompetence, shallowness, obtuseness, idiotism, fatuity, ineptitude, dementia, futility, senility, inaptness, inaptitude, ineptness, simplicity, irrationality, drivel, driveling.

genteel—*Syn.* polite, polished, well-bred, refined, cultured, pleasing, fashionable, graceful, sympathetic, well-mannered, well-behaved, elegant, mannerly, civil, courteous, accomplished, kind, kindly, bland, soft, congenial. *Ant.* rough, gruff, gross, coarse, thick, dense, stupid, dull, doleful, dolesome, boorish, sour,

surly, sulky, sullen, severe,
stern, harsh, rugged, dogged,
stubborn, clownish, rustic, rude,
ill-bred, ill-mannered, grouchy,
grumpy, harsh, morose, censorious, captious, snappish, snarling, growling, disagreeable,
forbidding, odious, repulsive,
repugnant, repelling.

gentle—*Syn.* placid, bland, mild,
peaceful, meek, tame, docile,
soft, suave, soothing, calm,
benign, pacific, serene, easy,
sweet, tender, kind, balmy,
light, yielding, pleasing, pleasant,
pliant, compliant, tractable. *Ant.*
rough, boorish, uncultured, uncouth, coarse, harsh, rude, wild,
unpolished, clownish, barbarous,
bluff, brutish, vulgar, churlish,
ill-mannered, gross, ill-tempered,
uncivil, ungracious, boisterous,
stormy.

genuine—*Syn.* real, veritable,
proven, tested, unadulterated, unmixed, true, natural, authentic,
unalloyed, unaffected, actual,
unquestioned, legitimate, right,
exact, honest, sincere, factual,
unquestionable. *Ant.* false,
meretricious, deceitful, deceptive, unreal, questionable, un-
acceptable, illegitimate, adulterated, mixed, compounded, al-
loyed, confused, clouded, jumbled, blended, deceiving, misleading, erroneous, fallacious,
spurious, bogus, counterfeit,
mock, sham, assumed.

germ—*Syn.* origin, source, beginning, fount, bud, embryo,
sprout, sprig, offshoot, root,
principle, rudiment, spore, microbe, microörganism, bacterium, element, organism.

gesture—*Syn.* attitude, action,
posture, motion, movement,
carriage, pose, manner, behavior,
deportment, demeanor, bearing,
conduct.

get—*Syn.* obtain, receive, procure,
gain, earn, attain, achieve, acquire, secure, win, beget, procreate, propagate, generate.
Ant. leave, quit, relinquish, renounce, forgo, surrender, repudiate, withdraw, retract,

vacate, desert, abjure, forswear,
forsake.

ghastly—*Syn.* pallid, wan, hideous, grim, shocking, deathlike,
ghostlike, corpselike, cadaverous, spectral, ghostly, unearthly, wan, weird, unnatural,
uncanny, terrible, hideous, terrifying, grisly, horrible, horrid,
frightful, dreadful, revolting,
awe-inspiring. *Ant.* pleasing,
pleasant, agreeable, nice, beautiful, fine, lovely, appealing,
attractive, captivating, delightful, alluring, enticing, compelling, fascinating, healthy, wholesome, rosy, roseate, rubicund,
blooming, vigorous, strong.

ghost—*Syn.* vision, specter,
wraith, apparition, shade, sprite,
manes, goblin, spirit, soul, fay,
fairy, banshee, phantom, image,
hallucination, delusion, appearance, elf, hobgoblin, imp. *Ant.*
reality, substance, matter, materiality, body, stuff, element,
solidity, substantiality, actuality,
being, existence, essence, fact.

giant, *adj.*—*Syn.* monster, huge,
large, enormous, immense, colossal, tremendous, stupendous,
gigantic, vast, jumbo, super,
whopping. *Ant.* pygmy, miniature, tiny, microscopic.

gibe—*Syn.* scoff, sneer, flout, jeer,
mock, taunt, deride, mimic,
ape, ridicule, harass, asperse,
banter, fool, tantalize, chaff,
plague, fleer, tease, twit, vex,
annoy, irritate, provoke, torment. *Ant.* praise, exalt, encourage, foster, laud, eulogize,
applaud, commend, inspirit, animate, incite, inspire, stimulate,
extol, elevate, forward, urge,
impel, instigate, approve, sanction, support, admire, advance,
recommend, honor, respect.

giddy—*Syn.* light, light-headed,
unsteady, doddering, shaky, uncertain, unreliable, thoughtless,
flighty, gay, romantic, careless,
sentimental, fanciful, chimerical, imaginative, wild, unbalanced, dizzy, tottering, frivolous, silly, fantastic, conceited,
vain. *Ant.* steady, solemn,

serious, thoughtful, reliable, firm, constant, consistent, uniform, undeviating, regular, equable, well-balanced, calm, cool, level-headed, calculating, conservative, dependable, grave, sober, sedate, earnest, stable, careful, attentive, settled, discreet, wise, prudent, sensible.

gift—*Syn.* presentation, donation, benefaction, largess, grant, gratuity, boon, present, alms, endowment, bequest, bounty, charity, provision, legacy, bequeathment, favor, bestowal, bestowment, benevolence, kindness, liberality, support, maintenance. *Ant.* loss, privation, deprivation, forfeit, forfeiture, detriment, damage, injury, penalty, amercement, mulct, indemnity, confiscation, sequestration, subtraction, divestment, bereavement, disinheritance.

gigantic—*Syn.* large, huge, immense, colossal, enormous, prodigious, monstrous, vast, amazing, extraordinary, marvelous, astonishing, great, extensive, bulky, mammoth, massive, stupendous. *Ant.* small, dwarfish, short, little, minute, Lilliputian, diminutive, contracted, abridged, petty, insignificant, slight, inconsiderable, limited, abbreviated, wizened, slender, emaciated.

gimmick, *n.*—*Syn.* contrivance, gadget, gizmo, point, angle, device, trick, swindle, fraud, adjunct.

girl, *n.*—*Syn.* miss, maid, maiden, damsel, virgin, filly, coed, lass, mademoiselle, señorita.

girth, *n.*—*Syn.* circumference, size, outline, boundary, measure.

gist, *n.*—*Syn.* substance, pith, meaning, core, point, essence, sense, basis, significance.

give—*Syn.* grant, bestow, confer, impart, yield, deliver, furnish, present, supply, cede, turn over, deliver. *Ant.* take, deprive, bereave, strip, divest, dispossess, take away, remove, seize, steal, rob, cheat, bare, keep, retain, hold.

glad——*Syn.* pleased, cheerful, joyful, gladsome, gratified, cheering, exulting, joyous, merry, inspiring, delighted, happy, pleasing, gay, blithesome, jolly, lively, sprightly, vivacious. *Ant.* sad, sorrowful, gloomy, dull, peevish, cranky, crotchety, censorious, dejected, melancholy, mournful, heavy, oppressed, depressed, cast down, dispirited, grieved, discouraged, grouchy, pessimistic.

glamour, *n.*—*Syn.* fascination, magic, aura, enchantment, charm, allure, spell, attraction.

glance, *v.*—*Syn.* peep, peek, sight, look, glimpse, view.

glare—*Syn.* glisten, scintillate, glitter, shine, flash, coruscate, glimmer, gleam, flicker, glister, sparkle, beam, shimmer, glow, twinkle, radiate, dazzle, stare.

glaring—*Syn.* staring, piercing, penetrating, obvious, outstanding, notorious, barefaced, shameless, impudent, audacious, gazing.

glassy—*Syn.* vitreous, smooth, polished, glabrous, brittle, transparent, crystalline, pellucid, limpid, glossy, bright, silken, lustrous, translucent. *Ant.* opaque, dull, lusterless, dim, obscure, rough, uneven, jagged, rugged, scabrous, cloudy, tarnished, dusky, dark.

gleam, *v.*—*Syn.* shine, flash, shimmer, glitter, sparkle.

glee—*Syn.* joviality, merriment, mirth, hilarity, joyfulness, gaiety, joy, exhilaration, jollity, liveliness, sprightliness, animation, vivacity, cheer, cheerfulness, fun, frolic, festivity. *Ant.* dulness or dullness, gloom, sadness, sorrow, misery, melancholy, listlessness, depression, dejection, heaviness, despondency, lamentation, wretchedness, unhappiness, abjection, grief.

glisten, *v.*—*Syn.* glitter, gleam, sparkle, shine, scintillate, flash, coruscate, twinkle.

gloom—*Syn.* darkness, duskiness, obscurity, woe, sadness, depression, dejection, heaviness, oppression, dulness or dullness, despondency, melancholy, the blues, misfortune, misery. *Ant.* rejoicing, fun, frivolity, mirth, joy, mirthfulness, merriment, delight, gladness, rapture, ecstasy, happiness, exultation, transport, bliss, festivity, jollity, hilarity.

gloomy—*Syn.* lowering, lurid, dark, dim, clouded, dusky, sad, glum, low-spirited, down-hearted, cast down, dejected, depressed, funereal, melancholy, oppressive, frowning, heavy, dull, morose, depressing, moody, sullen, pensive, sorrowful, downcast, unhappy, miserable, discontented, discouraged, pessimistic. *Ant.* joyful, joyous, gay, merry, rejoicing, light-hearted, buoyant, cheering, cheerful, animated, happy, contented, satisfied, uplifted, light, sparkling, scintillating, exalted, exulting, glad, gladdening, sportive, festive, vivacious, sprightly, blithe, blithesome, lively, jolly, sunny, serene, bright, clear, glowing.

glorify—*Syn.* magnify, exalt, extol, adore, celebrate, praise, worship, honor, reverence, revere, idolize, respect, venerate, esteem, appreciate, prize, value, laud, applaud, commend, elevate. *Ant.* abase, debase, lower, dishonor, disregard, disrespect, mock, despise, contemn, condemn, degrade, depress, disgrace, humble, humiliate, shame, censure, disparage, reproach.

glorious—*Syn.* famous, renowned, distinguished, noble, exalted, illustrious, splendid, resplendent, wonderful, wondrous, marvelous, showy, brilliant, pompous. *Ant.* infamous, disgraceful, shameful, shameless, ignominious, execrable, odious, opprobrious, scandalous, wicked, heinous, contemptible, ridiculous, flagrant, flagitious, atrocious, nefarious.

glory—*Syn.* honor, fame, renown, splendor, grandeur, celebrity, effulgence, radiance, brightness,

light, lucency, luminosity, brilliancy, illumination, blaze. *Ant.* disgrace, dishonor, abasement, degradation, humiliation, debasement, depression, baseness, degeneracy, deposition, ignominy, shame, infamy, blemish, opprobrium, darkness, opacity, dimness, blackness, gloom, obscurity.

glossy—*Syn.* shining, reflecting, lustrous, polished, smooth, even, plausible, calm, beguiling, bland, sleek, velvety, elegant, refined, polite. *Ant.* dull, lusterless, clouded, dimmed, tarnished, soiled, sullied, stained, rough, ruffled, uneven, rude, unpolished, boorish, unrefined, domineering, harsh, uncouth.

glow, *v.*—*Syn.* burn, flush, light, shine, flame, radiate, blaze, brighten, gleam, flare.

glum, *adj.*—*Syn.* morose, moody, blue, dismal, surly, dejected, sullen, gloomy, sulky, low. *Ant.* cheerful, happy, lighthearted, joyous.

glut—*Syn.* fill, cloy, stuff, gorge, cram, satiate, surfeit, feast, hog (*colloq.*) wolf (*slang*), satisfy, devour, consume, raven, eat greedily. *Ant.* abstain, fast, mortify, restrain, reduce, subdue, forbear, cease, relinquish, deny, repress, curb, moderate, control, lessen, refrain from.

gluttony, *n.*—*Syn.* greed, voracity, hoggishness, indulgence, rapacity, avarice, covetousness.

go—*Syn.* move, pass, proceed, step, walk, depart, get out, disappear, vamose or vamoose (*slang*), decamp, travel, stir, budge, run, abscond, leave, retire, retreat, withdraw, recede, relinquish, cease, desert, desist, abandon. *Ant.* come, become, begin, approach, appear, arrive, enter, come hither, come near, move forward, draw near, come out, show up (*colloq.*), heave in sight (*colloq.*).

goal, *n.*—*Syn.* aim, object, intention, end, ambition, destination.

God—*Syn.* Lord, Ruler, Creator,

Almighty, Omnipotence, Providence, Author, Divinity, Supreme Being, Deity, Godhead, Jehovah, Maker, Master, King of Kings, Lord of Lords, Allah [*Ar.*].

godly—*Syn.* righteous, devout, holy, pious, religious, godlike, reverent, reverential, sincere, earnest, humble, submissive, saintly, moral, devotional, hallowed, consecrate, consecrated, divine, sinless, inviolate, pure, immaculate, stainless, incorrupt, sacred, devoted. *Ant.* sinful, wicked, bad, evil, profane, impious, godless, ungodly, irreverent, irreligious, unholy, unhallowed, unsanctified, worldly, corrupt, vile, immoral, lewd, lascivious, iniquitous, depraved, vicious, carnal, impure, lecherous, libidinous.

good, *adj.*—*Syn.* righteous, upright, virtuous, honest, true, just, benevolent, moral, chaste, pure, fine, incorrupt, unspotted, untainted, sinless, stainless, honorable, conscientious, sound, serviceable, real, valid, reputable, propitious, proper, fit, suitable, useful, valuable, agreeable, pleasant, satisfying, satisfactory, complete, strong, reliable, healthy, health-giving, invigorating, appropriate, gratifying. *Ant.* bad, evil, wicked, vile, sinful, depraved, impure, corrupt, unsound, dishonorable, disgraceful, contemptible, dishonest, vicious, abandoned, base, debased, abominable, foul, disgusting, execrable, hateful, abhorrent, horrid, horrible, odious, loathsome, nauseous, detestable, offensive, disagreeable, unpleasant, noxious, unhealthy, deleterious, injurious.

good, *n.*—*Syn.* benefit, weal, advantage, profit, boon, gain, blessing, virtue, prosperity, interest, welfare, health, happiness, wellbeing, favor, benediction, success, good luck, felicity, bliss, benison, commendation, approval, achievement, consummation, victory, enjoyment,

peace, plenty. *Ant.* evil, misfortune, bad luck, loss, sickness, deprivation, penury, adversity, catastrophe, ill, calamity, harm, injury, misadventure, disadvantage, obstacle, difficulty, drawback, danger, peril, hazard, risk, jeopardy, embarrassment, obstruction, impediment, perplexity, trouble, sorrow, distress, vexation, affliction, anxiety, misery, confusion, abashment, shame, disgrace, dishonor.

goods, *n.*—*Syn.* material, merchandise, chattels, effects, property, ware, freight, stock.

gorgeous—*Syn.* superb, grand, magnificent, stately, surpassing, glorious, splendid, great, resplendent, majestic, superb, imposing, pompous, princely, kingly, queenly, impressive, affecting, munificent, lavish, showy, flashy, garish, gaudy, gay, brilliant, dazzling, attractive. *Ant.* plain, simple, unpretentious, dull, common, ordinary, unimpressive, tawdry, modest, lowly, homely, unadorned, usual, customary, mean, poor, insignificant, unimposing, commonplace, unattractive, ragged.

govern—*Syn.* rule, direct, control, manage, command, moderate, guide, curb, influence, mold, reign, reign over, sway, restrain, administer, conduct, supervise, oversee, regulate, dominate, prevail, lead, check, adjust, order, keep in order. *Ant.* obey, submit, yield, comply, assent, accede, fulfil, perform, follow, acquiesce, surrender, cede, agree to, consent, conform, concede, allow, suffer, permit, give way, give up.

government—*Syn.* rule, order, control, sway, administration, constitution, state, kingdom, empire, sovereignty, polity, method, system, regulation, direction, law. *Ant.* anarchy, rebellion, revolution, chaos, confusion, disorder, lawlessness, tumult, riot, turbulence, insubordination, violence, revolt, insurrection, resistance, mutiny, sedition.

graceful—*Syn.* becoming, comely, elegant, beautiful, handsome, neat, fit, suitable, congruous, proper, regular, refined, pleasing, fitting, seemly, clean, trim, well-proportioned, clear-cut, clean-cut, symmetrical, proportioned, dignified, charming, easy, unaffected. *Ant.* awkward, uncouth, ungraceful, undignified, unpolished, vulgar, rude, boorish, slovenly, careless, loose, negligent, clumsy, lubberly, clownish, ungainly, rough, unrefined, coarse, bungling, blundering, bearish, beastly, bestial, swinish, gawky, maladroit, unhandy, unskilful.

gracious—*Syn.* merciful, kind, kindly, beneficent, nice, benevolent, munificent, mild, bland, congenial, courteous, benignant, compassionate, tender. *Ant.* rough, rude, domineering, coarse, dominating, vulgar, harsh, unkind, cruel, rigorous, hard, exacting, austere, severe, stern, bitter, ungracious, churlish, brutal, ill-tempered, uncivil, acrimonious, sarcastic, ironical, vituperative.

gradual—*Syn.* slow, creeping, progressive, continuous, unintermittent, gradational, regular, continual, perpetual, incessant. *Ant.* sudden, unexpected, unlooked for, unanticipated, precipitate, intermittent, hasty.

grand—*Syn.* majestic, stately, dignified, lofty, elevated, exalted, splendid, gorgeous, superb, magnificent, sublime, pompous, great, illustrious, imposing, striking, elegant, showy, brilliant, impressive. *Ant.* shabby, mean, inferior, beggarly, low, ragged, tattered, threadbare, pitiful, contemptible, poor, paltry, petty, trivial, trifling, insignificant, little, small, unimposing, ordinary, common, commonplace.

grant, n.—*Syn.* gift, boon, reward, present, allowance, stipend, donation, benefaction, gratuity, endowment, concession, bequest, privilege. *Ant.* loss, deprivation, deduction, decrement, detriment, damage, forfeiture.

grant, v.—*Syn.* permit, yield, cede, accede, allow, give, impart, bestow, confer, invest, transfer, comply, concur, present, arrange. *Ant.* refuse, withhold, withdraw, deny, decline, reject, repel, rebuff, disavow, disclaim, disown, renounce, oppose, forbid.

graphic—*Syn.* forcible, telling, picturesque, vivid, pictorial, illustrative, descriptive, intelligible, comprehensible, clear, explicit, definite, lucid, striking, distinct, precise, unequivocal, expressive. *Ant.* obscure, confused, ambiguous, mixed, uncertain, unintelligible, perplexing, enigmatic, incomprehensible, doubtful, dubious, crytographic, jumbled, involved, intricate, complex, complicated, abstruse.

grasp—*Syn.* catch, clutch, seize, clasp, grapple, retain, grip, gripe, take, capture, apprehend, comprehend, understand, perceive, infer, discern, recognize, deduce. *Ant.* lose, slip, let go, miss, unclasp, release, free, liberate, loose, disengage, extricate, misapprehend, misconstrue, misconceive, misunderstand.

grateful—*Syn.* thankful, appreciative, beholden, obliged, acceptable, gratifying, delicious, agreeable, pleasing. *Ant.* ungrateful, thankless, unmindful, forgetful, unacknowledged, unrequited, unrewarded, heedless, careless, harsh, rough, rude, abusive.

gratification—*Syn.* satisfaction, enjoyment, pleasure, delight, reward, comfort, happiness, content, contentment, compensation, recompense, choice, self-indulgence, voluptuousness, preference, will, inclination, purpose, determination, favor, indulgence. *Ant.* denial, self-denial, sacrifice, self-sacrifice, asceticism, abstinence, fasting, castigation, mortification, submission, humiliation, penance, vexation, chagrin, disappointment, subjection, suffering, forbearance, persecution, contumely, shame.

gratify—*Syn.* indulge, humor, satisfy, please, satiate, placate, pamper, yield, favor, comply, acquiesce, grant, coddle, pet, fondle, treat. *Ant.* displease, deprive, disgust, offend, vex, annoy, disturb, provoke, dissatisfy, pique, mock, taunt, scoff, ridicule, censure, blame.

gratuitous, *adj.*—*Syn.* unprovoked, voluntary, spontaneous, groundless, wanton, unfounded. *Ant.* deserved, warranted, called-for.

grave, *adj.*—*Syn.* serious, solemn, heavy, sober, important, momentous, sedate, weighty, thoughtful, earnest, intense, forcible, ponderous, consequential, far-reaching. *Ant.* light, airy, volatile, buoyant, gay, capricious, vain, frivolous, thoughtless, unimportant, inconsequential, idle, fruitless, trifling, trivial, nugatory, futile.

grave, *n.*—*Syn.* tomb, sepulcher, vault, pit, hollow, burial place, crypt, mausoleum, catacomb, hole, cenotaph, long home, last home, death.

great—*Syn.* big, large, huge, majestic, gigantic, vast, noble, grand, august, dignified, extensive, extraordinary, bulky, extended, wide, strong, powerful, puissant, eminent, commanding, famous, illustrious, famed, celebrated, noted, distinguished, renowned, gallant, conspicuous, elevated, prominent, high, glorious, exalted, honorable, influential, brave, heroic, courageous, fearless, intrepid, valiant, daring, authoritative, lordly, princely, kingly, stately, imperial, generous, magnanimous, chivalrous, high-minded, high-souled, excellent, splendid. *Ant.* small, little, dwarfish, wee [*Sc.*], short, stunted, wizened, withered, diminutive, Lilliputian, min-

ute, petty, mean, low, footy (*dial*), contemptible, shallow, ordinary, common, asinine, stupid, silly, pusillanimous, weak, powerless, ignorant, despicable, despised, poor, unknown, infamous, vile, evil, wicked, bad, obtuse, doltish, dense, addlepated, worthless, good-for-nothing, useless, obscure, abject, base, beggarly, undignified, wretched, vulgar, ignoble, slavish, groveling, spiritless, degraded, sordid, degenerate, servile, paltry, menial, shameful, dishonorable.

greed—*Syn.* greediness, avidity, eagerness, voracity, excess, rapacity, gluttony, piggishness, indulgence, hoggishness, gormandism, or gourmandism, ravenousness, voraciousness, intemperance, cupidity, graspingness, covetousness, desire. *Ant.* generosity, liberality, munificence, bounty, moderation, temperance, fast, abstinence, self-denial, asceticism, austerity, mortification, rigor.

greedy—*Syn.* avid, avaricious, grasping, rapacious, gluttonous, voracious, devouring, edacious, parsimonious, miserly, close, close-fisted, grudging, sordid, mercenary, illiberal, stingy, covetous. *Ant.* liberal, open-handed, charitable, philanthropic, prodigal, profuse, improvident, lavish, squandering, spendthrift, extravagant, wasteful.

greet, *v.*—*Syn.* hail, address, welcome, accost, salute.

gregarious, *adj.*—*Syn.* social, convivial, neighborly, companionable, accessible, amicable. *Ant.* solitary, unsociable, unfriendly.

grief—*Syn.* sorrow, sadness, affliction, trial, regret, woe, tribulation, melancholy, vexation, mourning, misfortune, adversity, catastrophe, calamity, evil, distress, misery, trouble, pain, hardship, worry, worriment, harassment, anxiety, anguish. *Ant.* joy, gladness, rejoicing, happiness, ecstasy, delight, gratification, satisfaction, exultation, rapture, transport, triumph, victory, merriment, exhilaration, pleasure.

grievous—*Syn.* painful, afflicting, heavy, baleful, sad, unhappy, woeful, sorrowful, oppressive, burdensome, distressing, distressful, outrageous, flagitious, heinous, calamitous. *Ant.* light, lightsome, trivial, harmless, salutary, advantageous, innocuous, good, serviceable, pleasant, pleasurable, gratifying, delightful, agreeable, comforting, delectable, beneficial, advantageous.

grim—*Syn.* sullen, stern, austere, severe, sour, harsh, threatening, repellent, terrifying, crabbed, crusty, cranky, rigid, rigorous, ugly, ill-looking, gloomy, obstinate, resolute, intractable, sulky, cross, morose, splenetic, churlish, glum, grumpy, scowling, grouchy, glowering, dogged, stubborn, cantankerous. *Ant.* pleasant, mild, bland, smiling, laughing, blithe, merry, gay, suave, calm, agreeable, charming, winning, winsome, attractive, chipper, amiable, cordial, cheerful, cheering, buoyant, light-hearted, enlivening, soothing, debonair, sunny, serene, jocund, jovial, gleeful, inspiriting, mirthful, jocose, rollicking.

grimace, *n.*—*Syn.* contortion, scowl, face, leer, squint, smirk.

grind—*Syn.* crush, oppress, harass, tire, worry, annoy, afflict, tyrannize, dominate, domineer, bully, inflict, ill-treat, override, coerce, trample, overpower, overcome, burden, overwhelm, treat harshly, put on the screws, grate, reduce, pulverize, sharpen, grate to an edge. *Ant.* lighten, relieve, succor, help, assist, solace, comfort, encourage, alleviate, diminish, mitigate, assuage, ameliorate, allay, soften, lessen, soothe, mollify, console, cheer, enliven, inspirit, gladden, support, refresh, blunt, dull, make blunt or dull.

grip, *v.*—*Syn.* grasp, clasp, hold, clutch, grab, seize.

grisly—*Syn.* horrible, terrible, disgusting, sickening, loathsome, frightful, abhorrent, detestable, odious, repellent, forbidding, repulsive, shocking, revolting, repugnant, abominable. *Ant.* pleasing, attractive, compelling, nice, handsome, beautiful, lovely, sweet, dainty, refined, alluring, charming, captivating, fascinating, agreeable, good-looking, personable, well-favored, comely, symmetrical, graceful, shapely.

grit, *n.*—*Syn.* nerve, courage, fortitude, mettle, guts, pluck, decision, spirit. *Ant.* cowardice, faintheartedness, cravenness, timidity.

groan, *v.*—*Syn.* moan, lament, cry, sob, sigh, growl, suffer.

gross—*Syn.* coarse, indelicate, rough, vulgar, corrupt, obscene, lewd, impure, sensual, thick, dense, bulky, enormous, monstrous, fat, corpulent, large, unwieldy, obese, fleshy, ponderous, clownish, rude, low, vulgar, unbecoming, repulsive, total, whole. *Ant.* fine, delicate, dainty, refined, comely, fair, slender, thin, svelte, lithe, graceful, easy, appealing, attractive, handsome, well-bred, choice, proper, purified, moral, clean, spiritual, virtuous, intellectual, pure, chaste.

grotesque, *adj.*—*Syn.* fantastic, misshapen, absurd, odd, unnatural, bizarre, incongruous, strange. *Ant.* normal, usual, customary.

ground—*Syn.* land, estate, property, section, quarter, part, surface, possession, place, region, territory, country, locality, habitat, origin, foundation, base, basis, support, cause.

group—*Syn.* assembly, cluster, collection, clump, order, class, assemblage, bunch, crowd, audience, gang, company, throng, knot, meeting.

grovel—*Syn.* crawl, cringe, fawn, sneak, stoop, kneel, crouch, truckle, toady, sponge, cower, snivel, beg, beseech, implore, wheedle, blandish, flatter, prostrate, reverence. *Ant.* command, order, control, govern, direct, rule, lead, master, discipline, dictate, spurn, despise, scorn, disdain, contemn, mock, ridicule, deride, taunt, jeer, provoke, delude, gibe, tantalize, fool.

grow—*Syn.* expand, swell, enlarge, increase, augment, vegetate, wax, dilate, stretch, spread, develop, thicken, incrassate, extend, bud, burgeon, amplify, tumefy, turgesce, inflate, puff, gemmate, germinate, intumesce, *Ant.* decrease, diminish, detumesce, lessen, abate, reduce, lower, sink, wither, fade, fail, decline, droop, dwindle, vanish, blanch, etiolate, wizen, decay, pass away, die.

growl—*Syn.* grumble, snarl, mumble, complain, murmur, mutter, bemoan, groan, rumble, speak harshly, utter indistinctly, talk imperfectly.

grub, *n.*—*Syn.* food, victuals, vittles, eats, chow, groceries, tucker.

grudge—*Syn.* spite, rancor, malice, hatred, aversion, pique, animosity, enmity, ill-will, hardfeeling, malevolence, malignity, hostility, antipathy, antagonism, repugnance, abhorrence, disgust, dislike, detestation, contrariety, opposition, resistance, maliciousness, evil-mindedness. *Ant.* good-will, benevolence, friendliness, brotherliness, fraternalism, kindness, tenderness, benignity, beneficence, charity, bounty, generosity, kindheartedness, philanthropy, sympathy, affection, love, admiration, graciousness, munificence, devotion, liberality, fondness, congeniality, affinity, fellow-feeling, agreement.

gruesome, *adj.*—*Syn.* ghastly, hideous, ugly, grim, horrifying, fearful, macabre, grisly, frightful, appalling.

gruff—*Syn.* abrupt, blunt, rugged, rough, bluff, sour, churlish, rude, unceremonious, short, snappish, cross, crabbed, morose, surly, stern, snarling, harsh, bearish, uncivil, acrimonious. *Ant.* free, easy, pleasant, sunny, serene, civil, courteous, polite, obliging, condescending, respectful, attentive, affable, conciliating, urbane, complaisant, benign, friendly, gracious, cheerful, genial, ready, kind, kindly, kindhearted.

guarantee—*Syn.* certify, testify, aver, vouch, attest, verify, declare, assure, indorse, secure, warrant, guard, insure, obligate, make sure, bear witness, support, confirm, affirm, asseverate, assert, allege, avow, depose. *Ant.* deny, disown, decry, ignore, deprecate, disapprove, condemn, censure, disclaim, oppose, reject, contradict, gainsay, disprove, depreciate, detract, disparage, disavow, renounce.

guard—*Syn.* watch, protect, guide, secure, defend, safeguard, keep, preserve, shield, care for, observe, superintend, supervise, tend, attend. *Ant.* neglect, forsake, abandon, disregard, desert, leave, quit, relinquish, forego, withdraw, cease, stop, resign, go away.

guess, *v.*—*Syn.* believe, surmise, reckon, assume, imagine, suppose, conjecture, opine, fancy.

guide—*Syn.* lead, direct, control, conduct, regulate, persuade, induce, command, dispose, order, contrive, manage, sway, train, educate, influence. *Ant.* see ANTONYMS for **guard** above.

guile—*Syn.* craft, cunning, artifice, duplicity, deceit, doubledealing, trickery, knavishness, dishonesty, fraud, wiliness, cleverness, artfulness, craftiness, astuteness, slyness, subtlety, subtleness, dissimulation, knavery, deception, rascality, trickishness, imposture, stratagem, hypocrisy, false pretension. *Ant.* honesty, openness, candor, fair-dealing, square-shooting (*slang*), frankness, ingenuousness, fairness, sincerity, truth-

fulness, genuineness, uprightness, righteousness, artlessness,
integrity, probity, rectitude,
straightness, rightness, reliability, unreservedness, unaffect-
edness, plainness, simplicity.

guiltless—*Syn.* harmless, innocent, free, sinless, crimeless, upright, honest, blameless, faultless, undefiled, spotless, pure,
unstained, untainted, innocuous,
truthful. *Ant.* guilty, sinful,
criminal, corrupt, wicked, liable,
tarnished, stained, faulty, blame-
ful, culpable, blamable, blameworthy, censurable, wrong, unworthy, immoral.

guilty—*Syn.* see ANTONYMS for
guiltless above. *Ant.* see
SYNONYMS for **guiltless** above.

gumption, *n.* — *Syn.* common
sense, sagacity, penetration,
acumen, astuteness, discernment, cunning, judgment,
shrewdness.

gusto, *n.*—*Syn.* relish, pleasure,
enthusiasm, delight, ardor, zest,
appetite, enjoyment.

gyp, *v.*—*Syn.* cheat, swindle, defraud, bamboozle, trick.

gyrate, *v.*—*Syn.* spin, whirl, rotate, swirl, turn, spiral, revolve.

H

habit—*Syn.* custom, practice,
tendency, fashion, form, manner, habitude, routine, addic-
tion, use, usage, rule, regularity,
repetition, wont, mode, method,
manner, way, style, continuation, garb, covering, dress, raiment, costume, clothes. *Ant.*
irregularity, disuse, desuetude,
rarity, infrequency, uncommon-
ness, nonconformity, unconventionality, uncertainty, unpunc-
tuality, fitfulness, capriciousness.

habitation—*Syn.* house, abode,
dwelling, occupancy, domicile,
residence, home, abiding-place,
sojourn, stay, roof-tree, dwell-
ing-place.

habitual—*Syn.* regular, ordinary,
perpetual, usual, customary,

familiar, accustomed, wonted,
established, normal, general,
recurrent, systematic, periodical, stated, formal. *Ant.* rare,
uncommon, unusual, seldom,
infrequent, remarkable, unwonted, not often, extraordinary.

hack, *n.*—*Syn.* worn-out horse,
prad (*colloq.*), drudge, slave,
literary drudge, impecunious
writer, ghost writer, hackney-
coach, coach for hire, healed
cut, dry wound, cicatrice, scar.

hack, *v.*—*Syn.* cut, chop, hag,
mangle, tear, split, break, mutilate, lacerate, botch, notch,
chip, drudge, toil, slave, cough
faintly.

hackneyed, *adj.*—*Syn.* stereotyped, trite, inane, flat, vapid,
stale, banal, commonplace, ordinary. *Ant.* original, fresh,
novel.

Hades—*Syn.* hell, underworld,
inferno, infernal regions, Sheol,
Tartarus, gehenna, abyss, Tophet,
Styx, Acheron, Cocytus, Aver-
nus, Abaddon, realm of Pluto,
bottomless pit, jahannan [*Hind.*],
Satan's kingdom. *Ant.* heaven,
paradise, New Jerusalem, Land
of Beulah, Beulah Land, Holy
City, Elysium, Elysian fields,
Zion, Valhalla, Heavenly
Home, abode of the blessed,
God's kingdom.

hag, *n.*—*Syn.* crone, witch, harpy,
beldam, virago, termagant, harridan, battle-ax, bat.

haggard—*Syn.* gaunt, careworn,
fretted, worried, wrinkled, lean,
meager, thin, emaciated, hunger-
stricken, wasted, harassed,
weary, tired, exhausted, worn-
out, weak, debilitated. *Ant.*
strong, robust, healthy, blooming, exuberant, lively, playful,
vigorous, active, forcible, powerful, muscular, lusty, hearty.

haggle, *v.*—*Syn.* chaffer, bargain,
wrangle, cavil, stickle, dicker,
negotiate, deal.

hail—*Syn.* call, address, salute,
speak to, accost, greet, compliment, apostrophize, approach,
woo, court, welcome, honor,

acclaim, applaud, cheer, entertain. *Ant.* ignore, neglect, disregard, pass over, slight, scorn, spurn, disdain, deride, despise, contemn, shun, avoid, elude, eschew.

hair-trigger, *adj.—Syn.* touchy, quick, hasty, jittery, prickly, jumpy, hot. *Ant.* calm, cool, deliberate.

halcyon, *adj.—Syn.* golden, tranquil, placid, peaceful, calm, serene, unruffled, quiet, still, happy. *Ant.* stormy, turbulent, rough, tempestuous.

hale, *adj.—Syn.* healthy, vigorous, well, stout, chipper, robust, lusty. *Ant.* infirm, decrepit, feeble, weak.

hall—*Syn.* entrance, vestibule, passage, house, manor, building, residence, mansion, manor house, castle, room, auditorium, meeting place, headquarters, public building.

hallucination, *n.—Syn.* delusion, illusion, aberration, fantasy, fancy, fantod, mirage, chimera, pipe dream.

halt—*Syn.* pull up, stand, stop, check, linger, limp, falter, stammer, demur, hesitate, doubt, pause, stammer, stutter, scruple, desist, cease, rest, suspend, intermit, discontinue. *Ant.* go, proceed, advance, continue, walk, run, progress, emanate, move, go on, persevere, endure, carry on, keep going, pursue.

hamper—*Syn.* impede, thwart, embarrass, perplex, confuse, annoy, disconcert, entangle, embroil, obstruct, delay, prevent, retard, fetter, check, spancel, shackle, clog, hinder, prevent, encumber, restrict, restrain, oppilate, oppress. *Ant.* facilitate, make easy, help, assist, encourage, succor, befriend, favor, comfort, relieve, support, second, aid, co-operate, forward, promote, cheer, embolden, inspirit.

handicap, *n.—Syn.* encumbrance, dope, cap, hindrance, burden, penalty, bug, impost, impedi-, ment, odds, allowance. *Ant.*

advantage, asset.

handle, *v.—Syn.* manipulate, wield, operate, manage, finger, use, ply, direct.

handsome—*Syn.* beautiful, graceful, lovely, pretty, elegant, comely, fair, well-favored, well-proportioned, bonny, shapely, agreeable, liberal, large, ample. *Ant.* ugly, ill-favored, ungraceful, offensive, repulsive, repugnant, revolting, mean, poor, niggardly, miserly, small, insignificant.

handy—*Syn.* near, convenient, useful, helpful, ready, ingenious, skilful, skilled, fitting, inventive, clever, resourceful, apt, dexterous. *Ant.* unhandy, unskilful, clumsy, stupid, useless, unskilled, ignorant, untrained, awkward, bungling, inexpert, fumbling, clownish, ineffectual.

hang, *v.—Syn.* suspend, depend, lean, droop, hover, attach, swing, dangle, drape.

haphazard — *Syn.* accidental, chancy, risky, sudden, careless, unconsidered, unexpected, casual, fortuitous, contingent, incidental, random. *Ant.* considered, premeditated, deliberate, designed, purposed, intentional, determined, planned, intended, contemplated, studied.

hapless—*Syn.* unfortunate, miserable, luckless, unlucky, ill-fated, jinxed (*slang*), Jonahed (*slang*), hoodooed (*colloq.*), unhappy. *Ant.* fortunate, lucky, favored, fortuitous, successful, prosperous, happy, satisfied, flourishing, well-off, contented.

happen—*Syn.* bechance, occur, chance, fall, supervene, betide, befall, take place, fall out, come to pass, arrive, meet with, come after, turn, up, ensue, result, eventuate.

happily—*Syn.* fortunately, contentedly, gracefully, luckily, successfully, felicitously. *Ant.* unfortunately, unluckily, unsuccessfully, calamitously, disastrously, ungracefully.

happiness—*Syn.* bliss, beatitude,

blessedness, aptness, felicity, joy, contentment, satisfaction, sanctity, ecstasy, rapture, peace, mirth, mirthfulness, merrymaking, delight, gladness, exultation, transport. *Ant.* misery, misfortune, unhappiness, grief, sorrow, abandonment, sadness, melancholy, gloom, distress, despondency, despair, dejection, depression, heaviness, calamity, wretchedness, mournfulness, lamentation, adversity, catastrophe, disaster.

happy—*Syn.* joyous, joyful, merry, mirthful, glad, delighted, delightful, cheerful, cheering, gay, contented, satisfied, prosperous, rapturous, felicitous, cheery, blithe, blithesome, jolly, blessed, blissful, rejoiced, rejoicing, jovial, jocund, gladsome, propitious, favorable, pleased, gratified, pleasing, fortunate, peaceful, comfortable, light, bright, buoyant, vivacious, sunny, dexterous, smiling, successful, sprightly, lucky, lively, animated, spirited, exhilarated, exhilarating, smiling, laughing, satiated. *Ant.* sad, sorrowful, unhappy, moody, morose, sour, discontented, dissatisfied, mortified, disappointed, calamitous, blue, unfortunate, unlucky, gloomy, dejected, despairing, melancholy, depressed, cast down, disheartened, discouraged, embarrassed, poverty - stricken, wretched, weeping, wailing, moaning, bemoaning, mournful, miserable, grieved, anguished, aggrieved, tormented, abject, forlorn, pitiable, disconsolate, abandoned, cheerless, comfortless, destitute, hopeless, forsaken, afflicted, distressed, woeful, woebegone, troubled.

harass—*Syn.* annoy, vex, irritate, plague, tantalize, taunt, provoke, worry, exacerbate, exasperate, disturb, discommode, molest, pester, fret, tease, agitate, excite, rouse, ruffle, discompose, anger, inflame, enrage, incense, chafe, nettle, trouble,

embarrass, twit, torment, jeer, deride, flout, mock, upbraid, revile, ridicule, reproach, defame, vilify, traduce, calumniate, sneer, fleer, disconcert, arouse, infuriate, gibe, banter, fool, delude. *Ant.* cheer, inspirit, embolden, appease, encourage, aid, help, assist, advise, exhort, animate, succor, befriend, comfort, compose, console, calm, promote, forward, facilitate, support, favor, cooperate, tranquilize or tranquillize, second, incite, urge, impel, stimulate, revive, gladden, enliven, refresh, abet, countenance, instigate, contribute, strengthen, embolden, solace, sustain, alleviate, lighten, allay, relieve, assuage, abate, soothe.

harbor, *v.*—*Syn.* shelter, foster, house, cherish, nurture, protect, shield. *Ant.* eject, expel, banish, exile.

hard—*Syn.* firm, compact, solid, unyielding, resisting, strong, substantial, stable, stout, thick, fixed, steady, compressed, close, dense, unimpressible, condensed, concrete, pressed, adamantine, adamantean, impervious, stony, rocky, rigid. *Ant.* soft, yielding, impressible, malleable, light, weak, pliant, pliable, susceptible, penetrable, muddy, watery, wet, moist, damp, humid.

hard—*Syn.* arduous, difficult, laborious, toilsome, troublesome, unaccommodating, harsh, stiff, unconventional, constrained, unfeeling, severe, austere, stern, pitiless, exacting, obdurate, cruel, unrelenting, perverse, vengeful, unforgiving. *Ant.* soft, tender, mild, gentle, kind, kindly, tender-hearted, feeling, pitying, merciful, sensitive, delicate, effeminate, weak, feeble, frail, compassionate, affectionate, indulgent, tractable, clement, gracious, tolerant.

hard-boiled, *adj.*—*Syn.* tough, callous, fixed, determined, obstinate, unfeeling, crude, thickskinned. *Ant.* lily-livered, soft, effeminate, weak.

hardihood—*Syn.* fearlessness, effrontery, boldness, courage, resolution, impudence, impertinence, scoffing, audacity, audaciousness, presumption, daring, spirit, confidence, assurance, shamelessness, barefacedness, intrepidity, dauntlessness, bravery, fortitude, firmness, coolness, resistance. *Ant.* weakness, faltering, cowardice, fear, pusillanimity, poltroonery, dastardliness, fearfulness, timorousness, timidity, apprehension, faintheartedness, misgiving, trepidation, dismay, consternation, dread, awe, reluctance, cowardliness.

hardship—*Syn.* trial, burden, privation, affliction, injury, oppression, adversity, misfortune, injustice, disaster, calamity, distress, unhappiness, misery, harm, misadventure, catastrophe, trouble, sorrow, grief, regret, sadness, tribulation. *Ant.* advantage, benefit, good, profit, gain, utility, vantage, help, emolument, interest, favor, blessing, boon, benefit, improvement, aid, assistance, coöperation, friendship, support, sustenance.

hardy—*Syn.* strong, enduring, tenacious, unyielding, fearless, courageous, intrepid, brave, resisting, inured, robust, stouthearted, vigorous, dauntless, bold, confident, assured, impudent, audacious, daring, spirited, resistant, valorous, firm, forcible, undaunted. *Ant.* weak, yielding, soft, tender, timid, delicate, puny, feeble, enfeebled, debilitated, impaired, enervated, infirm, invalid, sickly, cowardly, fearful, apprehensive, timorous, timid, shrinking, craven, pliant, submissive.

harm—*Syn.* injury, wrong, damage, infliction, hurt, detriment, evil, mischief, bane, deterioration, impairment, loss, deprivation, forfeiture. *Ant.* good, welfare, prosperity, benefit, advantage, advancement, interest,

happiness, boon, benefit, weal, gain, blessing, profit.

harmless—*Syn.* innocuous, innoxious, inoffensive, innocent, blameless, guiltless, faultless, artless, simple, irreproachable, unblemished, spotless, pure, undefiled, incorrupt, easy-going, gentle, good-natured, manageable, obedient, docile, good. *Ant.* harmful, hurtful, injurious, noxious, poisonous, evil, bad, evil-minded, malicious, malignant, wicked, sinful, pernicious, baneful, · noisome, unwholesome, pestilential, pestiferous, deleterious, prejudicial, detrimental, damaging.

harmonious—*Syn.* agreeable, accordant, concordant, corresponding, congruous, suitable, fit, adapted, melodious, musical, dulcet, tuneful, answerable, consonant, similar, like. *Ant.* discordant, disagreeable, unlike, opposed, incongruous, unsuitable, dissonant, harsh, jarring, inharmonious, disagreeing, clashing, jangling, jangly, incompatible, inappropriate.

harmony—*Syn.* concord, agreement, unison, accord, accordance, concordance, concurrence, union, unanimity, consonance, congruity, unity, uniformity, melody, consistency, symmetry, concert, conformity, amity, music, tune, suitableness, agreeableness. *Ant.* discord, jangle, disagreement, dissonance, discordance, opposition, inconsistency, strife, clashing, variance, difference, incongruity, unsuitableness, disunion, changeableness, wavering, variation, deviation, mutation, alteration, innovation, interchange, alternation, change, antagonism, conflict, contention, dissension.

harry, *v.*—*Syn.* harass, hector, persecute, snipe, afflict, annoy, badger, hound, worry, torment, trouble, pester. *Ant.* comfort, relieve, console, assuage.

harsh—*Syn.* rough, rigorous, severe, austere, stern, gruff, morose, hard, exacting, cruel, sharp, cutting, keen, acrimonious, bitter, ungracious, uncivil, churlish, brutal, ill-tempered, jarring, censorious, rigid, strict, unrelenting, pitiless, inexorable, merciless, unfeeling, selfish, surly, sour, crabbed, snarling, rude, cross, overbearing, crusty. *Ant.* gentle, mild, forbearing, easy, unselfish, meek, placid, even, good-tempered, sweet-tempered, kind, kindly, indulgent, moderate, peaceful, quiet, unassuming, backward, bashful, beneficent, charitable, benevolent, merciful, patient, calm, humble, unostentatious, soft, unpretentious, tender, yielding, commiserating, sympathetic, feeling, agreeable, pleasant, congenial, compassionate, consoling, encouraging.

harvest—*Syn.* produce, result, fruitage, profit, product, proceeds, return, yield, crop, store, storage, growth, intake, ingathering, amount, corn, grain, reaping.

hassle, *n.*—*Syn.* argument, controversy, contention, dispute, fight, quarrel, brawl, disagreement, scrap, rhubarb.

haste—*Syn.* hurry, despatch, speed, nimbleness, rapidity, rapidness, celerity, swiftness, bustle, fleetness, quickness, flurry, acceleration, speediness, promptness, exertion, expedition, velocity, agility, scramble, urgency, bustle, scurry, rush, activity, briskness. *Ant.* slowness, tardiness, laziness, lagging, loitering, lingering, delay, delaying, tarrying, lateness, stay, procrastination, indolence, inaction, leisure, ease, rest, repose, collapse, convenience, postponement, dilatoriness.

hasten—*Syn.* accelerate, despatch, speed, expedite, hurry, drive, push, quicken, move quickly, rush, run, sprint, dash, spurt, scamper, scurry, race, skip. *Ant.* delay, procrastinate, postpone, loiter, linger, idle, defer, put off, prolong, retard, creep, crawl, lag, drawl, saunter, plod,

trudge, drag, dawdle, slouch, shuffle, shamble, hobble, limp, totter, stagger, wobble.

hasty—*Syn.* hurried, ill-advised, rash, eager, inopportune, easy, quick, speedy, excited, precipitate, headlong, rushing, sudden, foolhardy, thoughtless, headstrong, heedless, indiscreet, impulsive, careless, adventurous, reckless, incautious. *Ant.* thoughtful, patient, slow, deliberate, careful, cautious, considerate, intentional, purposed, heedful, watchful, circumspect, provident, anxious, wary, prudent, discreet, judicious, serious, meditative, contemplative, calculating, politic, scrupulous, vigilant, observing, foxy, wily, calm, cool, collected.

hate—*Syn.* abhor, abominate, loathe, detest, dislike, despise, execrate, curse, anathematize, denounce. *Ant.* love, regard, like, approve, praise, value, admire, commend, esteem, adore, respect, revere, reverence, worship.

hateful—*Syn.* odious, detestable, repugnant, putrid, revolting, repulsive, disgusting, nauseating, disagreeable, distasteful, shocking, ungenial, uncongenial, repellent, offensive, rotten, sickening, obnoxious, execrable, corrupt. *Ant.* lovable, winsome, amiable, attractive, estimable, agreeable, engaging, enticing, charming, delightful, alluring, fascinating, captivating, magnetic, seductive, pleasing, satisfying, entrancing, bewitching, overpowering, enchanting, pure, chaste, moral, incorrupt.

hatred—*Syn.* enmity, ill-will, rancor, antipathy, abhorrence, aversion, detestation, dislike, hostility, loathing, loathsomeness, spite, malevolence, malignity, malice, umbrage, pique, grudge, resentment, acrimony, execration, abomination, implacability, bitterness, repugnance, animosity. *Ant.* love, kindness, friendship, good-feeling, benevolence, fondness, regard, admiration, devotion, fervor, enthusiasm, adoration, idolatry, worship, infatuation, rapture, enchantment, attractiveness, affection, reverence, sympathy, fellow-feeling, approval, veneration, brotherly love.

haughtiness—*Syn.* arrogance, disdain, pride, presumption, contemptuousness, vanity, conceit, conceitedness, self-love, pretension, affectation, overbearance, egoism, egotism, insolence, bumptiousness, assumption, swagger, cheek (*colloq.*), insolence, nerve (*colloq.*), effrontery, gall (*slang*), ostentation. *Ant.* modesty, servility, bashfulness, timidity, backwardness, unobtrusiveness, diffidence, humility, coyness, meekness, mildness, gentility, docility, submissiveness, gentleness, graciousness, benignity, condescension, obsequiousness, shyness, subserviency, deference, timorousness, sycophancy, flattery, parasitism.

haughty—*Syn.* arrogant, disdainful, supercilious, proud, highminded, high-hat (*slang*), imperious, pompous, hightoned, high-flown, bumptious, toplofty, swollen, puffed up, stuck up (*colloq.*), affected, straitlaced, prim, consequential, stiff. *Ant.* lowly, humble, unassuming, bashful, backward, servile, submissive, timid, afraid, down in the mouth (*slang*), unobtrusive, unpretentious, unpretending, abashed, ashamed, confused, mortified, browbeaten, crushed, dumbfoundered, flabbergasted (*colloq.*), chapfallen, crestfallen.

haywire, *adj.*—*Syn.* disordered, disorganized, confused, chaotic, pied, crazy, wacky, tangled, makeshift. *Ant.* ordered, neat, harmonious, shipshape.

hazard—*Syn.* risk, venture, chance, danger, accident, peril, casualty, fortuity, fortune, jeopardy, luck, fate, adventure, contingency, fluke, probability, possibility, gamble, uncertainty, likelihood, presumption. *Ant.* certainty, surety, assurance, fact, reality, determination, decision, confidence, conviction, proof, trust, faith, reliance, security, truth, actuality, actualization, realization, plan, necessity, protection, safeguard.

hazy—*Syn.* cloudy, foggy, murky, misty, nebulous, filmy, gauzy, vaporous, smoky, nubilous, obfuscated, thick, dim, dull, adiaphanous, fuliginous, obscure, uncertain, wavering. *Ant.* clear, transparent, translucent, bright, diaphanous, luminous, light, vivid, distinct, perspicuous, lucid, brilliant, effulgent, illuminated, radiant, pellucid, shining, obvious, manifest.

head—*Syn.* summit, top, crown, peak, crest, cap, acme, apex, culmination, pinnacle, tip, termination, guide, leader, commander, ruler, chief, boss, foreman, master, overseer, source, beginning, intellect, mind, brain, faculty, reason, understanding, mentality, intelligence, reasoning, instinct, capacity, cognition. *Ant.* base, bottom, foot, foundation, plinth, dado, substructure, substratum, ground, groundwork, basis, level, support, rest, servant, slave, follower, disciple, pupil, attendant, valet, footman, adherent, dependent, imitator, imbecility, weakness of intellect, idiocy, shallowness, silliness, incapacity, stupidity, incompetence.

headlong, *adj.*—*Syn.* precipitate, heedless, thoughtless, imprudent, reckless, foolhardy, hasty, impetuous, rash. *Ant.* cautious, wary, careful, deliberate.

headstrong, *adj.*—*Syn.* ungovernable, self-willed, wayward, unruly, obstinate, willful, stubborn, bull-headed. *Ant.* submissive, docile, tractable, biddable.

heal, *v.*—*Syn.* cure, repair, knit, soothe, restore, remedy, fix, mend, amend.

healthy—*Syn.* sound, salubrious, robust, strong, salutary, wholesome, hale, vigorous, virile, healthful, well, hearty, unimpaired, lusty, invigorating, prophylactic, bracing, nutritious, sanative, sanitary, sanatory, healing, hygeian, hygienic. *Ant.* unhealthy, insalubrious, bad, corrupt, rotten, mephitic, noisome, pestilential, septic, deadly, unsound, noxious, morbific, morbiferous, deleterious, azotic, wasted, weak, worn, emaciated, sick, unsound, ill, fragile, frail, diseased, delicate, fainting, exhausted, sickly, indisposed, infirm, ailing, disordered, distempered, languishing, valetudinarian.

heap, *n.—Syn.* pile, accumulation, mass, quantity, load, collection, aggregation, abundance, profusion, cargo, bulk, volume, fulness, plenty, lump, total, sum, whole. *Ant.* modicum, minimum, atom, molecule, speck, dot, jot, iota, handful, fragment, chip, piece, trifle, morsel, mite, bit.

heap, *v.—Syn.* pile, aggregate, accumulate, amass, collect, gather, build up, increase, hoard, lay up, add, augment, enlarge, swell, expand. *Ant.* lessen, abate, diminish, reduce, decrease, curtail, minimize, lower, dwindle, shrivel, shrink, constrict, contract, compress.

hear, *v.—Syn.* listen, heed, attend, regard, hearken, learn, judge.

heart, *n.—Syn.* core, center, pith, nucleus, kernel, nub, essence, focus, midpoint.

heartbroken, *adj.—Syn.* disconsolate, disheartened, wretched, desolate, despairing, miserable, forlorn, discouraged.

hearty—*Syn.* cordial, warm, zealous, sincere, cheery, cheerful, vivacious, gay, healthy, animated, jovial, jolly, friendly, ardent, genial, fervid, glowing, enthusiastic. *Ant.* insincere, false, dissembling, deceitful, hypocritical, deceptive, pharisaical, sanctimonious, smug, mincing, mealy, unctuous, simpering, affected, self-righteous, make-

believe, simulating, pretending, feigned, spurious, counterfeit, sham, mock, perfidious.

heat—*Syn.* warmth, calidity, fire, flame, blaze, furnace, bonfire, fireworks, incandescence, ardor, passion, excitement, temperature, fever, intensity, fervor, zeal, agitation, emotion, flush, glow, bloom, blush, redness. *Ant.* cold, gelidity, coolness, ice, snow, frost, chilliness, frigidity, cold-heartedness, apathy, unconcern, unfeelingness, disinterestedness, impassiveness, stoicism, lethargy, repression, heedlessness, carelessness.

heathen, *adj.—Syn.* pagan, infidel, godless, unbelieving, unconverted.

heave, *v.—Syn.* raise, elevate, hoist, rise, lift, toss, fling, throw, vomit.

heaven—*Syn.* see ANTONYMS for **Hades** above. *Ant.* see SYNONYMS for **Hades** above.

heavy—*Syn.* weighty, ponderous, burdensome, massive, cumbersome, unwieldy, bulky, large, troublesome, dull, stupid, embarrassing, pressing, vexatious, afflicting, grievous, severe. *Ant.* light, slight, trivial, inconsequential, trifling, inconsiderable, unimportant, shallow, insignificant, little, small, nugatory, paltry, immaterial, petty.

heckle, *v.—Syn.* bait, challenge, badger, pester, harass, hector, taunt, flout, jeer.

hectic, *adj.—Syn.* feverish, restless, nervous, agitated, excited, fretful, flustered. *Ant.* calm, cool, unhurried, serene.

heed—*Syn.* care, attention, devotion, attachment, watch, circumspection, observation, notice, application, consideration, watchfulness, concentration, concern, anxiety, solicitude, caution, precaution, forethought, regard, oversight, vigilance, heedfulness, supervision. *Ant.* heedlessness, carelessness, neglect, negligence, disregard, remissness, default, omission, thoughtlessness, inattention, oversight, absent-mindedness, inconsiderateness, unconcern, inadvertence, insouciance, indifference, apathy, disinterestedness, nonchalance.

heel, *n.*—*Syn.* cad, blackguard, dog, louse, swine, scoundrel, wretch, rascal, scamp.

hegemony, *n.*—*Syn.* ascendancy, leadership, predominance, authority, rule, supremacy.

height, *n.*—*Syn.* elevation, eminence, prominence, altitude, stature, loftiness.

heighten—*Syn.* enhance, emphasize, intensify, strengthen, increase, augment, aggravate, amplify, advance, exaggerate, magnify, vivify, raise, elevate, exalt, acclaim. *Ant.* lower, weaken, lessen, deprecate, depreciate, disapprove, diminish, impair, decrease, reduce, abate, decry, disparage, undervalue, underrate, traduce, detract.

heinous—*Syn.* atrocious, flagitious, flagrant, awful, terrible, infamous, wicked, nefarious, hateful, depraved, profligate, immoral, bad, evil, vile, outrageous, monstrous, grievous, criminal, villainous, shameful, satanic, devilish, infernal, corrupt, vicious, sinful, odious, iniquitous, dissolute, disgraceful, disreputable, loathsome, degrading, unnatural, notorious, glaring, aggravated, abominable, execrable, abhorrent, detestable, foul. *Ant.* virtuous, moral, meritorious, good, righteous, deserving, worthy, creditable, fine, laudable, praiseworthy, excellent, commendable, admirable, exemplary, saintly, ideal, ethical, spiritual, chaste, pure, exalted, perfect, sterling, approved, acceptable, proper, fit, noble, high, glorious, honorable, elevated, dignified, splendid, magnificent, grand, upright, just.

hell—see **Hades.**

help—*Syn.* assist, aid, succor, relieve, support, uphold, sustain, second, encourage, advise, befriend, abet, foster, co-operate,

nurture, nourish, maintain, prop, incite, instigate, countenance, favor, benefit, stand by, intercede for. *Ant.* oppose, hinder, obstruct, impede, check, retard, injure, annoy, bother, clog, arrest, stop, embarrass, combat, withstand, resist, oppugn, contradict, contravene, thwart, frustrate, fetter, hamper, counteract, discourage.

hereditary, *adj.*—*Syn.* inherited, constitutional, congenital, innate, inherent, transmitted.

heretic—*Syn.* schismatic, sectary, sectarian, dissenter, nonconformist, heresiarch, secularist, separatist, deserter, nonjuror, apostate, recusant, renegade, traitor, pervert.

heritage, *n.*—*Syn.* inheritance, legacy, patrimony, birthright.

heroic—*Syn.* fearless, intrepid, valiant, brave, courageous, gallant, daring, bold, undaunted, valorous, chivalrous, spirited, resolute, firm, hardy, dauntless, plucky. *Ant.* cowardly, craven, timid, timorous, fearful, pusillanimous, mean, base, dastardly, cringing, crawling, slinking, effeminate, shy, spiritless, pigeon-hearted, lily-livered.

hesitate—*Syn.* doubt, falter, pause, scruple, stammer, stutter, waver, fluctuate, fear, vacillate, question, ponder, think, defer, delay, wait, demur, shrink, hang fire (*colloq.*), duck (*slang*), dodge, shirk, fight shy of (*slang*). *Ant.* embrace eagerly, act willingly, go ahead, tackle, try, persevere, continue, hold to, cling to, decide, resolve, carry on, stick to.

heterogeneous—*Syn.* unlike, mixed, miscellaneous, variant, nonhomogeneous, mingled, discordant, dissimilar, conglomerate, confused, various, different, promiscuous. *Ant.* alike, homogeneous, like, same, pure, uniform, similar, identical, agreeing conforming, unvarying, unchanging, unchanged.

hew, *v.*—*Syn.* chop, cut, cleave, slash, lop, fell, track, trim, shape.

hide—*Syn.* conceal, secrete, mask, dissemble, protect, disguise, screen, cover, bury, cloak, veil, suppress, overwhelm, inter, entomb, curtain, shield, shade, shelter. *Ant.* expose, lay bare, uncover, exhibit, show, display, offer, present, open, unclose, disclose, reveal, make known, divulge, unveil, impart, discover, admit, advertise, avow, lay open, exhume, unmask, tell, manifest, publish, disinter, promulgate, betray, confess.

hideous—*Syn.* ghastly, grisly, frightful, horrible, terrible, awful, dreadful, revolting, fierce, abominable, abhorrent, disgusting, grim, shocking, terrifying, repulsive, forbidding, repellent, monstrous, Gorgonian, gorgonesque, terrific, loathsome, odious, detestable, cadaverous, corpse-like, putrid, foul, mephitic, pestilential. *Ant.* beautiful, lovely, attractive, handsome, appealing, pleasing, satisfying, nice, exquisite, fine, alluring, charming, fascinating, grand, compelling, captivating, soothing, assuaging, anodynous, comforting, agreeable, softening, delightful, enticing, gratifying, lovable, bewitching, ravishing, graceful, splendid.

high—*Syn.* lofty, tall, elevated, towering, raised, eminent, exalted, noble, haughty, proud, arrogant, boastful, ostentatious, bumptious, conceited, self-assertive, high-hat (*slang*), vain. *Ant.* low, short, stunted, dwarfed, depressed, deep, inferior, weak, mean, contemptible, despicable, groveling, base, degraded, worthless, dishonorable, vile, ignoble, lowminded.

highway, *n.*—*Syn.* road, avenue, route, turnpike, parkway, thoroughfare, street, drive.

hilarious, *adj.*—*Syn.* mirthful, merry, jocund, lighthearted, blithe, gay, gleeful, jolly, joyful. *Ant.* glum, morose, somber, cheerless.

hinder—*Syn.* impede, obstruct, prevent, check, retard, block, thwart, bar, clog, embarrass, oppose, counteract, encumber, inhibit, stop, debar, repress, interrupt, arrest, delay, restrain, curb, baffle, balk, resist, prolong, foil, frustrate, hamper, defer, deter, postpone. *Ant.* help, assist, aid, encourage, facilitate, further, advance, promote, urge, expedite, speed, hurry, despatch, drive, hasten, press on, impel, stimulate, instigate, forward, incite, cheer, hearten, enthuse, inspirit, animate, accelerate, push, hasten.

hint, *n.*—*Syn.* suggestion, intimation, allusion, innuendo, inkling, whisper, insinuation, reference, advice, information, communication, notice, observation. *Ant.* repression, concealment, secrecy, latency, obscurity, mystery, silence.

hint, *v.*—*Syn.* allude, refer, suggest, insinuate, intimate, imply, notify, tell, warn, apprise, inform, acquaint, remind, mention, impart. *Ant.* conceal, cover, veil, mask, refrain, disguise, camouflage, befog, stifle, reserve, withhold, ignore, suppress.

hip, *adj.*—*Syn.* gone, knowledgeable, aware, cool, up-to-date, modern, appreciative, discerning, perceptive. *Ant.* square, corny, unaware, unenlightened.

history—*Syn.* story, recital, chronicle, account, narrative, narration, record, register, annals, archives, muniments, title deeds, memoir, memorial, biography, autobiography, events, facts. *Ant.* legend, romance, myth, novel, invention, imagery, imagination, figment, fabrication, fable, falsehood, allegory, apologue, parable, fiction, mythology, Apocrypha.

hit, *v.*—*Syn.* strike, smite, reach, contact, attain, succeed, knock, rap, beat, batter, slap, punch.

hoard, *n.*—*Syn.* store, accumulation, savings, collection, stock, pile, heap, treasure, supply, lot, set.

hoax, *n.*—*Syn.* trick, deception,

fraud, imposture, delusion, fakery, canard, humbug, spoof.

hobby, *n.—Syn.* avocation, pursuit, recreation, pastime, diversion, enjoyment.

hold—*Syn.* have, retain, keep, own, occupy, maintain, detain, continue, sustain, consider, regard, think, judge, reserve, restrain, confine, contain, persevere, resist, affirm. *Ant.* lose, let go, drop, suspend, adjourn, give up, relinquish, cede, convey, part with, bestow, present, confer, free, renounce, leave, quit, abandon, forsake, desert.

hole, *n.—Syn.* cavity, opening, hollow, void, orifice, aperture, cave, gap, excavation, pit.

holiness—*Syn.* sanctity, piety, sacredness, godliness, devotion, veneration, unction, consecration, sanctification, grace, reverence, humility. *Ant.* ungodliness, wickedness, sin, profanation, blasphemy, hypocrisy, cant, sanctimoniousness, irreverence, profanity, impiety, indifferentism, infidelity, materialism, rationalism, agnosticism, hylotheism, atheism.

hollow—*Syn.* incomplete, concave, empty, vacant, depressed, insincere, unsound, unsubstantial, weak, infirm, flimsy, artificial, transparent, false, faithless, curved, rounded, unfilled. *Ant.* full, solid, convex, raised, material, hard, firm, stable, strong, substantial, dependable, sincere, truthful, earnest, faithful, honest, upright, frank, elevated, upraised, high.

holy—*Syn.* devout, pious, religious, saintly, divine, blessed, consecrated, hallowed, devoted, sacred, set apart, pure, immaculate, unstained, unspotted, righteous, sinless, virtuous, incorrupt, godly, dedicated, devout, reverent, devotional, spiritual, sanctified, seraphic. *Ant.* wicked, sinful, depraved, vicious, evil, vile, contaminated, obscene, immoral, impure, lewd, lascivious, profane, blasphemous, sacrilegious, impious,

fiendish, infernal, satanic, reprobate, abandoned, graceless, iniquitous, unholy, nefarious, godless, irreverent, unsanctified, unregenerate, abominable, polluted, cursèd, diabolical.

home—*Syn.* house, abode, residence, dwelling, domicile, apartment, habitation, ingle, ingleside, fireside, roof, rooftree, hearth, hearthstone, haven, rest, grave, birthplace, country, native land, habitat, heaven.

homely—*Syn.* plain, rough, rude, ugly, uncouth, awkward, coarse, ungainly, unadorned, common, ordinary, thick, vulgar, blunt. *Ant.* beautiful, handsome, refined, polished, suave, polite, nice, attractive, stately, dignified, graceful, agreeable, inviting, charming, captivating.

homogeneous, *adj.—Syn.* uniform, alike, consonant, same, similar, identical. *Ant.* heterogeneous, miscellaneous, mixed, variegated.

honest—*Syn.* frank, open, truthful, sincere, upright, straightforward, candid, reliable, true, trustworthy, honorable, trusty, just, equitable, fair, ingenuous, genuine, faithful, good, aboveboard, incorrupt, scrupulous, reputable, creditable, estimable. *Ant.* dishonest, dishonorable, unjust, unfair, crooked, tricky, deceptive, deceitful, fraudulent, faithless, ignoble, knavish, unfaithful, perfidious, misleading, artful, shifty, delusive, elusive, illusive, false, traitorous, untrustworthy, lying, hypocritical, treacherous, disingenuous, mendacious.

honesty—*Syn.* integrity, probity, honor, uprightness, rectitude, self-respect, straightforwardness, trustiness, trustworthiness, confidence, faithfulness, responsibility, fairness, justice, just-dealing, frankness, openness, sincerity. *Ant.* dishonesty, double-dealing, double-crossing, cheating, trickery, false pretense, chicanery, quibble, stratagem, flimflam, cajolery, fraud, deceit, artifice, deception, imposition, swindle, swindling, stealing, thieving, theft, larceny, chiseling (*slang*).

honor—*Syn.* respect, reverence, esteem, admiration, dignity, reputation, renown, adulation, laudation, praise, commendation, recommendation, regard, trust, confidence, faith, reliance, glory, glorification, worship, adoration. *Ant.* dishonor, disgrace, degradation, derision, contumely, opprobrium, shame, ignominy, reproach, blemish, censure, disrespect, abasement, debasement, contempt, denunciation, infamy, humiliation, baseness, meanness, corruption, venality, prostitution.

hoot, *v.*—*Syn.* jeer, boo, hiss, denounce, gibe, scoff, fleer, twit, razz.

hope—*Syn.* confidence, expectation, trust, desire, anticipation, prospect, aspiration, optimism, presumption, reliance, assumption. *Ant.* hopelessness, despair, despondency, dejection, pessimism, abandonment, discouragement, disappointment, fear.

hopeless—*Syn.* despairing, desperate, reckless, rash, irretrievable, lost, abandoned, gone, inconsolable, brokenhearted, dejected, condemned, undone, ruined, remediless, irreparable, irremediable, irrecoverable, irredeemable, impracticable, irrevocable, immitigable, incurable. *Ant.* hopeful, encouraging, cheering, reassuring, confident, sanguine, elated, dauntless, enthusiastic, propitious, promising, probable, bright, sunny, roseate, glowing, plucky, daring, expectant, courageous, animating, emboldening, stimulating, inciting.

horizontal—*Syn.* level, flat, even, plane, plain, parallel, straight, linear. *Ant.* rough, rugged, uneven, irregular, broken, hilly, lumpy, slanting, sloping, rolling, inclined.

horrible, *adj.*—*Syn.* hateful, repulsive, loathsome, abominable,

dreadful, horrid, detestable, appalling, awful, fearful, terrible, frightful, alarming. *Ant.* pleasing, attractive, lovable, alluring.

horror, *n.*—*Syn.* dismay, consternation, dread, loathing, disgust, awe, aversion, alarm, terror, antipathy, fear, fright. *Ant.* delight, pleasure, fascination.

horse, *n.*—*Syn.* steed, mount, nag, dobbin, hackney, hayburner, pony, gee-gee.

hospitable, *adj.*—*Syn.* receptive, companionable, gregarious, friendly, convivial, sociable, neighborly, cordial, kind. *Ant.* inhospitable, solitary, reserved, unsociable.

host, *n.*—*Syn.* landlord, publican, boniface, innkeeper, tavernkeeper. *Ant.* guest, visitor, patron.

hostile, *adj.*—*Syn.* unfriendly, contrary, antipathetic, adverse, inimical, antagonistic, rancorous, belligerent, malevolent. *Ant.* friendly, devoted, loyal, amicable.

hot—*Syn.* ardent, burning, fiery, flaming, calescent, incalescent, incandescent, blazing, glowing, heated, passionate, excited, eager. *Ant.* cold, frigid, freezing, chilling, chilly, gelid, algid, bleak, raw, biting, stiff, distant, rigid, affected, insensitive, calm, cool, apathetic.

hotheaded, *adj.*—*Syn.* impetuous, headstrong, unruly, hasty, precipitate, fire-eating, peppery. *Ant.* deliberate, cool, steady, equable.

hound, *v.*—*Syn.* pursue, harass, persecute, hector, afflict, chase, dog, harry, track, hunt.

however—*Syn.* nevertheless, notwithstanding, yet, still, though, although, but, in spite of, as if.

hug, *v.*—*Syn.* embrace, press, hold, cling, cuddle, clasp, cherish.

huge, *adj.*—*Syn.* immense, great, giant, bulky, vast, colossal, enormous, tremendous, monstrous, gigantic. *Ant.* tiny, wee, Lilliputian, miniature.

humane—*Syn.* kind, benevolent,

sympathetic, merciful, pitying, compassionate, kind-hearted, human, tender-hearted, forgiving, gracious, charitable, benignant, gentle, clement, benign, indulgent, lenient. *Ant.* barbarous, atrocious, uncivilized, savage, pitiless, inhuman, cruel, brutal, merciless, barbaric, barbarian, rude, uncouth, untamed, ferocious, brutish, wild, fierce, murderous, unmerciful.

humble, *adj.*—*Syn.* lowly, meek, mild, docile, unassuming, submissive, unpretentious, unpretending, simple, backward, bashful, modest, retiring, unselfish, restrained, unobtrusive, diffident, reserved, shy, coy, timid, shrinking, hesitating, yielding, unostentatious, forbearing, enduring, plain. *Ant.* proud, haughty, arrogant, ostentatious, boastful, masterful, tyrannical, overbearing, domineering, sneering, sarcastic, ironical, censorious, presumptuous, pretentious, conceited, vain, insolent, imperious, assuming, blustering, boisterous, self-assertive, arbitary, dogmatic.

humble, *adj.*—*Syn.* lowly, meek, ten, abase, lower, depress, cast down, degrade, mortify, shame, debase, disgrace, reduce, depose, dishonor. *Ant.* raise, elevate, exalt, praise, extol, laud, applaud, commend, recommend, glorify, heighten, promote, eulogize, approve, admire, encourage, sanction, support, abet.

humdrum, *adj.*—*Syn.* tedious, dull, monotonous, routine, prosaic, boring, wearisome, tiresome, commonplace, everyday. *Ant.* lively, exciting, stimulating, gay.

humor, *n.*—*Syn.* wit, pleasantry, mood, disposition, temper, caprice, fancy, badinage, banter, chaff, jesting, raillery, drollery, jocosity, jocularity, waggery, whimsicality, comicality, shenanigans (*slang*), jest, joke, quip, *Ant.* dullness, heaviness, moroseness, flatness, stupidity, slowness, taciturnity, obtuseness, dejection, depression, sad-

ness, gloom, sullenness, spleen, melancholy, the blues, the dumps.

humor, *v.*—*Syn.* indulge, pamper, coddle, satiate, pet, please, appease, placate, gratify, spoil, fondle, caress, satisfy. *Ant.* provoke, taunt, irritate, annoy, pique, fret, tease, roil, twit, chafe, nettle, gall, sting, exasperate, enrage, rile, insult, affront.

hunch, *n.*—*Syn.* premonition, presentiment, feeling, impression, omen.

hungry, *adj.*—*Syn.* avid, voracious, thirsting, greedy, covetous, ravening, famished. *Ant.* replete, sated, satiated, surfeited.

hunt, *n.*—*Syn.* pursuit, search, chase, quest, investigation, probe, seeking, inquiry.

hunt, *v.*—*Syn.* seek, chase, follow, pursue, search, investigate, inquire, expel, banish, dismiss.

hurry, *v.*—*Syn.* hasten, rush, scurry, move, press, force, accelerate, speed, impel, drive, quicken. *Ant.* delay, dawdle, dally, procrastinate.

hurt, *n.*—*Syn.* wound, injury, damage, harm, bruise, rupture, cut, laceration, blow, stroke, detriment, wrong, impairment, bane, disadvantage, drawback, annoyance, mishap, accident, misfortune, infliction, grief, grievance, suffering, irritation, pain, painfulness, dolor, discomfort. *Ant.* pleasure, delight, joy, comfort, ease, relief, content, contentment, enjoyment, solace, refreshment, consolation, balm.

hurt, *v.*—*Syn.* wound, injure, damage, harm, bruise, cut, tear, pain, impair, deteriorate, spoil, abuse, tarnish, mar, maltreat, ill-treat, molest, victimize, maul, smite, outrage. *Ant.* heal, cure, benefit, restore, remedy, make well, serve, reward, assist, succor, aid, comfort, console, assuage, abate, alleviate, soothe.

hurtful—*Syn.* harmful, injurious, bad, noxious, pernicious, destructive, baneful, damaging, detrimental, unwholesome, deleterious, mischievous, disadvantageous, distressing, poisonous, unhealthy, weakening, enervating, noisome. *Ant.* beneficial, advantageous, good, healthy, health-giving, bracing, stimulating, energizing, wholesome, healthful, salutary, salubrious, nutritious, healing, useful, helpful, vitalizing, invigorating, strengthening.

husbandry—*Syn.* agriculture, tillage, culture, cultivation, land management, crop production, farming, farm management, floriculture, gardening, arboriculture, horticulture, kitchen-gardening, market-gardening, field management, field-culture, agronomy, cattle-raising, stock-feeding, frugality, thrift, good management, domestic economy. *Ant.* waste, destruction, bad management, prodigality, mismanagement, loss, squandering, misuse, decrement.

hustle—*Syn.* hurry, rush, run, act quickly, move quickly, push on, drive on, display eagerness, haste, hasten, expedite, accelerate, go ahead, bustle, stir quickly, advance rapidly, get a move on (*slang*), work eagerly. *Ant.* slow up, take it easy (*slang*), dawdle, trifle, waste time, hold your horses (*slang*), procrastinate, laze (*colloq.*), loaf, idle, lounge about, bum around (*colloq.*), sponge, dissipate, loll, toddle.

hygiene, *n.*—*Syn.* sanitation, cleanliness, salubrity, health, prophylaxis.

hypocrisy—*Syn.* deceit, deception, pharisaism, sanctimony, sanctimoniousness, false pretension, dissimulation, pretense, counterfeit, imitation, simulation, formalism, pietism, affectation, cant. *Ant.* honesty, truth, openness, candor, sincerity, truthfulness, frankness, ingenuousness, genuineness, transparency, plainness, clearness, impartiality, fairness, righteousness, uprightness, earnestness, artlessness, integrity, rectitude, probity.

hypocrite—*Syn.* impostor, dissembler, pretender, deceiver, cheat, swindler, knave, rascal, crook, humbug, adventurer, four-flusher (*slang*), rogue, charlatan, quack, empiric, mountebank, fraud, malingerer, crimp, stool-pigeon, decoy-duck, informer, traitor, faker, spieler, confidence man, bunko steerer (*slang*), capper (*slang*), ringer (*slang*), trickster. *Ant.* the antonymns of this term occur in substantive phrases in which personal nouns are preceded by such qualifying adjectives as *honest, true, sincere, just, reliable, reputable, fair, square, white, upright,* or the like, as *upright* judge, *honest* official, *white* man (*colloq.*), etc.

hypocritical—*Syn.* dishonest, deceptive, deluding, deceiving, measly, Pharisaical, double-dealing, pretending, assuming, pretentious, false, sanctimonious, unctuous, dissimulating, dissembling, feigning, shuffling, two-faced (*colloq.*). *Ant.* honest, truthful, reliable, reputable, just, fair, righteous, upright, square, on the level (*slang*), trustworthy, faithful, steadfast, dependable, ingenuous, frank, open, sincere, straightforward, unimpeachable, candid, earnest, artless.

hypothesis—*Syn.* theory, supposition, scheme, system, conjecture, assumption, presumption, condition, suggestion, thesis, proposal. *Ant.* evidence, fact, proof, certainty, conviction, demonstration, discovery, confirmation, manifestation, assurance, affirmation, result, settlement, ratification, consequence, inference.

hypothetic—*Syn.* supposed, suppositious, imagined, imaginary, postulated, conditional, conjectural, assumed, vague, indeterminate, problematical, equivocal, speculative, indefinite, contingent. *Ant.* proved, proven, demonstrated, confirmed, affirmed, approved, real, true, factual, literal, exact, genuine, actual, authentic, indisputable, certain, reliable, credible, veritable, undoubted, unquestionable.

I

icon, *n.—Syn.* image, effigy, statue, representation, portrait.

icy, *adj.—Syn.* cold, frigid, chilling, chilled, frosty, forbidding, distant, cool, unemotional. *Ant.* fiery, torrid, hot, passionate.

idea—*Syn.* all *synonyms* of this term relate to the mind or its functioning, as image, impression, concept, conception, imagination, thought, conceit, notion, fancy, fantasy, supposition, ideal, abstraction, mental picture or representation, etc. For instance, when one thinks of an object, the mind sees, as it were, a representation of the object—this is a *conception*, which should not be identified with *perception*, as the latter is a visual representation of an object, as seen by the eyes. *Ant.* all *antonyms* of this term relate to matter or its attributes, as actuality, reality, fact, body, corporeality, substance, matter, material, stuff, element, compound, thing, object, anything, something, substantiality, solidity, density, denseness, firmness, weight, etc.

ideal—*Syn.* imaginary, fancied, visionary, fanciful, unreal, mental, intellectual, subjective, metaphysical, psychical, spiritual, psychological, excellent, exemplary, consummate, fitting, perfect, supreme. *Ant.* actual, real, material, common, commonplace, ordinary, imperfect, disappointing, undesirable, vulgar, mean.

identical, *adj.—Syn.* same, equal, indistinguishable, coincident, uniform, equivalent, synonymous. *Ant.* different, distinct, diverse, separate.

idiocy—*Syn.* imbecility, insanity, folly, foolishness, madness, senselessness, incapacity, fatuity, stupidity, feebleness of mind, paranoia, dementia, mania, lunacy, derangement, alienation, delirium, frenzy, monomania. *Ant.* sense, acuteness, sharpness, wisdom, intelligence, sagacity, brilliancy, capacity, soundness, astuteness, perception, understanding, acumen, penetration, judgment, shrewdness, discernment, sapience, prudence, knowledge, common sense.

idiomatic, *adj.—Syn.* colloquial, dialectal, vernacular, peculiar, special, proper.

idle—*Syn.* unemployed, inactive, workless, unused, unoccupied, waste, barren, fallow, untilled, uncultivated, lazy, shiftless, slothful, trifling, sluggish, indolent, listless, ineffectual, inert, futile, frivolous, vain, useless, unprofitable, unimportant. *Ant.* busy, industrious, hustling, bustling, diligent, employed, working, active, occupied, settled, productive, cultivated, fruitful, assiduous, sedulous, laborious, unremitting, untiring, indefatigable.

ignoble—*Syn.* mean, base, debased, dishonorable, despicable, contemptible, degraded, reproachful, scandalous, cowardly, shameful, worthless, disgraceful, abject, immodest, degenerate, depraved, scurrile, scurrilous, indecent, ribald, coarse, vulgar. *Ant.* noble, high, highminded, highsouled, stately, dignified, majestic, magnanimous, august, generous, grand, exalted, modest, honorable, decent, ennobled, decorous, respectable, admirable, estimable, reputable, venerable, worthy, gracious, kind, charitable, refined.

ignominious — *Syn.* shameful, scandalous, disgraceful, infamous, heinous, execrable, wicked, offensive, opprobrious, vile, abusive, hateful, despicable, low, mean, base, cowardly, flagrant, flagitious, atrocious, nefarious, abhorrent, abominable, disgusting, detestable, revolting, dishonorable, humiliating, disreputable, inglorious, debasing, ribald, shocking, outrageous, notorious, cowardly. *Ant*. reputable, stately, dignified, gracious, creditable, glorious, worthy, praiseworthy, noble, fine, illustrious, commendable, laudable, laudatory, commendatory, encomiastic, eulogistic, popular, estimable, distinguished, meritorious, good, splendid, exemplary, excellent, honorable, admirable, respectable, pleasing, gratifying, virtuous, high, exalted, lofty, grand, magnificent.

ignominy—*Syn*. shame, disgrace, scandal, obloquy, infamy, reproach, contumely, contempt, contemptuousness, opprobrium, dishonor, scurrility, abasement, degradation, blemish, depravity, humiliation, censure, disrespect, debasement, baseness, degeneracy, lowness, meanness, sordidness, odium, defamation, dislike, hatred, detestation. *Ant*. honor, respect, fame, glory, renown, reputation, grandeur, splendor, nobility, dignity, respectability, stateliness, credit, praise, exaltation, admiration, glorification, regard, esteem, reverence, celebrity, distinction, eminence, loftiness, praise, laudation, approval, commendation, eulogy, applause, appreciation, estimation, character, repute, superiority.

ignorance—*Syn*. illiteracy, nescience, darkness, sciolism, bewilderment, dullness, stupidity, denseness, benightedness, unenlightenment, incapacity, thickness, stolidity, dumbness, shallowness. *Ant*. knowledge, enlightenment, cognition, cognoscence, learning, education, scholarship, erudition, information, lore, culture, attainment, accomplishments, menticulture, proficiency, understanding, acquirements, omniscience, pantology.

ignorant—*Syn*. uneducated, stupid, dense, obtuse, uncultured, uncultivated, untaught, unlearned, uninstructed, unlettered, illiterate, shallow, superficial, unenlightened, empty-headed, thick (*colloq*.), thick-headed (*colloq*.), thick-skulled (*colloq*.), benighted, low-brow (*slang*), nescient, gross, coarse, vulgar. *Ant*. enlightened, learned, scholarly, cultured, cultivated, educated, trained, instructed, informed, well-informed, skilled, wise, sage, literate, lettered, erudite, efficient, competent, able, well-read, accomplished, talented.

ilk, *n.*—*Syn*. kind, character, type, nature, sort, breed, genus, class.

ill, *adj.*—*Syn*. sick, unwell, poorly, complaining, indisposed, disordered, distempered, ailing, impaired, weak, feeble, morbid, diseased, valetudinarian, bad, evil, wicked, iniquitous, disgusting, nauseating. *Ant*. well, fine, bright, cheery, merry, healthy, robust, strong, powerful, muscular, sound, whole, wholesome, hale, hearty, vigorous, lusty, lively, sprightly, forcible, good, pleasing, comforting, consoling.

ill, *n.*—*Syn*. evil, wickedness, misfortune, harm, mischief, danger, accident, mishap, calamity, pain, trouble, misery, sorrow, disease, distress, grievance, vexation. *Ant*. good, luck, fortune, privilege, welfare, advantage, prosperity, happiness, benefit, boon, emolument, gain, weal, blessing, profit, attainment, achievement, favor, benediction.

illegal—*Syn*. unlawful, illicit, contraband, prohibited, banned, proscribed, outlawed, interdicted, proclaimed, illegitimate, irregular. *Ant*. legal, permitted, permissible, sanctioned, confirmed, allowed, lawful, conformable, judicial, right, authorized, approved, countenanced.

illiterate, *adj.*—*Syn.* unlettered, ignorant, unlearned, uneducated, nescient. *Ant.* taught, lettered, literate, schooled.

illuminate, *v.*—*Syn.* enlighten, brighten, elucidate, illustrate, clarify. *Ant.* darken, obscure, complicate, obfuscate.

illusion—*Syn.* fantasy, phantasm, phantom, image, imagination, dream, vision, fancy, apparition, specter, spirit, ghost, manes, shade, ghoul, spook, sprite, fairy, poltergeist, revenant. *Ant.* reality, fact, actuality, occurrence, happening, certainty, incident, circumstance, event, episode, materiality, materialization, corporeality, corporeity.

illustration, *n.*—*Syn.* example, comparison, case, instance, specimen.

illustrious—*Syn.* celebrated, noble, eminent, exalted, famous, renowned, glorious, brilliant, distinguished, conspicuous, acclaimed, applauded, great, superior, superlative. *Ant.* lowly, mean, obscure, humble, poor, unpretentious, unassuming, meek, abject, debased, degraded, menial, ignoble, groveling, spiritless, depraved, despicable, degenerate.

image—*Syn.* representation, similitude, appearance, form, show, conception, likeness, effigy, figure, picture, portrait, photograph, copy, imitation, resemblance, semblance, drawing, duplication, counterpart, facsimile, model, pattern, depictment, reproduction, illustration.

imaginary—*Syn.* ideal, fanciful, illusory, unreal, non-existent, fancied, visionary, shadowy, suppositious, hypothetical, assumed, conceived, pictured, false, deceptive, fantastic, chimerical, whimsical, phantasmal, dreamy. *Ant.* real, true, factual, genuine, substantial, physical, corporeal, material, existing, known, proven, visible, tangible, sensible, natural, cosmical, regular, normal, palpable, evident, definite, percep-

tible, apprehensible, comprehensible, regular, determined.

imagination—*Syn.* fancy, conception, thought, fantasy, mental image, idea, notion, impression, concept, conceit, reflection, supposition, contemplation. *Ant.* reality, actuality, existence, substance, substantiality, materiality, being, entity.

imagine—*Syn.* conceive, fancy, apprehend, think, presume, suppose, guess, prognosticate, prophesy, foretell, infer, conclude, picture, visualize, believe, conjure up, vision, envision. *Ant.* be inert, be passive, be lethargic, be dormant, sleep, doze, drowse, be torpid, be unconscious.

imbecile—*Syn.* weak-minded, deranged, feeble-minded, silly, senile, moronic, doting, simple, puerile, childish, fatuous, idiotic, foolish, driveling, demented. *Ant.* strong-minded, sane, wise, sapient, sagacious, acute, sharp, subtle, longheaded, cunning, witty, discerning, discriminating, rational, sound, intellectual, intelligent.

imbecility—*Syn.* feeble-mindedness, foolishness, idiocy, brainlessness, hebetude, dulness or dullness, stupidity, idiotism, incapacity, incompetency, dotage, simplicity, fatuousness, irrationality, fatuity, dementia, senility, ineptitude. *Ant.* wisdom, sageness, sagacity, intelligence, capacity, comprehension, understanding, gumption, longheadedness, subtlety, sapience, judgment, profundity, acuteness, perspicacity, discernment, discrimination.

imbue, *v.*—*Syn.* pervade, color, suffuse, animate, saturate, inspire.

imitate—*Syn.* copy, mimic, ape, mock, counterfeit, duplicate, reduplicate, reproduce, paraphrase, parody, transcribe, quote, simulate, personate, travesty, caricature, burlesque, repeat, match, parallel, represent, take pattern by. *Ant.* differ from, vary, alter, change, modify, mismatch, diverge, disagree, conflict, oppose, dispute, bicker, clash, wrangle, deviate from, reverse.

immaculate—*Syn.* unstained, untainted, unsullied, spotless, pure, virgin, undefiled, clean, untarnished, innocent, incorrupt, stainless. *Ant.* defiled, unclean, tarnished, spotted, dirty, filthy, impure, corrupt, tainted, vile, soiled, sullied, stained, foul, blackened, defamed, infamous.

immature, *adj.*—*Syn.* unripe, green, undeveloped, callow, raw, precocious, imperfect. *Ant.* mature, ripe, mellow, adult.

immediately—*Syn.* instantly, forthwith, directly, presently, straightaway, right away, right off, at once, instanter, now, this instant, without delay. *Ant.* by and by, after a while, some time, in the future, tomorrow, next week, when convenient, shortly, not at all.

immense—*Syn.* colossal, huge, great, large, bulky, vast, enormous, titanic, mighty, gigantic, monstrous, Cyclopean, Brobdingnagian, Gargantuan, stupendous. *Ant.* small, little, wee [*Sc.*], insignificant, petty, trifling, pigmy, dwarfish, elfin, puny, runty (*slang*), diminutive, trivial, light, minute, tiny, Lilliputian, paltry, stinted, microscopic.

immerse—*Syn.* immerge, submerge, sink, dip, douse, plunge, bury, duck, overwhelm, involve, engage deeply, put under, drown, cover with water. *Ant.* raise up, take up, rescue, uncover, release, recover, regain, restore, retrieve.

imminent—*Syn.* impending, threatening, menacing, hanging over, overhanging, about to happen, approaching, near, destined, coming, in store, at hand, brewing. *Ant.* distant, afar, receding, retrograding, retiring, retreating, withdrawing, regressing, departing, unsettled, un-

steady, fluctuating, wavering, changing, unlikely, doubtful, unexpected, improbable, problematical.

immodest, *adj.*—*Syn.* indelicate, bold, indecent, shameless, coarse, brazen, obscene, unreserved, unconstrained. *Ant.* decorous, shamefaced, reserved, bashful.

immoral, *adj.*—*Syn.* unprincipled, loose, corrupt, evil, wrong, indecent, profligate, depraved, licentious, vicious, dissolute, abandoned, lecherous. *Ant.* chaste, pure, highminded, noble, virtuous.

immortal, *adj.*—*Syn.* undying, eternal, permanent, deathless, perpetual, everlasting, sempiternal, abiding, imperishable. *Ant.* mortal, transitory, fleeting, ephemeral.

immovable, *adj.*—*Syn.* steadfast, fixed, rooted, stable, immobile, constant, firm, obdurate. *Ant.* movable, yielding, plastic, inconstant.

immunity—*Syn.* exemption, privilege, prerogative, release, exoneration, discharge, exculpation, acquittal, clearance, respite, compurgation, reprieve. *Ant.* condemnation, conviction, proscription, sequestration, attainder, disapprobation, blame, censure, interdiction, debarment, exclusion, preclusion.

impact, *n.*—*Syn.* collision, shock, percussion, concussion, brunt, clash, contact, slam.

impair—*Syn.* injure, diminish, decrease, deteriorate, weaken, taint, infect, contaminate, corrupt, defile, degrade, vitiate, pollute, prostitute, demoralize, debauch, adulterate, damage, harm, hurt, blemish, deface, despoil, ravage, disfigure, cripple, blight, corrode, mar. *Ant.* improve, better, restore, renew, revive, revivify, redress, heal, mend, repair, cure, rally, renovate, rectify, redeem, reclaim, remedy, reanimate, resuscitate, refresh, reëstablish, regenerate, rejuvenate.

impalpable, *adj.*—*Syn.* intangible, vague, imperceptible, shadowy, tenuous, attenuated, refined, rarefied. *Ant.* material, tangible, solid, definite.

impart—*Syn.* reveal, divulge, disclose, discover, bestow, afford, inform, tell, enlighten, notify, signify, specify, mention, communicate, intimate, acquaint, advise, instruct. *Ant.* conceal, secrete, hide, deny, mystify, puzzle, keep, hold, seal, screen, suppress, stifle, veil, curtain, mask, camouflage, shroud, befog, reserve, withhold, cloak, cover.

impartial—*Syn.* fair, just, equitable, unbiased, right, square, fair and square, justifiable, good, equal, equable, even-handed, reasonable, unprejudiced, disinterested, indifferent. *Ant.* partial, biased, prejudiced, unjust, unfair, onesided, unequal, unreasonable, wrong, inequable, unwarrantable, unfit, unjustified, improper, illegal, unmoral.

impassioned—*Syn.* glowing, burning, fiery, vehement, intense, ardent, warm, fervid, thrilling, stirring, soul-stirring, heart-stirring, exciting, raging, fuming, flaming, raving, ranting, frantic, wild, hysterical, furious, violent. *Ant.* cool, collected, calm, undisturbed, placid, composed, quiet, patient, reserved, modest, retiring, bashful, backward, staid, steady, level-headed, coolheaded, restrained, stoical, solemn, serious, grave, tranquil, forbearing, longanimous, dull, phlegmatic, cloying.

impassive, *adj.*—*Syn.* phlegmatic, insensitive, imperturbable, apathetic, reserved, calm, unimpassioned, stolid. *Ant.* responsive, tender, sympathetic, compassionate.

impatient—*Syn.* eager, restless, fretful, fidgety, fussy, excitable, irascible, mercurial, chafing, unquiet, hasty, hurried, feverish, clamorous, turbulent, highstrung, nervous, agitated. *Ant.* patient, calm, cool, self-pos-

sessed, self-controlled, coldblooded, cool-headed, easy-going, peaceful, tranquil, serene, collected, forbearing, content, resigned, chastened, meek, tolerant, unperturbed.

impeach—*Syn.* accuse, charge, arraign, censure, blame, impugn, denounce, indict, discredit, reprehend, chide, admonish, berate, brand, reprimand, bring to book, call to account. *Ant.* defend, protect, approve, support, uphold, vindicate, commend, praise, favor, admire, benefit, assist, indorse, acclaim, eulogize, laud, honor, appreciate, sanction.

impeccable, *adj.*—*Syn.* spotless, immaculate, perfect, precise, faultless, accurate, irreproachable. *Ant.* defective, flawed, imperfect, blameworthy.

impede—*Syn.* hinder, retard, obstruct, prevent, offset, counteract, check, delay, embarrass, fetter, hamper, entangle, shackle, derange, clog, thwart, cross, contravene, oppose, arrest, stop, block, bar, encumber, weaken, oppose, neutralize, resist, restrain, repress. *Ant.* help, assist, facilitate, abet, support, encourage, stimulate, instigate, back, forward, advance, second, endorse, coöperate, serve, subserve, favor, aid, succor, sustain, further, expedite, uphold.

impediment—*Syn.* obstruction, hindrance, obstacle, barrier, bar, clog, encumbrance, difficulty, check, retardment, oppilation, stoppage, infarction, restriction, stricture, restraint, embarrassment, block, blockage, barricade, prohibition, inhibition, blockade. *Ant.* aid, assistance, help, support, benefit, succor, relief, advantage, sustenance, maintenance, coöperation, coadjuvancy, concurrence, conformity, consent, encouragement, indorsement, recommendation, commend, commendation.

impel—*Syn.* instigate, incite, induce, animate, actuate, drive, force, push, move, urge, press, boom, thrust, prod, start, set going. *Ant.* recoil, react, revulse, rebound, ricochet, reverberate, balk, jib, rebuff, repulse, repercuss, recalcitrate.

impending—see **imminent** above.

impenetrable, *adj.*— *Syn.* impervious, unfathomable, adamant, dense, stolid, dull, impassive, obtuse, esoteric. *Ant.* comprehensible, transparent, indulgent, soft.

imperative—*Syn.* commanding, despotic, urgent, authoritative, irresistible, dictatorial, compulsory, obligatory, mandatory, dominant, inexorable, peremptory, absolute, preponderant, paramount, decretive, decretory, jussive, necessary, requisite, essential, indispensable, exigent, pressing. *Ant.* voluntary, optional, discretional, free, discretionary, unconstrained, spontaneous, original, willing, intentional, deliberate, purposed, unrestrained, premeditated, designed, contemplated.

imperfection—*Syn.* fault, blemish, stain, defect, failing, drawback, weakness, vice, deficiency, frailty, incompleteness, immaturity, infirmity, transgression, depravity, sin, sinfulness, wrong, viciousness. *Ant.* advantage, perfection, completeness, goodness, improvement, blessing, favor, popularity, esteem, admiration, loyalty, confidence, respect.

imperil—*Syn.* endanger, hazard, jeopardize, peril, expose, risk, chance, venture. *Ant.* safeguard, protect, care for, guard, watch, preserve, defend, shield, secure.

imperious—*Syn.* authoritative, dictatorial, stern, commanding, overbearing, tyrannical, lordly, domineering, imperative, insolent, arrogant, presumptuous, self-assertive, swaggering, bullying, saucy, nervy, toplofty, bumptious. *Ant.* obsequious, subservient, cringing, fawning, crouching, sycophantic, truckling, toadying, servile, grov-

eling, mealymouthed, mean, sneaking, base, abased, pliant, soapy, oily, dough-faced (*colloq.*), parasitical, abject, slavish, beggarly.

impertinent—*Syn.* saucy, impudent, insolent, rude, officious, meddling, intrusive, contumelious, irrelevant, forward, bold, brazen, underbred, insulting, audacious, abusive, contemptuous, gross, coarse, vulgar. *Ant.* polite, suave, flattering, appeasing, mollifying, meek, humble, gentle, refined, courteous, civil, obliging, condescending, conciliating, respectful, polished, affable, urbane, submissive, mild, bland, pleasant, complaisant, pleasing, well-mannered.

imperturbable, *adj.*—*Syn.* unruffled, calm, serene, placid, cool, nonchalant, sedate, composed. *Ant.* touchy, irritable, irascible.

impervious, *adj.*—*Syn.* impenetrable, impermeable, obdurate, resistant, frustrating. *Ant.* open, susceptible, sensitive, exposed.

impetuous—*Syn.* furious, boisterous, vehement, violent, headlong, headstrong, rash, rushing, hasty, precipitate, impulsive, fiery, passionate, fierce, ungovernable, obstinate, intractable, heady, unruly, fervid, ardent, burning. *Ant.* calm, steady, slow, thoughtful, careful, considerate, meek, mild, patient, hesitant, diffident, doubtful, peaceful, placid, quiet, tranquil, composed, bashful, modest, backward, retiring, unobtrusive.

impetus, *n.*—*Syn.* force, momentum, stimulus, impulse, motive.

impinge, *v.*—*Syn.* touch, strike, hit, smite, infringe.

impious—*Syn.* profane, sinful, blasphemous, irreligious, godless, wicked, pharisaical, sacrilegious, irreverent, desecrating, canting, sanctimonious, unsanctified, reprobate, unregenerate, hypocritical, unholy, Satanic, devil-ridden, fiendish. *Ant.* inspired, consecrated, pious, devout, prayerful, holy, spiritual, pietistic, religious, saintly, saintlike, seraphic, cherubic, pure, righteous, sanctified, regenerated, redeemed.

implacable, *adj.—Syn.* unrelenting, pitiless, inexorable, vindictive, grim, ruthless, inflexible, obdurate, uncompromising. *Ant.* lenient, tolerant, merciful.

implement, *v.—Syn.* effect, perform, execute, effectuate, achieve, realize, expedite.

implicate—*Syn.* involve, accuse, incriminate, charge, tax, impute, criminate, entangle, embarrass, compromise, stigmatize, impeach, indict, arraign, blame, attack, inculpate, imply, denounce, cite, challenge. *Ant.* defend, assist, help, free, absolve, pardon, palliate, condone, support, plead for, speak for, stand up for, excuse, minimize, indorse, sanction, approve, ratify, countenance, authorize.

implicit, *adj.—Syn.* implied, tacit, inferred, presupposed, understood. *Ant.* explicit, expressed, specific, stated.

imply, *v.—Syn.* connote, mean, suggest, signify, involve, hint, infer, include, comprise. *Ant.* express, state, describe.

important—*Syn.* significant, influential, weighty, grave, material, considerable, relevant, dignified, momentous, essential, serious, substantial, great, prominent, decisive, critical, determining, determinative, powerful, earnest, imposing, urgent, pressing, chief, paramount, primary, foremost, principal. *Ant.* slight, trivial, trifling, light, paltry, petty, unimportant, subordinate, frivolous, nonessential, commonplace, inconsiderable, puerile, shallow, weak, mean, contemptible, pitiful, shabby, farcical, cheap, worthless, inconsiderable, powerless, meagre, poor, beggarly, insignificant, nugatory, inane, piddling, trashy, wishywashy, namby-pamby.

importunate, *adj.—Syn.* pressing, urgent, demanding, persistent, pertinacious.

imposing—*Syn.* impressive, striking, majestic, grand, noble, august, sublime, lofty, towering, supreme, superlative, commanding, solemn, paramount, surpassing, overruling, leading, capital, chief, principal, foremost, dignified, stately, illustrious, eminent, high, mighty, splendid, awe-inspiring. *Ant.* mean, small, meagre, poor, wretched, ridiculous, unimportant, petty, paltry, insignificant, absurd, subordinate, ordinary, commonplace, light, trivial, shabby, worthless, despicable, contemptible, weak, tawdry, gimcrack, trumpery, cheap, trashy, scurvy, beggarly, one-horse (*slang*), useless, negligible, inconsiderable, feeble, foolish.

imposture, *n.—Syn.* deception, ruse, pretense, hoax, fake, fraud, counterfeit, cheat.

impotent—*Syn.* weak, feeble, powerless, unable, enfeebled, nerveless, useless, disabled, infirm, incapacitated, frail, puny, delicate, enervated, debilitated, exhausted, sterile, incapable, inefficient, ineffectual, barren. *Ant.* strong, potent, powerful, mighty, forcible, robust, efficient, effectual, virile, puissant, efficacious, energetic, vigorous, manly, productive, fertile, sturdy, lusty, capable, able, masterful, masterly, dominating, active.

imprecation, *n.—Syn.* malediction, execration, denunciation, objurgation, vituperation, abuse, profanity. *Ant.* blessing, benediction, benison.

impregnable, *adj.—Syn.* invulnerable, invincible, secure, insuperable. *Ant.* exposed, liable, open, susceptible.

impressive—*Syn.* forcible, affecting, moving, stirring, exciting, deep, profound, soul-stirring, thrilling, penetrating, absorbing, notable, remarkable, prominent, momentous, vital, commanding, grave, serious, solemn. *Ant.* light, trivial, trifling, petty, paltry, unimpressive, unimportant, shallow, inconsequential, common, ordinary, regular, normal, insignificant, slight, frivolous, inane, commonplace, uninteresting, cheap.

imprison—*Syn.* immure, incarcerate, confine, restrain, lock up, impound, circumscribe, keep, hold, detain, inclose, limit, jug (*slang*), pen, constrain, debar. *Ant.* free, liberate, release, discharge, let go, loose, loosen, unchain, dismiss, unbind, acquit, extricate, reprieve, disenthrall, unbar, deliver, set free.

impromptu, *adj.*—*Syn.* extemporaneous, improvised, spontaneous, devised, ad lib, offhand, impulsive, off the cuff. *Ant.* rehearsed, premeditated, considered, deliberate.

improper, *adj.*—*Syn.* unsuitable, unbecoming, wrong, discourteous, incorrect, misplaced, indelicate, indecent, incongruous. *Ant.* fitting, proper, seemly, correct.

improve—*Syn.* mend, amend, better, reform, rectify, apply, ameliorate, use, employ, emend, advance, revise, correct, refine, purify. *Ant.* deteriorate, degrade, impair, vitiate, damage, injure, corrode, ravage, blight, wither, decay, fade, degenerate, decline, droop, sink, weaken.

improvident—*Syn.* careless, incautious, prodigal, imprudent, wasteful, reckless, spendthrift, extravagant, lavish, unthrifty, thriftless, dissipated, profuse, squandering. *Ant.* parsimonious, niggardly, miserly, thrifty, penurious, stingy, close-fisted, close, tight-fisted, tight, grudging, gripping, sordid, mercenary, avaricious, greedy.

improvise, *v.*—*Syn.* extemporize, invent, concoct, ad-lib, dream up, devise, contrive.

impudence—*Syn.* assurance, impertinence, confidence, insolence, rudeness, boldness, effrontery, sauciness, presumption, incivility, pertness, forwardness, officiousness, intrusiveness, brazenness, assumption, cheek

(*slang*), audacity, nerve (*slang*), overbearance, sycophancy, toadeating, flunkeyism, subserviency, timeserving, truckling, knuckling, cringing, crawling, coyness, bashfulness, diffidence, submissiveness, lowliness, modesty, meekness, abasement, servility, obsequiousness, abjectness, slavishness.

impudent—*Syn.* saucy, brazen, bold, impertinent, audacious, forward, rude, insolent, immodest, shameless, bumptious, toplofty, high-hat (*slang*), uncivil, caustic, sarcastic, presumptuous, pert, officious, arrogant, self-assertive, haughty, supercilious, flippant, blustering, swaggering, hectoring, domineering, fresh (*slang*). *Ant.* retiring, modest, humble, backward, coy, bashful, mealy-mouthed, groveling, sycophantic, cringing, servile, slavish, abject, parasitical, lowly, fearful, timid, self-effacing, apprehensive, cowardly, dough-faced (*colloq.*), crouching, crawling, truckling, fawning, afraid, soapy (*slang*), lily-livered (*slang*).

impulsive—*Syn.* rash, hasty, forcible, violent, excitable, high-strung, impatient, vehement, fiery, hot-headed, clamorous, impellent, precipitate, incautious, indiscreet, imprudent, temerarious, heedless, careless, reckless, wild, headstrong, foolhardy, devil-may-care. *Ant.* cautious, careful, prudent, steady, thoughtful, cool, calculating, wary, guarded, watchful, circumspect, patient, discreet, self-possessed, cool-headed, level-headed, deliberate, hesitant, heedful, politic, leery (*slang*).

impure, *adj.*—*Syn.* unclean, sullied, defiled, smutty, corrupt, adulterated, loose, coarse, immodest, obscene, indecent, foul. *Ant.* spotless, immaculate, clean, pure.

impute—*Syn.* count, reckon, attribute, ascribe, charge, estimate, blame, assign, allege, reproach, stigmatize, implicate, denounce, indict, brand, inculpate, call to account. *Ant*. defend, advocate, extenuate, palliate, gloze, bolster up, excuse, justify, exculpate, clear, exonerate, vindicate, support, countenance, indorse, stand up for.

inactive, *adj.—Syn*. idle, inert, passive, quiescent, latent, motionless, dormant, inanimate, lazy, torpid, indolent, dilatory. *Ant*. active, live, dynamic, busy.

inadequate, *adj.—Syn*. wanting, unfit, lacking, partial, ill-adapted, scanty, incompetent, deficient. *Ant*. adequate, sufficient, suitable, competent.

inane, *adj.—Syn*. empty, pointless, insipid, trifling, banal, foolish, frivolous, absurd, silly, asinine. *Ant*. expressive, meaningful, significant.

inappropriate, *adj.—Syn*. unsuitable, inapt, discordant, infelicitous, incongruous, improper, tasteless. *Ant*. suitable, becoming, fitting, proper.

inaugurate, *v.—Syn*. begin, install, originate, open, institute, induct, introduce, initiate, commence.

incarnate, *adj.—Syn*. embodied, substantialized, exemplified, personified, materialized.

incentive—*Syn*. motive, inducement, impulse, spur, goad, reason, ground, magnet, enticement, allurement, consideration, stimulus, fillip, whip, bribe, lure, decoy, temptation, bait, charm, spell, stimulation. *Ant*. discouragement, dissuasion, scruple, caprice, monition, warning, dehortation, reluctance, curb, restraint, admonition, expostulation.

inception, *n.—Syn*. inauguration, beginning, start, origin, initiation, commencement, opening, onset. *Ant*. termination, end, finish, close.

incessant, *adj.—Syn*. unending, eternal, ceaseless, perpetual, interminable, continual, endless, unremitting. *Ant*. intermittent, periodic, recurrent, occasional.

incident, *n.—Syn*. event, occasion, affair, episode, chance, occurrence, happening.

incidental, *adj.—Syn*. subordinate, accidental, fortuitous, minor, occasional, chance, casual, contingent, secondary, associated. *Ant*. fundamental, cardinal, essential, basic.

incite—*Syn*. excite, instigate, stimulate, urge, encourage, impel, provoke, inspirit, rouse, arouse, animate, actuate, spur, goad, exhort, force, persuade, influence, sway, coax, wheedle, induce, prick, taunt, egg on. *Ant*. deter, hold back, dishearten, dissuade, admonish, check, discourage, remonstrate, expostulate, warn, dehort, restrain, damp, dampen, depress, dispirit, frustrate, stop, prevent.

inclination—*Syn*. leaning, slope, disposition, tendency, bent, bias, affection, attachment, wish, desire, liking, fancy, allurement, hobby, fascination, attraction, proneness, aptness, predilection, propensity, animus, partiality, penchant. *Ant*. unconcern, indifference, neutrality, nonchalance, apathy, inappetence, supineness, coldness, inattention, impotence, insouciance, heedlessness.

include, *v.—Syn*. contain, incorporate, embody, encompass, comprise, involve, embrace, comprehend. *Ant*. exclude, eliminate, debar, omit.

incommode—*Syn*. annoy, plague, molest, disturb, inconvenience, trouble, vex, disarrange, inhibit, disquiet, tease, worry, bother, pester, bore, harass, harry, badger, heckle, bait. *Ant*. please, satisfy, gratify, indulge, humor, flatter, enliven, amuse, regale, comfort, refresh, gladden, delight, charm, captivate, fascinate, attract, benefit, exhilarate.

incompatible, *adj.—Syn*. inharmonious, discordant, discrepant, incongruous, contrary, opposing, inconsonant, unsympathetic, antipathetic, inconsistent, opposite. *Ant.* compatible, congenial, harmonious, attuned.

incompetent—*Syn.* unskilful, inexpert, bungling, unable, incapable, inadequate, unfit, inefficient, insufficient, ineffectual, unhandy, maladroit, unqualified, disqualified, stupid, floundering, stumbling, ignorant, unskilled, inept, unsuitable, benighted. *Ant.* skilful, dexterous, expert, proficient, competent, deft, adroit, clever, talented, capable, knowing, masterly, skilled, erudite, informed, able, experienced, practical, efficient, effectual, qualified, trained, apt, handy, adept.

incongruous—*Syn.* inconsistent, inappropriate, absurd, incompatible, inharmonious, disagreeing, unsuitable, inapposite, contrary, repugnant, mismated, irreconcilable, mismatched, incoherent, discordant, discrepant, ill-matched, incommensurable, contradictory, conflicting, different, heterogeneous, divergent, disparate, inconformable, unconformable, modified, diversified, differential, variform. *Ant.* accordant, suitable, matched, harmonious, consistent, agreeing, compatible, identical, coinciding, homogeneous, uniform, homologous, same, selfsame, connatural, consonant, invariable, unvarying, unchanging, undeviating, analogous, cognate, corresponding, allied, congeneric, apposite.

inconsistent, *adj.*—*Syn.* unsteady, vacillating, inconstant, contrary, inconsonant, unsuitable, incompatible, varying.

inconstant, *adj.*—*Syn.* unstable, inconsistent, changing, mutable, uncertain, capricious, vacillating, perfidious. *Ant.* constant, reliable, steadfast, loyal.

increase, *n.*—*Syn.* augmentation, addition, accession, enlargement, extension, increment, accretion, growth, development, inflation, gain, multiplication,

expansion, turgescence, **amplification**, dilation, spread, dilatation, intumescence, distension. *Ant.* decrease, contraction, shrinkage, decrement, compression, deflation, attenuation, diminution, lessening, reduction, decimation, decrescence, atrophy, abridgment, deterioration, abstraction, subtraction, curtailment, abbreviation.

increase, *v.*—*Syn.* augment, extend, enlarge, dilate, expand, amplify, raise, enhance, magnify, grow, develop, lengthen, broaden, double, triple, quadruple, etc., produce, spread, inflate, widen, swell, accresce, burgeon, bud, germinate, fructify, tumefy, distend, protuberate, reinforce, add, supplement. *Ant.* diminish, lessen, contract, shrink, wither, fade, atrophy, dwindle, shrivel, narrow, decrease, compress, deflate, condense, squeeze, pucker, reduce, abridge, curtail, subtract, deduct, abstract, consume, subside, decay, crumble, erode, wear away, fall off.

inculcate, *v.*—*Syn.* instill, impress, imbue, implant, teach, impart, instruct, urge.

incumbent—*Syn.* pressing, urgent, obligatory, binding, devolving, coercive, necessary, imperative, stringent, behooving, peremptory, unavoidable, persistent, inescapable. *Ant.* free, immune, exempt, released, unencumbered, excusable, irresponsible, unaccountable, unamenable, liberated, privileged, absolved, clear, cleared.

incursion, *n.*—*Syn.* raid, inroad, foray, attack, infringement, trespass, invasion, violation.

indecent, *adj.*—*Syn.* improper, indelicate, unbecoming, offensive, immoral, immodest, lewd, coarse, shameless. *Ant.* decent, chaste, virtuous, modest.

indefatigable, *adj.*—*Syn.* tireless, diligent, pertinacious, assiduous, dogged, persevering, unremitting, sedulous, vigorous.

indefinite—*Syn.* vague, uncertain,

unsettled, loose, lax, indeterminate, indistinct, undefined, unlimited, inexact, inconclusive, ambiguous, equivocal, confused, undefinable, obscure, oracular. *Ant.* clear, definite, exact, apparent, certain, indubitable, indisputable, conclusive, unquestionable, evident, sure, reliable, infallible, assured, positive, absolute, decided, ascertained, known.

indemnify, *v.*—*Syn.* recompense, repay, guarantee, compensate, remunerate, reimburse, satisfy.

independent, *adj.*—*Syn.* free, separate, unrestricted, alone, unconfined, sovereign, autonomous, self-reliant, self-sufficient. *Ant.* dependent, subordinate, subservient, relative.

indicate—*Syn.* show, disclose, mark, tell, point out, designate, denote, reveal, manifest, testify, evidence, determine, differentiate, specify, imply, signify, connote. *Ant.* confuse, disconcert, discompose, perplex, bewilder, moider, lead astray, fluster, flurry, humbug, rattle (*colloq.*), distract, derange, confound, embarrass.

indifference—*Syn.* apathy, carelessness, listlessness, insensibility, nonchalance, insouciance, inattention, coldness, unconcern, phlegm, impassibleness, impassibility, impassivity, hebetude, supineness, callousness, neutrality, stoniness, insusceptibility. *Ant.* feeling, warmth, sympathy, sensitiveness, enthusiasm, tender-heartedness, compassion, softness, sentimentality, desire, inclination, attention, heed, carefulness, vivacity, tenderness, vivaciousness, impressibility, passion, liveliness, cordiality, sincerity, zeal, application, assiduity.

indigence—*Syn.* poverty, want, need, hunger, privation, starvation, penury, destitution, misery, insufficiency, dearth, scarcity, famine, stint, scantiness, pauperism, distress, necessity, mendicancy, mendicity, beggary. *Ant.*

plenty, plenitude, fullness, repletion, wealth, opulence, affluence, fortune, independence, money, capital, resources, property, substance, competence, riches, luxury, abundance, sufficiency.

indigenous, *adj.*—*Syn.* native, natural, domestic, aboriginal, inborn, endemic, innate. *Ant.* imported, naturalized, foreign, alien.

indignation—*Syn.* anger, wrath, ire, resentment, scorn, fury, displeasure, umbrage, rage, passion, animosity, exasperation, pique, huff, temper, irascibility, spleen, sulks, tantrums, acrimony, virulence, bitterness, agitation, excitement. *Ant.* calmness, coolness, benignity, quiet, gentleness, modesty, humility, patience, forbearance, imperturbability, toleration, sang-froid [*Fr.*], tranquillity, dispassion, restraint, equanimity, self-possession, self-control, self-restraint, hebetation, poise, passiveness.

indignity—*Syn.* insult, affront, disrespect, dishonor, contumely, outrage, obloquy, opprobrium, reproach, ignominy, discourtesy, disparagement, irreverence, scurrility, scoffing, sibilation, jeering, mocking, mockery, slight, taunt, vituperation. *Ant.* esteem, praise, honor, reverence, obeisance, courtesy, consideration, admiration, respect, veneration, fealty, deference, approbation, homage, regard, obsequiousness, appreciation.

indirect, *adj.*—*Syn.* devious, roundabout, crooked, tortuous, oblique, implied, inferred. *Ant.* straightforward, direct, unswerving, explicit.

indiscreet, *adj.*—*Syn.* unwise, rash, reckless, foolhardy, heedless, imprudent, thoughtless, foolish.

indiscriminate, *adj.*—*Syn.* promiscuous, mixed, wholesale, heterogeneous, uncritical, unselective.

indispensable—*Syn.* essential, necessary, requisite, imperative, needful, fundamental, basic, expedient, required, prerequisite.

Ant. unnecessary, superfluous, supernumerary, useless, redundant, needless, uncalled for, unwanted.

indisputable—*Syn.* undeniable, undoubted, incontestable, indubitable, irrefutable, unquestionable, unassailable, impregnable, incontrovertible, positive, unmistakable, certain, sure, infallible, assured, definite, unequivocal. *Ant.* doubtful, uncertain, dubious, questionable, vague, unreliable, indeterminate, equivocal, undefined, unauthentic, untrustworthy, controvertible, disputable, indefinite, changeable, casual, ambiguous, cryptic, undetermined.

indistinct—*Syn.* vague, uncertain, confused, indefinite, indistinguishable, obscure, ambiguous, shadowy, blurred, ill-fated, dim, misty, muddy, nebulous, darkened. *Ant.* clear, distinct, plain, visible, conspicuous, manifest, perceptible, definite, obvious, palpable, luminous, explicit, lucid, intelligible, positive, apparent, evident.

individual, *adj.*—*Syn.* peculiar, separate, special, distinct, particular, singular, specific, characteristic, personal, idiosyncratic, *Ant.* general, universal, common, ordinary.

indolent—*Syn.* lazy, idle, slothful, sluggish, sleepy, drowsy, slack, inert, torpid, dull, remiss, supine, dronish, otiose, ineffectual, lethargic, soporous, soporific, languid, listless, lackadaisical, shilly-shally. *Ant.* active, quick, keen, eager, vivacious, lively, prompt, ardent, anxious, sleepless, plodding, laboring, laborious, hustling, bustling, spry, alert, smart, sharp, indefatigable, busy, earnest, intent, energetic, vigilant, zealous, sedulous, enthusiastic, diligent, persevering.

indorse—*Syn.* ratify, confirm, superscribe, sanction, approve, subscribe, accept, guarantee, O.K., sign, commend, praise, recommend, uphold, support,

vouch for, stand up for, defend. *Ant.* condemn, depreciate, disparage, blame, censure, reprehend, disapprove, denounce, reprove, reprimand, admonish, frown upon, ignore, chide, berate, stigmatize, rebuke, decry, protest, deprecate, objurgate.

induce, *v.*—*Syn.* impel, instigate, persuade, actuate, cause, move, incite, motivate, spur.

indulge—*Syn.* foster, cherish, fondle, gratify, please, pamper, humor, favor, placate, concede, spoil, satisfy, satiate, endear, nourish, nurture, sustain, coddle, pet. *Ant.* torment, torture, rack, harrow, annoy, trouble, disquiet, molest, plague, bother, pester, displease, mortify, harass, harry, badger, faze, grieve, sadden, afflict, distress, pain, hurt, thwart, tease, tire, worry, vex.

industrious—*Syn.* diligent, busy, active, engaged, sedulous, laborious, occupied, assiduous, zealous, indefatigable, intent, plodding, working, laboring, business-like. *Ant.* inactive, idle, indolent, careless, slothful, sluggish, lethargic, slack, remiss, otiose, inert, languid, supine, laggard, dilatory, lazy, unoccupied, workless, drowsy, oscitant, listless, lackadaisical.

industry—*Syn.* activity, diligence, sedulousness, assidulity, labor, laboriousness, exertion, persistence, effort, attention, application, patience, intentness, perseverance, pains, constancy, plodding, indefatigability, pursuit, enterprise, business, undertaking. *Ant.* idleness, indolence, laziness, sloth, sluggishness, neglect, negligence, fickleness, changeableness, inertness, inattention, remissness, inconstancy, dawdling, languor, otiosity, ergophobia, lethargy, drowsiness, statuvolence, torpor, torpidity, heaviness, procrastination, shirking, relinquishment.

inebriated, *adj.*—*Syn.* drunk, intoxicated, soused, tipsy, tight. *Ant.* sober, teetotal.

ineffective, *adj.—Syn.* inadequate, ineffectual, useless, impotent, futile, unfruitful, vain, inconsequential. *Ant.* effective, efficacious, forceful, potent.

inefficient, *adj.—Syn.* ineffective, weak, unproductive, wasteful, incapable, inept, unskillful, maladroit.

inept, *adj.—Syn.* awkward, maladroit, unfit, unhandy, clumsy, foolish, inappropriate, asinine. *Ant.* apt, competent, skillful, adroit.

inevitable—*Syn.* unavoidable, indefeasible, sure, certain, necessary, avoidless, irresistible, ineluctable, imminent, ineludible, inescapable. *Ant.* uncertain, unlikely, doubtful, vague, casual, indeterminate, contingent, incidental, fortuitous, questionable, indefinite, problematical.

inexorable, *adj.—Syn.* implacable, severe, pitiless, inflexible, resolute, grim, firm, obdurate, unyielding. *Ant.* merciful, lenient, compassionate, forbearing.

infamous—*Syn.* wicked, heinous, disgraceful, atrocious, abhorrent, shameful, execrable, ignominious, disreputable, despicable, unmentionable, opprobrious, outrageous, shocking, notorious, abandoned, profligate, arrant, foul, base, vile, blackguard, perfidious, scandalous, rascally, corrupt, immoral, iniquitous, malevolent, depraved, demoralized, vicious, sinful, dissolute, villainous, flagitious, flagrant, foul, evil. *Ant.* virtuous, good, pure, noble, worthy, meritorious, righteous, faultless, spotless, sinless, stainless, immaculate, unblemished, moral, incorruptible, whole-souled, fine, perfect, innocent, high, exalted, sublime, glorious, admirable, exemplary, true, constant, straightforward, honest, clean, frank, candid, undefiled, conscientious, high-principled, just, square (*slang*), honorable, white (*slang*), trustworthy, dignified, reputable, respectable, beloved.

infatuated, *adj.—Syn.* fascinated, doting, fond, foolish, beguiled, captivated, silly. *Ant.* sensible, prudent, wise, judicious.

inference—*Syn.* deduction, conclusion, assumption, judgment, consequence, corollary, result, resultant, sequence, reason, argument, enthymeme, epagoge, solution, derivation, upshot, illation, moral, implification, application. *Ant.* preconception, prejudgment, anticipation, prenotion, predilection, foretelling, foreknowledge, foregone conclusion, foreboding, presentiment, foresight, forethought.

inferior, *adj.—Syn.* subordinate, poorer, secondary, inadequate, lesser, lower, deficient. *Ant.* superior, top-drawer, first-class.

infernal—*Syn.* diabolical, fiendish, hellish, devilish, malicious, satanic, demoniacal, flagitious, atrocious, horrible, hellborn, incarnate, accursed, Mephistophelian, wicked, unspeakable. *Ant.* heavenly, angelic, divine, pure, seraphic, cherubic, celestial, rapturous, sanctified, hallowed, consecrated, holy, sacred, sacrosanct, predestined, godlike, glorious, saintly.

infinite—*Syn.* unlimited, boundless, illimitable, immeasurable, interminable, unbounded, eternal, countless, immense, numberless, innumerable, incalculable, indefinite, endless, incomprehensible, termless, perpetual, continual, continuing. *Ant.* limited, definite, particular, circumscribed, numbered, terminable, measurable, finite, bounded, confined, momentary, hourly, daily, etc., restricted, transient, transitory, narrow, brief, ephemeral, evanescent, fleeting, small, short, shallow, moderate, little, fixed, positive, determinate.

infirm—*Syn.* weak, feeble, enfeebled, decrepit, debilitated, tottering, invalid, sickly, drooping, enervated, exhausted, frail, doddering, languid, spent, wasted, sapless, seedy, worn, anaemic, adynamic, asthenic. *Ant.* strong, robust, stout, vigorous, sturdy, husky, lusty, powerful, potent, puissant, energetic, forceful, hale, healthy, hearty, sound, active, brisk, husky, muscular, tough, sinewy, virile.

inflame—*Syn.* anger, irritate, enrage, chafe, incense, nettle, aggravate, embitter, exasperate, arouse, kindle, excite, stir, provoke, incite, gall, vex, taunt, tease, pester, plague, harass, worry, ruffle, roil, heckle, infuriate, madden, craze, goad, spur. *Ant.* soothe, mollify, pacify, palliate, calm, assuage, appease, lull, compose, still, alleviate, allay, smooth, smooth over, hush, quell, quiet, soften, repress, reconcile, restrain, cool down, mitigate, please, placate, tranquillize.

inflate, *v.*—*Syn.* distend, expand, swell, exaggerate, dilate, enlarge, elate. *Ant.* deflate, shrink, condense, compress.

inflexible, *adj.*—*Syn.* stiff, firm, obdurate, strict, stubborn, obstinate, rigid, tenacious, intractable, inexorable. *Ant.* flexible, elastic, resilient, yielding.

influence, *n.*—*Syn.* power, control, sway, authority, weight, supremacy, superiority, pull (*slang*), patronage, credit, favor, reputation, character, ascendancy, importance, preponderance, prominence, prestige, predominance, command, leadership, absolutism, despotism, mastery, mastership, domination, prerogative, rule. *Ant.* unimportance, uselessness, lack of power, powerlessness, subordination, inefficacy, pettiness, smallness, littleness, subserviency, inferiority, obsequiousness, servility, meanness, contemptibleness, worthlessness, lowness, lowliness, submissiveness, inutility, weakness, shabbiness, inefficiency, incapacity, subjection.

influence, *v.*—*Syn.* sway, control, prejudice, modify, bias, act upon, direct, counteract, regulate, rule, restrain, compel, af-

fect, actuate, dominate, predominate, outweigh, carry weight. *Ant.* lack power, carry no weight, be of no importance, produce no effect, get no result.

information, *n.*—*Syn.* knowledge, learning, news, data, lore, intelligence.

infrequent, *adj.*—*Syn.* rare, odd, unusual, scarce, sporadic, irregular, isolated. *Ant.* common, usual, customary, ordinary.

infringe—*Syn.* transgress, violate, trespass, invade, break, encroach, infract, contravene, intrude, pirate, trample upon, discard, repudiate, attack, assault, aggress. *Ant.* observe, obey, fulfil, carry out, comply with, perform, keep faith, redeem, promise, discharge, satisfy, acquiesce, concur, agree, defend, repel, resist, repulse, submit, surrender, retreat.

infuriate, *v.*—*Syn.* enrage, anger, exasperate, incense, inflame, madden.

infuse, *v.*—*Syn.* instill, permeate, implant, imbue, inspire, inoculate, animate, steep.

ingenious—*Syn.* skilful, clever, resourceful, handy, ready, original, inventive, productive, fertile, imaginative, witty, keen, talented, expert, apt, deft, slick (*slang*), proficient, capable, trained, competent, qualified, able, gifted, endowed, dexterous, adroit, sagacious. *Ant.* unskilful, unskilled, bungling, inapt, incompetent, unable, ungainly, clumsy, awkward, dull, stupid, inexperienced, amateurish, puerile, fumbling, floundering, maladroit, unfit, unqualified, unhandy, green, immature.

ingenuous—*Syn.* open, frank, fair, undisguised, candid, unequivocal, honest, artless, sincere, plain, generous, natural, simple, unsophisticated, naïve, guileless, unsuspicious, unreserved, straightforward, aboveboard, outspoken, blunt, simple-minded, unaffected. *Ant.* cunning, sly, tricky, subtle, crafty, double-dealing, shifty, artful, wily, scheming, intriguing, foxy, feline, vulpine, designing, insidious, underhand, shrewd, strategic, diplomatic, politic, deceptive, Machiavellian, deceitful, crooked, stealthy.

ingratiate, v.—*Syn.* captivate, disarm, flatter, cajole, blandish, seduce, attract.

ingress, n.—*Syn.* entrance, adit, access, entry, door, gate, opening.

inhabit—*Syn.* dwell, occupy, sojourn, stay, remain, abide, reside, live, room, nestle, roost (*colloq.*), bunk perch, lodge. *Ant.* be absent, withdraw, stay away, slip out, retreat, retire, vacate, give up, exit, go away, desert, forsake, abandon.

inherent—*Syn.* inbred, inborn, innate, latent, natural, inseparable, indwelling, native, internal, intrinsic, infixed, ingrained, inwrought, immanent, subjective, congenital, indispensable. *Ant.* superfluous, superficial, extrinsic, incidental, superimposed, supplemental, supplementary, adscititious, ulterior, transient, unconnected, subsidiary, fortuitous, casual, external, outward, accidental, foreign to.

inhibit—*Syn.* restrain, hinder, check, repress, suppress, curb, prohibit, interdict, hold back, restrict, impede, block, obstruct, prevent, obtrude, interfere, oppose, discourage, veto, proscribe, forbid, bar, disallow, exclude, shut out, suspend, stop, abrogate, abolish, nullify, rescind, annul, repeal. *Ant.* permit, warrant, authorize, approve, accord, vouchsafe, empower, allow, grant, charter, license, consent, assent, yield, liberate, emancipate, affranchise, free, deliver, unbind, unchain, unharness, aid, help, succor, sustain, maintain, support, adopt, patronize, countenance, commend.

inhuman—*Syn.* cruel, savage, bloodthirsty, pitiless, barbarous, unfeeling, ruthless, malignant, malevolent, brutal, ferocious, truculent, venomous, cold-blooded, cold-hearted, ruffianly, evil-disposed, rancorous, harsh, fiendish, fiendlike, hellish, demoniacal, diabolical, devilish, infernal, Satanic. *Ant.* humane, feeling, sympathetic, mild, indulgent, warm-hearted, kind-hearted, tender, compassionate, considerate, obliging, gracious, kindly, amiable, helpful, affectionate, brotherly, fraternal, charitable, philanthropic, benignant, bounteous, beneficent, generous, cordial, accommodating, complacent, comforting.

iniquitous—*Syn.* wicked, nefarious, vicious, sinful, sinning, unrighteous, unjust, unfair, wrong, criminal, unprincipled, lawless, dissolute, immoral, blackguard, profligate, recreant, disreputable, disgraceful, shameful, shameless, degrading, flagitious, reprobate, foul, infamous, villainous, diabolical, hellborn, satanic, fiendish, infernal. *Ant.* good, virtuous, pure, innocent, moral, upright, honest, decent, worthy, creditable, fine, exemplary, praiseworthy, admirable, noble, excellent, blameless, lovable, kind, true, harmless, saintly, saintlike, exalted, just, equitable, square, reputable, respectable, honorable, high-principled, white (*slang*).

initiate, v.—*Syn.* begin, start, introduce, commence, institute, establish, inaugurate, invest.

injurious—*Syn.* noxious, hurtful, harmful, baneful, pernicious, mischievous, damaging, wrongful, deleterious, prejudicial, detrimental, destructive, disadvantageous. *Ant.* beneficial, helpful, advantageous, good, salutary, profitable, wholesome, salubrious, useful, inoffensive, healing, constructive, favorable, serviceable.

injury—*Syn.* hurt, harm, damage, detriment, wrong, injustice, disadvantage, outrage, prejudice, evil, impairment, blemish, injustice, loss, mischief, evil. *Ant.* good, benefit, emolument, help, advantage, profit, gain, avail, vantage, utility, boon, service, favor, blessing, assistance, succor, aid, relief, remedy.

injustice—*Syn.* wrong, grievance, unfairness, iniquity, violation, injury, foul play, partiality, favor, favoritism, nepotism, partisanship, encroachment, inequality, onesidedness, infringement, illegality, unlawfulness, unrighteousness. *Ant.* justice, right, privilege, equity, fairness, fair play, propriety, equitableness, honesty, square deal (*colloq.*), morality, morals, ethics, rectitude, integrity, honor, equality, sanction, warranty, recompense, reward, impartiality, lawfulness, squareness, uprightness, righteousness.

innate—see **inherent** above.

innocent—*Syn.* good, artless, guiltless, blameless, faultless, undefiled, pure, sinless, virtuous, spotless, immaculate, innoxious, harmless, inoffensive, right, righteous, guileless, upright, clear, exemplary, clean, innocuous, simple, plain, unsophisticated, unaffected, frank, sincere, open, honest, straightforward, candid, simple-minded, unsuspicious, simple-hearted. *Ant.* guilty, criminal, sinful, blamable, culpable, reprehensible, blameworthy, corrupt, bad, unrighteous, villainous, devilish, sadistic, evil, delinquent, impenitent, hard, hardened, sensual, licentious, wild, dissolute, carnal, debauched, orgiastic, voluptuous, Corybantic, drunken, immoral, impure, lewd, lascivious, intemperate, artful, tricky, treacherous, cunning, evasive, sly, foul.

innocuous—*Syn.* harmless, innoxious, inoffensive, beneficial, salutary, salubrious, safe, wholesome, healthy, prophylactic, bracing, tonic, invigorating, stimulating, energizing, strengthening, nutritious, hygienic, profitable, uninjurious, improving, refreshing, reviving, restorative, resuscitating, curative, useful,

advantageous, helpful. *Ant.* noxious, poisonous, deleterious, bad, injurious, maleficent, malefic, impairing, degenerative, detrimental, deteriorating, blighting, insalubrious, unhealthy, morbific, pestilent, pestilential, envenomed, toxic, deadly, baneful, tainted, toxemic, luetic, noisome, unwholesome, damaging, prejudicial, destructive, pernicious, morbiferous, harmful.

inordinate—*Syn.* overmuch, excessive, immoderate, undue, intemperate, disorderly, irregular, unlimited, superabundant, redundant, crammed, profuse, lavish, overwhelming, overflowing, overcharged, extravagant, profuse, prodigal. *Ant.* moderate, meager or meagre, insufficient, stinted, scanty, sparse, inadequate, incomplete, deficient, exhausted, expended, depleted, short, exigent, spent, squandered.

inquire—*Syn.* ask, seek, solicit, demand, search, question, interrogate, pursue, examine, sift, analyze, interpellate, catechize, probe, sound, rummage, ransack, peer, look, pry, pump, cross-question, hunt, trail, track, explore, reconnoitre, scrutinize. *Ant.* answer, respond, retort, reply, rebut, counterstate, contradict, neglect, ignore, pass over, disregard, shun, shelve, wink at, discard, postpone, defer, delay, procrastinate, put off, abandon.

inquiry—*Syn.* quest, request, pursuit, search, examination, investigation, research, exploration, question, questioning, scouting, inquisition, catechism, discussion, reconnaissance or reconnoissance, survey, analysis, inspection. *Ant.* neglect, abandonment, supineness, indisposition, carelessness, negligence, disregard, adjournment, postponement, procrastination, delay, nonchalance, insouciance, inactivity, inattention.

inquisitive—*Syn.* searching, scrutinizing, peeping, prying, inquiring, intrusive, curious, meddling, meddlesome, peering, nosey (*colloq.*), sniffing, intruding, forward, aggressive. *Ant.* careless, backward, bashful, inattentive, abstracted, absent-minded, indifferent, listless, unheeding, undiscerning, neglectful, supine, scatter-brained, inadvertent, hen-headed (*colloq.*), harum-scarum, regardless, negligent.

insane—*Syn.* mad, deranged, demented, delirious, distracted, frenzied, frenetic, unsound, disordered, lunatic, crazy, daft, cracked (*colloq.*), fanatical, maniacal, possessed, moon-struck, shatterbrained, scatter-brained, crack-brained, rabid, wild, giddy, addle-pated, addle-brained, muddled, nutty (*slang*), screwy (*slang*), distraught, idiotic, unhinged, unsettled, rambling, driveling, paranoiac, furious, raging, Corybantic, orgiastic. *Ant.* sane, sound, lucid, normal, whole, common-sense, rational, right-minded, sober, sober-minded, self-possessed, steady, reasonable, healthy, regular, stable, calm, cool, cool-headed, level, imperturbable, ordinary, hard-headed, un-ruffled, practical, natural, wholesome, unimpaired, solid, right, correct, sensible, hearty, vigorous, wise, intelligent, sedate, settled, solemn.

insanity—*Syn.* frenzy, mania, delirium, derangement, lunacy, madness, dementia, dementia præcox, aberration, alienation, idiocy, craziness, hallucination, monomania, phrenitis, amentia, delusion, fanaticism, dipsomania, the horrors (*colloq.*), the jimjams (*slang*), bats in the belfry (*slang*), paranoia, imbecility. *Ant.* clearness, lucidity, common sense, sanity, rationality, normalcy, sobriety, steadiness, normality, regularity, healthiness, saneness, firmness, constancy, reasonableness, intelligence, mentality, wisdom, discernment, judgment, sagacity, understanding.

inscrutable, *adj.*—*Syn.* mysterious, incomprehensible, hidden, arcane, baffling, unfathomable, enigmatic, secret. *Ant.* obvious, plain, manifest, evident.

insensible, *adj.*—*Syn.* stuporous, numb, torpid, unfeeling, impassible, apathetic, stolid, insentient. *Ant.* conscious, aware, awake, feeling.

insidious—*Syn.* crafty, cunning, artful, designing, intriguing, deceitful, guileful, wily, foxy, tricky, elusive, illusory, treacherous, subtle, sly, cunning, deceptive, crafty, artful, feline. *Ant.* open, frank, candid, aboveboard, sincere, unsophisticated, plain, honest, fair, fair and square, honorable, simple, straightforward, unreserved, guileless.

insight—*Syn.* discernment, judgment, introspection, penetration, cleverness, perspicacity, acumen, shrewdness, inspection, keenness, intuition, consciousness, perception, apperception, comprehension, apprehension. *Ant.* ignorance, mental obscurity, darkness, mental blindness, unconsciousness, nescience, shallowness, bewilderment, incapacity, unenlightenment, illiteracy, perplexity, confusion, incomprehensibility, muddiness, doubt, lack of judgment.

insinuate—*Syn.* suggest, intimate, hint, introduce, ingratiate, infuse, mean, signify, connote, convey, imply, purport, denote, allude, whisper, mention, communicate, disclose, tip off (*slang*), tip the wink (*slang*), inform, indicate. *Ant.* conceal, hide, mask, camouflage, veil, cloud, cloak, screen, evade, reserve, befog, withhold, disguise, suppress, cover, stifle, shade, keep secret, dissemble, muffle, shroud, beguile, bamboozle.

insipid—*Syn.* tasteless, flat, dull, stale, vapid, flavorless, uninteresting, characterless, lifeless, inanimate, mawkish, unsavory, jejune, wishy-washy, sloppy, trashy, nauseating, dull, slow, uninteresting. *Ant.* tasty, piquant, pungent, tart, savory, flavored, spiced, sapid, palatable, dainty, delectable, delicious, pleasing, luscious, appetizing, toothsome, tempting, ambrosial, sharp, keen, interesting, lively, quick, energetic, enterprising, brisk, up-to-date.

insolent—*Syn.* impudent, impertinent, offensive, rude, unmannerly, overbearing, arrogant, saucy, bold, contemptuous, defiant, haughty, bumptious, presumptuous, contumelious, swaggering, self-assertive, imperious, supercilious, toplofty (*colloq.*), high-hat (*slang*), domineering, brazen, blustering, audacious, flippant, fresh (*slang*). *Ant.* fawning, sponging, truckling, obsequious, abject, servile, sycophantic, cringing, base, mealymouthed, toadying, parasitic, groveling, slavish, beggarly, sniveling, sneaking, mean, time-serving, abased, reptilian, dough-faced (*colloq.*), hen-hearted, chicken-livered, cowardly.

insolvent—*Syn.* bankrupt, ruined, impoverished, indigent, beggared, penniless, indebted, poverty-stricken, fortuneless, destitute, impecunious, reduced, straitened, moneyless, fleeced, stripped. *Ant.* solvent, opulent, affluent, independent, wealthy, well-to-do, substantial, rich, moneyed, well-off, warm, comfortable, snug (*colloq.*), propertied.

insouciant—*Syn.* careless, heedless, gay, reckless, unconcerned, devil-may-care, happy-go-lucky, light-hearted, carefree, thoughtless, indifferent, supine, abstracted, woolgathering, dreamy, flighty, giddy, absent-minded, harum-scarum, rantipole, harebrained, hen-headed. *Ant.* careful, cautious, watchful, attentive, observant, heedful, mindful, serious, prudent, preoccupied, circumspect, alert, vigilant, thoughtful, cognizant, advertent, absorbed, engrossed, contemplative, deliberate, wary, guardful, cool, self-possessed, discreet.

inspection, *n.*—*Syn.* examination, overseeing, supervision, scrutiny, study, investigation, survey, observation, inquiry.

inspiration—*Syn.* grasp, acumen, subtlety, penetration, acuteness, long-headedness, discrimination, perspicacity, sagacity, mother wit, understanding, comprehension, apprehension, gumption, savvy (*colloq.*), imagination, invention, impulse, flash, impression, sensation, feeling, predilection, emotion, revelation, manifestation, theopneusty. *Ant.* silliness, foolishness, hebetude, dullness or dulness, stupidity, incapacity, inability, fatuity, idiocy, idiotism, senility, anility, driveling, dementia, folly, nugacity, futility, trifling, insensibility, inappetency, insusceptibility, apathy, coldness, callousness, stupor, unconcern, insouciance, nonchalance, unconsciousness, indifference, impassiveness, impassivity, inertness, numbness, dumbness.

instance—*Syn.* case, precedent, example, type, point, illustration, occurrence, exemplification, antecedent, pattern, specimen, sample, elucidation, object lesson. *Ant.* exception, peculiarity, breach, anomaly, rarity, freak, abnormity, abnormality, irregularity, eccentricity, aberration, noncomformity, heterogeneity, singularity.

instantaneous, *adj.*—*Syn.* immediate, abrupt, sudden, direct, prompt, lightning. *Ant.* slow, delayed, deliberate, gradual.

instantly, *adv.*—*Syn.* immediately, directly, abruptly, suddenly, anon, now, presto.

instigate—*Syn.* incite, urge, force, stimulate, encourage, animate, persuade, influence, sway, bias, prevail upon, overcome, inspirit, rouse, arouse, induce, predispose, entice, tempt, impel, prompt, press, exhort, insist.

Ant. dissuade, discourage, expostulate, remonstrate, warn, threaten, deter, dampen, deprecate, admonish, avert, prevent, hold back, dishearten, turn aside, constrain, restrain, suppress, repress, check, subdue, crush, overwhelm, stifle, smother, stop.

instil—*Syn.* infuse, diffuse, suffuse, transfuse, intermix, immix, combine, imbue, inject, infiltrate, medicate, blend, alloy, interject, inoculate, impregnate, implant, introduce, inculcate, insinuate, indoctrinate, disseminate. *Ant.* eliminate, take out, remove, extract, draw, uproot, extirpate, eradicate, expel, leave out, dislodge, exclude, get rid of, clear, purify, excrete, free from, eject, discard, effuse, spill, shed, void, egest, extrude, detrude, pour out, clear off.

instruct — *Syn.* teach, inform, guide, direct, initiate, enlighten, educate, train, advise, tutor, prepare, qualify, school, coach, grind, cram, exhort, counsel, warn, tell, convey, impart, regulate, model, form, promulgate, proclaim, announce, indoctrinate, expound, interpellate. *Ant.* misrepresent, pervert, falsify, misdirect, misinstruct, misinform, misguide, deceive, delude, lead astray, misinterpret, neglect, ignore, abandon, forget, withhold, withdraw, dispute, impugn, repudiate, refuse, deny.

instrumental, *adj.*—*Syn.* contributory, promoting, conducive, helping, auxiliary, serving, accessory.

insubordination, *n.*—*Syn.* disobedience, intractability, contumacy, rebellion, revolt, defiance, mutiny.

insubstantial, *adj.*—*Syn.* imaginary, groundless, incorporeal, inane, unfounded, flimsy, tenuous, trifling, rarefied. *Ant.* substantial, real, material, solid.

insufferable—*Syn.* unbearable, intolerable, unendurable, unallowable, unpermissible, agonizing, grievous, heartrending, insupportable, shocking, appalling, dreadful, frightful, excruciating, harrowing, fearful, crushing. *Ant.* pleasant, agreeable, delightful, refreshing, comfortable, comforting, delicious, soothing, healing, palliative, easing, emollient, enjoyable, cheering, dainty, delicate, satiating, satisfying, pleasurable, delectable, purifying, healthy, healthful, ameliorating, salubrious, salutary, wholesome, invigorating, restorative.

insult—*Syn.* indignity, outrage, affront, abuse, insolence, contempt, contumely, disdain, impudence, impertinence, discourtesy, incivility, disrespect, blackguardism, rudeness, acerbity, bitterness, spleen, gall, mockery, scoffing, scurrility, derision, sneering, sarcasm, jeer, fleer, taunt, derision. *Ant.* respect, regard, reverence, homage, tribute, admiration, fealty, obeisance, deference, courtesy, humility, friendship, cordiality, fraternity, fellowship, culture, polish, politeness, gentility, amenity, urbanity, suavity, esteem, benevolence, benignity, brotherly love, kindness, sympathy.

intact, *adj.*—*Syn.* whole, untouched, complete, entire, unbroken, sound, perfect, undamaged. *Ant.* defective, impaired, marred, spoiled.

integration, *n.*—*Syn.* unification, amalgamation, merger, joining, fusion, mingling, consolidation, blending, desegregation.

integrity—*Syn.* uprightness, honesty, incorruptness, moral soundness, purity, honor, righteousness, probity, rectitude, constancy, candor, faithfulness, trustworthiness, loyalty, merit, worth, morality, virtue, fidelity. *Ant.* improbity, dishonor, dishonesty, pretension, sham, corruption, falsity, unfaithfulness, disloyalty, treason, turpitude, knavery, roguery, infidelity, perfidiousness, faithlessness, unfairness, double-dealing, infamy, disgrace, shame.

intellectual—*Syn.* mental, cultured, learned, inventive, creative, talented, accomplished, ideal, metaphysical, cogitative, reflective, meditative, speculative, thoughtful, studious, deliberative, contemplative, thinking, keen, sharp, acute, precocious, skilled, learned. *Ant.* dull, stupid, brainless, thoughtless, inane, fatuous, foolish, vacuous, silly, unintellectual, unreasoning, irrational, weak-minded, loony (*slang*), moonstruck, wool-gathering, harum-scarum, flighty, pigeon-brained, harebrained, driveling.

intelligence, *n.*—*Syn.* acumen, penetration, intellect, perspicacity, discernment, brains, grasp, insight.

intelligible—*Syn.* comprehensible, plain, clear, obvious, distinct, perceptible, lucid, unequivocal, vivid, expressive, graphic, definite, positive. *Ant.* unintelligible, bewildering, perplexing, hard, difficult, abstruse, muddled, obscure, incomprehensible, inscrutable, unknowable, puzzling.

intemperate—*Syn.* drunk, drunken, unrestrained, immoderate, excessive, inordinate, dissipated, sottish, tipsy, inebriated, beery (*colloq.*), groggy (*colloq.*), intoxicated, flush, lit up (*slang*), stewed (*slang*), spiffy (*slang*), bibacious, spifflicated (*slang*), top-heavy (*slang*), raddled (*slang*), pickled (*slang*), tight (*slang*), boozy (*colloq.*), maudlin, muzzy (*colloq.*), muddled, obfuscated, fuddled (*colloq.*), full (*colloq.* and *vulgar*), lushy (*slang*), mellow (*slang*), half seas over (*slang*), three sheets in the wind (*slang*). *Ant.* sober, temperate, teetotal, abstemious, abstinent, steady, serious, sedate, moderate, wellbehaved, dependable, reliable, self-denying, nephalic, ascetic, nonindulgent, rigorous.

intend, *v.*—*Syn.* mean, propose, design, aim, try, conceive, destine, plan, purpose, scheme.

intensity—*Syn.* eagerness, ardor, energy, tension, attention, concentration, force, strain, earnestness, hustle, vehemence, rush, pressure, vigor, ginger (*slang*), pep (*slang*), ferment, perturbation, bustle, stir. *Ant.* inactivity, inaction, sloth, sluggishness, listlessness, laziness, inertness, passivity, torpor, languor, latency, dullness, or dulness, moderation, slowness, flatness, apathy, carelessness, indolence, idleness.

intent, *n.*—*Syn.* intention, design, plan, aim, motive, desire, purpose, meaning, object.

intentional—*Syn.* intended, designed, purposed, deliberate, premeditated, studied, contemplated, meant, meditated, projected, determined, calculated, aimed at. *Ant.* chancy, accidental, speculative, tentative, fortuitous, undesigned, unpremeditated, purposeless, causeless, random, aimless, indiscriminate, unthought of, haphazard, casual, incidental, occasional.

interchange, *n.*—*Syn.* crossroads, exchange, cloverleaf, intersection.

intercourse—*Syn.* communication, intercommunication, connection, commerce, correspondence, acquaintance, fellowship, fraternity, sorority, intercommunion, comradeship, companionship, intimacy, familiarity, sociableness. *Ant.* unfriendliness, bitterness, enmity, hatred, animosity, estrangement, hostility, malice, loggerheads, alienation, seclusion, eremitism, aversion, isolation, solitude, aloofness, loneliness.

interest, *n.*—*Syn.* profit, share, portion, advantage, benefit, gain, concern, business, attention, curiosity, behalf, inquisitiveness, stake, right, title, claim, premium. *Ant.* unconcern, disconnection, apathy, indifference, insouciance, carelessness, loss, nonpayment, default.

interest, *v. — Syn.* entertain, amuse, enliven, please, divert, delight, cheer, beguile, occupy, recreate, gratify, disport. *Ant.* bore, weary, tire, annoy, disturb, disgust, disquiet, bother, vex, worry.

interminable, *adj. — Syn.* endless, infinite, boundless, everlasting, perpetual, limitless, unceasing, eternal, incessant, permanent, continuous. *Ant.* intermittent, periodic, ended.

intermittent, *adj. — Syn.* broken, occasional, periodic, infrequent, spasmodic, interrupted, fluttering, discontinuous, recurrent, fitful. *Ant.* incessant, continual, perpetual, constant.

internal, *adj. — Syn.* interior, inward, inherent, intrinsic, inner, innate, enclosed, domestic. *Ant.* external, outer, foreign, alien.

interpose — *Syn.* interfere, intervene, intercede, meddle, intermeddle, come between, mediate, obtrude, arbitrate, intrude, interpolate, intercept, intersperse, interrupt, interject, negotiate. *Ant.* remain inactive, do nothing, keep off, refrain from, withhold, withdraw, refuse, ignore, neglect, disregard, overlook, forbear, omit, retire, keep out, keep clear, hold off, stand back, stand aside, shun, avoid.

interpret — *Syn.* translate, elucidate, clear, decipher, unravel, unfold, solve, expound, explain, construe, render, define, enucleate, manifest, describe, disentangle, paraphrase, illuminate. *Ant.* misinterpret, misconstrue, misapply, distort, travesty, burlesque, misapprehend, twist, confuse, tangle, mystify, puzzle, misstate, pervert, exaggerate, falsify, parody, garble, subvert, jumble.

interrogation, *n. — Syn.* examination, inquiry, investigation, test, inquisition, probe.

interrupt, *v. — Syn.* break, divide, discontinue, interfere, delay, cut, disturb, disconnect, sever, stop, hinder, check, arrest.

intimate, *adj. — Syn.* close, affectionate, friendly, familiar, private, near, confidential, secret, internal. *Ant.* formal, distant, conventional, ceremonious.

intimate, *n. — Syn.* comrade, friend, partner, pal, mate, crony, buddy, chum, fellow. *Ant.* stranger, outsider.

intimate, *v. — Syn.* hint, allude, insinuate, whisper, suggest, betoken, imply. *Ant.* state, declare, specify, vouch.

intimidate — *Syn.* scare, frighten, abash, daunt, terrify, cow, threaten, browbeat, dismay, bully, overawe, astound, bulldoze, alarm, shock, unnerve, domineer, hector, terrorize, dictate, coerce, drive, menace, abuse, fulminate, curse, accuse, denounce, bluster, shout, roar. *Ant.* encourage, hearten, inspirit, inspire, comfort, console, assuage, mollify, soften, embolden, buoy up, praise, laud, gratify, please, animate, incite, cheer, rouse, stimulate, stir up, instigate, assure, reassure.

intolerable — *Syn.* insufferable, unendurable, unbearable, insupportable, shocking, appalling, agonizing, harrowing, horrifying, horrible, dire, heart-breaking, heart-rending, terrible, maddening. *Ant.* consoling, soothing, allaying, assuaging, healing, comforting, pleasant, pleasing, pleasurable, satisfying, delightful, charming, felicitous, cheering, alluring, captivating, fascinating.

intrepid — *Syn.* brave, fearless, bold, courageous, dauntless, unafraid, undaunted, firm, valiant, doughty, chivalrous, gallant, daring, heroic, aweless, lionhearted, nervy, plucky, valorous, unshrinking, unflinching, self-reliant. *Ant.* afraid, timid, shrinking, skulking, awestruck, cowardly, craven, cringing, diffident, nervous, faint-hearted, shaky, panic-stricken, frightened, scared, trembling, tremulous, intimidated, discouraged, hesitant.

intricate — *Syn.* complex, tangled,

twisted, involved, confused, convoluted, difficult, irregular, disordered, chaotic, mixed, disarranged, labyrinthine, raveled, knotted, complicated, inextricable. *Ant.* tidy, methodical, arranged, orderly, systematic, regulated, shipshape, plain, easy, trim, proper, clear, not difficult, uniform, normal, untangled, ordinary, unmixed.

intrigue—*Syn.* plot, scheme, secret, complication, combination, conspiracy, artifice, dodge, ruse, wire-pulling, connivance, design, plan, craft, arrangement, collusion, craftiness, subtlety, maneuvering, chicanery, trickery, duplicity, doubledealing, machination, jugglery, finesse, Machiavellianism, circumvention, cunning. *Ant.* artlessness, innocence, fair-play, honor, honesty, guilelessness, straightforwardness, sincerity, simplicity, candor, unreservedness, matter-of-fact, bluntness, plainness, plain speaking, simplemindedness, openness.

intrinsic—*Syn.* true, real, genuine, aboveboard, honest, indwelling, subjective, fundamental, native, natural, inward, internal, radical, innate, inborn, essential, ingrained, inbred, immanent, inherited, congenital, syngenic. *Ant.* extrinsic, objective, without, extraneous, incidental, accidental, casual, subsidiary, adventitious, fortuitous, occasional, contingent, dependent, by chance, foreign, external, exterior.

introduction, *n.*—*Syn.* presentation, preface, prelude, overture, preamble, beginning, commencement, inception, interjection, interpolation.

intrusive, *adj.*—*Syn.* interfering, trespassing, obtrusive, meddlesome, infringing, invading, inquisitive, snooping, nosy. *Ant.* retiring, bashful, diffident, shy.

invasion—*Syn.* entrance, attack, incursion, inroad, fray, foray, outbreak, aggression, raid, irruption, ingress, intrusion, ingression, investment. *Ant.* defense, protection, guard, safeguard, fortification, escarpment, rampart, bulwark, stockade, blockade, rampart, breastwork, stronghold.

invective—*Syn.* raillery, scurrility, opprobrium, censure, condemnation, denouncement, accusation, reproach, sarcasm, satire, railing, abuse, contumely, disapprobation, disparagement, depreciation, denunciation, reprehension, remonstrance, reproof, reprimand, disapproval, obloquy. *Ant.* approbation, approval, sanction, admiration, commendation, eulogy, eulogium, encomium, praise, laudation, acclaim, acclamation, applause, appreciation, tribute.

invent—*Syn.* devise, discover, fashion, form, fabricate, design, plan, frame, contrive, outline, sketch, draft, project, scheme, carry out, lie, falsify, misrepresent, imagine, simulate, deceive, humbug, mystify, misstate, equivocate, conjure up, visualize, romance, fancy, conceive.

investigation—*Syn.* inquiry, examination, search, research, scrutiny, inquisition, review, interrogation, cross-examination, discussion, catechism, catechesis, exploitation, quest, pursuit.

invidious—*Syn.* odious, hateful, envious, malignant, provoking, galling, heart-breaking, vexatious, troublesome, irksome, irritating, wearisome, painful, annoying, obnoxious. *Ant.* pleasant, pleasurable, delightful, gratifying, satisfying, consoling, soothing, comforting, cordial, refreshing, delectable, attractive, benevolent, charitable.

invigorate—*Syn.* strengthen, animate, energize, vitalize, brace, nerve, fortify, harden, refresh, vivify, stimulate, pep up (*slang*), nerve, embolden. *Ant.* weaken, enervate, enfeeble, unnerve, sap, debilitate, impair, attenuate, paralyze, waste, injure, cripple, reduce, devitalize.

invincible—*Syn.* unconquerable,

insuperable, resistless, impregnable, insurmountable, irresistible, indomitable, incontestable, mighty, overpowering, all-powerful, all-sufficient, sovereign. *Ant.* weak, puny, deficient, defective, frail, fragile, flimsy, effeminate, faint, enervated, unnerved, crippled, languishing, languid, sickly, feeble, wasted, emaciated, spent.

invitation, *n.*—*Syn.* summons, bid, request, challenge, call, provocation, solicitation, proposition.

involve—*Syn.* entangle, implicate, imply, embarrass, compromise, overwhelm, contain, include, connect with, signify, denote, betoken, mean. *Ant.* separate, disconnect, explicate, remove, distinguish, disentangle, free, unravel, clear, extricate, disengage, untwist.

irate, *adj.*—*Syn.* angry, incensed, mad, infuriated, raging, nettled, irritated, enraged, wrathful.

irk, *v.*—*Syn.* annoy, upset, discompose, vex, trouble, fret, bother, perturb.

irony—*Syn.* sarcasm, satire, burlesque, ridicule, mockery, raillery, skit, quip, twit, banter, parody, travesty, derision, persiflage, buffoonery, scoffing, jeering, gibe, sneer, taunt. *Ant.* respect, regard, worship, reverence, veneration, attention, homage, courtesy, deference, obsequiousness, admiration, consideration, obeisance, submission, approbation, approval.

irrational—*Syn.* foolish, demented, ridiculous, absurd, silly, imbecile, fatuous, stupid, feebleminded, brutish, illogical, queer, evasive, odd, strange, unreasonable, loony (*slang*), crazed, crazy, perverted, weak-minded, paralogical, paralogistic, daft, nutty (*slang*), unsound, vacuous. *Ant.* rational, logical, sound, steady, reliable, intellectual, reasoning, judicial, thoughtful, reflective, meditative, studious, cultured, accomplished, talented, sane, wise, sober, soberminded, lucid, self-possessed,

normal, common-sense, ordinary.

irregularity, *n.*—*Syn.* abnormality, caprice, inconstancy, unevenness, deviation, aberration, variation, anomaly, disorderliness, fitfulness, unruliness.

irrelevant, *adj.*—*Syn.* unrelated, extraneous, inapposite, foreign, unessential, inappropriate, inconsequent, inapplicable, immaterial.

irreligious—*Syn.* impious, wicked, ungodly, profane, sacrilegious, desecrating, irreverent, blasphemous, unholy, unregenerate, reprobate, hardened, perverted. *Ant.* pious, godly, saintly, devout, devoted, reverend, prayerful, spiritual, pietistic, pietistical, consecrated, regenerated, sacred, solemn.

irrepressible—*Syn.* insuppressible, unrepressible, free, uncontrollable, irresistible, unconfined, excitable, unconstrained, independent, unshackled, unfettered, unrestricted, absolute, ebullient, high-strung, tumultuous, effervescing. *Ant.* passive, calm, placid, quiet, flat, dull, coldblooded, grave, serious, melancholy, solemn, imperturbable, cool, collected, composed, meek, patient, tolerant, submissive, resigned.

irresolute—*Syn.* wavering, doubting, undecided, shaky, undetermined, vacillating, fickle, uncertain, fluctuating, unsettled, lukewarm, hesitant, hesitating, shilly-shally, drifting, unstable, half-hearted, wabbly, wobbling, volatile. *Ant.* resolute, firm, determined, purposed, unvarying, resolved, unflinching, decided, definite, game, courageous, indomitable, inexorable, relentless, unhesitating, wilful, gritty, unyielding, tenacious, obstinate.

irresponsible—*Syn.* arbitrary, irresolute, shilly-shally, wobbly, unstable, undecided, hesitating, fluctuating, unsettled, faltering, wavering, infirm of purpose, unreliable, excusable, vacillating, weak, foolish, devil-may-care, not accountable, exempt, capricious, frothy, light, light-minded, feeble-minded, giddy, flighty, harum-scarum, rash, thoughtless. *Ant.* responsible, accountable, steady, firm, reliable, trustworthy, answerable, amenable, liable, unexempt, susceptive, subject, open to, dependent on, resolute, determined, strong-willed, self-reliant, earnest.

irritable—*Syn.* sensitive, susceptible, irascible, excitable, thin-skinned, fretful, fidgety, ill-tempered, touchy, testy, huffy, querulous, captious, peevish, petulant, fractious, snappy, waspish, cantankerous, hasty. *Ant.* pleasant, agreeable, suave, gentle, mild, calm, cool, passive, composed, enduring, good-tempered, tranquil, dispassionate, patient, tolerant, submissive, serene, imperturbable, self-possessed, forbearing.

irritate—*Syn.* provoke, exasperate, exacerbate, excite, foment, sting, pique, agitate, ruffle, embitter, fluster, flurry, disturb, annoy, madden, infuriate, inflame, aggravate, anger, enrage, vex, harass, worry, perplex, nettle, chafe, irk, plague. *Ant.* soothe, calm, mollify, comfort, console, ease, alleviate, mitigate, palliate, assuage, salve, allay, ameliorate, moderate, soften, appease, placate, pacify, conciliate, please.

isolate, *v.*—*Syn.* separate, segregate, disconnect, dissociate, quarantine, seclude, insulate, sequester.

issue, *n.*—*Syn.* result, consequence, effect, aftermath, denouement, event, eventuality, occurrence, incident, circumstance, casualty, contingency, termination, conclusion, upshot, resultant, finish, culmination, product, publication, progeny, offspring, fruits, family, brood, seed, children, emanation, outpouring, effusion, exudation, egression.

issue, *v.*—*Syn.* flow, emanate, exude, proceed, emerge, rise, spring, break out, begin, arise, start, eventuate, ensue, result, originate, publish, promulgate, spread, bring out, get out, go forth, send out, express, utter, circulate paper money or coin, publish, distribute, send out, deliver.

itinerary, *n.*—*Syn.* route, guidebook, plan, record, course, trip.

J

jabber, *v.*—*Syn.* gabble, babble, chatter, prate, prattle.

jar, *v.*—*Syn.* jolt, shock, clash, shake, jangle, rattle, jounce, quake, vibrate.

jargon, *n.*—*Syn.* cant, slang, patois, dialect, lingo, argot, jive.

jealous—*Syn.* envious, covetous, invidious, suspicious, jaundiced, yellow-eyed, distrustful, mistrustful, doubting, doubtful, dubious. *Ant.* honorable, righteous, trusting, faithful, true, loyal, trustworthy, incorrupt, clean, faithful, candid, square, aboveboard, honest.

jeer, *v.*—*Syn.* sneer, mock, gibe, contemn, scoff, deride, flout, ridicule, taunt, boo, hoot.

jest, *n.*—*Syn.* joke, witticism, wisecrack, gag, quip, humor, prank, play, banter.

jewel, *n.*—*Syn.* gem, treasure, stone, brilliant.

join, *n.*—*Syn.* connect, unite, bind, link, combine, cement, associate, marry, affiliate, merge, consolidate, unify, tie, knit. *Ant.* separate, sever, sunder, detach.

jolly, *adj.*—*Syn.* merry, humorous, gay, jocose, jocular, jocund, jovial, joyous, blithe, witty, frolicsome, playful, cheerful. *Ant.* solemn, sober, grave, dour.

journey—*Syn.* trip, voyage, travel, transit, tour, expedition, excursion, pilgrimage, passage, itinerary, course, peregrination, roving, wandering, traversing.

jovial—*Syn.* merry, gay, happy, joyous, jolly, frolicsome, cheerful, lively, animated, hilarious, blithe, lighthearted, vivacious, sparkling, sprightly, sportive, jocund, buoyant, riant, debonair, rollicking. *Ant.* sad, solemn, serious, morose, morbid, doleful, sorrowful, cast down, dejected, heavy, melancholy, cheerless, spiritless, gloomy, dull, dismal, somber, downcast, depressed, pensive, lugubrious, splenetic, atrabilious, grim, sober, demure, desolate, disconsolate.

joy—*Syn.* gladness, ecstasy, exultation, rapture, delight, happiness, enjoyment, felicity, glee, cheer, transport, cheerfulness. *Ant.* grief, sorrow, trouble, worry, distress, affliction, misery, heartache, unhappiness, wretchedness, gloom, despair, misfortune, tribulation.

jubilant—*Syn.* gay, rejoicing, celebrating, boastful, joyous, triumphant, exultant, cheerful, rollicking, happy, buoyant, highspirited, delighted. *Ant.* downcast, gloomy, sorrowful, sad, disappointed, dejected, forlorn, joyless, despondent, cheerless, unhappy, melancholy.

judge—*Syn.* referee, umpire, arbitrator, arbiter, adjudicator, justice, magistrate, master, warden, interpreter, judiciary, protector, custodian, guardian.

judgment—*Syn.* discernment, discrimination, penetration, decision, sagacity, understanding, intuition, mentality, intelligence, reason, rationality, conception, intellectuality, reasoning. *Ant.* thoughtlessness, vacuity, inanity, misunderstanding, incogitancy, fatuity, vacancy of mind, want of discernment, indiscrimination, imbecility, foolishness, lack of intelligence, stupidity, misjudgment, misconception.

judicious—*Syn.* discerning, wise, thoughtful, just, prudent, sensible, well-advised, well-guided, well-judged, discreet, cautious, sagacious, politic, sensible, intelligent, wary, circumspect. *Ant.* foolish, silly, fatuous, idiotic, driveling, senseless, imbecile, irrational, nonsensical, maudlin, puerile, anile, inept, shallow, asinine, ill-judged, ill-advised, injudicious.

jump, *v.*—*Syn.* skip, leap, hop, spring, bounce, bound, vault, caper.

junction, *n.*—*Syn.* connection, meeting, attachment, fusion, merger, union, linkage, joint, seam. *Ant.* separation, severance, detachment.

just—*Syn.* honest, impartial, exact, upright, proper, precise, right, good, reasonable, fair, equable, equitable, square, fair and square, evenhanded, rightful, righteous, lawful, legitimate. *Ant.* wrong, unjust, unfair, inequitable, partial, unequal, unwarrantable, iniquitous, unjustified, one-sided, unreasonable, illegal, knavish, dishonest, base, villainous.

justice—*Syn.* fairness, impartiality, fair play, square deal, equity, propriety, uprightness, integrity, desert, reasonableness, justness, lawfulness, truth, faith, fulness, legality, honor, right, rightfulness, righteousness, rectitude, virtue, law. *Ant.* injustice, wrong, foul play, crooked deal, unfairness, partiality, favoritism, dishonesty, perfidy, perfidiousness, knavery, rascality, corruption, barratry, venality, dishonor, graft (*colloq.*), unlawfulness, unreasonableness, inequity.

justify—*Syn.* vindicate, warrant, maintain, excuse, defend, exculpate, clear, exonerate, acquit, whitewash, advocate, plead for, support, countenance, extenuate, bolster up, gloss over, varnish. *Ant.* accuse, incriminate, impute, charge, tax, blame, censure, reproach, denounce, brand, impeach, indict, arraign, stigmatize, slur, implicate, condemn.

juvenile—*Syn.* young, youthful, immature, puerile, boyish, childish, infantine, girlish, tender, undeveloped, adolescent, growing, green, callow, beardless, juvenescent, infantile, babyish. *Ant*. old, senile, senescent, old-womanish, anile, sere, withered, wrinkled, hoary, decrepit, doddering, doting, declining, waning, venerable, time-worn, antiquated, superannuated.

K

katatonia—*Syn*. gloom, gloominess, periodic mania, depressive insanity, extreme depression, morbid, fanaticism, deep dejection, lassitude, dulness or dullness, heaviness, pensiveness. *Ant*. abandon, mirth, rapture, joy, joyfulness, sprightliness, vigor, cheer, cheerfulness, gaiety, merriment, blithesomeness, conviviality, jollity, liveliness, vivacity, gladness.

keen—*Syn*. sharp, eager, penetrating, acute, piercing, acrimonious, bitter, acrid, poignant, enterprising, energetic, intense, mettlesome, incisive, pointed, vivid, lively, sagacious, witty, cute, perspicacious, discerning, quick. *Ant*. blunt, dull, thick, stupid, driveling, lazy, fatuous, obtuse, pointless, insipid, deadened, insensate, stolid, doltish, loutish, morose, sour, flat, depressed, spiritless, sluggish, slothful, dilatory, slow, tardy, dawdling, careless, heedless, uninterested, apathetic.

keep—*Syn*. hold, retain, preserve, maintain, save, guard, support, supply, fulfill, detain, confine, conserve, defend, carry, carry on, sustain, withhold, obey, observe, conduct, protect, refrain, restrain, uphold, observe, continue, persevere, imprison, secure, reserve. *Ant*. relinquish, give up, resign, drop, forego, renounce, cede, abandon, dispose of, throw away, cast off, release, surrender, forsake, leave, desert, discard, desist, depart, withdraw, stop, quit, drop,

set aside, consume, spend, waste, deplete, exhaust, disperse, retreat, retire, vacate, go away.

keepsake, *n*.—*Syn*. souvenir, memento, reminder, token, memorial, emblem.

ken, *n*.—*Syn*. sight, compass, knowledge, range, view, scope, cognizance, purview, domain.

kill—*Syn*. slay, murder, assassinate, destroy, massacre, butcher, hang, electrocute, slaughter, immolate, dispatch, burke, shoot, strangle, stifle, choke, suffocate, asphyxiate, drown, smother, garrote, execute, behead, guillotine, disembowel, bayonet, saber. *Ant*. preserve, guard, safeguard, protect, watch, watch over, defend, uphold, save, deliver, sustain, free, set free, pardon, vindicate.

kin, *n*.—*Syn*. family, kinsfolk, kinsmen, relatives, siblings, kindred, clan, tribe.

kind, *adj*.—*Syn*. benevolent, good, affectionate, loving, caring, beneficent, generous, charitable, kindly, amiable, gracious, cordial, obliging, indulgent, warm-hearted, kind-hearted, humane, good-intentioned, well-meaning, well-meant, fatherly, motherly, brotherly, sisterly, paternal, maternal, fraternal, sororal, merciful, friendly, sympathetic, considerate, accommodating, soft-hearted, tender. *Ant*. malevolent, malignant, harsh, cruel, inhuman, grinding, bitter, acrimonious, ill-disposed, stony, stony-hearted, ill-conditioned, ill-intentioned, evil-disposed, evil-minded, rancorous, spiteful, unamiable, uncharitable, unfriendly, invidious, cold-hearted, cold-blooded, ruthless, merciless, spiteful, treacherous, caustic, virulent, barbarous, overbearing, truculent, venomous, hard-hearted, brutal, ferocious, unkind.

kind, *n*.—*Syn*. class, sort, genus, race, kin, kindred, family, connection, blood, progeny, offspring, relation.

kindle, *v.*—*Syn.* ignite, inflame, light, enkindle, arouse, awaken, incite, excite, stir, provoke. *Ant.* quench, douse, smother, stifle.

kindness, *n.*—*Syn.* generosity, goodness, grace, benevolence, benignity, sympathy, cordiality, complaisance, friendliness.

kindred—*Syn.* relation, relationship, consanguinity, affinity, blood, descent, kind, birth, race, family, genus, species, variety, tribe, sept, clan, caste, breed, type, progeny, stock, alliance.

king—*Syn.* sovereign, ruler, potentate, pope, prince, autocrat, czar, emperor, master, lord, commander, chief, chieftain, dictator, sahib, sirdar, sheik, boss, governor, leader. *Ant.* subject, serf, slave, henchman, follower, liege, servant, servitor, flunky (*colloq.*), menial, dependent, bondman, bondslave, hireling, helot, mercenary, vassal, parasite.

kingdom, *n.*—*Syn.* dominion, demesne, domain, empire, sovereignty, rule, realm, country.

knack, *n.*—*Syn.* skill, facility, faculty, ability, dexterity, adeptness, expertness, aptitude. *Ant.* ineptitude, gaucherie, awkwardness, clumsiness.

knave, *n.*—*Syn.* scoundrel, villain, rascal, rogue, scamp, miscreant, churl, blackguard, trickster.

knit, *v.*—*Syn.* weave, unite, link, join, tie, fasten, interlace, intertwine, bind.

knock, *v.*—*Syn.* rap, tap, clap, slap, hit, strike, beat, collide, rattle.

knot—*Syn.* bond, tie, connection, tangle, snarl, bunch, collection, gathering, perplexity, protuberance, ligature, entanglement, group.

know—*Syn.* perceive, understand, realize, believe, credit, effectuate, apprehend, comprehend, think, hold, entertain, profess, imply, recognize, learn, interpret, discern, conceive. *Ant.* doubt, disbelieve, discredit, reject, mistrust, misbelieve, suspect, misdoubt, differ, dissent, demur, deny, dispute, misapprehend, misunderstand, misinterpret, misconstrue.

knowledge—*Syn.* information, learning, erudition, skill, lore, understanding, scholarship, comprehension, science, wisdom, experience, cognition, intuition, apprehension, recognition, cognizance, perception, light, acquaintance, conscience, consciousness, apperception. *Ant.* ignorance, darkness, blindness, stupidity, shallowness, nescience, incapacity, incomprehension, inexperience, illiteracy, unenlightenment, benightedness, obscurity, unconsciousness, misconception, mystery, incomprehensibility, mysteriousness, misunderstanding, misapprehension, unfamiliarity.

L

labor—*Syn.* toil, work, exertion, undertaking, effort, drudgery, travail, task, pains, painstaking, employment, execution, achievement, exercise, operation, transaction, performance, striving, plodding, exercitation, industry, diligence. *Ant.* idleness, sloth, slothfulness, inertia, inactivity, laziness, indolence, ergophobia, bumming (*U.S. slang*), dawdling, remissness, inaction, relaxation, otiosity, inertness, loafing, loitering, panhandling (*slang*), ease, unemployment.

laborious—*Syn.* arduous, hard, difficult, stiff, heavy, toilsome, wearisome, backbreaking, crushing, pressing, tedious, hardworking, tiresome, burdensome, grievous, wearing, grinding, painstaking, indefatigable, cruel, oppressive, diligent, assiduous, plodding, troublesome, uphill, strenuous, herculean, tough, irksome, onerous. *Ant.* easy, facile, light, trivial, smooth, petty, paltry, piddling, ordinary, common, slight, inconsiderable, frivolous, insignificant, small, trifling, immaterial, puerile, childish, inconsequential, nugatory, unimportant, mean, contemptible, make-believe, rambling, loose, desultory, abortive, inefficient, inept, vain, fiddle-faddle (*colloq.*), namby-pamby (*colloq.*), wishy-washy (*colloq.*).

lack—*Syn.* want, destitution, need, failure, loss, absence, deprivation, deficiency, scarcity, insufficiency, incompleteness, depletion, scantiness, inadequacy, paucity, neediness, necessity, privation, distress, poverty. *Ant.* plenty, plenteousness, abundance, copiousness, fullness, satiation, satisfaction, satiety, surfeit, repletion, sufficiency, luxuriance, profusion, provision, supply.

lackadaisical, *adj.*—*Syn.* languishing, indolent, apathetic, spiritless, listless, inert, carefree, indifferent. *Ant.* energetic, lively, spirited, enthusiastic.

laconic—*Syn.* pithy, curt, brief, epigrammatic, terse, concise, short, condensed, exact, pointed, succinct, compendious, sententious. *Ant.* diffuse, rambling, dilated, profuse, wordy, copious, long-winded, prolix, diffusive, frothy, long-spun, excursive, discursive, loose, flatulent.

lag—*Syn.* delay, linger, loiter, tarry, retard, saunter, lounge, slacken, slow up, drawl, plod, trudge, toddle, waddle, slouch, shuffle, falter, stagger, hobble, limp, shamble. *Ant.* haste, hasten, speed, quicken, sprint, scurry, hustle, scamper, run, spurt, bound, trot, gallop, race, scorch, scuttle, dash, dart, outstrip, accelerate, scour, sweep on, skim over, wing over.

lambent, *adj.*—*Syn.* radiant, brilliant, flickering, shimmering, beaming, gleaming, bright, luminous.

lame—*Syn.* crippled, defective, deformed, halt, hesitating, weak, hobbling, faltering, impotent, ineffective, imperfect. *Ant.* agile, quick, active, forceful, perfect, impetuous, dashing, athletic, swift, speedy, efficient.

lament—*Syn.* grieve, sorrow, weep, wail, mourn, bewail, moan, caoine (*Ir.*, keen), cry, bemoan, deplore, regret, anguish, snivel, whimper, sob, sigh, greet (*Sc.*), weep over, howl, ululate, yammer (*dial.*). *Ant.* rejoice, laugh, snicker, crow, cheer, simper, smirk, smile, hurrah, snigger, exult, skip for joy, shake with laughter, make merry.

lampoon—*Syn.* satire, invective, abuse, censure, reproach, contumely, disparagement, reflection, obloquy, reprehension, taunt, denunciation, tirade, insinuation, innuendo, diatribe, jeremiad. *Ant.* approbation, approval, applause, praise, plaudit, adulation, flattery, tribute, acclaim, commendation, sanction, panegyric, eulogium, acclamation, compliment, admiration, encomium.

land—*Syn.* ground, soil, dirt, earth, field, lot, section, quarter, property, estate, country, continent, province, coast, shore, beach, globe, clay, loam, region, tract, part, realty, real estate. *Ant.* air, atmosphere, stratosphere, ether, sky, cloud, mist, fog, ocean, sea, lake, water, river, rain, wave, billow, deep, brine, fluid, waterfall, cataract.

landscape—*Syn.* scenery, view, appearance, spectacle, show, aspect, feature, outline, contour, panorama.

language—*Syn.* speech, utterance, expression, words, tongue, vocabulary, lingo, idiom, dialect, diction, brogue, patois, vernacular, phraseology, glossary, glossology, philology, linguistics, glottology, letters, literature.

languid—*Syn.* drooping, pensive, lethargic, weak, flagging, feeble, slow, dull, heartless, listless, apathetic, inert, slow, torpid, inactive, remiss, weary, sluggish, dronish, laggard, drowsy, slack, shilly-shally, heavy. *Ant.* brisk, lively, animated, eager, vigorous, quick, vivacious, nimble, alert, spry, sharp, smart, peppy (*slang*), agile, bustling, hustling, restless, indefatigable, unwearied, unwearying, wide-awake, zealous, strenuous, assiduous, spirited.

languor, *n.*—*Syn.* listlessness, inertia, lassitude, ennui, sluggishness, indolence, torpidity, torpidness. *Ant.* vigor, energy, vitality, vivacity.

lanky, *adj.*—*Syn.* gaunt, spare, rawboned, gangling, lean, bony, thin. *Ant.* husky, brawny, burly, portly.

lapse, *n.*—*Syn.* error, mistake, slip, oversight, fault, blunder, boner, bobble, fluff, butch.

larceny—*Syn.* theft, thievery, robbery, appropriation, pillage, plunder, abstraction, peculation, embezzlement, fraud, pilfering, purloining. *Ant.* restoration, return, disgorgement, reimbursement, compensation, indemnification, restitution, atonement, recoupment, reversion.

large—*Syn.* big, vast, massive, immense, great, huge, colossal, gigantic, capacious, spacious, grand, bulky, extensive, wide, plentiful, copious, populous, comprehensive, abundant, ample, liberal, diffuse, titanic, cyclopean, giant, Brobdingnagian, monstrous, towering, mighty, magnificent, long, commodious, broad, enormous, grand, bloated, turgid, swollen, tumid, edematous, puffy, blowzy, extended, corpulent, obese. *Ant.* small, little, insignificant, wee [*Sc.*], thin, attenuated, minute, tiny, slight, petty, paltry, mean, inconsiderable, infinitesimal, slender, short, microscopic, limited, brief, diminutive, scanty, narrow, meagre, trifling, trivial, wasted, shriveled, shrunken, withered, contracted, Lilliputian, dwarfish, abbreviated, puny, emaciated.

lascivious—*Syn.* lewd, immoral, unchaste, loose, wanton, lustful, impure, lecherous, impudicious, unclean, immodest, carnal, polluted, prurient, concupiscent, ribald, Sadistic, Masochistic, bawdy, aphrodisiac, coarse, adulterous, salacious, pornographic, risqué, nympholeptic, nymphomaniacal, sexual, gross, libidinous, licentious, dissolute, rakish, obscene, incestuous, stupratic, fornicative, shameless. *Ant.* good, pure, virtuous, clean, uncontaminated, unsullied, unstained, modest, retiring, virginal, undefiled, continent, chaste, ascetic, innocent, unblemished, immaculate, untarnished, holy, sinless, saintly, angelic, spotless, incorrupt, moral, righteous, exemplary, faultless, restrained, ascetic, self-denying.

lassitude—*Syn.* languor, faintness, weariness, tiredness, fatigue, heaviness, stupor, dullness, drowsiness, yawning, exhaustion, prostration, drooping, torpor, torpidity, lethargy, apathy, phlegm, hebetude, inappetency, supineness, inertia. *Ant.* vivacity, vivaciousness, sprightliness, liveliness, quickness, briskness, agility, keenness, activity, pep (*slang*), vigor, mirth, refreshment, animation, gaiety, alertness, nimbleness, levity, lightness, cheerfulness.

last—*Syn.* latest, ultimate, final, utmost, lowest, meanest, least, extreme, conclusive, hindermost, determinative, ulterior, once and for all. *Ant.* first, foremost, beginning, introductory, leading, commencing, initial, initiatory, primary, inaugural, front, preparatory, incipient.

lasting, *adj.*—*Syn.* stable, durable, unremitting, continuing, protracted, enduring, unceasing, permanent. *Ant.* temporary, fleeting, ephemeral, transitory.

late—*Syn.* past, gone, extinct, no more, lapsed, elapsed, foregoing, former, recent, slow, preterit, bygone, tardy, dead, deceased, demised, defunct, departed, remote, distant, ancient. *Ant.* prospective, expectant, future, next, near, coming, approaching, anticipated, eventual, impending, ulterior, alive, living, breathing, animated, alive and kicking (*colloq.*).

latent—*Syn.* concealed, unknown, hidden, invisible, secret, inherent, implied, undeveloped, unobserved, dormant, involved, unperceived, imperceptible, implicit, unseen, uncomprehended, recondite, potential, torpid, occult, esoteric, symbolic, mystic, abeyant, veiled, cryptic, cabalistic, unexplained. *Ant.* apparent, perceptible, active, evident, manifest, exposed, unconcealed, clear, developed, conspicuous, visible, known, plain, public, prominent, indubitable, unmistakable, conclusive, open, bare, obvious, undisguised, definite, distinct.

laudable—*Syn.* praiseworthy, commendable, worthy, deserving, good, true, pure, innocent, virtuous, honest, honorable, philanthropic, righteous, creditable, exemplary, moral, dutiful, right-minded, true-hearted, kind, kind-hearted, loyal, loving, obliging, self-sacrificing, admirable, excellent, grand, noble, perfect, saintly, angelic, holy, moral, sacred, hallowed, blessed. *Ant.* vile, vicious, base, mean, corrupt, dishonest, dishonorable, bad, depraved, dissipated, drunken, blameworthy, blamable, sinful, wicked, iniquitous, dissolute, criminal, immoral, disorderly, unrighteous, unprincipled, devilish, demoralized, degraded, contemptible, villainous, worthless, lawless.

laughable—*Syn.* ludicrous, ridiculous, comic, comical, funny, whimsical, droll, drollish, waggish, risible, semi-comic, tragi-comic, jocose, absurd, quaint, eccentric, bizarre. *Ant.* serious, solemn, impressive, awe-inspiring, fearful, depressive, sad, melancholy, sorrowful, funereal, painful, shocking, morbid, dead-ly, wretched, pitiful, pitiable, mournful.

lavish, *adj.*—*Syn.* profuse, abundant, superabundant, inordinate, excess, prodigal, exorbitant, overmuch, replete, exuberant, too much, free, costly, dear, spendthrift, exhaustive, wild, unrestrained, excessive, improvident. *Ant.* scarce, scanty, skimpy, curtailed, lessened, meagre, insufficient, stinted, empty, wanting, jejune, sparse, lacking, diminished, deficient, inadequate, few, unsupplied, empty-handed, unprovided.

lavish, *v.*—*Syn.* scatter freely, give much, squander, surcharge, gorge, inundate, deluge, flood, glut, load, overload, overrun, run over, brim over, waste, expend, dissipate, run riot, spend recklessly, deplete, disperse. *Ant.* hoard, treasure up, put by, hold back, husband, economize, stint, skimp, scrimp, curtail, conserve, preserve, limit, reduce, lower, pinch, grudge, begrudge, withhold, starve, skin a flint (*colloq.*).

law—*Syn.* order, rule, statute, ordinance, legislation, enactment, edict, code, canon, decree, regulation, formula, economy, command, commandment, mandate, polity, principle, jurisprudence, equity, constitution, constitutionalism, constitutionality, legality, rite, justice. *Ant.* lawlessness, anarchy, chaos, violence, barbarism, despotism, tyranny, savagery, barbarity, ferocity, inhumanity, confusion, tumult, disorder, illegality, mobocracy, brute force, outlawry.

lawful—*Syn.* legitimate, allowable, right, righteous, legal, permissible, authorized, permitted, licit, recognized, admitted, conceded, granted, judicial, warranted, constitutional, statutory, juridical, canonical, regular, legislative, official. *Ant.* illegal, prohibited, unlawful, arbitrary, unlicensed, taboo, unauthorized, unofficial, despotic, unconstitutional, unwarrantable, tyrannical, oppressive, lawless, summary, informal.

lawless—*Syn.* illegal, unauthorized, uncontrolled, unconformable, insurgent, mutinous, riotous, rebellious, unruly, ungovernable, recusant, contumacious, seditious, revolutionary, insubordinate, disobedient, piratical, transgressive, evasive, refractory, infringing, noncompliant, nonobservant, defiant, recalcitrant. *Ant.* law-abiding, obedient, observant, subjective, non-resistant, passive, faithful, submissive, loyal, devoted, compliant, controllable, resigned, restrainable, duteous, dutiful, subservient, amenable, answerable, accountable, responsible.

lax—*Syn.* loose, slack, remiss, soft, flabby, careless, insouciant, undutiful, unobservant, dishonorable, unconscientious, disingenuous, depraved, weak, immoral, unprincipled. *Ant.* tight, firm, hard, muscular, moral, upright, conscientious, reliable, determined, observant, faithful, true, righteous, honorable, honest, dutiful.

lay, *adj.*—*Syn.* popular, nonprofessional, common, profane, nonecclesiastical, secular. *Ant.* professional, ecclesiastical, clerical, spiritual.

layer, *n.*—*Syn.* fold, tier, stratum, thickness, bed, ply.

lazy—*Syn.* slow, indolent, slothful, sluggish, idle, inactive, slack, remiss, torpid, dull, laggard, dormant, comatose, lethargic, flagging, otiose, weary, tired, supine, lackadaisical, rusty, maudlin, drowsy, dopey (*colloq.*), dozy, dronish, inert, torpescent, leaden, dreamy, oscitant. *Ant.* lively, brisk, keen, sharp, quick, prompt, spry, alert, smart, diligent, assiduous, hardworking, sedulous, unwearied, fit, active, bustling, hustling, businesslike, sleepless, painstaking, forcible, impetuous, headlong, pushing, persevering, indefatigable.

lead—*Syn.* guide, conduct, precede, direct, command, govern, manage, supervise, superintend, control, survey, overlook, oversee, steer, handle, pilot, order, regulate, show the way, induce, influence, point the way. *Ant.* follow, obey, conform, comply, accede, assent, concur, acquiesce, concede, consent, perform, submit, carry out, attend, work for, serve, help, assist, wait on, submit, yield to.

leader, *n.*—*Syn.* chief, head, guide, superior, director, master, conductor. *Ant.* follower, disciple, adherent, henchman.

league, *n.*—*Syn.* alliance, entente, confederation, association, union, coalition, cartel, pool.

lean—*Syn.* incline, bend, hang, tend, depend upon, slope, slant, shelve, decline, sidle, sag, careen, cant, crook, be oblique. *Ant.* to be horizontal, to be parallel, to lie flat, to be upright, to be perpendicular, to be downright, to be at right angles.

leap, *v.*—*Syn.* spring, caper, jump, skip, gambol, romp, bound, frisk, frolic, vault.

learn—*Syn.* acquire, receive, imbibe, take in, drink in, gain, gather, pick up, read, study, wade through, gain information. *Ant.* teach, guide, inform, instruct, coach, cram, imbue, disseminate, inculcate, indoctrinate, enlighten, direct, impress.

learned—*Syn.* scholarly, erudite, profound, educated, accomplished, academic, philosophic, solid, instructed, lettered, well-informed, bookish, high-brow (*slang*), pansophic, omniscient. *Ant.* ignorant, shallow, illiterate, gross, empty-headed, dull, stupid, incapable, uninformed, low-brow (*slang*), crass, thick (*colloq.*), incompetent, nescient, uncultured, benighted.

leave, *n.*—*Syn.* permission, license, liberty, allowance, consent, withdrawal, absence, dispensation, furlough, holiday, vacation. *Ant.* retention, confinement, prohibition, restriction, proscription, injunction, interdict, interdiction, taboo, hindrance, disallowance, veto.

leave, v.—Syn. permit, let, allow, withdraw, depart, quit, relinquish, give up, go away, resign, back out, vacate, abandon, forsake, desert. Ant. stay, remain, continue, abide, tarry, rest, persist, hold, maintain, endure, keep, stand pat (colloq.), stand still, hold on.

lechery, n.—Syn. lasciviousness, lust, lubricity, concupiscence, lewdness, salacity.

lecture, n.—Syn. discourse, sermon, talk, address, speech, homily, lesson.

leftist, n.—Syn. radical, progressive, red, pink, communist, liberal, socialist, revolutionary. Ant. rightist, right-winger, reactionary, conservative.

legal—Syn. permissible, permitted, lawful, allowable, allowed, sanctioned, legitimate, licit, authorized, warranted, admitted, ordained, prescribed, right, just, equitable, fair, fair and square. Ant. unfair, unjust, unlawful, unsanctioned, illegal, illicit, disallowed, disbarred, wrong, unconstitutional, uncharted, prohibited, restricted, interdicted.

legendary, adj.—Syn. fictitious, traditional, fanciful, fabulous, mythical. Ant. historical, actual, real, true.

leisure, n.—Syn. rest, ease, idleness, relaxation, freedom, vacation, off-time. Ant. work, toil, travail, drudgery.

lengthen, v.—Syn. extend, increase, protract, stretch, prolong. Ant. shorten, cut, curtail, abbreviate.

lenient—Syn. indulgent, soft, softhearted, kind, kind-hearted, feeling, compassionate, merciful, forbearing, tender, tolerant, mild, moderate, reasonable, lenitive, assuaging, assuasive, emollient. Ant. harsh, cruel, rough, coarse, brutal, unfeeling, tyrannical, overbearing, severe, austere, rigorous, hard, exacting, acrimonious, churlish, irritable, irritating, inflaming, exasperating, exacerbating, furious, ferocious.

lessen, v.—Syn. decrease, curtail, abridge, shrink, abate, diminish, shorten, reduce, dwindle.

let—Syn. permit, allow, suffer, bear, tolerate, leave, admit, warrant, grant, empower, privilege, demise, authorize, sanction, accord, concede, lease, rent. Ant. prevent, hinder, hold, retain, keep, inhibit, obstruct, impede, preclude, contravene, oppose, debar, frustrate, counteract, balk, circumvent.

lethargy, n.—Syn. listlessness, torpor, apathy, passiveness, lassitude, stupor, languor. Ant. vigor, vitality, liveliness, vim.

level—Syn. uniform, equal, flat, horizontal, smooth, regular, of a piece, plane, flush. Ant. rough, uneven, rugged, lumpy, irregular, hilly, mountainous, unequal, vertical, perpendicular, upright, plumb.

levis, n.—Syn. jeans, dungarees, pants, trousers, denims, breeches, coveralls, Levi Strauses, overalls.

levity, n.—Syn. lightness, jocularity, gaiety, frivolity, liveliness, flippancy, volatility, flightiness, buoyancy. Ant. gravity, sobriety, solemnity, austerity.

liable—Syn. responsible, answerable, bound, subject, accountable, chargeable, likely, apt. Ant. excusable, unbound, not accountable, exempt, freed, irresponsible, unamenable, released, clear, absolved.

liberal—Syn. generous, openhanded, lavish, free, ample, bounteous, munificent, princely, unselfish, bountiful, largehearted, magnanimous, nobleminded, extravagant, prodigal, profuse, Ant. niggardly, miserly, closefisted, narrow, parsimonious, penurious, gripping, grasping, sordid, mercenary, stingy, illiberal, greedy, close, venal, avaricious, mean, shabby, sparing.

liberate—Syn. free, deliver, set free, unchain, loose, unshackle, extricate, release, ransom, save, redeem, emancipate, rescue, manumit, discharge, dismiss, acquit, absolve, pardon, enfranchise, affranchise, reprieve, clear. *Ant*. hold, keep, confine, chain, shackle, bind, restrain, enchain, fetter, manacle, handcuff, hobble, debar, restrict, suppress, imprison, incarcerate, detain, limit, prohibit, shut up, lock in, constrain, leash, arrest, immure, jug (*slang*), jail, lock up.

liberty—*Syn*. freedom, privilege, exemption, right, immunity, emancipation, enfranchisement, affranchisement, license, permit, permission, release, allowance, dismissal, manumission, discharge, independence, acquittance, absolution. *Ant*. slavery, oppression, tyranny, serfdom, captivity, thraldom, servitude, compulsion, necessity, constraint, obligation, imprisonment, confinement, detention, restraint, incarceration, duress, arrest.

libidinous, *adj*.—*Syn*. lewd, lecherous, lascivious, wanton, lustful, carnal, salacious, licentious, obscene, abandoned.

license, *v*.—*Syn*. permit, commission, endorse, authorize, warrant, allow, approve, sanction. *Ant*. prohibit, ban, forbid, check.

licentious, *adj*.—*Syn*. wanton, profligate, libertine, libidinous, lustful, debauched, loose, lascivious, corrupt. *Ant*. continent, chaste, moral, virtuous.

lie, *v*.—*Syn*. prevaricate, equivocate, deviate, quibble, fib, evade, misrepresent, exaggerate, stretch.

life—*Syn*. existence, animation, vitality, source, vivacity, essence, origin, manner, conduct, custom, principle, nature, breath, being, entity, endurance, duration. *Ant*. death, dying, dissolution, passing, departure, mortality, rest, release, decease, demise, cessation, destruction, end, finish.

lifeless—*Syn*. dead, inanimate, departed, defunct, gone, no more, deceased, demised, dull, inert, heavy, slow, sluggish, lazy, dormant, stagnant, inactive, la-

tent. *Ant*. alive, living, breathing, animated, spirited, vital, vivified, vigorous, brisk, active, sprightly, lively, gay, merry, light-hearted, cheerful, cheery.

lift, *v*.—*Syn*. raise, hoist, boost, intensify, exalt, elevate, heighten.

light, *n*.—*Syn*. illumination, radiance, brightness, flame, glow, gleam, beam, blaze, effulgence, coruscation, luminosity, phosphorescence, scintillation, flash, shimmer, twinkle, twinkling, brilliancy, flare, shine, incandescence, gleam, lustre, sheen, sparkle, glitter, glimmer, glister, flicker, instruction, knowledge, instinct, reasoning, understanding, spirit, soul. *Ant*. darkness, dimness, blackness, obscurity, gloom, gloominess, shade, shadow, murk, murkiness, umbra, umbrageousness, obscuration, eclipse, tenebrosity, sombreness, night, caliginousness, adumbration, penumbra, dusk, duskiness, sadness, sorrow, depression, heaviness, benightedness, ignorance, soullessness.

light, *adj*.—*Syn*. buoyant, volatile, imponderable, slight, scanty, small, easy, airy, subereus, suberose, floating, frothy, ethereal, sublimated, fluffy, imponderous, weightless, downy, portable, bright, luminous, shining, scintillating, sparkling, lively, merry, gay, capricious, frivolous, vain, unsteady, frolicsome, giddy, wanton, thoughtless, unbalanced, short, inadequate, empty. *Ant*. heavy, ponderous, massive, weighty, cumbersome, burdensome, cumbrous, unwieldy, dense, solid, thick, dejected, depressed, sad, sorrowful, difficult, laborious, tedious, weary, wearied, tired, sullen, morose, dull, dark, obscured, hidden, opaque, gloomy, murky, misty, dusky, dim, concealed, ignorant, unenlightened.

lighten, *v*.—*Syn*. ease, alleviate, moderate, mitigate, diminish, temper, relieve, qualify.

like, *adj*.—*Syn*. similar, allied, akin, related, parallel, comparable, analogous, equivalent. *Ant.* different, dissimilar, unlike, diverse.

likely—*Syn.* credible, probable, possible, feasible, presumable, liable, conceivable, apt, reasonable, conjectural, practicable. *Ant.* impracticable, out of the question, beyond reach, unachievable, insuperable, insurmountable, unattainable, unobtainable, uncomeatable (*colloq.*).

likeness, *n.*—*Syn.* similarity, counterpart, representation, portrait, resemblance, analogy, equivalence.

limit, *n.*—*Syn.* boundary, confine, border, edge, end, brink, frontier, rim, terminus.

limp, *adj.*—*Syn.* limber, soft, lax, flabby, slack, drooping, flaccid, supple, *Ant.* stiff, rigid, tense, hard.

line—*Syn.* cord, thread, string, outline, length, row, direction, course, succession, sequence, span, extent, mileage, stroke, measure, extension, continuation, rank, descent, ancestry.

linger—*Syn.* tarry, loiter, saunter, lag, hesitate, delay, plod, trudge, traipse, falter, totter, stagger, dawdle, lumber, wamble, slouch, shuffle, hobble. *Ant.* hasten, quicken, hurry, run, scamper, spurt, dash, scurry, whiz, sprint, speed, dart, hustle, bustle, scramble, flurry, flutter, drive.

link, *v.*—*Syn.* join, connect, associate, fasten, tie, unite, couple, bind.

liquid—*Syn.* fluid, serous, flowing, splashing, sappy, juicy, ichorous, solvent, diluent, liquefied, watery, deliquescent, dissolved. *Ant.* solid, dense, solidified, imporous, impenetrable, impervious, firm, hard, indissoluble, undissolved, compact, close, frozen, coagulated, condensed, substantial.

liquor, *n.*—*Syn.* liquid, spirits, alcohol, whisky, beverage, fluid.

list, *n.*—*Syn.* roll, record, schedule, index, catalog, arrangement, enrolment, invoice, register, inventory, account, table, syllabus, tally, file, manifest, prospectus, bulletin, directory.

list, *v.*—*Syn.* record, set down, arrange, catalog, schedule, enter, note, place, chronicle, post, insert, enroll. *Ant.* cancel, erase, blot out, wipe out, efface, expunge, obliterate, delete.

listen—*Syn.* hark, harken, attend, heed, hear, overhear, give attention, lend an ear, pick up. *Ant.* ignore, shun, turn away, neglect, scorn, mock, slight, turn a deaf ear to, reject, pass by.

listless—*Syn.* careless, forgetful, inattentive, inactive, indifferent, drowsy, sleepy, languid, heedless, supine, indolent, spiritless, slack, inert, torpid, sluggish, leaden, dull, laggard, dilatory, lethargic, heavy, dreamy, shilly-shally. *Ant.* quick, active, brisk, eager, prompt, spry, alert, sharp, acute, expeditious, agile, nimble, bustling, hustling, restless, indefatigable, unweary, ardent, strenuous, attentive, hard-working, assiduous, diligent, sedulous.

literal—*Syn.* verbal, veritable, true, exact, accurate, precise, regular, conformable, real, according to Hoyle (*slang*), actual, undeviating, unerring, veracious, undisputed. *Ant.* wrong, erring, misleading, mistaken, false, erroneous, deceiving, untrue, delusive, beguiling, fallacious, unsound, lying, distorted, unreal, groundless, figurative, metaphorical, mythical, symbolical, figurative.

literature—*Syn.* learning, lore, education, erudition, belles-lettres (*Fr.*), knowledge, writings, compilations, treatises, books, languages, publications, literary productions, literary works, scholarship, instruction, reading, letters, bookishness, culture, book learning, menticulture, enlightenment. *Ant.* ignorance, darkness, blindness, chaos, confusion, barbarism, unenlightenment, nescience, illiteracy, benightedness, bewilderment, incomprehension, incomprehensiveness.

lithe, *adj.*—*Syn.* pliant, graceful, lissome, limber, flexible, supple. *Ant.* stiff, awkward, wooden.

little—*Syn.* small, diminutive, wee (*Sc.*), dwarfish, minute, meagre, light, scanty, inconsiderable, inappreciable, atomic, trifling, trivial, Lilliputian, microscopic, puny, tiny, runty, stunted, pygmy, elfin, undersized, exiguous. *Ant.* large, bulky, huge, capacious, big, great, much, enormous, mighty, immense, towering, ample, comprehensive, spacious, magnificent, massy, unwieldy, monstrous, colossal, Brobdingnagian, titanic, vast, gigantic, whopping.

live—*Syn.* dwell, exist, reside, inhabit, continue, subsist, endure, abide, remain, last, be, have being, prevail, breathe, act, do, perform, stay, sojourn, lodge, room. *Ant.* die, pass away, pass out, cease to exist, depart, vanish, fade, dissolve, disappear, expire, perish, pop off (*slang*), go off (*colloq.*), give up the ghost (*slang*), cash in (*slang*), pay the debt of nature, hop the twig (*slang*).

livelihood—*Syn.* maintenance, support, sustenance, subsistence, circumstances, condition, living, means, resources, property, provision, money, lucre, riches, wealth, competence, capital, substance, affluence, independence, gratuity, fortune, dowry, legacy. *Ant.* mendicity, beggary, beggarliness, poverty, neediness, necessity, hunger, privation, starvation, need, distress, mendicancy, pauperism, indigence, penury, want, emptiness, pennilessness, impecuniosity.

liveliness—*Syn.* animation, spiritedness, briskness, gaiety, jollity, sprightliness, vigor, vigorousness, activity, vivacity, effervescence, keenness, cheerfulness, geniality, glee, joviality, levity, hilarity, exhilaration, merrymaking, rejoicing. *Ant.* gloom, melancholy, the blues (*slang*), spleen, mopes, dumps (*colloq.*), hypochondria, hypochondriasis, despondency, dejection, depression, heaviness, low spirits, torpor, drowsiness, lassitude, lethargy, stupor, oscitancy, yawning, pandiculation, stretching, weariness.

livid, *adj.*—*Syn.* black-and-blue, discolored, bruised; pale, ashen, lurid, ghastly. *Ant.* brilliant, radiant, effulgent.

load, *n.*—*Syn.* weight, burden, oppression, lading, cargo, incubus, incumbrance, freight, pack, charge, clog, contents, shipment, pressure, mass. *Ant.* lightness, buoyancy, weightlessness, imponderosity, imponderableness, imponderability, suberoseness, suberousness, unsubstantiality, insubstantiality.

load, *v.*—*Syn.* burden, oppress, lade, cumber, charge, press, encumber or incumber, surcharge, make heavy. *Ant.* lighten, make light, remove, take away, reduce, alleviate, lessen, render less heavy.

loathe—*Syn.* abhor, detest, abominate, hate, dislike, despise, execrate, curse, anathematize, damn, denounce, imprecate, disapprove, condemn. *Ant.* love, like, admire, approve, fancy, respect, revere, cherish, prize, foster, indulge, nourish, nurture, esteem, appreciate, honor.

location, *n.*—*Syn.* place, site, locale, situation, neighborhood, locality, region, post.

lock—*Syn.* fastening, hook, catch, latch, hasp, clasp, bolt, bar, junction, connection, attachment, fixture, link, barrier, canal gate, grip, grapple, tuft, curl.

lofty—*Syn.* high, elevated, exalted, proud, arrogant, stately, haughty, dignified, eminent, towering, tall, soaring, vain, conceited, ostentatious, bombastic, inflated, pretentious. *Ant.* low, depressed, under, nether, beneath, below, modest, diffident, retiring, bashful, timid, timorous, coy, sheepish, unobtrusive, unpretentious, unassuming, shy, reserved, demure.

loiter, v.—*Syn.* linger, tarry, wait, idle, loaf, lag, dally, dawdle, poke, delay, stall. *Ant.* hasten, hurry, speed.

lonesome, adj.—*Syn.* lonely, forsaken, alone, isolated, desolate, solitary, forlorn.

long—*Syn.* lengthy, extended, outstretched, elongated, endless, interminable, protracted, drawn out, prolonged, enduring, perpetual, eternal, lasting, prospective, eventual, profuse, diffuse, longspun, continued, stretched out, distant, far-off, far-away, remote. *Ant.* short, shortened, abridged, abbreviated, transient, fleeting, evanescent, ephemeral, cursory, brief, concise, condensed, curt, curtailed, epitomized, terse, compact, compressed, pithy.

look, n.—*Syn.* appearance, face, condition, expression, aspect, air, mien, manner, behavior, conduct, deportment, bearing, carriage.

look, v.—*Syn.* see, view, gaze, glance, scan, stare, behold, contemplate, descry, watch, survey, regard, inspect, discern, perceive, spy, glimpse, speculate, recognize, distinguish, observe.

loose, adj.—*Syn.* free, lax, unconfined, flowing, indefinite, unattached, independent, careless, slack, vague, diffuse, rambling, dissolute, licentious. *Ant.* tight, taut, precise, strict.

loquacity, n.—*Syn.* volubility, talkativeness, prolixity, fluency, glibness, garrulity, facility. *Ant.* taciturnity, reticence, reserve, silence.

lore, n.—*Syn.* learning, knowledge, erudition, information, wisdom.

lose—*Syn.* miss, drop, mislay, forfeit, let slip, squander, waste, fail, falter, flounder, blunder, botch, stumble, fall short of, miscarry, be defeated, bite the dust (*slang*). *Ant.* gain, acquire, obtain, recover, procure, win, collect, pick up, reap, get,

inherit, increase, expand, extend, profit, advance, progress, forge ahead, proceed, improve, rally, mend, surmount, overcome.

loss—*Syn.* injury, damage, detriment, deprivation, forfeiture, disadvantage, privation, bereavement, mishap, misfortune, deterioration, impairment, degeneration, retrogression, retardation, decline. *Ant.* gain, profit, emolument, acquisition, improvement, elevation, advancement, amendment, return, inheritance, legacy, support, assistance, help, patronage, favor.

lot, n.—*Syn.* portion, fortune, fate, destiny, heritage, chance, award.

loud—*Syn.* clamorous, noisy, uproarious, sonorous, blatant, clangorous, deafening, earsplitting, shrill, piercing, high-sounding, trumpet-toned, blaring, vociferous, ringing, resonant, thundering, crashing, vulgar, ill-bred, gaudily dressed. *Ant.* faint, muffled, stifled, soft, low, quiet, murmuring, whispering, tinkling, soughing, sighing, purling, soothing, dulcet, sweet, inaudible, silent.

love—*Syn.* affection, emotion, sentiment, passion, feeling, gratification, tenderness, liking, fondness, attachment, charity, friendship, regard, attraction, devotion, benevolence, fervor, flame, transport, rapture, adoration. *Ant.* hate, hatred, disaffection, estrangement, enmity, bitterness, pique, grudge, antipathy, repugnance, revulsion, malice, implacability, umbrage, loathing, abhorrence, detestation, aversion, abomination, execration, contumely, scorn.

lovely—*Syn.* beautiful, attractive, inviting, nice, captivating, fascinating, charming, winsome, enticing, delightful, gratifying, satisfying, lovable, handsome, graceful, exquisite, comely. *Ant.* ugly, plain, homely, unseemly, uncomely, unprepossessing, ill-favored, hard-featured, ungraceful, cadaverous, grim, forbidding, repellent, repulsive, odious, hideous, shocking, repugnant, revolting.

low—*Syn.* below, beneath, under, depressed, sunken, nether, inferior, flat, squat, faint, soft, hushed, muffled, mean, debased, vulgar, disreputable, shameless, disgraceful, unbecoming, dishonorable, despicable, degraded, ill, sick, cheap, moderate, inexpensive. *Ant.* high, elevated, upper, lofty, tall, exalted, eminent, prominent, towering, loud, clamorous, noisy, blatant, thunderous, crashing, honest, honorable, decent, respectable, worthy, estimable, respected, well, healthy, vigorous, strong, dear, costly, expensive.

loyal, *adj.*—*Syn.* faithful, steadfast, constant, trustworthy, true, devoted. *Ant.* faithless, false, treacherous, perfidious.

lucid—*Syn.* bright, shining, resplendent, pellucid, serene, transparent, refulgent, luminous, clear, plain, diaphanous, translucent, vitreous, hyaline, glassy, limpid, sane, rational, sound, explicit, distinct, understandable, plain, evident. *Ant.* dark, murky, gloomy, obscure, dim, nebulous, dusky, shadowy, shady, gloomy, cloudy, nubilous, deranged, demented, screwy (*slang*), confused, unintelligible, incomprehensible, puzzling, enigmatical.

lucky—*Syn.* fortunate, successful, prosperous, victorious, triumphant, thriving, flourishing, healthy, wealthy, conquering, overcoming, winning, gaining, being benefited or rewarded. *Ant.* unlucky, unfortunate, ill-starred, ill-fated, unsuccessful, crushed, downtrodden, persecuted, wrecked, ruined, overwhelmed, defeated.

ludicrous—*Syn.* comical, odd, farcical, ridiculous, droll, drollish, funny, waggish, whimsical, laughable, screaming, queer, bizarre, quaint, baroque, outlandish, grotesque, eccentric, ridiculous, risible, fantastic, burlesque, absurd. *Ant.* serious,

solemn, sad, sorrowful, grievous, terrible, shocking, mournful, grave, depressing, pensive, doleful, grim, melancholic, sedate, earnest, demure, forlorn, disconsolate, heart-broken, broken-hearted, downtrodden, careworn.

lull, *v.*—*Syn.* quiet, tranquilize, mollify, hush, still, appease, calm, pacify.

luminous, *adj.*—*Syn.* radiant, lit, shining, bright, lucid, effulgent, incandescent, glowing, alight.

lunacy—*Syn.* madness, insanity, mania, furor, aberration, amentia, dementia, morosis, frenzy, delirium, delusion, hallucination, brainstorm. *Ant.* sanity, rationality, normalcy, common sense, steadiness, soundness, self-possession, right-mindedness, lucidity, reason, reasonableness, horse sense (*colloq.*).

lure—*Syn.* attract, entice, draw, pull, magnetize, decoy, charm, adduce, deceive, inveigle, coax, cajole, flatter, ensnare, trap, bait, delude, entangle, enmesh, trick, induce, persuade, overcome, prevail, bewitch, charm, fascinate, wheedle, seduce, vamp (*slang*). *Ant.* repel, repulse, antagonize, revolt, disgust, drive away, give the cold shoulder (*colloq.*), dissuade, dehort, discourage, dishearten, damp, deter, remonstrate, warn, keep back, turn aside, disenchant, admonish, deprecate.

lurk, *v.*—*Syn.* skulk, ambush, steal, slink, sneak, hide, prowl.

luscious—*Syn.* sweet, toothsome, palatable, pleasing, gratifying, satisfying, tasty, savory, agreeable, delectable, gusty, gustative, gustatory, gustful, appetizing, delicious, exquisite; ambrosial. *Ant.* unsavory, acrid, tart, sharp, sour, unpalatable, bitter, ill-flavored, nasty, nauseous, sickening, repulsive, disagreeable, insipid, savorless, acid, acidulous, acetose, astringent, sourish, vapid, flat.

lush, *adj.*—*Syn.* luxuriant, exuberant, abundant, profuse, opulent, juicy, teeming. *Ant.* sparse, barren, arid, meager.

lust, *n.—Syn.* concupiscence, desire, lechery, passion, avarice, craving, appetite, hankering, cupidity, wantonness.

luster, lustre—*Syn.* brightness, brilliancy, glossiness, gloss, splendor, glow, glare, sheen, effulgence, lucidity, luminosity, radiation, repute, renown, fame, distinction, celebrity, dignity, approbation, glory, honor, grandeur, reputation. *Ant.* darkness, gloom, obscurity, obscuration, murk, murkiness, shade, shadow, dimness, sombreness, cloudiness, duskiness, nebulosity, disrepute, dishonor, disgrace, humiliation, shame, baseness, stigma, reproach, turpitude, notoriety, infamy.

luxuriant—*Syn.* exuberant, abundant, superabundant, profuse, teeming, rank, dense, lush, copious, plenteous, uberous, proliferous, fertile. *Ant.* meagre, stunted, dwarfed, thin, shriveled, scanty, scarce, withered, barren, jejune, unproductive, infertile, fallow, unfruitful, sterile, arid.

lying—*Syn.* untruthful, mendacious, untrue, false, deceitful, fraudulent, dishonest, faithless, insincere, disingenuous, forsworn, evasive, hollow, deceptive, hypocritical, dissembling, pharisaical, mean, low, contemptible. *Ant.* true, truthful, candid, sincere, frank, open, honest, guileless, unreserved, ingenuous, undisguised, honorable, trustworthy, reliable, straightforward, true-blue (*colloq.*), veracious, scrupulous.

lyric, *adj.—Syn.* melodious, poetic, musical, emotional, singing. *Ant.* tuneless, harsh, grating, cacophonous.

M

macabre, *adj.—Syn.* gruesome, horrid, fearful, grim, deathly, lurid, appalling, ghastly, grisly, repulsive.

Machiavellian, *adj.—Syn.* intri-
guing, sly, subtle, insidious, cunning, deceitful, wily, tricky, crafty.

machination—*Syn.* scheme, plot, design, purpose, ruse, conspiracy, intrigue, cabal, artifice, dodge, plan, project, device, maneuver, stratagem. *Ant.* artlessness, simplicity, sincerity, candor, honesty, unsophistication, plainness, bluntness, openness, frankness, ingenuousness, naïveté, guilelessness, straightforwardness.

machine, *n.—Syn.* engine, apparatus, motor, appliance, instrument, contrivance, tool, mechanism, automatism.

mad—*Syn.* insane, crazy, deranged, distracted, wild, raging, furious, rabid, frantic, frenzied, violent, lunatic, cracked (*colloq.*), maniacal, frenetic, buggy (*slang*), bughouse (*slang*), cuckoo (*slang*), ravening, infuriate, raving, fierce, convulsed, unhinged, daft, demented, moonstruck, unsettled, crackbrained, scatterbrained, addlepated (*colloq.*), screwy (*slang*). *Ant.* normal, steady, settled, calm, cool, collected, self-possessed, sober, rational, lucid, sane, clear-headed, perspicacious, acute, sharp, smart, brainy, intelligent, discerning, wide-awake, bright, nimble-witted, clever, cunning, wise, sage, sapient, reasonable, rational, sound, sensible, sagacious, strong-minded.

madden, *v.—Syn.* infuriate, exasperate, inflame, enrage, irritate, anger, provoke.

magic—*Syn.* occultism, legerdemain, witchery, superstition, conjuring, sorcery, jugglery, presagement, prognostication, soothsaying, fortunetelling, omen, prediction, vaticination, forecast, augury, foreboding, horoscopes, horoscopy, astrology, astromancy, genethliacs, genethliacism, genethlialogy, divination. (To these may be added many terms covering different forms of divination, and expressive of ancient superstitions and beliefs, as aëromacy, crystallomancy, chiromancy, pyromancy, lithomancy, etc.)

magnanimous—*Syn.* high-minded, generous, noble, exalted, great-souled, honorable, lofty, dignified, noble-minded, princely, kingly, great-hearted, large-hearted, chivalrous, heroic, sublime. *Ant.* selfish, timeserving, mean, corrupt, depraved, ungenerous, venal, mercenary, covetous, miserly, narrow-minded, self-seeking, egotistical, illiberal, close, suspicious, doubting, self-interested, hoggish, grasping, greedy, self-indulgent.

magnificent—*Syn.* grand, splendid, noble, gorgeous, sublime, princely, kingly, royal, surpassing, transcendant, glorious, superb, stately, brilliant, radiant, beautiful, fine, artistic, ostentatious, showy, flashy, flashing, majestic, gaudy, garish, sumptuous, spectacular. *Ant.* plain, common, commonplace, ordinary, normal, informal, unpretentious, dull, ugly, inartistic, misshapen, misproportioned, dumpy, dowdy, uncouth, ungraceful, gross, offensive, repulsive, dingy, repellent, forbidding, grim, disfigured, dim, blurred, unshapely, smeared, blotted, discolored.

magnify, *v.*—*Syn.* enlarge, amplify, aggrandize, enhance, increase, expand, augment, exaggerate.

magnitude—*Syn.* size, volume, largeness, bulk, extent, greatness, bigness, highness, measure, extension, mass, quantity, amplitude, enormity, multitude, muchness, vastness, might, power, intensity, importance, grandeur, dignity, expanse, proportions. *Ant.* littleness, smallness, thinness, paucity, slenderness, insignificance, mediocrity, minimum, modicum, particle, grain, atom, molecule, handful, snip, bit, morsel, crumb, fragment, mite, chip, driblet, splinter, iota, speck.

maiden, *adj.*—*Syn.* unexperienced, virgin, vestal, youthful, pure, fresh, untouched, untried, unused.

maim, *v.*—*Syn.* cripple, damage, disfigure, lame, mangle, mutilate, spoil.

main, *adj.*—*Syn.* principal, chief, prime, necessary, leading, primary, foremost.

maintain—*Syn.* support, sustain, hold, uphold, defend, contend, assert, preserve, carry, bear, keep, continue, vindicate, prove, confirm, bear out. *Ant.* deny, reject, refuse, cast off, forsake, abandon, desert, leave, quit, depart, retire, withdraw, withhold, denounce, condemn.

majestic—*Syn.* stately, grand, impressive, noble, august, dignified, splendid, sublime, imposing, solemn, affecting, important, towering, high, mighty, eminent, renowned, distinguished, illustrious, prominent, exalted. *Ant.* mean, low, small, diminutive, little, inferior, humble, subordinate, shabby, petty, insignificant, trifling, common, obscure, unpretentious, ridiculous, paltry, imperfect, unadorned, contemptible, poor, flimsy, second-rate, dilapidated, defective.

major, *adj.*—*Syn.* greater, preponderant, principal, first, dominant, salient, chief, larger, superior.

make—*Syn.* do, form, construct, fabricate, forge, contrive, compose, produce, turn out, perform, execute, constitute, effect, originate, shape, create, build, cause, establish, frame, manufacture, generate, beget, complete, perfect, achieve, fashion, accomplish. *Ant.* break, burst, destroy, demolish, wreck, scatter, tumble, abolish, ruin, overthrow, overturn, pull down, smash, crash, batter, ravage, dismantle, raze, level, mutilate, disfigure, deform, distort, twist, warp, undo, injure, impair, damage, mar, deface, shatter, subvert, eradicate, exterminate, remove, obliterate, annihilate, end, extirpate, crack, crush, split, sunder.

makeshift, *adj.—Syn.* immediate, substitute, momentary, stopgap, expedient, temporary.

malady, *n.—Syn.* illness, disorder, infirmity, ailment, disease, indisposition, sickness.

male, *adj.—Syn.* masculine, virile, mannish, manlike, manful, manly, potent. *Ant.* female, womanly, effeminate.

malediction—*Syn.* curse, execration, imprecation, anathema, maranatha, proscription, excommunication, fulmination, denunciation, vituperation, wrath, damning, damnation, invocation of evil, condemnation, commination, vilification, disparagement. *Ant.* blessing, benediction, benison, commendation, approval, invocation of good, approbation, praise, esteem, estimation, admiration.

malefactor—*Syn.* evildoer, wrongdoer, transgressor, criminal, convict, villain, rascal, scoundrel, hellhound, rakehell, rounder (*slang*), wretch, jailbird, culprit, delinquent, felon, murderer, outlaw, scamp, scapegrace, outcast, vagabond, varlet, rapscallion, rogue, rowdy, ruffian, rough, black sheep, hoodlum, sinner, larrikin [*Aus.*], tough (*colloq.*), blackguard. *Ant.* model, example, exemplar, pattern, hero, helper, philanthropist, paragon, brick (*slang*), trump (*slang*), saint, white man (*slang*), virgin, innocent, Madonna, benefactor, lalapaloosa (*slang*), humdinger (*slang*), good man, good woman.

malevolent—*Syn.* malignant, spiteful, malicious, evil, evil-minded, ill-disposed, virulent, ill-intentioned, evil-disposed, malign, rancorous, bitter, envenomed, caustic, spiteful, treacherous. *Ant.* amiable, cordial, soft-hearted, kind, kindly, tender, considerate, warm-hearted, indulgent, gracious, complacent, kind-hearted, good-natured, sympathetic, beneficent, charitable, benevolent.

malice—*Syn.* spite, rancor, animosity, ill-feeling, grudge, enmity, implacability, bitterness, hatred, abhorrence, detestation, antipathy, umbrage, repugnance, dislike, resentment, venom, acerbity, malignance, malignity, evil disposition, bad blood. *Ant.* benevolence, unselfishness, kindliness, sympathy, charity, philanthropy, good will, warm-heartedness, affection, *bonhomie* [*Fr.*], goodness, kindness, amiability, consideration, indulgence, benignity, compassion, cordiality.

malicious—*see* **malevolent.**

malign, *adj.—Syn.* malevolent, inimical, pernicious, sinister, malicious, poisonous, malignant, baneful. *Ant.* benign, favorable, auspicious, kindly.

malign, *v.—Syn.* calumniate, traduce, blacken, besmirch, asperse, vilify, depreciate, revile, slander, libel, defame. *Ant.* defend, vindicate, justify, praise.

malodorous, *adj.—Syn.* stinking, rank, foul, fetid, noisome, rancid, musty, putrid, high, gamy, mephitic, noxious.

maltreat—*Syn.* injure, abuse, castigate, ill-treat, punish, maul, strike, harm, damage, smash, beat, pummel, hurt, bruise, misuse, oppress, scathe, persecute, scratch, victimize, tyrannize. *Ant.* benefit, treat kindly, soothe, encourage, favor, befriend, countenance, help, assist, aid, comfort, console, assuage, refresh, inspirit, appease, sustain, support, gratify, satisfy, cheer, enliven, animate, gladden.

mammoth, *adj.—Syn.* huge, gigantic, tremendous, colossal, immense, enormous, elephantine, titanic.

manage—*Syn.* regulate, govern, direct, show, control, conduct, administer, wield, influence, carry on, care for, take care of, hoard, husband, watch, sway, dominate, actuate, rule, master, prevail, pull the strings (*slang*), superintend, supervise, oversee, guide, advise, steer, run, head, experiment, officiate. *Ant.* mismanage, bungle, botch, blunder, fumble, muff, mar, misdirect, misapply, misconduct, misguide, make a mess of (*colloq.*), overshoot the mark, put one's foot in it (*colloq.*), make hash of, boggle, spoil, fall down, fail.

maneuver, *n.—Syn.* artifice, tactic, movement, feint, ruse, plot, wile, stratagem, scheme.

mangle—*Syn.* tear, mutilate, lacerate, wound, injure, cripple, maim, rend, hock, hamstring, disfigure, cut, slay, slit, slice, separate, carve, butcher, bruise.

maniac, *n.—Syn.* madman, lunatic, screwball, crank, nut, bat.

manifest, *adj.—Syn.* clear, visible, evident, plain, apparent, open, aboveboard, obvious, definite, defined, unmistakable, self-evident, explicit, undisguised. *Ant.* buried, concealed, hidden, disguised, covered, cloaked, obscured, puzzling, mystifying, complex, intricate, hard, difficult, twisted, warped, abstruse.

manifest, *v.—Syn.* reveal, show, discover, exhibit, display, declare, disclose, unveil, unfold, unmask, divulge, expose, tell, proclaim, publish, uncover, open up, lay bare. *Ant.* bury, conceal, hide, cover, cloak, screen, mask, cloud, curtain, disguise, dissemble, withhold, secrete, veil, obscure, puzzle, mystify.

manifold, *adj.—Syn.* diverse, numerous, multitudinous, several, various, many, sundry.

mankind, *n.—Syn.* humanity, man, men, humankind, mortality, people.

manly—*Syn.* brave, courageous, undaunted, fearless, firm, staunch, dignified, stately, noble, valiant, valorous, high-spirited, plucky, lion-hearted, intrepid, gallant, resolute, bold, audacious, stout-hearted, confident, self-reliant. *Ant.* cowardly, timid, afraid, nervous, shaky, apprehensive, restless, faint-hearted, bashful, retiring, old-womanish, anile, senile, diffident, vacillating, hesitant, craven, skulking, cringing, fawn-

ing, truckling, slavish, servile, effeminate, pigeon-hearted.

manner—*Syn.* habit, custom, behavior, appearance, aspect, look, way, air, style, mood, mien, mode, expression, description, character, stamp, means, method, fashion, demeanor, guise, deportment, carriage, bearing, approach.

manners—*Syn.* morals, conduct, behavior, habits, routine, practice, breeding, politeness, suavity, urbanity, affectation, vanity, mode, vogue, decorum, propriety, conventionality, taste, *savoir-faire* [*Fr.*], etiquette, form, formality. *Ant.* vulgarity, vulgarism, rudeness, boorishness, grossness, misconduct, misbehavior, coarseness, ill-breeding, rowdyism, blackguardism, barbarism, ruffianism, ribaldry.

manufacture—see **make.**

many, *adj.—Syn.* numerous, several, manifold, diverse, various, countless.

map, *n.—Syn.* chart, plot, scheme, plan, design, outline, graph, representation, program.

mar—*Syn.* deform, distort, impair, injure, hurt, botch, spoil, deface, disfigure, mutilate, twist, warp, control, harm, damage, despoil, dilapidate, waste, bungle, impede, obstruct. *Ant.* beautify, adorn, repair, improve, ornament, decorate, garnish, garland, mend, refresh, vivify, embellish, enrich, furbish, polish, gild, varnish, paint, lacquer, bedizen, prink, titivate (*colloq.*), spruce up (*colloq.*).

marauder, *n.—Syn.* raider, pillager, brigand, looter, free-booter, pirate, plunderer, sacker.

march, *n.—Syn.* journey, expedition, promenade, hike, saunter, tour, outing, walk, peregrination, trek, ramble, perambulation, constitutional (*colloq.*), stroll, airing, progress, advancement, course, progressiveness, itinerary, route.

march, *v.—Syn.* walk, move, advance, step out, go on, proceed, space, step, tread, tramp, travel, journey, stroll, saunter, ramble, roam, rove, patrol, prowl, range, promenade, peregrinate, progress, go ahead, forge ahead. *Ant.* rest, pause, halt, stand, stay, stop, remain, heave to, pull up, anchor, recede, retreat, return, revert, regrade, retrograde, back, back out, wheel, countermarch, turn round.

margin—*Syn.* brink, edge, border, verge, brim, lip, brow, skirt, rim, fringe, flange, bank, shore, strand. *Ant.* interior, surface, area, background, hinterland, extension, width, breadth, depth, superficies, thickness.

marital, *adj.*—*Syn.* connubial, wedded, matrimonial, nuptial, conjugal. *Ant.* single, celibate, bachelor, spinster.

maritime—*Syn.* nautical, naval, marine, oceanic, pelagic, seagoing, hydrographic, Neptunian, seafaring, aquatic, natatorial. *Ant.* earthy, earthly, terrestrial, terrene, geodetic, midland, inland, earthbound, landlocked, tellurian, telluric, alluvial.

mark, *n.*—*Syn.* sign, symbol, token, design, brand, badge, line, trace, tracing, drawing, impress, impression, stamp, note, engraving, device, representation, type, emblem, character, figure, stroke, score, stripe, imprint, letter, index.

mark, *v.*—*Syn.* stamp, impress, print, form, make, brand, label, sign, imprint, engrave, designate, note, trace, insert, enter, jot down, record, chronicle, commemorate, register, list, inscribe, represent, tick, nick, indicate, earmark, ticket, docket.

market, *n.*—*Syn.* marketplace, bazaar, shop, emporium, exchange, mart, store, sale.

marriage—*Syn.* espousal, espousals, spousals, union, wedlock, nuptials, wedding, conjugality, matrimony, match, nuptial knot, nuptial tie. *Ant.* celibacy, bachelorhood, spinsterhood, widowhood, singleness, single blessedness, maidenhood, virginity,

spouselessness, divorce.

marsh, *n.*—*Syn.* swamp, fen, bog, morass, slough, quagmire.

marshal, *v.*—*Syn.* arrange, assemble, order, organize, collect, rank, systematize.

martial—*Syn.* warlike, soldierly, hostile, brave, courageous, military, belligerent, bellicose, militant, combative, bristling, embattled, armor-bearing. *Ant.* peaceful, quiet, pacific, noncombatant, submissive, meek, mild, conciliatory, humble, pacificatory, yielding, unresisting, pliant.

marvel—*Syn.* miracle, prodigy, wonder, phenomenon, freak, monster, monstrosity, sensation, curiosity, amazement, astonishment, bewilderment.

marvelous—*Syn.* wonderful, wondrous, miraculous, phenomenal, curious, amazing, astonishing, astounding, surprising, unexpected, stupendous, mysterious, awful, overwhelming, prodigious, indescribable, unspeakable, inexpressible, ineffable. *Ant.* plain, common, normal, ordinary, simple, conventional, usual, natural, commonplace, matter-of-fact, insignificant, unimportant, little, small, inconsiderable, trifling, trivial, paltry, petty, piddling, frivolous, shallow, shabby, meagre, miserable, contemptible.

masculine—*Syn.* manly, mannish, manlike, manful, male, virile, strong, robust, brave, bold, daring. *Syn.* feminine, womanly, womanish, effeminate, female, delicate, modest, tender, compassionate.

mask—*Syn.* conceal, cloak, cover, hide, screen, disguise, dissemble, shade, curtain, veil, muffle, camouflage, hoodwink, mystify, befog, stifle, hush, smother, suppress. *Ant.* unmask, uncover, unveil, open up, make known, inform, tell, be plain, enlighten, explain, announce, disclose, relate, record, report, declare, proclaim, expose.

mass—*Syn.* bulk, heap, lump, whole, sum, total, amount, aggregate, quantity, density, gravity, size, muchness, volume, magnitude, fullness, body, dimension, amplitude, proportions, ponderosity, ponderousness, weight, solidity, consistence, viscosity, spissitude, thickness. *Ant.* buoyancy, lightness, imponderability, fluff, froth, air, airiness, rarity, rarefaction, tenuity, gas, light, electricity, magnetism, heat, vacuum, space, emptiness.

massage, *v.—Syn.* rub, knead, stroke, pound.

massive—*Syn.* huge, heavy, dense, ponderous, weighty, large, cumbrous, ponderable, unwieldy, cumbersome, bulky, static, solid. *Ant.* light, airy, imponderable, imponderous, sublimated, suberose, buoyant, volatile, foamy, soft, pliant, flexible.

master—*Syn.* chief, leader, ruler, governor, director, lord, principal, overseer, superintendent, supervisor, boss (*colloq.*), teacher, instructor, preceptor, pedagogue, guide, mentor, judge, arbiter, sage, savant, wizard, pundit, sahib, patriarch, chieftain, commander, commandant. *Ant.* servant, slave, follower, attendant, flunkey, valet, subject, menial, henchman, dependent, vassal, serf, subordinate, disciple, pupil, novice, neophyte, learner, beginner, retainer, operative, laborer, drudge, bondman, servitor, helot, mercenary, hireling, hanger-on.

masterpiece, *n.—Syn.* magnum opus, forte, chef d'oeuvre, masterwork, paragon, peak.

mastery—*Syn.* ascendancy, dominance, dominion, control, power, influence, superiority, rule, sway, government, success, advantage, conquest, victory, subjugation, walkover, triumph, exultation. *Ant.* failure, miscarriage, inefficiency, impotence, incapacity, blunder, blundering, stumble, stumbling, breakdown, mishap, defeat, subjugation, deathblow, downfall, wreck, ruin.

matchless—*Syn.* peerless, incomparable, inimitable, surpassing, consummate, unparalleled, unrivaled, supreme, unequaled, perfect, complete, faultless, superior. *Ant.* common, commonplace, ordinary, mean, meagre, petty, paltry, second-rate, cheap, poor, imperfect, impaired, damaged, mutilated, faulty, defective, secondary, inferior, one-horse (*slang*).

mate, *n.—Syn.* companion, spouse, intimate, pal, chum, comrade, associate, consort, husband, wife.

material, *adj.—Syn.* corporal, corporeal, bodily, physical, sensible, tangible, solid, substantial, ponderable, palpable, somatic. *Ant.* immaterial, incorporeal, airy, shadowy, misty, ethereal, bodiless, discarnate, unearthly, spiritual, spiritistic, disembodied, ghostly.

material, *n.—Syn.* substance, matter, provision, equipment, gear, outfit, stuff, fabric.

matrimonial, *adj.—Syn.* marital, nuptial, conjugal, wedded, connubial.

matter—*Syn.* substance, substantiality, body, corporeality, corporeity, stuff, element, materiality, materialness, materialization, object, article, thing, physical world or nature. *Ant.* nihility, nothingness, immateriality, immaterialness, incorporeity, spirit, soul, ego, astral body, ghost, apparition, vision, phantom, phantasm, vision, thought, fancy, imagination.

mature—*Syn.* adolescent, pubescent, ripe, nubile, adult, full-grown, full-blown, matronly, womanly, marriageable, prime, virile, ready, fit, perfect, complete, prepared, mellow, settled, seasoned, developed, man-like, maturated. *Ant.* immature, unripe, undeveloped, incomplete, green, fresh, new, unprepared, premature, rudimental, rudimentary, callow, raw, crude, unfitted, unready, imperfect, defective, faulty, weak, deficient, inexperienced.

maudlin, *adj.—Syn.* sentimental, emotional, mushy, effusive, silly.

mausoleum—*Syn.* tomb, crypt, vault, grave, sepulchre, catacomb, pit, tumulus, mound, barrow, cenotaph, last home, long home, narrow bed, tower of silence, *dokhma* [*Per.*].

maxim—*Syn.* text, aphorism, precept, proverb, adage, saw, saying, byword, apothegm, epigram, moral, *bon mot* [*Fr.*], witticism, repartee, truism, axiom. *Ant.* absurdity, blunder, nonsense, quibble, joke, extravaganza, bull, bathos, buncombe, jargon, gibberish, balderdash, fiddlefaddle (*colloq.*), flapdoodle (*colloq.*), bombast, claptrap, twaddle, tomfoolery, crap (*slang*), fudge, bunk, poppycock, palaver, piffle (*colloq.*), rigmarole, moonshine (*slang*).

maze—*Syn.* tangle, entanglement, twist, winding, convolution, intricacy, confusion, sinuosity, sinuousness, meandering, torsion, labyrinth, perplexity, coil, crookedness, difficulty, enigma, riddle, puzzle, ignorance, benightedness. *Ant.* simplicity, ease, easiness, facility, plainness, smoothness, flatness, roundness, circle, circularity, facility, disentanglement, clearness, disencumbrance, perception, knowledge, enlightenment.

meager, meagre—*Syn.* thin, poor, small, slender, emaciated, lank, scanty, barren, withered, dry, starved, diminutive, inconsiderable, short, incomplete, deficient, insufficient, scrimp, sparing, · stinted. *Ant.* sufficient, ample, abundant, luxuriant, lavish, plenteous, copious, abounding, replete, chock-full, liberal, unstinted, wide, extended, expanded, outspread, outstretched, large, fat, corpulent, big, complete, full, excessive, unlimited.

mean, *adj.—Syn.* low, base, debased, vile, despicable, degraded, contemptible, ignoble, abject, disgraceful, shameless, shameful, dishonorable, deceitful, paltry, pitiful, shabby, beggarly, stingy, miserly, scrubby, parsimonious, penurious, piddling, close-fisted (*colloq.*), ·tight-fisted (*colloq.*), sordid, mercenary, discreditable, disreputable, niggardly, selfish. *Ant.* generous, unselfish, liberal, openhearted, honorable, noble, noble-minded, charitable, philanthropic, helpful, compassionate, indulgent, bounteous, bountiful, unsparing, ungrudging, free, munificent, prodigal, extravagant, profuse, lavish, fullhanded, improvident, distinguished, respected, high, eminent.

mean, *v.—Syn.* intend, purpose, signify, indicate, design, denote, contemplate, decide, aim at, determine, predetermine, propose, undertake, pursue, purport, imply, drive at, allude to, speak of, touch on, point to. *Ant.* mean nothing, jabber, babble, palaver, talk childishly, humbug, confuse, bamboozle, mystify, puzzle, shuffle, waver, sidestep, speak foolishly, dissimulate, pretend, deceive, delude, beguile, mislead.

meaning, *n.—Syn.* significance, intent, aim, explanation, import, purpose, sense, denotation.

means, *n.—Syn.* resource, material, wealth, income, property, expedient, measure.

measure—*Syn.* quantity, magnitude, amplitude, measurement, degree, grade, amount, extent, range, scope, pitch, reach, plan, plot, design, scheme, outline, sketch, draft, bill, proposal, project, proposition, suggestion.

measureless — *Syn.* unbounded, unlimited, boundless, limitless, vast, infinite, unending, eternal, immense, immeasurable, illimitable, interminable, indefinite, incalculable, exhaustless, incomprehensible, endless, termless, unmeasured, illimited, perpetual. *Ant.* definite, precise, bounded, limited, terminable, comprehensible, short, transient, ephemeral, transitory, evanescent, passing, brief, temporary, restricted, shallow, confined, measured, meager, little, small, inconsiderable, trifling, trivial, circumscribed, contracted, measurable, defined, dimensional.

mechanical, *adj.*—*Syn.* instinctive, reflex, automatic, unreasoned, impulsive, involuntary, stereotyped.

meddle—*Syn.* interpose, interfere, intermeddle, mix, tamper with, obtrude, butt in (*slang*), horn in (*slang*), dip one's nose in (*slang*), take part in, put a finger in the pie (*slang*). *Ant.* keep off, shun, hang back, refrain from, steer clear, ignore, stay away, turn back to, avoid.

meddlesome—*Syn.* obtrusive, intrusive, meddling, audacious, impertinent, officious, obstructive, impedient, impeditive, hindering, encumbering, obstructing, interrupting, interfering, embarrassing. *Ant.* aiding, assisting, helping, encouraging, sustaining, supporting, ministering, obliging, accommodating, seconding, countenancing, advocating, cheering, stimulating, abetting.

medicine, *n.*—*Syn.* remedy, specific, treatment, medicament, simple, cure, drug.

mediocre, *adj.*—*Syn.* commonplace, passable, middling, fair, average, normal, ordinary.

meditate—*Syn.* study, contemplate, consider, ruminate, ponder, revolve, project, reflect, deliberate, cogitate, excogitate, speculate, reason, think, brood over, concentrate, study. *Ant.* relax the mind, take it easy (*colloq.*), divert attention, dismiss from mind, be inattentive, turn from, neglect, ignore.

medium, *adj.*—*Syn.* middle, middling, mediocre, intermediate, average, commonplace, ordinary, middle-class, normal, moderate, so-so (*colloq.*), fair to middling (*colloq.*). *Ant.* good, excellent, superior, fine, tran-

scendent, choice, rare, tiptop, topping, eminent, surpassing, bad, worthless, inferior, valueless, useless, cheap, low, base, mean, below par, under the standard, short of the mark.

medium, *n.*—*Syn.* means, channel, instrument, organ, agent, oracle, operator, performer, executor, go-between, soothsayer, fortune teller, prophet, sibyl, seer, clairvoyant, intermediary, representative, substitute.

medley—*Syn.* mixture, mingling, confusion, variance, variety, miscellany, diversity, disorder, diffusion, admixture, intermixture, derangement, hodgepodge. *Ant.* arrangement, order, uniformity, proportion, system, orderliness, simpleness, simplification, method, regularity, normality, normalcy, grouping, allotment.

meek—*Syn.* humble, mild, gentle, unassuming, unpretentious, unostentatious, modest, retiring, bashful, soft, yielding, compliant, deferential, lowly, submissive, subdued, demure, imperturbable, dispassionate, serene, tranquil, quiet, reserved, placid, tolerant, patient, resigned, forbearing, lamblike. *Ant.* harsh, cruel, overbearing, tyrannical, assertive, proud, haughty, disdainful, vain, conceited, bold, arrogant, presumptuous, presuming, wrathful, wilful, resentful, choleric, obstinate, fiery, furious, fierce, raging, revengeful, vengeful, vindictive, stubborn, high-spirited, lofty, contentious, contemptuous, impertinent, impudent, toplofty (*colloq.*), swanky (*slang*), pompous, self-important, high-toned, supercilious, bumptious, consequential.

meet, *v.*—*Syn.* encounter, find, fulfill, greet, gather, unite, intersect, collide, confront, touch.

melancholy, *adj.*—*Syn.* depressed, dispirited, low-spirited, gloomy, pensive, dejected, discontented, sad, sorrowful, glum, blue, despondent, sombre, downcast, heavy-hearted, dismal, funereal, spiritless, mournful, joyless, heavy, dull, dolesome, doleful, woe-begone, hypochondriac, chapfallen, saturnine, lugubrious, lackadaisical, bilious, jaundiced, discouraged, forlorn, dull, atrabilious, moody, sulky, hypped or hipped (*colloq.*). *Ant.* cheery, cheering, cheerful, gay, lively, merry, laughing, light-hearted happy, smiling, blithe, devil-may-care, careless, chippy (*slang*), chipper (*slang*), bully (*slang*), fine, buoyant, exhilarated, frolicsome, debonair, light, sprightly, hilarious, jovial, jolly, jocose, jocular, jaunty, sportive, vivacious, animated, spirited, breezy, brisk, fresh, gleeful, playful, rollicking, dashing, fun-loving, frisky, pleasant, agreeable, amiable, bright, elated, jubilant, entertaining, inspiriting.

mellow—*Syn.* ripe, mature, perfected, seasoned, rich, full-flavored, soft, aged, pleasing, refined, intoxicated, tipsy, hearty, genial, jolly, gay. *Ant.* immature, hard, harsh, sour, acrid, tart, pungent, flat, stale, insipid, dull, steady, sober, serious, temperate, solemn.

melodious—*Syn.* musical, harmonious, agreeable, pleasing, euphonic, sweet, tuneful, dulcet, accordant, assonant, unisonant, soft, clear, silvery, silvertoned, euphonious. *Ant.* harsh, grating, unmusical, dissonant, inharmonious, discordant, tuneless, cacophonic, cacophonous, jarring, ear-splitting, raucous, unmelodious, jangling, stridulous, shrill, skirling, strident, ear-piercing, hollow, sepulchral.

melody—*Syn.* music, harmony, symphony, unison, concord, agreement, measure, rhythm, tune, syncopation, orchestration, harmonization. *Ant.* discord, dissonance, disagreement, caterwauling, cacophony, charivari, harshness, stridor, stridulation, tunelessness, discordance.

melt—*Syn.* liquefy, dissolve, soften, mollify, thaw, render, deliquesce, decrease, diminish, pass away, vanish, waste, squander, spend. *Ant.* freeze, coagulate, thicken, densify, stick, adhere, take hold, solidify, solidate, consolidate, congeal, condense, inspissate, petrify, incrassate, regelate.

member, *n.*—*Syn.* constituent, segment, part, unit, adherent, element, limb, component.

memorable—*Syn.* extraordinary, uncommon, striking, vivid, important, surpassing, unforgettable, crucial, critical, remarkable, noticeable, prominent, conspicuous, illustrious, distinguished, famous, great, particular, momentous, notable, significant. *Ant.* unimportant, trifling, trivial, petty, foolish, frivolous, uneventful, uninteresting, ridiculous, absurd, idle, puerile, silly, farcical, insignificant, nugatory, light, inconsiderable, inconsequential, irrelevant.

memorial—*Syn.* memento, souvenir, remembrance, monument, tablet, slab, pillar, tombstone, headstone, column, shaft, obelisk, monolith, mausoleum, record, inscription.

memory—*Syn.* recollection, remembrance, retrospect, retrospection, reminiscence. *Ant.* oblivion, obliviousness, forgetfulness, oversight, unconsciousness, Lethe, obliteration, amnesia, effacement.

menace—*Syn.* threat, evil intention, intimidation, warning, vengeance, revenge, fear, trepidation, notice, forecast, prophecy, writing on the wall. *Ant.* peace, peace of mind, tranquillity, peacefulness, quietness, calmness, friendship, repose, passiveness, serenity, poise, equanimity.

mend—*Syn.* improve, repair, rectify, correct, amend, restore, patch up, reform, ameliorate, better, revise, refine, revive, refresh, renew, touch up, bolster up, enhance, put in order. *Ant.*

deteriorate, weaken, destroy, injure, hurt, ruin, impair, damage, mar, despoil, dilapidate, disfigure, mutilate, blemish, deface, deform, smash.

mendacity—*Syn.* lying, falsehood, prevarication, misrepresentation, calumny, perjury, deception, falsification, untruth, invention, fabrication, subreption, perversion, suppression, distortion. *Ant.* truth, truthfulness, veracity, candor, frankness, openness, honesty, probity, fidelity, faithfulness, sincerity, ingenuousness, artlessness, square dealing.

menial, *adj.*—*Syn.* servile, mean, lowly, abject, humble, ignoble, base, degrading.

mental—*Syn.* intellectual, psychical, psychological, metaphysical, rational, subjective, subliminal, percipient, appercipient, subconscious, telepathic, psychic, clairvoyant. *Ant.* incogitant, incogitative, fatuous, unreasoning, thoughtless, inane, vacuous, unintelligent, idiotic, imbecile, brainless.

mercenary, *adj.*—*Syn.* venal, sordid, selfish, hired, avaricious.

merchandise, *n.*—*Syn.* stock, wares, goods, produce, commodities.

merchant, *n.*—*Syn.* dealer, agent, businessman, trader, factor, shopkeeper.

merciful—*Syn.* kind, lenient, gentle, tender, gracious, feeling, compassionate, clement, kindhearted, pitiful, sympathetic, humane, soft-hearted, forbearing. *Ant.* unkind, cruel, inhuman, ruthless, cold-blooded, stony-hearted, barbarous, truculent, savage, tyrannical, pitiless, inclement, merciless, unmerciful, relentless.

merciless—*Syn.* see ANTONYMS for **merciful** above. *Ant.* see SYNONYMS for **merciful** above.

mercurial—*Syn.* changeable, variable, fluctuating, inconstant, unsteady, unstable, restless, erratic, excitable, fickle, capricious, uneasy, irresolute, wavering, feverish, fidgety. *Ant.* steady,

stable, settled, constant, unvarying, unchangeable, immutable, invariable, unyielding, fixed, steadfast, unalterable, obstinate, stubborn, imperturbable, tranquil, calm, dispassionate, patient, composed, cool, collected, easy-going, cool-headed.

mercy—*Syn.* pity, lenity, forbearance, charity, compassion, sympathy, humanity, clemency, leniency, soft-heartedness, indulgence, toleration, tolerance, forgiveness, favor, mildness, tenderness, gentleness, kindness, lenience, pardon, benignity, grace, benevolence, blessing. *Ant.* cruelty, severity, harshness, rigor, hardness, punishment, revenge, vengeance, sternness, justice, penalty, implacability, inclemency, tyranny, domination, arrogance, pitilessness, intolerance, coercion, oppression, despotism, austerity, terrorism, torture, maltreatment, chastisement, castigation, conviction, condemnation, proscription, banishment, sequestration, infliction, affliction, inhumanity, torment, vexation, pain.

meretricious, *adj.*—*Syn.* spurious, tawdry, pretentious, false, deceptive, misleading, sham. *Ant.* genuine, authentic, bona fide, true.

merge, *v.*—*Syn.* blend, unite, mix, unify, amalgamate, integrate, coalesce.

merit—*Syn.* worth, worthiness, desert, goodness, excellence, reward, regard, honor, appreciation, value, credit, virtue, nobleness, rectitude, morality, righteousness, character, manhood, stability, honesty, truth, candor, sincerity. *Ant.* vice, dishonor, demerit, shame, scandal, wrongdoing, wickedness, treachery, betrayal, immorality, laxity, depravity, demoralization, profligacy, flagrancy, badness, vileness, corruption, injustice, wrong, oppression.

meritorious—*Syn.* worthy, praiseworthy, generous, noble, commendable, estimable, admirable, good, excellent, honorable, fine, exemplary, laudable, disinterested, unselfish, magnanimous, liberal, chivalrous, spirited, heroic, honest, conscientious, straightforward, high-principled, righteous, self-denying, self-sacrificing, philanthropic, charitable. *Ant.* unworthy, dishonorable, shameless, treacherous, dishonest, blameworthy, reprehensible, vicious, improper, wrong, immoral, depraved, corrupt, demoralized, iniquitous, dissolute, profligate, disreputable, discreditable, unprincipled, unrighteous, infamous, villainous, scandalous, flagrant, flagitious.

merriment—*Syn.* gaiety, hilarity, frolic, jollity, joviality, mirth, cheer, cheerfulness, glee, light-heartedness, exhilaration, sport, sportiveness, merrymaking, joy, joyousness, jocularity, levity, laughter, fun, frolic, tomfoolery, buffoonery, mummery, mockery, *Ant.* sorrow, sadness, dullness, gloom, gloominess, melancholy, dejection, heaviness, blues (*colloq.*), dumps (*colloq.*), doldrums, woe, despondency, depression, hopelessness, despair, misfortune, hypochondriasis, dreariness, mourning, disconsolateness.

merry—*Syn.* gay, cheerful, happy, jovial, jocular, joyous, mirthful, lively, sprightly, boisterous, hilarious, tophole (*slang*), spirited, frolicsome, devil-may-care, rollicking, vivacious, animated, buoyant, light-hearted, lightsome, sportive, sporting, playful, jubilant, entertaining, laughable, festive, gleeful, elated, blithe, blithesome, revelling, rejoicing. *Ant.* sad, sorrowful, doleful, miserable, dull, wretched, gloomy, downcast, melancholy, moping, blue, mournful, scowling, frowning, crying, weeping, moaning, groaning, lamenting, grieving, weary, worried, tired, bored, pessimistic, drowsy, monotonous, tedious, splenetic, pensive, hypochondriacal, bilious, jaundiced, jaded, grim, for-

lorn, sombre, solemn, saturnine, tristful, doleful, woebegone, lachrymose, atrabilious, listless, languid, lackadaisical, morose, moody.

mess—*Syn.* mixture, combination, compound, glutinous mass, waxy lump, medley, olla-podrida, potpourri, omnium-gatherum, jumble, hotchpotch, hodgepodge, muss (*colloq.*), disorder, disorganization, confusion, difficulty, tough proposition (*colloq.*), allowance, portion, ration.

message, *n.*—*Syn.* communication, news, letter, note, dispatch.

metamorphosis, *n.*—*Syn.* transformation, conversion, transmutation, change, transfiguration.

metaphorical—*Syn.* symbolical, allegorical, figurative, catachrestic, referential, allusive, comparative, anagogic, contrastive, antonomastic, euphuistic, ironic, colloquial.

method—*Syn.* order, system, arrangement, style, manner, vogue, custom, way, rule, regularity, mode, procedure, process, course, routine, tenor, form, adjustment, regulation, means, fashion. *Ant.* disorder, derangement, irregularity, discord, disunion, confusion, topsy-turvy, disarrangement, entanglement, mixture, mess, complexity, complication, intricacy, huddle, shuffle, muddle, displacement, misplacement, involvement.

meticulous, *adj.*—*Syn.* scrupulous, fastidious, precise, punctilious, particular, prissy, fussy, finical. *Ant.* careless, sloppy, remiss, casual.

mettle—*Syn.* spirit, animation, character, stamina, physical, endurance, courage, bravery, temperament, ardor, grit, determination, backbone (*slang*), nerve, valor, gallantry, intrepidity, manliness, manhood, dash, vim, vigor, hardihood, tenacity, resoluteness, energy, earnestness, intensity. *Ant.* fear, weakness, cowardice, timidity, funk (*colloq.*), pusillanimity, poltroonery, faintheartedness, shyness, effeminacy, yellowness (*slang*), yellow streak (*slang*), trepidation, dastardliness, dormancy, laziness, inertness, languor, sloth, passiveness, dullness, irresolution, tiredness, weariness, inactivity, latency, passivity, sluggishness, cowardliness.

mettlesome—*Syn.* spirited, animated, dashing, bold, brave, gallant, unafraid, rash, venturesome, active, vigorous, energetic, fiery, excitable, dynamic, chivalrous, courageous, nervy, high-spirited, plucky, manly, resolute, lion-hearted, valiant, valorous, daring, dauntless, self-reliant. *Ant.* cowardly, shrinking, yellow (*slang*), white-feathered (*colloq.*), white-livered (*colloq.*), dastardly, skulking, sneaking, timid, effeminate, pusillanimous, abject, weak, irresolute, timorous, mean-spirited, weak-minded, pigeon-hearted, spiritless.

microbe, *n.*—*Syn.* germ, bacillus, bacterium, micro-organism, virus.

microscopic, *adj.*—*Syn.* infinitesimal, tiny, wee, minimal, minute.

middle, *adj.*—*Syn.* central, median, mean, average, mediocre, halfway, intermediate.

mien—*Syn.* manner, aspect, appearance, condition, look, air, outline, feature, contour, expression, carriage, deportment, seeming, demeanor, visage, phiz (*slang*).

mighty—*Syn.* strong, powerful, great, resistless, forceful, potent, lusty, muscular, vigorous, robust, hardy, husky, puissant, indomitable, invincible, overpowering, unconquerable, manful, virile, doughty, strapping, stalwart. *Ant.* weak, puny, poor, infirm, delicate, flaccid, feeble, debilitated, powerless, effeminate, frail, tottering, doddering, anæmic, asthenic, enervated.

migratory—*Syn.* wandering, unsettled, transient, roving, roaming, strolling, vagrant, changeable, casual. *Ant.* settled, permanent, fixed, steady, unchanging, stable,

lasting, established, irremovable, continuing.

mild—*Syn.* soft, gentle, tender, kind, bland, meek, easy, mellow, sweet, savory, quiet, smooth, tranquil, untroubled, calm, peaceful, pacific, summery, genial, tepid, lukewarm, clement, lenient, indulgent, tolerant, compassionate, complaisant, imperturbable, easy-going, patient, lamblike. *Ant.* rough, rude, uncouth, harsh, unkind, ungentle, bluff, boisterous, brusque, abrupt, blustering, bullying, tyrannical, irritating, exacerbating, turbulent, unruly, disorderly, cold, bitter, biting, austere, arrogant, domineering, forceful, despotic, arbitrary, ruffled, perturbed, angry, irritable, agitated, violent.

militant, *adj.*—*Syn.* contentious, combative, fighting, aggressive, belligerent, pugnacious, hostile, active, combating. *Ant.* peaceful, pacific, acquiescent, submissive.

mimic—*Syn.* imitate, repeat, echo, re-echo, mock, ape, simulate, parody, burlesque, caricature, counterfeit, personate, reproduce, copy, represent, parody, forge, emulate, follow suit, model after, take pattern by, tread in the steps of.

mind—*Syn.* soul, spirit, intellect, understanding, belief, inclination, desire, sentiment, judgment, purpose, choice, will, liking, impetus, remembrance, recollection, memory, thought, sense, reason, faculty, consciousness, instinct, disposition, intelligence, rationality, mentality, intuition, perception, conception, intellectuality, percipience, apperception, capacity, wisdom, brains, genius, talent, reasoning. *Ant.* matter, substance, materiality, corporeity, substantiality, corporeality, corporality, body, stuff, element, all material substance, the physical world, the physical universe, material creation.

mindful—*Syn.* attentive, thoughtful, heedful, observant, watchful, caring for, regardful, observing, alert, alive to, occupied with, engrossed in. *Ant.* inattentive, heedless, careless, inadvertent, absent-minded, woolgathering (*dial*), distrait, bemused, day-dreaming, moonraking (*dial.*), dreamy, engrossed, rapt, dazed, preoccupied.

miniature, *adj.—Syn.* diminutive, small, minikin, little, tiny, minute.

minimize, *v.—Syn.* belittle, depreciate, degrade, fault, detract, disparage, derogate. *Ant.* magnify, exalt, extol, praise.

minister, *n.—Syn.* priest, parson, clergyman, preacher, divine, dominie, padre [*Fr.*], soggarth [*Ir.*], ecclesiastic, sky-pilot (*slang*), pulpiteer, sin-shifter (*Aus. slang*), churchman, pastor, abbé [*Fr.*], confessor, reverend, curé [*Fr.*], shepherd, hierophant, servant, official, ambassador, plenipotentiary, consul, representative. *Ant.* layman, catechumen, secularist, parishioner, learner, tyro, disciple, follower, student, neophyte, probationer, novice, recruit, renegade, apostate, turncoat, pervert.

minister, *v.—Syn.* serve, act, perform, aid, assist, help, succor, relieve, rescue, support, sustain, uphold, nourish, nurture, administer, tend, attend, wait on. *Ant.* obstruct, impede, bar, interdict, stop, check, encumber, hinder, embarrass, counteract, interfere, hamper, incommode, restrain, oppose.

minor, *adj.—Syn.* lesser, subordinate, small, inferior, unimportant, junior, secondary, lower.

minstrel, *n.—Syn.* bard, rhymer, musician, player, poet, scald, scop, troubadour, minnesinger.

minute—Syn. small, microscopic, diminutive, little, wee [*Sc.*], insignificant, atomic, inconsiderable, miniature, tiny, puny, infinitesimal, exiguous, petty, microbic, molecular, exact, precise, fine, particular, critical, detailed,

comminuted, circumstantial. *Ant.* large, heavy, bulky, unwieldy, huge, immense, great, colossal, vast, massive, considerable, towering, big, enormous, mountainous, stupendous, capacious, extensive, commodious, spacious, infinite, comprehensive, ample, mighty, magnificent.

miraculous—Syn. wonderful, prodigious, marvelous, extraordinary, supernatural, curious, monstrous, freakish, spectacular, stupendous, surprising, wondrous, astonishing, incredible, strange, overwhelming, amazing, bewildering, astounding, indescribable, inexpressible, unimaginable, fearful, stupefying, awesome. *Ant.* common, commonplace, ordinary, everyday, expected, usual, unimportant, trivial, general, trifling, regular, habitual, customary, frequent, prevalent, current, hackneyed, familiar, natural, insignificant, petty, formal, normal, according to rule, *en régle* [*Fr.*], according to Hoyle (*colloq.*).

mirthful, *adj.—Syn.* merry, cheery, jolly, gay, glad, hilarious, gleeful, jovial, festive.

misanthrope, *n.—Syn.* cynic, pessimist, man-hater, churl, crab, grouch, bluenose.

miscellaneous—Syn. mixed, mingled, promiscuous, various, combined, commixed, commingled, heterogeneous, indiscriminate, intermingled, collective, compound, different, several, many, manifold, diverse, diversified. *Ant.* simple, uniform, unmixed, unblended, elemental, same, similar, like, single, common, of a kind, homogeneous, unadulterated, unalloyed.

mischief—Syn. damage, hurt, injury, detriment, evil, wrong, ill, harm, grievance, outrage, disaster, calamity, catastrophe, disaster, accident, disadvantage, disservice, prejudice, drawback, spoliation, mutilation, mishap, casualty, ruin. *Ant.* good, benefit, advantage, service, profit, improvement, betterment, kindness, favor, blessing, friendship, friendliness, assistance, support, countenance, help, aid, concession, good will, amity, defense, vindication, friendly disposition.

miscreant—*Syn.* wretch, villain, knave, rogue, ruffian, rascal, rapscallion, scamp, caitiff, sneak, scoundrel, culprit, delinquent, tough, bully, malefactor, felon, criminal, convict, outlaw, jailbird, panhandler (*slang*), drunkard, bootlegger, blackguard, outcast, scapegrace, scallawag, skeesicks, rake, rakehell, racketeer, hoodlum, pickpocket, dip (*slang*), loafer, bum (*colloq.*), rounder, rowdy, rough, roughneck, vagabond, ne'er-do-well, larrikin (*Aus. slang*). *Ant.* model, exemplar, pattern, hero, heroine, benefactor, philanthropist, brick (*slang*), trump (*slang*), rough diamond, salt of the earth, saint, angel, demigod, good example, white man (*slang*), good man, good woman, corker (*slang*), humdinger (*slang*), paragon, *beau ideal* [*Fr.*].

miser—*Syn.* curmudgeon, screw, shrew, skinflint, hunks (*slang*), hoarder, skimper, scrimp, niggard, churl, dimesqueezer (*slang*), pinchbelly (*slang*), money-grub (*slang*), codger (*dial.*), extortioner, usurer, rackrenter, pincher, pinchpenny (*slang*), lickpenny (*slang*), cheeseparer, nickel-snatcher (*slang*), muckworm, harpy. *Ant.* prodigal, waster, spendthrift, consumer, squanderer, broadcaster (*slang*), lavisher, spender, sugar-daddy (*slang*), butter-and-egg man (*slang*), blower-in (*slang*), high-roller (*slang*), scattergood, wastrel.

miserable—*Syn.* unhappy, pained, afflicted, distressed, unfortunate, uncomfortable, discontented, sick, sickly, ailing, friendless, woebegone, crushed, suffering, sorrowful, sad, heartbroken, broken-hearted, worried, small, scanty, meager, insufficient, contemptible, illiberal, mean, stingy, venal, covetous, mercenary, narrow-minded. *Ant.* happy, smiling, prosperous, comfortable, cheerful, blithe, gay, gelogenic, debonair, mirthful, contented, satisfied, lighthearted, buoyant, jovial, jocund, lively, high-spirited, merry, vivacious, vigorous, jocose, waggish, sprightly, sportive, hilarious, exhilarated, bully (*slang*), chipper (*colloq.*), riant, rejoicing.

misery—*Syn.* pain, worry, grief, sorrow, depression, distress, unhappiness, infelicity, wretchedness, despair, desolation, dolor, suffering, care, anxiety, uneasiness, trouble, trial, ordeal, anguish, agony, affliction, bother, annoyance, irritation, vexation, mortification, chagrin, heartache, heaviness, despondency. *Ant.* pleasure, gratification, enjoyment, well-being, ease, comfort, happiness, felicity, hedonism, cheerfulness, gaiety, gladness, fun, frolic, delight, amusement, bliss, beatitude, delectation, rapture, ecstasy, joy, rejoicing, jollity, mirth, merriment, jocularity, joviality, vivacity, vivaciousness, levity, animation, glee, hilarity, buoyancy, lightheartedness, elation, laughter.

misfortune—*Syn.* calamity, adversity, bad luck, injury, harm, hurt, accident, misadventure, evil, catastrophe, ill luck, ill fortune, sorrow, trial, trouble, affliction, bereavement, tribulation, mischance, mishap, misery, reverse, disappointment, blow, stroke, visitation, chastening, chastisement, disaster, hardship, eclipse, failure, casualty, infliction, backset, setback, ill, ruin, ruination. *Ant.* prosperity, success, advantage, joy, good luck, good fortune, happiness, welfare, consolation, gratification, boon, blessing, comfort, pleasure, relief, triumph, victory, godsend, stroke of luck, fair weather, happy days, serenity, satisfaction, contentment, bliss, ease, cheerfulness, peace of mind, well-being, legacy, donation, bounty, concession, consignment, assignment, promotion, reward, compensation, redress, indemnity, remuneration.

mishap, *n.—Syn.* accident, misadventure, contretemps, mischance, slip, reverse, misfortune.

misinterpret, *v.—Syn.* misconstrue, misunderstand, misconceive, falsify, distort, pervert.

misjudge, *v.—Syn.* mistake, misconstrue, misconceive, miscalculate, misestimate.

mislead—*Syn.* delude, deceive, misrepresent, defraud, cheat, bamboozle, humbug, cozen, hoodwink, bilk, take in, overreach, outwit, insnare, ensnare, trick, enmesh, entangle, bunko, diddle (*dial.*), victimize, lure, beguile, inveigle, hoax, barney (*slang*), blarney (*slang*), dupe, gull, bait, chouse (*colloq.*), jerry (*slang*), bluff. *Ant.* advise, befriend, encourage, assist, aid, help, succor, relieve, counsel, inform, suggest, prompt, direct, guide, conduct, steer, warn, instruct, teach, lead the way, point out, protect, safeguard, guard, watch over, favor, defend, uphold, support, sustain, benefit.

misrepresent, *v.—Syn.* falsify, distort, mislead, dissemble, pervert, belie, feign, simulate, exaggerate, caricature, misstate.

missive, *n.—Syn.* message, epistle, communication, dispatch, letter, report.

mistake—*Syn.* blunder, error, omission, fallacy, failure, oversight, miss, slip, trip, break, fall, downfall, check, mishap, miscarriage, misapprehension, misconception, lapse, delusion, illusion, flaw, misprint, oversight, laxity, aberration, aberrance, misstatement, false impression, misinterpretation, misunderstanding, catachresis. *Ant.* truth, reality, verity, veracity, fact, gospel, accuracy, exactitude, precision, answer, authenticity, knowledge,

exegesis, interpretation, explanation, success, mastery, triumph, perfection, certainty, certitude, surety, sureness, reliableness, assurance, clearness, correctness, definiteness, exactness, matter-of-fact statement.

mistreat, *v.—Syn.* abuse, wrong, injure, pervert, oppress, misuse, mishandle, outrage.

mistrust, *n.—Syn.* doubt, uncertainty, fear, misgiving, apprehension, suspicion, presentiment. *Ant.* trust, assurance, confidence, faith.

misty, *adj.—Syn.* foggy, dim, clouded, hazy, blurred, murky, faint, obscure, dark.

mite, *n.—Syn.* particle, bit, iota, trifle, smidgen, dab, sliver.

mitigate—*Syn.* assuage, abate, alleviate, lessen, lighten, moderate, soften, relieve, soothe, calm, mollify, temper, lull, deaden, allay, rebate, appease, slow down, palliate, subdue, weaken, decrease, diminish. *Ant.* aggravate, increase, excite, augment, strengthen, intensify, swell, inflate, stimulate, heighten, deepen, enrage, provoke, acerbate, exacerbate, exasperate, envenom, embitter, render worse.

mix—*Syn.* blend, mingle, confuse, unite, join, compound, combine, commix, intermix, immix, commingle, intermingle, shuffle, confound, incorporate, associate, medicate, amalgamate, adulterate, infiltrate, alloy. *Ant.* purify, separate, sift, eliminate, exclude, simplify, adjust, regulate, systematize, arrange, decompose, decompound, dissolve, disintegrate, disperse, unravel, resolve into elements, analyze, untangle, untwine, sort, sort out, remove, segregate, sunder, sever, part, disjoin, divide, detach, disconnect, disengage, disunite, discriminate, dissociate, assort, classify.

mixture, *n.—Syn.* compound, miscellany, blend, jumble, assortment, medley, variety.

mob—*Syn.* crowd, gathering, populace, people, rabble, ragtag, ragtag-and-bobtail (*slang*), plebeians, *canaille* [*Fr.*], *hoi polloi* [*Gr.*], disorderly element, flock, drove, herd, the multitude, the masses, *sans-culottes* [*Fr.*], small fry, horde, commonalty, yokels, bogtrotters [*Ir.*], proletariat, rank and file, the lower five, the submerged tenth, hayseeds (*slang*), hewers of wood and drawers of water; in Australia, sheep, horses, and domestic animals in general. *Ant.* nobility, gentry, quality, upper ten, the four hundred, bigwigs, grandees, the blue-bloods, aristocracy, high life, upper crust, squirarchy, better sort, samurai, royalty, gilded roosters (*U. S. slang*), notables, highflyers.

mobile, *adj.*—*Syn.* movable, free, variable, unstable, changeable, loose.

mock, *v.*—*Syn.* ridicule, defy, taunt, imitate, jeer, gibe, deride, satirize, flout.

mode—*Syn.* fashion, style, manner, custom, rule, method, kind, sort, state, habit, condition, decorum, convention, conventionality, breeding, etiquette, vogue, taste, wont, attitude, usage, practice, precedent, prevalence, tone, procedure, course, plan, scheme. *Ant.* disuse, desuetude, disusage, infringement, nonprevalence, obsolescence, nonconformity, dissidence, infraction of usage, nonobservance of custom.

model—*Syn.* archetype, prototype, original, standard, example, mold, form, facsimile, design, image, pattern, paradigm, representation, imitation, type, copy, likeness, tracing, duplicate, counterpart, outline, shape, figure, sketch, structure, illustration, delineation, depictment. *Ant.* misrepresentation, caricature, travesty, burlesque, parody, distortion, exaggeration, disfigurement, amorphism, defacement, shapelessness, mutilation, derangement, twist, deformity, disproportion, misproportion, contor-

tion, crookedness, grotesqueness.

moderate, *adj.*—*Syn.* limited, sparing, medium, reasonable, fair, middling, nonindulgent, abstemious, temperate, self-denying, modest, ordinary, abstinent, steady, sober, regulated, calm, dispassionate, lenient, tolerant, clement, compassionate, small, slight, scanty, meager, slow, tardy, gradual, deliberate, languid, sluggish, cheap, low-priced, inexpensive. *Ant.* large, great, considerable, extensive, extended, excessive, extravagant, outrageous, exorbitant, sufficient, full, complete, abundant, liberal, unstinted, ample, plenty, unlimited, fast, speedy, rapid, quick, fleet, dear, expensive, costly, high-priced, intemperate, indulgent, voluptuous, sensual, immoderate.

moderate, *v.*—*Syn.* check, curb, restrain, lessen, allay, temper, reduce, qualify, control, limit, soften, regulate, repress, govern, mitigate, blunt, calm, alleviate, tranquillize, assuage, tone down, quell, slake, smooth, check, palliate, throw a wet blanket on (*colloq.*), pour oil on the waters. *Ant.* excite, rouse, incite, exasperate, inflame, exacerbate, stir up, stimulate, quicken, urge, infuriate, madden, irritate, foment, swell, agitate, lash to fury, anger, enrage, craze, increase, strengthen, intensify, add fuel to flames, instigate, enthuse, goad, arouse, spur.

modern—*Syn.* recent, fresh, new, novel, late, newfangled, new-fashioned, up-to-date, fresh as paint (*colloq.*), spick-and-span, *fin-de-siècle* [*Fr.*], vernal, brand-new, just out, immature, virgin, green, untried, unhandled, renovated, up-to-the-minute, improved, fashionable, current, latest. *Ant.* ancient, antique, old, primitive, primordial, antediluvian, Adamic, Adamitic, fossil, prehistoric, paleozoic, antemundane, archaic, antiquated, hoary, time-honored, venerable, ancestral, olden, primigenial, patriarchal, immemorial, traditional, outworn, musty, fusty, timeworn, crumbling, out-of-fashion, out-of-date, obsolete, moth-eaten, old as the hills (*colloq.*).

modest—*Syn.* bashful, backward, retiring, reserved, diffident, unobtrusive, shy, coy, humble, small, inconsiderable, minute, insignificant, timid, sheepish, timorous, unpretentious, unassuming, demure, unostentatious, decent, decorous, chaste, pure, virtuous, virgin, continent, undefiled. *Ant.* extravagant, excessive, exorbitant, outrageous, imposing, towering, mighty, grand, big, huge, glaring, impressive, magnificent, bold, brazen, presumptuous, vain, conceited, self-confident, self-glorious, ostentatious, flaunting, inflated, puffed-up, priggish, egotistical, arrogant, assured, unabashed, proud, haughty, supercilious, indelicate, indecent, obscene, lascivious, unclean, impure, immodest, shameless, prurient, libidinous, concupiscent, erotic, unchaste, wanton.

modesty—*Syn.* reserve, timidity, shyness, coyness, restraint, diffidence, coldness, constraint, bashfulness, backwardness, unobtrusiveness, decency, purity, decorum, delicacy, chastity, virtue, cleanness, virginity, continence, decorum, innocence. *Ant.* boldness, confidence, audacity, insolence, pertness, defiance, effrontery, brazenness, hauteur, shamelessness, bumptiousness, arrogance, haughtiness, presumption, swagger, conceit, nerviness (*colloq.*), impudence, impertinence, self-assertion, impurity, lust, obscenity, lechery, Sadism, Sapphism, tribadism, Lesbianism, masochism, satyriasis, lewdness, nymphomania, carnality, prurience, venery, lubricity, salaciousness, salacity.

modify, *v.*—*Syn.* alter, soften, qualify, temper, vary, shape, lower, change, convert, transform.

moist—*Syn.* damp, wet, fresh, humid, dank, watery, aqueous, infiltrated, saturated, soaked, sodden, soppy, sloppy, swampy. *Ant.* dry, arid, waterless, barren, sandy, siccative, desiccative, desiccated, dehydrated, droughty, waterless, anhydrous, parched, scorched, dried up.

molest—*Syn.* damage, hurt, injure, annoy, disturb, worry, plague, bother, pester, harry, harass, discompose, badger, displease, irritate, vex, thwart, trouble, confuse, aggrieve, oppress, ill-treat, wrong, persecute, maltreat, misuse. *Ant.* comfort, console, soothe, aid, help, assist, befriend, hearten, encourage, cheer, benefit, praise, applaud, oblige, favor, commend, recommend, eulogize, approve, acclaim, indorse, defend, stand up for.

mollify—*Syn.* assuage, mitigate, lessen, soften, ameliorate, moderate, appease, soothe, compose, lull, smooth, alleviate, temper, tranquillize, moderate, calm, pacify, restrain, repress, reconcile, comfort, console, please, allay, flatter, gratify. *Ant.* anger, enrage, infuriate, taunt, tempt, excite, incite, disturb, annoy, harass, agitate, worry, plague, torment, vex, irritate, provoke, exasperate, exacerbate, arouse, stir up, inflame, incense, chafe, nettle, madden, lash to fury.

moment, *n.*—*Syn.* instant, minute, trice, wink, second, jiffy, flash.

momentous—*Syn.* important, far-reaching, serious, consequential, grave, solemn, weighty, memorable, notable, salient, eventful, stirring, signal. *Ant.* unimportant, slight, trivial, trifling, insignificant, small, immaterial, irrelevant, unessential, uninteresting, commonplace, ordinary.

monastic, *adj.*—*Syn.* secluded, cenobitic, monkish, conventual, ascetic, solitary.

money—*Syn.* gold, silver, coin, cash, currency, bills, notes, specie, funds, capital, property, bullion, wealth, stock, assets, finance, wherewithal, means, lucre, Mammon, opulence, treasure, resources, affluence, independence, riches, substance, supplies, securities, bonds—the needful, chink, rhino, jack, kale, dust, dough, long green, wampum, blunt, pile, bones, backbone, roll, wallet, shekels, quids, tin, brass, moss, rocks, spondulics, wad, filthy lucre—all *slang.*

monomania—*Syn.* insanity, madness, derangement, morbidity, morbidness, mania, lunacy, dementia, delirium, aberration, morosis, phrenitis, delusion, hallucination, paranoia, fanaticism, infatuation, obsession. *Ant.* sanity, lucidity, self-possession, common sense, normalcy, normality, soundness, steadiness, mental vigor, saneness, healthiness of mind, rationality, reasonableness.

monopoly, *n.*—*Syn.* trust, pool, combination, cartel, syndicate, corner, control.

monotonous—*Syn.* dull, tedious, wearisome, wearying, unvaried, undiversified, tiresome, irksome, uninteresting, humdrum, prosy, slow, dry, drowsy, heavy, depressive, flat. *Ant.* varied, versatile, interesting, witty, jocular, waggish, droll, pleasant, amusing, entertaining, festive, merry, gay, jolly, sportive, clever, keen, pungent, brilliant, humorous, facetious, whimsical, lively, pleasing, inviting, charming, delightful, attractive, refreshing, heartening, appealing, captivating, enticing, cheerful, cheering.

monstrous—*Syn.* abnormal, horrible, terrible, atrocious, horrent, dreadful, awful, frightful, shocking, preposterous, marvelous, stupendous, vast, prodigious, uncanny, wonderful, wondrous, unspeakable, terrifying, inconceivable, strange, incredible, huge, enormous, immense, anomalous, teratoid, teratogenetic, teratogenic, unnatural. *Ant.* common, commonplace, ordi-

nary, normal, natural, conventional, formal, small, little, diminutive, beautiful, nice, pretty, attractive, graceful, shapely, regular, usual, simple, plain, customary, expected, conformable, habitual, standard, average.

monument—*Syn.* tomb, shaft, column, pillar, vault, mausoleum, cenotaph, headstone, tombstone, grave-stone, memorial, shrine, statue, building, erection, pile, tower, obelisk, monolith, tablet, slab, stone, memento, record, scroll, testimonial, register. *Ant.* forgetfulness, oblivion, Lethe, obliteration, effacement, mindlessness, unmindfulness, extinction, annihilation.

mood—*Syn.* mode, manner, state, condition, temper, disposition, humor, vein, behavior, conduct, nature, principle, character, habit, constitution, quality, temperament, propensity, tendency, change, variation, mutation, proclivity, susceptibility, idiosyncrasy.

moral, *adj.*—*Syn.* ethical, good, honest, righteous, upright, noble, just, scrupulous, virtuous, decent.

morbid—*Syn.* abnormal, pathological, sick, sickly, diseased, ailing, affected, unsound, unhealthy, consumptive, phthisical, tubercular, chlorotic, drooping, flagging, seedy (*colloq.*). *Ant.* healthy, sound, vigorous, robust, normal, lively, cheerful, strong, well, wholesome, hardy, hearty, hale, stanch, blooming, lusty, spirited.

moron—*Syn.* fool, simpleton, boob (*slang*), booby (*slang*), milksop, lubber, dunderhead (*colloq.*), lunkhead (*colloq.*), chucklehead (*colloq.*), loony (*slang*), mutt (*slang*), nut (*slang*), chowderhead (*dial.*), imbecile, goose, tomfool, lout, addlepate, dullard, bonehead (*slang*), calf (*colloq.*), muttonhead (*colloq.*), saphead (*slang*), softy (*colloq.*), gawk, gowk, dunce, thickhead (*colloq.*), numbskull (*colloq.*). *Ant.* sage, philosopher, *savant* [*Fr.*], scholar, scientist, thinker, wizard, student, philologist, pedagogue, teacher, instructor, judge, prodigy, educator, genius, linguist, doctor, lexicographer, scholiast, commentator, annotator.

morose—*Syn.* gloomy, sour, sullen, splenetic, morbid, depressed, acrimonious, ill-natured, ill-humored, gruff, dolorous, melancholy, perversive, ill-tempered, sulky, crusty, grouchy, surly, moody, churlish, cantankerous, crabbed, cross, crossgrained, frowning, snappish, mournful, funereal, lugubrious. *Ant.* cheery, cheerful, bright, lively, animated, spirited, blithe, smiling, debonair, happy, lighthearted, buoyant, sprightly, vivacious, jolly, keen, jovial, breezy, rollicking, exhilarated, hilarious, rejoicing, gleesome, lightsome, joyous, high-spirited, amiable, benignant, pleasant, sympathetic, tender, mild, loving, kind, indulgent, good-natured, gentle, friendly, complacent, complaisant, genial, bland.

mortal—*Syn.* deadly, fatal, destructive, death-dealing, lethal, deathly, serious, extreme, human, transient, temporal, passing. *Ant.* life-giving, refreshing, reinvigorating, reviving, freshening, strengthening, vivifying, revivifying, curative, light, trivial, trifling, lasting, everlasting, perpetual, eternal.

motif, *n.*—*Syn.* figure, theme, design, leitmotiv, subject, topic, matter.

motion—*Syn.* movement, transition, change, transit, passage, act, action, move, motility, restlessness, changeableness, rate, stride, gait, pace, step. *Ant.* quiet, quiescence, rest, stillness, fixity, immobility, stop, pause, standstill, repose, lull, stagnation, deadlock, stoppage, halt, cessation.

motionless—*Syn.* still, unmoving, torpid, dead, inert, quiescent, motionless, moveless, fixed, stationary, immotile, stockstill, stagnant, immovable, unruffled, calm, becalmed, undisturbed, silent. *Ant.* moving, shifting, changing, movable, changeable, motile, restless, traveling, wandering, flowing, floating, sailing, gliding, skimming, flying, drifting, walking, tramping, dancing, marching.

motivate, *v.*—*Syn.* impel, prompt, stimulate, arouse, move, inspire, provoke, actuate, induce, excite.

motive, *n.*—*Syn.* reason, impulse, purpose, aim, principle, cause, end, intention, determinant.

motley, *adj.*—*Syn.* assorted, heterogeneous, disparate, diverse, incongruous, varied, miscellaneous, composite. *Ant.* uniform, homogeneous, similar, like.

mound—*Syn.* hill, pile, heap, cumulus, grave, knoll, elevation, eminence, hillock, fortification, defense, earth bank, protection, shield, mole, rampart, ditch, fosse, scarp, counterscarp, breastwork, moat, parapet, embankment, entrenchment.

mount—*Syn.* rise, ascend, climb, tower, scale, arise, uprise, aspire, scramble, shoot up, grow, increase, augment, add to, swell, soar, surge. *Ant.* descend, decline, drop, fall, subside, lapse, collapse, sink, slump, get down, dismount, alight, decrease, diminish, lessen, abate, curtail, abridge.

mourn—*Syn.* lament, deplore, grieve, bewail, fret, sorrow, bemoan, rue, regret, droop, languish, repine, weep over, caoine (*keen*, Ir.), sigh, cry, whimper, ululate, groan, wail. *Ant.* rejoice, exult, delight in, glory in, revel, make merry, be glad, cheer, shout, caper, frolic, gambol, play, express joy, triumph.

mournful—*Syn.* sorrowful, sad, heavy, doleful, lugubrious, downcast, down-hearted, unhappy, funereal, melancholy, sombre, joyless, cheerless, blue, heavy-hearted, low-spirited, pensive, tristful, disconsolate, forlorn, abandoned, heartsick, broken-hearted, despairing. *Ant.* joyful, cheerful, merry, gay, light, lightsome, light-hearted, buoyant, rejoicing, vivacious, lively, animated, high-spirited, enlivening, frolicsome, playful, jolly, exhilarated, gleeful, elated, sprightly, sparkling, hilarious, rollicking.

move—*Syn.* stir, advance, influence, actuate, instigate, convert, impel, budge, shift, glide, walk, run, sweep along, fly, travel, drift, go, keep going, propel, put in motion, go ahead, push forward, peg along, hustle, bustle, proceed, propose, induce, stimulate, rouse, arouse, persuade, agitate, excite, inspirit, wheedle, coax, bias, lure, inveigle, vamp (*slang*), whip, lash, spur, urge, prevail upon, bring round. *Ant.* stand, halt, pause, rest, cease, let up, pull up, stop, keep still, relax, sleep, doze, drowse, snooze (*colloq.*), calm, suppress, restrain, mollify, pacify, dissuade, dehort, discourage, dishearten, quell, settle, put on the brakes (*colloq.*), mark time (*slang*), heave to (*slang*), cast anchor (*slang*).

movement—*Syn.* motion, velocity, transition, change, motility, movableness, restlessness, flight, journey, transit, travel, progress, advancement, progression, speed, activity, action, nimbleness, quickness, hustle, bustle, hurry, flurry, scurry, work, labor, undertaking, act, enterprise. *Ant.* inactivity, abandonment, resignation, cessation, stop, stoppage, inaction, idleness, inertness, laziness, somnolence, stupor, insensibility, hypnosis, hibernation, slumber, sleep, indolence, sloth, remissness, quiescence, inaction, stagnation, passiveness.

movies—*Syn.* moving pictures, motion pictures, cinema, cinematograph, kinematograph, biograph, dissolving views, silver screen, talkies (*colloq.*), photodrama, panorama, diorama, cos-

morama, presentation, photoplay, entertainment.

muddle, *n.*—*Syn.* difficulty, confusion, dilemma, mixup, disarrangement, misarrangement, derangement, disorder, jumble, chaos, maze, turmoil, perplexity, mixture, complication, intricacy, entanglement, muss (*colloq.*), mess, botch, hodgepodge, farrago, ferment, complexity. *Ant.* order, arrangement, method, plan, conformity, unity, system, orderliness, uniformity, ease, easiness, smoothness, disencumbrance, plain sailing, regulation, organization, systematization, collocation, classification, allocation, schematism, disposition, outline, settlement, gradation, standardization, regularity.

muddle, *v.*—*Syn.* foul, stir up, confuse, misarrange, disarrange, disturb, mix, derange, disorder, jumble, perturb, huddle, splash, shake up, shuffle, toss, turn, ravel, ruffle, disorganize, muss, entangle, embroil, disconcert, embarrass, distract, confound, involve. *Ant.* clarify, explain, elucidate, interpret, expound, put in order, arrange, draw up, regulate, adjust, systematize, methodize, unravel, untangle, sort, classify, group, grade, allot, collocate, allocate, form, set to rights.

muddy, *adj.*—*Syn.* turbid, clouded, murky, unclear, dark, opaque, foul, obscure, vague. *Ant.* clear, transparent, lucid, limpid.

mulish, *adj.*—*Syn.* obstinate, stubborn, intractable, pertinacious, recalcitrant, headstrong, pigheaded, bullheaded. *Ant.* obedient, tractable, biddable, docile.

multitude—*Syn.* crowd, throng, swarm, gathering, congregation, aggregation, collection, assemblage, host, legion, large number, array, galaxy, army. *Ant.* fewness, scarcity, sparseness, small number, part, portion, paucity, fraction, zero, nothing, nobody, exiguity, minority, handful.

mundane, *adj.*—*Syn.* worldly, temporal, mortal, carnal, secular, earthly. *Ant.* heavenly, eternal, infinite, celestial.

munificent—*Syn.* bountiful, generous, liberal, helpful, bounteous, openhanded, lavish, charitable, philanthropic, large-hearted, hospitable, unselfish, freehanded, prodigal, princely, ample, unsparing, profuse. *Ant.* miserly, parsimonious, penurious, close-fisted (*colloq.*), selfish, chary, frugal, saving, niggardly, grudging, stingy, tight (*colloq.*), tightfisted (*colloq.*), sordid, avaricious, improvident, cautious, careful, chary, illiberal.

murder—*Syn.* kill, slay, butcher, slaughter, dispatch, assassinate, immolate, destroy, massacre, victimize, settle, put to death, deprive of life. *Ant.* restore, vivify, animate, refresh, reinvigorate, vitalize, reanimate, revive, keep alive, keep body and soul together, give birth to, quicken, propagate, produce, bring forth.

murky—*Syn.* obscure, dark, filmy, dim, gloomy, dull, flat, sable-colored, overcast, clouded, somber, lowering, funereal, dreary, dismal, umbrageous, tenebrous, shaded, darkling, dusky, dingy. *Ant.* light, clear, bright, sunny, lucent, lambent, unclouded, effulgent, shining, glittering, glistening, glistering, sparkling, glowing, luminous, radiant, brilliant, dazzling, unobscured, cloudless, lustrous, fulgurant, flashing, shimmering.

murmur—*Syn.* whisper, mutter, grumble, trickle, purl, gurgle, guggle, ooze, percolate, drip, hum, babble, tinkle, flow gently, meander. *Ant.* blow hard, storm, thunder, peal, clang, swell, fulminate, rend, split, roar, boom, resound, clatter, explode, detonate.

muscular, *adj.*—*Syn.* vigorous, powerful, husky, athletic, lusty, sinewy, brawny, stout, forceful, belligerent. *Ant.* puny, feeble, slight, infirm.

muse—*Syn.* think, ponder, meditate, reflect, deliberate, study, lucubrate, consider, cogitate, contemplate, speculate, reason, cerebrate, indulge in reverie, brood over. *Ant.* relax, unbend, divest the mind, put away thought, take it easy (*slang*).

music—*Syn.* harmony, melody, symphony, tune, air, vocalism, concord, rhythm, minstrelsy, jazz, syncopation, ragtime, orchestration, instrumentation, harmonization. *Ant.* discord, dissonance, cacophony, confusion, jangle, harshness, clash, jar, disagreement, variance, discordance, incongruity, inconsistence, inconsistency, dissidence.

musical—*Syn.* melodious, harmonious, dulcet, sweet, tuneful, pleasing, euphonic, euphonious, agreeable, symphonious, melic, canorous, melodic, lyric, lyrical, symphonic, vocal, choral, tonal, mellow, homophonous, unisonant, assonant. *Ant.* discordant, harsh, grating, jarring, jangling, disagreeable, cacophonous, tuneless, dissonant, unmusical, incongruous, inharmonious, conflicting, out of tune.

musty—*Syn.* moldy, stale, sour, mildewed, fusty, rank, foul, fetid, dirty, smudged, filthy, grimy, dusty, soiled, rusty, moth-eaten. *Ant.* clean, pure, stainless, unstained, fresh, sweet, green, spotless, new, purified, cleansed, renewed.

mute—*Syn.* dumb, speechless, silent, still, noiseless, soundless, hushed, calm, aphonic, inaudible, deathlike, tongueless, voiceless, wordless, deaf and dumb. *Ant.* vocal, articulate, distinct, oral, talkative, clear, accentuated, phonetic, voiced, spoken, uttered, eloquent, oratorical, loquacious, garrulous.

mutilate—*Syn.* maim, cripple, disable, disfigure, injure, impair, mangle, deface, lame, wound, hurt, cut, truncate, distort, spoil, despoil, mar, deform, damage. *Ant.* form, restore, fix, shape, patch, fashion, trim, mold, cast, model, build up, put in shape, replace, reconstitute, renovate, renew, touch up, brush up, remodel, revive, rectify, redintegrate, repair, rehabilitate, cure, heal, mend, reconstruct.

mutinous—*Syn.* rebellious insubordinate, riotous, revolutionary, seditious, turbulent, insurgent, violent, resistive, resistant, tumultuous, disobedient, recalcitrant, oppugnant, insubordinate, contumacious, unruly, unsubmissive, lawless, ungovernable, refractory, recusant. *Ant.* obedient, submissive, loyal, passive, subjective, resigned, subordinate, compliant, lawabiding, faithful, devoted, obsequious, peaceful, pacific, contented, satisfied, tranquil, observant, true, constant, incorruptible, trustworthy, firm, attached, stanch, consistent, yielding, dutiful, subservient, docile, orderly.

mutter, *v.*—*Syn.* mumble, murmur, rumble, moan, grumble.

mutual—*Syn.* reciprocal, interchangeable, joint, common, correlative, convertible, identical, coïncident, equivalent, self-same, similar, like, correspondent, analogous. *Ant.* separate, separated, unconnected, dissociated, sundered, disunited, distinct, unreciprocated, unrequited, detached, disconnected, unshared, severed, dissimilar, unlike, nonidentical, different, disparate, unequal, divergent, changeable, variant.

muzzle—*Syn.* bind, fasten, gag, restrain, trammel, restrict, repress, suppress, check, confine, prevent, stop, silence, keep within bounds. *Ant.* free, liberate, unbind, unfasten, foster, encourage, approve, stimulate, embolden, inspirit, impel, urge, instigate.

mysterious—*Syn.* mystic, occult, secret, obscure, enigmatic, enigmatical, covert, dark, incomprehensible, cabalistic, hidden, unintelligible, inconceivable, incredible, unaccountable, inexplicable, impenetrable, puzzling, transcendental, inexpressible, in-

effable, esoteric, abstruse, metempirical, ambiguous, equivocal, unrevealed, unfathomable, unknown, mystical, inscrutable, recondite, clandestine, surreptitious, latent, cryptic, oracular. *Ant.* clear, plain, definite, apparent, distinct, manifest, obvious, unambiguous, unequivocal, unmistakable, evident, intelligible, lucid, straightforward, perspicuous, explicit, graphic, vivid, comprehensible, precise, open, known, knowable, indubitable, conclusive, overt, patent, downright, undisguised, exoteric, ostensible, self-evident, axiomatic, palpable, discernible, indisputable, incontrovertible.

mystery, *n.*—*Syn.* puzzle, enigma, riddle, perplexity, secret.

mystic, *adj.*—*Syn.* esoteric, secret, abstruse, obscure, recondite, cabalistic, hidden, occult.

mystify—*Syn.* perplex, puzzle, confuse, humbug, bamboozle (*slang*), trick, dupe, deceive, delude, fool, hoodwink, dissemble, confound, embarrass, mislead, misguide, misrepresent, equivocate, obfuscate. *Ant.* clear, explain, illustrate, inform, declare, report, interpret, translate, define, render, elucidate, unravel, disentangle, enucleate, enlighten, disclose, tell, communicate, expound.

mythical, *adj.*—*Syn.* fabulous, legendary, imaginary, fictitious, apocryphal, visionary, traditional.

N

nab, *v.*—*Syn.* catch, bag, grab, arrest, trap, snatch, capture, seize, snag, snare, nail, collar, hook.

naive, *adj.*—*Syn.* artless, simple, unsophisticated, spontaneous, unaffected, ingenuous, fresh, plain.

naked—*Syn.* bare, uncovered, open, exposed, unclothed, nude, undressed, stripped, unconcealed, manifest, plain, evident, undisguised, simple, definite, distinct, explicit, express, literal, divested, unclad, threadbare, leafless, hairless. *Ant.* covered, clad, clothed, cloaked, dressed, arrayed, draped, robed, garbed, attired, appareled, gowned, habited, costumed, invested, enveloped, wrapped, swathed, swaddled, hidden, latent, concealed, secret, covert, unexposed, undisclosed, veiled.

name, *n.*—*Syn.* cognomen, appellation, designation, title, denomination, epithet, prenomen, surname, style, agnomen, reputation, repute, character, distinction, sign, signature, autograph, patronymic, eponym, nickname, *sobriquet*, pen name, pseudonym, *nom de plume* [*Fr.*], *nom de guerre* [*Fr.*], alias, stage name, pet name, good name, bad name.

name, *v.*—*Syn.* style, call, christen, denominate, term, title, entitle, head, specify, signify, denote, designate, mark, nickname, characterize, proclaim, label, baptize, define, dub (*colloq.*).

nameless—*Syn.* unnamed, unacknowledged, anonymous, obscure, inglorious, disreputable, despicable, shameful, degrading, humiliating, unmentionable, pseudo, bastard. *Ant.* named, acknowledged, signed, confirmed, designated, known, famous, celebrated, renowned, prominent, eminent, distinguished, well-known.

narcotic, *n.*—*Syn.* dope, soporific, opiate, drug, tranquillizer, anaesthetic, anodyne, sedative, hop, junk.

narrate—*Syn.* tell, relate, recite, make known, rehearse, detail, enumerate, describe, recount, set forth, portray, picture, proclaim, unfold, recapitulate, paint, disclose, reveal. *Ant.* screen, cover, shade, withhold, keep silent, veil, hide, conceal, disguise, suppress, repress, stifle, smother, restrain, stop.

narrow—*Syn.* restricted, close, cramped, contracted, shrunken, weazen, wizened, compressed, limited, scanty, miserly, parsimonious, constrained, tenuous, emaciated, slender, thread-like,

thin, scrawny, attenuated, shriveled, lanky, spindling, spindle-legged, spindle-shanked, spare, prejudiced, bigoted, illiberal. *Ant.* wide, expanded, ample, broad, extended, swollen, obese, expansive, turgid, tumid, pot-bellied, corpulent, edematous, puffy, bloated, fat, thick, dumpy, squat, thickset, stubby, adipose, adipous, fleshy, plump, portly, stout, dilated, liberal, broad-minded, generous, catholic.

nasty—*Syn.* dirty, filthy, foul, disgusting, nauseous, contaminated, offensive, unclean, tainted, defiled, impure, sloppy, slatternly, sluttish, slimy, gurry, soiled, gross, grimy, sozzly (*dial.*), smutty, squalid, lousy, pediculous, reeky, putrid, fetid, mucky, feculent, excremental, excrementious, putrescent, rotten, putrefied, fecal, saprogenic, saprogenous, ordurous, stercoraceous, beastly, stercoricolous, corrupt, impetiginous, polluted. *Ant.* clean, pure, sweet, untainted, uncontaminated, pleasing, unstained, unsoiled, unsullied, spotless, pleasurable, gratifying, attractive, winsome, purified, stainless, disinfected, cleansed, bright, shiny, glittering, attractive, washed, elutriated, bathed, scrubbed, perfumed, scented, fumigated, whitewashed, flushed, sponged, scoured, swabbed, scraped, brushed, laundered, unblemished, perfect.

nation—*Syn.* state, realm, country, commonwealth, republic, empire, kingdom, principality, colony, body politic, people, population, populace, persons, folk, society, community, public.

native—*Syn.* indigenous, original, natal, aboriginal, natural, innate, inborn, vernacular, domestic, home-grown, domesticated, naturalized, domiciliary, autochthonal, autochthonous. *Ant.* foreign, alien, extraneous, outside, extrinsic, strange, distant, remote, external, outward, not inherent, artificial, assumed, unnatural, acquired.

natural—*Syn.* intrinsic, original, regular, normal, spontaneous, essential, true, consistent, probable, artless, cosmical, subjective, implanted, fundamental, inborn, innate, inbred, ingrained, immanent, inherited, congenital, genetic, incarnate, bred in the bone, unintentional, simple, unaffected, plain. *Ant.* extrinsic, objective, extraneous, casual, contingent, adventitious, incidental, subsidiary, outward, external, unessential, intentional, contemplated, intended, prepared, ready, cut-and-dried, ornamented, embellished, elaborated, decorated, beautified, unnatural.

nature, *n.*—*Syn.* character, quality, kind, humor, mood, essence, disposition, sort.

naughty, *adj.*—*Syn.* perverse, bad, contrary, disobedient, wanton, froward, mischievous, wicked, wayward.

nauseous—*Syn.* disgusting, disgustful, abhorrent, loathsome, unsavory, unpleasant, distasteful, abominable, disagreeable, offensive, revolting, repulsive, repellent, fulsome, nasty, unpalatable, sickening. *Ant.* pleasing, pleasant, agreeable, sweet, savory, delectable, toothsome, gustful, delicious, luscious, ambrosial, nectareous, palatable, dainty, tasty, satisfying, desirous, desirable, refreshing, appetizing.

nautical—*Syn.* marine, maritime, naval, oceanic, aquatic, sailing, seafaring, seagoing, navigable, floating, natatorial, natatory, boating, yachting, rowing. *Ant.* peripatetic, wandering, ambulatory, vehicular, itinerant, sauntering, rambling, gadding, walking, running, jumping, flying, skating.

navigate, *v.*—*Syn.* guide, sail, govern, steer, control, conduct, manage, pilot.

near—*Syn.* nigh, close, intimate, adjacent, bordering, neighboring, adjoining, proximal, proximate, at hand, approaching, next,

prospective, expectant, imminent, impending, contiguous, immediate, coming, brewing, looming, forthcoming, approximate, converging, miserly, niggardly, stingy, penurious, parsimonious. *Ant.* far, distant, far away, remote, past, gone, expired, extinct, late, posthumous, behindhand, adjourned, shelved, reserved, prorogued, postponed, deferred, stopped, suspended, put off, untimely, inopportune, inexpedient, out of date, regressive, lavish, prodigal, extravagant, liberal, generous.

neat—*Syn.* tidy, shapely, proportioned, clean-cut, trim, prim, spruce, clean, cleanly, natty, dapper, orderly, nice, becoming, suitable, regular, correct, shipshape, well-dressed, symmetrical, uniform, methodical, systematic, spotless. *Ant.* slovenly, ungainly, unkempt, ragged, untidy, careless, dirty, awkward, irregular, disordered, disorderly, straggling, negligent, scampish, sluttish, sloppy, slatternly, loose, slipshod, lax, clumsy, gawky, inept, slouchy, lubberly, dowdy, rough, ill-fitting, sloshy.

necessary—*Syn.* essential, requisite, expedient, needful, indispensable, needed, required, unavoidable, undeniable, urgent, wanted, imperative, prerequisite, pressing, exigent, compulsory, inexorable, obligatory, binding. *Ant.* unnecessary, redundant, inexpedient, useless, overmuch, prodigal, exorbitant, casual, extravagant, overflowing, crammed, inoperative, inefficacious, ineffectual, inadequate, unsuitable, superfluous, undesirable, objectionable, unfit, inadmissible, disadvantageous, unsatisfactory, needless, contingent, optional, worthless.

necessity—*Syn.* need, want, emergency, privation, hunger, starvation, poverty, penury, pauperism, destitution, distress, indigence, exigency, urgency, compulsion, duress, enforcement, constraint, restraint, stress, obligation. *Ant.* free will, voluntarism, determination, desire, wish, will, volition, willingness, inclination, assent, compliance, propensity, readiness, zeal, enthusiasm, earnestness, ardor, wealth, fortune, opulence, riches, affluence, means, resources, income, easy circumstances.

necromancy, *n.—Syn.* magic, witchery, wizardry, witchcraft, thaumaturgy, enchantment, sorcery, diablerie.

need, *n.—Syn.* want, distress, privation, misery, destitution, penury, indigence, extremity, emergency, necessity, exigency. *Ant.* plenty, fulness, comfort, luxury, competence, wealth, riches, property, fortune, opulence, independence.

nefarious—*Syn.* wicked, sinful, detestable, abominable, atrocious, villainous, vile, iniquitous, base, sinister, vicious, corrupt, depraved, sinful, foul, gross, disgraceful, shameful, scandalous, outrageous, dishonorable, shameless, brazen, immodest, immoral, recreant, improper, flagrant, flagitious, heinous, hellish, infernal, infamous, inexcusable, disreputable, unpardonable. *Ant.* virtuous, good, innocent, right, righteous, praiseworthy, noble, commendable, creditable, exemplary, worthy, inoffensive, blameless, irreproachable, meritorious, excellent, fine, upright, honest, honorable, reputable, candid, frank, sincere, dependable, high-minded, high-principled, just, scrupulous, true, square (*colloq.*), incorruptible, unselfish, magnanimous, self-denying, fair-and-square (*colloq.*).

negate, *v.—Syn.* controvert, abrogate, confute, deny, cancel, revoke, refuse, nullify.

neglect, *n.—Syn.* negligence, remissness, slight, omission, carelessness, default, failure, indifference, disregard, thoughtlessness, disrespect, scorn, oversight, inadvertence, slackness, neglectfulness, inattention, evasion, in-

dolence, supineness, deferment, procrastination, nonchalance, disuse, disusage, desuetude, relinquishment, forbearance, nonfulfilment, incompleteness, nonobservance, nonperformance, dereliction. *Ant.* performance, execution, achievement, perpetration, work, labor, toil, vigilance, watchfulness, surveillance, alertness, concern, heedfulness, vigil, carefulness, attention, observance, fulfilment, obligation, action, briskness, eagerness, zeal, ardor, enthusiasm, dash, pep (*slang*), agility, application, perseverance, anxiety, caution, circumspection, heed, forethought, foresight, prudence, wariness, precaution, management, solicitude.

neglect, *v.—Syn.* omit, forbear, slight, overlook, disregard, contemn, despise, ignore, pass by, pass over, defer, procrastinate, suspend, dismiss, discard, depreciate, spurn, underestimate, undervalue, shake off, turn one's back upon, detest, scorn, disdain, turn a cold shoulder to (*colloq.*), pooh-pooh, set at nought, forget. *Ant.* do, perform, carry out, care for, watch, guard, safeguard, protect, warn, advise, use, handle, manipulate, accomplish, achieve, consummate, complete, finish, conclude, effect, execute, fulfil, satisfy, discharge, make good (*colloq.*), undertake, exercise, practice, work, serve, hustle (*colloq.*), keep going (*colloq.*), go ahead, stir, bestir, rouse, arouse, toil, labor, plod, drudge, move, exert, try, bring about, act, persevere, continue, peg away (*slang*).

negligent—*Syn.* careless, inattentive, thoughless, remiss, inconsiderate, unmindful, woolgathering (*slang*), neglectful, heedless, perfunctory, dreamy, unwary, unwatchful, indifferent, insouciant. *Ant.* careful, watchful, keen, sharp, quick, heedful, regardful, thoughtful, considerate, alert, vigilant, wide-awake, mindful, Argus-eyed, sharp-eyed, lynx-eyed, on the *qui vive*, on the alert.

negotiate, *v.—Syn.* bargain, confer, consult, contract, arrange, treat, dicker, compromise.

neighborhood—*Syn.* environs, vicinity, vicinage, locality, proximity, purlieus, district, adjacency, nearness, propinquity. *Ant.* distance, remoteness, farness, background, hinterland, outpost, outskirt, foreign parts, *ultima Thule* [L.].

neophyte, *n.—Syn.* novice, beginner, probationer, apprentice, student, tyro, trainee.

nerve, *n.—Syn.* courage, grit, hardihood, audacity, fortitude, intrepidity, pluck, guts.

nervous—*Syn.* timid, shaky, timorous, excitable, jumpy (*slang*), apprehensive, restless, afraid, quivering, shaking, trembling, perturbed, aghast, fidgety, frightened, panic-stricken, hysterical, alarmed, shocked, tremulous, awe-stricken, terror-stricken, weak. *Ant.* brave, fearless, strong, hardy, inured, bold, seasoned, courageous, manly, spunky (*colloq.*), plucky, valiant, valorous, resolute, daring, stout-hearted, lion-hearted, mettlesome, dauntless, aweless, audacious, spirited, heroic, confident, unshirking, strongwilled, doughty.

nestle, *v.—Syn.* cuddle, snuggle, shelter, nuzzle, lodge.

net, *v.—Syn.* snare, trap, catch, capture, entangle, charm, captivate.

nettle, *v.—Syn.* irk, vex, irritate, fret, exasperate, sting, provoke, annoy, agitate.

neutral, *adj.—Syn.* indifferent, disinterested, indeterminate, unconcerned, impartial, nonpartisan, unallied. *Ant.* positive, decided, biased, predisposed.

new—*Syn.* novel, fresh, recent, late, renewed, restored, green, raw, immature, virgin, young, inexperienced, untried, modern, up-to-date. *Ant.* old, ancient, medieval, dilapidated, worn, worn-out, time-worn, deteriora-

ted, olden, antique, time-honored, venerable, primeval, primordial, prehistoric, antediluvian, immemorial, antiquated, archaic, out-worn, out-of-date, old-fashioned, obsolete.

news—*Syn.* information, tidings, intelligence, story, copy, message, telegram, cable, wire (*colloq.*), radio (*colloq.*), radiogram, broadcast, marconigram, bulletin, report, despatch, flash (*colloq.*).

newspaper — *Syn.* publication, press, fourth estate, public press, journal, sheet, tabloid, magazine, gazette, budget, daily, weekly, Sunday edition, monthly, quarterly, annual.

next, *adj.—Syn.* nearest, adjacent, contiguous, beside, adjoining, later, after.

nice—*Syn.* fine, handsome, pretty, comely, beautiful, lovely, attractive, fascinating, captivating, exquisite, dainty, refined, delicate, charming, fair, graceful, elegant, good-looking, well-favored, well-formed, pleasing, amiable, agreeable, winning, winsome, precise, particular, punctilious, fastidious, squeamish, exact, correct, prepossessing. *Ant.* ugly, coarse, repellent, repulsive, revolting, abhorrent, displeasing, unpleasant, rough, rude, boorish, ill-favored, pockmarked, scarred, misshapen, ill-looking, grim, grim-faced, sour, unseemly, disfigured, unprepossessing, dumpy, dowdy, squat, dwarfish, homely, deformed, hulking, ungainly, odious, forbidding, horrid, shocking, hideous, unmannerly, slovenly.

niggardly—*Syn.* miserly, parsimonious, penurious, stingy, sparing, close, close-fisted (*colloq.*), tight-fisted (*colloq.*), chary, grudging, avaricious, illiberal, mercenary, venal, covetous, mean, sordid. *Ant.* generous, liberal, open-handed, prodigal, lavish, unsparing, profuse, extravagant, wasteful, bounteous, munificent, spendthrift, dissipated.

nimble—*Syn.* alert, lively, quick, brisk, swift, spry, active, prompt, bustling, hustling, speedy, rapid, agile, sprightly, fast, expeditious. *Ant.* slow, dull, tardy, slack, dilatory, leisurely, languid, wearisome, weary, apathetic, sluggish, gradual, creeping, snail-like, reptatorial, sluggish.

nobility—*Syn.* rank, gentility, blue blood, peerage, Upper Ten (*slang*), Upper Tendom (*slang*), aristocracy, notables, the Four Hundred (*colloq.*), bigwigs (*slang*), the Fashionables (*colloq.*), gilded roosters (*U. S. slang*), élite [*Fr.*], haut monde [*Fr.*]. *Ant.* commonalty, Lower Five (*slang*), Lower Fivedom (*slang*), Brown, Jones and Robinson, the common herd, the masses, the Great Unwashed, John Q. Public (*slang*), the public, proletariat, hewers of wood and drawers of water, the rabble, hoi polloi [*Gr.*], sans culottes [*Fr.*], the working class, canaille [*Fr.*], the scum, the riffraff, rag-tag-and-bob-tail, small fry.

noble—*Syn.* grand, high, exalted, majestic, august, stately, imperial, princely, generous, magnanimous, magnificent, courtly, lofty, elevated, splendid, supreme, eminent, lordly, dignified, sublime, great, superior, A1, first-rate, honorable, honored, titled, distinguished, patrician, aristocratic, loyal, incorrupt, trustworthy, candid, sincere, truthful, constant, faithful, upright, square (*colloq.*). *Ant.* base, mean, corrupt, ignoble, treacherous, low, vile, contemptible, lying, deceitful, depraved, dishonest, faithless, perfidious, disreputable, disloyal, degraded, turpid, immoral, villainous, unfaithful, deceptive, untrustworthy, debased, infamous, ignominious, shameful, disreputable, disgraceful, dishonorable, scandalous, plebeian, proletarian, common, indecent, commonplace, subordinate, inferior.

noise—*Syn.* clamor, clatter, din, tumult, uproar, cry, outcry, sound, resonance, clangor, roar, racket, bomb, explosion, detonation, blare, blast, bombardment, loudness, peal, boom, tinkling, tintinnabulation, murmuring, cooing, singing, shouting, music, yelling, discussion, talk, speechifying. *Ant.* silence, muteness, stillness, lull, calm, hush, stop, soundlessness, speechlessness, peace, peacefulness, oblivion, deadness, grave, tomb.

noiseless—*Syn.* silent, still, hushed, lulled, stilly, calm, quiet, stifled, muffled, gagged, smothered, dead, deadened, stilled, stifled, stopped. *Ant.* sounding, sonorous, noisy, resonant, audible, distinct, phonic, stertorous, resounding, phonetic, tinkling, booming, shouting, bellowing, yelling, roaring.

noisome—*Syn.* bad, noxious, putrid, rotten, mephitic, mischievous, offensive, disgusting, malodorous, fetid, stinking, foul, strong-smelling, rancid, olid, musty, fusty, frowsy, tainted, rank, fulsome, moldy, reasty (*Eng. dial.*), empyreumatic, evil-smelling. *Ant.* good, fragrant, redolent, perfumed, aromatic, odorous, sweet, sweet-smelling, pleasing, spicy, balmy, scented, thuriferous, health-giving, delightful, pleasurable, refreshing, comforting, delectable, agreeable, gratifying.

nomad, *n.*—*Syn.* wanderer, gypsy, migrant, itinerant, vagabond, vagrant, rover, roamer.

nominal—*Syn.* suppositious, formal, mere, sheer, simple, named, mentioned, suggested, bare, ostensible, pretended, professed, trivial, trifling, low, inconsiderable, insignificant, cheap, inexpensive, low-priced, reduced, marked down. *Ant.* dear, costly, expensive, substantial, practical, extravagant, exorbitant, high, choice, precious, high-priced, above ordinary, unusual, valuable, prized, uncommon, beyond price, priceless, unreasonable, at a premium.

nominate, v.—*Syn.* name, present, propose, designate, elect, suggest, offer.

nonchalant—*Syn.* careless, indifferent, unconcerned, negligent, uncaring, neglectful, trifling, insouciant, untroubled, supine, heedless, thoughtless, inconsiderate, perfunctory, remiss, devil-may-care, reckless, unheeding, frivolous, scampish, apathetic, cold, frigid, unfeeling, impassive, imperturbable, easygoing, listless, lackadaisical. *Ant.* careful, considerate, thoughtful, patient, cautious, wary, solicitous, anxious, eager, spirited, enthusiastic, emotional, attentive, heedful, earnest, fervent, fervid, zealous, ardent, hardworking, impressionable, precautious, prudent, quick, active, perturbed, excitable, agitated, vigilant, watchful, alert, on the *qui vive*.

nonobservance—*Syn.* inattention, negligence, inadvertence, abstraction, preoccupation, woolgathering, absence of mind, insouciance, absorption, desuetude, disuse, obsolescence, infraction, omission, neglect, disobedience, violation, repudiation, retraction, casualness, laxity, dereliction, noncoöperation, failure, evasion, transgression. *Ant.* obligation, liability, responsibility, duty, observance, conscientiousness, fealty, allegiance, compliance, fulfilment, acquiescence, performance, obedience, habit, custom, usage, practice, prevalence, conventionalism, attention, consideration, mindfulness, alertness, circumspection, heed, heedfulness, steadfastness, conformity, performance.

nonsense—*Syn.* balderdash, absurdity, pretense, folly, trash, jest, joke, piffle (*dial.*), bosh, buncombe, twaddle, flapdoodle (*colloq.*), fustian, extravaganza, humbug, braggadocio, bluster, pomposity, rhodomontade, anticlimax, blather, blathering, galimatias, jargon, medley, Irishism, bull, gibberish, moonshine, tomfoolery, mummery, muddle, monkeyshine (*U. S. slang*), amphigory, farrago, fiddle-faddle (*colloq.*), hifalutin (*slang*), stultification, claptrap, stuff, paradox, hocus-pocus, jabber, palaver, silliness, foolishness, shallowness, senselessness, rigmarole, babble, babbling, rant, poppycock (*U.S. colloq.*), fudge, rubbish, fiddlestick (*colloq.*), fiddledeedee (*colloq.*), chaff (*slang*), smoke (*slang*), froth (*slang*), frippery (*slang*), inconsistency, empty talk. *Ant.* wisdom, sense, common sense, truth, fact, reality, veracity, exactness, verity, gospel, matter of fact, orthodoxy, actuality, accuracy, authenticity, certainty, sureness, reliability, positiveness, dogmatism, meaning, significance, sincerity, signification, intelligibility, clarity, clearness, lucidity, comprehensibility, perspicuity, understanding, literality, import, perception, discernment, prudence, sapience, discrimination, truism, axiom, proverb, maxim, dictum, apophthegm, adage, saw, epigram, theorem, postulate, evidence, plainness, aphorism, true account, true saying, precision, exactitude, doctrine, principle, affirmation, attestation, declaration, pronunciamento, statute, law.

normal—*Syn.* regular, ordinary, conventional, usual, natural, common, typical, average, sane, rational, reasonable, rightminded, orderly, methodical, habitual, medium, middle, intermediate, uniform, customary, commonplace. *Ant.* irregular, unusual, extraordinary, unnatural, queer, eccentric, odd, abnormal, unconventional, diversified, anomalous, uncomfortable, exceptional, arbitrary, aberrant, uncustomary, strange, singular, peculiar, unprecedented, uncommon, rare.

nosy, *adj.* — *Syn.* inquisitive, snoopy, intrusive, meddling, curious, prying.

notable—*Syn.* remarkable, well-known, famous, notorious, celebrated, renowned, distinguished, clever, skilled, skilful, eminent, illustrious, popular, significant, rare, striking, manifest, apparent, pronounced, extraordinary, eventful, evident, explicit, plain, signal, conspicuous, prominent, great, worthy, heroic, foremost, honored, dignified, stately, imposing, exalted. *Ant.* unknown, obscure, humble, low, lowly, mean, debased, contemptible, unworthy, cheap, false, hypocritical, lying, sordid, sinister, abject, common, plebeian, unimportant, insignificant, petty, trivial, inconsequential, immaterial, commonplace, slight, ordinary, usual, uneventful, uninteresting.

note—*Syn.* sign, symbol, token, index, mark, figure, type, representation, device, trace, record, indication, register, explanation, commentary, interpretation, rendering, translation, letter, postal, postcard, dispatch, epistle, paper, paper money, order, promissory note, repute, renown, fame, celebrity, distinction, reputation, tone, semitone, breve, semibreve, minim, crotchet, quaver, semiquaver, demisemiquaver, hemidemisemiquaver.

nothing—*Syn.* nonexistence, not anything, nullity, nihility, inexistence, nonbeing, nothingness, nonentity, *non esse* [L.], obliteration, annihilation, extinction, oblivion, unreality, nullification, shadow, spectre, vision, illusion, ghost, phantom, unsubstantiality, dream, insubstantiality, naught, Nirvana. *Ant.* thing, something, anything, object, article, matter, reality, actuality, materiality, corporality, corporeity, materialness, existence, fact, positiveness, substance, substantiality, body, creature, person, stuff, element, corporeality, hypostasis, entity, being, life.

notice, *n.*—*Syn.* warning, intimation, notification, remark, note, heed, attention, respect, consideration, information, intelligence, instruction, direction, observation, cognizance, regard, civility, respectful treatment, hint, enlightenment, publicity, mention, advice. *Ant.* neglect, omission, forgetfulness, unmindfulness, evasion, laxity, exemption, disrespect, discourtesy, disfavor, contempt, slight, lack of esteem, disdain.

notice, *v.*—*Syn.* note, observe, heed, regard, attend to, mark, respect, mention, see, distinguish, treat civilly, speak to, warn, give attention, be attentive, look at, smile upon, bow to, salute, remember, compliment, greet, hail, welcome, shake hands. *Ant.* ignore, shun, avoid, despise, deprecate, pass by, turn back to, shut eyes to, reject, repel, repulse, scorn, contemnn, disdain, spurn, detest, elude, eschew, keep away from, hate, abominate, loathe, recoil from, shrink from, give the cold shoulder to, keep at a distance.

notify—*Syn.* declare, announce, publish, inform, make known, tell, acquaint, express, intimate, impart, communicate, signify, specify, convey, disclose, tip off (*slang*), tip the wink (*slang*), indicate, give the cue, proclaim, advertise, herald, blazon, circulate, spread, diffuse, disseminate, apprise, wire, 'phone, telegraph, cable, broadcast, promulgate, divulge, reveal, vent, whisper, let the cat out of the bag, blurt out, speak out, report. *Ant.* conceal, hide, keep silent, screen, cover, mask, secrete, camouflage, withhold, reserve, keep back, hold one's tongue, keep light under a bushel, cloak, bottle up, suppress, evade, smother, dissemble, disguise, mystify, confuse, shuffle, shift, prevaricate, lie, deny, quibble, equivocate, avoid, sidestep (*colloq.*), maneuver, dodge, procrastinate, put off, delay.

notion—*Syn.* thought, idea, conception, concept, sentiment, opinion, understanding, inkling, whim, conceit, inclination, mental apprehension, imagination, fancy, belief, knowledge, impression, perception, reflection, theory, claim, viewpoint, presumption, conviction, tenet, dogma, doctrine, principle, surmise, insight, consciousness, cogitation, meditation, cerebration, consideration.

notorious—*Syn.* ill-famed, infamous, disreputable, inglorious, shameful, disgraceful, arrant, opprobrious, discreditable, despicable, outrageous, ignominious, vile, base, debased, villainous, scandalous, dishonorable, dishonored, disgraced, vicious, immoral, depraved, profligate, flagrant, iniquitous, dissolute, unprincipled, unspeakable, diabolic, Satanic, hellish, flagitious, well-known in a sinister sense. *Ant.* good, virtuous, noble, high-minded, honorable, honest, decent, true, moral, law-abiding, chivalrous, manly, exalted, elevated, respected, reputable, praiseworthy, meritorious, righteous, right-minded, charitable, philanthropic, kind, commendable, fine, creditable, admirable, exemplary, sterling, famous, celebrated, distinguished, honored, renowned, notable, popular, well-known in a good sense.

notwithstanding, *adv.*—*Syn.* however, nevertheless, yet.

notwithstanding, *prep.*—*Syn.* despite, in spite of, for all that, on the other hand, after all.

notwithstanding, *conj.*—*Syn.* however, nevertheless, though, although, but, howbeit, still, yet.

nourish—*Syn.* feed, supply, sustain, support, nurture, cherish, foster, minister, administer, nurse, serve, attend, tend, wait on, care for, succor. *Ant.* starve, famish, deprive, take from, exhaust, weaken, debilitate, enervate, enfeeble, reduce, impair, attenuate, sap, neglect, abandon.

nourishment—*Syn.* food, supply, sustenance, nutrition, diet, upkeep, meal, repast, collation, refreshment, entertainment, regalement, maintenance, support, victuals, provisions. *Ant.* starvation, hunger, deprivation, destitution, detriment, injury, impairment, damage, want, deficiency, lack, scarcity, indigence, poverty, dearth, famine.

novel—*Syn.* new, unusual, strange, uncommon, rare, modern, recent, out of the ordinary, late, fresh, untried, unprecedented, unique, odd, w o n d e r f u l, unparalleled, dissimilar. *Ant.* old, olden, ancient, primitive, antiquated, old-fashioned, out-of-date, outworn, hoary, known, familiar, usual, habitual, customary, frequent, common, commonplace, ordinary, similar.

novice—*Syn.* beginner, learner, neophyte, tyro, pupil, undergraduate, schoolboy, schoolgirl, follower, disciple, recruit, catechumen, apprentice, probationer, *debutant* [*Fr.*], *debutante* [*Fr.*], bungler, blunderer, ignoramus—lout, lubber, duffer, muffer, dolt, blunderhead, woodenhead, dunderhead, bonehead, numskull, butter-fingers, dupe, flat, sucker, booby, clod, yokel, tenderfoot, greenhorn— all *slang* or *colloq.* *Ant.* master, instructor, trainer, tutor, teacher, professor, preacher, pedagogue, dominie, guide, director, mentor, adviser, *pundit* [*Sans.*], *guru* [*Sans.*], *sahib* [*Ar.*], expositor, exemplar, preceptor, scholar, *savant* [*Fr.*], wrangler, doctor, don, academician, philomath, philosopher, sophist, bookman, philologist, scientist, classicist, linguist, *m o o n s h e e* [*Ind.*], bibliophilist, bluestocking (*colloq.*), *bas-bleu* [*Fr.*], highbrow (*slang*).

noxious—*Syn.* harmful, baneful, pernicious, noisome, pestiferous, poisonous, injurious, deleterious, pestilential, dangerous, unwholesome, deadly, azotic, morbific, venomous, virulent, toxic, mephitic, offensive, putrid, rotten, smelling, malodorous, stinking, tainted, contaminated, septic, luetic, tabetic, zymotic, foul, bad, rank, fulsome, nocuous, unhealthy, insalubrious, hurtful, destructive. *Ant.* good, healthy, wholesome, salubrious, health-giving, bracing, curative, strengthening, invigorating, prophylactic, hygienic, harmless, innoxious, innocuous, sanative, sanatory, restorative, helpful, preservative, nutritious, beneficial, healing, remedial, advantageous, useful, profitable, valuable, healthful, energizing, forceful, stimulating, antiseptic, inoffensive, harmless.

nucleus, *n.*—*Syn.* core, focus, center, heart, middle, kernel, basis.

nude—*Syn.* bare, naked, unclothed, undraped, uncovered, denuded, stripped, disrobed, divested, undressed, exposed, in buff, in birthday suit (*colloq.*), Adamitic. *Ant.* clothed, clad, dressed, robed, covered, cloaked, screened, draped, habited, invested, liveried, attired, costumed, garbed, arrayed, appareled.

nullify—*Syn.* repeal, cancel, invalidate, quash, vacate, annul, make void, deprive of force, destroy, abrogate, counteract, upset, suppress, obliterate, erase, countermand, break down, delete, dispel, overthrow, set aside, revoke, rescind, ignore, infringe, discard, disobey, trample under foot. *Ant.* uphold, support, affirm, conform, consent, concur, agree, harmonize, pull together, keep pace with, coöperate, record, note, list, indorse, chronicle, commemorate, let stand, adhere to, observe, obey, respect, comply with, carry out, execute, perform, discharge, act up to, do one's office.

numb, *adj.*—*Syn.* dull, torpid, deadened, stupefied, insensitive, paralyzed, dazed, frozen, lifeless.

number—*Syn.* count, enumerate, estimate, reckon, compute, calculate, check, tell, score, call, call the roll, muster, sum up, take an account of, run over, recapitulate.

numerous—*Syn.* many, various, divers, sundry, manifold, profuse, multifold, crowded, multitudinous, teeming, populous. *Ant.* few, scarce, sparse, scant, lacking, reduced, diminished, small, fractional, decimated, thin, deficient, hardly any.

nuptials, *n.*—*Syn.* marriage, wedding, wedlock, matrimony.

nurse, *v.*—*Syn.* cherish, foster, tend, feed, encourage, nurture, suckle, nourish, pamper.

nurture, *v.*—*Syn.* nourish, nurse, train, rear, foster, support, cherish, uphold.

nutriment, *n.*—*Syn.* food, sustenance, aliment, provision, nourishment, nurture.

O

oaf—*Syn.* nitwit, giddy-head, beetlehead, bullhead, calf, numskull, addle-head, noodle-head, addlepate, chucklehead, nincompoop, thickhead, gaby, jolter head, stick, block, lunkhead, softy—all *colloq.*; mutt, loony, bonehead, spoon, spoony, saphead—all *slang;* chowderhead, ninny, loon, sawney, lummox— all *dial.;* dolt, idiot, blockhead, simpleton, ass, donkey, imbecile, goose, rattlepate, dullard, lubber, bungler, greenhorn, dunce, rube, gawk, ignoramus, fool, moron. *Ant.* wise man, sage, *savant* [*Fr.*], scientist, scholar, philosopher, teacher, mentor, instructor, professor, wiseacre, wizard, expert, oracle, connoisseur, judge, master, doctor, pedagogue, philomath, schoolman, philologist, lexicographer, sophist, leader, academician, scholiast, luminary, Solon, *pundit* [*Sans.*], lecturer, preacher, dominie, schoolmaster, schoolmistress, guide, director, expositor, apostle, tutor, adviser.

oath—*Syn.* affirmation, declaration, imprecation, assertion, malediction, curse, affidavit, blasphemy, denunciation, execration, swearing, profanity, cursing, reprobation, anathema, adjuration, blaspheming, sworn statement, profane swearing, ban, vow, maranatha, fulmination, malison. *Ant.* benediction, benison, blessing, approval, approbation, sanction, admiration, commendation, laudation, acclamation, praise, hosanna, pæan, acclaim, eulogy, encomium, eulogium, panegyric.

obdurate—*Syn.* stubborn, callous, hard, hardened, unyielding, self-willed, headstrong, obstinate, immovable, dogged, resolute, contumacious, perverse, dogmatic, tenacious, opinionative, case-hardened, sulky, inflexible, inexorable, pigheaded, mulish. *Ant.* susceptible, amenable, gentle, persuasible, tractable, yielding, changing, changeful, erratic, eccentric, volatile, freakish, fitful, whimsical, flighty, light-headed, careless, free-and-easy, devil-may-care, capricious, inconsistent, fantastic, fanciful, crotchety, frivolous, giddy.

obedient—*Syn.* compliant, dutiful, submissive, respectful, law-abiding, loyal, faithful, devoted, resigned, passive, sycophantic, subjective, pliant, acquiescent, yielding, conformable, prostrate, cringing, truckling, kowtowing, submitting, surrendering. *Ant.* obstinate, disobedient, contemptuous, rude, obdurate, contumacious, insubordinate, infringing, mutinous, insurgent, lawless, unruly, riotous, obstreperous, seditious, defiant, unyielding, insolent, impudent, impertinent, stubborn, unwilling, dour.

obeisance, *n.*—*Syn.* homage, fealty, salute, reverence, deference, allegiance, bow, curtsy, genuflection.

obese—*Syn.* fat, corpulent, adipose, plump, fleshy, rotund, stout, burly, bulky, ponderous, unwieldy, lumpish, lusty, whopping (*colloq.*), puffy, swollen, corn-fed (*colloq.*), fat as a pig. *Ant.* lean, thin, slender, attenuated, lanky, weazened, emaciated, delicate, consumptive, tabetic, atrophied, withered, shrunken, shriveled, scraggy, scrawny, pinched, skinny, weedy (*colloq.*), gaunt, skeletal.

obey—*Syn.* conform, comply, submit, answer, respond, assent, accede, concur, surrender, yield, act, perform, carry out, attend to orders, come at call, do one's bidding, serve.

object, *n.*—*Syn.* thing, anything, something, substance, substantiality, matter, materiality, article, person, body, element, part, earth, sky, heaven, sun, moon, star, world, creation, universe, everything. *Ant.* nothingness, insubstantiality, nihility, vision, shadow, spirit, ghost, appearance, dream, fancy, imagination, illusion, vacuity, vacuum, emptiness, space.

object, *v.*—*Syn.* oppose, discard, reject, dislike, loathe, detest, abhor, abominate, disrelish, shun, avoid, repugn, shrink from, hate, despise, repel, sicken, nauseate, deprecate, contravene, impeach, demur, disapprove, gainsay, hesitate, scruple, take exception. *Ant.* like, desire, wish, want, need, long for, hanker for, covet, aspire to, request, solicit, demand, beg, implore, sue for, ask, crave, entreat, petition, beseech, invite, assent, grant, gratify, accept, welcome, comply, concur, consent, applaud, approve, admire, admit, accede.

objective, *n.*—*Syn.* object, goal, aim, aspiration, purpose, end, intention, design, scheme, perspective, prospective, outlook, result, mark, butt. *Ant.* premise, beginning, introduction, preface, foreword, cause, origin, inception, initiation, initiative, preliminary.

objurgation, *n.*—*Syn.* rebuke, abuse, execration, condemnation, vituperation, reprobation, criticism. *Ant.* praise, applause, commendation, approval.

obligation, *n.*—*Syn.* responsibility, duty, pledge, liability, burden, debt, promise, agreement.

oblige—*Syn.* accommodate, gratify, please, constrain, compel, coerce, force, drive, enforce, insist, hinder, prevent, necessitate, restrain, command, commandeer. *Ant.* free, release, exempt, discharge, acquit, unbind, untrammel, unshackle, set free, excuse, renounce, accede, grant, absolve, spare.

oblique, *adj.*—*Syn.* indirect, devious, tilted, askew, crooked, diagonal, sidelong, sloping. *Ant.* direct, straightforward, immediate, forthright.

obliterate, *v.*—*Syn.* erase, delete, cancel, expunge, efface, nullify, raze.

oblivious, *adj.*—*Syn.* heedless, unmindful, inattentive, unaware, negligent, forgetful. *Ant.* mindful, aware, alert, watchful.

obloquy—*Syn.* contumely, odium, reproach, disgrace, defamation, shame, disrepute, disapprobation, abasement, debasement, dishonor, scandal, humiliation, stigma, brand, infamy, turpitude, vileness, opprobrium. *Ant.* repute, fame, character, dignity, stateliness, nobility, glory, celebrity, p o p u l a r i t y, reputation, renown, distinction, majesty, sublimity, prestige, approbation, eminence, worthiness.

obnoxious—*Syn.* offensive, disagreeable, displeasing, hurtful, reprehensible, blameworthy, detestable, hateful, pernicious, distressing, disgusting, abhorrent, abominable, odious, repulsive, repellent, revolting, shocking, irritating. *Ant.* pleasing, pleasurable, beneficial, attractive, inviting, fascinating, delightful, charming, seductive, winsome, satisfying, gratifying, welcome, gladsome, delectable, cordial, refreshing, gladdening, sweet.

obscene—*Syn.* impure, lewd, indelicate, coarse, indecent, im-moral, dirty, filthy, nasty, unclean, smutty, soiled, grimy, foul, beastly, abominable, offensive, defiled, polluted, contaminated, corrupt, rotten. *Ant.* pure, upright, honorable, clean, spotless, unstained, unspotted, virtuous, unsullied, unstained, immaculate, innocent, white (*slang*), decent, well-behaved, modest, particular, respectable, respected.

obscure—*Syn.* dim, dark, doubtful, mysterious, cloudy, complex, intricate, abstruse, indistinct, unknown, hidden, concealed, profound, ambiguous, incomprehensible, dense, deep, darksome, complicated, casual, indecisive, unintelligible, involved, difficult, enigmatical, uncertain, dubious, vague, indeterminate, indefinite, confused, cryptic, oracular, unknown. *Ant.* plain, clear, evident, axiomatic, undisputed, unquestionable, apparent, unimpeachable, conclusive, irrefutable, incontrovertible, indubitable, definite, intelligible, comprehensible, unequivocal, explicit, lucid, perspicuous, distinct, positive, absolute, clear-cut, graphic, easy, unambiguous, manifest, visible, perceptible, unmistakable, known, distinguished, famous, celebrated.

obsequious—*Syn.* cringing, slavish, sycophantic, deferential, kowtowing, servile, subject, enslaved, subordinate, parasitical, stipendary, toadying, fawning, truckling, groveling, reptilian, dough-faced (*slang*), spineless, crouching, mealy-mouthed, abject, beggarly, timeserving, sniveling, sneaking, soapy (*slang*), oily, toadeating, flunkeyish. *Ant.* insolent, impudent, bold, defiant, swaggering, presumptuous, presumptive, contemptuous, saucy, hardened, cheeky (*slang*), domineering, intimidating, bullying, arrogant, imperious, haughty, assertive, dictatorial, arbitrary, high-handed, highhattish (*slang*), supercilious, nervy (*colloq.*), overbearing, toplofty (*colloq.*), assuming, brazen, confident, audacious.

observant—*Syn.* attentive, watchful, careful, heedful, mindful, listening, alert, regardful, intent on, taken up with, engaged in, alive to. *Ant.* heedless, careless, unmindful, indifferent, abstracted, preoccupied, dreamy, woolgathering, moonraking (*dial.*), thoughtless, nonobservant.

obsolete—*Syn.* disused, old-fashioned, archaic, desuete, antique, ancient, antiquated, obsolescent, out of date, rare, old, traditional, obscure, neglected, outworn, hoary, primitive, timeworn, *passé* [*Fr.*], extinct. *Ant.* new, novel, recent, modern, newfangled, new-fashioned, up-to-date, fresh, green, evergreen, late, raw, just out (*colloq.*), brand-new, neoteric, neologic, neological, unused.

obstacle, *n.*—*Syn.* impediment, check, hindrance, barrier, snag, obstruction.

obstinate—*Syn.* stubborn, headstrong, opinionated, contumacious, pertinacious, inflexible, resolute, immovable, insusceptible, perverse, unaffected, unimpressible, determined, resolved, indomitable, intractable, firm, dogged, obdurate, persistent, refractory, unconquerable, unflinching, heady, mulish, unyielding, decided, firm, fixed. *Ant.* complaisant, courteous, obliging, yielding, tractable, docile, submissive, obedient, teachable, pliant, pliable, gentle, compliant, agreeable, amenable, undecided, wavering, irresolute, acquiescent, controllable, obsequious, subservient, humble, passive, dutiful, manageable, governable, easily led.

obstreperous, *adj.*—*Syn.* troublesome, turbulent, noisy, boisterous, recalcitrant, unruly, uproarious, refractory. *Ant.* quiet, peaceful, silent, harmonious.

obstruct—*Syn.* impede, oppose, retard, embarrass, stay, check, clog, arrest, stop, block, hinder, prevent, close, plug, shut, bar, bolt, lock, incumber, incommode, interrupt, circumvent, thwart, frustrate, baffle, barricade, counteract, contravene, cramp, hamper, handicap, cripple, inhibit. *Ant.* aid, assist, help, encourage, favor, succor, support, sustain, expedite, speed, second, accommodate, abet, espouse, countenance, patronize, advance, further, champion, advocate, promote, forward, uphold, re-enforce, accelerate, facilitate, clear the way.

obtain—*Syn.* acquire, procure, get, attain, gain, win, secure, retrieve, recover, collect, gather, earn, pick, pick up, purchase, inherit, salvage, effect, receive, compass, realize, save, hoard, lay up. *Ant.* disburse, scatter, spend, waste, squander, lose, mislay, forfeit, give, give away, expend, donate, bestow, dispense, present, consign, contribute, hand out, shell out (*slang*), award, subscribe, grant, bequeath, yield, distribute, allocate, assign, allot, apportion, divide.

obtrusive, *adj.*—*Syn.* interfering, officious, meddling, meddlesome, curious, forward, pushing. *Ant.* shy, diffident, modest, retiring.

obtuse, *adj.*—*Syn.* blunt, insensitive, impassive, stolid, blockish, dull, slow, stupid, phlegmatic. *Ant.* acute, sensitive, imaginative.

obviate, *v.*—*Syn.* avoid, prevent, avert, forestall, remove, evade, preclude, elude.

obvious—*Syn.* plain, clear, evident, self-evident, conclusive, manifest, apparent, distinct, lucid, intelligible, comprehensible, precise, definite, unequivocal, unambiguous, explicit. *Ant.* complex, complicated, mixed, confused, intricate, puzzling, unintelligible, obscure, indefinite, ambiguous, occult, esoteric, muddy, latent, mysterious, acroatic, abstruse, difficult.

occasion—*Syn.* opportunity, cause, reason, juncture, conjuncture, opening, ground, exigency, need, time, necessity, circumstance, situation, origin, contingency, emergency, occurrence, crisis, turn, plight, source, spring, wellspring, fountainhead. *Ant.* consequence, resultant, conclusion, aftermath, effect, outcome, outgrowth, development, fruit, fruitage, product, result, issue, event.

occasional—*Syn.* casual, accidental, incidental, irregular, contingent, uncertain, doubtful, dubious, vague, unstable, unsettled, indefinite, equivocal, indeterminate, questionable, precarious, problematical, dependent, provisional. *Ant.* certain, sure, dogmatic, authoritative, indubious, conclusive, incontestable, incontrovertible, indubitable, irrefutable, authentic, unquestionable, indefeasible, undeniable, beyond question, without doubt.

occult—*Syn.* latent, hidden, mysterious, esoteric, secret, unknown, unrevealed, dark, ambiguous, unintelligible, unknowable, obscure, enigmatic, unfathomable, impenetrable, metempirical, transcendental, elusive, undiscernible, mystical, inscrutable, inexplicable, incomprehensible, acroatic, abstruse, inconceivable, recondite. *Ant.* see SYNONYMS for **obvious** above.

occupation—*Syn.* calling, vocation, trade, profession, pursuit, business, craft, office, employment, undertaking, concern, mission, commission, sphere, engagement, incumbency, charge, care, duty, berth, billet, work, job, place, situation, enterprise, function, province, handicraft.

occurrence—*Syn.* happening, incident, accident, event, occasion, circumstance, emergency, juncture, conjuncture, provision, exigency, crisis, eventuality, proceeding, transaction, casualty, adventure, experience.

odd—*Syn.* uneven, single, singular, strange, queer, wonderful, occult, mysterious, mystifying, peculiar, quaint, marvelous, fantastic, unmatched, alone, sole, fragmentary, rare, ridiculous, absurd, erratic, remaining, residual, irregular, anomalous, eccentric, comical, funny, crazy, cracked (*colloq.*), touched, unhinged, awkward, vulgar, rococo, droll, laughable, bizarre, baroque, exaggerated, extraordinary, unusual, uncommon, abnormal. *Ant.* uniform, even, conformable, regular, formal, orderly, symmetrical, normal, methodical, ordinary, common, commonplace, conventional, standard, constant, sane, lucid, sober, steady, reliable, rational, reasonable, right-minded, cultivated, dainty, æsthetic, refined, artistic, everyday, usual, habitual.

odious—*Syn.* hateful, abhorrent, repellent, disgusting, abominable, offensive, foul, detestable, loathsome, disagreeable, invidious, nauseous, repugnant, revolting, execrable, hideous, shocking, horrible, horrid, obnoxious, repulsive, distasteful, displeasing, unclean, nasty, coarse, vulgar, unmoral, impure, reeky, beastly, putrid, rotten, purulent, saprogenous. *Ant.* pleasing, attractive, inviting, engaging, fascinating, winning, charming, enticing, seductive, alluring, entrancing, ravishing, captivating, delightful, cheerful, cheering, lovable, likable, dainty, delicious, refreshing, clean, pure, wholesome, moral, sound, honorable, amiable, agreeable, beautiful, handsome, graceful, lovely, refined, fine, splendid, gorgeous, magnificent, grand, sublime.

odor, *n.*—*Syn.* scent, smell, redolence, effluvium, perfume, fragrance, aroma, reek, fume, fetor.

offense—*Syn.* misdeed, misdemeanor, transgression, trespass, fault, affront, resentment, crime, scandal, sin, attack, assault, insult, onslaught, aggression, onset, battery, wrong, harm, hurt, injury, malfeasance, misconduct, felony, outrage, atrocity, corruption, guilt. *Ant.* innocence, harmlessness, goodness, good, conduct, morality, honor, decency, uprightness, righteousness, correctness, excellence, credit, good behavior, rectitude, nobility, magnanimity, heroism, generosity, character, self-denial, charity, philanthropy, altruism, large-heartedness, kindness, probity, worthiness, integrity, respectability, inoffensiveness.

offensive—*Syn.* insolent, impudent, impertinent, abusive, obnoxious, disagreeable, fetid, disgusting, saucy, displeasing, opprobrious, insulting, rude, scurrilous, abhorrent, detestable, reprehensible, infamous, hateful, audacious, aggressive, forward, brazen, arrogant, overbearing, low, foul, indecent, coarse, ribald, vulgar, nasty, unclean, filthy, feculent, lousy, verminous, putrid, stinking, rotten. *Ant.* humble, gentle, mild, docile, pliable, agreeable, conformable, ready, compliant, complaisant, willing, polite, courteous, pleasing, amiable, well-behaved, gentlemanly, ladylike, civil, gracious, deferent, deferential, genteel, polished, well-bred, refined, modest, retiring, bashful, backward, clean, immaculate, moral, virtuous, tidy, neat, well-dressed, affable, suave, bland, clean-cut, symmetrical, stylish, becoming.

offer, *v.*—*Syn.* present, tender, propose, advance, dare, volunteer, bid, proffer, move.

offhand, *adj.*—*Syn.* extempore, unpremeditated, impromptu, casual, impulsive, improvised, impetuous, hasty. *Ant.* studied, advised, considered, deliberate.

office—*Syn.* charge, function, place, business, calling, employment, business place, accounting room, clerical force, duty, performance, transaction, engagement, undertaking, mission, trade, craft, profession, vocation, avocation, service, appointment, post, station, agency, cue, tip (*slang*), action, activity,

praying, daily prayer, act of worship.

official—*Syn.* authoritative, authentic, trustworthy, genuine, true, proper, unquestionable, indubitable, veritable, real, certain, sure, reliable, assured, absolute, positive, clear, unequivocal, unmistakable, decided, decisive, conclusive, unimpeachable, irrefutable, incontestable, undeniable, governmental, indisputable, not to be questioned, definite. *Ant.* dubious, doubtful, indecisive, vague, indeterminate, equivocal, indefinite, disputable, questionable, confused, unauthentic, unauthorized, obscure, puzzling, cryptic, mysterious, perplexing, untrustworthy, unreliable, uncertain, apocryphal, problematical, contingent, ambiguous, suspicious, hypothetical, unofficial.

officious, *adj.*—*Syn.* meddling, obtrusive, presumptuous, nosy, intrusive, interfering.

offspring—*Syn.* progeny, issue, descendants, children, siblings, lineage, generation, posterity, brood, seed, family, heirs, offshoots, chips of the old block (*colloq.*), heredity, succession, successors. *Ant.* ancestry, ancestors, progenitors, forefathers, fathers, fatherhood, paternity, stem, line, stock, forbears or forebears, family, race, tribe, clan, sept, pedigree, lineage, genealogy, stirps, house, tree, trunk.

often, *adv.*—*Syn.* frequently, commonly, recurrently, repeatedly. *Ant.* seldom, rarely, infrequently.

oily—*Syn.* smooth, polished, lustrous, bright, brilliant, shining, greasy, smeary, oleaginous, slippery, servile, sycophantic, flattering, cajoling, coaxing, deceitful, plausible, sanctimonious. *Ant.* dull, dim, lustreless, rough, dry, coarse, cheeky (*slang*), impudent, nervy (*colloq.*), saucy, presumptuous, impertinent, flippant, insolent.

old—*Syn.* ancient, primitive, antique, antiquated, bygone, old-fashioned, obsolete, early, pre-historic, pristine, immemorial, antediluvian, hoary, venerable, time-honored, superannuated, timeworn, patriarchal, olden, re-mote, gray, decrepit, aged, se-nile. *Ant.* new, modern, up-to-date, of the present, recent, late, fresh, green, blooming, budding, young, juvenile, puer-ile, childish, youthful, new-fash-ioned, renovated, freshened, spick-and-span, unhandled, neo-teric, fresh as paint (*colloq.*).

omen—*Syn.* portent, augury, sign, indication, foreshadow, warning, prognostic, auspice, harbinger, precursor, presage, and many terms, mostly ending in the suf-fix, -*mancy* (from *Gr. manteia,* divination, from *Gr. mantis,* a diviner, seer, or prophet), de-noting different forms of divina-tion, expressive of early cus-toms and superstitions, as hiero-mancy, hydromancy, ichthyo-mancy, myomancy, pyromancy, crystallomancy, sciomancy, or-nithomancy, ophiomancy, dac-tyliomancy, Bibliomancy, an-thropomancy, austromancy, alec-tryomancy, catoptromancy, pse-phomancy, capnomancy, sidero-mancy, alphitomancy, molybdo-mancy, lithomancy, onycho-mancy, oneiromancy, chiro-mancy, aëromancy, rhabdo-mancy, cleromancy, aleuro-mancy, axinomancy, belomancy, tephramancy, etc., to which may be added aruspicy, orniscopy, genethliacs, sortilege, geloscopy, bletonism, extispicy, palmistry, table-tapping, spirit-rapping, and various superstitious practices indulged in on Walpurgis Night (May I, Germany) and Hal-lowe'en (Oct. 31, Ireland).

ominous—*Syn.* threatening, fore-boding, suggestive, portentous, premonitory, unpropitious, in-auspicious, presaging, indicating, augural, precursive, significant, prescient, prophetic, vatic, vatic-inal. *Ant.* cheerful, cheering, comforting, consoling, roseate, bright, appealing, heartsome, en-couraging, inspiriting, pleasing, exhilarating, good, auspicious, favorable.

omit—*Syn.* exclude, overlook, dis-regard, pass over, leave out, bar, except, preclude, repudiate, prohibit, reject, cast aside, elim-inate, neglect, discard, nullify, retract, cancel, void. *Ant.* in-sert, enter, set down, take in, include, record, put in, intro-duce, inject, interject, register, enroll, chronicle, accept, docket, inscribe, mark, indicate, com-memorate.

onerous—*Syn.* burdensome, trou-blesome, difficult, oppressive, responsible, heavy, serious, over-powering, galling, grinding, la-borious, toilsome, irksome, ar-duous, formidable, cumber-some, cumbrous. *Ant.* easy, light, trivial, trifling, agreeable, pleasant, facile, unimportant, immaterial, insignificant, little, small, unessential, common, un-necessary, normal, ordinary, commonplace, paltry, petty, in-considerable.

onlooker, *n.*—*Syn.* spectator, wit-ness, beholder, bystander, view-er, observer, kibitzer, rubber-neck.

only, *adv.*—*Syn.* exclusively, sole-ly, merely, simply, singly, just, but, barely.

onset, *n.*—*Syn.* beginning, attack, onslaught, assault.

opaque—*Syn.* dark, obscure, dark-ened, non-transparent, imper-vious to light, dim, dull, lustre-less, shady, obfuscated, smoky, murky, misty, nubilous, cloudy, filmy, fuliginous, sooty, dusky, adiaphanous. *Ant.* clear, trans-parent, lucid, pellucid, bright, shining, limpid, diaphanous, hyaline, glassy, crystalline, trans-lucent, vitreous, luminous, se-rene, undimmed, unclouded, lus-trous.

open, *adj.*—*Syn.* unclosed, acces-sible, unsealed, unobstructed, unrestricted, free of entrance, passable, ajar, gaping, agape, apart, unbarred, expanded, full-blown, clear, manifest, apparent, definite, plain, evident, conspicuous, unmistakable, ostensible, explicit, disclosed, candid, frank, straightforward, unreserved, simple, sincere, undisguised, unaffected, ingenuous, outspoken, unsophisticated, artless, naïve, simple-minded, guileless, innocent. *Ant.* closed, shut, barred, stopped, blocked, obstructed, tight, contracted, compressed, hidden, concealed, buried, latent, secret, underhand, steganographic, cryptographic, covert, involved, enigmatical, cryptic, insincere, hypocritical, equivocal, cunning, crafty, subtle, subtile, deep, intriguing, designing, foxy, artful, deceptive, deceitful, wily, tricky, shifty, astute, sharp, shrewd, canny [*Sc.*].

open, *v.*—*Syn.* unbar, unlock, unclose, expand, uncover, begin, start, inaugurate, admit, make known, put on sale, make accessible, give entrance, clear, cut through, render passable, split, divide, rend, separate, discover, make manifest, explain, speak, initiate. *Ant.* bar, lock, shut, close, refuse admittance, turn away, deny, stop, block, plug, screen, cover, hide, secrete, c o n c e a l, finish, terminate, conclude, end, exclude, reject, repudiate, preclude, prevent, hinder, restrain, prohibit, interdict, inhibit, disallow, debar.

operate—*Syn.* work, act upon, perform, carry on, sustain, execute, manipulate, transact, practice, buy, sell, manage, direct, guide, superintend, produce, manufacture, construct, contrive, constitute, accomplish, achieve. *Ant.* fail, suppress, abolish, dissolve, overthrow, smash, destroy, quash, squash (*colloq.*), batter down, wreck, scuttle, ruin, dismantle, disorganize, stamp out, disuse, relinquish, dispense with, neglect, leave off, discard.

operation—*Syn.* action, execution, performance, act, agency, effect,

process, production, work, procedure, surgical treatment, employment, labor, deed, proceeding, handiwork, manufacture, workmanship, transaction, achievement, result. *Ant.* failure, inaction, inactivity, inutility, powerlessness, uselessness, inefficiency, ineffectiveness, idleness, inertness, indolence, remissness, ergophobia, negligence, otiosity, sloth, slothfulness, relaxation, repose, rest, inexertion, inertia, exhaustion, collapse.

opinion—*Syn.* notion, view, judgment, belief, sentiment, conception, idea, estimation, conviction, impression, surmise, conclusion, inference, tenet, creed, principle, doctrine. *Ant.* unbelief, doubt, misgiving, incredibility, scepticism, scruple, dissent, demur, disbelief, discredit, suspicion, incredulity, distrust, mistrust, uncertainty, vagueness, perplexity, ambiguity, embarrassment, suspense, bewilderment.

opponent—*Syn.* rival, antagonist, competitor, emulator, claimant, disputant, challenger, attacker, assailant, invader, encroacher, intruder, infringer, violator, contestant, litigant, enemy, foe, foeman, adversary. *Ant.* friend, confidant, associate, pal (*slang*), buddy (*slang*), companion, comrade, ally, mate, colleague, assistant, helper, classmate, crony, schoolmate, roommate, shipmate, playfellow, partner, sidepartner, consort, helpmate.

opportunity, *n.*—*Syn.* chance, occasion, situation, contingency, time, opening, possibility.

oppose—*Syn.* resist, check, combat, oppugn, obstruct, contravene, withstand, restrain, deny, thwart, counteract, confront, retaliate, rebuff, snub, kick (*slang*), contradict, run counter, protest, countervail, face, dare, brave, taunt, defy, clash, cross, antagonize, frustrate, overpower, impede, hinder, neutralize, overcome, invert, reverse, turn the tables. *Ant.* coöperate, concur, side with, join hands, combine, fraternize, conspire, rally round, federate, ratify, vouch for, confirm, indorse, sanction, commend, recommend, certify, attest, support, sustain, approve, praise, flatter, laud, applaud, eulogize, acclaim, collude, connive, participate, coalesce, join forces, unite with, pull together.

opposite, *n.—Syn.* counterpart, reverse, antithesis, contrary, contradictory, antonym.

oppress, *v.—Syn.* afflict, crush, harass, persecute, overbear, overwhelm, maltreat, burden, tyrannize, aggrieve.

opprobrious—*Syn.* hateful, infamous, disgraceful, scandalous, shameful, scurrile, scurrilous, offensive, derogatory, abusive, reproachful, contemptuous, degrading, ingominious, dishonorable, abasing, base, humiliating, heinous, execrable, defamatory, slanderous, outrageous, flagrant, nefarious, wanton, flagitious, odious, atrocious, abhorrent, monstrous, villainous, abominable, detestable, shocking, notorious, despicable, disreputable. *Ant.* worthy, praiseworthy, commendable, deserving, creditable, estimable, meritorious, reputable, respectable, decent, honest, honorable, well-behaved, virtuous, noble, exalted, distinguished, famous, celebrated, popular, honored, eulogized, illustrious, eminent, proper, prominent, respected, esteemed, righteous, trustworthy, good, just, upright, dignified, incorruptible, straightforward, high-minded, high-principled, square (*colloq.*), fair and square (*colloq.*), aboveboard, staunch, true, dependable, white (*slang*).

oppugnant—*Syn.* opposing, resisting, unfavorable, unpropitious, hostile, inimical, unfriendly, adverse, obstructive, recalcitrant, renitent. *Ant.* coöperating, favorable, friendly, propitious, helpful, sympathetic, concilia-

tory, comforting, consolatory, solacing, condoling.

optimistic—*Syn.* hopeful, cheering, comforting, cheerful, sanguine, confident, elated, enthusiastic, promising, encouraging, heartening, inspiriting, rousing, arousing. *Ant.* pessimistic, gloomy, despairing, doleful, doubtful, afraid, anticipating evil, hopeless, dejected, inconsolable, down in the mouth (*slang*), heavy, melancholy, lugubrious, mournful, broken-hearted.

option, *n.—Syn.* choice, discretion, selection, preference, alternative, election.

oracular—*Syn.* ambiguous, obscure, mystical, cryptic, vague, hazy, equivocal, esoteric, unintelligible, obscured, incomprehensible, mysterious, mystifying, abstruse, dubious, doubtful. *Ant.* plain, easy, lucid, intelligible, clear, distinct, unequivocal, explicit, positive, definite.

oracular—*Syn.* positive, authoritative, grave, wise, sage, sapient, sound, prophetic, portentous, predictive, presageful, vaticinal, rational. *Ant.* foolish, senseless, fatuous, driveling, irrational, babbling, silly, nonsensical, inept, stupid, maudlin, idiotic, asinine, ridiculous.

oration—*Syn.* speech, harangue, discourse, address, disquisition, talk, declamation, tirade, panegyric, rhetoric, bombast, lecture, sermon. *Ant.* silence, muteness, taciturnity, reserve, reticence, stillness, hush, aphony, dumbness, suppression, speechlessness, voicelessness.

orbit, *n.—Syn.* circuit, path, sweep, ambit, gamut, scope, purview, ken, horizon.

ordain—*Syn.* install, institute, appoint, enact, decree, dictate, order, command, prescribe, impose, commission, delegate, assign, constitute, warrant, legalize, call, induct, consecrate. *Ant.* abrogate, cancel, revoke, rescind, repeal, depose, dismiss, bounce (*slang*), sack (*slang*), disallow, invalidate, prohibit, disqualify, annul, abolish, countermand, recall, quash, nullify, disestablish, retract, set aside, void, make void.

ordeal, n.—Syn. trial, test, judgment, scrutiny, strain, tribulation, gauntlet.

order, n.—Syn. command, mandate, instruction, injunction, direction, regulation, requirement, prohibition, rule, regularity, system, plan, method, precept, custom, condition, state, rank, class, management, arrangement. Ant. disorder, disorganization, confusion, chaos, derangement, irregularity, mixture, medley, tangle, perplexity, complexity, snarl, maze, labyrinth, huddle, muddle, muss, shuffle, disobedience, infringement, informality, unconformity, unconventionality, nonconformity, allowance, consent, leave, liberty, license, permission, permit.

order, v.—Syn. command, appoint, direct, rule, dictate, enjoin, bid, demand, instruct, request, decree, ordain, prescribe, charge, proclaim, impose, exact. Ant. beg, petition, solicit, crave, entreat, beseech, implore, supplicate, importune, seek, pray, appeal, humbly ask, ask deferentially, plead for.

orderly—Syn. methodical, regular, systematic, peaceable, quiet, correct, neat, tidy, systematical, arranged, adjusted, regulated, symmetrical, unconfused, classified, formal, normal. Ant. disorderly, disordered, confused, irregular, tangled, entangled, disorganized, promiscuous, gnarled, snarled, intricate, complex, untidy, straggling, slovenly, hugger-mugger.

ordinance, n.—Syn. statute, law, decree, regulation, prescript, rule, enactment, ceremony, order.

ordinary—Syn. common, commonplace, normal, regular, usual, conventional, formal, customary, conformable, typical, consistent, habitual, accustomed, wonted, familiar, trite, prevalent, stereotyped, current, simple, unaffected, natural, artless, unadorned, plain, ugly. Ant. uncommon, extraordinary, informal, unconventional, anomalous, eccentric, arbitrary, irregular, exceptional, strange, unnatural, unique, curious, wonderful, unusual, unaccustomed, egregious, exclusive, peculiar, funny (colloq.), sui generis [L.].

organ, n.—Syn. instrument, means, medium, vehicle, implement.

organization, n.—Syn. structure, arrangement, institution, establishment, association.

organize, v.—Syn. arrange, establish, systematize, co-ordinate, classify, form, plan, shape, frame, constitute, regulate.

origin—Syn. rise, beginning, alpha [Gr.], commencement, source, fountain, cause, outset, incipience, inception, start, outstart, birth, nativity, cradle, dawn, foundation, spring, causation, origination. Ant. end, termination, effect, result, consequence, resultant, product, harvest, upshot, issue, outcome, outgrowth, conclusion, finish, finality, close, goal, determination, completion, fulfillment, eschatology, omega [Gr.], destiny, destination, death, the grave.

original—Syn. first, primary, primeval, primordial, chief, principal, pivotal, rudimentary, causal, etiological, formative, aboriginal, constitutive, originative, protogenic, inceptive, creative, productive, generative, demiurgic, archetypal, non-imitative, unexampled, elemental, elementary, rudimental, rudimentary. Ant. individual, special, peculiar, formal, conventional, consequential, resulting, accruing, deriving, following, emanating, evolved, derivative, coming from, growing from, arising from, issuing, proceeding from, depending upon.

ornamental—Syn. decorative, embellishing, garnishing, garnished, decorated, embellished, ornate, gilt, begilt, inlaid, tesselated, adorned, emblazoned, embossed, embroidered, bespangled, arrayed, illuminated, painted, bedight, glittering, bright. *Ant.* dull, tarnished, soiled, discolored, disfigured, blotted, botched, patched, blurred, spotted, stained, unadorned, ugly, deformed, imperfect, injured, unseemly, misshapen, smudged, dirty, filthy, smeared, foul, nasty,

ornate, *adj.—Syn.* decorated, ornamented, rich, opulent, embellished, figured, florid, ostentatious. *Ant.* simple, chaste, austere, unadorned.

oscillate, *v.—Syn.* waver, sway, vibrate, vacillate, swing, fluctuate, undulate.

ostensible—*Syn.* apparent, avowed, specious, professed, manifest, demonstrative, notable, pronounced, striking, probable, likely, expected, anticipated, seeming, obvious, evident, plain, visible. *Ant.* improbable, unlikely, unexpected, obscure, shadowy, vague, latent, concealed, secret, unknown, unseen, invisible, covert, veiled, hidden, unapparent, indirect, abeyant, unrevealed, unexperienced.

ostentation—*Syn.* show, display, bravado, brag, vaunt, vaunting, boast, boasting, pomp, pomposity, pompousness, flourish, pageant, pageantry, parade, array, magnificence, splurge (*colloq.*), fuss, splash (*colloq.*), pretension, swank (*Eng. slang*), dash colloq.), claptrap, spectacle, exhibition, *mise en scène* [*Fr.*], scenic effect. *Ant.* modesty, humility, diffidence, timidity, unobtrusiveness, shrinking, retirement, quietness, reserve, backwardness, coyness, bashfulness, demureness, unostentation, restraint, constraint, shyness, abasement, humiliation, submissiveness, lowliness, humbleness.

ostracize, *v.—Syn.* banish, expel, blackball, exclude, bar, exile, deport.

oust—*Syn.* eject, dispossess, evict,

dislodge, remove, dismiss, deprive, expel, bounce (*slang*), fire (*slang*), depose, dethrone, sack (*slang*), distrain, disinherit, banish, discharge. *Ant.* restore, reinstate, commission, delegate, depute, instruct, install, induct, authorize, receive, admit, welcome, empower, appoint, ordain, constitute.

outbreak—*Syn.* eruption, violence, ebullition, boisterousness, fury, outburst, explosion, quarrel, brawl, row, rumpus (*colloq.*), riot, disturbance, fight, scrimmage, sudden attack, revolt, revolution, irruption, mutiny, rebellion, insurrection, uprising, *émeute* [*Fr.*]. *Ant.* peace, tranquillity, quiet, quietness, good will, brotherhood, fraternalism, friendship, obedience, compliance, subjection, allegiance, loyalty, passivity, nonresistance, fidelity, servility, concord, harmony, agreement, union, unanimity, understanding, tolerance, toleration, patience, submission, resignation, forbearance, endurance.

outcast—*Syn.* vagrant, vagabond, reprobate, castaway, tramp, hobo, loafer, lounger, blasphemer, sinner, scoffer, unbeliever, hooligan, bum (*U. S. slang*), larrikin [*Aus. slang*], sundowner [*Aus. slang*], dope fiend (*slang*), snow-sniffer (*slang*), panhandler, drunkard, wench, slut, prostitute, Jezebel, quean, hell-cat, tough (*colloq.*), rough (*colloq.*), jailbird, felon, rogue, thief, scamp, rowdy, scapegrace, scallawag, rapscallion, ne'er-do-well, rip (*slang*), hangdog, crook (*colloq.*), criminal. *Ant.* good man, man of honor, white man (*slang*), model, paragon, exemplar, hero, pattern, saint, seraph, angel, clergyman, leader, chief, prelate, bishop, god, goddess, virgin, queen, Madonna, lady, virtuous woman, philanthropist, gentleman, guardian, noble liver, brick (*slang*), trump (*slang*), rough diamond (*colloq*), worthy, celebrity, heroine, demi-god, benefactor, philosopher.

outcome, n.—Syn. result, effect, upshot, consequence, issue, end, termination, sequel.

outlandish—Syn. strange, odd, queer, peculiar, bizarre, grotesque, unfamiliar, fantastic, barbarous, uncouth, ridiculous, irregular, extraneous, foreign, vulgar, indecorous, ribald, unseemly, comic, ludicrous, whimsical, eccentric, quaint, rum (slang), baroque, rococo, unusual, abnormal, unconventional, unparalleled, unexampled, unprecedented. Ant. normal, regular, common, commonplace, usual, familiar, seemly, becoming, fashionable, conventional, decorous, plain, consistent, typical, formal, strict, natural, conformable, general, universal, customary, habitual, trite, current, simple, homely, unaffected, uniform, symmetrical, trim, neat, prevalent, appropriate, suitable, adapted, fit, apt, proper, meet, congruous.

outlaw, n.—Syn. criminal, outcast, excommunicant, fugitive, brigand, desperado, bandit, bad guy, Cain.

outline—Syn. delineation, sketch, drawing, draft, plan, contour, boundary, skeleton, profile, silhouette, perimeter, periphery, circumference, circuit, form, configuration, shape, figure, formation, lineament, aspect, appearance, representation, design, tracing, copy, alignment. Ant. distortion, misrepresentation, caricature, anamorphosis, misproportion, amorphism, disfigurement, defacement, formlessness, shapelessness, deformity, irregularity, contortion, crookedness.

outrage—Syn. insult, abuse, affront, offense, injury, indignity, rudeness, violence, assault, fury, wrong, grievance, foul play, illtreatment, misusage, oppression, persecution, maltreatment, ravage, pillage, rapine, transgression, malice, damage, malignity,

maliciousness, atrocity, enormity. Ant. innocence, benefit, favor, harmlessness, kindness, gentleness, feeling, benevolence, respect, regard, reverence, admiration, esteem, estimation, approbation, warm-heartedness, kindheartedness, friendship, amiability, consideration, unselfishness, love, praise, advantage, service, moderation, calm, calmness, tranquility, peace.

outrageous—Syn. wanton, flagrant, nefarious, atrocious, heinous, excessive, infamous, violent, scandalous, disgraceful, wicked, abusive, shameful, despicable, notorious, opprobrious, shocking, disreputable, ignominious, violent, turbulent, disorderly, insulting, unbearable, vehement, frenzied, furious, frantic, infuriate, desperate, fierce. Ant. calm, peaceful, quiet, quiescent, patient, tolerant, tranquil, dispassionate, passive, cool, imperturbable, self-controlled, submissive, cold-blooded, phlegmatic, inexcitable, composed, collected, meek, mild, unresisting, resigned, gentle, forbearing, unruffled, untroubled, peaceable, soft, soothing, even-tempered, good-natured.

outstanding, adj.—Syn. prominent, remarkable, striking, noticeable, superior, salient, exceptional, conspicuous. Ant. ordinary, commonplace, everyday.

outward—Syn. external, outside, superficial, exterior, outer, outermost, extraneous, foreign, ecdemic, exomorphic. Ant. inner, interior, inside, internal, inward, inmost, innermost, interstitial, endemic, endomorphic.

overbearing—Syn. tyrannical, oppressive, haughty, domineering, imperious, proud, arrogant, insolent, brazen, dictatorial, magisterial, supercilious, high-handed, contumelious, swaggering, blustering, browbeating, intimidating, toplofty (colloq.), high-brow (slang), high-hat (slang), pedantic, egoistic, egotistic, egomaniacal, megalomaniacal, vainglorious, audacious, jingoistic, chauvinistic, hectoring, saucy. *Ant.* meek, mild, humble, submissive, servile, cringing, fawning, sycophantic, cowardly, retiring, bashful, modest, backward, obsequious, soapy (*slang*), doughfaced (*colloq.*), parasitical, crouching, abject, cowering, truckling, groveling, sniveling, slavish, sneaking, mealymouthed, time-serving, toadying.

overcome, *v.*—*Syn.* subdue, beat, conquer, outdo, lick, crush, exceed, overwhelm, defeat, overpower, master, vanquish, suppress, surmount.

overflow—*Syn.* redundancy, exuberance, abundance, overproduction, superabundance, congestion, oversupply, superfluity, plethora, glut, inundation, deluge, engorgement, avalanche. *Ant.* scarcity, sparseness, meagreness, insufficiency, deficiency, depression, reduction, curtailment, retrenchment, shortening, shortage, want, dearth, inadequacy, depletion, emptiness, stint, scantiness.

overrun, *v.*—*Syn.* devastate, beset, ravage, infest, despoil, harry, harass.

oversight—*Syn.* supervision, management, inspection, superintendence, direction, guidance, control, watch, surveillance, watchfulness, government, regulation, bossism (*U.S. slang*), failure, omission, mistake, error, slip, inadvertence, inattention, heedlessness, abstraction, preoccupation, absence of mind, aberration, misapprehension, misconception, fault, flaw, stumble. *Ant.* attention, alertness, care, thought, advertence, consideration, circumspection, inspection, scrutiny, observance, observation, heed, heedfulness, intentness, accuracy, exactitude, precision, carefulness, exactness,

watchfulness, realism, truth, verity, fact.

overt, *adj.*—*Syn.* manifest, open, unconcealed, undisguised, obvious, patent.

overthrow—*Syn.* destroy, subvert, upset, overturn, ruin, demolish, defeat, rout, overcome, discomfit, invert, overset, reverse, abolish, extirpate, disrupt, disorganize, wreck, raze, level, break up, pull down, obliterate, smash, crush, shatter. *Ant.* construct, build up, rehabilitate, produce, form, make, fashion, manufacture, establish, organize, put together, develop, contrive, erect, constitute, fabricate, raise, uprear, set up, build, prove, verify, demonstrate, convince.

overweening, *adj.*—*Syn.* arrogant, egotistical, vain, proud, haughty.

overwhelm—*Syn.* overcome, crush, drown, submerge, inundate, defeat, vanquish, rout, ruin, destroy, ravage, lay waste, dismantle, disrupt, demolish, upset, conquer, overpower, master, suppress, triumph, overmatch, override, worst, swamp, subdue, subjugate, wipe out. *Ant.* fail, lose, miss, flounder, weaken, falter, give up, avoid, shun, flee, skedaddle, desert, turn tail (*colloq.*), cut and run (*colloq.*), run away, recede, decamp, restore, reproduce, recompense, assist, succor, help, befriend, save, rescue.

overwrought—*Syn.* emotional, affected, excited, tired, worn out, spent, exhausted, perturbed, inflamed, impassioned, agitated, ruffled, flustered, shaken, disturbed, hysterical. *Ant.* calm, collected, cool, unruffled, silent, quiet, composed, peaceful, content, tranquil, quiescent, reposeful, self-possessed, undisturbed, unimpassioned, restrained, satisfied, complacent, contented, resigned, patient, stoical.

own, *v.*—*Syn.* possess, hold, control, have, retain, confess, admit, concede, reveal, disclose.

P

pace, n.—*Syn.* speed, gait, velocity, rate, step, stride.

pacific—*Syn.* peaceable, peaceful, tranquil, calm, placid, untroubled, halcyon, smooth, gentle, quiet, still, appeasing, conciliating, composed, restful, unruffled, easygoing. *Ant.* rough, turbulent, warlike, quarrelsome, hostile, contentious, belligerent, militant, military, martial, bellicose, combative, sanguinary, bloodthirsty, armed, soldierly.

pacify, v.—*Syn.* compose, appease, tranquilize, reconcile, allay, relieve, placate, mollify, propitiate, assuage, settle. *Ant.* antagonize, anger, roil, stir.

pack, n.—*Syn.* bundle, blanket, swag [*Aus. slang*], kit, package, burden, parcel, load, baggage, impedimentum, grip, bag, handbag, valise, trunk, luggage, lot, amount, assemblage, concourse, gathering, number, group, collection, flock.

pack, v.—*Syn.* prepare, get ready, put in, stuff, squeeze, tie, bind, brace, girdle, gather, collect, go, depart, skedaddle, go away, be gone, hasten, condense, compress, contract, press, stow, arrange, put away. *Ant.* unpack, untie, unbind, loosen, scatter, disperse, dispose, sort, take out, muss, ruffle, rumple, derange, put aside, distribute, parcel out, allot, allocate, apportion, strew, bestrew.

package, n.—*Syn.* parcel, bundle, pack, packet.

pad, n.—*Syn.* bed, kip, flop, doss, hay.

padre—*Syn.* clergyman, priest, minister, monk, parson, divine, shepherd, pastor, black-coat (*slang*), confessor, reverend, curé [*Fr.*], abbé [*Fr.*], missionary, preacher, revivalist, Bible-reader, gospel sharp (*slang*), gospel-monger (*slang*), sin-shifter (*Aus. slang*), sky-pilot (*slang*), dean, deacon, arch-deacon, prebendary, chaplain.

pagan—*Syn.* idolater, gentile, pantheist, heathen, Pyrrhonist, doubter, scoffer, heretic, unbeliever, sceptic or skeptic, infidel, freethinker, atheist, paynim, Gheber, Zoroastrian, animist, fire-worshiper, Jaina [*Hind.*], agnostic. *Ant.* Christian, Jew, Mohammedan, believer, Catholic, Protestant, apostle, missionary, churchman, ritualist, theosophist, Christian Scientist, spiritualist, Puritan, Mormon, Unitarian, Lutheran, Baptist, Congregationalist.

pageantry—*Syn.* pomp, show, spectacle, exhibition, display, ostentation, parade, flourish, array, fuss, pretension, showing off, magnificence, glitter, splendor, Saturnalia, splurge (*colloq.*), splash (*colloq.*), coup d'oeil [*Fr.*], revel, revelry, carnival, festivity, merrymaking, junket. *Ant.* modesty, unobtrusiveness, diffidence, privacy, reserve, humility, humbleness, retirement, lowliness, backwardness, dulness or dullness, weariness, wearisomeness, boredom, tedium, tediousness, humdrum, monotony.

pain—*Syn.* suffering, torture, torment, agony, woe, anguish, distress, paroxysm, throe, ache, twinge, pang, rack, discomfort, misery, laceration, lancination, spasm, cramp, gripe, stitch, disorder, malady, sickness, mental suffering, and various morbid conditions of both body and mind, as gout, rheumatism, sciatica, toothache, grief, worry, anxiety, etc. *Ant.* good health, physical and mental well-being, pleasure, enjoyment, delectation, joy, gladness, bliss, felicity, transport, cheerfulness, ecstasy, happiness, delight, comfort, ease, rapture, contentment, peace, relief, solace.

pal, n.—*Syn.* comrade, buddy, chum, companion, crony, friend, mate, fellow.

pale—*Syn.* pallid, wan, white, colorless, spectral, ghastly, faded, bleached, hueless, blanched, etiolate, achromatic, leaden, ashy, ashen, cadaverous, lackluster, discolored, dim, tallow-faced, lurid. *Ant.* florid, roseate, red, flushed, blooming, bright, glowing, luminous, shiny, radiant, lambent, gleaming, rosy, rufous, rubious, crimson, pink, reddish, red-complexioned, ruddy, rubicund, hectic, red-faced, inflamed, blowzy, ruddy-faced, high-colored.

pall, *v.—Syn.* cloy, jade, dispirit, satiate, sicken, deject, surfeit.

palliate—*Syn.* apologize for, extenuate, make light of, screen, hide, conceal, cover, veil, gloss over, cloak, mitigate, varnish, veneer, whitewash, soften, excuse, moderate, gloze, bolster up, exculpate, vindicate, defend, justify, alleviate. *Ant.* charge, blame, accuse, censure, check, denounce, implicate, impute, reproach, tax, inculpate, brand, criminate, incriminate, indict, call to account, arraign, impeach, disapprove, condemn, reprove, upbraid, reprehend.

pallid, *adj.—Syn.* wan, pale, colorless, ashen, sallow, waxen, bloodless. *Art.* ruddy, flushed, pink, glowing.

palmy—*Syn.* prosperous, glorious, delightful, sunny, victorious, flourishing, pleasant, thriving, lucky, halcyon, calm, peaceful, bright, fortunate, enjoyable, auspicious, pleasurable, captivating, joyous, bewitching, mirthful, exhilarating, cheerful, hilarious, entrancing, happy. *Ant.* sad, gloomy, melancholy, irksome, annoying, deplorable, unlucky, mournful, lugubrious, dreary, pensive, doleful, comfortless, woeful or woful, irritating, painful, disagreeable, distressing, wearisome, tiresome, galling, bitter, intolerable, insufferable, heartbreaking, dire, unfortunate.

palpable—*Syn.* plain, manifest unmistakable, obvious, discernible, perceivable, apparent, clear, evident, open, visible, conspicuous, perceptible, distinct, definite, well-defined, striking, prominent, salient, ostensible, explicit, indubitable, self-evident. *Ant.* latent, obscure, occult, hidden, concealed, mystic, puzzling, involved, complex, intricate, esoteric, veiled, symbolic, inferential, indirect, implied, complicated, covert, delitescent, mysterious, anagogic, secret, cryptic, recondite.

palpitation, *n.—Syn.* throb, pulse, flutter, vibration, quivering.

paltry, *adj.—Syn.* insignificant, trifling, picayune, sorry, petty, mean, inconsequential, trivial, pitiable, puny. beggarly, measly.

pamper—*Syn.* indulge, spoil, pet, coddle, fondle, caress, cherish, nurse, cater to, gratify, humor, please, satisfy, satiate, glut, gorge, overfeed, cram, stuff, flatter, console, comfort. *Ant.* deny, suppress, refuse, punish, chastise, chasten, correct, spank, strap (*colloq.*), larrup (*colloq.*), displease, disappoint, discountenance, negative, withhold, harden, inure, season, train, educate, teach, guide, point the way.

pandemonium, *n.—Syn.* uproar, racket, ado, din, hubbub, bedlam, tumult.

pander, *v.—Syn.* procure, subserve, cater, gratify, truckle, cringe, pimp.

pang, *n.—Syn.* throe, spasm, anguish, gripe, twinge, pain, stitch.

panic—*Syn.* alarm, consternation, terror, fright, apprehension, awe, dread, horror, dismay, fear, tremor, quivering, trembling, perturbation, flutter, agitation, flustration or flusteration (*colloq.*), trepidation, nervousness. *Ant.* peace, peaceableness, peacefulness, quiet, quiescence, contentment, tranquility, calm, repose, pacification, placidity, calmness, restfulness, assurance, reassurance, security, hope, hopefulness, trust, optimism, confidence, bravery, cheerfulness, courage, self-reliance, intrepidity, boldness, grit, firmness, invincibility, nerve, pluck, stamina, daring, dauntlessness, stout-heartedness, fearlessness.

pant, *v.*—*Syn.* puff, gasp, thirst, yearn, desire, sigh.

par, *n.*—*Syn.* level, equality, norm, mean, balance, parity.

parade, *v.*—*Syn.* display, flaunt, vaunt, expose, publish, show.

paradox—*Syn.* contradiction, ambiguity, bull [*Ir.*], absurdity, mystery, enigma, difficulty, inconsistency, nonsense, blunder, muddle, claptrap, puzzle, bathos, sophism, perplexity, confusion, entanglement, embarrassment, uncertainty. *Ant.* proverb, saw, maxim, wise saying, axiom, truism, postulate, adage, moral, aphorism, lucidity, clearness, precision, intelligibility, comprehensibilty, vividness, clarity, explicitness, distinctness.

paragon, *n.*—*Syn.* pattern, nonpareil, model, ideal, standard, criterion.

parallel—*Syn.* correspondent, congruent, congruous, concurrent, correlative, analogous, concentric, similar, like, uniform, regular. *Ant.* irregular, distorted, askew, crooked, skewed, oblique, slanting, sloped, diagonal, zigzag, dissimilar, divergent, unlike.

paramount—*Syn.* supreme, eminent, preeminent, supereminent, chief, superior, excellent, superexcellent, principal, transcendent, transcendental, greatest, utmost, unequaled, unsurpassed, unapproachable, unique, inimitable, unparalleled, peerless, matchless, foremost, culminating. *Ant.* inferior, subordinate, minor, less, lesser, unimportant, secondary, deficient, least, smallest, secondrate, trifling, trivial, common, commonplace, ordinary, normal, poor, paltry, insignificant, petty, slight, inconsiderable, light, inconsequential, low, lower, meager, unessential, worthless.

paraphernalia, *n.*—*Syn.* equipment, apparatus, impedimenta, trappings, belongings, property, gear, tackle.

parasite—*Syn.* toady, flatterer,

slave, fawner, flunky, wheedler, sycophant, truckler, sponger, sucker (*slang*), tufthunter, toadeater, craven, lickspittle, doormat (*slang*), sniveler, groveler, lapdog, whiner (*colloq.*), hangeron, doughface (*slang*), timeserver, courtier, tout (*colloq.*), votary, devotee, pothunter, placehunter, panhandler (*slang*), mendicant, cadger, heeler (*slang*), puppet, dupe, tool, cat's-paw, jackal, loafer, dependent. *Ant.* master, director, ruler, taskmaster, leader, ringleader, driver, boss (*U.S. slang*), superior, dictator, bully, tyrant, blusterer, swaggerer, swashbuckler, roisterer, bulldozer (*slang*), terrorist, roughneck, hooligan (*slang*), rowdy, tough (*colloq.*), desperado, daredevil, slanderer, detractor, calumniator, reviler, cynic, critic, muckraker, knocker (*colloq.*), castigator, defamer, reprover, traducer.

parcel, *n.*—*Syn.* bundle, package, packet, pack.

parch, *v.*—*Syn.* dry, sear, burn, scorch, wither, desiccate, shrivel.

pardon, *n.*—*Syn.* forgiveness, mercy, acquittal, absolution, forbearance, amnesty, remission, exoneration, discharge, release, respite, reprieve, exculpation, immunity, impunity, condonation, deliverance, freedom. *Ant.* condemnation, conviction, punishment, proscription, penalty, chastisement, retribution, imprisonment, sequestration, infliction, restraint, arrest, confinement, incarceration, detention, prison, jail, donjon, penitentiary, duress, stir (*slang*), lockup, cell, cooler (*slang*), hoosegow (*slang*).

pardon, *v.*—*Syn.* forgive, absolve, remit, quash, reprieve, forget, exonerate, exculpate, excuse, condone, acquit, wipe out, overlook, efface, set free, bury the hatchet, pass over, pass by, liberate. *Ant.* avenge, punish, retaliate, smite, castigate, banish, expel, ostracize, boycott, chastise, convict, condemn, doom, sentence, damn, proscribe, exile, transport, imprison.

pariah—See **outcast** above.

parley, v.—*Syn.* confer, discuss, negotiate, debate, treat, talk.

paroxysm—*Syn.* violence, agitation, emotion, anger, fit, attack, spasm, convulsion, furor, fury, outbreak, outburst, berserk, passion, hysterics, eruption, explosion, tremor, quiver, tarantism, jactation, twitching, vellication, seizure, throe, subsultus, delirium, raving, frothing, whirl, whirling, fuming, rage, raging, excitation, perturbation, madness. *Ant.* tranquillity, equanimity, steadiness, restraint, coolness, composure, imperturbability, dispassion, repression, self-restraint, suppression, passiveness, unconsciousness, stupefaction, hebetude, quiet, quiescence, calm, calmness, inexcitability, repose, rest, restfulness, mildness, impassibility, impassiveness, stupor, torpor, apathy.

parsimonious, *adj.*—*Syn.* stingy, tight, penny-pinching, miserly, penurious, mean, niggardly, grasping, mercenary, avaricious. *Ant.* prodigal, profuse, lavish, generous.

part—*Syn.* portion, share, piece, fragment, section, component, constituent, member, division, particle, segment, subdivision, partition, element, fraction, instalment, detachment, bit, slice, scrap, chip, chunk, lump. *Ant.* whole, all, total, aggregate, sum, entirety, entireness, completeness, embodiment, bulk, mass, totality, amount, gross, combination, unity, integration, collectiveness, *tout ensemble* [*Fr.*], lock, stock, and barrel.

partial, *adj.*—*Syn.* prejudiced, imperfect, unjust, disposed, partisan, biased, limited.

participate, *v.*—*Syn.* share, use, partake, join, cooperate, mingle.

particle—*Syn.* atom, iota, jot, scrap, shred, mite, bit, corpuscle, molecule, morsel, piece, scintilla, whit, tittle, grain, ele-

ment. *Ant.* mass, quantity, lot, sum, total, whole, entirety, aggregate, totality, completeness.

particular—*Syn.* exact, distinct, exclusive, specific, definite, precise, actual, appropriate, careful, thoughtful, prudent, watchful, observant, attentive, singular, odd, strange, eccentric, erratic, capricious, whimsical, fastidious, squeamish, discriminating, finicky, meticulous, querulous, prudish, prim, strait-laced, hard to please. *Ant.* general, indefinite, inexact, unauthentic, inaccurate, erroneous, fallacious, careless, heedless, thoughtless, inconsiderate, unwary, unwatchful, unguarded, reckless, imprudent, undiscriminating, neglectful, insouciant, devil-may-care, supine, nonchalant, negligent, slovenly, untidy, unmethodical, irregular, out of kilter (*colloq.*), easy to please.

partisan, *n.*—*Syn.* adherent, henchman, assistant, follower, ally, supporter, backer.

partition—*Syn.* distribution, apportionment, separation, division, severance, inclosure, barrier, compartment, apartment, detachment, segregation, disunion, disconnection, fence, wall, dividing line. *Ant.* juncture, connection, conjugation, conjunction, attachment, union, unity, circumjacency, coalescence, combination.

partner, *n.*—*Syn.* colleague, sharer, confederate, associate, ally, accomplice.

party, *n.*—*Syn.* faction, clique, society, league, fellowship, ring, circle, side, set.

passage, *n.*—*Syn.* corridor, gateway, way, road, path, avenue.

passion, *n.*—*Syn.* intensity, ardor, excitement, emotion, zeal, fervor, fury, desire, frenzy, lust, urge, craving.

passionate, *adj.*—*Syn.* ardent, fervid, vehement, intense, burning, excited, precipitate, quickened, violent, intemperate. *Ant.* stolid, impassive, phlegmatic, apathetic.

passive, *adj.—Syn.* submissive, inert, quiescent, unresisting, quiet, receptive, indifferent, stoical. *Ant.* active, live, operative, dynamic.

pastoral, *adj.—Syn.* rural, bucolic, idyllic, provincial, georgic, rustic, arcadian.

pathetic, *adj.—Syn.* touching, pitiable, sad, melancholy, plaintive, poignant, affecting, pitiful, piteous, moving.

patience—*Syn.* resignation, forbearance, fortitude, composure, submission, endurance, calmness, passiveness, sufferance, long-suffering, leniency, perseverance, moderation, persistence, plodding, constancy, poise, equanimity, imperturbability, self-possession. *Ant.* impatience, uneasiness, petulance, fretfulness, restlessness, excitement, excitability, disquietude, perturbation, fuss, flurry, fluster, hurry, hurry-skurry, fidgets, anger, rage, passion.

patient—*Syn.* passive, submissive, meek, composed, cool, calm, enduring, long-suffering, quiet, serene, unruffled, resigned, imperturbable, placid, dispassionate, cold-blooded, easygoing, grave, philosophic, tolerant, gentle, unimpassioned. *Ant.* impatient, excitable, boisterous, vehement, irritable, fidgety, flustered, feverish, hysterical, fiery, hotheaded, clamorous, rampant, turbulent, fussy, chafing, irrepressible, ungovernable, furious, raging, high-strung, hasty, violent, passionate.

patron—*Syn.* benefactor, helper, protector, encourager, upholder, supporter, advocate, defender, guide, leader, friend, ally, sympathizer, champion, well-wisher, partisan, customer, client, purchaser, buyer, employer. *Ant.* enemy, opponent, adversary, detractor, backbiter, calumniator, foe, traitor, assailant, obstructionist, competitor, antagonist, rival, disputant, contender, seller, vendor, auctioneer, salesman, preëmptor.

pattern, *n.—Syn.* model, standard, paragon, mold, exemplar, ideal, conformation, prototype, blueprint, paradigm.

pause—*Syn.* rest, stop, intermission, cessation, halt, suspension, discontinuance, hitch, lull, truce, stay, respite, interregnum, standstill, deadlock, stillness, hesitancy, break, stoppage, interlude, interruption, recess. *Ant.* continuance, persistence, perseverance, endurance, prolongation, repetition, extension, carrying on, doing, up and doing, gradation, course, ceaselessness, continuity, progression.

pay, *n.—Syn.* compensation, recompense, salary, reward, requittal, payment, hire, remuneration, fee, wages, stipend, honorarium, earnings, allowance, indemnity, redress, reparation, acknowledgment, atonement, retribution, meed, perquisite, consideration, emolument, tribute, defrayment, settlement, reckoning, satisfaction, clearance, reciprocation, liquidation. *Ant.* penalty, fine, forfeit, forfeiture, damages, confiscation, seizure, amercement, execution, nonpayment, repudiation, default, failure, insolvency, bankruptcy, disbursement, dispersion, distribution, expense, expenditure, outlay, waste.

pay, *v.—Syn.* compensate, reward, recompense, expend, defray, remunerate, discharge, settle, satisfy, liquidate, refund, reimburse, indemnify. *Ant.* cheat, swindle, defraud, victimize, cozen, diddle (*dial.*), bilk, circumvent, overreach, embezzle, steal, bunko (*slang*), hold up, stick up (*colloq.*), bail up [*Aus. slang*].

peace—*Syn.* calm, repose, tranquillity, order, pacification, conciliation, reconciliation, concord, harmony, quiet, amity, contentment, agreement, sympathy, union, unity, fraternalism, fraternization, unanimity, equanimity, concordance, calmness, congeniality, silence, stillness, hush, lull, rest, love, brotherhood, friendship, armistice. *Ant.* discord, variance, difference, dissension, division, split, rupture, disruption, disunion, quarrel, brawl, row, fight, imbroglio, fracas, riot, scrimmage, dispute, disturbance, enmity, anger, disagreement, contention, conflict, battle, skirmish, sound, roar, uproar, noise, clamor, racket, clatter, explosion, detonation, clangor, belligerency, war, warfare.

peaceable—*Syn.* pacific, peaceful, quiet, tranquil, composed, calm, gentle, mild, serene, amiable, friendly, undisturbed, moderate, conciliatory, pacificatory, placid, temperate, inoffensive, civil, kind, well-disposed, harmless, sympathetic, orderly. *Ant.* turbulent, rough, roisterous, boisterous, violent, vehement, tumultuous, disorderly, furious, angry, impetuous, rampant, irritating, exasperating, raging, roaring, blustering, uproarious, fierce, ferocious.

peaceful, *adj.*—*Syn.* calm, quiet, serene, composed, unruffled, gentle, tranquil, pacific, still, placid, mild. *Ant.* turbulent, noisy, upset, agitated.

peculate, *v.*—*Syn.* embezzle, steal, defraud, rob, purloin, pilfer, appropriate.

peculiar, *adj.*—*Syn.* characteristic, particular, proper, specific, singular, individual, uncommon, distinctive; odd, queer, strange, abnormal, eccentric, idiosyncratic, unusual.

peep, *v.*—*Syn.* peek, spy, peer, pry, glimpse, glance.

peerless—*Syn.* unequaled, supreme, best, perfect, glorious, transcendent, nonpareil, unique, unrivaled, inimitable, unexampled, superior, maximum, culminating, paramount, preëminent, matchless, superlative, surpassing, superexcellent, prime, exquisite, A1, excelling, priceless, faultless, supereminent, incomparable, transcendental. *Ant.* inferior, subordinate, imperfect,

secondary, minor, second-rate, unimportant, poor, mean, trivial, trifling, common, commonplace, ordinary, paltry, petty, contemptible, worthless, inconsiderable, deficient, defective, faulty, incomplete, impaired, mediocre, indifferent, average, obscure, unknown, valueless, inadequate, deteriorated, decayed, frayed, adulterated, withered, battered, stale, dilapidated, secondhand, worn, blighted, worn-out, useless.

peeve, *v.*—*Syn.* provoke, annoy, fret, irk, exasperate, vex, irritate, nettle, bother, chafe.

peevish—*Syn.* fretful, fretting, captious, perverse, obstinate, thrawn [*Sc.*], twisted, cantankerous (*colloq.*), cross, ill-natured, growling, grumbling, pessimistic, repining, naggy (*colloq.*), critical, faultfinding, murmuring, censorious, irascible, irritable, churlish, ungracious, ill-conditioned, uncivil, grouchy (*slang*), gruff, touchy, petulant, thin-skinned, fractious, fidgety, tetchy, querulous, morose, sullen, moody, sulky, crabbed. *Ant.* good-tempered, suave, courteous, pleasant, agreeable, amiable, polite, civil, gentle, kind, good-mannered, refined, gentlemanly, well-behaved, winning, winsome, mild, bland, soft-spoken, unctuous, complaisant, mannerly, complacent, affable, goodhumored, benevolent, well-bred, polished, gracious, ingratiating, sympathetic, cordial, good - humored, conciliatory, charming, engaging, captivating, attractive, soothing.

pellucid, *adj.*—*Syn.* limpid, transparent, pure, bright, clear. *Ant.* turbid, muddy, roiled, dark.

pen, *n.*—*Syn.* penitentiary, prison, hoosegow, jail, lockup, stir, pokey.

penalize, *v.*—*Syn.* punish, fine, discipline, chasten, handicap.

penalty, *n.*—*Syn.* punishment, forfeit, fine, disadvantage, damages, handicap.

penetrate—*Syn.* bore, pierce, perforate, enter, insert, percolate, infiltrate, permeate, transude, pass through, push on, go through, interfere, butt in (*slang*), see through, comprehend, understand, grasp, absorb. *Ant.* pull out, emerge, exude, leak, ooze, filter, filtrate, drain, trickle, seep, discharge, gush, weary, tire, give up, turn back, recede, break down, lose ground, slump, misinterpret, fail to understand, misconstrue, muddle, not know, be blind to, miscomprehend, doubt, be perplexed, misapprehend.

penetrating—*Syn.* sharp, keen, subtle, astute, acute, shrewd, sagacious, pointed, piercing, boring, quick, clever, wideawake, clear-headed, nimblewitted, farseeing, farsighted, canny [*Sc.*], discerning, incisive, keen. *Ant.* dull, stupid, shallow, blunt, thick, heavy, obtuse, fatuous, idiotic, inept, thickskulled, foolish, feeble-minded, addlepated, muddled, confused, stolid, doltish, batty (*slang*), balmy (*slang*), nutty, (*slang*), asinine, sappy, (*slang*), silly, senseless, nonsensical.

penetration—*Syn.* entrance, ingress, ingression, infiltration, insertion, invasion, discernment, discrimination, perception, judgment, acuteness, intelligence, capacity, comprehension, understanding, sagacity, acumen, longheadedness, subtlety, subtility, perspicacity, gumption (*colloq.*), grasp. *Ant.* egress, egression, emergence, exit, emanation, evacuation, exudation, discharge, indiscrimination, lack of discernment, shallowness, incapacity, hebetude, dulness or dullness, shortsightedness, simplicity, ineptitude, silliness, foolishness, incompetence, asininity, fatuity, noncomprehension, incomprehensibility.

penitence, *n.*—*Syn.* contrition, remorse, scruples, compunction, qualms, repentance, sorrow, regret. *Ant.* obduracy, impenitence, contumacy.

pensive, *adj.*—*Syn.* thoughtful, solemn, musing, contemplative, sad, grave, reflective, meditative.

penury, *n.*—*Syn.* indigence, destitution, want, privation, need, straits, distress, poverty, lack. *Ant.* luxury, abundance, plenty, opulence.

people—*Syn.* persons, humanity, mankind, race, human race, populace, population, community, individuals, inhabitants, tribe, fellow-beings, fellow-creatures, nation, state, commonwealth, multitude, crowd, mass, mob, herd, commonalty, folks, residents, mortals, mortality, flesh, generation, society, world, *bourgeoisie* [*Fr.*], democracy, proletariat, *hoi polloi* [*Gr.*], *demos* [*Gr.*].

pep, *n.*—*Syn.* zest, fervor, gusto, ginger, energy, initiative, enthusiasm, keenness, vim, mettle, spirit, vitality. *Ant.* languor, lassitude, sloth, torpor.

perceive—*Syn.* note, observe, discern, distinguish, sense, comprehend, grasp mentally, conceive, understand, see, realize, apprehend, see through, infer, behold, discover, descry, recognize, savvy (*slang*). *Ant.* mistake, misconceive, misunderstand, misjudge, overlook, fail to grasp, lose sight of, grope, blink, search, feel, fumble, bungle, give up search, mizzle, confuse, jumble, muddle, fail of, ignore, pass by, miss, misapprehend, lose.

percussion, *n.*—*Syn.* collision, concussion, shock, encounter, clash, impact, striking.

peremptory—*Syn.* arbitrary, absolute, dictatorial, harsh, overbearing, decisive, assertive, authoritative, firm, compulsory, rigorous, dominant, imperious, imperative, stringent, hegemonic, paramount, strict, stern, rigid, uncompromising, positive, coercive, oppressive, unsparing, inflexible, inexorable, relentless, highhanded, exacting, exigent, austere, unmistakable, emphatic, insistent, determined, binding, obligatory, compelling, express, distinct, explicit, precise, unavoidable. *Ant.* mild, indulgent, lenitive, clement, easy, soft, moderate, tolerant, compassionate, easygoing, lax, loose, slack, careless, weak, feeble, wavering, shallow, wobbly, light, unexacting, indeterminate, irresolute, infirm of purpose, indecisive, negligible, vacillating, fluctuating, hesitating, irresponsible, capricious, half-hearted, indefinite, optional, discretional, discretionary, erratic, eccentric, inconsistent, foolish, freakish, whimsical, fantastic.

perennial, *adj.—Syn.* enduring, continual, perpetual, constant, unfailing, endless, lasting, persistent, permanent, ceaseless, everlasting. *Ant.* fleeting, fugitive, transient, evanescent.

perfect—*Syn.* complete, completed, consummate, conclusive, crowning, thorough, mature, exhaustive, elaborate, faultless, unblemished, uninjured, immaculate, spotless, impeccable, intact, culminating, entire, whole, absolute, plenary, full, unqualified, august, grand, dignified, sublime, supreme, ideal. *Ant.* imperfect, deficient, incomplete, unfinished, uncompleted, defective, wanting, lacking, short, poor, mean, meager, crude, jejune, scanty, injured, mutilated, damaged, spoiled, smashed, mangled, torn, faulty, mediocre, middling, tainted, spotted, stained, cracked, below par, inferior, secondary, second-rate, secondhand, one-horse (*U. S. slang*), rubbishy, tuppen-ha'penny (*Eng. colloq.*), lousy, worthless, useless, bad, rotten, decayed, putrid, putrescent, corrupt, deformed, ruined.

perfidious, *adj.—Syn.* treacherous, false, deceitful, venal, faithless, untrustworthy, disloyal.

perform, *v.—Syn.* do, act, play, achieve, execute, accomplish, fulfill, complete.

perfume—*Syn.* scent, fragrance, aroma, smell, odor, sweetness, redolence, bouquet, nosegay, incense, spray, garland, chaplet, flower, bloom, blossom, conservatory, garden. *Ant.* fetor, putridity, decay, rottenness, stink, stench, malodor, rancidity, reastiness, foulness, mephitis, fetidness, nastiness, uncleanness, latrine, privy, midden, sewer, cloaca, cesspool, feces.

perhaps—*Syn.* possibly, maybe, perchance, peradventure, mayhap, haply, by chance, probably. *Ant.* incredibly, untruly, unlikely, improbably, impossibly, not likely.

peril—*Syn.* danger, pitfall, snare, risk, jeopardy, hazard, exposure, insecurity, venture, defenselessness, openness to attack, apprehension. *Ant.* safety, carefulness, caution, foresight, invulnerableness, invulnerability, protection, safekeeping, guardianship, impregnability, security, safeguard.

period—*Syn.* epoch, age, era, cycle, circuit, term, duration, end, limit, conclusion, lifetime, generation, epact, semester, quarter, term, year, decade, decennium, recurrence.

periodical—*Syn.* regular, recurrent, recurring, intermittent, alternate, serial, cyclic, hourly, daily, weekly, monthly, yearly, annual, centennial, occasional, occurring now and them. *Ant.* irregular, uncertain, erratic, desultory, variable, fitful, capricious, anomalous, rambling, devious, eccentric, unsystematic, changeable, mutable, immethodical, constant, perpetual, continuing, lasting, permanent.

periphery, *n.—Syn.* perimeter, limit, boundary, circumference, bound, border, compass, ambit.

perky, *adj.—Syn.* jaunty, cocky, trim, tidy, animated, lively, chipper, irrepressible.

permanent—*Syn.* durable, lasting, abiding, constant, unchanging, unchangeable, changeless, indelible, irremovable, persistent, enduring, indestructible, perpetual, perdurable, imperishable, chronic, continual, settled, unalterable, confirmed, ineradicable, perennial, habitual, customary, invariable, wonted, everyday, stable, steadfast, usual, general. *Ant.* fleeting, evanescent, passing, short, brief, changing, changeable, uncertain, temporary, transitory, fugitive, momentary, flitting, flying, ephemeral, transient, impermanent, temporal, short-lived, inconstant, variable, mutable, unsettled, erratic, fitful, alternating, alterable, fluctuating, spasmodic, capricious, unsteady, vacillating.

permeate, *v.—Syn.* saturate, imbue, pervade, penetrate, infiltrate, drench, impregnate, animate, fire.

permission—*Syn.* leave, liberty, consent, license, permit, allowance, authority, tolerance, toleration, authorization, dispensation, warranty, sufferance, grace, connivance. *Ant.* prohibition, interdiction, proscription, injunction, embargo, restraint, inhibition, opposition, debarment, circumscription, taboo, exclusion, restriction, hindrance.

permit—*Syn.* allow, tolerate, warrant, authorize, empower, charter, license, sanction, intrust, accord, vouchsafe, legalize, let, grant, patent, suffer, concede, indulge, privilege, favor. *Ant.* deny, refuse, disallow, veto, proscribe, hinder, prevent, interdict, forbid, inhibit, ban, bar, debar, withhold, exclude, restrict, shut out, prohibit, enjoin, stop, restrain, circumscribe.

pernicious—*Syn.* destructive, hurtful, noxious, deadly, evil, noisome, mischievous, virulent, baneful, obnoxious, poisonous, ruinous, harmful, injurious, detrimental, pestiferous, baleful, deleterious, perverting, foul, insalubrious, unhealthful, perversive, pestilential, malignant, prejudicial, venomous, nocuous, disadvantageous, malefic, dire, bad, damnable, grievous, morbific, mephitic, putrid, rotten, toxic, toxiferous, unhealthy, unwholesome. *Ant.* good, healthy, salubrious, bracing, invigorating, wholesome, hygienic, pure, innocuous, innoxious, restorative, helpful, advantageous, harmless, inoffensive, excellent, fine, superfine, beneficial, profitable, favorable, propitious, benign, satisfactory, unobjectionable, salutary, tonic, sanative, remedial, curative, healing, cleansing, abstersive, abstergent, detersive, roborant, prophylactic, therapeutic, allopathic, useful, serviceable, efficacious, mitigating, reviving.

perpetual—*Syn.* continual, unceasing, constant, incessant, permanent, lasting, uninterrupted, eternal, everlasting, enduring, perennial, continued, endless, sempiternal, ceaseless, imperishable, undying, immortal. *Ant.* momentary, temporary, short, brief, inconstant, transient, fleeting, passing, ephemeral, transitory, fugitive, evanescent, impermanent, short-lived.

perplex—*Syn.* puzzle, mystify, bewilder, baffle, confound, disconcert, stump (*colloq.*), excite, flabbergast (*colloq.*), amaze, bother, worry, annoy, irk, irritate, trouble, agitate, embarrass, hamper, mock, entangle, daze, nonplus, astonish, confuse, mislead, abash, dismay, discompose, fluster, flurry, rattle (*colloq.*), moider (*dial.*), muddle, flusterate. *Ant.* render certain, make sure, clinch, assure, convince, guarantee, prove, ensure, determine, arrange, place, set in order, regulate, please, satisfy, gratify, delight, instruct, inform, enlighten, acquaint, disclose, impart, teach, tell, explain, interpret, expound, elucidate.

perplexity—*Syn.* doubt, embarrassment, distraction, disturbance, bewilderment, astonishment, confusion, amazement, complexity, complication, intricacy, ferment, agitation, uncertainty, doubtfulness, dilemma, suspense, botheration, quandary, contingency, hesitation, ignorance, nescience, incomprehension, inexperience, aporia, emergency, crisis, exigency. *Ant.* certainty, sureness, facility, easiness, smoothness, disentanglement, feasibility, capability, plain sailing, perception, familiarity, apprehension, foreknowledge, assurance, comprehension, intelligibility, capacity, clearness, explicitness, plainness, expressiveness, vividness, grasp, understanding, lucidity, precision, sense, enlightenment, understanding, conception, intelligence.

perquisite, *n.—Syn.* privilege, prerogative, due, right, reward, gratuity, tip.

persecute—*Syn.* oppress, torment, worry, afflict, annoy, harass, aggrieve, inflict, victimize, abuse, outrage, molest, maltreat, illtreat, punish, chastise, castigate, rack, torture, flog, strike, beat, imprison, scourge, pester, badger, bullyrag, irritate, provoke, roil, rile, gall, enrage, scarify, crucify, plague, grind, crush, banish, expel, exile, transport. *Ant.* reward, recompense, redress, remunerate, benefit, serve, favor, recommend, please, gratify, satisfy, gladden, indulge, comfort, refresh, help, assist, aid, support, sustain, succor, nourish, nurture, oblige, accommodate, cheer, encourage, patronize, indorse, approve, relieve, soothe, console, assuage, inspirit, enliven, solace, embolden, stimulate, instigate.

perseverance—*Syn.* steadfastness, tenacity, persistence, constancy, indefatigableness, indefatigability, continuance, continuation, perpetuation, pursuance, endurance, resolution, pertinacity, grit, determination, pluck (*colloq.*), stamina, sand (*slang*), backbone (*slang*). *Ant.* sloth, slothfulness, laziness, languor, torpidity, inactivity, idleness, remissness, otiosity, indolence, ergophobia, sluggishness, ennui, stupor, drowsiness, tiredness, lethargy, weariness, discontinuance, cessation, desistance, halt, standstill, stoppage, suspension, rest.

persiflage, *n.—Syn.* banter, frivolity, badinage, raillery, chaffing, rallying, pleasantry.

personality, *n.—Syn.* character, ego, temperament, individuality.

perspicacious, *adj.—Syn.* penetrating, discerning, astute, shrewd, acute, sharp, keen.

perspicuity—*Syn.* clearness, plainness, distinctness, explicitness, intelligibility, lucidity, clarity, comprehensibility, preciseness, transparency, discernment, perspicacity, definiteness. *Ant.* obscurity, unintelligibility, vagueness, imcomprehensibility, unknowableness, jargon, uncertainty, perplexity, mystification, riddle, enigma, paradox, puzzle, conundrum, bewilderment, confusion, embarrassment, intricacy, complexity.

persuade—*Syn.* coax, prevail upon, entice, urge, allure, convince, impel, win over, lead, influence, dispose, incite, move, incline, wheedle, bring over, exhort, prompt, instigate, lure, decoy, bribe, induce, seduce, provoke, actuate, stimulate, rouse, arouse, inspirit, prevail upon, inveigle, cajole, vamp (*slang*). *Ant.* dissuade, discourage, curb, restrain, remonstrate, expostulate, dishearten, deter, dampen, check, prevent, repress, hinder, coerce, stop, suppress, withhold, constrain, restrict, prohibit, divert from, admonish, dispirit, depress, scare, frighten, terrify, turn from.

pertinacious, *adj.—Syn.* tenacious, persevering, resolute, firm, persistent, dogged, inflexible, stubborn.

pertinent, *adj.—Syn.* relevant, material, apposite, apropos, appropriate, fit, germane, fitting, proper, applicable.

pertness—*Syn.* impertinence, flippancy, forwardness, self-assertion, vainglory, vaingloriousness, pride, pretension, assumption, presumption, self-glorification, self-admiration, egotism, self-conceit, vanity, self-confidence, self-sufficiency, selfishness, self-approbation, self-applause, self-gratulation, conceit, priggishness, arrogance, impudence, bumptiousness, boldness, sauciness, brazenness, insolence, swagger. *Ant.* bashfulness, shyness, modesty, humility, diffidence, demureness, timidity, unobtrusiveness, coyness, constraint, self-depreciation, self-condemnation, restraint, subserviency, abasement, servility, toadyism, obsequiousness, sycophancy, flunkyism, fawning, cringing, sniveling, groveling, truckling, sponging, timeserving, slavishness.

perturbation—*Syn.* discomposure, trepidation, worry, derangement, disorganization, excitation, agitation, ebullition, effervescence, fermentation, tremor, quiver, shock, succussion, turmoil, tumult, hubbub, racket, disturbance, commotion, flurry, fluster, rage, fury, furor, anger, choler, passion, excitement, paroxysm, frenzy, delirium, hysterics, violence, madness, terror, alarm, consternation, dread, horror. *Ant.* peace, quietness, quiescence, inexcitability, imperturbability, tranquillity, dispassion, calmness, composure, quietude, silence, self-control, self-possession, self-restraint, submission, resignation, forbearance, endurance, moderation, repression, restraint, fortitude, patience, suppression, stoicism, coolness, coldness, unconcern, hebetude, dulness, impassivity, apathy, coldbloodedness, insusceptibility, impassiveness, inertia, inertness, deadness.

perverse—*Syn.* obstinate, contrary, stiff, stiff-necked, opinionated, self-opinionated, stubborn, unyielding, cross, peevish, petulant, wayward, froward, ungovernable, fractious, untoward, factious, seditious, contrary, snappish, wilful, obdurate, resolute, dogged, self-willed, intractable, churlish, irascible, sullen, sulky,

crabbed, refractory, cantankerous, splenetic, grouchy, querulous, contentious, censorious, faultfinding, captious, sour, crusty, cranky, headstrong. *Ant.* tractable, docile, mild, amenable, gentle, irresolute, yielding, complacent, complaisant, spineless, soft, willing, capricious, changeable, weak-kneed, agreeable, conformable, harmonious, coöperative, acquiescent, condescending, assenting, conceding, pliant, compliant, consenting, manageable, governable, easily managed, good-tempered, infirm of purpose, wavering, shilly-shally, timorous.

pessimistic, *adj.*—*Syn.* gloomy, depressed, cynical, despondent, despairing, misanthropic. *Ant.* optimistic, hopeful, sanguine, confident.

pester, *v.*—*Syn.* harass, harry, torment, tease, bait, nettle, molest, disturb, chafe, heckle, bother, vex, provoke, fret, badger, plague, trouble.

pestilential—*Syn.* infectious, pestiferous, malignant, noxious, contagious, mischievous, destructive, troublesome, catching, communicable, smittle (*Eng. dial.*), virulent, contaminating, morbiferous, morbific, deadly, fermentative, zymotic, plague-bearing, septic, toxic, toxiferous, epidemic, endemic, pandemic. *Ant.* wholesome, healthful, salubrious, hygienic, antiseptic, aseptic, sanative, sanitary, innoxious, innocuous, uninfectious, healing, restorative, invigorating, stimulating, healthy, beneficial, advantageous, profitable, preservative, bracing, nutritious, nutritive, nourishing, alimental.

pet, *v.*—*Syn.* fondle, caress, embrace, cuddle, spoon, neck, smooch.

petition—*Syn.* appeal, request, supplication, entreaty, prayer, requisition, application, importunity, impetration, invocation, proposal, solicitation. *Ant.* deprecation, disapprobation, expostulation, protest, remonstrance, opposition, disapproval, condemnation, denunciation, censure, blame, denial.

petty—*Syn.* small, trivial, trifling, insignificant, puny, weeny, wishy-washy, weak, childish, puerile, frivolous, mean, meager, paltry, little, ignoble, contemptible, shallow, unimportant, worthless, slight, piffling, piddling, namby-pamby, scurvy, trumpery, pitiful, ridiculous, two-for-a-cent (*U. S. colloq.*), tuppenny-ha'penny (*Eng. colloq.*), cheap, tawdry, trashy, shabby, miserable, beggarly. *Ant.* large, great, important, significant, fine, prominent, leading, salient, beneficial, profitable, salutary, advantageous, useful, principal, essential, necessary, valuable, serious, grave, vital, consequential, impressive, commanding, absorbing, paramount, eminent, foremost, worthy, remarkable, capacious, corpulent, heavy, weighty, huge, enormous, massive, bulky, lusty, strapping (*colloq.*), brawny, immense, gigantic, thumping (*colloq.*), bully (*colloq.*), extraordinary.

petulant, *adj.*—*Syn.* peevish, fretful, cranky, pettish, cross, querulous, irritable, touchy.

phantom, *n.*—*Syn.* ghost, apparition, revenant, shade, vision, spook, wraith, specter.

philanthropic—*Syn.* kind, benevolent, public-spirited, humanitarian, well-disposed, considerate, feeling, generous, liberal, high-minded, man-loving, patriotic, endemonic, chivalrous, cosmopolitan, humane, large-hearted, good, helpful, charitable, beneficent, munificent, bountiful, bounteous, openhanded, altruistic, sympathetic, friendly, pitiful, compassionate. *Ant.* misanthropic, antisocial, cynical, egotistical, selfish, morose, cranky, grouchy, pitiless, hard-hearted, merciless, harsh, cruel, oppressive, tyrannical, miserly, sordid, niggardly, stingy, parsimonious, gripping, grasping, covetous, mean, contemptible,

penurious, beggarly, unpitying, distrustful, suspicious, greedy.

philosophical—*Syn.* thoughtful, calm, collected, cool, unmoved, impassive, patient, reflective, cogitative, studious, imperturbable, composed, level-headed, staid, steady, sober, grave, serious, solemn, tolerant, unimpassioned, resigned, content, placid, peaceful, wise, prudent, careful, considerate, sapient, sagacious, rational, judicious, well-balanced, sensible, strong-minded, solid, deep, profound, authoritative, erudite, oracular. *Ant.* imprudent, rash, precipitate, headlong, unthinking, thoughtless, foolish, silly, thick, inexperienced, green (*colloq.*), raw (*colloq.*), dull, stupid, shallow, harebrained, light, light-headed, careless, asinine, addlepated, blundering, sappy (*slang*), irrational, narrow-minded, inconsistent, unphilosophical, frivolous, injudicious, unreasonable, fatuous, idiotic, childish, puerile, narrow-minded, prejudiced, credulous, s i m p l e, eccentric, senseless; nutty, batty, loony, spoony, balmy, balmy in the crumpet—all *slang*.

phlegmatic—*Syn.* dull, indifferent, cold, sluggish, heavy, inexcitable, stolid, moody, morose, Boeotian, stupid, slow, apathetic, languid, lymphatic, slack, passive, tardy, dispassionate, cold-blooded, easy-going, insouciant, lackadaisical, half-hearted, unambitious, listless, careless, inappetent. *Ant.* lively, quick, keen, acute, sharp, fussy, up-to-date, impatient, eager, aggressive, fiery, passionate, excitable, explosive, feverish, restless, fidgety, vehement, demonstrative, hot-headed, enthusiastic, rampant, clamant, clamorous, urgent, turbulent, tempestuous, uproarious, boisterous, bumptious, assertive, self-assertive, impetuous, domineering.

physical—*Syn.* material, corporeal, corporal, visible, tangible, natural, substantial, sensible, fleshy, fleshly, bodily, somatic, palpable, concrete, ponderable, carnal, materialistic, vigorous, vital, lusty, sinewy, muscular, forcible, compelling, compulsory. *Ant.* immaterial, incorporeal, insubstantial, unsubstantial, spiritual, mental, sublimated, ethereal, intellectual, subjective, metaphysical, unreal, psychical, psychological, discarnate, disembodied, invisible, unearthly, intangible, asomatous, abstract, moral, spiritual, imaginary, visionary, unreal, delusive, ideal, dreamy, ghostly, fanciful.

pick, *v.*—*Syn.* select, gather, take, pluck, single, choose, cull, prefer.

pickle, *n.*—*Syn.* plight, jam, difficulty, quandary, dilemma, fix, predicament.

picture—*Syn.* image, likeness, portrait, painting, effigy, representation, appearance, description, spectacle, pageant, panorama, view, engraving, illustration, contour, silhouette, diorama, cosmorama, tableau, scene, scenery, landscape, seascape, prospect, vista, depiction, design, drawing, icon, statue, figure, figurehead, bust, outline, diagram, facsimile, tracing, copy, radiograph, sciagraph, map, plan, sketch, draft, cartoon, daguerreotype, woodcut, photo, photograph, lithograph, cut, glyptograph, xylograph, zincograph, half-tone, rotogravure, etching.

picturesque—*Syn.* artistic, pictorial, graphic, scenic, graceful, seemly, prepossessing, comely, attractive, pleasing, vivid, striking, compelling, lucid, bright, clear, alluring, elegant, pretty, personable, symmetrical, well-proportioned, æsthetic, becoming, inviting, pleasing. *Ant.* ugly, ungainly, forbidding, repulsive, repellent, ungraceful, ill-favored, unlovely, grim, gruesome, squalid, dingy, unprepossessing, uncouth, slovenly, awkward, deformed, sinister, distorted, inartistic, unsightly,

unseemly, homely, coarse, misshapen, haggard, odious, hideous.

piece, *n.*—*Syn.* part, bit, amount, portion, section, fraction, scrap, fragment, morsel, hunk.

piercing—*Syn.* loud, shrill, keen, acute, deafening, ear-splitting, sharp, penetrating, entering, perforating, boring, high-sounding, blatant, noisy, clangorous, harsh, strident, stridulant, stridulous, blaring, cacophonous, raucous, metallic, discordant. *Ant.* soft, low, murmuring, modulated, faint, purling, stifled, muffled, inaudible, hoarse, whispered, liquid, soothing, lulling, gentle, melodious, sussurant, mute, soundless, nonresonant, silent, inaudible.

pile, *n.*—*Syn.* stack, quantity, amount, heap, collection, mass, load, bank, assemblage, battery.

pillage—*Syn.* plunder, loot, rapine, spoil, booty, injury, damage, hurt, theft, spoliation, desecration, robbery, impairment, detriment, havoc, ravage, outrage, loss, wreck, ruin, sack, raid, foray, brigandage, holdup (*slang*), burglary, piracy, filibustering, housebreaking, thievery, depredation, seizure, confiscation, boodle, swag. *Ant.* restoration, repair, restitution, compensation, recompense, satisfaction, remuneration, reward, amends, return, indemnification, reparation, atonement, replacement, requital, retribution, repayment, expiation, indemnity, reimbursement, refund, recoupment, redress.

pinch, *n.*—*Syn.* crisis, difficulty, strain, strait, plight, emergency, predicament, stress, vicissitude.

pinnacle, *n.*—*Syn.* peak, top, zenith, apex, culmination, summit, climax. *Ant.* bottom, foot, depths, nadir.

pious—*Syn.* religious, reverent, devout, devotional, righteous, godly, saintly, pure, holy, spiritual, saintlike, humble, sanctified, sacred, solemn, seraphic, consecrated, unworldly. *Ant.*

impious, wicked, sinful, blasphemous, sacrilegious, profane, irreverent, evil, perverted, unhallowed, unholy, irreligious, unsanctified, unregenerate, hypocritical.

piquant—*Syn.* spirited, clever, smart, lively, charming, racy, bright, sparkling, interesting, sharp, savory, pungent, pricking, stimulating, high-flavored, biting, spicy, peppery, acrid, trenchant, impressive, incisive, caustic. *Ant.* unsavory, unpalatable, flat, insipid, tasteless, sweet, saccharine, honied, cloying, nauseating, dull, dry, languid, prosaic, vapid, monotonous, mawkish, wishy-washy, sketchy, colorless, trashy, rambling.

pique, *n.*—*Syn.* umbrage, resentment, offense, displeasure, grudge, irritation, indignation, anger, ire, wrath, annoyance, mortification, bitterness, acrimony, disaffection, dudgeon, exasperation, vexation. *Ant.* pleasure, gratification, enjoyment, satisfaction, complacency, contentment, delight, approval, comfort, happiness, gladness, cheerfulness, felicity, ease, delectation.

pique, *v.*—*Syn.* irritate, fret, goad, offend, displease, anger, provoke, rouse, taunt, inflame, agitate, ruffle, disturb, perturb, excite, fool, mock, annoy, trouble, plague, bother, pester, harry, badger, heckle, cross, irk, vex, torment, nettle, disgust, chafe, gall, roil, rile, affront, incense, embitter, exasperate, aggravate, insult, excite. *Ant.* please, delight, charm, interest, allure, attract, fascinate, captivate, indulge, amuse, entice, invite, satisfy, satiate, humor, tickle, flatter, propitiate, seduce, bewitch, gladden, refresh, comfort, entrance, enrapture, enamour, enchant, transport, ravish, gratify, rejoice.

pitiful—*Syn.* doleful, wretched, miserable, mournful, pitiable, piteous, sorrowful, compassionate, sad, woeful, distressed, distressing, rueful, cheerless, comfortless, lamentable, deplorable, joyless, dismal, afflicted, suffering, pathetic, moving, mean, paltry, abject, base, low, vile, contemptible. *Ant.* happy, cheerful, contented, wealthy, rich, well-to-do, high, exalted, honored, respected, respectable, famous, great, mighty, dignified, stately, powerful, superior, sublime, grand, commanding, noble, august.

pitiless—*Syn.* merciless, hardhearted, obdurate, unfeeling, revengeful, malevolent, ruthless, incompassionate, unpitying, unmerciful, bowelless, relentless, inexorable, unkind, austere, tyrannical, rigorous, spiteful, harsh, cruel, cold-blooded, unfeeling, savage, ferocious, truculent, barbarous, fiendish, diabolical, demoniacal, atrocious, bloodthirsty. *Ant.* merciful, kind, gentle, compassionate, benevolent, cordial, sympathetic, indulgent, warm-hearted, charitable, philanthropic, kindhearted, bountiful, beneficent, unselfish, good-natured, amiable, considerate, soft-hearted, tender, tenderhearted, friendly, clement, humane, bounteous, benignant, altruistic, well-intentioned, comforting, kindly.

pity—*Syn.* compassion, sympathy, kindness, soft-heartedness, charity, philanthropy, tenderness, goodness, commiseration, forbearance, humanity, clemency, mercy, devotion, large-heartedness, generosity. *Ant.* pitilessness, severity, inclemency, malevolence, hardheartedness, harshness, mercilessness, truculence, tyranny, ruthlessness, ferocity, cruelty, brutality, relentlessness, persecution, rigor, rancor, vindictiveness, sternness, revenge, vengeance, implacability, inhumanity, barbarity.

place, *n.*—*Syn.* locality, situation, spot, position, point, site, post, station, area, region, section, quarters, abode, house, town, country, residence, home, habitation, fatherland, motherland, retreat, haunt, resort, covert, habitat, encampment, headquarters.

place, v.—Syn. appoint, establish, settle, fix, put, set, induct, arrange, locate, dispose, allot, group, allocate, assign, distribute, deposit, plant, lodge, quarter, install, store, stow, invest. Ant. displace, remove, dislodge, unplace, misplace, disestablish, take away, empty, unload, discompose, disarrange, disorder, disorganize, disturb, eject, throw out, dismiss, unsettle, jumble, shuffle.

placid, adj.—Syn. quiet, gentle, even, calm, serene, cool, tranquil, unruffled, peaceful.

plain—Syn. open, evident, manifest, obvious, clear, visible, distinct, perceptible, exposed, conspicuous, discernible, apparent, glaring, staring, well-defined, definite, recognizable, striking, prominent, self-evident, pronounced, notable, unmistakable, indubitable, express, explicit, patent, intelligible, easily understood, comprehensible, lucid, positive, unequivocal, unadorned, undisguised, homely, ugly, ordinary, level, flat, even, smooth. Ant. obscure, complex, complicated, intricate, difficult, enigmatical, puzzling, hard, unintelligible, unknowable, invisible, illegible, inscrutable, undiscoverable, cryptic, cloudy, mystic, mystical, occult, incomprehensible, hazy, indistinct, imperceptible, unperceivable, latent, hidden, concealed, oracular, Delphic, involved, esoteric, symbolic, mysterious, anagogic, cabalistic, impenetrable, secret, profound.

plaintive, adj.—Syn. melancholy, doleful, piteous, sad, mournful, lugubrious, wistful, pathetic, woeful.

plan, n.—Syn. arrangement, scheme, design, drawing, sketch, cut, draft, delineation, device, map, project, scope, view, undertaking, plot, representation, outline, model, prospectus, proposal, proposition, course of action, policy, method, device, contrivance, program.

plan, v.—Syn. devise, shape, outline, delineate, depict, picture, sketch, represent, illustrate, trace, draw, design, map, chart, project, prepare, scheme, contrive, plot, draft. Ant. distort, misrepresent, twist, confuse, muddle, shuffle, falsify, render unintelligible, mix, derange, disorder, obscure, perplex, misapply, cut out, wipe out, delete, erase, cancel, tangle, obliterate, blot out, cast aside.

plastic, adj.—Syn. ductile, resilient, pliant, pliable, flexible, malleable.

platitude, n.—Syn. banality, truism, insipidity, nonsense, cliché, commonplace, inanity.

plausible, adj.—Syn. credible, acceptable, probable, reasonable, likely, believable, specious, suave, glib, colorable, fulsome.

play, n.—Syn. amusement, sport, game, contest, action, exhibition, show, drama, tragedy, comedy, melodrama, scene, act, representation, theatricals, vaudeville, pantomime, burlesque. Ant. work, toil, labor, slavery, oppression, drudgery, dulness or dullness, heaviness, weariness, boredom, tedium, tediousness, torpidity, tiredness, dreariness, melancholy, depression.

play, v.—Syn. act, perform, take part in, participate, represent, imitate, mimic, amuse, entertain, divert, revel, make merry, cheer, rejoice, skip, jump, gambol, frisk, sport, display, frolic, caper, dance, raise Cain (slang), paint the town red (slang). Ant. be morose, be sour, be glum, mope, whine, grieve, mourn, look downcast, brood over, give way, croak, despair, groan, put a damper on, throw a wet blanket on (colloq.), hang crepe on your nose (slang), pull a long face (slang), be sad, be funereal, sigh for your grandmother (slang).

playful, adj.—Syn. sportive, wanton, gay, jolly, prankish, roguish, lively, frisky, sprightly, frolicsome, mischievous.

plead—Syn. implore, beg, ask, solicit, argue, advocate, urge, press, beseech, entreat, request, petition, appeal, crave, supplicate, testify, depose, witness, vouch, adduce, attest, bear witness, give evidence, answer, reply, respond, defend, allege. Ant. deprecate, protest, reject, deny, expostulate, refuse, decline, forswear, turn down (slang), dissuade, remonstrate, discourage, dishearten, deter, warn, argue against, dampen, check, admonish, decry, turn from, denounce.

pleasant—Syn. agreeable, gratifying, satisfying, pleasing, enjoyable, cheerful, enlivening, obliging, pleasurable, kind, kindly, attractive, good-natured, sympathetic, welcome, cordial, refreshing, glad, gladsome, delectable, engaging, winning, winsome, alluring, enticing, fascinating, captivating, cheering, pleasure-giving, good-humored, gay, lively, jocose, humorous, amusing, jocund, merry, sportive, witty, charming, jovial, jolly, frolicsome, droll, funny, entertaining, diverting, laughable, festive, flattering, comforting. Ant. unpleasant, disagreeable, dissatisfying, dull, painful, irritating, vexing, annoying, disturbing, provoking, mocking, taunting, hurtful, dolorous, sad, sorrowful, disquieting, displeasing, saddening, bothersome, troublesome, mortifying, harassing, distressing, tormenting, torturing, untoward, unsatisfactory, inauspicious, exasperating, glum, ill-humored, ill-natured, crabbed, austere, severe, arrogant, unkind, harsh, cruel, offensive, repellent, repelling, hateful, afflicting, joyless, gloomy, cheerless, mournful, deplorable, bitter, unwelcome, undesirable, depressing, melancholy, forbidding,

dismal, dreary, woeful, rueful, comfortless, grievous, piteous, pitiful, galling, irksome, carking, grim, crushing, dreadful, fearful, dire, appalling.

please—Syn. gratify, satisfy, humor, delight, gladden, captivate, indulge, flatter, amuse, attract, allure, entice, comfort, console, cheer, oblige, comply with, serve, benefit, obey, satisfy, assent, acquiesce, conform, accede, accept, follow, praise, exalt, glorify, boost (colloq.), elevate. Ant. displease, offend, injure, hurt, pain, afflict, persecute, mortify, taunt, mock, shame, irritate, worry, annoy, chafe, bore, grieve, trouble, vex, plague, bother, torment, roil, rile, distress, pester, tease, provoke, pique, disgust, nauseate, shock, disobey, detract, calumniate, wrong, malign, defame, traduce, slander.

pleasure—Syn. gratification, enjoyment, satisfaction, indulgence, voluptuousness, sensuality, joy, choice, self-indulgence, preference, preferment, will, favor, determination, purpose, inclination, charm, delight, luxury, luxuriance, wealth, riches, amusement, diversion, entertainment, comfort, health, well-being, fulfillment, victory, satiety, completion, happiness, felicity, contentment, bliss, ease, rest, peace, peace of mind. Ant. displeasure, sorrow, woe, grief, suffering, dissatisfaction, uneasiness, vexation, worry, sickness, illness, misfortune, evil, pain, hurt, wound, disease, mourning, mournfulness, affliction, grievance, anguish, disappointment, plague, visitation, persecution, tyranny, slavery, tribulation, despair, hopelessness, misery, wretchedness, desolation, anxiety, care, burden, responsibility, discontentment, distress, mortification, heartbreak, heartscald, adversity, infelicity, trouble, unhappiness.

pledge, v.—Syn. guarantee, vow, promise, engage, contract, affirm, bind.

plentiful—*Syn.* abundant, copious, ample, plenty, plenteous, fruitful, abounding, profuse, lavish, full, sufficient, adequate, enough, liberal, unsparing, replete, chockfull, luxuriant, inexhaustible, rich, teeming, generous, large, overflowing, complete, bountiful, exuberant, affluent, bounteous, unstinted, unmeasured, well-provided. *Ant.* scarce, few, short, little, small, insufficient, deficient, scant, scanty, exhausted, impoverished, straitened, sparing, stingy, inadequate, drained, mean, miserly, niggardly, poor, skimpy, scrimped, empty, vacant, bare, dry, unsupplied, barren, depleted, illprovided, denuded, stripped, minute, exiguous, lacking, sparse.

pliant—*Syn.* limber, supple, bending, lithe, flexible, ductile, docile, obsequious, tractable, plastic, malleable, extensile, extensible, soft, yielding, inexperienced, youthful, green (*colloq.*), raw (*colloq.*), fickle, irresolute, weak, wavering, fluctuating, vacillating, submissive, capricious, unstable, feeble-minded, timid. *Ant.* hard, hardened, unbending, unyielding, stiff, rigid, determined, resolute, self-reliant, self-possessed, wise, experienced, tough, tenacious, indomitable, unconquerable, stable, strongminded, obstinate, obdurate, arrogant, domineering, inflexible, unchangeable, callous, stubborn, headstrong, contumacious, pertinacious, opinionated.

plight—*Syn.* difficulty, dilemma, predicament, state, condition, situation, position, lot, quandary, form, shape, fettle, mood, circumstance, emergency, exigency, doubt, doubtfulness, contingency, hesitation, embarrassment, perplexity. *Ant.* assurance, surety, certainty, regularity, plain sailing, security, confidence, firmness, boldness, courage, capability, ease, easiness, facility, easy circumstances, absence of worry, fearlessness.

plot, *n.*—*Syn.* intrigue, conspiracy, cabal, combination, plan, scheme, design, project, proposal, outline, sketch, draft, program, platform, plank, slate, machination, idea, forecast, prospectus, ground, land, area, patch, lot, section.

plot, *v.*—*Syn.* plan, scheme, contrive, sketch, devise, invent, frame, project, intrigue, concoct, draft, organize, conspire, map out, propose, put forward, suggest.

pluck—*Syn.* courage, boldness, bravery, determination, grit (*colloq.*), sand (*slang*), spunk (*colloq.*), mettle, spirit, resolution, decision, firmness, energy, tenacity, perseverance, gameness, intransigency, sticktoitiveness (*colloq.*), self-reliance, persistence, backbone (*slang*), willpower, dauntlessness, doggedness, stamina, endurance, indefatigability, obstinacy, manliness, guts (*vulgar slang*). *Ant.* tergiversation, fickleness, fluctuation, wavering, indecision, hesitation, weakness, cowardice, irresolution, indetermination, uncertainty, wabbling, vacillation, unstability, fear, apprehension, timidity, pulsillanimity, unwillingness, disinclination, reluctance, shyness, remissness, backwardness, bashfulness, abulia, feeble-mindedness, faltering, faint-heartedness, diffidence, cravenness, dastardliness, poltroonery, spiritlessness.

plump—*Syn.* fleshy, portly, full, chubby, round, fat, bouncing, well-conditioned, pot-bellied, stout, corpulent, lusty, burly, corn-fed (*colloq.*), dumpy, hulking, lubberly, puffy, swollen, florid. *Ant.* lean, thin, emaciated, puny, runty, spindly, skeletal, shrunken, spare, weazened, withered, wrinkled, wasted, consumptive, shriveled, tabescent, tabletic, atrophied, attenuated.

plunder, *n.*—*Syn.* booty, spoils, loot, pillage.

plush, *adj.*—*Syn.* luxurious, sybaritic, sumptuous, sensuous, rich, elegant, prodigal. *Ant.* wretched, miserable, poor, scanty.

ply, *v.*—*Syn.* work, exert, exercise, wield, employ, use, operate, urge, apply, handle, control, press, solicit.

poetry—*Syn.* poem, verse, song, numbers, rime, rhyme, rhythm, meter, metrical, composition, versification, poesy, stanza, epic, idyll, pastoral, rondeau, elegy, b a l l a d, lyric, ode, sonnet. *Ant.* prose, prosaic speech, prosaic writing, essay, story, history, sermon, speech, address, oration, common speech, ordinary writing.

poignant, *adj.*—*Syn.* keen, piercing, acute, pungent, biting, mordant, sharp, intense, bitter, painful, trenchant.

poise—*Syn.* balance, gravity, equilibrium, ballast, equality, evenness, equalization, equiponderance, adjustment, readjustment, calm, calmness, composure, steadiness, imperturbability, patience, mental calmness, coolness, stolidity, inexcitability. *Ant.* inequality, difference, disparity, levity, lightness, buoyancy, excitability, vehemence, violence, turbulence, anger, rage, fury, agitation, passion, excitement, paroxysm, frenzy, fierceness, ferocity, madness, insanity, outburst.

poisonous—*Syn.* bad, noxious, harmful, hurtful, dangerous, pestiferous, baneful, malignant, infective, venomous, virulent, peccant, vicious, corrupt, deleterious, noisome, morbid, morbific, morbiferous, fatal, pestilential, toxic, toxiferous, deadly, destructive. *Ant.* good, healthy, invigorating, stimulating, salubrious, wholesome, nourishing, tonic, bracing, sanitary, prophylactic, hygienic, preservative, preserving, curative, innocuous, harmless, remedial, strengthening, preventative.

polite—*Syn.* civil, courteous, genteel, polished, refined, well-bred, accomplished, finished, urbane, suave, amiable, good-mannered, complacent, attentive, obliging, cultured, cultivated, affable, agreeable, chivalrous, gallant, mannerly, well-behaved, winning, ingratiating, cordial, bland, unctuous, oily-tongued, obsequious. *Ant.* rude, rough, unmannerly, uncivil, gruff, snappish, peevish, discourteous, ill-bred, churlish, boorish, hoggish, piggish, grouchy, ungracious, impolite, vulgar, impudent, impertinent, insulting, abusive, brusque, foul-mouthed, scurrile, scurrilous, indecent, gross, underbred, disgusting, coarse, opprobrious, foul, obscene, low, filthy, offensive.

politic—*Syn.* cunning, wary, adroit, foxy, discreet, judicious, sagacious, diplomatic, wise, provident, prudent, well-devised, tricky, wily, watchful, calculating, sapient, sage, long-sighted, long-headed, crafty, subtle, artful, intriguing, designing, time-saving, Machiavellian, underhand, double-faced, shifty, deceptive, shrewd, sharp, astute, acute, canny [*Sc.*]. *Ant.* dull, stolid, stupid, blundering, simple, unsophisticated, blunt, dull-witted, slow, doltish, thick, shallow, addle-pated, obtuse, sappy (*slang*), spoony (*slang*), straightforward, artless, ingenuous, sincere, candid, specious, unreserved, fatuous, foolish, incautious, rash, foolhardy, hasty, indiscreet, heedless, careless, reckless, hot-headed, headstrong, stubborn, stiff-necked, devil-may-care.

pollute—*Syn.* deprave, soil, stain, taint, corrupt, defile, debase, tarnish, smear, smudge, smirch, befoul, begrime, contaminate, impair, prostitute, violate, disgrace, dishonor, debauch, defile, degrade, demoralize. *Ant.* cleanse, purify, wash, clean, deterge, edulcorate, fumigate, ventilate, deodorize, sweep, brush, tidy, improve, exalt, ennoble, refresh, reform, reclaim, refine, dignify, honor, respect, upraise, elevate, chasten.

pompous—*Syn.* arrogant, haughty, proud, domineering, boastful, ostentatious, vain, vainglorious, swaggering, showy, egotistical, blustering, bombastic, puffed up, inflated, grandiose, frothy, flashy, flamboyant, high-flown, hifalutin, affected, disdainful, bumptious, supercilious, high-handed, consequential, imperious, magisterial, high-hat(*slang*), top-hat (*slang*), pretentious, theatrical, dashing, jaunty, garish, gaudy, spectacular, flaunting, swanky (*Eng. dial.*). *Ant.* unobtrusive, retiring, unpretentious, mild, coy, shy, sheepish, diffident, timid, backward, bashful, unassuming, humble, meek, lowly, modest, shrinking, reserved, submissive, abashed, ashamed, chapfallen, flabbergasted (*colloq.*), plain, simple, ordinary, common, servile, obsequious, demure, deprecatory, unostentatious, unaspiring, shamefaced, confused, blushing.

ponder, *v.*—*Syn.* weigh, think, reflect, contemplate, deliberate, muse, consider, cogitate, study.

ponderous—*Syn.* dull, heavy, lifeless, inanimate, inert, massive, weighty, ponderable, burdensome, cumbrous, cumbersome, unwieldy. *Ant.* light, volatile, fluffy, airy, imponderable, ethereal, buoyant, subereus, suberose, suberous, subtile, feathery, corky, weightless.

poor—*Syn.* indigent, penniless, moneyless, impecunious, destitute, needy, poverty-stricken, fortuneless, starved, straitened, distressed, reduced, beggared, stinted, famine-stricken, empty-handed, pitiful, paltry, contemptible, meager or meagre, miserable, pitiable, scanty, wretched, dejected, unhappy, weak, puny, dwarfed, insignificant, diminutive. *Ant.* rich, wealthy, well-to-do, affluent, opulent, warm (*colloq.*), snug (*colloq.*), strong, robust, vigorous, husky, powerful, manly, courageous, important, promi-

nent, assertive, compelling, domineering, influential, commanding, happy, joyous, strong, large, great, fine, exalted, enviable.

popular—*Syn.* favorite, liked, well-liked, approved, recommended, well-received, pleasing, suitable, general, familiar, widespread, prevailing, common, current, demanded, sought, fashionable, customary, stylish, conventional, beloved, polished, refined, likable, lovable, attractive, alluring, inviting, deserving, engaging, famous, celebrated, admired, esteemed, commendable, loved, seductive, winning, winsome, estimable, captivating, bewitching, notable, renowned, worthy, praiseworthy. *Ant.* hateful, despicable, loathsome, abhorrent, disgusting, odious, execrable, abominable, detestable, repulsive, repellent, revolting, offensive, noxious, displeasing, disagreeable, troublesome, unwelcome, unpopular, undesirable, distasteful, depressing, annoying, provoking, repugnant, nauseous, sickening, antagonistic, forbidding, obnoxious, opprobrious, infamous, wicked, heinous, disgraceful, abandoned, exiled, shunned, ostracized, boycotted, banished.

portent, *n.*—*Syn.* omen, sign, token, wonder, augury, meaning, presentiment, presage, warning, phenomenon.

portion—*Syn.* division, share, part, fraction, parcel, quantity, allotment, dividend, fragment, detachment, subdivision, section, piece, slice, cutting, lump, consignment, allowance. *Ant.* whole, all, entirety, embodiment, aggregation, amount, sum, total, unity, completeness, mass, indivisibility, gross.

position—*Syn.* place, station, state, condition, circumstance, posture, attitude, rank, office, employment, situation, status, standing, footing, post, environment, ground, locality, location, site, seat, spot, whereabouts, bearings.

positive—*Syn.* certain, absolute, decided, peremptory, unequivocal, assertive, obstinate, stiff, opinionated, precise, real, strict, stubborn, actual, factual, substantive, well-grounded, rigid, uncompromising, sure, genuine, unquestionable, assured, unmistakable, definite, clear, dogmatic, dictatorial, obvious, distinct, express, explicit, emphatic, decided, immovable, inexorable, obdurate, arbitrary, imperative, veritable, exact, authentic. *Ant.* uncertain, doubtful, questionable, suspicious, fallible, incredulous, incredible, erroneous, erring, fallacious, groundless, unsound, unintelligible, ambiguous, obscure, enigmatic, puzzling, indefinite, loose, vague, incomprehensible, negative, contradictory, disputable, confutable, irresolute, veiled, changeable, inexplicable, irregular, anomalous, wandering, confused, indistinct, hazy, equivocal, complicated, involved, indeterminate, cryptic, untrustworthy, problematical, unauthentic.

possessor—*Syn.* holder, owner, proprietor, proprietress, inheritor, occupant, occupier, retainer, master, buyer, purchaser, sharer, partner, landlord, landowner, lessee, legatee, landlady, mistress, lord of the manor, master, laird [*Sc.*], trustee, beneficiary, inheritor, heir.

possible—*Syn.* feasible, likely, potential, practicable, contingent, indeterminate, fortuitous, casual, adventitious, incidental, liable, credible, conceivable, accessible, achievable, attainable. *Ant.* impossible, unlikely, impracticable, unattainable, insurmountable, improbable, incredible, absurd, ridiculous, unreasonable, visionary, inconceivable, contrary to reason.

postpone—*Syn.* defer, put off, delay, procrastinate, adjourn, suspend, prorogue, lay over, stave off, retard, waive, remand, protract, temporize, pigeonhole,

shelve, lay on the table. *Ant.* proceed, continue, carry on, accelerate, expedite, hasten, hurry, quicken, persist, uphold, sustain, persevere, prolong, pursue, maintain, extend, keep going.

potent—*Syn.* powerful, strong, forcible, influential, able, efficacious, strengthening, effective, effectual, dynamic, mighty, vigorous, sturdy, robust, irresistible, puissant, stalwart, virile, sinewy, able-bodied, brawny, muscular, strenuous, prevailing, dominant, authoritative, important. *Ant.* weak, puny, delicate, fragile, impotent, inept, inefficient, incompetent, powerless, disabled, invalid, effeminate, enervated, unfit, crippled, decrepit, emasculate, palsied, exhausted, paralytic, helpless, unimportant, uninfluential, subordinate, poor, unknown, obscure.

potential, *adj.*—*Syn.* latent, possible, quiescent, promising, hidden. *Ant.* actual, active, real.

pound, *v.*—*Syn.* strike, thump, buffet, batter, smite, hit, beat.

poverty—*Syn.* distress, beggary, mendicancy, pennilessness, want, penury, indigence, need, deficiency, destitution, pauperism, dearth, scarcity, insufficiency, inadequacy, exigency, privation, starvation, famine. *Ant.* wealth, riches, affluence, plenty, fortune, independence, means, resources, substance, opulence, capital, property, competence, money, lucre, abundance, plenty, plenteousness.

powder, *v.*—*Syn.* pulverize, abrade, grind, crunch, crumble, crush, triturate, granulate, bray, levigate, comminute.

power—*Syn.* efficacy, strength, vigor, vim, force, forcefulness, energy, potentiality, effectiveness, might, potency, capacity, capability, command, sway, authority, influence, jurisdiction, dominion, susceptibility, government, agency, faculty, caliber, ability, rule, qualification, skill, talent, expertness, dexterity, competence, competency, efficiency, energy, cogency, aptitude, cleverness, puissance, ascendancy, superiority, domination, mastery, predominance, ableness, control, supremacy, patronage, sovereignty, leadership, hegemony, prestige, prerogative, pull (*slang*). *Ant.* weakness, impotence, debility, infirmity, atomy, languor, lassitude, faintness, decrepitude, disability, disablement, ennui, weariness, tiredness, ineptitude, inability, collapse, helplessness, powerlessness, incapacity, inefficiency, unfitness, effeminacy, asthenia, cachexia, softness, debilitation, feebleness, prostration, enervation, impairment, fatigue, exhaustion, deterioration, degeneration, timidity, cowardliness, fear, trepidation, tremor, fright, nervousness, cravenness, abjectness, faintheartedness, cowardice, yellowness (*colloq.*), funk.

powerful, *adj.*—*Syn.* potent, forceful, capable, strong, muscular, mighty, vigorous, energetic, robust, effectual, sturdy, competent. *Ant.* feeble, impotent, fragile, decrepit.

praise, *n.*—*Syn.* laudation, eulogy, applause, adulation, encomium, blandishment, plaudit, panegyric, esteem, commendation, recommendation, appreciation, cheer, cheering, advocacy, admiration, tribute, compliment, eulogium, homage, acclaim, acclamation, sycophancy, flattery. *Ant.* condemnation, censure, blame, obloquy, sarcasm, satire, disapproval, contempt, disapprobation, dislike, disparagement, denunciation, hate, hatred, vituperation, umbrage, vilification, detraction, accusation, disfavor, boycott, ostracism, repudiation, rebuke, scorn, reproach, remonstrance, slander, reprimand, reproof, hissing, execration.

praise, *v.*—*Syn.* laud, commend, recommend, extol, applaud,

magnify, glorify, cheer, acclaim, indorse, sanction, exalt, admire, approve, eulogize, compliment, boost (*colloq.*), bepraise. *Ant.* censure, condemn, decry, disapprove, dislike, disfavor, reprehend, disparage, boycott, ostracize, shun, blame, reproach, admonish, berate, impugn, blacklist, blackball, objurgate, upbraid, snub, execrate, defame, denounce, backbite, deprecate.

prayer—*Syn.* supplication, entreaty, request, petition, suit, appeal, importunity, imploration, orison, imprecation, solicitation, postulation, invocation, act of devotion. *Ant.* deprecation, expostulation, remonstrance, protest, dissent, disapprobation, inhibition, prohibition, interdict, interdiction, restriction, proscription, negligence, disrespect, mockery, ridicule, contempt, godlessness, scoffing, irreverence, derision.

precarious—*Syn.* doubtful, uncertain, dubious, unsettled, unstable, unsteady, equivocal, risky, uncertain, unassured, hazardous, insecure, perilous, chancy. *Ant.* certain, assured, undoubted, unquestionable, undeniable, sure, steady, stable, infallible, real, settled, immutable, incontestable, firm, strong, actual.

preceding, *adj.*—*Syn.* foregoing, anterior, prior, previous, antecedent, earlier, former. *Ant.* subsequent, following, succeeding, later.

precept—*Syn.* doctrine, law, rule, principle, maxim, instruction, injunction, mandate, commandment, direction, form, model, formulary, regulation, adage, apothegm, aphorism, saw, saying, byword, proverb.

precious—*Syn.* valuable, costly, dear, inestimable, beloved, highpriced, expensive, superior, excellent, select, important, worthy, great, considerable, useful, invaluable, fine, priceless, firstclass, superfine, superexcellent, peerless, unequaled, superlative, bully (*slang*), crackerjack (*slang*), A1, exquisite, tiptop (*colloq.*). *Ant.* worthless, insignificant, inconsiderate, valueless, wishy-washy, trashy, trifling, useless, unimportant, immaterial, common, commonplace, ordinary, slight, trumpery, gimcrack, petty, two-for-a-nickel (*U.S. slang*), tuppeny-ha'penny (*Eng. slang*), one-horse (*U.S. slang*), cheap, imperfect, impaired, faulty, defective, deficient, indifferent, contemptible, despicable.

precise—*Syn.* accurate, definite, scrupulous, exact, punctilious, well-defined, authentic, genuine, strict, meticulous, rigid, rigorous, particular, exacting, inflexible, obdurate, strait-laced, austere, uncompromising, prudish, arbitrary. *Ant.* inexact, careless, negligent, slipshod, slapdash, faulty, stumbling, erroneous, misleading, deceiving, erring, unauthentic, loose, lax, false, fallacious, questionable, jumbled, mixed, ambiguous, uncertain, paradoxical, contradictory.

predicament—*Syn.* strait, quandary, plight, puzzle, perplexity, dilemma, difficulty, fix, scrape, corner, hole, *impasse* [*Fr.*], pickle, mess, muddle, imbroglio, hot water (*colloq.*) exigency, stew (*slang*), deadlock, pinch, crisis, pretty kettle of fish (*colloq.*). *Ant.* firmness, fixity, resolution, contentment, certainty, confidence, comfort, satisfaction, ease, decision, content, rest, assurance, calmness, self-confidence, self-satisfaction, self-reliance, ease, easiness, facility, smoothness, plain sailing (*colloq.*), nothing to worry about (*colloq.*).

prediction—*Syn.* prognostication, announcement, foretelling, presage, presagement, foreboding, preannouncement, prophecy, soothsaying, fortune-telling, divination, vaticination, augury, prognosis, forecast, horoscope.

predominant—*Syn.* supreme, prevailing, prevalent, ruling, overruling, reigning, controlling, ascendant, supervisory, directing, gubernatorial, arbitrary, hegemonic, authoritative, dominant, paramount, preponderant, imperious, peremptory, compulsory, absolute, executive, official, bureaucratic, potent, influential, weighty, effective, governing. *Ant.* humble, lowly, unimportant, petty, insignificant, puerile, light, slight, trivial, immaterial, powerless, weak, uninfluential, non-effective, trifling, submissive, obscure, obedient, subservient, servile, obsequious, sycophantic, subjective, subordinate, dependent, restricted, restrained, impotent, ineffective, inefficient, ineffectual.

prefer, *v.*—*Syn.* desire, fancy, approve, choose, pick, promote, select, favor.

prejudice—*Syn.* partiality, unfairness, spleen, bias, detriment, prepossession, enmity, prejudgment, objection, dislike, disgust, aversion, hatred, antipathy, disrelish, enmity, umbrage, pique, coolness, animosity, spite, contemptuousness, bad opinion, displeasure, repugnance, revulsion, preconception, foregone conclusion, quirk, warp, twist. *Ant.* appreciation, admiration, estimation, attraction, attractiveness, regard, esteem, good opinion, respect, approval, approbation, consideration, attachment, concern, care, friendship, confidence, sympathy, benevolence, kindness, warm-heartedness, benignity, brotherly love.

premature—*Syn.* untimely, precipitate, rash, unseasonable, unauthenticated, crude, hasty, precocious, early, impending, anticipatory, sudden, immature, unripe, unprepared, raw, green. *Ant.* late, delayed, retarded, kept back, ripe, mature, ready, prepared, expected, arranged, anticipated, made to order, cut and dried, deferred, tardy, slow, belated, backward, dilatory, behindhand, overdue.

premeditated, *adj.—Syn.* intended, meant, intentional, voluntary, calculated, planned, designed, plotted, deliberate. *Ant.* spontaneous, unforeseen, accidental, casual.

preoccupied, *adj.—Syn.* abstracted, engrossed, absorbed, absent, musing, intent, inattentive, unobservant, oblivious.

prepare, *v.—Syn.* arrange, dispose, provide, form, plan.

preposterous, *adj.—Syn.* absurd, extravagant, nonsensical, unreasonable, ridiculous, silly, fantastic.

presage, *v.—Syn.* foreshadow, forebode, portend, forecast, prophesy, augur, predict, prognosticate.

prescribed, *adj.—Syn.* destined, established, ordained, decreed, assigned, allotted.

presence, *n.—Syn.* carriage, appearance, mien, deportment, personality, demeanor, air, manner.

present, *v.—Syn.* bestow, award, endow, give, tender, confer, grant, proffer, deliver.

preserve, *v.—Syn.* maintain, keep, guard, secure, save, protect, uphold, sustain, support. *Ant.* abolish, destroy, abrogate, oppose.

presumptuous—*Syn.* arrogant, insolent, bold, rash, overconfident, presuming, reckless, impudent, haughty, brazen, impertinent, domineering, bullying, boisterous, bumptious, imperious, magisterial, supercilious, contumelious, dictatorial, overbearing, assuming, nervy, blustering, swaggering, toplofty (*colloq.*), high-hat (*slang*), fresh (*slang*), flippant, saucy, audacious, thrasonical, bragging, boastful, boasting, inflated, vainglorious, self-assertive, temerarious, unwarranted, unjustified. *Ant.* modest, backward, retiring, bashful, humble, timid, diffident, coy, unpretentious, unassuming, unostentatious, deprecatory, unobtrusive, meek, lowly, servile, submissive, obsequious, slavish, abject, pliant, groveling, sycophantic, parasitical, reserved, shy, hesitating, doubtful, reluctant, unwilling, fawning, truckling, toadying, cringing, sniveling, subservient, subordinate.

presupposition, *n.—Syn.* presumption, belief, conjecture, premise, guess, opinion, implication, surmise, assumption, inference, deduction.

pretense—*Syn.* subterfuge, pretext, excuse, trick, show, mask, cloak, appearance, seeming, semblance, imitation, copy, simulation, affectation, misrepresentation, falsification, falseness, falsehood, gloss, disguise, assumption, dissembling, deceit, excuse, dissimulation, perversion, equivocation, prevarication, wile, subreption, fabrication, trickery, ruse, double-dealing, quibbling, misstatement, shuffling, insincerity. *Ant.* candor, honesty, truth, openness, fairness, square dealing, probity, sincerity, truthfulness, veracity, straightforwardness, guilelessness, trustworthiness, outspokenness, plain dealing, exactness, ingenuousness, frankness, artlessness, simplicity, bluntness, plain speaking, unsophistication, inartificiality, simplemindedness, naivete, plainness, unreservedness, actuality, reality, fact.

pretty—*Syn.* handsome, beautiful, fine, nice, dainty, elegant, swell (*slang*), becoming, attractive, comely, appealing, fair, lovely, graceful, delicate, refined, exquisite, *svelte* [*Fr.*], prepossessing, flowerlike, good-looking. *Ant.* ugly, homely, ordinary, common, ill-favored, hard-visaged, hard-featured, grim-faced, grim-visaged, revolting, repellent, forbidding, repulsive, dumpy, dowdy, ungraceful, gawky.

prevailing—*Syn.* prevalent, general, predominant, universal, common, catholic, worldwide, sweeping, all-embracing, comprehensive, widespread, ecumenical. *Ant.* isolated, sporadic, particular, individual, definite, special, determinate, uncertain, partial, peculiar, private, exclusive, restricted, singular.

prevent—*Syn.* preclude, obviate, forestall, anticipate, block, stop, thwart, debar, repress, interrupt, halt, impede, check, avert, hinder, frustrate, balk, foil, retard, obstruct, counteract, inhibit, restrain, intercept, override, circumvent, corner. *Ant.* allow, permit, aid, help, succor, support, sustain, uphold, further, abet, encourage, accommodate, advocate, countenance, assist, serve, second, stand by, back up, patronize, favor, befriend, oblige, incite, instigate, stimulate.

previous—*Syn.* antecedent, prior, former, forerunning, preceding, anterior, preliminary, preparatory, introductory, foregoing, above-mentioned, above-named, aforesaid, precedent, earlier, front, forward, before, aforementioned, precursory, prefatory. *Ant.* succeeding, pursuant, sequent, following, consequent, concluding, after, latter, posterior, subsequent, later, hind, hinder, hindmost, ensuing, coming after, going after.

price—*Syn.* charge, expenditure, outlay, expense, cost, value, worth, figure, impost, dues, tariff, duty, tax, rate, valuation, appraisement. *Ant.* discount, allowance, concession, rebatement, abatement, reduction, salvage, tare, tret, cloff [Eng.], deduction, poundage.

pride—*Syn.* vanity, conceit, self-esteem, egotism, self-satisfaction, vainglory, self-respect, egoism, haughtiness, arrogance, presumption, pomposity, swank (*Eng. dial.*), side (*slang*), dog (*slang*), swagger, toploftiness (*colloq.*), high hat (*slang*), bumptiousness, superciliousness, disdain, contemptuousness, self-exaltation, assumption, self-conceit, self-complacency, reserve, insolence. *Ant.* humility, lowliness, self-effacement, self-

denial, humiliation, abasement, self-abasement, humbleness, self-distrust, meekness, modesty, timidity, backwardness, bashfulness, obsequiousness, subserviency, sycophancy, abashment, abjectness, flunkeyism, diffidence, reserve, hesitation, reluctance, sheepishness, unobtrusiveness, demureness, shyness.

primary, *adj.*—*Syn.* principal, chief, basic, primitive, original, fundamental, first, leading, initial, elementary, main. *Ant.* secondary, subordinate, subsequent, following.

primeval—*Syn.* ancient, primitive, primal, primary, pristine, primordial, old, olden, misty, prime, patriarchal, autochthonic, immemorial, uncreated, native, indigenous, original, antique, venerable, time-honored, hoary, prehistoric, traditional, antediluvian, fossil, remote, longgone, distant, early. *Ant.* modern, recent, late, present, prospective, future, expectant, eventual, approaching, impending, near, new, novel, fresh, green, up-to-date, coming, new-fashioned, new-born, neoteric, foreign, exotic, adventitious, new-made, upstart, young, youthful, newfangled.

princely—*Syn.* royal, regal, august, grand, fine, sublime, splendid, magnificent, superb, supreme, munificent, imperial, noble, exalted, titled, aristocratic, high-born, high-bred, patrician, noble-minded, magnanimous, chivalrous, heroic, lofty, great-hearted, large-hearted, celebrated, famous, renowned, far-famed, dignified, lordly, stately, high-minded, well-born. *Ant.* mean, contemptible, miserly, ignoble, low, lowly, underbred, vulgar, coarse, gross, plebeian, baseborn, low-born, rude, brutish, loutish, churlish, unpolished, clownish, tough (*colloq.*), cruel, cowardly, boorish, nasty, low-minded, vile, base, graceless, ribald, ungentlemanly, ill-bred, ill-mannered, uncivil, scurrilous, abusive, vicious, blackguard, ruffianly, cruel, despicable, abject, worthless.

principal—*Syn.* leading, chief, first, head, prime, main, foremost, cardinal, essential, capital, important, preëminent, highest, supreme, prominent, dominant, predominant, predominating, supereminent, controlling, superior, capital, prevailing, paramount, greatest. *Ant.* inferior, minor, negligible, secondary, supplemental, accessory, auxiliary, helping, subsidiary, contributory, added, additional, inconsiderable, subordinate, subject, dependent, unessential, nonessential, trivial, unimportant, insignificant, nugatory, immaterial.

principally—*Syn.* chiefly, mainly, essentially, above all, in the first place, to crown all. *Ant.* slightly, somewhat, tolerably, fairly well, pretty well, slightly, of no consequence.

principle—*Syn.* law, doctrine, precept, tenet, purpose, decree, rule, reason, motive, policy, ground, groundwork, foundation, character, nature, disposition, mood, attitude, habit, belief, inspiration, impulse, dogma, maxim, model, system, faith, constancy, honor, integrity, uprightness, rectitude, constitution, temperament, intrinsicality, naturalness, profession of faith, article of faith.

priority, *n.*—*Syn.* precedence, ascendancy, antecedence, supremacy, pre-eminence.

prison, *n.*—*Syn.* jail, keep, dungeon, penitentiary, reformatory, cage, lockup, brig, jug, stir, pen, hoosegow, calaboose, clink, cooler, can, pokey.

privation, *n.*—*Syn.* want, indigence, destitution, poverty, penury, need, exigency. *Ant.* plenty, wealth, riches, opulence.

privilege—*Syn.* favor, advantage, prerogative, exemption, immunity, claim, right, freedom, permission, due, license, full swing, liberty, tolerance, indulgence, dispensation, warranty, authorization, sanction. *Ant.* assumption, usurpation, illegality, defiance, prohibition, interdiction, inhibition, restriction, disallowance, injunction, embargo, service, servitude, slavery, thraldom, subjection, subordination, subjugation, serfdom, enslavement.

probable, *adj.*—*Syn.* likely, presumptive, presumable, rational, apparent, plausible, reasonable, credible.

probity—*Syn.* honesty, honor, integrity, trustiness, loyalty, rectitude, uprightness, trustworthiness, impartiality, fairness, fair play, justice, righteousness, principle, incorruptness, incorruptibility, sincerity, frankness. *Ant.* dishonor, dishonesty, knavery, trickery, deception, double-dealing, perfidy, perfidiousness, unfaithfulness, injustice, unfairness, roguery, rascality, foul play, corruption, fraud, improbity.

problematic—*Syn.* problematical, uncertain, doubtful, contingent, vague, possible, dubious, unreliable, casual, equivocal, undecided, indeterminate, indefinite, questionable, disputable, apocryphal. *Ant.* certain, sure, undoubted, indubitable, evident, apparent, authentic, reliable, authoritative, unerring, conclusive, irrefutable, incontestable, indisputable, dogmatic, doubtless, self-evident, axiomatic.

proceeding—*Syn.* action, process, transaction, deed, experiment, performance, measure, step, course, undertaking, venture, adventure, occurrence, incident, casualty, circumstance, happening, movement, operation, procedure, exercise, maneuver. *Ant.* inactivity, stagnation, quiescence, inertness, unemployment, loafing, passiveness, idling, idleness, remissness, cessation, standstill, stupor, unconsciousness, lethargy, torpidity, somnolence, insensibility.

proclaim, *v.—Syn.* declare, voice, promulgate, publish, advertise, announce, divulge, reveal, utter.

procure, *v.—Syn.* acquire, secure, get, gain, win, obtain, achieve, contrive, manage.

prodigious—*Syn.* huge, immense, monstrous, extraordinary, enormous, vast, wonderful, great, amazing, marvelous, astonishing, miraculous, surprising, stupendous, indescribable, inconceivable, incredible, phenomenal, overwhelming, impressive. *Ant.* common, commonplace, ordinary, small, meager, insignificant, petty, piddling, trivial, trifling, inconsiderable, mean, poor, unimpressive, minute, minor, slight, diminutive, dwarfed, microscopic, shrunken, contracted.

prodigy—*Syn.* marvel, portent, wonder, miracle, monster, monstrosity, enormity, spectacle, freak, curiosity, scholar extraordinary. *Ant.* normalcy, normality, regularity, commonness, generality, universality, matter of fact, plainness, state of being ordinary.

produce, *n.—Syn.* product, fruit, fruitage, harvest, result, resultant, return, effect, consequence, amount, profit, ingathering, outcome, outgrowth, crops, aftermath, gain, emolument, realization. *Ant.* cause, origin, beginning, source, agent, principle, element, loss, damage, detriment, deprivation, squandering, waste, privation.

produce, *v.—Syn.* bear, yield, impart, give, afford, occasion, effect, cause, make, breed, beget, increase, augment, swell, extend, dilate, originate, bring about, constitute, create, set on foot, operate, manufacture, bring out, issue, institute, organize, show, display, act, perform, dramatize. *Ant.* waste, consume, destroy, annihilate, demolish, overthrow, tear down, deny, refuse, decrease, diminish, shrink, reduce, wreck, abolish, break up, conceal, hide, shut, shut down,

close, close up, take off, discard, terminate.

profane, *adj.—Syn.* mundane, secular, temporal, worldly, earthly, lay, vulgar, unconsecrated. *Ant.* sacred, holy, spiritual, hallowed.

profession—*Syn.* calling, trade, business, avocation, vocation, employment, occupation, engagement, avowal, office, situation, billet, rôle, service, pursuit, undertaking, concern, post, incumbency, berth, craft, sphere, line, field, walk of life, pretense, assertion, declaration.

proficient, *adj.—Syn.* competent, able, skilled, adroit, adept, expert, dextrous, accomplished, practiced. *Ant.* awkward, clumsy, gauche, maladroit.

profit—*Syn.* gain, benefit, advantage, improvement, return, returns, proceeds, receipts, avail, good, utility, value, usefulness, service, expediency, emolument, acquisition, accumulation, aggrandizement, augmentation, interest, remuneration. *Ant.* loss, damage, detriment, deprivation, forfeiture, failure, ruin, bankruptcy, harm, hurt, injury, disadvantage, indebtedness, obligation, waste, ruin, destruction, subversion, overthrow, downfall.

profligate—*Syn.* dissolute, abandoned, depraved, shameless, corrupt, degenerate, blackguard, ruffianly, rascally, perfidious, wicked, sinful, lewd, vicious, demoralized, flagrant, casehardened, offensive, immoral, Lesbianic, erotic, debauched, Sadistic, loose, lax, iniquitous, disreputable, disgraceful, base, sinister, vile, evil, evil-minded, flagitious, atrocious, infamous, villainous, heinous, diabolic, Mephistophelian, satanic, hellish, hellborn, fiendlike, demoniacal, shameful, scandalous, nefarious, obscene, pornographic, incestuous, ribald, foul, foul-mouthed, libidinous, licentious, lustful, carnal, lecherous, sensual, unregenerate, unbridled, bad, voluptuous, unchaste, impure, indecent, indelicate, lascivious, wanton, dissipated. *Ant.* virtuous, upright, noble, magnanimous, refined, modest, pure, decent, God-fearing, innocent, uncorrupt, uncorrupted, undefiled, immaculate, unspotted, unstained, chaste, uncontaminated, virgin, moral, spiritual, clean, good, wholesome, continent, restrained, blameless, irreproachable, righteous, constant, commendable, exemplary, model, well-behaved, worthy, praiseworthy, meritorious, excellent, enviable, sterling, admirable, creditable, laudable, sinless, faultless, straightforward, incorruptible, high-principled, conscientious, honorable, respectable, trustworthy, religious, prayerful, saintlike, godly, pious, devout, devoted, devotional, reverent.

profound—*Syn.* deep, fathomless, mysterious, solemn, abstruse, recondite, learned, erudite, scholarly, deeply read (*colloq.*), accomplished, knowing, knowledgeable, intellectual, wise, sagacious, penetrating, intense, great, consummate, enlightened, experienced, well-informed, sage, discerning, comprehensive, serious. *Ant.* shallow, slight, light, superficial, flighty, unsettled, erratic, eccentric, simple, trifling, silly, foolish, unlearned, unenlightened, unlettered, ignorant, absurd, fatuous, stupid, frivolous, giddy, nonsensical.

profuse—*Syn.* lavish, prodigal, extravagant, abundant, liberal, improvident, excessive, plentiful, plenteous, copious, superabundant, overflowing, over-liberal, full-handed, redundant, superfluous. *Ant.* scarce, meager, stinted, insufficient, inadequate, scanty, beggarly, empty, bare, dry, wanting, lacking, limited, curtailed, deficient, barren, incomplete, small, short, scrimpy.

progress—*Syn.* advancement, progression, development, growth, improvement, advance, locomotion, attainment, increase, proficiency, motion, movement, progressiveness, headway, rate, pace, step, stride, velocity, transit, journey, voyage. *Ant.* rest, stillness, standstill, stagnation, fixity, immobility, retrogression, pause, stay, stop, stoppage, falling back, falling off, delay, relapse, check, decline, decrease, cessation, primitiveness, backwardness, decline, declination.

prohibit—*Syn.* bar, debar, hinder, prevent, block, check, forbid, interdict, preclude, disallow, inhibit, restrict, restrain, exclude, proscribe, ban, taboo, veto, refuse, deny, withhold. *Ant.* allow, permit, tolerate, license, concede, grant, warrant, indorse, sanction, encourage, authorize, empower, legalize, recognize, admit, command, direct, order, enjoin, empower, suffer, consent to, give consent, let, unrestrict, unrestrain, uncheck.

project, *v.*—*Syn.* plan, intend, devise, outline, plot, scheme.

proletariat, *n.*—*Syn.* masses, workingmen, plebeians, laborers, populace.

prolix—*Syn.* diffuse, wordy, tedious, tiresome, wearisome, prolonged, long, lengthy, prosy, verbose, prosaic, long-spun, long-winded, wandering, maundering, roundabout. *Ant.* short, concise, explicit, clear, brief, terse, condensed, pointed, laconic, compact, compressed, succinct, sententious, pithy, curt, crisp, summary, axiomatic, epigrammatic, snappy (*colloq.*).

prominent—*Syn.* protuberant, extended, jutting, conspicuous, embossed, relieved, extended, remarkable, bossy, notable, protruding, projecting, bossed, hummocky, hilly, important, eminent, well-known, popular, famous, striking, celebrated, leading, renowned, distinguished, preëminent. *Ant.* depressed, sunken, flat, level, concave, hollow, cup-shaped, dish-shaped, calathiform, pitted, alveolate, vuggy, discoid, homaloid, obscure, unknown, humble, retiring, backward, common, ordinary, mean, low, scrubby, rude, raffish, unpopular, vulgar, dissolute, contemptible, worthless.

promiscuous—*Syn.* confused, mixed, indiscriminate, confounded, undistinguished, mingled, commingled, irregular, composite, heterogeneous, miscellaneous, hybrid. *Ant.* select, unmixed, unblended, unadulterated, simple, homogeneous, regular, orderly, unconfused, arranged, uniform, discriminate, distinctive.

promise, *v.*—*Syn.* pledge, vow, engage, undertake, swear, guarantee, warrant, contract.

promote—*Syn.* advance, encourage, organize, equip, endow, further, forward, prefer, push, aid, assist, urge, urge on, foster, help, encourage, excite, foment, raise, elevate, exalt, build up, contribute. *Ant.* lower, reduce, sink, debase, humiliate, degrade, cast down, humble, dishonor, discredit, disgrace, impair, wreck, deteriorate, pervert, injure, demoralize, damage, harm, hurt, cripple, ravage, ruin, destroy.

prompt, *adj.*—*Syn.* quick, keen, swift, ready, early, alert, immediate, apt, instant, vigilant. *Ant.* remiss, lax, slow, negligent.

promulgate—*Syn.* publish, declare, proclaim, announce, spread, advertise, herald, blazon, circulate, disseminate, foretell, make known, broadcast. *Ant.* hide, conceal, keep secret, suppress, smother, keep back, withhold, cloak, disguise, veil, cover, dissemble, shut up (*slang*), silence, still, refrain, restrain.

propagate—*Syn.* beget, breed, engender, create, procreate, originate, generate, increase, spread, disseminate, diffuse, continue, multiply, produce, reproduce, develop, inculcate, impregnate, imbue, teach, implant, graft. *Ant.* destroy, kill, suppress, crush, exterminate, waste, extirpate, slaughter, slay, sacrifice, ruin, annihilate, devastate, stamp out, devour, sweep away, tram-

ple under foot, eradicate, ravage.

propel, *v.*—*Syn.* thrust, impel, force, urge, push, drive.

proper—*Syn.* just, right, fair, square, fair and square, decent, suitable, meet, fit, becoming, adapted, appropriate, pertinent, equitable, legitimate, expedient, reasonable, fitting, correct, seemly. *Ant.* improper, incongruous, inexpedient, wrong, unfit, inapplicable, inappropriate, unsuited, incorrect, inaccurate, unreasonable, objectionable, unsuitable, inopportune, unseemly, inadmissible, ineligible, inept, useless, worthless.

property, *n.*—*Syn.* possessions, estate, assets, resources, chattels, wealth, goods, appurtenances, belongings.

propitiate—*Syn.* conciliate, appease, atone, calm, assuage, soothe, mollify, satisfy, gratify, pacify, placate, tranquillize, compose, moderate, reconcile, allay, soften, mitigate, sympathize, expiate, make good, make amends, please, delight, fascinate, captivate. *Ant.* excite, annoy, anger, aggravate, taunt, mock, scoff, ridicule, laugh at, scorn, enrage, infuriate, irritate, provoke, nettle, agitate, ruffle, offend, shock, disgust, nauseate, displease, harass, badger, thwart, cross, pain, torment, torture, vex, plague, mortify, worry, bother, pester, distress.

propitiation—*Syn.* conciliation, reconciliation, expiation, atonement, reparation, indemnification, redress, amends, apology, penance, fasting, mortification, sacrifice, satisfaction, repentance, scourging, sackcloth and ashes, self-denial. *Ant.* impenitence, sinfulness, guilt, transgression, delinquency, guiltiness, wickedness, obduracy, stoniness, hardness of heart, depravity, scorn, mockery, ridicule.

propitious—*Syn.* favorable, pleasing, satisfactory, gracious, kind, kindly, friendly, benignant, benign, helpful, auspicious, merciful, clement, timely, beneficial, helping, prosperous, encouraging, hopeful, reassuring, heartening, uplifting, promising, cheering, inspiriting, bright, roseate, rose-colored, providential, lucky, fortunate, opportune. *Ant.* unfavorable, harmful, hurtful, unkind, hopeless, disastrous, unfortunate, unlucky, disconcerting, intimidating, alarming, discouraging, saddening, disquieting, unfriendly, aggravating, ill-omened, obstructive, malignant, evil, unsatisfactory, disadvantageous, pernicious, malefic, mischievous, inauspicious, direful, ill-fated, unpropitious, inexpedient, ill-timed, inopportune, untimely, ill-starred, antagonistic, adverse, hostile, repellent.

proportional, *adj.—Syn.* proportionate, commensurate, relative, corresponding, dependent.

proposal—*Syn.* scheme, design, offer, suggestion, plan, proposition, overture, project, program, outline, prospectus, measure, request, application, bid, appeal. *Ant.* protest, expostulation, deprecation, refusal, remonstrance, denunciation, disapprobation, renunciation, dissent, denial, negation, noncompliance, disapproval, rejection, repulse.

propose—*Syn.* purpose, plan, project, design, suggest, offer, put forward, move, state, proffer, advance, propound, contend, enunciate, assert, state. *Ant.* discount, belittle, denounce, renounce, deprecate, dispute, impugn, deny, repudiate, objure, contradict, protest.

propriety—*Syn.* decency, righteousness, modesty, becomingness, fitness, congruity, appropriateness, good manners, good behavior, seemliness, circumspection, correctness, justice, equity, fair play, duty, obligation, morality, decorum, gentlemanly, conduct, conventionality, good breeding, taste in dress, mould of form, grace, graceful-

ness, unison, harmony, concord, agreement. *Ant.* impropriety, misconduct, misbehavior, rudeness, vulgarity, unseemliness, boldness, wrong, injustice, foul play, double-dealing, trickery, cheating, partiality, illegality, unlawfulness, lawlessness, dereliction of duty, idleness, indolence, laziness, neglect, transgression, violation, moral turpitude, sin, sinfulness, immorality, bad manners, bad behavior, bad breeding, viciousness, sloth, slovenliness, awkwardness, filthiness, unfitness, disagreement, discord, incongruity, disparity.

proscribe—*Syn.* banish, outlaw, exile, prohibit, forbid, interdict, ostracize, boycott, shun, bar, debar, reject, repudiate, blackball, exclude, enjoin, restrict, disallow, circumscribe, inhibit, denounce, execrate. *Ant.* invite, induce, solicit, entreat, beseech, implore, appeal to, entertain, welcome, greet, receive hospitably, praise, laud, applaud, exalt, honor, respect, esteem, approve, admire, commend, recommend, support.

prospect, *n.—Syn.* outlook, probability, expectation, expectancy, presumption, likelihood, view.

prosperity—*Syn.* success, welfare, well-being, weal, good luck, good fortune, happiness, affluence, attainment, achievement, consummation, riches, fulfilment, victory, conquest, triumph, opulence, independence, money, property, possessions. *Ant.* adversity, failure, misfortune, misery, bad luck, calamity, misadventure, loss, ruin, ruination, sorrow, affliction, infliction, trouble, poverty, penury, pauperism, destitution, straits, privation, distress, neediness, necessity, difficulties.

prostrate, *adj.—Syn.* flat, powerless, recumbent, down, abject, humbled, fallen. *Ant.* upright, erect, proud, exalted.

protract—*Syn.* postpone, defer, procrastinate, prolong, lengthen, elongate, extend, draw out, continue, delay, put off, stretch, spin out. *Ant.* shorten, abbreviate, abridge, curtail, contract, limit, reduce, conclude, hurry, hasten, epitomize, lessen, condense, shrink.

proud, *adj.—Syn.* imperious, arrogant, dignified, lordly, lofty, majestic, haughty, exalted. *Ant.* humble, meek, lowly, modest.

prove, *v.—Syn.* show, test, verify, corroborate, demonstrate, sustain, examine, confirm, check, justify, establish, substantiate.

proverb—*Syn.* maxim, adage, aphorism, precept, saw, saying, motto, dictum, axiom, truism, apothegm, byword, epigram, *mot* [*Fr.*], moral. *Ant.* absurdity, nonsense, silliness, farrago, gibberish, balderdash, tomfoolery, mummery, bathos, inanity, flapdoodle (*colloq.*), piffle (*slang* or *dial.*), twaddle, jabber, hocus-pocus, rigmarole, fudge, poppycock (*colloq.*), bosh (*colloq.*).

proverbial—*Syn.* current, general, unquestioned, unquestionable, undoubted, notorious, acknowledged, familiar, noted, well-known, recognized, established, traditional, common, passable, circulating, oft-repeated. *Ant.* unknown, strange, unheard of, misleading, deceiving, deceptive, erroneous, false, untrue, fallacious, wrong, absurd, indefinite, uncertain, vague, indeterminate.

provident, *adj.—Syn.* prudent, economical, thoughtful, careful, frugal, foresighted, discreet, thrifty, cautious. *Ant.* extravagant, prodigal, wasteful, profuse.

province, *n.—Syn.* domain, office, department, field, métier, sphere, territory, bailiwick.

provoke—*Syn.* rouse, arouse, excite, stir, move, incite, exasperate, inflame, enrage, anger, taunt, tempt, mock, irritate, chafe, pique, incense, infuriate, aggravate, exacerbate, madden, agitate, perturb, sting, lash to fury. *Ant.* mollify, placate, please, pacify, flatter, soothe, calm, comfort, cheer, appease,

propitiate, restrain, moderate, tranquillize, quell, lull, allay, assuage, conciliate, please, soften, abate, mitigate, ameliorate, alleviate.

prowess—*Syn.* bravery, valor, intrepidity, gallantry, heroism, courage, boldness, chivalry, manliness, backbone (*colloq.*), grit (*colloq.*), hardihood, spunk (*colloq.*), nerve (*colloq.*), pluck. *Ant.* fear, vacillation, wavering, uncertainty, trepidation, pusillanimity, cowardliness, cowardice, poltroonery, funk (*colloq.*), weakness, cold feet (*slang*), yellow streak (*slang*), timidity, effeminacy, dastardliness, slinking, sneaking, skulking.

proximity, *n.—Syn.* nearness, propinquity, contiguity, vicinity, neighborhood.

prudence—*Syn.* discretion, caution, circumspection, judgment, providence, considerateness, judiciousness, forecast, deliberation, wisdom, foresight, forethought, care, c a r e f u l n e s s, frugality, watchfulness, precaution, heedfulness, c o n c e r n, gumption (*colloq.*), penetration, perspicacity, discernment, subtlety, discrimination, cunning, vigilance, coolness, calculation, presence of mind. *Ant.* negligence, carelessness, imprudence, rashness, improvidence, procrastination, deferment, supineness, inactivity, folly, silliness, shallowness, remissness, stupidity, stolidity, incompetence, ineptitude, shortsightedness, inconsistency, irrationality, indiscretion, foolhardiness, thoughtlessness, heedlessness, impetuosity, precipitancy, recklessness, prodigality, wastefulness.

prudent—*Syn.* wise, careful, discreet, cautious, thoughtful, provident, economical, frugal, judicious, considerate, circumspect, sagacious, heedful, particular, alert, wide-awake, surefooted, discriminate, discriminating, canny [*Sc.*], discerning, cool, far-sighted, sensible, levelheaded, penetrating, wary, guarded, suspicious, leery (*slang*), deliberate, self-possessed. *Ant.* rash, impetuous, foolish, silly, thoughtless, heedless, careless, imprudent, Quixotic, precipitate, foolhardy, hot-headed, shallow, stupid, doltish, simple, shiftless, negligent, supine, inactive, incautious, reckless, inconsiderate, unconcerned, unmindful, hasty, headstrong, indiscreet, adventurous, injudicious, unwise, improvident, wasteful, prodigal, extravagant, lavish, spendthrift.

prurient—*Syn.* itching, longing, hankering, craving, desiring, desirous, fain, wishful, wistful, solicitous, sedulous, eager, avid, ardent, fervent, impure, lecherous, lewd, wanton, dissolute, debauched, depraved, salacious, lickerish, rampant, lustful, concupiscent, erotic, pornographic, indecent, unclean, bestial, incestuous, libidinous, immoral, rakish, carnal, dissipated, indecorous, smutty, voluptuous, foul, licentious, lascivious, coarse, gross, beastly, adulterous. *Ant.* cold, frigid, lukewarm, indifferent, neutral, easygoing, phlegmatic, supine, listless, halfhearted, lacking desire, impotent, anaphrodisiac, unfeeling, modest, chaste, pure, continent, undesirous, decent, decorous, virtuous, moral, spiritual, undefiled, uncontaminated, clean, self-denying, guileless, innocent, exemplary, well-behaved, model, immaculate, unspotted, pious, religious, God-fearing.

pseudonym, *n.*—*Syn.* alias, pen name, nom de plume, nom de guerre.

psychiatrist, *n.*—*Syn.* psychoanalyst, alienist, psychopathologist, psychologist, psychotherapist, head-shrinker.

publish, *v.*—*Syn.* communicate, disseminate, issue, utter, impart, emit, promulgate, circulate, proclaim, divulge, announce.

puerile—*Syn.* boyish, inexperienced, immature, foolish, feeble, trifling, weak, puny, youthful, childish, silly, fatuous, impo-

tent, simple, frivolous, giddy, inept, shallow, unphilosophical, rattle-brained, hare-brained, light-headed, asinine, nutty (*slang*), talkative, long-winded, rambling, wandering, slight, piffling, fribbling, frothy, paltry, trashy, finicky. *Ant.* experienced, wise, sensible, old-fashioned, veteran, patriarchal, aged, wide-awake, brainy, sharp, sage, sapient, rational, judicious, strong-minded, sagacious, clear-headed, farsighted, philosophical, shrewd, cunning, discerning, perspicacious, canny [*Sc.*], shrewd, forcible, impressive, great, important, grave, serious.

pugnacious, *adj.*—*Syn.* belligerent, bellicose, aggressive, contentious, warlike, combative, quarrelsome, militant. *Ant.* peaceful, pacific, placid, peaceable.

pulchritude, *n.*—*Syn.* beauty, loveliness, attractiveness, grace, comeliness. *Ant.* ugliness, repulsiveness, loathsomeness.

pull, *v.*—*Syn.* draw, drag, tug, pluck, tow, pick, haul.

pulse, *n.*—*Syn.* throb, vibration, beat, palpitation, oscillation.

punch, *v.*—*Syn.* hit, cuff, smite, pound, swat, poke, slug, clout, strike, pummel.

punctilious—*Syn.* formal, particular, exact, finicky, precise, scrupulous, definite, careful, cautious, observant, constant, dutiful, loyal, faithful, strict. *Ant.* careless, negligent, neglectful, heedless, uncaring, inattentive, omissive, omitting, unmindful, regardless, unobservant, absent-minded, woolgathering (*colloq.*).

punctual—*Syn.* prompt, precise, particular, exact, timely, seasonable, expeditious, periodic, regular, cyclic, recurrent, constant, steady, definite, scrupulous, punctilious, meticulous, faithful, honorable, loyal, true. *Ant.* unpunctual, careless, unreliable, desultory, rambling, uncertain, irregular, unsettled, wavering, flighty, jumpy, fickle, inconstant, changeable, variable, fluctuating, vacillating, unstable, unsteady.

pungent—*Syn.* sharp, acid, tart, biting, stinging, penetrating, severe, acute, painful, poignant, burning, throbbing, gnawing, twinging, twitching, mordant, piquant, high-flavored, caustic, strong. *Ant.* sweet, mild, pleasant, soothing, saccharine, pleasing, agreeable, alkaline, wishy-washy (*colloq.*), insipid, tasteless, vapid, cloying, sloppy, watery, weak, sugary, syrupy, flat, stale, flavorless, unseasoned, honey-sweet, melliferous, nectareous, candied, sweetened.

punish—*Syn.* chastise, correct, lash, discipline, beat, whip, scourge, kick, cuff (*colloq.*), pummel, trounce (*colloq.*), flog, castigate, inflict, afflict, chasten, correct, strike, smash, horse-whip, thump, thwack, buffet, spank, drub, thresh, leather (*colloq.*), wallop (*colloq.*), strap, lick (*colloq.*), larrup (*colloq.*), dress down (*colloq.*), lambaste (*slang*), ribroast (*slang*), pickle (*slang*), dust one's jacket (*slang*), pelt, stone, sandbag, bastinado, take for a ride (*slang*), welt, cowhide, baste, lace (*colloq.*), belabor, cudgel, warm (*colloq.*), warm one's jacket (*slang*), tar and feather, keelhaul, blackjack, warm one's hide (*slang*), hamstring, crack his bean (*slang*), smash his coco (*slang*), lay him out (*slang*), cook his goose (*slang*), put him on the spot (*slang*). *Ant.* clear, free, acquit, exculpate, exonerate, whitewash (*colloq.*), defend, praise, cheer, laud, applaud, commend, recommend, pardon, release, reward, recompense, indemnify, compensate, redress, comfort, cherish, befriend, aid, help, assist, support, sustain, uphold, serve, oblige, accommodate, humor, encourage, favor, indorse, succor, relieve, rescue, patronize, inspirit, animate, incite, urge, impel, stimulate, instigate, promote, advance, forward, inspire, foster, indulge, nurture,

nourish, benefit, advance, care for, guard, protect.

puny, *adj.*—*Syn.* feeble, small, trivial, diminutive, stunted, petty, frail, tiny, weak, little, slight, inferior. *Ant.* robust, sturdy, strong, mighty.

purchase—*Syn.* obtain, acquire, get, procure, secure, buy, barter for, bargain for, gain, win, earn, gather, collect, pick up, glean. *Ant.* lose, miss, mislay, sell, squander, scatter, spend, waste, exchange, dispose of, barter, swap (*colloq.*), take, deprive, bereave, pilfer, steal.

pure—*Syn.* chaste, immaculate, spotless, stainless, unspotted, unstained, undefiled, innocent, virtuous, guiltless, guileless, unblemished, untainted, unsullied, untarnished, unpolluted, continent, clean, incorrupt, holy, heavenly, divine, Godlike, upright, virgin, angelic, unadulterated, unmixed, unmingled, simple, perfect, clear, genuine, classic, sheer, real, true. *Ant.* impure, lewd, lascivious, defiled, libidinous, gross, coarse, unclean, dirty, filthy, foul, immodest, indecent, unchaste, unclean, obscene, polluted, corrupt, rotten, putrid, tainted, spotted, mixed, mingled, adulterated, sullied, tarnished, ribald, immodest, indelicate, vulgar, lustful, licentious, pornerastic, pornographic, dissolute, profligate, vile, abandoned.

purify—*Syn.* cleanse, chasten, clear, refine, wash, disinfect, fumigate, deodorize, depurate, clarify, deterge, edulcorate, purge, filter, revise, correct, improve. *Ant.* soil, tarnish, stain, smirch, corrupt, besmear, pollute, defile, debase, contaminate, begrime, blot, blur, putrefy, taint, sully, debauch, vitiate, befoul, render unclean.

purpose—*Syn.* design, intention, goal, finality, end, consummation, meaning, object, objective, view, aim, scope, resolve, wish, desire, mind, inclination, determination, ambition, lookout, expectation, realization. *Ant.* chance, indefiniteness, speculation, gamble, risk, uncertainty, doubt, wavering, vacillation, fortuity, accident, hazard, random, casualty, fortune, unreasonableness, negligence, carelessness.

pursue, *v.*—*Syn.* follow, persist, track, chase, hound, hunt, trail.

push—*Syn.* impel, propel, shove, press, urge, accelerate, thrust, drive, expedite, butt, force, advance, go ahead, proceed, progress. *Ant.* idle, lag, dawdle, recede, regrade, retrograde, back out (*colloq.*), fall down (*colloq.*), retreat, withdraw, stand still, halt, falter.

pusillanimity—*Syn.* weakness, timidity, effeminacy, cowardice, cowardliness, apprehension, fear, cravenness, weakmindedness, baseness, dastardy, dastardliness, funk (*colloq.*), cold feet (*slang*), yellow streak (slang), poltroonery, dunghill bravery (*slang*), Dutch courage (*colloq.*), white-liveredness (*colloq.*), vacillation, faint-heartedness, meanspiritedness. *Ant.* boldness, bravery, determination, resolution, confidence, self-reliance, manliness, mettle, grit, spunk, nerve, pluck, firmness, hardihood, fortitude, intrepidity, gallantry, chivalry, derring-do, courage, backbone (*slang*), guts (*vulgar slang*), manhood, valor, daring, audacity, fearlessness, stout-heartedness, dauntlessness, bulldog courage, tenaciousness, tenacity.

pusillanimous, *adj.*—*Syn.* timorous, spiritless, timid, craven, cowardly, weak, contemptible, feeble, sorry, fearful. *Ant.* courageous, brave, stouthearted.

put—*Syn.* place, lay, set, deposit, seat, settle, station, lodge, quarter, install, establish, fix, lay down, plant, insert, imbed, invest in. *Ant.* move, remove, displace, misplace, shift, take up, tear up, scatter, dislodge, drive out, transfer, take away, disestablish, abstract, oust, trans-

port, carry off.

putrefy—*Syn.* rot, decay, decompose, corrupt, putresce, taint, defile, pollute, contaminate, beslime. *Ant.* cleanse, purify, renew, restore, freshen, invigorate, strengthen, heal, refresh, revive.

putrid—*Syn.* corrupt, rotten, decayed, polluted, putrescent, contaminated, rancid, mucid, fecal, feculent, disgusting, saprogenic, purulent, loathsome, pustular, impetiginous, stercoraceous, excrementitious, mephitic, bad-smelling, ulcerous. *Ant.* clean, pure, whole, wholesome, sound, uncontaminated, fresh, undecayed, blooming, hardy, healthy, health-giving, restorative, sanitary, sanatory, incorrupt, healing, stimulating, invigorating, pleasing, odoriferous, fragrant, sweet-scented.

puzzle, *n.*—*Syn.* perplexity, difficulty, mystery, confusion, embarrassment, doubt, uncertainty, bewilderment, mystification, conundrum, enigma, vagueness, ambiguity, obscurity, labyrinth, intricacy, complication, complexity, muddle, quandary, incertitude, riddle, maze. *Ant.* certainty, plainness, clearness, perspicuity, certitude, sureness, lucidity, explicitness, fact, truth, simplicity, understanding, comprehension, distinctness, discernment, conception, perception, penetration, comprehensibility, intelligibility, clarity, positiveness, definitiveness, actuality, reality.

puzzle, *v.*—*Syn.* perplex, confuse, confound, mystify, bewilder, embarrass, nonplus, complicate, involve, muddle, rattle (*colloq.*), derange, jumble, disorder, disconcert, abash, baffle, discompose, mix, mingle, intermingle, distract, entangle. *Ant.* clarify, illustrate, explain, assure, certify, demonstrate, evince, manifest, prove, confirm, elucidate, exemplify, reveal, show, exhibit, display, interpret, expound, unravel, unfold, solve.

puzzling—*Syn.* obscure, ambiguous, uncertain, perplexing, extraordinary, mystifying, confused, mixed, complicated, complex, involved, jumbled, intricate, vague, indefinite, enigmatical, transcendental, cryptic, mystical, hidden, concealed, occult, latent, mysterious, secret, equivocal, doubtful, hazy. *Ant.* clear, lucid, plain, evident, factual, explicit, precise, intelligible, comprehensible, perspicuous, positive, unequivocal, definite, obvious, undisguised, unreserved, open, manifest, apparent, discernible, accurate, correct, certain, sure, assured, undoubted, indubitable, indisputable, true, real.

Q

quack—*Syn.* impostor, charlatan, mountebank, Cagliostro, humbug, sophist, pretender, empiric, boaster, deceiver, dissembler, faker, fourflusher (*slang*), swindler, knave, cheat, rogue, capper (*U. S. slang*), spieler (*Aus. slang*), shuffler, bunko steerer (*U.S. slang*), carpetbagger (*slang*), stool pigeon (*slang*), confidence man. *Ant.* sucker (*slang*), simpleton, fool, greenhorn, ignoramus, dupe, victim, boob (*slang*), booby (*slang*), lubber, lout, know-nothing, ass (*colloq.*), jackass (*colloq.*), block, blockhead, dolt, jay, hayseed (*slang*), bumpkin, rustic, clown, cat's-paw, come-on (*slang*), easy-mark (*colloq.*), gudgeon (*slang*), flat (*slang*), laughingstock.

quail, *v.*—*Syn.* cower, flinch, shrink, wince, recoil, hesitate, blench, quake, falter.

quaint—*Syn.* odd, queer, curious, old, old-fashioned, freakish, informal, singular, far-fetched, fanciful, ancient, peculiar, bizarre, antique, whimsical, affected, unconventional, anomalous, grotesque, eccentric, baroque, rum (*slang*), rummy (*slang*), rococo. *Ant.* up-to-date, ordinary, common, commonplace, normal, conformable, consistent, regular, natural, habitual, usual, formal, artistic, attractive, becoming, modern, fashionable, conventional, decorous, fitting, appropriate, customary, prevailing.

quake, *v.*—*Syn.* tremble, shiver, shudder, quiver, vibrate, quail, waver.

qualification, *n.*—*Syn.* modification, restriction, proviso, reservation, limitation, consideration, exception, condition, allowance; mitigation, diminution.

qualified—*Syn.* capable, equal to, able, effectual, adequate, competent, efficacious, efficient, proficient, skilful, clever, expert, adept, talented, accomplished, experienced, fitted, equipped. *Ant.* inept, incapable, incompetent, stupid, unfit, ineffectual, inefficient, deficient, unsuitable, unable, disqualified, impotent, disabled, helpless, decrepit, inefficacious, ignorant, powerless, crippled.

quality—*Syn.* nature, character, peculiarity, characteristic, attribute, essence, soul, heart, backbone, state, condition, endowment, qualification, property, faculty, capability, tendency, proneness, proclivity, propensity, inclination, susceptibility, idiosyncrasy, temperament, tone, disposition, personality.

qualm, *n.*—*Syn.* compunction, scruple, misgiving, twinge, pang, apprehension, uncertainty.

quandary, *n.*—*Syn.* dilemma, perplexity, predicament, plight, puzzle, pickle, pass, doubt, uncertainty.

quantity, *n.*—*Syn.* amount, mass, lot, volume, aggregate, total, measure, batch, bulk.

quarrel—*Syn.* wrangle, dispute, contention, feud, strife, altercation, brawl, bickering, argument, fuss, disagreement, dissension, dissidence, clash, contradiction, rupture, disruption, split, squabble, row, tiff, barney (*slang*), embroilment, fracas, riot, disturbance, rumpus (*col-*

loq.), hubbub, bear garden, commotion, Kilkenny cats, Donnybrook Fair. *Ant.* peace, quiet, quietness, quietude, rest, repose, tranquillity, agreement, agreeableness, concord, concordance, harmony, accord, unanimity, friendliness, consonance, congeniality, mutual understanding, *entente cordiale* [*Fr.*], unity, alliance, conciliation, friendship, sympathy, coöperation.

quarrelsome—*Syn.* factious, fractious, turbulent, unruly, pugnacious, litigious, contentious, irritable, peevish, snappish, hot-tempered, fiery, excitable, irascible, choleric, petulant, brawling, bickering, churlish, bad-tempered, disputatious, thin-skinned, touchy, hasty, huffy, quick, rash, cantankerous (*colloq.*), cross-grained, waspish, peppery, passionate, hot-headed, vehement, violent, impassioned, furious, impetuous, tempestuous, uproarious, tumultuous, rampant, boisterous, clamorous. *Ant.* peaceful, quiet, inoffensive, modest, retiring, bashful, backward, agreeable, good-natured, good-tempered, friendly, fraternal, kind, kindly, pacific, sympathetic, tolerant, patient, submissive, humble, resigned, imperturbable, easy-going, placid, calm, composed, unruffled, steady, staid, philosophic, cool, collected, tranquil, dispassionate, passive, level-headed, cool-headed, cold-blooded, forbearing, unresisting, indulgent, forgiving.

quaver, *v.*—*Syn.* tremble, vibrate, shake, quake, quiver, shudder, shiver, falter, oscillate, waver.

queer—*Syn.* odd, strange, peculiar, uncommon, abnormal, extraordinary, astonishing, unique, wonderful, singular, erratic, eccentric, droll, comical, quaint, cross, whimsical, crotchety, unmatched, unusual, grotesque, preposterous, ridiculous, ludicrous, funny, fantastic, laughable, curious, bizarre, freakish, anomalous, irregular, nonde-

script, arbitrary, egregious, exceptional, oulandish, unnatural, unexampled, unfamiliar, unparalleled, unprecedented. *Ant.* common, commonplace, normal, regular, usual, ordinary, familiar, natural, customary, conventional, conformable, consistent, original, general, habitual, prevalent, wide-spread, typical, universal, worldwide, simple, plain, current, constant, steady, orderly, symmetrical, according to rule, according to Hoyle (*colloq.*), *en règle* [*Fr.*], unvarying, invariable, systematic, established, recognized, accepted, orthodox, formal.

quell—*Syn.* subdue, put down, stop, reduce, allay, quiet, check, silence, disperse, scatter, surmount, overcome, stem, conquer, vanquish, defeat, override, beat, rout, moderate, pacify, calm, tranquillize, curb, restrain, subjugate, demolish, overthrow, crush, hush, stay, still, lull. *Ant.* foment, excite, inflame, encourage, incite, urge, stimulate, promote, stir up, kindle, aggravate, exasperate, exacerbate, infuriate, madden, goad, spur, lash to fury, agitate, perturb, disturb, irritate, ruffle, rouse, arouse, add fuel to the flames, instigate, anger, incense, enrage, embitter, envenom, roil, rile, taunt, mock.

querulous—*Syn.* fretful, fretting, peevish, touchy, tetchy, complaining, repining, censorious, fidgety, faultfinding, disagreeable, irritable, murmuring, dissatisfied, resentful, irascible, petulant, contentious, disputatious, sensitive, testy, cross, choleric, perverse, obstinate, thrawn [*Sc.*], crabbed, grumbling, plaintive, querimonious, finicky, hypercritical, meticulous, exacting, squeamish, fastidious, queasy, ticklish, thin-skinned. *Ant.* cheerful, happy, joyous, merry, gay, dashing, careless, devil-may-care, laughing, smiling, carefree, jubilant, triumphant, rejoicing, elated, chuckling, indifferent, calm, insouciant, lackadaisical, unconcerned, satisfied, content, easygoing, serene, glad, unperturbed, exhilarated, light-hearted, bright, buoyant, vivacious, brisk, animated, spirited, free-and-easy, smug, canty [Sc.], sprightly, blithe.

query, v.—Syn. question, quiz, ask, interrogate, examine.

quest, n.—Syn. expedition, journey, search, seeking, pursuit, enterprise, adventure, trek.

question, n.—Syn. query, quest, inquiry, interrogatory, subject, interrogation, examination, disquisition, controversy, discussion, debate, topic, proposition, problem, inquisition, investigation, catechism, consideration, theorem, argument, dissertation, thesis, essay, analysis, scrutiny, issue, contention, search, research, exploitation. Ant. answer, response, reply, result, rejoinder, retort, contradiction, plea, acknowledgment, explanation, return, counterstatement, admission, avowal, affirmation, confirmation, acquiescence, ratification, corroboration, approval.

question, v.—Syn. ask, inquire, interrogate, examine, cross-examine, pry into, seek, search, put, propose, propound, demand, require, query, catechize, grill (colloq.), roast (colloq.), probe, investigate, scrutinize, analyze, fathom, track, hunt, pursue, sound (colloq.), dissect. Ant. answer, reply, depose, state, volunteer, inform, asseverate, swear, affirm, assent, acknowledge, aver, avow, avouch, declare, attest, testify, put forward, put forth, advance, confirm, adjure, allege, maintain, contend, pronounce, make affidavit, take oath, kiss the Book.

questionable—Syn. uncertain, dubious, doubtful, equivocal, disputable, suspicious, obscure, indecisive, controvertible, vague, unsettled, indeterminate, debatable, unconfirmed, problemati-

cal, apocryphal, hypothetical, mysterious, cryptic, oracular, occult, enigmatic, ambiguous, indefinite, contingent, provisional, paradoxical, dependent on, open to question, hard to believe, incredible, unbelievable, disreputable, notorious, opprobrious, evil, shameful, degrading, scandalous, infamous, outrageous, unmentionable, disgraceful. Ant. certain, sure, unequivocal, plain, obvious, assured, reliable, positive, indubitable, definite, determinable, proven, determinate, decisive, unmistakable, demonstrable, unquestionable, ascertainable, matter of fact, dogmatic, evident, cocksure (colloq.), undoubted, trustworthy, credible, satisfying, satisfactory, axiomatic, believable, straightforward, aboveboard, beyond doubt, self-evident, clear, convincing, logical, veracious, dependable, unimpeachable, precise, exact, authentic, genuine, legitimate, true, correct.

quibble—Syn. evade, tergiversate, prevaricate, equivocate, shuffle, dodge, sidestep (colloq.), straddle, blow hot and cold, hold with the hare and run with the hounds (colloq.), shift, intershift, cavil, dissemble, palter, practice doubledealing, play the hypocrite, beat about the bush (colloq.), speak deceitfully. Ant. speak truly, be sincere, face the issue, be honorable, tell the truth and shame the Devil (colloq.), keep faith, play the game (colloq.), stand pat (colloq.), be firm, act conscientiously, act squarely, be on the square, speak plainly, be guileless.

quick—Syn. swift, nimble, agile, active, brisk, alert, lively, sharp, ready, intelligent, prompt, expeditious, fleet, rapid, impetuous, sagacious, nimble-witted, speedy, mercurial, instantaneous, posthaste, winged, flying, quick-tempered, irascible, fiery, peppery, light-footed, nimble-footed, quick as lightning, swift as an arrow, quick as thought, express, fast. *Ant.* slow, creeping, crawling, tardy, dilatory, languid, sluggish, apathetic, phlegmatic, lymphatic, snail-like, lazy, indolent, slothful, reptatorial, reptatory, weary, drowsy, humdrum, tiresome, irksome, heavy-footed, dull, flat, leaden, stupid, doltish.

quicken—*Syn.* accelerate, expedite, stimulate, refresh, revive, speed, urge, urge on, hurry, hasten, make haste, despatch, advance, drive, drive on, facilitate, further, press on, press forward, force, excite, incite, animate, inspire, wake up, stir up, enthuse, inspirit, sharpen, whet, impel, goad, spur, egg on, hurry on, whip, lash, prick, propel, infuse life into, give new life to. *Ant.* hinder, impede, obstruct, retard, drag, delay, clog, check, embarrass, counteract, cumber, encumber, handicap, cramp, hamper, thwart, frustrate, baffle, circumvent, cripple, dishearten, balk, foil, prevent, restrain, constrain, repress, suppress, inhibit, override, overcome, oppose, curb, intercept, preclude, block, discourage.

quiescent, *adj.*—*Syn.* still, resting, placid, undisturbed, unagitated, tranquil, serene, motionless, unruffled, quiet, calm, silent, inactive, latent, dormant. *Ant.* active, dynamic, stirring.

quiet—*Syn.* peaceful, calm, tranquil, still, unruffled, smooth, pacific, placid, pleased, contented, meek, satisfied, gentle, moderate, cool, untroubled, peaceable, halcyon, reposeful, silent, quiescent, motionless, stationary, hushed, soundless, muffled, mute, noiseless, solemn. *Ant.* noisy, sonorous, high-sounding, loud, clangorous, tinkling, blatant, thunderous, thundering, shrieking, screaming, deafening, ear-splitting, shrill, piercing, uproarious, trumpet-tongued, trumpet-toned, explosive, detonating, ringing, jingling, reverberating.

quintessential, *adj.*—*Syn.* purest, basic, essential, radical, fundamental.

quip, *n.*—*Syn.* sally, retort, jest, witticism, sarcasm.

quit—*Syn.* abandon, leave, forsake, relinquish, cease, stop, depart, go away, vacate, evacuate, withdraw, remove, vamoose or vamose (*slang*), skip (*slang*), cut (*slang*), decamp, cut and run (*colloq.*), abscond, flee the coop (*slang*), take French leave (*slang*), cut stick (*slang*), desert, give in the gun (*slang*), shut up shop (*slang*), yield, surrender, resign. *Ant.* remain, stand still, retain, hold, keep, occupy, appropriate, monopolize, corner, possess, cling to, engross, forestall, safeguard, defend, protect, guard, watch, preserve, secure, hold the fort (*colloq.*), don't give up the ship (*colloq.*), be firm, stand fast, stand pat (*colloq.*), make good, settle down, make sure, keep the old flag flying (*colloq.*).

quiver, *v.*—*Syn.* shiver, shudder, shake, vibrate, tremble, oscillate, quake, flutter, quaver.

quixotic, *adj.*—*Syn.* chimerical, visionary, imaginary, fantastic, fanciful, mad.

quiz, *n.*—*Syn.* test, examination, interrogation, questioning, puzzle, riddle, questionnaire.

quota, *n.*—*Syn.* ration, proportion, portion, allotment.

quotation, *n.*—*Syn.* extract, excerpt, selection, citation, quote, passage, reference.

quote—*Syn.* cite, adduce, repeat, note, exemplify, illustrate, recite, paraphrase, plagiarize, excerpt, extract, elucidate, explain, instance, refer to, appeal to, evidence, bring forward, allege, verify, attest, bear witness, ratify, confirm, corroborate, endorse, establish, authenticate, circumstantiate, detail, substantiate.

R

rabble, *n.—Syn.* mob, canaille, scum, rout, riffraff, trash, herd, crowd.

rabid—*Syn.* insane, mad, frantic, furious, infuriated, berserk, amuck or amok, raging, fanatical, deranged, crazy, lunatic, unhinged, cracked (*colloq.*), maniacal, frenzied, scatterbrained, daft, daffy, (*slang*), nutty (*slang*), crackbrained (*colloq.*), corybantic, distracted, distraught, frenetic, moonstruck, screwy (*slang*), having a screw loose (*slang*), wandering, imbecile, idiotic, touched. *Ant.* sane, normal, lucid, right-minded, sound-minded, common-sense, rational, reasonable, normal, self-possessed, sober-minded, capable, regular, ordinary, steady, consistent, sound, wise, intelligent, brainy (*colloq.*), clever, discerning, sagacious, perspicacious, nimble-witted, sapient, sharp, clear-headed.

race—*Syn.* breed, family, nation, stock, tribe, people, order, class, division, genus, species, variety, caste, sept, kind, type, coterie, clique, phylum, assortment, set, house, ancestry, lineage, pedigree, paternity, parentage, tribe.

rack—*Syn.* torture, torment, harass, punish, excruciate, annoy, pain, distress, irritate, afflict, rend, oppress, strain, stretch, lacerate, wring, crucify, agonize. *Ant.* cheer, encourage, sustain, support, enliven, animate, inspirit, embolden, stimulate, soothe, assuage, compose, calm, comfort, alleviate, entertain, refresh, regale.

racket—*Syn.* noise, clamor, commotion, confusion, uproar, clatter, din, brawl, shindy (*colloq.*), squabble, scuffle, wrangle, agitation, stir, turmoil, turbulence, tumult, hubbub, fuss, perturbation, disturbance, quarrel, strife, hurly-burly, hullabaloo, bobbery, outcry, clangor, scuffle, fracas, row, scrimmage, riot, caterwauling, charivari, shivaree (*slang*), jar, jarring, clash, clashing, discord, disagreement, imbroglio, dispute, rumpus, wrangle, loggerheads, squall, breeze (*colloq.*), fight, fisticuffs, bear garden, Donnybrook Fair, corroboree [*Aus.*], intrigue, conspiracy, plot, faction, cabal, unlawful combination, gangsterism, underworld activity, rowdyism, rascality, blackguardism, lawlessness. *Ant.* peace, quietude, good behavior, lawfulness, concord, harmony, unison, love, agreement, sympathy, understanding, union, unanimity, calm, calmness, concordance, fraternalism, conciliation, tranquillity, composure, tolerance, imperturbability, coolness, patience, equanimity, poise, self-control, self-possession, self-restraint, endurance, benignity, meekness, resignation, submission, repression, moderation, forbearance, good conduct, good behavior, quiescence, reconciliation, pacification, pacifism, truce, let-up (*colloq.*), law observance.

racy—*Syn.* pungent, piquant, spicy, sharp, flavorous, smart, clever, keen, bright, ready-witted, lively, interesting, entertaining, rich, saucy, spirited, forcible, animated, soulful, savory, tasty, gustful, appetizing, palatable, poignant, caustic, incisive, trenchant. *Ant.* dull, insipid, tasteless, watery, vapid, unsavory, flavorless, unpalatable, flat, nauseating, disgusting, sour, acrid, acid, bitter, ill-flavored, repulsive, nasty, offensive, nauseous, heavy, coarse, phlegmatic, dull-witted, stupid, thick (*slang*), morose, doltish, languid, languorous.

radiance—*Syn.* brightness, brilliance, brilliancy, splendor, resplendence, glow, sheen, shine, shimmer, luster, effulgence, refulgence, burnish, glare. *Ant.* dullness or dulness, darkness, shade, shadow, shading, dimness, obscurity, obscuration, adumbration, cloud, cloudiness, murk, murkiness, glimmer, umbra, penumbra.

radical, *adj.*—*Syn.* basic, innate, ingrained, organic, native, fundamental, essential, natural, original, positive, complete, entire, perfect, primitive, thorough, thoroughgoing, extreme, constitutional, total, intrinsic, inherent, implanted, inborn, inbred, genetic, immanent, indigenous, incarnate, inherited, congenital, internal, instinctive, indwelling. *Ant.* incomplete, partial, slight, tentative, superficial, moderate, weak, conservative, inadequate, palliative, subordinate, trivial, shallow, extrinsic, extraneous, casual, subsidiary, objective, nonessential, incidental, accidental, fortuitous, deficient, imperfect, defective, short, insufficient, meager or meagre, scarce, empty, barren, jejune.

radical, *n.*—*Syn.* red, commie, pinko, fellow traveler.

radius, *n.*—*Syn.* orbit, scope, field, compass, reach, span, range, sweep.

rag, *v.*—*Syn.* rally, kid, banter, ridicule, rib, taunt, guy, needle, josh, haze, chaff.

rage, *n.*—*Syn.* anger, choler, fury, ferocity, excitement, violence, wrath, temper, tantrum, excitation, passion, bluster, ire, agitation, ferment, perturbation, tumult, frenzy, madness, raving, hysterics, paroxysm, storm, burst, uproar, explosion, flare, fuming, ebullition. *Ant.* calm, calmness, coolness, composure, forbearance, fortitude, patience, resignation, submission, sufferance, endurance, restraint, peace, tranquillity, quietness, peacefulness, serenity, repose, stillness, rest, good-will, impassiveness, quiescence, apathy, stoicism, indifference, unconcern.

rage, *v.*—*Syn.* rave, storm, fume, shout, splutter, swear, foam, flash, flare, seethe, flame, shake,

shock, disturb, excite, boil, rant, roar, explode, rampage, fulminate, run amuck. *Ant.* soothe, calm, placate, soften, allay, alleviate, assuage, appease, tranquillize, lull, pacify, hush, quell, moderate, curb, mollify, chasten, attemper, mitigate, subdue.

raid, *n.*—*Syn.* foray, assault, invasion, incursion, onset.

rail, *v.*—*Syn.* berate, vituperate, denounce, chide, revile, rebuke, upbraid, reprobate, reprove, scold.

raillery, *n.*—*Syn.* chaff, persiflage, satire, badinage, jest, banter, ribbing.

raiment, *n.*—*Syn.* dress, attire, clothes, clothing, array, garb, costume, apparel, garments.

raise—*Syn.* lift, uplift, elevate, hoist, heighten, set up, boost (*colloq.*), erect, exalt, grow, aggrandize, increase, rear, produce, call forth, aggravate, arouse, excite, cause, collect, levy, heave, construct, build, establish, acquire, procure, gather, borrow, pawn, appropriate, excite, affect, stimulate, animate, inspire, augment, intensify, magnify. *Ant.* lower, reduce, decrease, curtail, abridge, abate, lessen, diminish, depreciate, demolish, overthrow, ravage, tumble, destroy, smash, shatter, level, raze, depress, debase, upset, pull down, pacify, quell, compose, appease, assuage, repress, subdue, impair, injure, damage, lessen, calm, placate, mollify, compose, reconcile, conciliate.

ramble—*Syn.* rove, roam, wander, range, stroll, stray, prowl, saunter, patrol, traverse, gad about, trudge, p r o m e n a d e, straggle, drift, digress, rave, dote, drivel, talk foolishly, diverge, warp, wind, twist, meander. *Ant.* lead, steer, direct, guide, act sanely, talk rationally, be sober, be steady, go direct, be concise, cool down, settle down, come to the point, be brief, be clear, be explicit, be definite, speak sensibly, clarify, condense, illuminate, illustrate, instruct, enlighten.

rampant—*Syn.* violent, vehement, brusque, abrupt, impetuous, turbulent, blustering, tumultuous, boisterous, furious, infuriate, unruly, rife, prevalent, dominant, predominant, clamorous, fanatical, impulsive, impassioned, intolerant, lickerish, lustful, lewd, carnal, ruttish, nymphomaniacal, satyriac, libidinous, prurient, concupiscent, lascivious, lecherous. *Ant.* mild, meek, modest, gentle, unobtrusive, quiet, tranquil, bland, calm, cool, patient, tolerant, hesitant, imperturbable, dispassionate, impassive, submissive, forbearing, composed, level-headed, easygoing, retiring, bashful, chaste, continent, virtuous, decorous, decent, moral, undefiled, incorrupt, pure.

rancid—*Syn.* rank, tainted, fetid, stinking, fulsome, sour, foul, impure, offensive, disagreeable, putrid, decaying, rotten, malodorous, mephitic, noisome, stercoraceous, ordurous, fecal, feculent, nasty, contaminated, putrescent, saprogenic, saprogenous, noxious, reasty (*Eng. dial.*), reeky, cloacal, disgusting, slimy, musty, stale, frowsty (*Eng. colloq.*), evil-smelling. *Ant.* sweet, fresh, sound, untainted, pure, wholesome, enjoyable, innoxious, innocuous, good, pleasing, nutritious, nourishing, satisfying, healthful, odorous, luscious, savory, tasty, pungent, tempting, dainty, delectable, appetizing, gustful, sugary, nectareous, fragrant, aromatic, spicy, sweet-smelling.

rancor—*Syn.* malignity, spite, hatred, malice, enmity, ill-will, harshness, malevolence, ill-feeling, animosity, hostility, bitterness, unfriendliness, antagonism, variance, antipathy, aversion, uncharitableness, vindictiveness, hardness of heart. *Ant.* friendship, love, brotherhood, regard, respect, sympathy, fellow-feeling, fellowship, affection, confidence, neighborliness, association, fraternization, favoritism, companionship, good will, benevolence, benignity, kindness, kind-heartedness, *camaraderie* [*Fr.*], charity, charitableness, warm-heartedness, *bonhomie* [*Fr.*], unselfishness, brotherly love.

random, *adj.*—*Syn.* casual, fortuitous, vagrant, haphazard, unplanned, chance, desultory, stray, aimless. *Ant.* planned, designed, intentional.

range—see **ramble.**

rank, *n.*—*Syn.* line, range, series, row, file, division, picket, aggregate, reputation, prestige, class, order, dignity, eminence, excellence, station, position, grade, degree, distinction, nobility, royalty, consideration, glory, standing, precedence, caste, condition, descent, birthright, Upper Tendom. *Ant.* disrepute, debasement, abjectness, humbleness, humiliation, shame, reproach, stigma, blot, obscurity, commonalty, proletariat, common herd, *sans culottes* [*Fr.*], great unwashed, *hoi polloi* [*Gr.*], *canaille* [*Fr.*], rabble, riffraff, ragtag, tagrag (*Eng. dial.*), Lower Fivedom.

rank, *adj.*—*Syn.* musty, fusty, frowsty (*Eng. dial.*), smelling, stinking, rancid, foul, fetid, noisome, reasty, offensive, luxuriant, dense, lush, wild, jungly. *Ant.* fresh, green, new, verdurous, satisfying, satisfactory, pleasing, wholesome, healthy, healthful, fragrant, sparse, thin, withered, barren, scanty.

ransack—*Syn.* pillage, plunder, ravish, rummage, overhaul, search, seek, sack, raid, rifle, loot, strip, spoil, despoil, hold up (*U.S. slang*), stick up (*U.S. slang*), bail up (*Aus. slang*), filibuster. *Ant.* restore, return, recoup, repair, compensate, reinstate, make good, atone for, give back, redress, indemnify, square (*colloq.*), make up for, make amends, reward, recompense, remunerate.

ransom—*Syn.* free, release, rescue, deliver, redeem, emancipate, manumit, unchain, unfetter, buy off, extricate, reprieve, liberate, save. *Ant.* enslave, confine, jail, lock up, incarcerate, imprison, enthrall or enthral, restrict, repress, immure, shackle, trammel, manacle, handcuff, bind, impound, jug (*slang*).

rant, *n.*—*Syn.* noise, noisy jollification, foolish talk, bombast, fustian, cant, piffle, bunk, buncombe, rot (*slang*), rotgut (*slang*), flapdoodle (*colloq.*), rigmarole, rodomontade, balderdash, jargon, rubbish, flummery (*slang*), twaddle, persiflage, moonshine, fiddle-faddle (*colloq.*), palaver, fudge, trash, poppycock (*colloq.*), bosh (*colloq.*), hocus-pocus, patter, fudge, nonsense, blah (*slang*), absurdity, fiddlesticks. *Ant.* wisdom, sapience, knowledge, genius, earnestness, intelligence, sense, common sense, meaning, significance, signification, purport, sagacity, wit, gumption, comprehension, head, brains, gray matter, acumen, acuteness, judgment.

rapacious—*Syn.* grasping, greedy, avaricious, plundering, wolfish, depredatory, pillaging, ransacking, cruel, relentless, predatory, predaceous, piratical, merciless, marauding, thievish, raptorial, ravening, ravenous, devouring, extortionate, mercenary, voracious. *Ant.* liberal, free-handed, bountiful, bounteous, munificent, princely, prodigal, profuse, extravagant, lavish, generous, improvident, full-handed, unsparing, ungrudging, free, charitable, hospitable, open-hearted, unselfish, self-denying, moderate, satisfied, lenient.

rapid—*Syn.* quick, swift, speedy, accelerated, flying, expeditious, fast, fleet, galloping, hell-for-leather (*slang*), agile, nimble, light-footed, express, mercurial,

electric, telegraphic, eagle-winged. *Ant.* slow, tardy, creeping, crawling, slack, dilatory, languid, sluggish, inactive, inert, indolent, idle, slothful, otiose, lazy, leaden, laggard, listless, torpid, sleepy, lethargic, drowsy, somniferous, soporiferous, somnolent, oscitant.

rapt—*Syn.* ravished, transported, entranced, bewitched, enchanted, charmed, ecstatic, abstracted, impressed, meditative, thoughtful, reflective, cogitative, contemplative, wistful, preoccupied, absorbed, engrossed, dreaming, dreamy, moonstruck (*colloq.*), moonraking (*dial.*), woolgathering (*Eng. dial.*), bemused, absent-minded, day-dreaming, enraptured. *Ant.* distracted, unthinking, incogitant, thoughtless, diverted, unreasoning, fatuous, inattentive, inconsiderate, unheeding, regardless, listless, flighty, giddy, giddy-headed, light-headed, scatterbrained, heedless, hen-headed (*colloq.*), harumscarum (*colloq.*), unreflecting, careless, volatile, muzzy (*colloq.*), dizzy, hare-brained.

rapture—*Syn.* ecstasy, delight, joy, bliss, transport, gladness, delectation, felicity, beatitude, happiness, glee, cheer, rejoicing, enjoyment, gratification, ravishment, enchantment, pleasure, hedonism, passion, infatuation, enthusiasm, fervor, devotion. *Ant.* sorrow, suffering, distress, privation, melancholy, hatred, disaffection, downheartedness, disillusion, growling, grumbling, worry, discontentment, ennui [*Fr.*], languor, lassitude, bitterness, enmity, acrimony, pain, annoyance, irritation, grief, affliction.

rare—*Syn.* uncommon, scarce, singular, infrequent, unique, unparalleled, unprecedented, unusual, odd, peculiar, curious, extraordinary, strange, unequaled, superlative, matchless, peerless, crackajack (*slang*), incomparable, remarkable, exceptional, choice, inimitable, unexampled, original, *sui generis* [*L.*], anomalous, exclusive, select. *Ant.* common, commonplace, ordinary, general, ubiquitous, universal, typical, normal, formal, usual, habitual, regular, numerous, profuse, many, various, manifold, frequent, constant, recurring, current, periodic, incessant, cheap, worthless, trivial, paltry, trashy, trumpery, gimcrack, tawdry, inexpensive.

rarefied, *adj.—Syn.* thin, attenuated, tenuous, refined, purified, diluted. *Ant.* dense, thick.

rascal—*Syn.* knave, trickster, sharper, cheat, rogue, villain, blackguard, traitor, betrayer, deceiver, swindler, fraud, hypocrite, Judas, impostor, liar, perjurer, delinquent, blackmailer, forger, informer, sneak, snake, snake in the grass, confidence man, bunko-steerer, counterfeiter, card-sharper, pickpocket, thief, robber, marauder, cutthroat, murderer, assassin, slayer, criminal, culprit, rowdy, ruffian, scoundrel, renegade, burglar, housebreaker, highwayman, freebooter, bandit, thug, gunman, desperado, cracksman, baby-snatcher, kidnapper, felon, caitiff, jailbird or gaol bird, reprobate, vagabond, outcast, runagate, convict, rapscallion, rascallion, cullion, cutpurse, fence, footpad, incendiary, evildoer, hell-hound, miscreant, rustler, shoplifter, tramp, loafer, scamp—black sheep, scallawag, second-story man, strong-arm man, gun-toter, ugly customer, shyster, wolf in sheep's clothing, shuffler, tough, blackleg, knight of the road—all *colloq.*—panhandler, thimble-rigger, bum, yegg, dip, shark, crook, spieler [*Aus.*], squealer, capper, stoolpigeon, rakehell, gutter-rat, guttersnipe, four-flusher — all *slang*—quack, charlatan, mountebank, humbug, pretender, adventurer, Cagliostro. *Ant.* philanthropist, benefactor, good man, virtuous man, honest man,

man of character, example, exemplar, model, guide, leader, uplifter, savior, redeemer, good Samaritan, faithful friend, comforter, consoler, protector, sympathizer, well-wisher, counselor, humanitarian, supporter, guardian, welldoer, defender, hero, helper, eudemonist, patriot, martyr, demigod, paragon, seraph, saint, pattern, noble liver, godly person, white sheep (*colloq.*), white-haired boy (*colloq.*), holy man, harmless person, fine fellow (*colloq.*)—corker, brick, white man, jim-dandy, lalapaloosa, bonzer [*Aus.*], bonzer lad [*Aus.*], glory-snatcher [*Aus.*], toff [*Aus.*], sin-shifter [*Aus.*], sky-pilot—all *slang*—priest, minister, rabbi, clergyman, divine, ecclesiastic, churchman, pastor, *curé* [*Fr.*], curate, deacon, archdeacon, bishop, archbishop, cardinal, Pope, padre, chaplain, dean, rector, preacher, *abbé* [*Fr.*], soggarth [*Ir.*], prebendary, vicar, parson.

rash—*Syn.* hasty, precipitate, foolhardy, reckless, careless, thoughtless, headstrong, impetuous, unthinking, heedless, inconsiderate, headlong, indiscreet, incautious, adventurous, imprudent, impulsive, madcap, hot-headed, hare-brained, Quixotic, devil-may-care. *Ant.* careful, cautious, prudent, slow, thoughtful, vigilant, watchful, circumspect, deliberate, guarded, discriminating, leery (*slang*), wary, chary, heedful, considerate, alert, wakeful, attentive, mindful, observant, painstaking, scrupulous, discerning, wise, cool, level-headed, calculating, sensible.

rate—*Syn.* ratio, proportion, degree, price, valuation, allowance, estimate, tax, taxation, assessment, measure, amount, figure, cost, duty, toll, levy, impost, tariff, brokerage, motion, movement, velocity, flow, stride, pace, tread. *Ant.* discount, rebate, concession, reduction, percentage, poundage, abatement, deduction, depreciation, tare and tret, rest, quiescence, repose, silence, lull, pause, calm.

ratify—*Syn.* confirm, indorse, approve, sanction, establish, substantiate, warrant, vouch for, O. K., sign, seal, certify, attest, bear witness to, support, second, corroborate, subscribe to, testify to, uphold, consent, acquiesce, accede, agree to. *Ant.* refuse, oppose, object to, renounce, denounce, counteract, contravene, contradict, deny, protest, refute, subvert, dissent, disagree, differ, revoke, disclaim, disavow, recant, abjure, forswear, abrogate, repudiate, ignore, rebut, negative, confute.

ration, *n.*—*Syn.* portion, share, quota, allotment, dole, measure, allowance, meed.

rational—*Syn.* wise, sensible, judicious, sane, reasonable, sagacious, sound, intelligent, conscious, mental, subjective, ratiocinative, logical, deductive, synthetic, analytical, subtle, perspicacious, brainy, sage, sapient, cool, discerning, impartial, calculating, thoughtful, level-headed, far-sighted, reflective, clear-headed. *Ant.* foolish, silly, absurd, ridiculous, weak, weak-minded, feeble-minded, erratic, eccentric, shallow, puerile, infantile, babyish, imbecile, fatuous, senseless, irrational, narrow-minded, unreasonable, nonsensical, blundering, crazy, incompetent, inconsistent, stupid, driveling, idiotic, fantastic, frivolous, giddy, trifling, witless, reasonless, brainless, visionary.

rattle, *v.*—*Syn.* confuse, discomfit, upset, embarrass, fluster, middle, disconcert, distract.

ravage—*Syn.* pillage, overrun, devastate, destroy, crush, desolate, despoil, overspread, damage, wreck, waste, disrupt, disorganize, demolish, annihilate, overthrow, overwhelm, break up, pull down, smash, crash, shatter, scatter, batter down,

exterminate, extinguish, prostrate, trample down, dismantle, stamp out, lay waste, lay in ruins, sweep away, raze, ruin. *Ant.* upraise, uprear, upbuild, restore, make good (*colloq.*), raise, rear, erect, build, set up, institute, organize, achieve, accomplish, construct, perform, produce, improve, mend, amend, better, reinstate, refresh, renew, rehabilitate, replace, revive, repair, reconstruct, renovate, assemble, bring together, put up, establish, constitute.

ravenous, *adj.*—*Syn.* rapacious, grasping, gluttonous, ravening, ferocious, insatiable, voracious, devouring, greedy.

ravish—*Syn.* charm, enchant, enthral or enthrall, bewitch, delight, cheer, gladden, rejoice, captivate, attract, enrapture, transport, gratify, allure, take, seize, bear away, swoop down upon, snatch, abuse, rape. *Ant.* displease, disgust, annoy, harass, worry, grieve, distress, trouble, sadden, beset, persecute, disturb, pain, bother, cross, molest, plague, mortify, torment, irritate, provoke, pique, rile, nettle, chafe, gall, aggrieve.

raw, *adj.*—*Syn.* green, unprepared, immature, callow, inexperienced, rude, unripe, rough, crude. *Ant.* mature, ripe, adult, seasoned.

raze—*Syn.* destroy, demolish, dismantle, ruin, scatter, overthrow, tumble, pull down, level, overturn, knock down, flatten, topple, breakdown, break-up, subvert, smash, crash. *Ant.* build, upbuild, raise, upraise, erect, rear, uprear, construct, contrive, restore, put together, set up, repair, put back.

reach—*Syn.* arrive, attain, enter, gain, land, descend, get to, come to, meet, overtake, join, rejoin, terminate, end, finish, alight, dismount, return, debark, disembark. *Ant.* start, go, depart, embark, begin, commence, go away, weigh anchor, set sail, set out, leave, march, take wing, break away, take leave, vamose (*slang*), cut (*slang*), cut stick (*slang*).

ready—*Syn.* prompt, prepared, suitable, proper, fit, equipped, apt, ripe, adroit, handy, willing, active, skilful, expectant, eager, enthusiastic, desirous, waiting. *Ant.* unprepared, unsuitable, improper, remiss, unfit, tardy, slow, slack, dilatory, deficient, immature, unripe, undeveloped, raw, crude, green, unseasoned, unready, disqualified.

real—*Syn.* actual, genuine, true, certain, solid, firm, substantive, positive, practical, literal, veritable, unquestionable, substantial, essential, authentic, developed, demonstrable, demonstrative, existent, existing. *Ant.* nonexistent, unreal, baseless, false, fabulous, mythological, imaginary, ideal, supposititious, fallacious, erroneous, untrue, deceptive, hypothetical, illusive, dreamy, fanciful, fancied, fantastic, visionary, mythical, shadowy, unsubstantial, illusory, theoretical, feigned, fictitious, supposed.

realize—*Syn.* achieve, effect, acquire, comprehend, gain, get, accomplish, perfect, complete, compass, consummate, execute, discharge, dispose of, fulfil, make good, conceive, believe, imagine, conjure up, fancy, apprehend, recognize, discern, perceive, experience. *Ant.* fall short, fail, slip, neglect, undo, flounder, falter, halt, hang fire, collapse, topple, tumble, blunder, botch, miscarry, lose, trip, stumble, miss, relax, leave undone, flunk (*colloq.*), fall down (*colloq.*), succumb, hit a snag (*colloq.*), bite the dust (*colloq.*), lose ground, misfire.

reap—*Syn.* gain, get, acquire, obtain, mow, cut, win, procure, gather, collect, glean, receive, recover, retrieve, raise funds, raise the wind (*slang*), realize, draw, produce, profit, salvage, earn, scrape, secure, derive, harvest. *Ant.* sow, scatter, disperse, forfeit, lose, miss, mis-

carry, break down, fail, fail to attain, fall, decline, decay, sink, lag, totter, tumble, go wrong, take wrong turn, quit, relinquish, give up, abandon, slip, let slip, waver, go to the wall (*colloq.*), go to the dogs (*colloq.*), succumb.

rear, *adj.*—*Syn.* back, posterior, after, hind, hinder, hindmost, following. *Ant.* front, forward, advance, leading.

rear, *v.*—*Syn.* raise, nurture, nurse, foster, train, erect, elevate, lift, boost.

reason, *n.*—*Syn.* motive, end, object, purpose, view, design, proof, ground, cause, aim, consideration, principle, account, argument, inducement, allurement, magnet, fascination, enticement, foundation, fountain, source, origin. *Ant.* aimlessness, folly, capriciousness, chance, venture, speculation, haphazard, gamble, risk, plunge, random, purposelessness, recklessness, heedlessness, carelessness, insouciance, negligence, apathy, imbecility, incogitance, thoughtlessness, vacuity, equivocation, evasion, shallowness, folly, silliness, space to let (*slang*), lack of intelligence.

reason, *v.*—*Syn* conclude, deduce, draw from, infer, trace, question, argue, contend, dispute, discuss, wrangle, prove, establish, debate, demonstrate, point out, discourse, converse, explain, speak logically, think logically, think, reflect, cogitate, deliberate, consider, contemplate, muse, meditate, ponder, study, investigate. *Ant.* quibble, equivocate, sidestep (*colloq.*), put off, hedge, dodge, evade, elude, shuffle, beat about the bush (*colloq.*), prevaricate, shift, split hairs (*colloq.*), misrepresent, mislead, lie, beguile, bewilder, confuse, trick, deceive, impose upon, delude, humbug, cheat, fool.

reasonable—*Syn.* fair, just, right, square (*colloq.*), honest, rational, wise, agreeable, tolerable, modest, probable, judicious, cheap, sane, sound, sensible, equitable, lenient, moderate, prudent, politic, inexpensive, low-priced, reduced, equitable, fair, square (*colloq.*), fair and square (*colloq.*), justifiable, just, lawful, legitimate. *Ant.* outlandish, excessive, immoderate, unreasonable, ridiculous, outrageous, inordinate, preposterous, extreme, excessive, prodigious, stupendous, monstrous, unconscionable, expensive, dear, high-priced, costly, exorbitant, extortionate.

rebellion—*Syn.* insurrection, revolt, revolution, debacle, overthrow, uprising, mutiny, *coup d'état* [*Fr.*], rising, upheaval, riot, outbreak, tumult, insubordination, disorder, disturbance. *Ant.* peace, peacefulness, quiet, quietness, quietude, calm, calmness, tranquillity, tolerance, patience, resignation, submission, forbearance, repression, endurance, conciliation, reconciliation, amnesty, armistice, truce, pacification.

rebellious—*Syn.* mutinous, unmanageable, recalcitrant, uncontrollable, revolutionary, pugnacious, quarrelsome, resistive, resistant, resisting, ungovernable, refractory, seditious, insubordinate, intractable, disobedient, contumacious. *Ant.* docile, dutiful, obedient, submissive, subservient, tractable, yielding, manageable, gentle, compliant, controllable, deferential, respectful, willing, agreeable, loyal, law-abiding, satisfied, contented.

rebuke, *v.*—*Syn.* reproach, criticize, chide, berate, admonish, censure, scold, reprove, upbraid, reprimand.

recalcitrant, *adj.*—*Syn.* headstrong, obstinate, refractory, intractable, rebellious, factious, willful, stubborn, disobedient, ungovernable. *Ant.* amenable, docile, biddable, obedient.

recall, *v.*—*Syn.* remember, reminisce, bethink, review, recollect, remind.

recant—*Syn.* recall, retract, abjure, deny, take back, revoke, cancel, renounce, disavow, disclaim, back down, back out, withdraw, rescind, abrogate, forswear, contradict, repudiate, abnegate, annul, nullify, void, countermand. *Ant.* acknowledge, admit, proclaim, commission, accredit, indorse, sanction, confirm, strengthen, authorize, warrant, carry on, persevere, persist, hold on, maintain, uphold, support, stick to, follow up, affirm, avouch, assert, emphasize, insist, cling to, asseverate, avow, sustain, defend.

recede—*Syn.* regrade, retrograde, retreat, retire, fall back, retrocede, withdraw, turn tail, retrace, back out, regress, shrink from, recoil, drift away, ebb, turn, return. *Ant.* press on, go forward, proceed, advance, approach, come, forge ahead, gain ground, step forth, progress, forge ahead, go full steam ahead, follow up, move on, get a gait (*slang*), pursue.

receive—*Syn.* accept, admit, take, entertain, acquire, get, gain, win, gather, collect, pick up, glean, reap, retrieve, procure, inherit, imbibe, inhale, absorb, ingest, include, incorporate, believe, credit, assent, agree, acquiesce, appropriate, derive, commandeer, seize, abstract, take possession, welcome. *Ant.* reject, refuse, renounce, exclude, expel, dislodge, discard, banish, bounce (*slang*), turn out, oust, sack (*slang*), fire (*slang*), deport, doubt, retract, disbelieve, discredit, distrust, question, challenge, dispute, deny, dissent, protest, demur, repudiate, lose, forfeit, miss, give, deliver, contribute, hand out, let go, restore, return, recoup, compensate, disgorge, pay, spend, advance, lend, disburse, expend, lavish, shell out (*slang*), fork out (*slang*), ante, ante up (*poker*), open the purse strings (*colloq.*).

recess—*Syn.* receptacle, corner, niche, cell, hole, nook, inclosure, pigeonhole, cove, crypt, cupboard, closet, cellaret, drawer, locker, fork, angle, oriel, crutch, hiding place, ambush, seclusion, vacation, intermission, interlude, interregnum, respite, congé [Fr.], cessation, pause, rest, interval. Ant. space, extension, range, expansion, room, void, waste, tract, level, plain, continuance, continuation, prolongation, persistence, pursuance, perseverance.

recidivism, n.—Syn. lapse, backsliding, deterioration, degeneration, regression, relapse, decadence. Ant. reform, reformation, progress, advance.

recite, v.—Syn. repeat, declaim, state, deliver, report, particularize, rehearse, narrate, relate, tell, recount.

reckless, adj.—Syn. rash, hasty, careless, foolhardy, wild, daring, impetuous, heedless, venturesome, precipitate, desperate. Ant. cautious, circumspect, prudent, wary.

reckon, v.—Syn. consider, deem, think, suppose, imagine, conceive, guess, value, esteem, believe, regard.

recluse, n.—Syn. hermit, ascetic, solitary, anchorite, eremite, cenobite.

recognize, v.—Syn. perceive, acknowledge, distinguish, concede, realize, accept, remember, admit, know, apprehend.

recoil, v.—Syn. rebound, reflect, react, echo, return, kick, ricochet, carom, bounce, boomerang.

recollect, v.—Syn. recall, remember, bethink, review, reminisce, reflect.

recompense, n.—Syn. compensation, reward, remuneration, indemnification, payment, reimbursement, salary, wages, requital.

recondite, adj.—Syn. esoteric, learned, profound, erudite, deep, abstruse, obscure, occult, hidden, mystic. Ant. popular, common, general, familiar.

record—Syn. career, course, treatment, walk, life, conduct, campaign, policy, management, government, stewardship, history, chronicle, schedule, experiences, performances, register, registry, docket, memorandum, scroll, archive, report, statistics, legend, inventory, memorial, entry, enrolment, catalog, inscription, document. Ant. erasure, obliteration, cancellation, extinction, oblivion, suppression, neglect, repudiation, forgetfulness, disregard, deferment, disremembrance, default, negligence, omission, exclusion, nonobservance, rejection, exception, elimination, debarment, preclusion, remissness.

recount, v.—Syn. report, recite, tell, describe, relate, detail, narrate, enumerate.

recover—Syn. regain, obtain, improve, mend, amend, increase, rally, pick up, revive, renew, restore, renovate, come round, pull through (colloq.), acquire, procure, profit, get, gain, win, redeem, salvage, realize, retrieve, inherit, purchase, collect, resume, regain, recuperate, reanimate, repossess, recruit, heal, cure. Ant. lose, miss, mislay, forfeit, squander, waste, let slip, fall back, retrograde, relapse, deteriorate, degenerate, decline, droop, wane, fall off, break down, injure, impair, harm, hurt, damage, contaminate, debase, corrupt, spoil, break up, destroy, sink, fall, totter, tumble, perish, die.

recreant—Syn. cowardly, craven, false, base, low, mean-spirited, faithless, unfaithful, apostate, erring, timid, fearful, dastard, dastardly, skulking, sneaking, weak-minded, pigeon-hearted, peacock-brained (colloq.), white-livered (colloq.), chicken-livered (colloq.), unmanly, spiritless, poor-spirited, false-hearted, double-faced, arrant, perfidious, treacherous, vile. Ant. constant, true, truthful, brave, courageous, gallant, lion-hearted, frank, straightforward, conscientious, unafraid, honorable, honest, just, square (*colloq.*), fair and square (*colloq.*), aboveboard, manly, high-minded, high-principled, open-hearted, candid, incorruptible, noble, reliable, upright, daring, good, trustworthy, staunch, faithful, true-hearted, dependable.

recreation—*Syn.* pastime, amusement, s p o r t, g a m e, play, fun, diversion, relaxation, jollity, joviality, jollification, jocosity, jocoseness, masquerade, drollery, pleasantry, pleasure, tomfoolery, merrymaking, merriment, frolic, skylarking (*colloq.*), monkeyshines (*colloq.*). *Ant.* drudgery, toil, slavery, plodding, hard labor, struggle, struggling, weariness, tiredness, boredom, lassitude, *ennui* [*Fr.*], heaviness, dullness, monotony, tedium, tediousness, wearisomeness, humdrum, drowsiness, somnolence, irksomeness, morbidness, morbidity, moroseness.

rectify, *v.*—*Syn.* emend, remedy, correct, revise, adjust, fix, regulate, amend, better, reform, ameliorate.

redeem—*Syn.* buy back, ransom, purchase, repurchase, rescue, liberate, set free, recover, deliver, free, reclaim, recoup, make good, atone, expiate, propitiate, make amends, satisfy, redress, repair, retrieve, extricate, emancipate, regain, replevy, pay, repay, prepay, defray, discharge, settle, release, regenerate, reform, perform, discharge, keep faith, save. *Ant.* sell, lose, barter, dispose of, part with, change, interchange, exchange, swap (*colloq.*), return, yield, give up, give away, lose, mislay, forfeit, let slip, fail, muddle, stumble, falter, fall down, miss, weaken, evade, neglect, discard, omit, elude, shun, ignore, defer, overlook, disregard.

redolence, *n.*—*Syn.* odor, fragrance, perfume, aroma, bouquet, smell.

redress—*Syn.* restoration, amendment, repair, remedy, relief, reparation, remission, abatement, diminution, replacement, rehabilitation, reëstablishment, reproduction, revival, renewal, renovation, reorganization, restitution, reconstruction, atonement, amends, propitiation, indemnification, compensation, satisfaction, payment, reward, remuneration, indemnity, retribution, requital, return, recompense, allowance. *Ant.* penalty, amercement, retribution, confiscation, forfeiture, assessment, increase, augmentation, intensification, fine, mulct, pecuniary punishment, tax, levy distraint, demand, appropriation, deprivation, distress, attachment, execution, sequestration, reprisal, seizure, disseizin, taxation, duty, toll, impost, tithe, exactment, capitation, tariff, cost, charge, damage, expenditure, disbursement, expenses, subsidy, outgoings, tribute.

reduce—*Syn.* lower, lessen, decrease, diminish, abate, abridge, modify, curtail, subdue, conquer, impoverish, shorten, degrade, thin, decimate, eliminate, weaken, debilitate, enervate, enfeeble, epitomize, condense, contract, abbreviate, overturn, subvert, master, surmount, overcome, defeat, override, outgeneral, outmaneuver, beat hollow (*colloq.*), lick (*colloq.*), rebate, mark down, discount. *Ant.* increase, augment, enlarge, expand, swell, mount, grow, spread, extend, amplify, inflate, incrassate, thicken, dilate, stretch, develop, magnify, puff, distend, strengthen, sustain, invigorate, refresh, raise, heighten, reinforce, add to, animate, reanimate, inspirit, brace, nerve, fortify, harden, gird, exalt, raise, aggrandize, intensify, enhance, advance, enrich, improve.

redundant, *adj.*—*Syn.* extra, supernumerary, plethoric, superfluous, tautological, wordy, verbose, repetitious, prolix, excessive. *Ant.* concise, terse, laconic, succinct.

refer, v.—*Syn.* allude, cite, appeal, consult, quote, point.

refinement—*Syn.* culture, civilization, scholarship, learning, erudition, elegance, politeness, cultivation, clarification, purification, enlightenment, polish, *savoir faire* [Fr.], *savoir vivre* [Fr.], good manners, breeding, suavity, courtesy, grace, graciousness, civility, courteousness, affability, complaisance, urbanity, condescension, taste, discrimination, discernment, nicety, compassion, finesse, delicacy, menticulture. *Ant.* rudeness, roughness, coarseness, grossness, piggishness, sulkiness, boorishness, brutality, clownishness, savagery, vulgarity, ignorance, rusticity, barbarism, blackguardism, swinishness, hooliganism, rowdyism, stupidity, asininity, larrikinism [Aus.], illbreeding, ribaldry, ruffianism, bad taste, discourtesy, bad manners, disrespect, incivility, impudence, moodiness, churlishness, sullenness, moroseness, cynicism.

reflect—*Syn.* contemplate, consider, ponder, think, concentrate, revolve, turn over, muse, cogitate, excogitate, reason, meditate, ruminate, study, deliberate, speculate, brood over, mull over (*colloq.*), censure, disapprove, frown upon. *Ant.* relax, overlook, disregard, ignore, neglect, be inattentive, dream, idle, waste time, indulge in pipe dreams, be indifferent, be abstracted, be absentminded, daydream, have head in the clouds, be bewildered, gad about, gossip, speak heedlessly, indulge in folly, act thoughtlessly, perform rashly, be precipitate, jump before looking.

reform—*Syn.* mend, amend, correct, improve, better, restore, convert, resolve, remodel, reorganize, transmute, revise, repair, renew, reconstruct, renovate, freshen. *Ant.* deteriorate, retrograde, relapse, degenerate, decline, droop, wither, waste, weaken, shrivel, shrink, break down, shake, totter, tumble, corrupt, contaminate, infect, taint, pollute, vitiate.

refractory, adj.—*Syn.* recalcitrant, unruly, disobedient, headstrong, stubborn, willful, contrary, dogged, obstinate, perverse, unmanageable. *Ant.* docile, tractable, amenable.

refresh, v.—*Syn.* revive, strengthen, renovate, renew, animate, brace, stimulate, restore, reinvigorate.

refuge—*Syn.* shelter, retreat, asylum, protectory, haven, harbor, protection, fastness, stronghold, fortress, home, almshouse, poorhouse, ambush, anchorage, covert, sanctuary, *sanctum* [L.], seclusion, solitude, privacy, retirement. *Ant.* abyss, chasm, pitfall, snare, trap, exposure, danger, peril, hazard, risk, jeopardy, venture, defenselessness, chance, haphazard, casualty, fortuity, contingency.

refuse, n.—*Syn.* offal, dregs, scum, scourings, leavings, remains, rubbish, residue, waste, trash, dross, junk, litter, shoddy, sweepings, rubble, *débris* [Fr.], rags, odds and ends. *Ant.* goods, valuables, merchandise, effects, belongings, property, possessions, assets, movables, chattels, stocks, bonds, currency, money, wealth, resources, supplies.

refuse, v.—*Syn.* decline, reject, repel, rebuff, disavow, disown, deny, repudiate, decline, withhold, turn down (*slang*), discountenance, renounce, protest. *Ant.* accept, acquiesce, accede, acknowledge, assent, admit, acquire, comply, conform, consent, yield, concede, allow, grant, agree to, approve, sanction, dispose, tender, proffer, offer, present, bestow, give, give away.

refute—*Syn.* disprove, overthrow, repel, confute, confound, show up, rebut, explode, parry, invalidate, knock the bottom out of (*colloq.*), knock into a cocked hat (*colloq.*), stultify, dumbfound, expose, not leave a leg to stand on. *Ant.* support, sustain, indorse, encourage, sanction, bolster up, defend, demonstrate, establish, prove, approve, confirm, affirm, ratify, subscribe to, commend, praise, stand up for, uphold, corroborate, strengthen.

regal, *adj.*—*Syn.* royal, imperial, majestic, sublime, stately, imposing, kingly, noble, magnificent, splendid.

regard—*Syn.* observe, consider, estimate, mind, heed, esteem, value, approve, prize, admire, respect, honor, revere, reverence, cherish, praise, exalt, appreciate, notice, mark, see, view, attend, give attention to, watch, look at, contemplate. *Ant.* disregard, overlook, shun, ignore, neglect, avert, turn away, shut eyes to, pass by, pay no attention, run away, reproach, vilify, defame, hate, detest, execrate, scowl at, disrespect, gibe, mock, taunt, disparage, dishonor, insult, affront, outrage.

regarding, *prep.*—*Syn.* about, respecting, apropos, re, concerning, touching, anent.

region, *n.*—*Syn.* area, district, territory, sphere, tract, province, quarter, sector, orbit, section, precinct, domain, part, beat.

regression, *n.*—*Syn.* reversion, deterioration, recession, retrogression, return, recidivism, backsliding, ebb, reflux.

regret—*Syn.* grief, sorrow, lamentation, remorse, repentance, concern, pain of mind, penitence, compunction, twitchings, self-condemnation, penance, self-reproach, sting of conscience, heartburning, dissatisfaction, worry, worriment, trouble, anxiety, disappointment, vexation. *Ant.* contentment, satisfaction, serenity, comfort, well-being, ease, easy conscience, peace of mind, tranquillity, cheerfulness, heart's ease, hardness of heart, impenitence, remorselessness, irrepentance, induration, obduracy, stiffness, want of feeling.

regular—*Syn.* customary, ordinary, orderly, stated, uniform, homogeneous, homologous, consistent, natural, invariable, methodical, proper, shipshape, systematic, graded, arranged, allotted, allocated, assigned, classified, filed, indexed, exact, symmetrical, normal, habitual, according to Hoyle (*colloq.*), conventional, usual, serial, recurrent, cyclic, successive, periodic. *Ant.* irregular, inconstant, inconsistent, nonconformable, variable, varied, heterogeneous, changing, rare, infrequent, sporadic, uncommon, extraordinary, unconformable, anomalous, wandering, eccentric, out of place, unusual, strange, peculiar, confused, complex, complicated, deranged, shuffled, mixed, muddled, topsy-turvy, disorderly, chaotic.

regulate—*Syn.* arrange, adjust, organize, govern, rule, methodize, dispose, direct, order, manage, supervise, superintend, overlook, control, look after, keep in order, classify, systematize, put in order, allocate, collocate, distribute, allot, coördinate, readjust, adapt, reconcile. *Ant.* disorder, disarrange, confuse, mix, muddle, derange, disarray, jumble, litter, muss, tangle, entangle, involve, unsettle, scatter, misplace, commingle, intermingle, disjoin, disconnect, dissociate, divide, sunder, separate, disrupt, detach, disorganize, disunite.

reimburse, *v.*—*Syn.* repay, recompense, indemnify, remunerate, refund.

reject, *v.*—*Syn.* exclude, refuse, repudiate, deny, spurn, eliminate, discard, veto, except, dismiss, jilt, blackball. *Ant.* accept, admit, choose, select.

rejoice, *v.*—*Syn.* exult, celebrate, glory, revel, gloat. *Ant.* grieve, sulk, lament, mourn.

rejoinder, *n.*—*Syn.* answer, retort, defense, reply, rebuttal, response.

relate, *v.*—*Syn.* recount, tell, narrate, recite, describe, report, state.

related, *adj.—Syn.* allied, associated, leagued, correlative, analogous, cognate, akin, kindred, connected, common, affiliated. *Ant.* dissociated, dissimilar, alien, foreign.

relaxation, *n.—Syn.* rest, leisure, ease, comfort, abatement, relief, repose, amusement, recreation.

release, *n.—Syn.* freedom, liberation, absolution, discharge, surrender, emancipation, acquittal, relinquishment, deliverance.

relent, *v.—Syn.* abate, yield, defer, forbear, soften, subside, submit, bow, refrain.

relentless, *adj.—Syn.* implacable, obdurate, strict, rigorous, hard, inexorable, pitiless, stringent, fierce, vindictive, inflexible, rigid. *Ant.* merciful, compassionate, lenient, gentle.

relevant—Syn.* suitable, appropriate, fit, proper, pertinent, becoming, pertaining to, apt, applicable, important, fitting, congruous, apposite, cognate, associated, allied, relative, approximate, affinitive, connected. *Ant.* disparate, separate, discrepant, antagonistic, opposed, irrelevant, unrelated, inconsistent, irrelative, unconnected, isolated, inapposite, heterogeneous, irreconcilable, arbitrary, different, separate.

reliable—Syn.* dependable, true, faithful, trusty, trustworthy, loyal, devoted, attached, certain, sure, undoubted, indubitable, positive, absolute, unquestionable, unequivocal, assured, definite, clear, explicit, decisive, dogmatic, gospel, conclusive, unimpeachable, indefeasible, irrefutable, indisputable, authoritative, authentic, axiomatic, evident, self-evident, undeniable, incontestable, incontrovertible. *Ant.* unreliable, flimsy, false, fallacious, doubtful, uncertain, dubious, unsound, vague, indeterminate, equivocal, confused, circumstantial, contingent, questionable, problematical, mysteri-

ous, cryptic, shaky, apocryphal, hypothetical, unstable, casual, random, aimless, obscure, oracular, changeable, unsettled, unauthentic, unauthoritative, wavering, fluctuating, shilly-shally.

reliance—Syn.* confidence, trust, hope, faith, optimism, conviction, anticipation, expectation, belief, assurance, encouragement, security, reassurance, prospect, presumption. *Ant.* hopelessness, despair, abandonment, despondency, gloom, evil foreboding, distrust, lack of confidence, ill-omen, suspicion, fear, dread, apprehension, doubt, suspense, uncertainty.

relief—Syn.* succor, help, assistance, alleviation, support, sustenance, maintenance, mitigation, redress, remedy, comfort, consolation, aid, exemption, release, extrication, deliverance, refreshment, palliation, easement, encouragement, rescue, reënforcement, nourishment, supplies. *Ant.* hindrance, impediment, obstruction, obstacle, interference, inhibition, restriction, embarrassment, stricture, barrier, drawback, check, incumbrance, drag, load, weight, burden, incubus, restraint, discouragement, disapproval, disapprobation.

religion—Syn.* godliness, piety, devotion, holiness, morality, righteousness, theology, theosophy, theism, deism, divinity, sect, persuasion, faith, profession of faith, worship, pietism. *Ant.* atheism, unbelief, godlessness, irreligion, ungodliness, wickedness, sacrilege, impiety, profanity, blasphemy, scoffing, indifference, infidelity, skepticism, disbelief, nihilism, agnosticism, passivity, laxity, apathy.

relinquish—Syn.* renounce, forego, leave, abandon, quit, resign, forsake, surrender, give up, abjure, withdraw from, forswear, back out, desert, secede, drop, discard, deny, break off, desist, disclaim, abdicate, vacate. *Ant.* hold, keep, grip, cling to, persevere, continue, persist, stick to, adhere to, carry on, bear up, maintain, keep going (*colloq.*), keep up, perpetuate, prolong, keep the ball rolling (*colloq.*), plug along (*slang*), march, advance, proceed, do your bit (*slang*), don't give up the ship (*colloq.*), keep the home fires burning (*colloq.*).

relish, *n.*—*Syn.* gusto, flavor, liking, delight, tang, appreciation, partiality, taste, zest, enjoyment.

reluctant—*Syn.* disinclined, loath, unwilling, averse, opposed, slow, tardy, backward, repugnant, adverse, laggard, remiss, slack, squeamish, demurring, grudging, involuntary, indisposed, disheartened, discouraged, disliking, queasy. *Ant.* willing, eager, disposed, favorable, desirous, inclined, ready, enthusiastic, predisposed, amenable, tractable, docile, compliant, persuasible, bent upon, voluntary, fain, wishful, longing, anxious, sedulous, solicitous.

rely, *v.*—*Syn.* depend, confide, bank, count, trust.

remain—*Syn.* continue, endure, tarry, last, wait, abide, dwell, stay, exist, prevail, go on, persist, protract, prolong, draw out, survive, outlast, outlive, stand, dwell, reside, inhabit, sojourn. *Ant.* go away, decamp, depart, vamose or vamoose (*slang*), vanish, beat it (*slang*), flit, fade, fade away, pass on, evaporate, melt, change, shift, move, run, skedaddle (*colloq.*), scud (*colloq.*), hook it (*slang*), be on your way (*colloq.*), cut and run (*colloq.*), stir your stumps (*slang*), scurry, turn tail (*colloq.*), beat a retreat, sheer off, give leg bail (*slang*), take French leave, slope (*slang*), bolt, levant (*Eng. slang*).

remainder, *n.*—*Syn.* rest, balance, surplus, excess, relics, remnant, dregs, leavings.

remarkable, *adj.*—*Syn.* notable, extraordinary, peculiar, memorable, famous, rare, striking, signal, important, prominent,

wonderful, uncommon.

remedy—*Syn.* cure, restorative, counteractive, reparation, redress, relief, help, specific, antidote, corrective, stimulant, panacea, cure-all, elixir, nostrum, pick-me-up (*colloq.*), bracer, drug, draft, dose, physic, pill, sedative, electuary, plaster, potion, salve, lotion, ointment, purgative, medical treatment. *Ant.* pain, agony, torment, torture, sickness, ill-health, weakness, disease, indisposition, malady, disorder, discomfort, plague, distemper, affliction, epidemic, shock, prostration, pestilence, infirmity, complaint, decline, invalidism.

remiss, *adj.*—*Syn.* careless, negligent, backward, lax, lazy, slow, thoughtless, slack, dilatory, unmindful. *Ant.* careful, scrupulous, mindful.

remit—*Syn.* release, relax, absolve, pardon, acquit, exonerate, forgive, relinquish, discontinue, surrender, leave off, desist, moderate, mitigate, alleviate, soften, relent, excuse, overlook, exempt, release, set free, discharge, restore, replace, send, forward, dispatch, transmit, convey, transfer, cohsign, deliver. *Ant.* hold, withhold, keep, retain, reserve, tie up, persist, continue, exact, control, command, sway, dominate, avenge, take revenge, get the upper hand, impose a duty on, bind, enjoin, render obligatory, make responsible, put under obligation, repress, suppress, restrain, restrict, prohibit.

remnant—*Syn.* remainder, residue, leavings, rest, balance, strip, piece, fragment, relic, fag-end, surplus, refuse. *Ant.* whole, entire, total, all, principal part, completeness, the altogether, full amount, entirety, bulk, mass, body, major part, addition, increment, augmentation, complement, supplement.

remonstrate—*Syn.* expostulate, check, criticize, find fault, pick flaws, animadvert, censure, scold, nag, deprecate, upbraid, reprimand, discourage, recriminate, objurgate, decry, frown upon, disparage, blame, protest, disapprove, chide, knock (*colloq.*), reproach. *Ant.* commend, praise, indorse, sanction, laud, eulogize, favor, support, sustain, encourage, stick up for (*colloq.*), stand up for, defend, boost (*colloq.*), admire, esteem, appreciate, advocate, uphold, give credit, recommend, acclaim, applaud, compliment.

remorse—*Syn.* compunction, regret, repentance, contrition, penitence, self-reproach, sorrow, self-reproof, sting of conscience, seared conscience. *Ant.* impenitence, hardness of heart, obduracy, induration, effrontery, shamelessness, pretension, braggadocio, vanity, ostentation, recusancy, gracelessness, consciencelessness, complacency, lack of repentance, deadness of conscience.

remorseless—*Syn.* casehardened, brazenfaced, shameless, stonyhearted, obdurate, indurate, indurated, braggart, boastful, impenitent, relentless, graceless, cruel, ruthless, tyrannical, merciless, pitiless, hard-hearted, unforgiving, vengeful, inhuman, barbarous, vindictive, avenging, rigorous, implacable, inexorable, sanguinary. *Ant.* feeling, tenderhearted, gentle, kind, pitiful, commiserative, forgiving, lenitive, merciful, tender, pitying, compassionate, humanitarian, sympathetic, clement, humane, consolatory, comforting, soothing, condolatory, conciliatory, sensitive, emotional, benevolent, indulgent, gracious, soft-hearted, kind-hearted, good-natured, affectionate, well-intentioned, amiable.

remote—*Syn.* distant, faraway, far off, far from, foreign, unconnected, unrelated, alien, separate, indirect, unconnected, heterogeneous, secluded, inaccessible, out-of-the-way, yonder, beyond, uttermost, over the hills and far away (*colloq.*), God-forgotten (*colloq.*), God-forsaken (*colloq.*). *Ant.* near, proximate, nigh, close, close at hand, neighboring, contiguous, adjoining, adjacent, handy, intimate, abutting, touching, bordering, related, connected, homogeneous, associated, affiliated, allied, approximate, cognate, kindred, congenial, homologous.

remove—*Syn.* move, displace, transfer, transport, separate, abstract, dislodge, eject, carry, oust, depart, migrate, shift, unseat, displant, take, lift, switch, shunt, push, leave, withdraw, go away, vacate, evacuate, skip (*slang*), retire, vamose or vamoose (*slang*), cut (*slang*), cut and run (*slang*), beat it (*slang*), scram (*slang*), mizzle (*slang*), quit, extract, draw, wrench, pull, uproot. *Ant.* place, settle, abide, remain, stay, stop, replace, establish, fix, strengthen, root, imbed, plant, post, stow, deposit, rest, pause, anchor, tarry, dwell, stand fast, stand firm, stand pat (*colloq.*), endure, continue, persist, persevere, last, linger, carry on, maintain, sustain, conserve, preserve, hold on, renew, prolong, confirm, institute, constitute.

remunerate—*Syn.* compensate, recompense, reward, requite, reimburse, repay, pay, satisfy, indemnify, return, acknowledge, atone, redress, bribe, tip (*colloq.*), give, grease one's palm (*slang*). *Ant.* deprive, take away, penalize, amerce, mulct, forfeit, escheat, confiscate, fine, levy, tax, blackmail, extort, distrain, appropriate, abstract, wrest, wring from, seize, grasp, bereave, despoil, strip, fleece, divest, ravish.

rend—*Syn.* rive, rip, tear, sever, sunder, slit, lacerate, mangle, cleave, rupture, burst, break, split, crack, separate, disjoint, dislocate, mince, break up, dissect, dismember. *Ant.* join, mend, reunite, secure, fasten, weld, stitch, solder, brace, put together, replace, renew, connect, conjoin, bind up, fuse, cement, graft, dovetail, mortise, rabbet, splice, tighten, attach, fix, affix, heal, inosculate, anastomose.

render—*Syn.* give, present, return, restore, give up, apportion, assign, distribute, surrender, dispense, pay, requite, deliver, impart, allot, assign, communicate, hand over, pass over, dispose of, fork over (*slang*), fork over the swag (*slang*), come across (*slang*), come across with the b o o d l e (*slang*), fork out (*slang*), shell out (*slang*), interpret, translate, explain, record, report, state, specify, convert into, resolve into, make, mold, form. *Ant.* withhold, withdraw, keep, retain, hold, secure, take, appropriate, seize, receive, get, obtain, abstract, carry off, take away, deduct, retrench, curtail, cast off, refuse, neglect, ignore, forget, hoard, scrimp, store, stow away, store up, garner, save, amass, accumulate, misinterpret, misconstrue, blunder, confuse, mix, muddle.

renew, *v.*—*Syn.* refresh, restore, continue, renovate, revive, repeat, iterate, regenerate, replenish, resuscitate. *Ant.* exhaust, deplete, diminish, enfeeble.

renounce—*Syn.* repudiate, recant, refuse, forswear, reject, abjure, abandon, deny, disavow, revoke, retract, recall, disclaim, disown, abdicate, apostatize, rescind, abrogate, relinquish, desert, quit, discard, break off, secede, forsake, throw up, give up, forego, abnegate. *Ant.* hold on, persist, conserve, maintain, remain, stay, keep, continue, carry on, uphold, keep the pot boiling (*colloq.*), plug along (*slang*), persevere, cling to, own, prize, value, commend, praise, retain, stick to, defend, sustain, support, preserve, advocate, assert, cherish, vindicate, claim, acknowledge, avow, proclaim.

renowned—*Syn.* famous, celebrated, illustrious, distinguished, eminent, exalted, remarkable, well-known, extraordinary, great, powerful, noble, goodly, august, grand, mighty, stupendous, prodigious, immense. *Ant.* obscure, unknown, trivial, trifling, humble, small, insignificant, puny, diminutive, inconsiderable, poor, lowly, forgotten, forsaken, abandoned, degraded, shameful, disgraced, nameless, unhonored.

reparation—*Syn.* atonement, satisfaction, return, repair, remuneration, compensation, indemnity, recompense, reward, restoration, restitution, rehabilitation, indemnification, redress, expiation, amends, propitiation, retribution, requital, emolument, payment. *Ant.* confiscation, mulct, amercement, levy, tax, impost, poundage, penalty, appropriation, extortion, deprivation, diversion, distraint, disinheritance, theft, robbery, blackmail, piracy, swag, loot, spoil, plunder, pillage, swindle, hold-up (*slang*), embezzlement, fraud.

repay, *v.*—*Syn.* recompense, reimburse, remunerate, requite, indemnify, refund, reward, retaliate.

repeat, *v.*—*Syn.* iterate, duplicate, reproduce, recite, tell, relate, echo, recapitulate, quote.

repel, *v.*—*Syn.* repulse, disperse, parry, refuse, reject, rebuff, resist, scatter, disgust, sicken.

repentance—*Syn.* sorrow, remorse, regret, penitence, contriteness, contrition, compunction, self-denunciation, self-abasement, self-reproach, self-condemnation, self-humiliation, prick of conscience, sting of conscience. *Ant.* self-complacency, self-congratulation, self-approval, hardness, hardness of heart, obduracy, impenitence, comfort, approval, content, contentment, obstinacy, stubbornness, gracelessness, recusancy, induration, unrepentance.

replace—*Syn.* restore, substitute,

reinstate, rearrange, rehabilitate, refund, reconstruct, reconstitute, repair, mend, supplant, put in place of, supersede. *Ant.* change, exchange, interchange, barter, swap (*colloq.*), bandy, shuffle, alternate, alter, vary, transform, shift, turn, modify, swerve, deviate, diversify.

replete, *adj.*—*Syn.* full, sated, stuffed, charged, abundant, gorged, surfeited, glutted. *Ant.* starved, hungry, empty.

reply, *v.*—*Syn.* answer, respond, retort, echo, rejoin, counter.

report, *n.*—*Syn.* story, statement, account, description, narrative, record, recital, narration, tale, rumor, relation, rehearsal, tidings, announcement, communication, rumor, news, chronicle, intelligence, despatch, communiqué [*Fr.*], wire, cable, 'phone, telephone, telegram, broadcast, radio, radiobroadcast, radiotelegram, radiotelephone, radiocast, newscast, message, information, pronouncement. *Ant.* concealment, secrecy, secret, reserve, suppression, evasion, latency, cancellation, reticence, furtiveness, deletion, effacement, misrepresentation, misstatement, distortion, understatement, exaggeration, travesty, caricature, extravaganza, lying, falsification, perversion, misleading statement, false account.

report, *v.*—*Syn.* announce, relate, tell, recite, describe, detail, communicate, declare, record, chronicle, note, hand down, set down, jot down, inform, apprise, publish, make known, disclose, impart, express, mention, specify, telegraph, telephone, radio, radiobroadcast, radiotelegraph, radiotelephone, radiocast, newscast. *Ant.* conceal, hide, secrete, veil, screen, keep back, cloak, mask, camouflage [*Fr.*], befog, confuse, reserve, suppress, withhold, delete, expunge, cancel, efface, blot out, stifle, hoodwink, bamboozle, puzzle, mystify, stop, squelch (*colloq.*), shut up (*slang*).

repose, *n.*—*Syn.* rest, ease, calm, respite, quiet, comfort, relaxation, serenity, leisure, peacefulness.

represent, *v.*—*Syn.* depict, describe, imitate, portray, picture, delineate, draw, personate.

reprimand, *v.*—*Syn.* admonish, scold, censure, reprove, berate, reproach, rebuke, reprehend, chide, blame.

reproach, *v.*—*Syn.* reprove, admonish, blame, chide, censure, rebuke, caution, reprimand.

reprobate, *adj.*—*Syn.* abandoned, dissolute, immoral, lewd, lascivious, blasphemous, sinful, depraved, degraded, vitiated, corrupt, wicked, profligate, vile, base, castaway, vicious, bad, immoral, demoralized, flagrant, iniquitous, unrighteous, disreputable, degenerate, Sadistic, diabolical, infernal, hellish, satanic, Mephistophelian, flagitious, demoniacal, hellborn, fiendish, devilish. *Ant.* good, honest, honorable, noble, respectable, God-fearing, virtuous, moral, pure, undefiled, worthy, commendable, praiseworthy, sterling, incorrupt, pure, righteous, right-minded, innocent, sinless, faultless, exemplary, blameless, irreproachable, unexceptionable, guiltless, fine, upright, conscientious, wholesome, whole-souled, straight, straightforward, trustworthy, peerless, matchless, perfect, saintly, sincere.

reprobate, *n.*—*Syn.* wretch, sinner, transgressor, law-breaker, criminal, jailbird, rascal, ruffian, demon, devil, hell-cat, hellbender (*colloq.*), hell-hound, rakehell, rake, roué [*Fr.*], Sadist, villain, scoundrel, seducer, profligate, prodigal, renegade, waster, rounder (*slang*), black sheep (*colloq.*), wastrel, mauvais sujet [*Fr.*], bad man, bad woman, viper, cockatrice, basilisk, monster, betrayer, scold, vixen, vampire, defaulter, embezzler, Jezebel, Judas, traitor, spy, bully, drunkard, sot, toper, debauchee, malefactor, felon, convict, blackguard, scamp, rogue, tough, culprit, outlaw, bawd, pimp, pander, procurer, procuress, white slaver (*colloq.*), adulterer, adulteress, libertine, scandalmonger, whore, whoremonger, whoremaster, sodomite, lecher, paramour, satyromaniac, nymphomaniac, prostitute, slut, streetwalker, Sapphist, Lesbian, trollop, tribadist, concubine, wench, drab, mistress, courtesan, strumpet, doxy (*slang*), harlot, *hetaira* [*Gr.*]. *Ant.* good man, good woman, model, exemplar, guide, paragon, angel, saint, seraph, cherub, virgin, Madonna, pattern, holy person, philanthropist, humanitarian, benefactor, uplifter, good Samaritan, good shepherd, ascetic, penitent, vestal, nun, pure maiden, anchorite, hermit, puritan, martyr, hero, worthy, churchman, clergyman, priest, prelate, minister, rabbi, parson, ecclesiastic, ecclesiarch, seer, prophet, rector, vicar, chaplain, patriarch, hierarch, sacrist, sacristan, divine, presbyter, sexton, communicant, devotee, confessor, apostle, religious, *religieuse* [*Fr.*], priestess, spiritual director, novice, postulant, Levite, acolyte, thurifer, evangelist, evangelizer, missionary, instructor, teacher, preacher, *abbé* [*Fr.*], *curé* [*Fr.*], bishop, archbishop, cardinal, pontiff.

reproof—*Syn.* censure, reprehension, chiding, rebuke, blame, condemnation, disapproval, reproach, admonition, check, comment, criticism, animadversion, reflection, denunciation, reproval, upbraiding, scolding, objurgation, disapprobation, disparagement, objection, sarcasm, satire, reprimand, invective, contumely, vituperation, dressing down (*colloq.*). *Ant.* credit, commendation, recommendation, approval, indorsement, appreciation, praise, adulation, flattery, acclaim, approbation, sanction, eulogy, eulogium, cheer, encomium, acclamation, tribute,

panegyric, esteem, estimation, advocacy, regard, encouragement, support, admiration, boost (*colloq.*), applause, greeting, welcome, favor, popularity, confirmation, O.K.

reprove—*Syn.* disapprove, berate, scold, chide, disparage, knock (*colloq.*), condemn, rebuke, reproach, blame, censure, frown upon, objurgate, snub, dress down (*colloq.*), criticize, admonish, chasten, upbraid, call down (*colloq.*), reprimand, check, remonstrate with, warn, find fault with, take to task, expostulate with. *Ant.* approve, abet, applaud, acclaim, proclaim, sanction, indorse, countenance, encourage, instigate, excite, incite, urge on, stimulate, cheer, impel, animate, inspirit, embolden, nerve, comfort, congratulate, promote, praise, eulogize, flatter, inspire, induce, egg on, importune.

repudiate—*Syn.* disavow, disown, discard, abjure, renounce, reject, disclaim, divorce, bar, exclude, debar, expel, banish, protest, demur, contradict, dissent, disagree, spurn, cast out, fling to the winds (*colloq.*), toss to the dogs (*colloq.*), revoke, cancel, repeal, rescind, dismiss, abrogate, annul, retract, reverse, void, quash, overrule, abolish, nullify, countermand, recall, evade, dodge, omit, ignore, infringe, violate. *Ant.* acknowledge, avow, affirm, assert, asseverate, profess, admit, take in, embody, incorporate, concede, ratify, own, approve, assent, acquiesce, yield, give in, espouse, select, choose, coöpt, countersign, prefer, observe, comply, adhere, carry out, fulfil, perform, keep faith, stick to, defend, obey, discharge, settle, clear off, repay, refund, reimburse, compensate, satisfy.

repugnant—*Syn.* antagonistic, antipathetic, disagreeable, disgusting, distasteful, inimical, hostile, disobedient, unwilling, opposed, contrary, inconsistent, offensive, incongruous, resistant, counter, averse, adverse, converse, reverse, antagonistic, conflicting, contradictory, unconformable, oppugnant. *Ant.* a g r e e a b l e, pleasing, pleasant, compatible, conformable, harmonious, suitable, congruent, apposite, allied, identical, equivalent, coinciding, concordant, concomitant, accordant, sympathetic, congenial, conciliatory, compliant, apt, correspondent, matched, fit, adapted, proportionate, commensurate, agreeing.

repulsive—*Syn.* forbidding, odious, horrible, horrid, hideous, ugly, repellent, disagreeable, revolting, detestable, queasy, abhorrent, nauseating, nauseous, abominable, grisly, gruesome, frightful, terrible, hateful, offensive, shocking, disgusting, fulsome, loathsome. *Ant.* pleasing. agreeable, enticing, inviting, attractive, refined, delicate, nice, beautiful, graceful, elegant, goodly, splendid, magnificent, alluring, captivating, fascinating, artistic, picturesque, enchanting, ornamental, handsome, radiant, sparkling, superb, grand, entrancing, bewitching.

reputable—*Syn.* honorable, estimable, worthy, trustworthy, creditable, respectable, famous, celebrated, distinguished, popular, dignified, straightforward, gentlemanly, constant, faithful, scrupulous, righteous, candid, upright, loyal, true, incorrupt, truthful, conscientious, square (*colloq.*), fair and square (*colloq.*), just, aboveboard, highprincipled, frank, open-hearted, chivalrous, staunch, reliable, dependable, virtuous, truehearted, noble. *Ant.* base, dishonorable, disloyal, untrue, foul, arrant, knavish, dishonest, unscrupulous, treacherous, depraved, tricky, undignified, untrustworthy, ungentlemanly, unbecoming, debased, selfish, crooked, Machiavellian, slippery, abject, mean, contemptible, low-bred, underbred, recreant, inglorious, shameless, false-hearted, disreputable, infamous, vile, despicable, unworthy, notorious, scandalous.

request, *v.*—*Syn.* ask, beg, appeal, invite, entreat, sue, implore, petition, importune, pray, supplicate, beseech.

require, *v.*—*Syn.* claim, ask, demand, crave, exact, urge, want, need.

requite—*Syn.* remunerate, repay, exchange, recompense, reciprocate, compensate, reward, satisfy, pay, pay off, settle with, retaliate, return, revenge, punish, quit. *Ant.* slight, pass over, pardon, overlook, neglect, forgive, excuse, extenuate, justify, absolve, acquit, release, set free, discharge, clear, exculpate, exempt, exonerate, remit, vindicate.

rescind—*Syn.* abrogate, revoke, annul, cancel, reverse, void, vacate, discard, dissent, disclaim, abolish, repeal, recall, reverse, quash, dissolve, set aside, countermand. *Ant.* commission, delegate, command, accredit, appoint, inaugurate, proffer, propose, advance, present, tender, permit, allow, ordain, order, propose, establish.

rescue—*Syn.* save, deliver, preserve, recover, recapture, liberate, free, set free, redeem, manumit, extricate, release, emancipate, reprieve, ransom, retrieve, snatch, take away. *Ant.* prevent, imprison, incarcerate, impede, check, bar, debar, hinder, retain, block, constrict, inhibit, hamper, thwart, obstruct, stop, preclude, bind, shackle, tie, chain, impound, confine, jail, jug (*slang*), enslave.

resemblance—*Syn.* likeness, similitude, similarity, match, companion, twin, counterpart, effigy, form, double, *alter ego* [*L.*], simile, facsimile, type, parallel, image, imitation, duplicate, representation, replica, copy, portrait, cast, mould, chip of the old block (*colloq.*), prototype, archetype, matrix, model, figure, negative, pattern. *Ant.* difference, variance, divergence, dissimilarity, disparity, dissimilitude, distinction, contradistinction, variety, discrepancy, oppositeness, heterogeneity, contrast, inconformity, inconsistency, diversity, contrast, antithesis, deviation, contradiction, antagonism, contrariness, disagreement, discrepancy.

resentment—*Syn.* anger, wrath, ire, perturbation, indignation, ill-feeling, displeasure, animosity, vexation, exasperation, exacerbation, acerbity, choler, passion, soreness, bitterness, acrimony, spleen, umbrage, dudgeon, pique, asperity, rankling, sulks, dander (*colloq.*), bile, gall. *Ant.* cheer, cheerfulness, urbanity, suavity, good will, friendship, friendliness, kindly feeling, affection, amity, concord, harmony, happiness, docility, geniality, cordiality, enthusiasm, willingness, readiness, compliance, good nature, good humor, joviality, mirth, vivacity, jollity, lightsomeness, animation, levity, laughter, exhilaration, lightheartedness.

reserved, *adj.*—*Syn.* restrained, shy, cautious, diffident, cold, secretive, aloof, demure, unsociable, close, taciturn, detached, distant, bashful. *Ant.* affable, friendly, uninhibited, expansive.

reside—*Syn.* dwell, abide, live, inhabit, stay, sojourn, remain, lodge, bunk (*colloq.*), room, roost (*slang*), tenant, people, frequent, occupy, take up, fill, populate, domicile. *Ant.* absent, keep from, shun, vacate, retire, leave, abandon, go away, stay away, withdraw, retract, skip (*slang*), vamoose or vamose (*slang*), flee, fly, fly the coop (*slang*), skedaddle (*colloq.*), avoid, run away, evade, elude, steer clear of, give up, move out, quit.

resign, *v.*—*Syn.* quit, yield, renounce, vacate, surrender, es-

chew, relinquish, forgo, abandon, cede, waive, abjure, withdraw.

resilient, *adj.*—*Syn.* elastic, supple, flexible, springy, buoyant, spirited. *Ant.* rigid, stiff, tense, inflexible.

resist—*Syn.* oppose, hinder, check, withstand, obstruct, baffle, thwart, disappoint, disobey, refuse, counteract, run counter to, impede, frustrate, react, rebuff, repulse, snub, kick against, recalcitrate, strike back, revolt, mutiny, infringe, secede, rebel, defy, kick over the traces (*colloq.*). *Ant.* comply, concur, coöperate, collaborate, help, assist, contribute, conform, submit, consent, obey, observe, subscribe to, adapt oneself to, defer, yield, give in, surrender, accede, bend, come to terms, kiss the rod (*colloq.*), eat humble pie (*colloq.*), lay down, capitulate, back down (*colloq.*), be obedient, answer the helm, come at call, acknowledge, assent, acquiesce, ratify, confirm.

resolute—*Syn.* steady, steadfast, firm, determined, decided, unshaken, bold, persevering, constant, fixed, brave, unwavering, resolved, intransigeant, intransigent, uncompromising, courageous, militant, game, plucky, intrepid, manly, defiant, valorous, valiant, high-spirited, lion-hearted, stout-hearted, daring, heroic, audacious, fearless, dauntless, dashing, undaunted, undismayed, confident, strong-minded, strong-willed, dogged, unflinching, indomitable, self-reliant. *Ant.* irresolute, weak, wavering, vacillating, unsteady, timorous, afraid, cautious, cowardly, pusillanimous, mean-spirited, poor-spirited, weak-minded, effeminate, hen-hearted (*colloq.*), chicken-hearted (*colloq.*), pigeon-livered (*colloq.*), puny, piffling, unmanned, dastard, dastardly, craven, white-livered (*colloq.*), unstable, hesitant, wobbly, unsteady, undecided, undetermined, shilly-shally, pliant, soft, shuffling, fickle, fidgety, lax, yielding, vague, uncertain, addled, addlepated, changeable, rattled (*slang*).

resolve, *v.*—*Syn.* decide, will, persist, purpose, determine, intend, plan, conclude, mean.

resort, *v.*—*Syn.* turn, go, use, try, address.

respect, *n.*—*Syn.* deference, esteem, fealty, admiration, reverence, consideration, regard, honor. *Ant.* contempt, scorn, disdain, contumely.

respective, *adj.*—*Syn.* individual, specific, particular, special.

respite—*Syn.* reprieve, suspension, commutation, delay, postponement, pause, interval, stop, intermission, deferment, acquittal, exculpation, pardon, forgiveness, discharge, immunity, halt, stay, deliverance, truce, extrication, exemption, cessation, interregnum, deadlock, interruption, protraction, adjournment, release. *Ant.* condemnation, conviction, sentence, proscription, damnation, punishment, penalty, banishment, exile, infliction, retribution, chastisement, castigation, correction, strain, stress, struggle, trouble, misery, annoyance, oppression, hard labor, exertion, wear and tear, continuance, continuation, persistence, prolongation, extension.

responsible—*Syn.* accountable, answerable, amenable, liable, subject, susceptive, binding, imperative, incumbent on, under obligation, obligatory, bound by, beholden to. *Ant.* irresponsible, exempt, immune, unbound, excusable, uncontrolled, lawless, unrestrained, unfettered, arbitrary, unconditioned, unlimited, free, supreme, absolute.

rest—*Syn.* repose, quiet, quietude, quietness, ease, tranquillity, intermission, cessation, slumber, sleep, stop, stay, pause, stillness, standstill, recreation, peace, peacefulness, peaceableness, calm, calmness, stay, pacification,

quiescence, lull, relaxation, discontinuance, release, decease, demise, mortality, death. *Ant.* unrest, movement, commotion, stir, tumult, work, strain, restlessness, disturbance, excitement, motion, disquiet, disquietude, agitation, toil, rush, bustle, activity, hustle (*colloq.*), wakefulness, confusion, uproar, hubbub, action, fuss, flurry, ferment, outcry, rattle, rattling, continuance, persistence, perturbation, crash, clamor, noise, racket, clatter, din.

restful, *adj.*—*Syn.* serene, easy, quiet, comfortable, tranquil, cozy, soothing.

restive—*Syn.* restless, fidgety, fractious, impatient, fretful, skittish, frisky, unruly, balky, stubborn, refractory, recalcitrant, rebellious, resentful, mutinous, mulish, obstinate, perverse, moody, splenetic, wayward, crossgrained, cantankerous (*colloq.*), averse, reluctant, arbitrary, headstrong, disobedient, insubordinate. *Ant.* quiet, peaceable, docile, tractable, submissive, passive, yielding, gentle, obedient, manageable, willing, agreeable, ready, amenable, pliant, compliant, resigned, easily-managed, suant, genial, cordial, well-disposed, satisfied, acquiescent, quiescent, patient, unresisting, tolerant, calm.

restless—*Syn.* agitated, disturbed, uneasy, fidgety, nervous, unquiet, disquieted, flurried, unsettled, anxious, excited, worried, peeved, annoyed, flustered, agitated, changeable, twitching, perturbed, tremulous, shaking, trembling, rattled (*slang*), on the go (*colloq.*), moving, moving to and fro, roving, wandering. *Ant.* unmoved, steady, tranquil, calm, composed, cool, quiet, inexcitable, stoical, coolheaded, level-headed, placid, peaceful, unperturbed, imperturbable, grave, solemn, sober, sober-minded, undemonstrative, undisturbed, resigned, content.

restore, v.—*Syn.* refresh, replace, renovate, revive, renew, regain, reform, reinstate, redeem, rebuild, mend, repair.

restrain—*Syn.* check, curb, bridle, restrict, suppress, keep, keep back, keep down, keep in, keep under, constrain, confine, circumscribe, hold, hold in, hold back, withhold, repress, hinder, abridge, call a halt (*colloq.*), prevent, coerce, stop, debar. *Ant.* loosen, unfetter, unchain, unbind, free, set free, liberate, release, emancipate, incite, let loose, arouse, aid, animate, inspirit, encourage, impel, manumit, dismiss, disband, discharge, disenthral, enfranchise, deliver from.

restrict, v.—*Syn.* limit, restrain, impede, confine, check, circumscribe, bind, curb, fence, crimp, squelch. *Ant.* widen, expand, extend, enlarge.

retain—*Syn.* hold, keep, cling to, secure, maintain, employ, hire, engage, preserve, detain, withhold, grasp, clutch, clinch, bind, reserve. *Ant.* relinquish, give up, throw away, cast aside, dismiss, surrender, cede, dispense, let go, let slip, cast off, pitch to the dogs (*colloq.*), sweep away, jettison, dispose of, discard, fling away, pitch overboard, forego, surrender.

retaliate, v.—*Syn.* requite, revenge, reciprocate, return.

retard, v.—*Syn.* hinder, delay, clog, hamper, check, arrest, postpone, impede, interrupt.

reticence, n.—*Syn.* taciturnity, reserve, silence, shyness. *Ant.* talkativeness, prolixity, frankness, forwardness.

retract—*Syn.* abjure, revoke, deny, recant, disown, recall, withdraw, annul, forswear, unsay, back down, back out, repudiate, cancel, quash, nullify, rescind, reverse, abrogate, renounce, disclaim, discard, negative, contradict, gainsay, abnegate, ignore, set aside. *Ant.* affirm, confirm, assert, reassert, depose, asseverate, declare, avouch, advance, put forward, propound, announce, avow, contend, emphasize, indorse, approve, corroborate, ratify, acknowledge, admit, commend, praise, uphold.

retreat, n.—*Syn.* refuge, seclusion, shelter, resort, den, recess, asylum, retirement.

retribution, n.—*Syn.* retaliation, reparation, compensation, requital, reprisal, reciprocation, penalty, revenge, redress, restitution. *Ant.* clemency, forgiveness, mercy, grace.

retrogress, v.—*Syn.* regress, retreat, backslide, relapse, degenerate, deteriorate, revert.

return, v.—*Syn.* recur, revert, reappear, reply, restore, reciprocate, yield, render.

reveal—*Syn.* divulge, unveil, disclose, show, impart, discover, expose, unmask, disburden, confess, uncover, unfold, betray, inform, publish, blab (*colloq.*), peach (*slang*), squeal (*slang*), let the cat out of the bag (*colloq.*). *Ant.* screen, veil, hide, conceal, cover, shade, curtain, blind, keep back, mask, dodge, juggle, evade, deceive, disguise, delude, blind, cheat, trick, hoodwink, mystify, impose upon, bunco or bunko (*slang*), spoof (*slang*), outwit.

revenant, n.—*Syn.* ghost, apparition, phantom, specter, wraith, spook, spirit.

revenge, n.—*Syn.* vengeance, retaliation, requital, retribution, avenging, avengement, vindictiveness, rancor, implacability, malevolence, eye for an eye, tooth for a tooth, *vendetta* [*It.*], day of reckoning. *Ant.* forgiveness, pardon, absolution, amnesty, reprieve, propitiation, conciliation, exoneration, exculpation, forbearance, love, brotherly love, indulgence, reconciliation, reconcilement, compassion, excuse, mercy, pity, acquittal, burying the hatchet (*colloq.*).

revenue—*Syn.* income, return, result, wealth, receipts, proceeds, resources, funds, stocks, dividends, credits, interest, graft (*slang*), perquisites, salary, means, profits, fruits, earnings, emolument, acquirements, annuity. *Ant.* expenditure, expenses, disbursements, costs, donations, gifts, fees, upkeep, waste, rent, taxes, levy, toll, payments, settlements, satisfaction, reckoning, liquidation.

reverence—*Syn.* honor, respect, admiration, homage, regard, esteem, veneration, approbation, obsequiousness, prostration, genuflection. *Ant.* disrespect, irreverence, contumely, affront, discourtesy, dishonor, mockery, execration, sarcasm, irony, satire, ridicule, affront, insult, indignity, outrage, superciliousness, scurrility, jeering, scoffing.

reverse, *v.*—*Syn.* transpose, upset, undo, nullify, repeal, void, revoke, overturn, annul.

review, *v.*—*Syn.* reconsider, inspect, survey, rehearse, retrace, criticize, analyze, commentate.

revile, *v.*—*Syn.* upbraid, calumniate, execrate, rail, malign, vilify, slander, berate, asperse, curse, scold. *Ant.* praise, laud, extol, eulogize.

revise—*Syn.* review, reconsider, edit, correct, reëxamine, look over, change, alter, amend, improve, develop, compare, scan, scrutinize, overhaul. *Ant.* neglect, dismiss, discard, ignore, set aside, disregard, botch, bungle, distort, twist, render nonsensical, pervert, derange, jumble, confuse, complicate, tangle, ball up (*slang*).

revive—*Syn.* refresh, renew, renovate, animate, resuscitate, vivify, cheer, comfort, revivify, reanimate, reproduce, recall, reinforce, invigorate, freshen, improve, touch up, repair. *Ant.* weaken, lessen, deteriorate, wither, decay, decline, droop, waste, run to seed, perish, fade, sink, shrink, molder, go from bad to worse, crumple, rankle, shrivel, rot, pass away.

revolting, *adj.*—*Syn.* nauseating, offensive, repellent, loathsome, odious, abominable, repugnant, obnoxious, repulsive, sickening.

revolution—*Syn.* revolt, rebellion, insurrection, insubordination, lawlessness, destruction, mutiny, sedition, tumult, riot, disorder, anarchy, confusion, disintegration, rising, uprising, outbreak, *émeuté* [*Fr.*]. *Ant.* government, sovereignty, domination, dominion, obedience, authority, command, law, loyalty, order, rule, supremacy, control, constancy, fidelity, faithfulness, peace, tranquillity, submission, submissiveness, fealty, constancy, devotion.

reward—*Syn.* remuneration, recompense, gain, compensation, reparation, retribution, amends, return, requital, meed, guerdon, satisfaction, indemnity, indemnification, recoupment, redress, reckoning, atonement, acknowledgment, consideration, payment. *Ant.* penalty, mulct, amercement, damages, confiscation, appropriation, abstraction, deprivation, divestment, disherison, distraint, attachment, plunder, spoliation, blackmail, pillage, robbery, seizure, forfeiture, fine, levy, toll, tax, loss.

rhythm, *n.*—*Syn.* cadence, regularity, swing, meter, periodicity, measure, beat, tempo.

rib, *v.*—*Syn.* chaff, banter, kid, lampoon, deride, twit, haze.

ribald—*Syn.* low, mean, base, filthy, dirty, foul-mouthed, obscene, lewd, lascivious, vulgar, depraved, sluttish, blackguard, blackguardly, scurrile, scurrilous, uncouth, brutish, indecorous, unbecoming, rude, raffish, outlandish, coarse, vile, contemptible, ungentlemanly, unladylike. *Ant.* graceful, refined, polished, courteous, polite, suave, clean, decent, pure, undefiled, courtly, elegant, chaste, charming, dainty, virtuous, cultivated, cultured, precise, artistic, tasty, modest, well-bred, well-mannered, gentlemanly, ladylike, decorous, genteel.

rich—*Syn.* wealthy, opulent, affluent, ample, copious, sumptuous, abundant, plentiful, plenteous, precious, generous, gorgeous, luscious, spicy, racy, exuberant, fruitful, fertile, superb, independent, moneyed, flush (*slang*), superabundant, profuse, luxuriant, lavish, bejeweled, embellished, ornate, gilt, tesselated, inlaid, bedizened, beautiful, swell (*slang*), swanky (*slang*). *Ant.* poor, impoverished, mean, lowly, humble, indigent, reduced, mendicant, starved, starving, penniless, seedy (*colloq.*), poverty-stricken, pinched, straitened, moneyless, beggared, beggarly, destitute, short (*colloq.*), ill-provided, depleted, needy, famine-stricken, jejune, empty-handed, trumpery, rubbishy, frippery, trashy, gimcrack.

riddle—*Syn.* conundrum, paradox, puzzle, obscurity, problem, enigma, charade, rebus, secret, intricacy, difficulty, maze, labyrinth, strait, entanglement, quandary, dilemma, embarrassment, perplexity, tough proposition (*colloq.*). *Ant.* answer, solution, explanation, interpretation, meaning, exposition, exegesis, elucidation, disentanglement, rendering, plainness, simplicity, information, openness, knowledge, clearness, perspicuity, lucidity, explicitness.

ridicule, *n.*—*Syn.* mockery, derision, sarcasm, persiflage, satire, irony.

ridiculous, *adj.*—*Syn.* ludicrous, preposterous, laughable, absurd, odd, droll, grotesque, foolish, nonsensical, comic, bizarre, silly.

right, *adj.*—*Syn.* true, correct, suitable, lawful, proper, straight, just, undeviating, regular, truthful, honest, sincere, accurate, precise, actual, real, unimpeachable, veracious, exact, definite, scrupulous, particular, meticulous, authentic, genuine, legitimate, sterling, sound, clear, clear-cut, valid, undisguised, undisputed, unrefuted, irrefutable, equitable, square (*colloq.*), fair, fair and square (*colloq.*), aboveboard, axiomatic, equal, equable,

reasonable, legitimate. *Ant.* wrong, false, untrue, erring, lying, unbelievable, unjust, unfair, foul, partial, unequitable, unwarrantable, unjustifiable, iniquitous, sinful, vile, shameful, disgraceful, improper, illegitimate, unbecoming, unlawful, preposterous, ridiculous, erroneous, misleading, fallacious, groundless, illogical, inexact, inaccurate, delusive, incorrect, unauthentic, untrustworthy, incredible, unreliable, uncertain, inconceivable, suspicious, doubtful, questionable.

right, *n.*—*Syn.* privilege, prerogative, franchise, immunity, claim, exemption, license, liberty, freedom, independence, emancipation, self-determination, enfranchisement, ownership, proprietorship, possession, dower, jointure, inheritance, domain, territory, chattels, fixtures, equity, justice, fair play, square deal, impartiality, title, birthright, duty, fealty, allegiance, responsibility, accountability, honor, faith, rectitude, uprightness, candor, truth, principle, trustworthiness. *Ant.* dishonor, disgrace, betrayal, perfidy, faithlessness, treachery, perfidiousness, baseless, turpitude, villainy, rascality, knavery, roguery, graft (*slang*), corruption, venality, evasion, nonobservance, transgression, infringement, sloth, sinfulness, breach, impropriety, illegality, imposition, violation, subjection, servility, slavery, thraldom, subjugation, serfdom, servitude, captivity, bondage, oppression.

righteous—*Syn.* just, upright, virtuous, godly, good, honorable, honest, deserving, worthy, moral, meritorious, exemplary, saintly, angelic, godlike, pure, noble, right-minded, well intentioned, good-hearted, philanthropic, charitable, dutiful, right-living, commendable, praiseworthy. *Ant.* wrong, unjust, unrighteous, sinful, vile, depraved, base, unprincipled, immoral, corrupt, vicious, shameless, slanderous, lying, perjured, criminal, dissolute, disreputable, recreant, profligate, blackguard, demoralized, degraded, evil-minded, sinister, infamous, villainous, foul, gross, flagitious, flagrant, diabolic, devilish, fiendish, atrocious, felonious, nefarious, dishonest, rascally.

rigid—*Syn.* stiff, inflexible, unyielding, inelastic, hard, firm, unbending, indurate, petrified, stony, stern, austere, severe, exact, exacting, rigorous, strict, scrupulous, precise, arrogant, arbitrary, despotic, dictatorial, obdurate, inexorable, dour [*Sc.*], relentless, strait-laced, Spartan, Draconian, grinding. *Ant.* soft, pliant, plastic, ductile, tractile, flexible, flexile, mobile, extensile, elastic, mollient, yielding, limber, putty-like, spongy, tolerant, indulgent, mild, compassionate, clement, merciful, lenient, complaisant, easy-going, forbearing, considerate, kind, kindly.

rigorous, *adj.*—*Syn.* stern, exacting, rigid, stringent, harsh, inflexible, severe, strict, stiff, oppressive. *Ant.* lax, easygoing, lenient, easy.

ripe—*Syn.* mature, mellow, complete, finished, perfect, ready, prepared, cut and dried (*colloq.*), fully developed, maturated, seasoned, fully grown, consummate. *Ant.* immature, young, soft, tender, green, raw, infantile, childish, crude, unprepared, unripe, unready, unseasoned, innocent, inexperienced, recent, fresh, new, unfledged, callow, budding, sappy, unfit, undeveloped.

rise—*Syn.* arise, ascend, mount, climb, scale, issue, emanate, flow, proceed, spring, begin, grow, progress, commence, originate, uprise. *Ant.* decline, descend, sink, settle, set, fall, drop, go down, recede, return, regrade, retrograde, tumble, topple, slide, slump.

risky, *adj.*—*Syn.* hazardous, chan-

cy, dangerous, perilous, precarious, uncertain.

rite, *n.*—*Syn.* ceremony, ritual, formality, liturgy, ordinance, solemnity.

rival, *n.*—*Syn.* opponent, competitor, antagonist, enemy, emulator, contestant, adversary, oppositionist, disputant, entrant, obstructionist, wrangler, combatant, corrival, controversialist. *Ant.* patron, helper, assistant, coworker, cooperator, coaid, helpmate, mate, matey (*Aus. slang*), comate, colleague, partner, confrère, coadjutor, auxiliary, recruit, ally, chum (*colloq.*), friend, backer, supporter, abettor, upholder, advocate, champion.

rival, *v.*—*Syn.* oppose, compete, contest, dispute, strive, emulate, envy, clash, collide, conflict, counteract, resist, confront, oppugn, antagonize, thwart, countermine, contend, encounter, s t r u g g l e, combat, wrestle, fight. *Ant.* aid, assist, help, uphold, support, strengthen, champion, coöperate, combine, participate, side with, unite with, join hands with, sustain, succor, second, abet, back, stand by, favor, encourage, patronize, defend.

road—*Syn.* route, path, way, highway, course, street, avenue, roadway, viaduct, right of way, track, thoroughfare, pathway, parkway, boulevard, byroad, boreen [*Ir.*], crossroad, byway, speedway, railroad, anchorage, roadstead, towpath, tramway, tramroad, trolley track.

roam—*Syn.* ramble, range, stroll, rove, wander, stray, prowl, saunter, patrol, walk, traverse, perambulate, peregrinate, scour, gad about, straggle, shuffle along, hike (*colloq.*). Ant. rest, cease, stop, stay, remain, stand, stand still, stand fast, repose, tarry, halt, pause, lie to, anchor, draw up, settle, settle down, put on the brakes (*colloq.*), stop short.

rob, *v.*—*Syn.* steal, purloin, rifle,

burglarize, thieve, pilfer, plunder, loot, despoil.

robber—*Syn.* thief, rogue, plunderer, burglar, highwayman, stick-up man (*slang*), bail-up man (*Aus. slang*), marauder, raider, pirate, footpad, pillager, buccaneer, brigand, bandit, freebooter, depredator, despoiler, forager, thug, knight of the road, desperado, gangster, bunco steerer (*slang*), thimblerigger, cutpurse, pickpurse, dip (*slang*), crook (*slang*), pickpocket, rustler, cattle thief, bushranger [*Aus.*], blackleg (*colloq.*), yegg (*slang*), forger, swindler, diddler (*slang*), welsher (*slang*), housebreaker, bank robber, sharper, card-sharper, cracksman (*slang*).

robust—*Syn.* strong, lusty, vigorous, sinewy, stout, sturdy, stalwart, ablebodied, muscular, virile, athletic, brawny, stalwart, strapping, powerful, manly, hardy, husky (*colloq.*). *Ant.* weak, feeble, debilitated, puny, frail, shaky, infirm, faint, fragile, nervous, languid, wasted, wishy-washy (*colloq.*), anæmic, reduced, effeminate, unmanly, flaccid, flabby, soft.

romantic, *adj.*—*Syn.* visionary, sentimental, mushy, picturesque, fanciful, heroic, idealistic, fictional, poetic, ideal, dreamy, imaginary.

romp, *v.*—*Syn.* gambol, play, frolic, sport, caper, frisk.

rookie, *n.*—*Syn.* beginner, tyro, recruit, novice, neophyte, apprentice.

root, *v.*—*Syn.* cheer, applaud, encourage, acclaim, plug.

roster, *n.*—*Syn.* list, roll, table, inventory, catalogue, register, directory.

rot, *v.*—*Syn.* decay, spoil, crumble, decompose, waste, disintegrate, degenerate, molder, putrefy.

rotate, *v.*—*Syn.* spin, revolve, turn, gyrate, circulate, swirl, eddy, whirl, circle, wheel.

rough, *adj.*—*Syn.* uneven, coarse, rank, hard, harsh, rugged, gross, unrefined, crude, austere, blunt, impolite, unpolished, indecent.

round, *adj.*—*Syn.* globular, circular, spherical, rotund, orbicular.

rouse, *v.*—*Syn.* animate, awaken, provoke, arouse, inflame, stir, raise, excite, stimulate.

rout—*Syn.* overcome, overthrow, scatter, hunt, beat, defeat, conquer, discomfit, surmount, overpower, overmaster, overmatch, beat, lick (*colloq.*), drub, lick to a frazzle (*colloq.*), outmanoeuvre or outmaneuver, swamp, vanquish, drive off, put to flight, repulse, subjugate, subdue. *Ant.* fail, lose, miss, succumb, fall a prey to, suffer defeat, run, run away, falter, flounder, turn tail (*colloq.*), go back, recede, regrade, shrink from, withdraw, wheel, countermarch, retire, turn back upon, regress, retreat, retrace, back out (*colloq.*), back down (*colloq.*).

route—*Syn.* road, course, passing, way, direction, journey, path, track, beat, tack, march, order of march, line of march, guidance, trend. *Ant.* deviation, diversion, divergence, drift, detour, digression, divagation, disorientation, deflection, twist, meandering, rambling, loss of direction, loss of way.

royal—*Syn.* kingly, princely, princelike, majestic, magnificent, splendid, regal, august, impressive, monarchical, noble, superb, magnanimous, dignified, commanding, regnant, dominant, ruling, paramount, authoritative, absolute, imperious, sovereign, imperial, aristocratic, overruling, lordly, supreme. *Ant.* low, mean, poor, contemptible, humble, plebeian, vulgar, coarse, indecorous, squalid, tawdry, rude, frippery, gimcrack, tinsel, boorish, clownish, outlandish, rustic, unbecoming, common, proletarian, scrubby, beggarly, loutish, upstart, rough, rowdy, undignified, ignoble, sorry, despicable, lousy, servile, slavish, vile.

rude—*Syn.* rough, uneven, shapeless, rugged, uncouth, inelegant, unfashionable, coarse, rustic, ignorant, illiterate, vulgar, clownish, currish, churlish, unskilful, uncivilized, savage, brutal, barbarous, raw, untaught, turbulent, boisterous, saucy, insolent, impudent, impertinent, surly, sullen, brutal, harsh, fierce, inclement, tumultuous, bullying, impetuous, severe, swashbuckling, domineering, profane, gruff, unpolished, flippant, violent, scoffing, disrespectful, insulting, scurrile, scurrilous, scornful, discourteous, unenlightened, uneducated, boorish, ill-bred, ill-mannered, impolite, foulmouthed, bearish, bad-tempered, crabbed, crusty, acrimonious, ungracious, repulsive. *Ant.* polite, polished, refined, genteel, gentlemanly, ladylike, well-bred, cultured, cultivated, courteous, urbane, complaisant, complacent, bland, suave, softspoken, civil, cordial, gracious, amiable, civilized, honeytongued, oily-tongued, complimentary, winning, ingratiating, graceful, pleasing, pleasant, mild, gentle, kindly, modest, retiring, gallant, chivalrous, elegant, nice, captivating, charming, fascinating, alluring, respectful, decorous, becoming, deferential, courtly, unselfish, dignified, benign, considerate, good-natured, sympathetic, attractive, noble, stately, highminded, friendly, well-disposed, amicable, sociable, Chesterfieldian, affable, tactful, mannerly, soft-spoken, congenial, winsome, engaging, seductive, magnetic.

rueful, *adj.*—*Syn.* melancholy, lugubrious, doleful, sorrowful, depressed, sad, pitiful, plaintive, mournful, despairing, dismal.

ruffian, *n.*—*Syn.* thug, roughneck, desperado, gangster, rowdy, bully, tough, rascal, hoodlum, mugger.

rugged, *adj.*—*Syn.* harsh, robust, hard, rough, arduous, craggy, irregular, hardy, difficult, brawny, husky.

rule—*Syn.* government, sway, control, regulation, direction, order, method, canon, precept, guide, maxim, system, formula, standard, test, authority, power, command, jurisdiction, sovereignty, prerogative, preponderance, prestige, mastery, dominion, supremacy, influence. *Ant.* misrule, misgovernment, violence, revolt, revolution, rebellion, insubordination, licentiousness, mob-rule, lynch law, ochlocracy, confusion, insurrection, uprising, strife, war, conflict, pillage, plunder, disorder, riot, rapine, slaughter, anarchy, chaos.

ruminate, *v.*—*Syn.* deliberate, muse, cogitate, meditate, think, ponder, reflect, weigh, chew, brood.

rumor—*Syn.* report, story, tale, news, gossip, tattle, tittle-tattle, talk, hearsay, bruit, whisper, canard, suggestion, supposition, tidings, intelligence, dispatch, cable, cablegram, wire, radiogram, telegram, marconigram, broadcast, radiocast, newscast. *Ant.* silence, aphony, muteness, lull, rest, hush, stillness, suppression, secret, mystery, concealment, reticence, reserve, reservation, latency, mystification, taciturnity, secrecy, mysticism, evasion, secretiveness, privacy.

ruse, *n.*—*Syn.* artifice, wile, trick, stratagem, shift, device, subterfuge, deception, expedient.

rustic—*Syn.* countrified, bucolic, pastoral, agricultural, rural, sylvan, rude, clownish, outlandish, boorish, hoydenish or hoidenish, uncouth, unadorned, unpolished, verdant, awkward, artless, coarse, country, inelegant, untaught, plain, unsophisticated, rough, honest, simple. *Ant.* accomplished, cultured, refined, elegant, urban, urbane, well-bred, polished, polite, charming, attractive, æsthetic, artistic, grand, magnificent, fashionable, stylish, gentlemanly, suave, unctuous, courteous, sophisticated, swell (*slang*), swanky (*slang*), aristocratic, dignified, lordly.

ruthless—*Syn.* savage, brutal, cruel, tyrannical, merciless, remorseless, relentless, unrelenting, barbarous, inhuman, pitiless, revengeful, harsh, unkind, unfriendly, tigerish, ferine, feral, ferocious, truculent, hard-hearted, cold-blooded, surly, unpitying, unmerciful, grim, inexorable, vengeful, vindictive, rancorous, rigorous, implacable, unforgiving, malevolent. *Ant.* kind, forgiving, amiable, kindhearted, soft, tender, pitiful, placable, conciliatory, compassionate, sympathetic, lenient, tender-hearted, merciful, indulgent, cordial, benevolent, humane, charitable, philanthropic, benign, benignant, good-humored, gracious, affectionate, loving, appreciative, obliging, accommodating, friendly, well-disposed, considerate, unselfish, beneficent, bountiful, good.

S

sack, *v.*—*Syn.* pillage, despoil, ravage, loot, devastate, plunder, strip.

sacrament—*Syn.* Lord's Supper, communion, eucharist, ordinance, rite, ceremony, observance, service, solemnity, formulary, function, ministration, liturgy, the Mass, incantation, ceremonial, act of divine worship.

sacred—*Syn.* holy, hallow, hallowed, consecrated, sanctified, dedicated, divine, religious, reverend, devoted, pious, pure, undefiled, sacrosanct, heavenly, celestial. *Ant.* unholy, desecrated, defiled, impure, impious, profane, irreverent, sacrilegious, blasphemous, unsanctified, unhallowed, reprobate, sinful, perverted.

sacrifice, *n.*—*Syn.* offering, oblation, hecatomb, libation, abnegation, self-denial, surrender, loss.

sacrilegious, *adj.*—*Syn.* impious, profaning, blasphemous, profane, polluting, desecrating.

sad, *adj.*—*Syn.* unhappy, sorrowful, blue, dejected, despondent, depressed, gloomy, disconsolate, dismal, melancholy, heavy, cheerless.

safety, *n.*—*Syn.* security, preservation, asylum, refuge, surety, escape, custody. *Ant.* danger, peril, risk, hazard, jeopardy.

sagacious—*Syn.* keen, keen-witted, keen-sighted, clear-sighted, sharp-witted, quick, quick-scented, discerning, perspicacious, intelligent, apt, judicious, shrewd, sensible, rational, able, sage, wise, acute, subtle, penetrating, discriminating, nimble-witted, farsighted, cunning, ready, brainy, long-headed, cute (*colloq.*), prudent, tactful, circumspect, cautious, discreet, discerning, careful. *Ant.* foolish, silly, shortsighted, vacuous, stupid, thoughtless, careless, simple, fatuous, dull, doltish, blockish, bovine, asinine, inapprehensive, irrational, inept, incapable, undiscerning, shallow, stolid, senseless, stultified, slow, slow-witted, heavy, flat, unimaginative, driveling, sap-headed (*colloq.*), feebleminded, addled, thick-skulled, thick-headed, sottish, obtuse, absurd, ignorant, unintelligent.

sage, *n.*—*Syn.* savant, intellectual, pundit, philosopher.

salary, *n.*—*Syn.* remuneration, wages, payment, stipend, compensation, income, pay, emolument, hire, fee.

sale—*Syn.* change, exchange, barter, trade, bargain, deal, disposal, auction, vendue, traffic, commerce, enterprise, speculation, roup [*Sc.*], auction, transaction, business, jobbing, negotiation. *Ant.* purchase, emption, preëmption, buying, shopping, marketing, dealing, trading, investment, acquisition, expenditure, procurement, procuration, care, management, acquirement.

salient, *adj.*—*Syn.* outstanding, conspicuous, impressive, prominent, signal, notable, noticeable, striking, significant.

salutary—*Syn.* wholesome, healthful, salubrious, beneficial, advantageous, useful, good, profitable, tonic, remedial, healthy, bracing, prophylactic, invigorating, hygienic, Hygeian, sanitary, nutritious. *Ant.* deleterious, harmful, noxious, poisonous, insalubrious, detrimental, innutritious, unhealthy, unwholesome, morbific, septic, pestilent, pestilential, bad, virulent, toxic, toxiferous, deadly, contagious, infectious, catching, zymotic, epidemic, endemic, pandemic.

salvation—*Syn.* preservation, deliverance, extrication, ransom, reprieve, redemption, respite, liberation, acquitance, emancipation, release, absolution, exemption, sanctification, sanctity, regeneration, justification. *Ant.* punishment, penalty, condemnation, damnation, execration, anathema, curse, *maranatha* [*Aram.*], excommunication, judgment, proscription, conviction, malediction, malison, doom, imprecation, denunciation.

sample, *n.*—*Syn.* specimen, exemplar, prototype, example, model, illustration, case, instance.

sanction, *n.*—*Syn.* confirmation, approval, commendation, authority, ratification, permission, permit, warrant, authorization, liberty, indulgence, *carte blanche* [*Fr.*], privilege, license, approbation, advocacy, appreciation, encouragement. *Ant.* disapproval, disapprobation, disparagement, denunciation, stricture, objection, blame, censure, obloquy, prohibition, injunction, interdict, interdiction, inhibition, restraint, hindrance, embargo, exclusion.

sanction, *v.*—*Syn.* confirm, encourage, support, sustain, ratify, authorize, countenance, indorse, approve, favor, commend, praise, recommend, promote, admire, eulogize, compliment,

acclaim, boost (*colloq.*), appreciate, applaud, proclaim. *Ant.* denounce, disparage, disapprove, frown upon, disfavor, object to, censure, blame, reproach, stigmatize, execrate, prohibit, inhibit, veto, disallow, interdict, forbid, exclude, shut out, ban, prevent, hinder.

sane—*Syn.* rational, normal, lucid, sensible, wholesome, rightminded, sound-minded, sober, steady, reasonable, self-possessed, sound. *Ant.* insane, irrational, demented, idiotic, loony (*slang*), wandering, delirious, mad, deranged, unsound, odd, eccentric, lunatic, crazy, crackbrained, scatterbrained, moonstruck, unhinged, cracked (*colloq.*), unsettled, frenetic, maniacal, distraught, Corybantic.

sanguine—*Syn.* hopeful, expectant, buoyant, optimistic, enthusiastic, trustful, trusting, confident, elated, reassured, emboldened, inspirited, expecting, keyed up (*colloq.*), on tiptoe (*colloq.*), looking forward, calculating, anticipative, prognostic. *Ant.* despairing, downcast, hopeless, despondent, pessimistic, dejected, depressed, heavy, melancholy, cheerless, somber, lugubrious, downhearted, heavyhearted, sad, pensive, morose, chapfallen, discouraged, hypped (*colloq.*), crestfallen, cut up (*colloq.*), disconsolate, low-spirited, disheartened.

sap, *v.*—*Syn.* undermine, debilitate, weaken, tunnel, drain, enfeeble, exhaust, impoverish.

sapient, *adj.*—*Syn.* wise, sagacious, acute, sage, prudent, knowing, judicious, discerning, sane, learned.

sarcasm—*Syn.* satire, irony, banter, derision, jeer, contempt, scoffing, flouting, superciliousness, ridicule, jibe, sniggering, burlesque, disparagement, criticism, scurrility, cynicism, invective, censure, lampooning, aspersion, sneering, mockery. *Ant.* flattery, soft soap (*slang*), fawning, cajolery, flunkeyism, toadyism, sycophancy, unctuousness, flummery (*colloq.*), wheedling, soft sawder (*slang*), obsequiousness, respect, admiration, commendation, appreciation, approval, encomium, eulogy, eulogium.

sarcastic—*Syn.* scornful, mocking, ironical, satirical, taunting, severe, derisive, sardonic, bitter, saucy, hostile, sneering, snickering, quizzical, arrogant, Rabelaisian, Hudibrastic, disrespectful, scurrile, scurrilous, jollying (*colloq.*), chaffing, twitting, guying (*colloq.*), captious, sharp, acrimonious, pert, saucy, brusque, caustic, biting, bitter harsh, austere, contumelious, grim. *Ant.* pleasant, pleasing, polite, courteous, civil, agreeable, honey-tongued, gentlemanly, complaisant, chivalric, bland, suave, well-mannered, amiable, deferential, respectful, decorous, condescending, complimentary, mannerly, urbane, ingratiating, obsequious, unctuous, flattering, soft-spoken, conciliatory, winning, affable, gracious, cordial.

sardonic, *adj.*—*Syn.* scornful, ridiculing, derisive, sarcastic, mocking, bitter, ironic.

satanic—*Syn.* malicious, vicious, devilish, hellish, bad, vile, infernal, wicked, slanderous, evil, sinful, blasphemous, impious, irreverent, profane, sacrilegious, reprobate, unhallowed, abandoned, diabolical, demoniacal, hellborn, iniquitous, dissolute, profligate, immoral, impure, corrupt, infamous, fiendish, fiendlike, Mephistophelian, Tartarean. *Ant.* good, virtuous, holy, sacred, blessed, saintly, saintlike, angelic, seraphic, pious, religious, devout, pure, heavenlyminded, prayerful, sanctified, consecrated, reverent, just, right, righteous, upright, innocent, praiseworthy, exemplary, pure, noble, sterling, right-minded, charitable, benevolent, benignant, moral, godly, godlike.

sate, *v.*—*Syn.* satiate, satisfy, cloy,

gorge, surfeit, glut.

satellite, *n.*—*Syn.* attendant, adherent, subordinate, follower, moon, sputnik, rocket.

satire, *n.*—*Syn.* ridicule, mockery, lampoon, sarcasm, irony, burlesque, derision, humor.

satisfy—*Syn.* pay, repay, settle, disburse, bestow, lend, give, confer, bequeath, defray, liquidate, foot the bill (*colloq.*), accommodate, befriend, redeem, reimburse, comfort, relieve, smooth, remedy, cure, allay, cheer, elate, exhilarate, rejoice, delight, brighten up, amuse, tickle, flatter, make merry, make cheerful, gladden, please, content, gratify, indulge, humor, conciliate, propitiate, enrapture, enthral, enliven, animate, captivate, fascinate, fill, sate, surfeit, gorge, glut, cloy, satiate. *Ant.* deny, stint, deprive, starve, discourage, displease, dissatisfy, delude, wrong, persecute, annoy, worry, vex, disgust, nauseate, repel, revolt, sicken, grieve, aggrieve, trouble, chafe, gall, anger, enrage, taunt, mock, deprecate, depreciate, harass, pain, fret, sadden, disconcert, disappoint, plague, afflict, distress, torment, provoke, taunt, mock, deride, scorn, restrain, restrict, refuse, check, tantalize, rile (*colloq.*), ridicule, jeer, sneer at, irritate, thwart, perplex, bother, discompose, sadden, injure, molest, ill-treat, maltreat, appal, shock, frighten, scare, doubt, discredit, disbelieve, weary, tire, betray, defraud, cheat, swindle.

saturate, *v.*—*Syn.* permeate, drench, impregnate, soak, imbue, fill.

saturnine, *adj.*—*Syn.* gloomy, morose, leaden, dour, glum, sullen, somber, crabbed. *Ant.* cheerful, genial, mercurial, gay.

saucy—*Syn.* impudent, impertinent, insolent, rude, flippant, forward, toplofty (*colloq.*), swaggering, presumptuous, jingoistic (*slang*), nervy (*slang*), brazen, domineering, self-assertive, disdainful, arrogant, swanky (*slang*), cheeky (*slang*), bullying, haughty, supercilious, overbearing, dictatorial, imperious, high-hat (*slang*), high-handed, assuming, magisterial, bumptious, discourteous, contumelious, sarcastic. *Ant.* backward, modest, retiring, bashful, meek, humble, servile, obsequious, cringing, craven, sycophantic, parasitic, toadeating (*slang*), unctuous, oily, oily-tongued, doughfaced (*slang*), sucking (*slang*), truckling, groveling, abject, mealy-mouthed (*colloq.*), fawning, toadying, timorous, timid, cowardly, mean-spirited, base, lily-livered (*colloq.*), afraid, diffident, daunted, abashed, panic-stricken, terrified, discouraged, faint-hearted.

savage—*Syn.* wild, barbarous, cruel, inhuman, fierce, ferocious, merciless, unmerciful, pitiless, brutal, brutish, murderous, terrible, rude, riotous, untamed, uncultivated, untaught, uncivilized, unpolished, heathenish, furious, violent, ravening, frenzied, infuriate, frantic, crazy, ungovernable, incontrollable, uncontrollable. *Ant.* meek, mild, gentle, genteel, soft, lenitive, tranquil, peaceful, moderate, modest, backward, calm, cool, sober, temperate, quiet, unobtrusive, yielding, tame, subdued, civil, courteous, easygoing, indulgent, complaisant, clement, merciful, patient, tolerant, forbearing, placid, serene, dispassionate, resigned, suave, urbane, amiable, polished, polite, kind, kindly, compassionate.

savory—*Syn.* palatable, pleasing, appetizing, piquant, pungent, spicy, flavorous, rich, tasty, tempting, delectable, gustful, luscious, dainty, toothsome, nectareous, exquisite, ambrosial, good. *Ant.* unsavory, tasteless, insipid, flat, vapid, unpalatable, bitter, acrid, offensive, sickening, nauseating, nasty, repulsive, ill-flavored, loathsome, nauseous, wishy-washy (*colloq.*).

savvy, n.—*Syn.* know-how, savoir-faire, understanding, sophistication, aplomb, ease, dexterity.

saying, n.—*Syn.* byword, maxim, quotation, proverb, aphorism, adage, epigram, saw, apothegm, dictum.

scan, v.—*Syn.* scrutinize inspect, examine, study, observe, survey, contemplate.

scandal—*Syn.* shame, disgrace, infamy, turpitude, crime, discredit, slander, disrepute, detraction, obloquy, calumny, defamation, opprobrium, reproach, censure, aspersion, scurrility, backbiting, evildoing, muckraking, gossip, eavesdropping, rumor, hearsay, bad news. *Ant.* praise, adulation, flattery, admiration, laudation, obsequiousness, flunkeyism, sycophancy, fawning, cajolery, truckling, pandering, currying favor, tuft-hunting, toadyism, unctuousness, oiliness—blarney, buncombe, soft soap, soft sawder, flummery, butter, buttering the parsnips, sprinkling the rose water —all *colloq.*

scandalize—*Syn.* calumniate, detract, defame, traduce, backbite, vilify, revile, malign, slander, offend, shock, disgust, asperse, libel, disparage, run down, lampoon, hold up to scorn, severely criticize, decry, dishonor, belittle, sneer at, blackball, blacken, knock (*U.S. colloq.*), blackguard, deprecate, condemn, depreciate, speak ill of. *Ant.* praise, laud, applaud, uphold, defend, support, aid, assist, speak well of, flatter, curry favor with, pander to, commend, recommend, honor, exalt, boost (*colloq.*), blarney (*colloq.*), butter (*colloq.*), bepraise, beslaver, fawn upon.

scanty—*Syn.* scarce, few, pinched, meager or meagre, little, small, bare, ragged, insufficient, slender, narrow, thin, scrimp, scrimpy, starved, emaciated, stinted, underfed, spare, slim, delicate, attenuated, scrawny, shriveled, skeletal, dwarfed, puny, pygmy, runty (*U.S. colloq.*), tiny, wee [*Sc.*], elfin, sparse, diminutive. *Ant.* big, large, grand, great, many, much, rich, luxuriant, fine, imposing, ample, sufficient, plenty, plentiful, plenteous, unstinted, abundant, abounding, chock-full, loaded, liberal, well-provided, broad, wide, extended, squat, thick, bulky, unwieldy, huge, whopping (*colloq.*), thumping (*colloq.*), massive, monstrous, fat, plump, profuse, bulky, burly, strapping (*colloq.*).

scare, v.—*Syn.* frighten, intimidate, daunt, alarm, dismay, startle, terrify, surprise, affright, cow.

scathing, *adj.*—*Syn.* mordant, caustic, cutting, scorching, ferocious, fierce, trenchant, searing, savage, blasting.

scatter—*Syn.* spread, strew, disseminate, sow, disperse, dispel, derange, dissipate, diverge, diffuse, disband, shed, distribute, intersperse, separate. *Ant.* collect, gather, assemble, unite, meet, converge, center, concur, pack, crowd, rally, throng, rush, press, group, clump, cluster, foregather, convene.

scheme, v.—*Syn.* plot, contrive, plan, intend, project, design, aim, intrigue, aspire.

schism, n.—*Syn.* split, sectarianism, division, dissension, disunion, faction, separation, breach.

scholar—*Syn.* disciple, learner, pupil, savant, sage, student, alumnus, alumna, exhibitioner, wrangler [*Eng.*], graduate, postgraduate, professor, teacher, pedagogue, instructor, dominie, guide, mentor, tutor, philosopher, *savant* [*Fr.*], lexicographer, *litterateur* [*Fr.*], philomath. *Ant.* ignoramus, blockhead, dunce, dolt, fool, idiot, idler, illiterate person, pretender, stupid fellow, clown, churl, buffoon, merry-andrew, quack, charlatan, impostor, deceiver.

school, v.—*Syn.* train, teach, educate, instruct, coach, prepare, tutor, discipline, indoctrinate, govern.

science—*Syn.* art, knowledge, skill, craftsmanship, comprehension, apprehension, cognition, enlightenment, erudition, lore, scholarship. *Ant.* ignorance, nescience, illiteracy, incomprehension, darkness, blindness, shallowness, sciolism, charlatanism, superficality.

scintillate, v.—*Syn.* sparkle, flash, gleam, coruscate, glint, twinkle, shimmer.

scoff, v.—*Syn.* jeer, sneer, mock, fleer, flout, scout, gibe, taunt, deride.

scold, v.—*Syn.* berate reprove, chide, censure, upbraid, tonguelash, rebuke, reprimand.

scope, n.—*Syn.* latitude, space, compass, gamut, field, sphere, room, orbit, purview, liberty, range, radius, domain.

scorn, v.—*Syn.* disdain, reject, slight, despise, spurn, flout, contemn, gibe.

scrap, n.—*Syn.* brawl, melee, fracas, tussle, rumpus, row, ruckus, hassle.

scrape, n.—*Syn.* predicament, pickle, difficulty, quandary, fix, plight, dilemma.

scrawny, *adj.*—*Syn.* lean, skinny, gaunt, rawboned, lanky. *Ant.* brawny, muscular, stout, fleshy.

screen, v.—*Syn.* winnow, sift, sort, examine, analyze, separate, inspect.

scruple, v.—*Syn.* doubt, balk, boggle, protest, demur, stick, vacillate, hesitate, falter.

scrupulous, *adj.*—*Syn.* punctilious, cautious, meticulous, conscientious, exact, precise, rigorous, fastidious, finical. *Ant.* remiss, negligent, careless.

scrutiny, n.—*Syn.* inspection, survey, examination, sifting, research, probe, inquiry, observation, investigation.

scurrilous, *adj.*—*Syn.* abusive, coarse, opprobrious, vituperative, offensive, insulting, vulgar, low, indecent, foul.

second, *n.—Syn.* moment, instant, trice, jiffy, flash, tick, twinkling, shake, sec, mo.

secondary, *adj.—Syn.* subordinate, accessory, subsidiary, tributary, minor, collateral, incidental, auxiliary, inferior.

secret—*Syn.* concealed, hidden, secluded, private, latent, underhand, clandestine, occult, mystic, unexplained, covert, unknown, ambiguous, cabalistic, veiled, symbolic, esoteric, cryptic. *Ant.* open, unconcealed, apparent, evident, obvious, plain, conspicuous, indubitable, unmistakable, undisguised, express, explicit, self-evident, manifest, transparent, clear, defined.

secrete, *v.—Syn.* hide, conceal, screen, disguise, mask.

section, *n.—Syn.* part, sector, fraction, segment, fragment, portion, region, division, field, piece, parcel.

security—*Syn.* pledge, surety, gage, bail, safety, protection, watch, watchfulness, shelter, guaranty, guarantee, certainty, promise, warranty, contract, compact, bond, covenant, pact, agreement, understanding, stipulation. *Ant.* uncertainty, doubt, perplexity, difficulty, contingency, fallibility, hesitation, suspense, possibility, timidity, vacillation, unreliability, untrustworthiness, unlikelihood, improbability, precariousness, incredibility.

sedate, *adj.—Syn.* sober, serious, solemn, serene, staid, proper, tranquil, calm, dignified, grave, decorous. *Ant.* flighty, mercurial, frivolous, lively.

seditious, *adj.—Syn.* insubordinate, rebellious, perfidious, mutinous, insurgent, faithless, treacherous, disloyal.

seduce—*Syn.* decoy, allure, inveigle, entice, abduct, attract, tempt, bait, bribe, lure, induce, excite, stimulate, inspirit, persuade, wheedle, coax, vamp (*slang*), attract, charm, defile, deprave, violate, prostitute, debauch, deflower. *Ant.* protect,

guide, preserve, warn, advise, dishearten, dissuade, expostulate, discourage, admonish, keep back, remonstrate, restrain, dispirit, deter, turn aside, hold back, safeguard, care for, watch over, guard.

sedulous—*Syn.* attentive, assiduous, unremitting, active, desirous, unwearied, industrious, diligent, busy, hustling, keen, eager, brisk, vivacious, stirring, painstaking, sleepless, avid, anxious, persevering, alert, spry, ardent. *Ant.* dull, careless, insouciant, indifferent, unconcerned, lethargic, somnolent, sleepy, weary, tired, exhausted, drowsy, dormant, comatose, lazy, indolent, idle, slothful, languid, supine, sluggish, remiss, otiose, shiftless, listless, lackadaisical, laggard.

seeming, *adj.—Syn.* apparent, ostensible, evident, specious, manifest.

seize—*Syn.* grasp, take, catch, apprehend, lay hold of, comprehend, appropriate, grip, clasp, clutch, swipe (*slang*), abstract, carry off, bear away, commandeer, grab, snatch, kidnap, abduct, pounce upon, steal, loot, pillage, plunder, sack, hold up (*U.S. slang*), bail up (*Aus. slang*), purloin, crib (*colloq.*), rifle, ransack, stick up (*U.S. slang*), filibuster, rustle, strip, maraud, fleece, defraud. *Ant.* restore, return, compensate, recompense, reward, repair, disgorge, give up, remit, repay, indemnify, redress, remunerate, satisfy, acknowledge, atone, make amends, reimburse, pass by, let alone, free, liberate, let slip, acquit, forgive, avoid, shun, keep off, refrain, spare, turn away, leave, relinquish, quit, desist, back down (*colloq.*), keep hands off.

select, *v.—Syn.* choose, prefer, pick, elect, opt, specify, designate.

semblance, *n.—Syn.* appearance, form, likeness, look, aspect, shape, figure.

send—*Syn.* transmit, despatch, forward, delegate, depute, project, propel, fling, hurl, emit, discharge, sling, throw, impel, drive, dart, cast, transfer, transport, consign, carry, convey, deliver, hand over, tote (*U.S. colloq.*). *Ant.* give, get, receive, hold, keep, retain, clutch, grasp, gripe, grip, cling to, withhold, secure, maintain, hide, conceal, put away.

senile, *adj.*—*Syn.* doddering, ancient, aged, superannuated, decrepit, infirm.

sensation—*Syn.* sense, feeling, emotion, perception, mental apprehension, impression, sensibility, susceptibility, sensitiveness, consciousness, wonder, awe, amazement, surprise, astonishment, admiration, sympathy, stupefaction, bewilderment, fear, terror, ecstasy, transport, joy. *Ant.* apathy, insensibility, stupor, stupidity, stupefaction, torpor, inertia, coma, lethargy, paralysis, narcosis, hypnosis, anæsthesia, sleep, *Dämmerschlaf* [*Ger.*], inactivity, fainting, asphyxia, unconsciousness, swoon, syncope, hebetude, impassiveness, trance, torpidity, stoicism.

sense—*Syn.* understanding, reason, mind, instinct, intellect, intelligence, spirit, soul, thought, brains, consciousness, perception, discernment, feeling, meaning, purport, sensibility, view, opinion, significance, import, susceptibility, judgment, appreciation, knowledge, insight, reasonableness, attainment, prescience, foresight, enlightenment, erudition, learning, sagacity, discretion, comprehension, capacity, gumption (*colloq.*), grasp, discrimination, penetration, perspicacity, acumen, *nous* [*Gr.*], genius, talent. *Ant.* imbecility, incapacity, vacuity, simplicity, idiocy, idiotism, folly, foolishness, fatuity, absurdity, silliness, senselessness, nonsense, irrationality, stupidity, unmeaningness, babble, babbling, bosh, balderdash, hocus-pocus, palaver, pat-

ter (*colloq.*), rigmarole, jargon, gibberish, flapdoodle (*colloq.*), rant, flummery (*colloq.*), rodomontade, piffle (*colloq.*), buncombe, highfalutin or hifalutin (*slang*), bombast, bluster, fanfaronade, stuff (*colloq.*), drivel, dementia, fatuousness, dotage, anility, jobbernowlism (*Eng. colloq.*).

sensible—*Syn.* wise, intelligent, sagacious, perspicacious, thoughtful, sharp, acute, penetrating, rational, reasonable, subtle, bright (*colloq.*), quick (*colloq.*), shrewd, sane, cool, hard-headed, longheaded, farsighted, sage, sapient, judicious, prudent, soundminded, astute, clear-headed, keen, brainy (*colloq.*), quick-witted, discerning, discriminative, cunning, cautious, calculating, level-headed, politic, canny [*Sc.*], cute (*colloq.*). *Ant.* foolish, shallow, simple, idiotic, maniacal, demented, imbecile, feeble-minded, deranged, *non compos mentis* [*L.*], stupid, stolid, fatuous, irrational, senile, doting, screwy (*slang*), childish, dippy (*slang*), driveling, crazy, insane, mad, lunatic, loony (*slang*), daft, daffy (*colloq*), unhinged, unsettled, distraught, frenzied, moonstruck, scatter-brained, crack-brained, frenetic, cracked (*colloq.*), touched, addle-brained, muddy (*colloq.*), thick-skulled, asinine, inept, senseless, nonsensical, maudlin, silly.

sensible—*Syn.* material, physical, corporeal, corporal, tangible, ponderable, substantial, embodied, fleshly, bodily, somatic, solid, palpable. *Ant.* immaterial, airy, ethereal, spiritual, disembodied, incorporeal, incorporal, imponderable, intangible, decarnated, psychic, psychical, subjective.

sensitive, *adj.*—*Syn.* predisposed, susceptible, perceptive, subject, prone, impressionable, liable, tender.

sensual—*Syn.* voluptuous, luxurious, pleasure-loving, carnal, fleshly, lewd, unspiritual, hedonic, apolaustic, self-loving, self-indulgent, epicurean, intemperate, gluttonous, Sybaritical, rakish, debauched, orgiastic, Corybantic, sensuous, piggish (*colloq.*), hoggish (*colloq.*), bestial. *Ant.* ascetic, self-denying, chaste, temperate, self-sacrificing, unselfish, chastened, rigorous, moderate, abstemious, abstinent, disinterested, stoical, self-controlled, sparing, frugal, economical, saving, humble, penitent, devotional, contrite, repentant, remorseful.

sententious, *adj.*—*Syn.* meaningful, succinct, pithy, didactic, laconic, pregnant, terse, curt, significant, concise.

sentimental, *adj.*—*Syn.* romantic, emotional, overemotional, passionate, mushy, tender.

separate, *adj.*—*Syn.* apart, disunited, disjoined, disjointed, divergent, diverging, radial, unconnected, disarranged, individual, lone, alone, parted, distant. *Ant.* joined, united, tied, buckled, connected, bound, attached, hooked, spliced, clinched, welded, fused, coupled, linked, mortised, dovetailed, grafted, twined, entwined, interlaced, commingled, mixed, tangled, entangled, associated, intermingled.

separate, *v.*—*Syn.* divide, disjoin, disunite, sever, sunder, dissolve, disengage, part, detach, disconnect, undo, unbind, unbuckle, unlock, unchain, disentangle, unravel, snap, wrench, rupture, break, disintegrate, dismember, dislocate, disperse, dissect, scatter, isolate. *Ant.* combine, collect, gather, assemble, lump, lump together, put together, yoke, bracket, fasten, bind, hitch, attach, mingle, mix, alloy, commingle, intermingle, blend, compound, fuse, interfuse, twine, intertwine, weld, mortise, dovetail.

sequel, *n.*—*Syn.* consequence, upshot, aftermath, continuation, result, issue, outcome, event, effect.

serene, *adj.*—*Syn.* clear, pellucid, limpid, unruffled, translucent, undisturbed, undimmed, tranquil, composed, imperturbable, dispassionate, calm, cool, coolheaded, sedate, level-headed, content, satisfied, patient, reconciled, easy-going, placid, comfortable, cheerful. *Ant.* confused, disturbed, ruffled, violent, foaming, boiling, effervescing, flaming, furious, passionate, excited, tumultuous, vehement, hot-headed, irascible, impassioned, fiery, rampant, clamorous, tempestuous, uproarious, boisterous, discontented, dissatisfied, glum, sullen, sulky, opaque, cloudy, dim, adiaphanous, obfuscated, smoky, nubilous, murky.

serious, *adj.*—*Syn.* solemn, grave, thoughtful, earnest, sober, profound, austere, deep, weighty, critical, important, momentous.

settle—*Syn.* regulate, adjust, straighten, arrange, decide, determine, conclude, dispose, array, group, put in order, shape, classify, allocate, distribute, rule, pass upon, judicate, adjudicate, arbitrate, establish, prove, confirm, place, locate, install, station, lodge, quarter, domesticate, colonize, sink, drop, fall, fall to bottom, coalesce. *Ant.* derange, discompose, disturb, perturb, disorganize, disarrange, displace, unsettle, shuffle, jumble, confuse, muddle, disorder, involve, entangle, ravel, shift, misjudge, distort, twist, move, remove, depart, go away, forsake, quit, leave, stir up, mix, mingle, intermingle.

sever, *v.*—*Syn.* divide, split, dissolve, separate, rend, disunite, part, divorce, sunder, detach, disconnect, cleave.

several—*Syn.* diverse, sundry, various, plural, different, distinct, some, restricted, few, certain, divers. *Ant.* many, numerous, multiple, manifold, teeming, populous, crowded, profuse, multiplied.

severe—*Syn.* harsh, cruel, tyrannical, overbearing, rigid, strict, stringent, rigorous, relentless, unyielding, stiff, unmitigated, unrelenting, austere, hard, inflexible, uncompromising, exacting, autocratic, domineering, despotic, arrogant, inexorable, oppressive, grinding, obdurate. *Ant.* lenient, lenitive, easy, complacent, gentle, tractable, yielding, pliable, soft, tender, sweet, mild, indulgent, genial, bland, affable, courteous, kind, compassionate, clement, merciful, tolerant, feeling, meek, moderate, easy-going, forbearing, placid.

shabby—*Syn.* mean, low, poverty-stricken, abject, meager, faded, ill-dressed, reduced, impoverished, down at heel (*colloq.*), paltry, beggarly, contemptible, ragged, threadbare, poor, pitiful, miserable, wretched, scrubby, weedy, deteriorated, degenerated, dilapidated, downhill (*colloq.*), decayed, worn, wasted, piffling, piddling, stingy, miserly, illiberal, tight (*colloq.*), tight-fisted, (*colloq.*), sordid, ungenerous, mercenary, on one's uppers (*colloq.*), down and out (*colloq.*). *Ant.* flourishing, well-to-do, prosperous, thriving, well-off, comfortable, cosy, warm (*colloq.*), fortunate, affluent, well-dressed, imposing, grand, splendid, magnificent, elaborate, lavish, extravagant, prodigal, liberal, over-liberal, squandering, wasteful, fashionable, distinguished, notable, important, opulent, moneyed, flush (*slang*), independent, rich, influential, wealthy, impressive, showy, flamboyant.

shackle, *v.*—*Syn.* chain, clog, impede, fetter, bind, curb, manacle, limit, trammel, check.

shade, *n.*—*Syn.* shadow, dimness, umbrage, obscurity, gloom, darkness, veil.

shady, *adj.*—*Syn.* dishonest, crooked, unethical, devious, suspicious. *Ant.* straight, square, honest, aboveboard.

shake—*Syn.* tremble, vibrate, quiver, quaver, shiver, flutter, oscillate, shudder, quake, wave, waver, agitate, fluctuate, reel, rock, sway, swing, joggle, jolt, flap, jounce, brandish, tremble, totter, thrill, jar, vary, move, wobble, wabble (*colloq.*), wamble (*dial.*), waggle, stagger. *Ant.* fix, place, fasten, tie, settle, solidify, set, stabilize, establish, confirm, strengthen, steady, stand still, hold down, resist, stick, keep back, restrain, bind, consolidate, cohere, condense, compress, thicken, incrassate, coagulate, congeal, freeze, render solid, harden, vitrify, petrify, indurate, cement, lapidify, ossify, lithify.

shallow—*Syn.* superficial, slight, flimsy, shoal, trifling, simple, unprofound, weak-minded, foolish, silly, empty, trivial, unintellectual, uintelligent, ignorant, idle, frivolous, piddling, fribbling, inane, farcical, namby-pamby, petty, wishy-washy (*colloq.*), small, inconsiderable, dribbling, paltry, unimportant, childish, half-baked (*colloq.*), low-brow (*slang*), illiterate. *Ant.* deep, profound, unfathomable, abysmal, bottomless, sunken, depressed, wise, sage, learned, scholarly, philosophic, strong-minded, educated, erudite, lettered, enlightened, shrewd, accomplished, talented, high-brow (*slang*), well-versed, academic, scientific, intelligent, intellectual, sapient, keen, keen-witted, sharp, quick, quick-witted, perspicacious, discerning, discriminative, farsighted, sagacious, sensible, long-headed, level-headed.

sham, *n.*—*Syn.* imitation, counterfeit, fake, deceit, pretense, cheat, trick, dissimulation, fraud, wile, humbug, phony.

shame—*Syn.* disgrace, dishonor, ignominy, infamy, reproach, derision, contempt, disrepute, obloquy, opprobrium, scandal, humiliation, vileness, turpitude, degradation, stigma, brand, blot, blur, bar sinister, bend sinister, tarnish, taint, pollution, execration, disrespect, censure, condemnation, impurity, indelicacy, immodesty, impudicity, indecency. *Ant.* respect, nobility, dignity, stateliness, fame, celebrity, exaltation, praise, applause, appreciation, reputation, popularity, goodness, virtue, illustriousness, modesty, magnanimity, approval, approbation, commendation, tribute, eulogy, encomium, panegyric, acclamation, boost (*colloq.*), admiration, honor, honesty, truth, truthfulness, purity, chastity, decency, good behavior.

shameful—*Syn.* disgraceful, dishonorable, vile, evil, bad, contemptible, dishonest, knavish, sinister, sinful, degrading, scandalous, outrageous, reprehensible, unworthy, blamable, villainous, contumelious, ignominious, reproachful, disreputable, base, opprobrious, infamous, discreditable. *Ant.* creditable, worthy, praiseworthy, virtuous, righteous, commendable, reputable, respectable, honorable, honest, fine, stately, dignified, celebrated, renowned, famous, glorious, illustrious, sublime, meritorious, deserving, well-intentioned, sterling, exemplary, excellent, admirable.

shameless—*Syn.* disgraceful, immodest, impudent, brazen, brazen-faced, forward, bold, rude, vulgar, indecent, lewd, indelicate, ribald, gross, incontinent, fornicative, lustful, carnal, fleshly, impure, unclean, indecorous, risqué [*Fr.*], obscene, libidinous, erotic, concupiscent, voluptuous, ruttish, smutty, dirty, filthy, debauched, corrupt, drunken, intemperate, profligate, sinful, immoral, abandoned, flagrant, flagitious, infamous, foul, villianous, diabolical, hellish, satanic, infernal, despicable, discreditable, evil, disreputable, shameful, reprobate, disgusting. *Ant.* decent, upright, righteous, respectable, respected, honorable, clean, pure, chaste, modest,

moral, guileless, innocent, undefiled, continent, virtuous, honest, noble, decorous, creditable, meritorious, praiseworthy, admirable, sterling, refined, exemplary, saintly, angelic, straightforward, truthful, high-minded, good, undefiled, irreproachable, unexceptionable, worthy, deserving, uncorrupted, unstained, unspotted, loyal, staunch, true, faithful, white (*slang*), high-principled, sinless, undefiled, chivalrous, square (*colloq.*), fair, commendable, proper, candid, conscientious.

shape, *n.*—*Syn.* form, fashion, model, mold, stamp, type, aspect, appearance, conformation, configuration, construction, frame, outline, structure, trim, cut of jib (*colloq.*), contour, cast. *Ant.* amorphism, amorphousness, shapelessness, deformity, disfigurement, mutilation, malformation, freak, malconformation, distortion, contortion, oddity, irregularity, unconformity, anomaly, abnormality, teratism, monstrosity.

shape, *v.*—*Syn.* form, mould, cast, regulate, fashion, make, create, design, construct, carve, chisel, cut, sketch, block out, hammer out, model, build, erect. *Ant.* deface, disfigure, deform, mutilate, cut, hack, chip, twist, distort, contort, warp, mangle, maim, impair, damage, ruin, destroy.

shapeless—*Syn.* amorphic, amorphous, misshapen, unshapely, formless, unformed, unsymmetrical, unfashioned, anomalous, deformed, disfigured, mutilated, irregular. *Ant.* shapely, symmetrical, regular, uniform, well-set, classic, chaste, proportionate, well-formed, adjusted, regulated, proportioned, fitting, proper, even, equal, well set up.

share, *n.*—*Syn.* part, portion, lot, allotment, quantity, quota, contingent, consignment, residue, remainder, allowance, apportionment, division, participation, contribution, assignment, amount, appropriation, partition, dividend, measure, dole, ratio, proportion, donation, legacy, gift. *Ant.* total, totality, entire, entirety, whole, all, combine, combination, aggregate, aggregation, agglutination, fusion, synthesis, unity, unification, compound, consolidation, conjunction, composition, amalgamation.

share, *v.—Syn.* give, allot, divide, apportion, part, partake, participate, appropriate, dispense, distribute, deal, partition, assign, administer. *Ant.* amass, aggregate, combine, unite, build up, form a whole, secure, keep, retain, hold, preserve, maintain, withhold.

sharp—*Syn.* acute, keen, keen-edged, penetrating, biting, sharp-edged, cutting, pointed, edged, peaked, prickly, acicular, muricate, thorny, pungent, piquant, acrid, high-flavored, stinging, spicy, m o r d a n t, peppery, intelligent, quick (*colloq.*), quick-witted, keen-witted, sagacious, wise, sapient, observing, brilliant, scintillating, sparkling, bright, wide-awake, discerning, on one's toes (*slang*), clear-headed, comprehending, sharp-eyed, brainy (*colloq.*), level-headed. *Ant.* dull, blunt, obtuse, pointless, rough, uneven, jagged, ragged, knurled, gnarled, notched, dented, indented, crenate, ribbed, grooved, sulcated, dull-edged, blunt-edged, flat, insipid, tasteless, unsavory, vapid, stale, unpalatable, nauseous, nasty, sickening, nauseating, dull-witted, heavy, unintelligent, unintellectual, shortsighted, half-baked (*colloq.*), stultified, balmy (*slang*), soft (*colloq.*), spoony (*slang*), clownish, thick (*colloq.*), thick-skulled, apathetic, inappetent, feeble-minded, shallow, stupid, fatuous, asinine, addlebrained, nutty (*slang*), batty (*slang*), bone-headed (*colloq.*), fat-headed (*colloq.*), foolish, nonsensical, inept, muddled.

shelter—*Syn.* screen, cover, hide, conceal, guard, take in, ward, harbor, defend, protect, shield, watch over, take care of, secure, preserve, safeguard, surround, enclose, house. *Ant.* expose, turn out, evict, send away, endanger, proscribe, banish, jeopardize, neglect, ignore, imperil, uncover, strip, exclude, put out, prohibit, restrain, shut out, disallow, bar, debar, inhibit, forbid, interdict, betray, expel, give up, refuse, reject, surrender.

shield, *v.—Syn.* protect, cover, preserve, defend, shelter, avert, guard, forfend.

shimmer, *v.—Syn.* gleam, coruscate, flash, sparkle, glow, glint, twinkle, glitter, scintillate.

shine—*Syn.* glare, glitter, radiate, sparkle, scintillate, coruscate, gleam, shimmer, glow, beam, glister, glisten, glimmer, flicker, illumine, irradiate, illuminate. *Ant.* shade, cloud, veil, darken, cover, curtain, obscure, dim, shadow, lower, overcast, eclipse, obfuscate, adumbrate, becloud, extinguish, shut out, overshadow, cast into shade, bedim, bedarken, darkle.

shiver, *v.—Syn.* shake, shudder, tremble, quake, quiver, wobble, splinter, shatter, disintegrate.

shock, *n.—Syn.* concussion, percussion, impact, collision, crash, blow, stroke, whack, thwack, thump, explosion, outrage, violence, excitement, ferocity, rage, fury, passion, outburst, agitation, jar, tumult, disturbance, racket. *Ant.* peace, calm, quietness, quietude, tranquillity, rest, silence, hush, lull, harmony, concord, stillness, repose, ease, comfort, content, contentment, contentedness, quiescence.

shock, *v.—Syn.* agitate, horrify, frighten, scare, alarm, dismay, terrify, affright, awe, daunt, startle, shake, unman, astound, appall, abash, overawe, intimidate, disquiet, terrorize, threaten. *Ant.* soothe, calm, lull, pacify, soften, mitigate, tranquillize, assuage, quiet, allay, alleviate, solace, comfort, console, palliate, please, inspirit, relieve, reconcile, compose, humor.

shocking, *adj.—Syn.* appalling, distressing, horrible, dreadful, odious, awful, frightful, terrible, ghastly, repellent, fearful.

short—*Syn.* brief, concise, succinct, summary, incomplete, insufficient, abridged, abbreviated, curtailed, epitomized, condensed, reduced, truncated, squat, pudgy, tubby (*colloq.*), stumpy · (*colloq.*), thickset, chunky (*colloq.*), dumpy, stunted, dwarfed, curtate, stocky, terse, compact, compressed, compendious, succinct, laconic, scarce, wanting, ill-provided, bare, denuded, impoverished, inadequate, deficient, jejune, meager, lopped, garbled, imperfect, deleted, cut down, unfinished. *Ant.* long, attenuated, lengthened, prolonged, protracted, extended, elongated, longish, lengthy, sesquipedalian, interminable, unending, profuse, lavish, spendthrift, wasteful, sufficient, luxuriant, flourishing, ample, abundant, redundant, prodigal, diffuse, superabundant, exuberant, superfluous, inexhaustible, unstinted, complete, entire, abounding, replete, full, adequate, plenteous, copious, well-stocked, plenty, plentiful, unexhausted, unmeasured, full up (*colloq.*), enough, chockfull, overflowing, excessive, overstocked.

shortsighted—*Syn.* myopic, nearsighted, purblind, partial, one-sided, superficial, undiscerning, indiscriminate, narrow-minded, conceited, dogmatic, fanatical, lacking judgment, positive, opinionated, opinioned, opinionative, misjudging, shallow, wrongheaded, pig-headed, stubborn, inflexible, irrational, foolish, inept, silly, unthinking, unreasoning, imprudent, rash. *Ant.* farsighted, thoughtful, prudent, reasoning, circumspect, careful, wise, farseeing, subtle, acute, sagacious, comprehending, perspicacious, long-headed, cun-

ning, foxy (*colloq.*), brainy (*colloq.*), alert, slick (*colloq.*), cautious, deliberative, vigilant, watchful, wary, observant, heedful, reflective, cogitative, studious, contemplative, steady, meditative.

showy—*Syn.* flashy, glaring, garish, gaudy, radiant, gorgeous, pompous, sumptuous, dressy (*colloq.*), stylish, magnificent, bright, vivid, variegated, flaunting, flaring, many-colored, brilliant, parti-colored, bright-colored, tinseled, jeweled, embroidered, ornate, begilt, glossy, tessellated, burnished, polished, gilded, glowing. *Ant.* dull, lustreless, lacklustre, dim, colorless, pale, achromatic, etiolated, withered, weazened, wan, sallow, ashen, leaden, corpse-like, death-like, cadaverous, waxen, hueless, squalid, dismal, gloomy, foul, dingy, besmeared, discolored, grim, ghastly, tarnished, bedraggled, drab, clouded, monotonous.

shrewd—*Syn.* knowing, cunning, clever, discerning, farseeing, calculating, cool, reflective, cautious, prudent, careful, observant, watchful, mindful, wary, guarded, sly, circumspect, canny [Sc.], politic, sure-footed, self-possessed, deliberate. *Ant.* rash, unthinking, unreasoning, silly, impetuous, slap-dash (*colloq.*), thoughtless, foolish, stultified, obtuse, dense, thick (*colloq.*), undiscerning, frivolous, indifferent, simple, ignorant, stupid, unintelligent, sottish, absurd, senseless, thick-skulled.

shrink, *v.—Syn.* dwindle, diminish, lessen, wither, withdraw, contract, shrivel, wizen, decrease, deflate.

shun, *v.—Syn.* eschew, avoid, disdain, evade, refuse, scorn, ignore, elude, balk, cut, escape.

shy, *adj.—Syn.* bashful, cautious, fearful, modest, wary, timid, reserved, diffident, circumspect, timorous, chary.

sick—*Syn.* ill, ailing, unwell, disordered, diseased, feeble, weak, impaired, sickly, unhealthy, morbid, valetudinarian, indisposed, distempered, infected, invalid, delicate, infirm, poorly, seedy (*colloq.*), confined, bedridden, unhealthy, under the weather (*colloq.*), sick of, disgusted, gorged, fed up (*colloq.*), tired of, nauseated, satiated. *Ant.* healthy, hearty, fine, strong, vigorous, healthful, robust, blooming, hale, hardy, unimpaired, sound, whole, chipper (*colloq.*), active, lusty, powerful, staunch, tiptop (*colloq.*), forceful, muscular, sinewy, sturdy, stout, rugged, brawny, thewy, athletic, mighty, stalwart, well, wholesome, dashing, impetuous, unconquerable, valiant.

sift, *v.*—*Syn.* screen, probe, analyze, discuss, winnow, sound, sort, examine.

sign, *n.*—*Syn.* omen, symbol, portent, token, emblem, symptom, prognostic, signal, indication, mark, manifestation, identification, presage, index, note, augury, type, cipher, device, motto, figure, representation, track, trail, footprint, clew.

sign, *v.*—*Syn.* affix, append, write, print, signal, convey, attract, contract, pledge, agree, guarantee, indicate, mark, note, imprint, score, impress, engrave, stamp, trace, gesture, gesticulate, tip the wink (*slang*).

signal, *adj.*—*Syn.* conspicuous, important, outstanding, momentous, famous, memorable, remarkable, prominent.

significant—*Syn.* important, material, momentous, critical, grave, prominent, outstanding, weighty, suggestive, meaningful, expressive, notable, remarkable, memorable, serious, paramount, vital. *Ant.* unimportant, trivial, trifling, petty, piddling, shallow, weak, childish, boyish, puerile, paltry, insignificant, contemptible, mean, meager, idle, farcical, ridiculous, worthless, wishy-washy (*colloq.*), fiddle-faddle (*colloq.*), namby-pamby (*colloq.*).

silent, *adj.*—*Syn.* quiet, still, soft, noiseless, calm, reticent, placid, hushed, faint, mute, inaudible, soundless, tacit, taciturn, uncommunicative.

silly, *adj.*—*Syn.* foolish, vacuous, preposterous, ridiculous, stupid, dumb, simple, absurd, witless, asinine, unreasonable, dense, empty, inane, shallow, frivolous.

similar, *adj.*—*Syn.* resembling, like, analogous, close, faithful, identical, akin, corresponding, comparable, reciprocal.

simple—*Syn.* plain, easy, single, artless, common, ordinary, unmixed, uncompounded, pure, unadorned, isolated, absolute, inartificial, unblended, unalloyed, unaffected, silly, undesigning, weak, humble, lowly, elementary, mere, homely, credulous, ignorant, elemental, childish, shallow, confiding, trustful, dumb (*colloq.*). *Ant.* sage, wise, sapient, knowing, alert, experienced, sensible, farsighted, discerning, discriminating, deep, profound, learned, philosophical, shrewd, sharp, strong-minded, level-headed, perspicacious, incredulous, skeptic, unbelieving, doubtful, suspicious, scrupulous, mixed, confused, compound, complex, involved, entangled, complicated, difficult, hard, puzzling.

simulate—*Syn.* pretend, dissemble, imitate, cheat, deceive, misrepresent, prevaricate, equivocate, shuffle, pervert, distort, feign, assume, quibble, shuffle, fence, play fast and loose (*colloq.*), gloss over, fabricate, disguise, concoct, exaggerate, play the hypocrite, beat about the bush (*colloq.*), act the faker, counterfeit, sham, invent, fabricate, lie. *Ant.* speak the truth, act courageously, be straightforward, speak one's mind, tell the truth the whole truth and nothing but the truth, be candid, be sincere, be honest, be frank, be open and aboveboard, speak beyond suspicion, deal squarely, make a clean breast of (*col-*

loq.), avoid deception, shun falsehood, be just, be righteous, tell the truth and shame the devil (colloq.).

simultaneous, adj.—Syn. concurrent, synchronous, concomitant, coincident, contemporaneous. Ant. preceding, following, foregoing, subsequent.

sin—Syn. evil, vice, transgression, guilt, fault, wrong, wickedness, falsification, falsehood, lying, cheating, chicanery, double-dealing, double-crossing, hypocrisy, immorality, ill-doing, evildoing, lust, perjury, criminality, depravity, vice, viciousness, iniquity, delinquency, crime, offense, wrongdoing, felony, misfeasance, misconduct, atrocity, atrociousness, ungodliness, profligacy, corruption. Ant. virtue, goodness, purity, morality, decency, righteousness, sinlessness, right, rectitude, innocence, holiness, godliness, excellence, blamelessness, uprightness, integrity, noble-mindedness, highmindedness, chivalry, spirituality, merit, worth, welldoing, honesty, honor, truth, truthfulness, impeccability, self-sacrifice, charity, charitableness, philanthropy, kindness, nobleness, straightforwardness.

sincere—Syn. honest, truthful, honorable, frank, open (colloq.), aboveboard, unreserved, true, veracious, candid, trustworthy, hearty, pure, genuine, real, bonâ fide [L.], outspoken, fair, just, true-blue (colloq.), truth-loving, ingenuous, faithful, unfeigned, undisguised, upright, conscientious, artless, simple, innocent, natural, incorruptible, inartificial, unsophisticated, plain, guileless, childlike, blunt, downright, direct, straightforward, impressive, earnest, serious. Ant. false, faithless, lying, perjured, insincere, hypocritical, deceitful, unfair, dishonest, uncandid, mendacious, disingenuous, artful, tricky, untruthful, hollow, canting, jesuitical, pharisaical, evasive, deceptive, deceiving,

untrue, corrupt, bad, evil, dishonorable, fraudulent, treacherous, base, unreliable, uncertain, vacillating, doubtful, traitorous, foul, malicious, malevolent, wicked, disreputable, untrustworthy, degraded, depraved.

sing—Syn. chant, carol, warble, chirp, chirrup, hum, celebrate in song, utter melodious sounds, raise the voice in musical regularity, sound words harmoniously, lift up the voice in measured utterance. Ant. cry, shout, howl, roar, shriek, bellow, bawl, yell, screech, whine, growl, grunt, yawp, hiss, squeal, snarl, utter discordant sounds.

single—Syn. one, only, sole, solitary, individual, separate, uncombined, uncompounded, unmarried, companionless, celibate, unwedded, wifeless, spouseless, virgin, secluded, private, simple, unmixed, elemental, unaccompanied, isolated. Ant. many, numerous, accompanied, attended, associated, coupled, mixed, blended, amalgamated, joined, combined, compounded, intermixed, mingled, intermingled, intertwined, composite, attached, corporate, united, hitched, jumbled, entangled, married, wedded, spliced (colloq.), yoked (colloq.).

singular, adj.—Syn. extraordinary, exceptional, unique, unusual, particular, strange, queer, fantastic, odd, uncommon, remarkable, quaint, curious, eccentric, rare, abnormal.

sinister—Syn. evil, bad, corrupt, perverse, dishonest, inauspicious, foreboding, disastrous, malign, malignant, hurtful, harmful, injurious, baneful, baleful, obnoxious, dire, woeful, morbific, pernicious, mischievous, deleterious, noisome, nocuous, noxious, poisonous, hoodooed (colloq.), jinxed (colloq.), adverse, unlucky, unfortunate, unfavorable, unpropitious. Ant. auspicious, lucky, fortunate, opportune, hopeful, timely, providential, propitious, favorable, promising, roseate, encouraging, inspiriting, heartening [*Sc.*], good, excellent, expedient, desirable, befitting, suitable, adventitious, inspiring, satisfying, friendly, benignant, kindly, benign, clement, gracious, benevolent, beneficent, salutary, wholesome.

situation, *n.—Syn.* condition, place, whereabouts, state, site, case, circumstances, spot, status, plight.

size, *n.—Syn.* magnitude, dimension, extent, expanse, bulk, mass, greatness, bigness, volume, space, amplitude.

skeptic—*Syn.* doubter, unbeliever, infidel, heathen, freethinker, idolator, atheist, agnostic, deist, disbeliever, Pyrrhonist, pagan, anti-Christian, dissenter, latitudinarian, misbeliever, disbeliever, rationalist, materialist, positivist, nihilist, somatist, theophobist, profaner, scoffer, blasphemer, apostate. *Ant.* believer, Christian, theist, pietist, devotee, worshiper, adorer, prayer, penitent, pilgrim, monotheist, priest, prelate, minister, clergyman, evangelist, preacher, religious, religious teacher, apostle, penitent.

sketch—*Syn.* portrayal, picture, draft, drawing, design, outline, form, shape, delineation, representation, plan, painting, skeleton, figure, figuration, configuration, depiction, illustration, tracing, copy, likeness, description, report, summary, brief, monograph, memoir. *Ant.* erasure, effacement, deletion, cancellation, obliteration, blot, defacement, distortion, misrepresentation, travesty, burlesque, caricature, daub, derangement, shapelessness, disfigurement.

skilful—*Syn.* skilled, handy, proficient, efficient, apt, clever, dexterous, ingenious, adroit, practiced, trained, deft, adept, expert, masterful, panurgic, accomplished, capable, smart, slick (*slang*), masterly, experienced. *Ant.* unskilful, unskilled,

bungling, blundering, clownish, boobyish, slovenly, inept, inapt, inexpert, unhandy, lubberly, maladroit, heavy-handed, unfit, unqualified, untrained, incompetent, clumsy, awkward, inexperienced.

skin, *n.—Syn.* epidermis, hide, pelt, integument, husk, veneer, bark, cuticle, surface, rind.

skittish, *adj.—Syn.* restive, nervous, jittery, restless, jumpy, shy, timorous, fidgety, feverish, volatile.

slack, *adj.—Syn.* lax, negligent, dilatory, indifferent, remiss, tardy, careless, stagnant, backward, inactive, slow, flaccid.

slander—*Syn.* asperse, defame, decry, malign, calumniate, traduce, vilify, revile, libel, disparage, detract, backbite, depreciate, defame, belittle, sneer at, criticize, blacken, derogate, run down (*colloq.*), falsify, belie, speak evil of. *Ant.* praise, applaud, extol, exalt, eulogize, vindicate, defend, laud, flatter, magnify, uphold, pander to, truckle to, court, curry favor, esteem, admire, advocate, justify, speak for, commend, recommend, acclaim, boost (*colloq.*), glorify, approve.

slang—*Syn.* cant, argot, colloquialism, vulgarism, vulgarity, caconym, antiphrasis, pseudology, lingo, thieves' Latin, peddlers' French, jargon, Billingsgate, Biddy Moriarty's vocabulary, bog Latin [*Ir.*], dog Latin, St. Giles' Greek. *Ant.* correct speech, classic language, proper words, literal interpretation.

slant, *n.—Syn.* pitch, angle, slope, inclination, grade, gradient, tilt, bias, divergence, leaning.

slavery—*Syn.* servitude, thraldom, enthralment, drudgery, hard labor, hard work, hard toil, bondage, captivity, subjection, toil and moil, serfdom, subjugation, restraint, constraint, enslavement, involuntary servitude. *Ant.* freedom, license, liberty, free will, prerogative, immunity, exemption, right, privilege, liberation, emancipation, manumission, idleness, independence, pleasure, enjoyment, gratification, diversion, amusement, entertainment, delight, comfort, ease.

sleazy, *adj.—Syn.* flimsy, tenuous, fragile, thin, limp, feeble, flabby, trashy, flaccid, weak, trumpery, gimcrack, slack.

sleek, *adj.—Syn.* glossy, lustrous, smooth, silky, oily, bland, ingratiating, satiny, velvety.

sleep—*Syn.* slumber, doze, drowse, nap, snooze, hibernate, dream, snore, nod, yawn, languish, flag, relax, go to bed, rest in the arms of Morpheus, close the eyelids, hit the hay (*slang*). *Ant.* be active, go ahead, keep busy, run along, hustle, bustle, elbow your way, press onward, push on, work, labor, toil, play, exercise, walk, run, keep a-going.

slender, *adj.—Syn.* slight, slim, tenuous, thin, feeble, flimsy, lean, spare, skinny, trivial, meager.

slight, *adj.—Syn.* little, small, petty, frail, trifling, puny, tenuous, trivial, slim, scant.

slip, *n.—Syn.* error, fault, mistake, misstep, blunder, indiscretion, boner, lapse, howler, fluff.

slope, *n.—Syn.* slant, incline, gradient, tilt, cant, pitch, grade.

slothful, *adj.—Syn.* lazy, leisurely, inactive, torpid, indolent, passive, lax, slow, sluggish, inert, idle. *Ant.* industrious, energetic, strenuous, active.

slow—*Syn.* tardy, sluggish, dawdling, drowsy, slack, lingering, inert, inactive, delaying, deliberate, dilatory, gradual, moderate, procrastinating, delaying, dull, heavy, belated, behindhand, late, backward, stolid, stupid, latent, passive, tame, lifeless, dead, languid, apathetic, easy, lymphatic, phlegmatic, imperceptible, creeping, crawling, torpid, torpescent, otiose, lazy, remiss, leaden, lumpish, dronish, weary, wearisome, tired, tiresome, monotonous, humdrum, flat, soporific, uninteresting. *Ant.*

fast, quick, active, agile, swift, spry, speedy, sprightly, lively, alert, brisk, bustling, hustling, prompt, energetic, vigorous, forcible, go-ahead (*colloq.*), intense, keen, sharp, ready, dashing, speedy, peppy (*slang*), vehement, violent, rushing, blustering, storming, stormy, dynamic, strenuous, irresistible, rapid, nimble, expeditious, light-footed, winged, mercurial, bounding, galloping, flying, scurrying, sprinting, wakeful, vigilant, vivacious, animated, frisky, assiduous, diligent, restless, busy, fussy, fidgety, sedulous, industrious, wide-awake.

sly, *adj.—Syn.* crafty, shrewd, secret, stealthy, cunning, furtive, insidious, underhand, wily, artful, knowing, foxy, tricky, subtle.

small, *adj.—Syn.* little, wee, slight, mean, tiny, paltry, unimportant, diminutive, trivial, minute.

smart, *adj.—Syn.* clever, bright, intelligent, alert, keen, quick, adroit, sharp, apt, knowing, ready, acute, shrewd. *Ant.* dull, dense, crass, stupid.

smell—*Syn.* fragrance, odor, scent, perfume, exhalation, emanation, effluvium, redolence, fetor or foetor, stench, stink, malodor, fetidness, empyreuma, reastiness, mephitis, foulness, mustiness, uncleanness, frowziness, filth, filthiness, rancidity, rottenness, corruption, putridity, pollution. *Ant.* inodorousness, deodorization, cleanness, cleanliness, purity, lustration, purification, ablution, disinfection, spotlessness, detersion, abstersion, incorruption.

smooth, *adj.—Syn.* even, level, mild, uniform, regular, invariable, undeviating, unvarying, flat, plane, flush, horizontal, sleek, glossy, silky, unwrinkled, tranquil, calm, still. *Ant.* rough, rugged, rugous, uneven, notched, gnarly, gnarled, nodular, bristly, pilose, scraggy, jagged, corrugated, furrowed, crinkled, prickly, rumpled, knurled, craggy, rocky, jagged, fluted, grooved, striated, sulcated, corduroy.

smooth, v.—*Syn.* to make level, make even, free from obstruction, free from harshness, palliate, gloze, gloze over, calm, quiet, make pleasant, settle argument, allay strife, throw oil on the water. *Ant.* rough, roughen, ruffle, crumple, corrugate, crinkle, render uneven, aggravate, torment, annoy, incite, exasperate, irritate, taunt, provoke.

snag, n.—*Syn.* knot, protuberance, obstacle, bar, hindrance, block, difficulty.

snappy, adj.—*Syn.* acute, crisp, poignant, animated, pungent, prompt, keen, piquant, quick, spicy, lively.

snare, n.—*Syn.* trap, net, pitfall, artifice, ambush, subterfuge, ruse.

sneer—*Syn.* mock, scoff, jeer, gibe, fling, taunt, disparage, blame, knock (*colloq.*), slight, scorn, despise, underrate, neglect, ignore, overlook, disapprove, censure, reprove, upbraid, scold, contemn, condemn, admonish, rebuke, reprimand, reproach, decry, belittle, asperse, detract, backbite, excoriate, execrate, vilify, lampoon, defame, calumniate. *Ant.* flatter, laud, applaud, praise, exalt, puff (*colloq.*), boost (*colloq.*), cheer, encourage, commend, justify, defend, advocate, befriend, uplift, uphold, counsel, advise, sustain, support, succor, assist, help, comfort, approve, esteem, hearten, inspire, reassure, inspirit, embolden, rally.

snide, adj.—*Syn.* mean, underhanded, insincere, oblique, sneaky, low, stealthy, contemptible, devious.

snoop, v.—*Syn.* pry, probe, peer, nose, investigate, ferret, gumshoe, mooch.

soak—*Syn.* drench, imbrue, steep, wet, immerse, merge, immerge, dip, water, sponge, infiltrate, saturate, sink into, drink, tipple, booze (*colloq.*), swill (*slang*),

guzzle, imbibe, lap up (*colloq.*). *Ant.* dry, dry up, wring, wring out, remove, press, press out, squeeze, squeeze out, desiccate, drain, dehydrate, evaporate, arefy, abstain, be temperate, deny oneself, refrain, keep sober.

soar, v.—*Syn.* fly, rise, tower, ascend, mount.

sober, adj.—*Syn.* temperate, moderate, solemn, calm, reasonable, unruffled, serious, cool, quiet, steady, sedate. *Ant.* drunk, excited, overwrought, passionate.

social—*Syn.* sociable, friendly, communicative, companionable, convivial, festal, jolly, merry, intimate, familiar, free and easy, hospitable, courteous, affable, pleasant, agreeable, urbane, chivalrous, polished, mannerly, complaisant, gracious, benign, benignant, complacent, kindly, civil, suave, polite. *Ant.* unsociable, disagreeable, discourteous, inhospitable, secluded, sequestered, cynical, morose, sullen, sour, cross, hermitic, hermitical, erimitical, solitary, forlorn, friendless, estranged, peevish, churlish, ill-tempered, stern, severe, austere, acrimonious, captious, scowling, rude, cold, uncomplaisant, vulgar, hoggish, doggish, currish, crusty, mean, ungracious, ill-mannered, underbred, impolite, unpolished, crude, ungentlemanly.

soft—*Syn.* gentle, meek, mild, pliant, yielding, impressible, smooth, plastic, pliable, bland, civil, complaisant, courteous, kind, mellow, tender, supple, flexible, flaccid, spongy, lenient, tolerant, indulgent, easy, clement, merciful, compassionate, sensitive, susceptible, tenderhearted, warm-hearted, weak, effeminate, docile, amenable, tractable, easy-going, irresolute, wobbly, faint-hearted, credulous, gullible, childish. *Ant.* hard, rocky, rigid, stubborn, stiff, unbending, unyielding, indurate, adamantine, severe, tyrannical, overbearing, domineering, cruel, callous, strict, stern, harsh, dour

[*Sc.*], sour, morose, sullen, arbitrary, absolute, pitiless, merciless, arrogant, presumptive, presumptuous, unkind, unsympathetic, brutal, unfeeling, hardhearted, insensible, resolute, determined, strong-willed, indomitable, self-possessed, gritty (*colloq.*), rough, obstinate.

solace, *v.*—*Syn.* allay, soothe, cheer, soften, calm, console, mitigate, lighten, comfort.

solemn—*Syn.* grave, serious, formal, ceremonial, sober, devout, important, notable, outstanding, weighty, momentous, salient, prominent, memorable, impressive, leading, chief, main, principal, prime, first, head, foremost, primary, imposing, distinguished, dignified, stately, commemorative, religious, holy, sacred, ritualistic, never-to-be-forgotten, sad, sorrowful, doleful, melancholy, mournful, lamentable, dire, direful, portentous, dread. *Ant.* unimportant, common, commonplace, ordinary, mean, paltry, undignified, trivial, unworthy, vulgar, low, lowly, humble, beggarly, contemptible, despicable, slight, uneventful, passing, transitory, light, insignificant, petty, lively, cheerful, jolly, merry, bright, breezy, buoyant, joyful, sprightly, sparkling, playful, rollicking, enlivening, hilarious, inspiriting, gay, animated, boisterous, rejoicing.

solicit—*Syn.* ask, request, beseech, beg, importune, implore, crave, entreat, desire, plead, petition, adjure, conjure, invoke, supplicate. *Ant.* protest, deprecate, remonstrate, expostulate, disapprove, argue against, oppose.

solid, *adj.*—*Syn.* dense, compact, substantial, hard, sound, unbroken, close, firm, stable, whole, rigid, concentrated, intact.

solitary—*Syn.* sole, only, alone, single, lonely, separate, retired, desolate, individual, secluded, isolated, singular, companionless. *Ant.* several, sundry, divers, various, many, numerous, manifold, crowded, thick, galore

(*colloq.*), accompanied, attended, associated, coupled with.

sophisticated, *adj.*—*Syn.* worldly, polished, knowledgeable, blasé, jaded. *Ant.* naïve, simple, artless, ingenuous.

sorcery, *n.*—*Syn.* magic, conjuration, enchantment, witchcraft, necromancy, thaumaturgy, wizardry.

sordid, *adj.*—*Syn.* mean, contemptible, base, ignoble, squalid, dirty, foul, cheap, low, venal, abject, filthy, degraded.

sorrow, *n.*—*Syn.* sadness, woe, suffering, heartache, distress, remorse, affliction, regret, grief, contrition, penitence, anguish.

sorry—*Syn.* grieved, poor, paltry, insignificant, dismal, mournful, sad, melancholy, pitiful, worthless, mean, despicable, trifling, small, unimportant, base, beggarly, menial, scrubby. *Ant.* glad, joyous, rejoicing, happy, contented, high, noble, exalted, important, significant, prominent, respectable, influential.

sort, *v.*—*Syn.* separate, order, select, classify, segregate, size, arrange, match, assort, grade, screen, sift.

soul—*Syn.* mind, spirit, intellect, life, force, essence, genius, principle, reason, mentality, intelligence, intellectuality, conception, thought, understanding, ego, psyche. *Ant.* matter, materiality, substance, body, corporeity, corporality, corporeality, materialization, material existence, substantiality, flesh and blood, physical nature, element, essence, stuff.

sound, *adj.*—*Syn.* healthy, wholesome, unimpaired, whole, entire, vigorous, hearty, hale, undecayed, strong, hardy, muscular, stanch, robust, sturdy, husky (*colloq.*), able-bodied, brawny, stalwart, perfect, unblemished, intact, stable, durable, unyielding, sterling, substantial, good, prime, excellent, genuine, reliable, true-blue (*colloq.*), faithful. *Ant.* decayed, impaired, injured, defective, deficient, unwholesome, broken, cracked, weak, delicate, unhealthy, affected, diseased, infirm, unsound, sick, sickly, wasted, consumptive, weak-minded, silly, crazy, screwy (*colloq.*), mad, insane, loony (*slang*), deteriorated, dilapidated, contaminated, rotten.

sound, *n.*—*Syn.* noise, tone, note, resonance, intonation, sonorousness, din, clamor, clangor, rattle, uproar, blare, outcry, shout, roar, racket, hullabaloo, fanfare, peal, jangle, boom, explosion, detonation, bellow, thunder. *Ant.* silence, hush, lull, muteness, soundlessness, stillness, oblivion, deadness, quiet, quietness, calmness, stagnation, rest.

sour—*Syn.* acid, tart, bitter, acetous, acidulated, acetic, astringent, crabbed, vinegary, morose, ill-natured, crusty, austere, severe, embittered, discontented, grouchy, sulky, sullen, glum, sore, sore-headed (*slang*), grumbling, dissatisfied, querulous, complaining, peevish, irritable, bad-tempered, grumpy, moody, surly, cynic, snarling. *Ant.* sweet, saccharine, syrupy, sugary, honeyed, nectareous, pleasant, agreeable, cheerful, complacent, serene, contented, satisfied, civil, courteous, polished, polite, urbane, kind, chivalrous, cordial, obliging, affable, friendly, good-humored, ingratiating, winning, gracious, amiable, bland, suave, attractive, magnetic.

source—*Syn.* origin, fountain, cause, spring, beginning, primogenitor, ancestor, forefather, commencement, incipience, rise, font, well-spring, foundation. *Ant.* effect, result, consequence, derivation, aftermath, upshot, *dénouement* [*Fr.*], issue, outcome, end, termination, conclusion, finish.

soused, *adj.*—*Syn.* drunk, inebriated, intoxicated, tight, cock-eyed, liquored, polluted, sickled, ossified, crocked, blind, blotto, corked, stewed, boiled, lush, high, glowing, fried, looped, full, hooched, loaded, lit, one-eyed, pie-eyed, tanked, fractured, illuminated, oiled, raunchy, mellow, plastered.

sovereign, *adj.*—*Syn.* paramount, dominant, ruling, supreme, predominant, ultimate, ascendant, absolute, authoritative, royal, regal, arbitrary, free, autonomous, independent.

sparkle, *v.*—*Syn.* glitter, coruscate, scintillate, flash, twinkle, glint, effervesce, shimmer, gleam, glisten.

speak—*Syn.* talk, utter, deliver, discourse, tell, say, express, pronounce, enunciate, chat, declare, declaim, chatter, articulate, converse, announce, communicate, proclaim, report, make known, voice, lecture, speechify, spout (*slang*). *Ant.* be silent, keep silence, say nothing, refrain, stop, put on the bridle (*slang*), shut your trap (*slang*), keep quiet, shut up (*slang*), button your lips (*slang*), keep a stiff upper lip (*slang*).

special—*Syn.* specific, particular, distinctive, especial, exceptional, appropriate, peculiar, extraordinary, proper, uncommon, individual, determinate, definite, marked, typical, characteristic. *Ant.* general, embracing, all-embracing, comprehensive, prevalent, prevailing, wide, world-wide, broad, ecumenical, all, every, catholic, universal.

specific, *adj.*—*Syn.* particular, definite, express, special, explicit, especial, exact, individual, categorical, concrete, precise. *Ant.* vague, general, indefinite.

specious—*Syn.* plausible, colorable, beguiling, ostensible, probable, presumable, presumptive, credible, likely, apparent, sophistical, flattering, apparently right, seemingly just, showy, garish, pretentious, ostentatious, pompous, gaudy. *Ant.* improbable, unlikely, incredible, unexpected, inconceivable, unreasonable, doubtful, obscure, dubious, dark, mysterious, implausible.

speech—*Syn.* speaking, utterance,

language, discourse, harangue, disquisition, talk, oration, oratory, address, sermon, homily, dissertation, delivery, lecture, communication, eloquence, recitation, palaver, prattle, parlance, talkativeness, verbal intercourse, oral communication, chatter, conversation. *Ant.* speechlessness, silence, stillness, taciturnity, hush, inarticulateness, mumble, mumbling, mutter, muttering, splutter, spluttering, gabble, gabbling, gibber, gibbering, gibberish, jargon, unintelligible talk, lingo, abracadabra.

speed, *n.*—*Syn.* swiftness, celerity, quickness, urgency, velocity, haste, expedition, dispatch, alacrity, hurry, rapidity.

spend—*Syn.* expend, exhaust, consume, waste, dissipate, squander, lay out, dispose of, drain, empty, deplete, disperse, scatter, fritter away, dispense, contribute, subscribe, donate, give, shell out (*slang*), fork out (*slang*), pony up (*slang*), disburse, discharge, pay, ante up (*poker*), liquidate, defray, distribute, settle, foot the bill (*colloq.*). *Ant.* save, hoard, collect, gather, take in, acquire, get, receive, recover, gain, profit, win, earn, inherit, regain, retrieve, realize, clear, treasure up, procure, seize, take, obtain, derive, benefit, pocket, appropriate, accept, commandeer, pick up.

spirit, *n.*—*Syn.* disposition, mood, intent, mettle, temper, enthusiasm, vivacity, resolution, humor, dash, verve, vitality, pluck, grit, zeal, ardor, energy.

spiteful, *adj.*—*Syn.* vindictive, rancorous, mean, malicious, vengeful, antagonistic, malevolent, malign, hostile, bitchy.

splendid, *adj.*—*Syn.* glorious, brilliant, showy, gorgeous, bright, excellent, grand, magnificent, refulgent, superb, sumptuous, eminent.

sponsor, *n.*—*Syn.* advertiser, patron, subscriber, angel, backer.

spontaneous—*Syn.* involuntary, instinctive, unbidden, unintentional, impulsive, automatic, unforced, natural, inevitable, irresistible, unavoidable, resistless, unwilling, avoidless, unconscious, uncontrollable, disinclined. *Ant.* willing, wilful, intended, inclined, unconstrained, voluntary, designed, devised, determined, premeditated, calculated, considered, volitional, forced, compelled, coerced, urged, driven.

sporadic—*Syn.* infrequent, rare, uncommon, isolated, separate, occurring here and there, scattered. *Ant.* grouped, clustered, conglomerate, concentrated, frequent, constant, continual, habitual, prevalent, general.

sport—*Syn.* play, game, diversion, amusement, fun, frolic, mockery, mirth, jest, joke, entertainment, festivity, merry-making, revel, revelry, jollification, carnival, Saturnalia, recreation, jollity, gambol, spree, pastime, tomfoolery, antics, mummery, enjoyment, pleasure, chase, hunt, hunting, shooting, fishing, angling, football, tennis, cricket, baseball, lacrosse, skating, skiing, running, racing, jumping, boxing. *Ant.* boredom, weariness, lassitude, ennui, tedium, dullness, melancholy, monotony, heaviness, moroseness, moodiness, pain, dolor, sickness, suffering, imprisonment, confinement, dejection, care, anxiety, trouble, heartache, unhappiness, infelicity, despair, desolation, misery, gloom, prostration, despondency, slough of despond, melancholia, grief, sorrow, distress, affliction, anguish, agony, worry, bother, burden.

sportive—*Syn.* gay, playful, merry, romping, sprightly, jolly, jocund, jovial, jesting, frolicsome, lively, cheerful, buoyant, lighthearted, debonair, jaunty, spirited, animated, sparkling, blithe, breezy, riant, vivacious. *Ant.* sad, sorrowful, dull, melancholy, blue, lethargic, weary, tired, flat, heavy, dejected, cast down, gloomy, moping, brooding, cheerless, joyless, mournful, lugubrious, depressed, unhappy, miserable, doleful, moody, glum, discouraged, disheartened, pensive, woebegone, s p l e n e t i c, grim, demure, sour, solemn, downhearted, disconsolate, forlorn.

spread—*Syn.* disperse, diffuse, scatter, expand, extend, propagate, disseminate, prepare, lay, cover, circulate, dispense, distribute, strew, intersperse, shed, sow, increase, deepen, heighten, lengthen, enlarge, widen, develop, diverge, radiate, branch off, publish, circulate, promulgate, herald, blazon, proclaim, announce. *Ant.* assemble, collect, muster, unite, herd, crowd, bring together, press together, combine, colligate, bind, concentrate, cluster, shorten, decrease, contract, diminish, lessen, shrink, subside, wane, ebb, abate, compress, condense, circumscribe, tighten, draw in, suppress, conceal, exclude, kill (*news, colloq.*), expunge, delete, squash (*slang*).

spring—*Syn.* fountain, source, beginning, origin, cause, principle, rise, commencement, inception, start, outset, opening, initiation, inauguration, fount, arising, causation. *Ant.* end, finish, effect, result, termination, completion, consummation, goal, limit, outcome, issue, finale, consequence, conclusion, fulfilment, expiration, cessation, terminus, extremity, uttermost, close.

sprite—*Syn.* elf, fairy, goblin, spirit, soul, wraith, incorporeal being, ethereal being, shade, spook, vision, phantom, ghost, spectre, etheric body, banshee [*Ir.*], White Lady [*Ir.*], witch, warlock, siren, jinnee, genius, familiar, dæmon, demon, imp, dæva, succubus, ghoul, flibbertigibbet, oaf, ouphe, hobgoblin, gnome, pixie, bogie, nymph, afrit or afreet [*Ar.*], barghest, *lamia* [*Gr.*], vampire, dryad, naiad, nereid, fay, brownie,

kelpie, mermaid, faun, peri, apparition. *Ant.* body, being, existence, incarnation, corporality, corporeality, corporeity, matter, materialness, materialization, substance, substantiality, substantialness, flesh and blood, physical being.

spry—*Syn.* nimble, active, vigorous, quick, agile, vivacious, lively, frisky, light-footed, smart, swift, fast, keen, alert, brisk, spirited, blithe, breezy, chipper (*colloq.*), debonair, buoyant, sprightly, sportive, lightsome, blithesome, free and easy, gay, gay and gallant, playful, rollicking, hearty, jaunty. *Ant.* dull, dejected, weary, depressed, gloomy, heavy, drooping, sad, melancholy, grave, serious, sullen, sulky, moody, sour, sorrowful, downcast, blue (*colloq.*), low-spirited, splenetic, woebegone, cheerless, spiritless, unhappy, lugubrious, doleful, weak, tottering, sickly, delicate, unhealthy, ailing, infirm, ill, seedy (*colloq.*).

spurious—*Syn.* counterfeit, fictitious, apocryphal, false, adulterate, fraudulent, dishonest, erroneous, deceptive, sham, faked, hollow, concocted, fabricated, misrepresented, make-believe, pretended, claptrap (*colloq.*), punk (*slang*), fishy (*slang*), phony (*slang*), delusive, deceiving, feigned, snide (*slang*), meretricious, misleading, illusory. *Ant.* genuine, real, true, hall-marked, proven, tested, true-blue (*colloq.*), A¹ or A1, actual, accurate, exact, authentic, pure, Simon-Pure (*colloq.*), valid, veritable, honest, good, first-class, excellent, up to the mark, unexceptionable, sound, perfect, standard, faultless, unblemished, intact, accredited, certain, trustworthy, authorized, substantial, unquestionable, positive, incontestable, assured, undoubted, undeniable, immutable, indisputable.

spurn, *v.*—*Syn.* disdain, repel, repulse, reject, contemn, refuse, flout, repudiate, scorn, decline.

squabble, *v.*—*Syn.* wrangle, dispute, contend, quarrel, argue, battle, brawl, spat, fight, bicker, struggle, scrap.

squalid—*Syn.* dirty, filthy, unclean, poor, poverty-stricken, mean, grimy, soiled, foul, reeking, ordurous, nasty, abominable, slimy, slummocky, sloshy, ill-smelling, feculent, odious, repellent, gruesome, horrid, horrible, besmeared, sloppy, smutty, muddy, miry, lutose, dingy, reeky, fetid, moldy or mouldy, musty, fusty, offensive. *Ant.* clean, pure, spotless, unsullied, sweet, attractive, spruce, neat, tidy, trim, washed, scoured, bright, shining, clean as a pin (*colloq.*), purified, disinfected, fumigated, airy, nice, fine, appealing, inviting, satisfactory, artistic, polished, adorned, ornamented, trig, up-to-date, comfortable, pleasant, suitable, beautiful, pretty, cosy, light, sunny.

square, *adj.*—*Syn.* corny, old-fashioned, conventional, schmaltzy, hokey, unaware. *Ant.* sophisticated, hep, hip, cool.

squeamish—*Syn.* finicky, fussy, censorious, hard to please, fastidious, hair-splitting, fault-finding, meticulous, scrupulous, querulous, hypercritical, particular, exacting, discriminating, prim, prudish, strait-laced, carping, critical, captious, easily nauseated, annoyed by trifles, readily disgusted, delicate, queasy. *Ant.* easy, easy to please, satisfied, contented, approving, admiring, commendatory, complimentary, uncritical, appreciative, acclamatory, pleased, gratified, delighted, charmed, indulgent, free and easy, good-natured, careless, sympathetic, generous, complaisant, complacent, liberal, spleenless, considerate, amiable, cordial, broad-minded, voracious, gluttonous, avid, greedy, swinish.

stable—*Syn.* unchanging, lasting, abiding, fixed, durable, endur-

ing, steady, constant, firm, established, steadfast, immutable, settled, anchored, moored, deep-rooted, riveted. *Ant.* movable, unsteady, wobbling, shaking, unfixed, unsettled, mobile, wavering, fluctuating, mutable, variable, restless, agitated, fickle, erratic, mercurial.

staid, *adj.*—*Syn.* serious, sober, demure, sedate, decent, steady, earnest, grave, cool, calm, decorous, complacent.

stain—*Syn.* blot, speck, spot, tarnish, blur, blotch, mark, tinge, color, discolor, soil, tint, dye, sully, disgrace, dishonor, blemish, impair. *Ant.* clean, wash, purify, clarify, deterge, depurate, clear, sponge, scour, polish, decorate, ornament, gild, embellish, whiten, bleach, honor, dignify, exalt, elevate.

state, *n.*—*Syn.* commonwealth, realm, government, empire, monarchy, republic, sovereignty, kingship, dominion, domination, territory, principality, command, sway, rule, property, estate, assets, means, chattels, resources, condition, character, stamp, predicament, dilemma.

state, *v.*—*Syn.* declare, testify, tell, inform, avow, certify, asseverate, assert, avow, specify, depose, allege, pronounce, claim, say, protest, set forth, swear, propound, aver, affirm, express, maintain, avouch, assure, predicate, report, mention, communicate, signify, disclose, announce. *Ant.* contradict, repudiate, disprove, gainsay, dispute, deny, refute, waive, retract, contravene, controvert, oppose, conceal, hide, suppress, bottle up, withhold, disclaim, disown, renounce, forswear, abnegate, abjure, confute, rebut, negative, impugn, ignore, recant, dissent.

stately—*Syn.* dignified, imposing, lofty, lordly, elevated, proud, pompous, majestic, grand, magnificent, high-minded, imperious, arrogant, toplofty (*colloq.*), haughty, stiff, purseproud, disdainful, masterful, high-toned, stuck-up (*colloq.*), stiff-necked, strait-laced, majestic, ceremonial, formal, ritualistic, dramatic, solemn. *Ant.* humble, poor, obscure, modest, retiring, abashed, timid, timorous, bashful, unassuming, unpretending, submissive, lowly, meek, coy, sheepish, demure, unostentatious, reserved, constrained, diffident, unpretentious, unobtrusive, downcast, backward, ashamed.

status, *n.—Syn.* condition, state, standing, situation, station, rank, footing, caste, posture.

steady, *adj.—Syn.* even, constant, firm, regular, uniform, enduring, continuing, secure, stable, perpetual, lasting, persevering.

steal, *v.—Syn.* rob, pilfer, thieve, take, filch, plunder, purloin, burglarize, pinch, loot, swipe.

stereotype, *n.—Syn.* pattern, convention, standard, repetition, copy, custom, orthodoxy.

sterile—*Syn.* barren, unproductive, fallow, unfruitful, destitute, bare, abortive, flat, ineffective, ineffectual, inefficacious, impotent, incomplete, unfinished, unprofitable, fruitless, unfertile, infertile, arid, jejune. *Ant.* fertile, productive, fruitful, bearing, prolific, copious, plentiful, fecund, teeming, plenteous, proliferous, luxuriant, profuse, generative, pregnant, uberous, *enceinte* [*Fr.*].

stern—*Syn.* severe, austere, rigid, rigorous, harsh, cruel, unrelenting, uncompassionate, unfeeling, determined, resolute, unyielding, unbending, grim, resolved, relentless, inexorable, earnest, firm, strict, exacting, inflexible, peremptory, uncompromising, oppressive, grinding, obdurate. *Ant.* gentle, kind, considerate, lenient, compassionate, indulgent, easy, easy-going, clement, tolerant, merciful, amiable, courteous, complacent, agreeable, affable, suave, compliant, free and easy, social, sociable, condescending, neighborly, urbane, friendly.

stiff, *adj.—Syn.* severe, conventional, unbending, punctilious, inflexible, tense, firm, wooden, stilted, rigid, frigid, formal, austere, awkward.

still, *adj.—Syn.* silent, calm, motionless, noiseless, hushed, quiet, soft, serene, peaceful, mute, unruffled, tranquil.

stimulate, *v.—Syn.* stir, rouse, awaken, provoke, excite, energize, invigorate, instigate, animate, urge, incite, impel, kindle.

stingy, *adj.—Syn.* miserly, greedy, thrifty, close, sordid, niggardly, avaricious, mean, covetous, tight, skimpy, parsimonious, meager, penurious. *Ant.* generous, liberal, bountiful, prodigal.

stink, *n.—Syn.* stench, miasma, smell, rancidity, fetor, effluvium, rankness, outcry.

stop, *v.—Syn.* cease, halt, arrest, hinder, suspend, check, frustrate, quit, stay, block, impede, interrupt, defer, desist, thwart. *Ant.* start, begin, commence, initiate.

storm—*Syn.* agitation, tempest, hurricane, disturbance, commotion, perturbation, turmoil, turbulence, tumult, racket, hubbub, violence, ebullition, rage, fury, paroxysm, outbreak, passion, hysterics. *Ant.* tranquillity, calm, calmness, quiet, quietness, quietude, rest, cessation, silence, repose, stillness, hush, muteness, solemnity, peace, pacifism, imperturbability, placidity, coolness, serenity, dullness or dulness, suppression, composure.

stormy—*Syn.* rough, boisterous, tempestuous, raging, violent, excitable, angry, excited, fierce, furious, agitated, turbulent, passionate, mad, frenzied, raving, fuming, flaming. *Ant.* cool, calm, collected, composed, quiet, peaceful, tranquil, patient, repressed, inexcitable, unpassionate, cold-blooded, grave, demure, steady, philosophic, sedate, meek, tolerant, gentle, forbearing, content.

story—*Syn.* novel, tale, anecdote, fable, fiction, myth, legend, narrative, sketch, account, incident. *Ant.* annals, history, biography, memoirs, chronicle, autobiography, essay, commentary.

stout, *adj.*—*Syn.* fat, obese, thickset, large, corpulent, rotund, portly, stocky, fleshy, burly, plump, chubby. *Ant.* lean, spare, lanky, scrawny.

straight—*Syn.* direct, right, rectilinear, undeviating, unswerving, vertical, perpendicular, upright, erect, unbent, regular, honest, reliable, honorable, good. *Ant.* crooked, distorted, twisted, bent, curved, deviating, swerving, wavering, sloping, angular, deformed, hunchbacked, bowlegged, grotesque, misshapen, dishonest, unreliable, knavish, thievish, tricky, deceptive, underhand, untrustworthy.

strange—*Syn.* unrelated, irrelevant, remote, far-fetched, detached, apart, inapplicable, dissociated, abnormal, unconformable, anomalous, irregular, wandering, uncustomary, unaccustomed, misplaced, funny (*colloq.*), queer, quaint, nondescript, supernormal, extraordinary, unfamiliar, grotesque, bizarre, fantastic, odd, out-of-the-way, baroque, whimsical, eccentric, wonderful, amazing, astonishing, surprising, bewildering, stupefying, startling, wondrous, striking, overwhelming, awesome, indescribable, ineffable, unutterable, fearful, stupendous, marvelous, electrifying. *Ant.* common, commonplace, ordinary, trite, expected, unimportant, trivial, trifling, usual, well-known, plain, regular, formal, conventional, typical, invariable, unvarying, simple, homely, matter-of-fact, natural, habitual, customary, general, frequent, everyday, hackneyed, familiar, normal, mediocre, average, current, prevailing, according to rule, in conformity with.

strict, *adj.*—*Syn.* severe, rigorous,

accurate, stern, inflexible, rigid, onerous, stringent, oppressive, austere, unyielding, harsh.

strike, *v.*—*Syn.* hit, beat, bang, clash, smite, pummel, swat, pound, slog, rap, slug, punch, clout, thrash, knock, cudgel, slap, cuff, buffet, belabor, whip.

strong—*Syn.* robust, sturdy, powerful, forceful, mighty, muscular, sinewy, thewy, vigorous, stout, solid, firm, hardy, energetic, tough, virile, stout, athletic, able-bodied, stalwart, brawny, wiry, strapping, invincible, indomitable, strenuous, forcible, resistant, resolute, plucky, self-willed, self-reliant, determined, game, gritty, unflinching, manly, manful, courageous, healthy, sound, hale, hearty, stanch, unimpaired. *Ant.* weak, feeble, delicate, ailing, infirm, ill, emaciated, consumptive, fragile, sickly, enervated, effeminate, invalid, anæmic, debilitated, unnerved, unstrung, languid, spent, wasted, languishing, wishy-washy (*colloq.*), shattered, shaken, trembling, tottering, doddering, torpid, heavy, languorous, irresolute, fickle, wavering, fluctuating, unsettled, shilly-shally, vacillating, wabbly, frail, timid, faltering, tremulous, hesitating.

strong—*Syn.* tainted, malodorous, fetid, smelling, decaying, decayed, putrid, diseased, rotten, sour, unsavory, unpalatable, high-flavored, acrid, pungent, peppery, overproof, bitter, biting, sharp, acid. *Ant.* fresh, good, wholesome, healthful, fragrant, odorous, savory, delectable, palatable, flat, insipid, wishy-washy (*colloq.*), nauseous, stale, weak, milk and water.

stubborn, *adj.*—*Syn.* obstinate, adamant, perverse, dogged, intractable, pertinacious, headstrong, recalcitrant, unyielding, obdurate, stiff, tough.

stupid—*Syn.* dull, foolish, obtuse, witless, doltish, senseless, stolid, heavy, sluggish, stupefied, besotted, insensate, dull-witted, addle-pated, prosy, prosaic, unintelligent, feeble-minded, nutty, (*slang*), batty (*slang*), sappy (*slang*), shallow, borné [*Fr.*], asinine, inapt, inept, childish, slow, sottish, thick-skulled, moronic, heavy, flat. *Ant.* quick, sharp, keen, alert, comprehensive, comprehending, wideawake, brainy (*colloq.*), clever, perspicacious, sagacious, sage, wise, sapient, acute, discerning, canny [*Sc.*], smart, witty, ready, brilliant, keen-witted, intelligent, bright, clear-headed, sharpsighted, acute, arch, cunning, thoughtful, solid.

stupidity—*Syn.* stupor, stupefaction, slowness, apathy, dulness or dullness, obtuseness, inertia, heaviness, flatness, insensibility, sluggishness, feeble-mindedness, childishness, fatuity, imbecility, shallowness, asininity, stultification, silliness, incompetence, jobbernowlism (*colloq.*), ineptitude, stolidity, stolidness, sappiness (*slang*), sapheadedness (*slang*). *Ant.* quickness, keenness, sense, sensibility, sagacity, sagaciousness, cleverness, alertness, acuteness, intelligence, wit, brilliancy, animation, readiness, comprehension, discernment, sapiency, sharp-sightedness, canniness [*Sc.*], nous [*Gr.*], penetration, discrimination, cunning, shrewdness, subtlety, longheadedness, gumption (*colloq.*), perspicacity, acumen, grasp.

stupor—*Syn.* insensibility, lethargy, apathy, stupefaction, asphyxia, swoon, coma, fainting, swooning, unconsciousness, numbness, torpor, syncope, narcosis, anæsthesia, trance, hypnosis, inertness, analgesia, suspended animation, amazement, bewilderment. *Ant.* feeling, susceptibility, consciousness, sensibility, sensitiveness, sensation, activity, vivacity, vivaciousness, excitability, liveliness, sprightliness, verve, rapture, enthusiasm, animation, spiritedness, emo-

tion, agitation, perturbation.

sturdy, *adj.*—*Syn.* stalwart, robust, durable, powerful, stout, sound, hardy, tough, strong, vigorous, lusty, husky.

subdue, *v.*—*Syn.* overcome, conquer, master, subjugate, vanquish, control, tame, surmount, beat, suppress, defeat.

subject—*Syn.* liable, exposed to, submissive, obedient, susceptible, open to, answerable, responsible, accountable, dependent on, subjugate, servile, slavish, subservient, parasitic, cringing, inferior, subordinate, secondary, lower. *Ant.* unconstrained, uncontrolled, untrammeled, unrestricted, unlimited, enfranchised, absolute, free, free from, independent, superior, above, exempt, freeborn, autonomous, unrestrained.

submit, *v.*—*Syn.* defer, abide, bend, resign, yield, surrender, bear, relent, obey, capitulate, succumb, suffer.

subsequent—*Syn.* succeeding, following, after, afterward, consequent, secondary, proximate, next, posterior, ensuing, later. *Ant.* preceding, prior, anterior, antecedent, earlier, previous, former, aforesaid, aforegoing, aforementioned, above-mentioned.

subsidy—*Syn.* grant, premium, indemnity, gift, bonus, tribute, gratuity, allowance, aid, bounty, support, pension, reward. *Ant.* check, barrier, prevention, restraint, hindrance, restriction, disapproval, opposition, objection, drawback, impediment, snag, difficulty, damper, wet blanket (*colloq.*).

substantial—*Syn.* solid, durable, lasting, strong, firm, material, ponderable, physical, dense, condensed, pressed, compressed, compact. *Ant.* unsubstantial, immaterial, bodiless, incorporal, incorporeal, airy, ethereal, astral, visionary, rare, fluffy, porous, spongy, tenuous, uncompressed, intangible, gaseous, invisible, spectral, phantasmal, unreal.

subvert—*Syn.* overturn, overthrow, suppress, supplant, supersede, ruin, destroy, extinguish, invert, depress, upset, demolish, tumble, topple, capsize, reverse, level, throw down, pull down, raze. *Ant.* erect, lift up, elevate, raise, heighten, uplift, rear, hoist, upheave, form, construct, build, put together, organize, make good, accomplish, establish, constitute, institute, perpetuate, preserve, conserve, sustain, uphold.

succeed—*Syn.* prevail, accomplish, get, obtain, achieve, attain, flourish, prosper, win, thrive, acquire, procure, profit, realize, recover, retrieve, reap, benefit, receive, gain, overcome, surmount, conquer, vanquish, overpower, overthrow, triumph, possess, follow after, take the place of. *Ant.* fail, lose, forfeit, give up, abandon, miss, blunder, fall down, slip, trip, stumble, succumb, be deprived of, stick in the mud (*colloq.*), drop behind, go wrong, go amiss, be unfortunate, come to misfortune, lack, want, need, go to the dogs (*colloq.*).

suffer—*Syn.* feel, bear, experience, undergo, sustain, permit, allow, tolerate, submit, endure, support, abide, bear with, put up with, acquiesce, allow, admit, ache, writhe, smart, twinge, bleed, collapse, fall down, gasp, groan, languish, droop, flag, sicken, be tortured. *Ant.* cast off, throw off, set aside, conquer, vanquish, banish, exclude, discard, overcome, laugh, smile, rejoice, make merry, exult, cheer, shout, sing, hurrah, triumph, celebrate, rollick, revel, jubilate.

sufficient, *adj.*—*Syn.* adequate, suitable, enough, satisfying, plentiful, proper, ample, fitting, meet, abundant, satisfactory.

suggestion—*Syn.* hint, allusion, intimation, insinuation, proposal, innuendo, implication, plan, scheme, advice, opinion, project,

design, proposition, outline, sketch, skeleton, draft, copy, prospectus, recommendation, charge, exhortation, injunction, instruction. *Ant.* reserve, sneer, silence, closeness, suppression, concealment, taciturnity, secrecy, reticence, reservation, remonstrance, reproof, disapproval, reproach, reprimand, reprehension, expostulation.

sullen, *adj.*—*Syn.* dour, morose, lowering, glum, cross, sour, sulky, grumpy, stubborn, surly, ill-tempered, saturnine, crusty, somber. *Ant.* cheerful, smiling, jocund, jovial.

superficial—*Syn.* flimsy, cursory, hasty, desultory, shallow, summary, short-sighted, purblind, ignorant, narrow-minded, prejudiced, warped, partial, untrustworthy, outward, external, exterior, unenlightened, unschooled, half-baked (*colloq.*), empty-headed, low-brow (*slang*), uneducated. *Ant.* deep, unfathomable, bottomless, abysmal, submerged, sunken, profound, learned, accomplished, scholarly, philosophic, knowing, cognitive, informed, shrewd, astute, discerning, cunning, sagacious, proficient, intelligent, well-informed, experienced, educated.

superfluous—*Syn.* unnecessary, excessive, superabundant, overflowing, redundant, overmuch, very great, abounding, inordinate, needless, exorbitant, extravagant, profuse, saturated, luxuriant, inexhaustible, turgescent, pleonastic, lavish, overcharged. *Ant.* scarce, scanty, few, little, small, wanting, lacking, insufficient, inadequate, short of, devoid of, incomplete, empty, bare, unprovided, meager, poor, indigent, starved, famine-stricken, moneyless, penniless, impoverished.

superior, *adj.*—*Syn.* higher, important, better, chief, greater, excellent, unsurpassed, foremost, distinguished, champion, sovereign, pre-eminent.

supernatural—*Syn.* preternatural,

superhuman, spectral, ghostly, occult, hidden, mysterious, secret, unknown, unrevealed, dark, mystic, mythical, mythological, fabulous, legendary, misty, unintelligible, unfathomable, inscrutable, incomprehensible, undiscernible, transcendental, metempiric, obscure, unknowable, impenetrable, invisible, concealed. *Ant.* natural, plain, common, commonplace, ordinary, known, usual, explainable, intelligible, manifest, evident, unconcealed, open, simple, obvious, apparent, undeniable, definite, demonstrable, provable, clear, revealed, explicit, indubitable, undoubted, unmistakable, self-evident, certain, visible, solvable, distinct, indisputable, sensible, physical, material.

supplicate, *v.—Syn.* importune, beg, plead, implore, pray, entreat, request, petition, beseech, appeal, adjure.

support—*Syn.* prop, maintain, uphold, hold up, sustain, keep, keep up, bear, carry, cherish, back up, bolster up, upbear, preserve, guard, take care of, aid, assist, help, contribute, subscribe, forward, advance, expedite, second, stand by, stick up for (*colloq.*), side with (*colloq.*), advocate, defend, plead for, vindicate. *Ant.* abandon, desert, give up, betray, overthrow, wreck, demolish, destroy, throw down, cast down, break down, drop, let go, hinder, impede, obstruct, embarrass, counteract, encumber, block, overwhelm, thwart, frustrate, circumvent, cripple, dishearten, discourage, check, prevent, inhibit, disconcert, undermine, oppose, block, defeat.

suppose—*Syn.* conjecture, guess, deem, think, surmise, imagine, presume, infer, deduce, count upon, take for granted, suspect, assume, fancy, speculate, dare say, presuppose. *Ant.* ascertain, find out, know, prove, discover, conclude, be sure of, determine, evolve, trace, detect,

decide, define, resolve, settle, discern, learn, uncover.

supreme, *adj.—Syn.* paramount, transcendent, chief, incomparable, highest, foremost, dominant, superlative, sovereign, utmost, first.

surprise, *v.—Syn.* astound, amaze, astonish, startle, bewilder, flabbergast, disconcert, stun, stupefy, confound, rattle.

surrender—*Syn.* sacrifice, yield, capitulate, cede, give, give in, give over, give up, give way, relinquish, let go, abandon, submit, comply, backdown (*colloq.*), deliver up, hand in the sword, lay down arms, beat a retreat, strike the colors, turn tail (*colloq.*), swallow the leek (*slang*), eat humble pie (*slang*), eat crow (*slang*). *Ant.* conquer, drive off, chase, overcome, triumph, succeed, surmount, defeat, outdo, lick (*slang*), lick to a frazzle (*slang*), leather (*slang*), rout, worst, override, overpower, overreach, overmatch, outmaneuver, repulse, rebuff, drub, thrash, wallop, trounce, larrup, (*slang*), lambaste (*slang*), pitch into (*slang*), beat back, tan their hides (*slang*), settle, vanquish.

surround—*Syn.* compass, encompass, circle, encircle, environ, enclose, gird, girdle, beset, besiege, beleaguer, blockade, invest, circumscribe. *Ant.* intervene, interpenetrate, permeate, interfere, interplace, insert, put between, interject, intersperse, introduce, throw in, run in, leave, abandon, desert, shun, flee, move from.

suspend—*Syn.* discontinue, cease, desist, break off, check, halt, interrupt, put a stop to, put an end to, shut up, delay, postpone, hang fire (*colloq.*), hang around (*colloq.*), put off, defer, adjourn, shelve, table, lay on the table, reserve, stall (*slang*), hang, hitch, hook up, append, fasten to. *Ant.* continue, persist, go on, keep going, maintain, keep the ball rolling (*colloq.*), expedite, accelerate, support, hold up, sustain, prop, brace, upbear, act, carry on, persevere.

sustain—*Syn.* maintain, support, bear, uphold, prop, assist, relieve, suffer, undergo, endure, nourish, keep, keep up, succor, contribute, relieve, minister to, attend on, stand by, back up, side with (*colloq.*), espouse cause of, favor, befriend. *Ant.* hinder, impede, prevent, interfere with, thwart, frustrate, injure, impair, weaken, balk, disconcert, obstruct, stop, block, oppose, contravene, contradict, check, suspend, leave, abandon, forsake, shun, avoid, denounce.

sway, *n.*—*Syn.* authority, rule, influence, government, power, superiority, dominion, control, bias, preponderance, domination, force, weight, ascendancy, mastery, supremacy, prestige, prerogative, jurisdiction, patronage, command, predominance, magnetism, strength, potency. *Ant.* impotence, inability, disability, incapacity, weakness, ineptitude, helplessness, powerlessness, futility, inferiority, uselessness, fatuity, ignorance, inefficiency, inefficacy, incompetence, asininity, stupidity, shallowness, baseness, misconduct, indecency, unrighteousness.

sweet—*Syn.* pleasant, pleasing, agreeable, toothsome, mild, luscious, fragrant, wholesome, winning, pure, fresh, amiable, gentle, melodious, musical, harmonious, lovely, beautiful, attractive, captivating, enticing, dulcet, sugary, saccharine, honeyed, cloying, nectareous, candied, melliferous, tuneful, canorous, euphonious, engaging, winning, winsome, alluring, charming, delightful, affectionate, tender, loving, amorous, sympathetic, lovable, seductive, bewitching. *Ant.* sour, acid, acetic, acidulous, acetous, astringent, vinegary, green, unripe, rough, evil-smelling, inodorous, fetid, stinking, foul, malodorous, discordant, disson-

ant, tuneless, inharmonious, unharmonious, cacophonous, unmusical, unmelodious, harsh, jarring, jangling, earsplitting, grating, repellent, repulsive, revolting, sickening, irritating, exasperating, intolerable, unbearable, hateful, execrable, offensive, disgusting, rude, bearish, brutal, discourteous, ill-bred, ungracious, boorish, unmannered, gross, coarse, churlish.

swindler—*Syn.* thief, cheat, impostor, con. man, pretender, charlatan, mountebank, conjuror, prestidigitator, trickster, villain, ruffian, rogue, rascal, ringer, spieler (*Aus. slang*), bunko-steerer (*slang*), capper (*slang*), decoy duck (*slang*), fraud, deceiver, four-flusher (*slang*), sharper (*colloq.*), blackleg (*colloq.*), bunko man (*slang*), diddler (*slang*), peculator, counterfeiter, forger. *Ant.* victim, dupe, mark, easy mark, Mr. Easy Mark (*slang*), Mr. Shallow (*slang*), come-on (*slang*), rustic, hayseed (*slang*), countryman, Johnny Raw (*slang*), plucked pigeon (*colloq.*), greenhorn, fool, cat's-paw, Silly Billy (*slang*), gull, gudgeon, *gobemouche* [*Fr.*], Simple Simon (*slang*), Mother's Boy (*slang*), Mr. Far-from-Home (*slang*), jay, sucker (*slang*), flat (*slang*), puppet, laughing-stock, clown, ass, donkey, clay-hog, bumpkin, flatfoot (*slang*), clod-hopper, Innocent Abroad.

sycophant—*Syn.* parasite, toady, flatterer, toadeater, tufthunter, lickspittle, flunkey, timeserver, cringer, crawler, truckler, slave, heeler (*pol. cant*), ward heeler (*pol. cant*), doughface (*slang*), sucker (*slang*), doormat (*slang*), rubber stamp (*pol. cant*), sponger, tool, hanger-on, puppet, cat's-paw, boot-licker (*slang*), groveler, spaniel, lap-dog, sniveler, dead-beat (*slang*). *Ant.* master, boss (*colloq.*), ruler, dictator, commander, chief, despot, overlord, leader, director, manager, tyrant, overseer, supervisor, taskmaster, ringleader, demagogue, driver, head, headsman, gang leader, censor, critic, fault-finder, knocker (*colloq.*), castigator, slanderer, backbiter, defamer, detractor, carper, lampooner, opponent, adversary, assailant, enemy.

symmetry—*Syn.* proportion, arrangement, order, equality, regularity, conformity, agreement, finish, shapeliness, centrality, evenness, balance, equivalence, equilibrium, equipoise, similarity. *Ant.* disproportion, inequality, irregularity, disparity, difference, disagreement, disarrangement, confusion, deformity, malformation, misproportion, contortion, distortion, unevenness, unconformity, crookedness.

sympathy — *Syn.* commiseration, compassion, condolence, cordiality, unity, harmony, alliance, concord, understanding, tenderness, pity, friendliness, friendship, kindness, fellow-feeling, consolation, sorrow-sharing, humanity, mercy, clemency, softheartedness, brotherly love, warm-heartedness, unselfishness, kindliness, charity. *Ant.* hate, hatred, unfriendliness, enmity, animosity, bitterness, aversion, dislike, hostility, coldness, hardheartedness, antagonism, rancor, spleen, malice, estrangement, discord, misunderstanding, difference, variance, feud, faction, disruption dissension, dissidence, jarring, wrangling, quarreling.

synonymous—*Syn.* same, like, similar, equivalent, identical, correspondent, corresponding, alike, interchangeable, synonymic, convertible, apposite, compatible, coincident. *Ant.* unlike, dissimilar, diverse, different, opposed, opposite, contrary, conflicting, divergent, unidentical, disparate, counter, contradictory, converse, reverse, antithetical, incongruous.

system—*Syn.* method, plan, order, regularity, rule, manner, mode, scheme, way, policy, artifice, operation, arrangement, program. *Ant.* chaos, confusion, disorder, derangement, disarrangement, topsy-turvy, jumble, mess, irregularity, complication, tangle, entanglement, medley, muddle, maze, intricacy, complexity, promiscuity.

systematic—*Syn.* regular, orderly, methodical, precise, punctual, formal, uniform, steady, constant, habitual, customary, conventional, stated, periodical, recognized, recurrent, normal, ordinary, certain. *Ant.* confused, irregular, informal, rare, unconventional, desultory, disorderly, uncertain, casual, random, vague, indeterminate, equivocal, contingent, changeable, unreliable, aimless, questionable, unstable, unsettled, enigmatic, indefinite, untrustworthy, fickle.

systematize—*Syn.* plan, arrange, organize, order, contrive, project, devise, design, frame, establish, institute, put in order. *Ant.* confuse, jumble, disorder, disarrange, derange, mess, muss, unsettle, disorganize, shuffle, complicate, involve, entangle, muddle.

T

table, *n.*—*Syn.* chart, catalogue, list, tabulation, schedule, index, roll, compendium, register, synopsis, roster.

taboo—*Syn.* prohibit, inhibit, interdict, forbid, prevent, debar, disallow, exclude, circumscribe, ban, frown upon, hinder, restrict, veto. *Ant.* permit, allow, sanction, license, grant, privilege, tolerate, suffer, authorize, warrant, favor, admit, concede, accord, bear with, wink at (*colloq.*), shut one's eyes to (*colloq.*),

taciturn—*Syn.* reserved, reticent,

uncommunicative, silent, mute, speechless, close, dumb, mum, curt, close-mouthed, laconic, sententious, sparing. *Ant.* garrulous, talkative, loquacious, multiloquent, chatty, chattering, gabbing (*colloq.*), fluent, voluble, cackling (*colloq.*), letting off steam (*colloq.*), gabbing (*colloq.*), gossiping, gassing (*slang*), freeing hot air (*slang*), verbose, wordy, argumentative.

tact—*Syn.* gumption (*colloq.*), perception, discrimination, judgment, acuteness, penetration, intelligence, cuteness (*colloq.*), acumen, longheadedness, perspicacity, subtlety, horse sense (*colloq.*), clear thinking, discernment, cunning, prudence, cleverness, ability, aptness, sharpness, good taste, refinement, delicacy, finesse. *Ant.* vulgarity, rudeness, coarseness, misconduct, misbehavior, blunder, blundering, thoughtlessness, carelessness, folly, foolishness, dullness or dulness, heaviness, stupidity, imbecility, folly, stolidity, hebetude, short-sightedness, giddiness, indiscrimination, shallowness, weak-mindedness, incompetence, fatuity, fatuousness, driveling, simplicity, silliness, misunderstanding, lack of intelligence.

tainted—*Syn.* infected, diseased, decayed, corrupt, vitiated, contaminated, fetid, smelling, stinking, putrid, rank, rancid, graveolent, rotten, polluted, impaired, damaged. *Ant.* pure, fresh, clean, sound, wholesome, good, excellent, untainted, uninfected, unblemished, incorrupt, blooming, unspotted, green, flourishing, strong, vigorous, healthy.

take—*Syn.* accept, receive, acquire, pocket, appropriate, seize, abstract, snatch, capture, collar, bear away, carry away, get, get hold of, clutch, grab (*colloq.*), recover, remove, obtain. *Ant.* give, donate, contribute, bestow, present, deliver, allow, bequeath, leave, hand out, dole out, grant, relinquish,

restore, return, disgorge, redeem, bring back, render, repair, compensate, indemnify.

talent, *n.*—*Syn.* aptitude, capacity, skill, power, knack, genius, turn, faculty, endowment, bent, gift, craft.

talkative—*Syn.* see ANTONYMS for **taciturn** above. *Ant.* see SYNONYMS for **taciturn** above.

tall, *adj.*—*Syn.* high, towering, lofty, elevated, stretched, exaggerated.

tame, *adj.*—*Syn.* submissive, domesticated, pliant, subdued, obedient, amenable, broken, tractable, timid, docile, meek, flat, spiritless, uninteresting. *Ant.* wild, fierce, spirited, unruly.

tardy, *adj.*—*Syn.* late, backward, overdue, delayed, dilatory, retarded, slow, detained. *Ant.* prompt, punctual, quick, ready,

tarnish, *v.*—*Syn.* stain, smudge, blemish, dishonor, defame, taint, soil, besmirch, sully, discolor.

task, *n.*—*Syn.* work, job, enterprise, burden, duty, office, mission, stint, charge, province, chore, function, assignment.

tasteful—*Syn.* delicious, delectable, pleasing, gratifying, tasty, nice, fine, elegant, esthetic, esthetical, delicate, artistic, dainty, chaste, exquisite, fastidious, classical, cultivated, refined, precise, pure, unaffected. *Ant.* coarse, vulgar, rough, rude, harsh, low, ribald, gaudy, gross, clumsy, unseemly, unbecoming, slovenly, dowdy, ungraceful, uncouth, rustic, barbarous, outlandish, uncultivated, unpolished, shabby, rugged, tawdry, grotesque, displeasing, inharmonious, inartistic, meretricious, deformed, disgusting, distasteful, offensive, fulsome, horrid, hideous.

taunt, *v.*—*Syn.* mock, deride, insult, ridicule, jeer, rally, offend, scoff, flout, twit, gibe, scorn.

tawdry, *adj.*—*Syn.* showy, garish,

flamboyant, pretentious, coarse, flashy, gross, cheap, gaudy, vulgar, florid, meretricious, phony, loud.

tax—*Syn.* custom, duty, impost, excise, toll, levy, assessment, rate, tribute, contribution, tariff, dues, tithe, exactment, capitation, dunnage. *Ant.* discount, rebate, allowance, poundage, concession, abatement, reduction, deduction, indulgence, tare, tare and tret, grace, favor, good-will.

teach—*Syn.* educate, instruct, tutor, train, school, enlighten, inculcate, indoctrinate, initiate, instil or instill, inform, nurture, discipline, drill, imbue, disseminate, expound, prepare, qualify, coach, cram (*colloq.*), prime, grind (*colloq.*), stuff (*colloq.*), illustrate, explain. *Ant.* learn, acquire, gain, receive, take in, drink in, study, read, cultivate, follow, imbibe, pore over, master, burn the midnight oil, plug (*slang*), copy, imitate, peruse, glean, wade through, translate.

tear, *v.*—*Syn.* rend, sever, split, part, rip, lacerate, rive, separate, mangle, sunder, cleave.

tease—*Syn.* taunt, tantalize, torment, vex, disturb, annoy, irritate, plague, harass, mortify, chagrin, spite, aggravate, bother, pester, harry, badger, irk, trouble, cross, anger, thwart, distress, displease, discomfort, provoke, exasperate. *Ant.* comfort, console, solace, please, satiate, satisfy, indulge, flatter, gratify, amuse, regale, refresh, stimulate, encourage, inspirit, animate, embolden, praise, laud, applaud, mollify, delight, charm, gladden, humor, interest, captivate, fascinate, allure.

tedious—*Syn.* slow, wearisome, tiresome, fatiguing, irksome, tardy, lingering, dilatory, sluggish, uninteresting, stupid, dull, humdrum, monotonous, soporific, drowsy, prosy. *Ant.* light, lightsome, heartsome, hearty, cheery, cheerful, cheering, lively, exhilarating, inspiring, animating, inspiriting, amusing, entertaining, diverting, jolly, jovial, merry, gay, interesting, captivating, charming, compelling, fascinating, enthralling.

tell, *v.*—*Syn.* reveal, impart, declare, divulge, communicate, disclose, discover, relate, inform, betray, recount.

telling, *adj.*—*Syn.* effective, convincing, forceful, decisive, cogent, efficacious, valid, powerful, definitive, sound.

temerity—*Syn.* audacity, boldness, hardihood, rashness, presumption, over-confidence, recklessness, venturesomeness, precipitancy, precipitation, hastiness, heedlessness, foolhardiness, thoughtlessness, carelessness, indiscretion, imprudence, impetuosity. *Ant.* caution, foresight, forethought, deliberation, care, prudence, discretion, coolness, self-command, self-possession, vigilance, watchfulness, circumspection, calculation, wariness, precaution, heed, heedfulness, prescience, worldly wisdom, watchful waiting, cowardice, hesitation, timidity.

temperament, *n.*—*Syn.* character, nature, disposition, constitution, temper, kind, personality, humor, individuality, complexion, composition.

temperate—*Syn.* cool, calm, impassionate, mild, moderate, genial, quiet, tranquil, still, smooth, tame, lenitive, reasonable, unruffled, pacific, halcyon, composed, dispassionate, easy-going, cool-headed, unperturbed, resigned, unexcited, patient, sober, frugal, sparing, abstinent, abstemious. *Ant.* forceful, boisterous, rude, rough, bullying, blustering, uproarious, violent, vehement, shocking, outrageous, furious, mad, angry, infuriate, raging, tempestuous, stormy, enraged, exasperated, boiling, rampaging, ranting, raving, roaring, uncontrolled, passionate, rabid, impetuous, frenzied, frantic, frenetic.

temporary—*Syn.* transitory, transient, fleeting, short, brief, ephemeral, evanescent, fugitive, volatile, shifting, passing, summary, momentary, fugacious, impermanent, changeable, vicarious, vicarial, substitutional. *Ant.* lasting, permanent, unchangeable, fixed, durable, persistent, long-standing, chronic, protracted, eternal, sempiternal, persistent, prolonged, immortal, undying, unperishing, imperishable, long extended, endless, perpetual, unremitting.

tempt, *v.*—*Syn.* invite, attract, fascinate, entice, allure, inveigle, woo, prompt, lure, solicit, seduce, incite, draw, decoy, court, appeal.

tenacious—*Syn.* tough, pertinacious, perverse, stubborn, obstinate, persistent, purposeful, unyielding, retentive, sticky, adhesive, cohesive, inseparable, waxy, resisting, gummy, cartilaginous, leathery, coriaceous, viscous, viscid, glutinous, clammy, persevering, resolute, determined, uncompromising, intransigent. *Ant.* loose, lax, nonadhesive, slack, immiscible, detached, brittle, breakable, delicate, crumbling, crisp, friable, fragile, frail, fissile, splitting, shattery, splintery, irresolute, wavering, vacillating, shilly-shally, infirm of purpose, fickle, unstable, giddy, light, light-headed, easy-going, timid, cowardly, faltering.

tend, *v.*—*Syn.* lean, lead, gravitate, dispose, incline, verge, trend.

tendency—*Syn.* aim, drift, scope, leaning, bias, tone, bent, turn, warp, propensity, susceptibility, mood, trend, disposition, predisposition, inclination, temperament, aptness, aptitude, aim, direction, object, goal, aspiration, purpose. *Ant.* aimlessness, thoughtlessness, oversight, purposelessness, negligence, heedlessness, neglect, carelessness, avoidance, supineness, omission, default, nonchalance, insensibility, forgetfulness, inattention, apathy, inanity.

tender, *adj.*—*Syn.* gentle, kind, compassionate, lenient, warm, humane, mild, loving, merciful, soft, delicate, sympathetic, benevolent. *Ant.* harsh, severe, unfeeling, callous.

tenet—*Syn.* view, conviction, belief, position, faith, trust, opinion, impression, doctrine, system, dogma, principle, profession, *credo* [L.], conception, self-conviction, presumption, assumption. *Ant.* disbelief, misbelief, misgiving, mistrust, scruple, qualm, doubt, scepticism, demur, unbelief, agnosticism, distrust, suspicion, uncertainty, vagueness, bewilderment, incredulity.

term—*Syn.* expression, phrase, word, name, denomination, member, article, condition, time, period, limit, boundary, end, finish, season, course, cycle, interval, interim, confine, bourne, border, verge, terminal, landmark, margin, line of demarcation, appellation, designation, title, head, caption, cognomen, patronymic, nickname, nomenclature, station, rank, degree, status, standing.

terminal, *adj.*—*Syn.* final, last, limiting, concluding, ending, terminating, ultimate. *Ant.* initial, first, beginning, opening.

terrible, *adj.*—*Syn.* frightful, horrible, terrifying, terrific, alarming, fearful, dire, appalling, dreadful, awful, horrid, shocking.

terse—*Syn.* short, succinct, pithy, laconic, sententious, compact, compendious, neat, concise, brief, close to the point, exact, pointed, trenchant, epigrammatic. *Ant.* prolix, tedious, wearisome, vapid, tiresome, profuse, verbose, wordy, long, lengthy, diffuse, confused, loose, meaningless, absurd, redundant, pleonastic, roundabout, tautological, ambiguous, rambling, long-winded, discursive, maundering.

test, *v.*—*Syn.* try, examine, substantiate, assay, prove, verify, experiment, inspect, scrutinize.

testimony—*Syn.* proof, evidence, affirmation, confirmation, affidavit, witness, deposition, certification, attestation, declaration, *data* [*L.*], warrant, credentials, voucher, testification. *Ant.* counterevidence, counter-protest, protestation, refutation, subversion, contravention, disproof, opposition, rebuttal, overthrow, denial, dissent.

thankful—*Syn.* grateful, obliged, gratified, contented, satisfied, beholden, indebted to, pleased, kindly disposed, mollified, assuaged. *Ant.* ungrateful, thankless, unmindful, careless, insensible, ingrate, forgetful, unsatisfied, grumbling, critical, censorious, faultfinding, repining, dissatisfied, grumpy, moody, morose, discontented.

thaw—*Syn.* melt, liquefy, dissolve, flow, run, deliquesce, liquate, calm, calm down (*colloq.*), cool, cool off (*colloq.*), curb one's temper, take it easy (*colloq.*), keep on one's shirt (*vulgar slang*). *Ant.* freeze, solidify, congeal, refrigerate, glaciate, chill, petrify, regelate, foment, incite, become excited, rage, rampage, storm, act violently, become furious.

theatrical—*Syn.* dramatic, showy, ceremonious, meretricious, affected, high-hat (*slang*), top-hat (*slang*), spectacular, ostentatious, melodramatic, high-toned (*colloq.*), pretentious, pedantic, stagy, big-sounding, canting, self-conscious, foppish, priggish, pragmatical, chesty (*slang*), stiff, starched, formal, prim, prudish, simpering, sentimental, jaunty, grandiose, imposing, flaunting, flashy, demonstrative, pompous, swaggering, vainglorious, arrogant, overbearing. *Ant.* humble, modest, reserved, retiring, bashful, diffident, coy, sheepish, timid, unassuming, unpretentious, unaffected, unobtrusive, unosten-

tatious, demure, shy, unpretending, deprecatory, constrained, deprecative, meek, lowly, submissive, subdued, mild, deferential, demure, gentle, compliant, cast down, abashed, mortified, embarrassed, ashamed, chastened, disciplined, suppliant, shamefaced, blushing, timorous, nervous.

theft—*Syn.* robbery, depredation, spoliation, pillage, plunder, swindle, appropriation, holdup (*slang*), burglary, brigandage, rapine, piracy, freebooting. *Ant.* restoration, amends, restitution, return, recoupment, compensation, indemnification, indemnity, equivalent, offset, set off, *quid pro quo* [*L.*].

theme—*Syn.* subject, topic, text, essay, writing, dissertation, proposition, matter, thesis, discourse, composition, conversation, tale, story, legend, talk, feature, *motif* [*Fr.*], point at issue, statement, report, narrative, description.

theory—*Syn.* hypothesis, conjecture, speculation, scheme, plea, supposition, surmise, attribution, ascription, apperception, perception, intuition, conscience, apprehension, precognition, condition, presumption, assumption. *Ant.* ignorance, darkness, blindness, nescience, unacquaintance, unconsciousness, haphazard, chance, probability, possibility, guess, indetermination, contingence, contingency, fortuity.

therefore—*Syn.* accordingly, consequently, hence, whence, thence, because, wherefore, for, since, on account of, forasmuch as, inasmuch as, by reason, for this reason, on account of.

thick—*Syn.* dense, close, crowded, solid, compact, coagulated, solidified, imporous, consolidated, petrified, indurated, lapidified, muddy, miry, heavy, turbid, dirty, filthy, feculent, foul, grimy, dreggy, slimy, gelatinous, viscous, glutinous, gummous, ropy, opaque, smoky, vitrified, ossified, numerous, packed, swarming, populous, heaped, profuse, multitudinous, dumpy, stubby, tubby, squat, thickset, friendly, familiar, fraternal, cordial, intimate, stupid, obtuse, crass, gross, coarse, ignorant, stultified, dull, doltish, clownish, stolid. *Ant.* rare, rarefied, airy, ethereal, thin, tenuous, subtle, filmy, gossamery, unsubstantial, light, spongy, porous, hollow, compressible, clear, transparent, diaphanous, limpid, pellucid, unsullied, foamy, frothy, immaterial, gaseous, shadowy, imponderable, vaporous, spectral, bodiless, incorporeal, disembodied, fragile, flaccid, frail, flimsy, plastic, flabby, flexible, flexile, yielding, limp, pliant, tensile, elastic, few, scarce, sparse, scant, unfriendly, inimical, hostile, estranged, alienated, disaffected, irreconcilable, smart, sharp, acute, intelligent, intellectual, sagacious, wise, sage, brainy (*colloq.*), sensible, level-headed.

thin—*Syn.* slight, slender, slim, flimsy, lean, scraggy, skeletal, *svelte* [*Fr.*], wasted, lank, gaunt, haggard, emaciated, attenuated, tenuous, rare, meagre or meager, spare, scrimpy (*colloq.*), scarce, scanty. *Ant.* thick, fat, ample, solid, abundant, profuse, plenteous, full, plethoric, heavy, massive, ponderous, dumpy, squat, roly-poly, pudgy, obese, swollen, inflated, ventricose, puffed.

think—*Syn.* cogitate, muse, ponder, imagine, suppose, expect, fancy, guess, conjecture, consider, meditate, reckon, deem, believe, contemplate, reflect, conceive, regard, opine, apprehend, hold, esteem, deliberate, study, speculate, reason, ruminate, brood over, mull over (*colloq.*). *Ant.* put away thought, relax the mind, let the mind lie fallow.

thorough—*Syn.* complete, perfect, reliable, trustworthy, accurate, correct, full, plenary, absolute, exhaustive, sweeping, radical, thoroughgoing. *Ant.* shallow, superficial, incomplete, inadequate, inefficient, unsatisfactory, unreliable, sketchy, crude, perfunctory, deficient, imperfect, garbled.

thought—*Syn.* sentiment, conception, consideration, reflection, imagination, supposition, care, opinion, view, idea, reflection, fancy, notion, provision, conceit, deliberation, cogitation, cerebration, meditation, speculation, lucubration, image, impression, perception, sentiment, apprehension, contemplation, brooding, mental exercitation. *Ant.* thoughtlessness, vacuity, vacancy, inanity, fatuity, incogitance, inattention, nonunderstanding, unreasoning, emptiness, non-intelligence, heedlessness, moonraking (*dial.*), woolgathering (*dial.*), abstraction, absent-mindedness, insouciance, indifference, giddiness, pipedream, brain-storm, fluster, flurry, distraction, light-headedness.

thoughtful—*Syn.* thinking, meditative, cogitative, engrossed, wistful, absorbed, rapt in, pensive, philosophic, contemplative, studious, museful, speculative, deliberative, reflective, sedate, introspective, clear-headed, clear-brained, acute, sharp, quick, level-headed, cautious, canny [*Sc.*] perspicacious, rational, intelligent, farsighted, keen, brainy (*colloq.*), wide-awake, cool, prudent, calculating, discerning, penetrating, politic, wise, sagacious, shrewd, cunning, discriminating, heedful, provident, pensive, dreamy, careful. *Ant.* thoughtless, heedless, careless, indifferent, shallow, feeble-minded, rattled (*colloq.*), stupid, heavy, obtuse, dull, loony (*slang*), addle-pated, muddy-brained (*dial.*), stolid, thick-skulled, doltish, asinine, inapt, inept, puerile, senseless, senile, fatuous, idiotic, nutty (*slang*), balmy (*slang*), foolish, silly, inane, driveling, incogitant, vacuous, empty, empty-headed, unintellectual, incomprehensive, wandering, irrational, absent-minded, unreasoning, witless, bovine, undiscerning, thick-headed, sappy (*slang*), spoony (*slang*), babbling, bewildered, confused.

thoughtless—*Syn.* see ANTONYMS for **thoughtful** above. *Ant.* see SYNONYMS for **thoughtful** above.

thrift, *n.*—*Syn.* economy, saving, frugality, prudence, providence, conservation. *Ant.* waste, prodigality, extravagance.

throng—*Syn.* multitude, mass, concourse, assembly, assemblage, crowd, host, jam, press, muster, gathering, meet, meeting, congregation, group, convocation, company, flock, swarm, mob, horde, body, gang, band, herd, aggregation, clan, posse, company, collection, cluster, pack, mass, agglomeration, conglomeration. *Ant.* scarcity, fewness, sparseness, sparsity, paucity, fraction, handful, scattering, dispersion, dissemination, diffusion, distribution, interspersion, spread, aspersion.

throw, *v.*—*Syn.* cast, project, fling, sling, hurl, impel, propel, thrust, pitch, push, toss, chuck, shy.

thrust, *v.*—*Syn.* shove, penetrate, drive, stab, push, fling, throw, enter, pierce, propel, move, cast.

thwart, *v.*—*Syn.* baffle, block, curb, prevent, oppose, outwit, frustrate, defeat, impede, hinder, balk, foil, check.

tidy, *adj.*—*Syn.* neat, spruce, orderly, snug, trim, systematic. *Ant.* slovenly, sloppy, messy, unkempt.

tie, *n.*—*Syn.* band, ligament, ligature, yoke, fastening, security, link, connection, bond, coupling, strap, tackle, bandage, brace. *Ant.* separation, sunderance, division, break, severance, detachment, disjunction, looseness.

tie, *v.*—*Syn.* bind, restrain, restrict, secure, unite, join, shackle, tether, hitch, fetter, fasten, fix, engage, moor, attach. *Ant.* loose, free, set free, unloose, unbind, unfasten, untie, detach, displace, unfix, loosen, change, disarrange, disturb, disunite, separate.

tight, *adj.*—*Syn.* taut, snug, close, firm, strict, constricted, tense, condensed, compact, compressed, narrow.

time—*Syn.* duration, age, period, season, era, eon, epoch, term, sequence, while, course, succession, date, span, spell, stage, interval, interim, cycle, present, past, future.

timely, *adj.*—*Syn.* opportune, proper, happy, well-timed, suitable, seasonable, appropriate, providential.

timid—*Syn.* fearful, shy, diffident, timorous, afraid, faint-hearted, humble, cowardly, spiritless, weak, poor-spirited, effeminate, hen-hearted, craven, sneaking, dunghill, skulking, frightened, nervous, shaky, apprehensive, discouraged, daunted, scared, terrified, sheepish, shamefaced, mean-spirited, irresolute, wavering, faltering, wabbly. *Ant.* brave, bold, courageous, undaunted, resolved, determined, resolute, unflinching, plucky, gritty (*colloq.*), unbending, unyielding, dashing, daring, unafraid, valiant, valorous, mettlesome, gallant, intrepid, manly, manful, stout, stout-hearted, fearless, dauntless, lion-hearted, chivalrous, doughty, indomitable, unshrinking, self-reliant, self-possessed, hardy, venturous, venturesome, bold as a lion, bold as brass (*colloq.*).

tiny, *adj.*—*Syn.* small, little, minute, wee, miniature, diminutive.

tire—*Syn.* weary, exhaust, jade, harass, fatigue, fag, wear out, worry, bore, irk, strain, overwork, overtax, prostrate, pall, disgust. *Ant.* refresh, brace, invigorate, inspirit, embolden, regale, enliven, freshen, stimulate, incite, energize, inspire, encourage, amuse, entertain, divert, cheer, comfort, solace, interest, relax, relieve, rest, restore, rouse, animate.

toil, *n.*—*Syn.* work, labor, trouble, task, grind, drudgery, travail, pains, occupation. *Ant.* leisure, rest, relaxation, repose.

tolerate—*Syn.* permit, allow, suffer, endure, admit, let, abide, indulge, concede, recognize, accord, vouchsafe, license, authorize, warrant, sanction, submit, submit to, bide, stand, bear, swallow, pocket, stomach, repress one's feelings. *Ant.* prohibit, inhibit, forbid, taboo, interdict, frown upon, bar, debar, disallow, hinder, prevent, restrict, veto, disapprove, deprecate, censure, remonstrate, reprehend, decry, protest, call down (*colloq.*), check, curb, stop, preclude, restrain, discountenance, oppose, obstruct, put a stop to.

tool—*Syn.* utensil, implement, machine, instrument, mechanism, weapon, apparatus, appliance, engine, motor, wheel, pinion, pulley, crank, jack, hammer, sledge, lever, bar, crowbar, winch, cam, turbine, loom, shuttle, derrick, crane, plane, screw, propeller, equipment, dupe, hireling, cat's-paw, stool-pigeon (*slang*), jay, hayseed (*slang*), greenhorn (*slang*), sucker (*slang*), puppet, gudgeon, fool, come-on (*slang*), gobemouche [*Fr.*], easy mark, Mr. Easy Mark (*slang*), heeler, wardheeler (*pol. cant*).

top, *n.*—*Syn.* summit, head, surface, apex, crown, culmination, pinnacle, acme, zenith.

topic—*Syn.* question, theme, subject, text, thesis, theorem, material, proposition, resolution, motion, argument, field of inquiry, point, point in question, matter, matter in hand, problem, moot point, affair, division, head, issue.

torment, *v.*—*Syn.* afflict, trouble, badger, provoke, annoy, torture, harass, bait, gull, try, plague, agonize, harry, distress.

torture—*Syn.* pain, anguish, agony, torment, rack, crucifixion, cruciation, martyrdom, pang, dolor, ache, twinge, physical suffering, mental suffering. *Ant.* enjoyment, delight, gratification, comfort, ease, luxury, purple and fine linen, bliss, entertainment, refreshment, health, bodily pleasure, mental pleasure.

tough—*Syn.* stubborn, hardened, refractory, unmanageable, tenacious, strong, firm, seasoned, wiry, hard, unyielding, fibrous, resisting, difficult, inseparable, coherent, adhesive, cohesive, turbulent, disorderly, rampageous (*colloq.*), rampant, unruly, boisterous, bullying, impetuous, savage, uproarious, immitigable, fierce, desperate, brutal, ruffianly, raging, ferocious, troublesome, laborious, rigorous, onerous, intricate, puzzling. *Ant.* mild, amenable, gentle, kind, good, tractable, yielding, complaisant, compliant, submissive, dutiful, obedient, docile, controllable, quiet, deferential, subservient, passive, peaceable, affable, bland, soft, genial, easy, easy-going, brittle, fragile, crumbling, friable, frail, crisp, splintery, nonadhesive, noncoherent, orderly, patient, humble, calm, serene, dispassionate, tranquil, peaceloving, composed, moderate, modest, forbearing, self-controlled, self-restrained.

trace—*Syn.* sign, mark, impression, trail, footprint, footstep, footmark, remains, vestige, memorial, track, remnant, token, record, indication, index, indicator, symbol, clew, scent, spoor, wake, representation, monument, memento, characteristic. *Ant.* obliteration, erasure, effacement, deletion, extinction, cancellation, suppression, oblivion, nonexistence, annihilation, extinguishment, destruction, demolition, abolition, dissolution, devastation, extirpation.

tractable, *adj.*—*Syn.* amenable,

docile, pliant, compliant, obedient, manageable, submissive, yielding, acquiescent, adaptable. *Ant.* unruly, ungovernable, intractable, obstinate.

trade—*Syn.* business, exchange, barter, traffic, speculation, sales, commerce, dealing, employment, office, occupation, calling, profession, line, job, situation, position, trading, undertaking, pursuit, province, function, craft, vocation, affair, concern, case, matter, art, handicraft, work, transaction, duty, avocation.

traduce, *v.*—*Syn.* calumniate, defame, malign, slander, libel, vilify, disparage, revile, asperse.

train, *n.*—*Syn.* series, sequel, sequence, trail, procession, retinue, line, tail, succession, attendants, henchmen, retainers, followers, following.

train, *v.*—*Syn.* lead, rear, accustom, habituate, inure, drill, exercise, practice, discipline, instruct, bend, educate, aim, direct, teach, prepare, qualify, initiate, familiarize with, inculcate, indoctrinate, instil, infuse, imbue, implant, guide, school, enlighten, prime, coach, inform, cram (*colloq.*), grind (*colloq.*), equip, fit out, make ready. *Ant.* misteach, misinform, misguide, misrepresent, mislead, misdirect, misinstruct, misdescribe, pervert, deceive, lie, falsify, dupe, hoodwink, fool, gull, hoax, delude, cheat, trick, mystify, puzzle, misinterpret, humbug, impose upon, confuse, bewilder, rattle (*slang*), misstate, distort, twist, garble, disguise, equivocate, lead astray, beguile, make false impression.

traitorous, *adj.*—*Syn.* perfidious, seditious, disloyal, treacherous, recreant, treasonable, faithless, apostate, mutinous, false, renegade, rebellious. *Ant.* loyal, faithful, constant, steadfast.

trammel—*Syn.* impede, hinder, obstruct, clog, hamper, shackle, fetter, spancel, hobble, restrain, check, encumber, cramp, retard,

oppose, cumber, incommode, discommode, discompose, thwart, frustrate, circumvent, enchain, bridle, muzzle, gag, pinion, manacle, restrict, bind, tether, tie, handcuff, curb. *Ant.* help, assist, succor, encourage, animate, incite, inspirit, stimulate, aid, advance, sustain, support, reënforce, relieve, uphold, serve, minister to, nurture, tend, oblige, cheer, accommodate, second, stand by, stick up for (*colloq.*), countenance, favor, befriend, lend a helping hand, free, set free, liberate, release, manumit, emancipate, enfranchise, unbind, deliver from, extricate, unloose.

tranquil—*Syn.* calm, peaceful, unruffled, quiet, still, hushed, undisturbed, restful, composed, smooth, tame, untroubled, pacific, sedative, moderate, gentle, assuaging, assuasive, soft, low, reposeful, soothing, placid, serene, temperate, halcyon, quiescent, faint, murmuring, whispering, stifled, muffled, purling, unexcited, softened, dulcet, unstirred, pleasing, agreeable, comforting, solacing. *Ant.* noisy, tumultuous, violent, rough, unquiet, clamorous, uproarious, blaring, disturbing, raging, raving, furious, loud, blatant, clangorous, deafening, ear-splitting, rackety, tempestuous, distracting, distressing, excited, raving, frenzied, boiling, agitated, ruffled, rampant, rampageous, perturbed, flustered, turbulent, flaming, ravening, uncontrollable, frantic, hysterical.

transact—*Syn.* do, act, perform, accomplish, treat, negotiate, conduct, carry on, achieve, execute, enact, perpetrate, prosecute, practice, hustle (*colloq.*), work, operate, officiate, exercise. *Ant.* idle, loaf, lounge, dawdle, slouch, loll, lag, loiter, dally, piddle, putter, dabble, sleep, slumber, snooze (*colloq.*), dream, languish, remain inactive, waste time.

transaction—*Syn.* doing, proceeding, business, act, affair, matter, deed, action, event, step, happening, deal, sale, selling, buying, purchase, purchasing, disposal, activity, performance, execution, undertaking.

transcendental—*Syn.* transcendent, primordial, original, intuitive, intellectual, beyond grasp, unintelligible, innate, vague, obscure, fantastic, supereminent. *Ant.* plain, clear, evident, obvious, intelligible, manifest, distinct, perspicuous, unequivocal, transparent, comprehensible, definite, unmistakable, positive, simple.

transform, *v.*—*Syn.* convert, change, modify, transfigure, evolve, transmute, vary, alter, develop.

transgression, *n.*—*Syn.* infringement, violation, fault, breach, invasion, sin, trespass, misdeed, crime, infraction, error, encroachment.

transient—*Syn.* brief, transitory, temporary, fugitive, passing, evanescent, ephemeral, momentary, short, fleeting, flying, flitting, impermanent, volatile, cursory, vanishing, short-lived. *Ant.* lasting, permanent, durable, enduring, persistent, chronic, protracted, perpetual, ceaseless, imperishable, unending, undying, everlasting, interminable, incessant, deathless, never-ending, never-dying, immortal, eternal.

transparent, *adj.*—*Syn.* clear, diaphanous, obvious, pellucid, lucid, serene, glassy, translucent, crystalline, patent, limpid, guileless. *Ant.* turbid, muddy, opaque, roiled.

trap, *n.*—*Syn.* snare, net, intrigue, stratagem, plot, pitfall, ruse, artifice, wile, ambush.

trash—*Syn.* waste, stuff, rubbish, rags, garbage, refuse, dross, dregs, frippery, dirt, filth, scum, offal, scourings, junk, leavings, shoddy, sweepings, rubble, *débris* [*Fr.*], slag, deads, litter, odds and ends, cast-off garments, residue, residuum, hog-

wash (*colloq.*), swill, sediment, slag, recrement, scoria, sordes, lees, rinsings, cheese-parings, worthless matter, worthless person or persons, *hoi polloi* [*Gr.*], *canaille* [*Fr.*], *sans culottes* [*Fr.*], guttersnipe (*slang*), gutter-rat (*slang*). *Ant.* goods, valuables, benefits, emoluments, advantages, perquisites, acquisitions, gifts, legacy, inheritance, gains, profits, earnings, income, salary, winnings, proceeds, prizes, acquirements, returns, accruements, money, wealth, riches, filthy lucre, Upper Ten (*colloq.*), Upper Crust (*colloq.*), Quality, Four Hundred, Society, swankdom (*slang*), swelldom (*slang*).

travel—*Syn.* journey, tour, voyage, expedition, excursion, pilgrimage, trip, tramp, ramble, peregrination, wandering, itinerary, march, migration, exodus, course, circuit, wayfaring. *Ant.* rest, repose, cessation, sleep, slumber, stop, pause, halt, inaction, stability, permanence, stoppage, unchangeableness, intermission, discontinuance, dead stand, dead stop, desistance, interruption.

treacherous—*Syn.* false, faithless, perfidious, traitorous, treasonable, false-hearted, unfaithful, untrustworthy, ill-disposed, unreliable, unfriendly, deceitful, ill-intentioned, malign, malicious, malignant, malevolent, spiteful, venomous, rancorous, base, foul, inglorious, evil, vile, ignominious, recreant, undependable, disloyal, trustless. *Ant.* true, faithful, trustworthy, reliable, dependable, magnanimous, fraternal, brotherly, warm-hearted, kindly disposed, friendly, charitable, sympathetic, affectionate, kind, loving, considerate, well-intentioned, loyal, honorable, honest, square (*colloq.*), white (*slang*), constant, staunch, upright, aboveboard, true-hearted, trusty, straightforward, conscientious, high-principled, frank, candid, open-hearted.

treat—*Syn.* talk of, write of, speak of, discourse upon, handle, arrange, manipulate, doctor, prescribe, comment, interpret, explain, descant upon, criticize, discuss, review, deal with, negotiate, bargain, make terms, entertain, indulge, satisfy, amuse, divert.

tremble, *v.*—*Syn.* shake, shiver, oscillate, quiver, pulsate, totter, quake, wobble, vibrate, shudder, quail, teeter.

tremendous, *adj.*—*Syn.* huge, prodigious, appalling, enormous, colossal, stupendous, vast, monstrous, immense, gigantic.

trenchant—*Syn.* sharp, keen, severe, cutting, critical, unsparing, energetic, emphatic, assertive, vigorous, strong, powerful, important, censorious, sarcastic, ironical, forcible, strenuous, dynamic, pointed, intense, vivid, impressive, incisive, poignant, positive, unmistakable, express, graphic, explicit, decided, dogmatic, salient, weighty, grave, serious, significant, spirited, pungent, piquant, pithy, sententious, ponderous, crushing. *Ant.* weak, feeble, vacillating, light, unimportant, shallow, simple, unimpressive, obscure, ambiguous, diffuse, pointless, languid, wishy-washy (*colloq.*), insipid, maundering, rambling, inflated, senseless, nonsensical, frothy, trite, trifling, silly, nonessential, petty, frivolous, worthless, rubbishy, puerile, childish, senile, inane, insignificant, paltry, inopportune, objectionable, futile, ridiculous.

trial, *n.*—*Syn.* test, experiment, attempt, touchstone, examination, effort, demonstration, scrutiny, proof, tribulation, endeavor, ordeal, assay.

tribulation, *n.*—*Syn.* suffering, oppression, agony, distress, wretchedness, trouble, trial, affliction, adversity, grief.

trick, *n.*—*Syn.* artifice, deception, illusion, maneuver, cheat, ruse, humbug, swindle, subterfuge, fraud, stratagem, caper.

trifle, *n.*—*Syn.* nothing, particle, jot, morsel, triviality, bit, fig, trace, iota, bagatelle, bean.

trite—*Syn.* hackneyed, common, commonplace, ordinary, dull, stupid, oft-repeated, wearisome, old, ancient, stale, out-of-date, antediluvian, whiskered (*slang*), graybearded (*slang*), fossil, familiar, known, well-known, conventional, archaic, hoary, venerable, worn-out, banal, uninteresting, driveling, piddling, senile. *Ant.* fresh, keen, sharp, up-to-date, interesting, pointed, new, novel, modern, fitting, suitable, appealing, moving, proper, opportune, becoming, seemly, desirable, expedient, rousing, bracing, heartening, enlightening, agreeable, apposite, pertinent, germane, felicitous, seasonable, applicable, relevant, apt, effectual, impressive.

triumph, *n.*—*Syn.* victory, conquest, mastery, achievement, jubilation, ovation, exultation, success, boast, celebration, ascendancy, walkover (*colloq.*), subdual, gain, advantage, trophy, prize. *Ant.* defeat, failure, vanquishment, subjection, subjugation, repulse, loss, rout, ruin, destruction, adversity, misfortune, downfall, ruination, calamity, catastrophe, reverse, backset, setback, disaster, hard luck.

trivial—*Syn.* petty, trifling, small, piddling, wee [*Sc.*], little, insignificant, frivolous, unimportant, mean, diminutive, slight, scanty, meager, inappreciable, microscopic, atomic, dribbling, inconsiderable, minute, unessential, paltry, beggarly, tuppenny (*Eng. slang*), worthless, useless, scurvy, mangy, gimcrack, frippery. *Ant.* great, large, massive, ponderous, heavy, important, serious, grave, consequential, far-reaching, mighty, powerful, precious, valuable, big, ample, weighty, significant, grand, paramount, paragon, essential, vital, necessary, useful, serviceable, advantageous, beneficial, momentous.

trouble, *v.—Syn.* distress, perturb, plague, embarrass, upset, annoy, agitate, concern, distract, vex, bother, worry.

truculent, *adj.—Syn.* savage, barbarous, fierce, ruthless, belligerent, ferocious, cruel, inhuman. *Ant.* harmless, tame, mild, inoffensive.

true—*Syn.* real, accurate, veracious, reliable, trustworthy, straight, honorable, honest, dependable, sincere, true-hearted, exact, correct, authentic, veritable, unaffected, actual, sincere, loyal, genuine, precise, factual, literal, positive, absolute, legitimate, unimpeachable, uncontradictable, definite, valid, well-founded, well-defined, truthful, faithful, leal, punctilious, scrupulous, square (*colloq.*), fair and square (*colloq.*), just, incorrupt, upright, righteous, rightful. *Ant.* false, fickle, treacherous, disloyal, unreal, fictional, lying, fabulous, mythical, ideal, imaginary, incorrect, erroneous, spurious, illusive, illusory, unauthentic, wrong, astray, inaccurate, inexact, unexact, mistaken, absurd, nonsensical, ridiculous, contradictory, self-contradictory, preposterous, fantastic, deceptive, untrue, fraudulent, misrepresented, sham, mock, bogus (*colloq.*), illegitimate, bastard, counterfeit, fishy (*colloq.*), unbelievable, deceitful, baseless, visionary, shadowy, unwarranted, crooked, traitorous, false-hearted, double-faced, perfidious, perjured, faithless, debased, evasive, slippery (*colloq.*), dishonorable, evil, dishonest, untrustworthy, trustless, evil-minded.

trust, *n.—Syn.* belief, confidence, credit, faith, hope, dependence, assurance, reassurance, expectation, reliance, opinion, conviction, security, estate, holding, benefit, interest. *Ant.* unbelief, disbelief, discredit, distrust, misgiving, demur, doubt, scruple, suspicion, incredibility, skepticism, debt, arrears, liability, default, deficit, insolvency, relinquishment, surrender, dereliction, abandonment, renunciation.

trust, *v.—Syn.* believe, credit, consider, esteem, rely on, place confidence in, confide in, depend upon, intrust, put hope in, swear by, intrust or entrust. *Ant.* distrust, disbelieve, doubt, impugn, assail, discredit, suspect, dispute, demur, smell a rat (*colloq.*), scruple, hesitate, waver, call in question, challenge, dispute.

trustworthy—*Syn.* reliable, honest, honorable, true, veracious, candid, sincere, true-hearted, loyal, leal, faithful, dependable, steady, constant, square (*colloq.*), four-square (*colloq.*), true-blue (*colloq.*), truthful, upright, righteous, decent, incorrupt, conscientious, reputable, respectable, staunch, high-principled, sincere. *Ant.* faithless, unfaithful, inconstant, unreliable, undependable, false, corrupt, mean, underhand, contemptible, sneaking, irregular, unsteady, drunken, intoxicated, perfidious, treacherous, traitorous, disloyal, unfriendly, inimical, base, mean, dishonorable, dishonest, ignominious, infamous.

truth—*Syn.* truthfulness, veracity, probity, honor, ingenuousness, sincerity, candor, openness, honesty, fidelity, artlessness, frankness, verity, authenticity, gospel, orthodoxy, accuracy, exactness, exactitude, precision, rectitude, uprightness, faithfulness, constancy, loyalty, incorruptibility, trustworthiness. *Ant.* falsehood, lying, prevarication, mendacity, fabrication, falsification, deception, invention, misrepresentation, perversion, suppression, exaggeration, equivocation, evasion, side-stepping (*colloq.*), beating about the bush (*colloq.*), duplicity, double-dealing, insincerity, hypocrisy, dishonesty, perfidy, bosh, flim-flam (*slang*), nonsense. twaddle, bunk, flap-doodle, (*colloq.*), poppy-cock (*U.S. colloq.*), rigmarole, rodomontade, absurdity, fiddle-faddle (*colloq.*), flummery (*slang*), fudge.

try—*Syn.* attempt, essay, assay, endeavor, aim, strive, make effort, risk, tackle, test, experiment, venture, adventure, speculate, take a chance, use, ply, handle, manipulate, put in operation, make trial of, judge, adjudge, inquire, examine, undertake. *Ant.* disuse, dispense with, lay aside, leave off, cast aside, pitch to the winds, throw overboard, prejudge, jump to a conclusion, look only at one side, neglect, avoid, shun.

tumid, *adj.*—*Syn.* turgid, swollen, pompous, protuberant, distended, ostentatious, inflated, dilated, bulging, expanded, grandiloquent. *Ant.* shrunken, deflated, reduced, concise.

tumultuous—*Syn.* agitated, disturbed, turbulent, violent, boisterous, disorderly, uproarious, lawless, riotous, noisy, excited, rowdy, vehement, blustering, rude, obstreperous, tempestuous, stormy, rough, raging, wild, rampant, perturbed, foaming, clamorous, passionate, uncontrolled, shaking, tremulous, mutinous, rebellious, demonstrative, vociferous. *Ant.* peaceful, quiet, restful, faint, gentle, muffled, tame, subdued, unexcited, unperturbed, easy-going, restrained, silent, quiescent, modest, pacific, moderate, soft, tranquil, mild, still, calm, unruffled, passive, resigned, repressed, inexcitable, cool, cool-headed, placid, staid, dispassionate, undemonstrative, composed, temperate, patient, meek, unimpassioned, grave.

turbid—*Syn.* foul, swollen, muddy, sedimentary, mixed, muddled, thick, impure, unsettled, unclean, slobbery, filthy, smudgy,

mired, befouled, grimy, messy, reeky, murky, dirty. *Ant.* clear, transparent, crystal, pellucid, translucent, limpid, glassy, hyaline, pure, purified, purged, clarified, settled, strained, filtered, filtrated, cleared, unsoiled, unsullied.

turbulent, *adj.*—*Syn.* disturbed, tumultuous, restless, violent, wild, brawling, boisterous, insurgent, agitated, stormy, riotous.

turn, *v.*—*Syn.* rotate, swing, revolve, spin, gyrate, whirl, pivot, twirl, circle, oscillate, reel, wheel, reverse.

type—*Syn.* symbol, emblem, figure, character, letter, representative, representaton, sign, sort, kind, pattern, form, class, model, standard, original, example, sample, copy, design, genus, species, variety, caste, clan, sept, phylum, breed, assortment, cast, mould, shape. *Ant.* amorphism, misproportion, deformity, monstrosity, abnormality, deviation, malformation, distortion, unconformity, peculiarity, teratism, freak, anomaly, anomalousness, shapelessness.

tyrant, *n.*—*Syn.* despot, oppressor, sovereign, dictator, autocrat, emperor.

tyro—*Syn.* novice, beginner, learner, neophyte, ignoramus, dunce, duffer (*colloq.*), bonehead (*slang*), numbskull (*slang*), blockhead, dabbler, smatterer, lubber, bungler, fumbler, muff (*colloq.*), lout (*slang*), butterfingers (*colloq.*), dolt, yokel, clod, booby, greenhorn, galoot (*slang*). *Ant.* expert, proficient, adept, scholar, connoisseur, master, *mahatma* [Sans.], philosopher, teacher, guide, leader, tribune, *doyen* [Fr.], seer, *savant* [Fr.], wizard, genius, prodigy, veteran, old stager, sage, thinker, oracle, luminary, star, Solomon, Solon.

U

ugliness, *n.—Syn.* unsightliness, distortion, unloveliness, uncomeliness, deformity, sordidness, hideousness, homeliness, sight, blemish, eyesore, fright. *Ant.* beauty, loveliness, pulchritude, handsomeness.

ugly—*Syn.* homely, ill-favored, plain, unsightly, unseemly, offensive, repulsive, hideous, deformed, forbidding, uncomely, hard-featured, ill-looking, grimvisaged, unprepossessing, dour, unbeauteous, ill-made, ill-shaped, unshapely, lumpish, lumpy, hulking, unpleasant, tough, hardboiled (*slang*), quarrelsome, illgrained, stiff-necked, rude, rough, pugnacious, cantankerous (*colloq.*), disagreeable, disorderly. *Ant.* beautiful, handsome, nice, comely, fair, pretty, lovely, charming, captivating, fascinating, graceful, elegant, flower-like, good-looking, wellfavored, roseate, rosy, rosycheeked, blooming, radiant, splendid, appealing, attractive, gorgeous, magnificent, elegant, exquisite, refined, delicate, dainty, shapely, well-informed, symmetrical, well-developed, tidy, neat, trim, jaunty, natty (*slang*), sleek, grand, gorgeous, dazzling.

ultimate, *adj.—Syn.* extreme, maximum, last, final, remotest, terminal, eventual, elemental, farthest, concluding, absolute.

umbrage—*Syn.* dissatisfaction, displeasure, resentment, offense, suspicion, hatred, contempt, harsh feeling, estrangement, grudge, antipathy, bitterness, resentment, aversion, alienation, enmity, malice, detestation, animosity, spite, rancor, repugnance, bad blood (*colloq.*). *Ant.* love, sympathy, affection, esteem, admiration, respect, regard, tenderness, brotherly love, attachment, devotion, fervor, infatuation, benevolence, friendship, cordiality, friendliness, fellowfeeling, fraternalism, fraternization, brotherhood, amity, good-will, comity, harmony, unselfishness, consideration, kindly feeling, warm-heartedness.

umpire—*Syn.* arbiter, arbitrator, judge, referee, justice, moderator, mediator, negotiator, peacemaker, propitiator, compromiser, settler, inspector, assessor, censor. *Ant.* partisan, adherent, follower, client, sycophant, parasite, heeler, (*slang*), toady, sympathizer, patron, backer, advocate, enemy, foe, opponent, antagonist.

unanimity—*Syn.* accord, agreement, unity, unison, concord, concordance, sympathy, congruence, conformity, correspondence, apposition, fitness, aptness, suitableness, aptitude, compatibility. *Ant.* discord, disagreement, dissonance, discord, dissidence, break, shock, jar, jarring, jostling, difference, variance, rupture, disruption, division, dispute, quarrel.

uncertain, *adj.—Syn.* doubtful, precarious, insecure, undecided, vacillating, irresolute, equivocal, indistinct, indefinite, ambiguous, problematical, unsettled.

unclean, *adj.—Syn.* dirty, filthy, soiled, grimy, smutty, slimy, unwashed, nasty, impure, foul, offensive, beastly, repulsive, squalid, obscene, fetid, abominable.

unconforming, *adj.—Syn.* aberrant, abnormal, irregular, erratic, peculiar, eccentric, singular, odd, offbeat, exceptional, incongruous.

unconstrained, *adj.—Syn.* free, spontaneous, natural, impulsive, unsophisticated, primitive, easy, voluntary, willful, autonomous.

uncouth—*Syn.* clumsy, ungainly, awkward, odd, strange, gawky, slouching, ungraceful, lumpish, hulking, graceless, ill-proportioned, vulgar, boorish, rude, homely, rustic. *Ant.* handsome, symmetrical, well-built, wellproportioned, easy, graceful, shapely, becoming, attractive, pleasing, neat, elegant, refined, genteel, mannerly, courteous.

understand—*Syn.* comprehend, take in, learn, apprehend, know, perceive, discern, recognize, conceive, imply, interpret, note, be aware of, experience, see through (*colloq.*), savvy (*slang*), make out, grasp. *Ant.* not know, be ignorant of, have no idea of, be blind to, be in ignorance of, mistake, misunderstand, misinterpret, misconstrue, garble, muddle, twist, render obscure, involve, tangle, jumble, mix, confuse.

understanding—*Syn.* intellect, intelligence, reason, rationality, faculty, knowledge, mind, comprehension, brains, mentality, capacity, reasoning, apperception, conception, gumption (*colloq.*), penetration, discernment, perspicacity, grasp of intellect, wisdom, sapience, genius, intuition, inspiration. *Ant.* noncomprehension, lack of intellect, cloudiness of intellect, incapacity, vacancy of mind, unwisdom, silliness, foolishness, imbecility, idiocy, aberration, incapacity, anility, senility, dotage, stupidity, simplicity, fatuity, vacuity.

undertaking, *n.*—*Syn.* venture, project, business, enterprise, task, effort.

undoing—*Syn.* ruin, ruination, downfall, reversal, destruction, misfortune, trouble, grief, hoodoo (*colloq.*), calamity, catastrophe, casualty, accident, mishap, infliction, bad luck, adversity, reverse, blow, trial, defeat, visitation, affliction, loss, woe, sorrow, mischance, failure, misadventure, jinx (*slang*). *Ant.* good luck, prosperity, fortune, blessing, godsend, wealth, happiness, pleasure, enjoyment, sunshine, fame, renown, glory, delight, success, triumph, victory, advantage, ascendancy, exaltation, honor, emolument, gain, mastery.

uneasy—*Syn.* unquiet, restless, fidgety, disturbed, anxious, troubled, fearful, irascible,

alarmed, afraid, timid, apprehensive, nervous, frightened, shaky, suspicious, unsettled, irritable, petulant, peevish, fretful, worried, harried. *Ant.* steady, firm, sober, constant, staid, undismayed, calm, cool, collected, peaceful, quiet, reserved, settled, stable, immobile, unchangeable, unalterable, immutable, content, satisfied, pleased, glad, gladsome, joyful, resigned, cheerful.

unequal—*Syn.* uneven, irregular, unlike, insufficient, inadequate, ill-matched, different, disparate, unbalanced, top-heavy, lopsided, one-sided, short, deficient, wanting, lacking. *Ant.* equal, balanced, even, full, sufficient, same, matched, equivalent, homologous, synonymous, coequal, invariable, regular, constant, steady, unchanging.

unfit, *adj.*—*Syn.* unsuitable, improper, inappropriate, unqualified, unhealthy, unconditioned, incapable, incompetent.

unfortunate—*Syn.* unlucky, disastrous, calamitous, ill-fated, unhappy, wretched, miserable, undone, lost, abandoned, deserted, ruined, overwhelmed, downhearted, sorrowing, sorrowful, unprosperous, unfavorable, doomed, ill-fated, ill-starred, unpropitious, evil, bad, jinxed (*slang*), hoodooed (*colloq.*), prostrate, desolate, ill, sick, poverty-stricken. *Ant.* fortunate, happy, blessed, successful, prosperous, healthy, wealthy, triumphant, affluent, victorious, conquering, advantageous, beneficial, thriving, lucky, halcyon, flourishing, opportune, timely, providential, propitious, auspicious, comfortable, well-to-do, contented, satisfied, delighted, pleasurable, joyous, cheerful, blithe, smiling, rejoiced, rejoicing, lighthearted, buoyant, animated, glad, exhilarated, breezy, bully (*slang*), gay, chipper (*colloq.*), jovial, elated, gleeful, exulting, exultant, rollicking, playful, hilarious, vigorous, vivacious, lively.

ungainly—*Syn.* clumsy, awkward, uncouth, inexpert, unskilled, lumbering, unfit, cumbrous, hulky, unwieldy, cumbersome, incompetent, bungling, lubberly, unhandy, slovenly, gawky, slatternly, unqualified, raw, inexperienced, green, inept, inapt, stupid, ugly, unseemly, ungraceful, slouching, stiff, rude, rough, ungracious, ill-mannered, discourteous underbred, unmannerly, gruff, churlish, clownish, vulgar, impolite, foul, foulmouthed, brutish, brutal, boorish. *Ant.* smart, quick, active, trim, neat, attractive, refined, skillful, expert, handsome, appealing, symmetrical, elegant, comely, fair, dainty, delicate, lovely, beautiful, graceful, fit, good-looking, alert, bright, keen, acute, handy, skilled, experienced, shapely, appealing, well-proportioned, trig, lively, polished, courteous, gentlemanly, good-mannered, cultured, gentle, well-bred, suave, polite, civil, bland, clever, talented, expert, adroit, slick (*slang*), proficient, masterly, competent, efficient, capable, qualified, trained, artistic, nimble-fingered, accomplished, apt, deft, able, up to snuff (*slang*).

unhappy, *adj.*—*Syn.* sad, dejected, sorrowful, dolorous, wretched, gloomy, miserable, distressed, despondent, disconsolate, dismal.

uniform—*Syn.* even, alike, symmetrical, equal, regular, unvaried, agreeing, conformable, consistent, unchanging, homogeneous, homologous, equable, unvarying, normal, undiversified, constant, stable, steady, agreeable, harmonious, proportionate, proportional. *Ant.* irregular, uneven, distorted, askew, awry, crooked, misproportioned, grotesque, jumbled, confused, twisted, contorted, slabsided, lobsided, unconformable, dissimilar, diversified, divergent, disjoined, heterogeneous, indis-

criminate, chaotic, anomalous, unarranged, topsy-turvy, deranged, formless, amorphous, tangled, disordered, straggling, unsystematic, misshapen, shapeless.

unimportant, *adj.*—*Syn.* trivial, slight, inferior, ordinary, small, mediocre, poor, unessential, frivolous, trifling, inconsequential, insignificant, paltry, indifferent, fair.

union—*Syn.* unity, unification, unison, oneness, junction, combination, conjunction, coöperation, coalition, concert, connection, concord, alliance, harmony, confederacy, association, attachment, marriage, wedlock, agreement, concurrence, concordance, unanimity, congruence, concinnity, conjugation, annexion, blending, absorption, amalgam, compound, alloy, amalgamation, commixture, affinity. *Ant.* disunion, difference, divergence, opposition, disagreement, discord, discordance, dissidence, disunity, unconformity, incongruity, disparity, inequality, disproportion, variance, clash, conflict, inconcinnity, irregularity, irrelevancy, disjunction, disconnection, dissociation, separation, division, rupture, break, severance, disseverance, segregation, contrariety, disintegration, analysis, dispersion, counteraction, antagonism.

unique—*Syn.* rare, uncommon, choice, matchless, different, unlike, unmatched, unprecedented, novel, original, unparalleled, unexampled, unrivaled, nonpareil, anomalous, individual, unusual, strange, remarkable, sole, bizarre, outlandish, baroque. *Ant.* common, commonplace, ordinary, normal, everyday, regular, like, alike, resembling, close, twin, equal, agreeing, accordant, congruous, conventional, customary, general, universal, formal, conformable, familiar, prevailing, well-known, trite, hackneyed.

unity, *n.*—*Syn.* integrity, oneness,

entity, identity, uniformity, concert, union, harmony. *Ant.* diversity, variety, multiplicity, dissimilarity.

universal—*Syn.* general, entire, whole, all-embracing, complete, comprehensive, total, unlimited, boundless, exhaustive, all, catholic, sweeping, widespread, world-wide, ecumenical, prevailing. *Ant.* special, private, individual, sectional, distinctive, unique, limited, narrow, particular, definite, certain, partial, singular, restricted, bounded, confined, small, circumscribed, terminable, defined, ringed, abbreviated, curtailed.

universe, *n.*—*Syn.* cosmos, macrocosm, creation, infinity, world, heavens, sky, firmament, galaxy.

unnerve, *v.*—*Syn.* upset, unman, discourage, weaken, confound, enfeeble.

unruly, *adj.*—*Syn.* fractious, disobedient, ungovernable, willful, headstrong, recalcitrant, obstreperous, refractory, mutinous, violent, wanton, rebellious, lawless.

unseemly—*Syn.* unbecoming, unfit, undesirable, unsuitable, inapt, inept, objectionable, ill-advised, inappropriate, inopportune, improper, ugly, forbidding, unsightly, inartistic, homely, vulgar, indecorous, ribald, gross, ungraceful, slovenly, dowdy, unkempt, uncouth, unpolished, boorish, clownish, rowdy, brutish, depraved, disorderly, vicious, dissolute, immoral, disgraceful, worthless. *Ant.* desirable, expedient, acceptable, convenient, fitting, becoming, seemly, practicable, goodly, symmetrical, well-favored, good-looking, comely, attractive, handsome, shapely, refined, cultured, polished, suave, courteous, artistic, cultivated, correct, proper, decorous, right, worthy, praiseworthy, commendable righteous, moral, well-intentioned, admirable, excellent, meritorious, deserving, unexceptionable.

unskilled, *adj.*—*Syn.* unpracticed, inexperienced, awkward, clumsy, inept, rusty, maladroit, ignorant.

unutterable, *adj.*—*Syn.* ineffable, unpronounceable, indescribable, inexpressible, incommunicable.

upright, *adj.*—*Syn.* upstanding, vertical, erect, honest, true, honorable, virtuous, faithful, trustworthy, straight, conscientious. *Ant.* prone, horizontal, dishonest, devious.

urgent—*Syn.* pressing, compelling, necessary, imperative, important, serious, momentous, wanted, required, demanded, solemn, grave, weighty, salient, earnest, impressive, chief, paramount, essential, primary, principal, critical, vital, absorbing, all-absorbing, hasty, precipitate, breathless, importunate, clamorous. *Ant.* leisurely, slow, dilatory, uncalled for, unnecessary, desultory, trifling, trivial, slight, shallow, foolish, puerile, unimportant, unessential, irrelevant, nonessential, piddling, petty, frivolous, farcical, nonsensical, immaterial, insignificant, uninteresting, inconsiderable, uneventful, common, subordinate, inferior, paltry, poor, mere, commonplace, ordinary.

use, *v.*—*Syn.* employ, apply, utilize, ply, manipulate, exploit, wield, handle, manage.

useful, *adj.*—*Syn.* serviceable, advantageous, helpful, valuable, applicable, suitable, practical, profitable, utilitarian.

useless, *adj.*—*Syn.* worthless, futile, unserviceable, valueless, unproductive, ineffectual, idle, empty, fruitless.

usual—*Syn.* general, habitual, normal, wonted, accustomed, frequent, familiar, ordinary, prevalent, regular, everyday, common, commonplace, public, prevailing, customary, conventional, prosaic, formal, stereotyped, trite, well-known, recognized, current. *Ant.* unusual, rare, infrequent, unwonted, strange, unconventional, odd, out-of-the-way, unique, uncommon, extraordinary, wonderful, remarkable, noteworthy, unexpected, queer, quaint, singular, abnormal, exceptional, anomalous, arbitrary, informal, unaccustomed, nonprevalent, unfashionable.

usurp—*Syn.* assume, arrogate, appropriate, seize, lay hold of, assume, claim, take from, encroach, take, bully, domineer, exact, wrest, wreak, oppress, override, trample, take advantage, put on the screws (*slang*), violate, clamp down (*colloq.*), overawe, dominate, infringe, commandeer (*colloq.*), take possession of. *Ant.* indulge, tolerate, bear with, spare, be merciful, give back, restore, recoup, compensate, indemnify, reinstate, rehabilitate, return, sanction, allow, grant, be lenient, permit, exempt, concede, stretch a point (*colloq.*), accord, favor, trust.

utility—*Syn.* use, usefulness, service, advantage, convenience, benefit, serviceableness, expediency, avail, benefit, profit, favor, efficacy, efficiency, adequacy, productiveness, utilitarianism. *Ant.* inutility, unprofitableness, folly, futility, inexpediency, impolicy, inanity, disadvantage, unfitness, inefficiency, disservice, ineptitude, inaptitude, inefficacy, uselessness, unfruitfulness, worthlessness.

utter, *adj.*—*Syn.* extreme, complete, entire, sheer, pure, unqualified, absolute, consummate, perfect, thorough, excessive, extravagant, exorbitant, outrageous, preposterous. *Ant.* little, diminutive, paltry, trifling, small, dribbling, piddling, inconsiderable, insignificant, limited, meager, simple, inappreciable, infinitesimal, microscopic.

utter, *v.*—*Syn.* speak, express, talk, articulate, pronounce, issue, voice, declare, say, assert, enunciate, deliver, emit, ejaculate, vocalize, blurt out, give tongue, recite, proclaim, declaim, acclaim, harangue, disclose, divulge, reveal, breathe, blab, inform, tell, publish, circulate, diffuse, disseminate, forge, counterfeit. *Ant.* keep silent, muffle, suppress, keep mouth

shut, shut up (*vulgar slang*), mump, mouth, gabble, chatter, gibber, splutter, croak, groan, snuffle, screen, cover, shade, mask, keep secret, keep mum (*colloq.*).

utterly—*Syn.* completely, entirely, totally, fully, wholly, altogether, quite, exclusively, absolutely, unreservedly, assuredly, positively.

V

vacant—*Syn.* empty, void, unoccupied, untenanted, idle, uncrowded, unfilled, unemployed, encumbered, free, inane, thoughtless, silly, daft, daffy (*slang*), foolish, giddy, wanting, blithering, irrational, vacuous, emptyheaded, blank, waste, deserted, null, uninhabited, tenantless, absent. *Ant.* full, filled, occupied, substantial, tangible, corporeal, solid, tenanted, inhabited, peopled, stuffed, crammed, congested, thoughtful, meditative, studious, bright, clever, accomplished, cultured, learned, scholarly, contemplative, wise, cogitative, reflective, introspective, brimful, replete, crowded, busy, jammed, packed, overflowing, brimming.

vagabond, *n.*—*Syn.* vagrant, tramp, wanderer, hobo, bum, stiff, bindle-stiff, idler.

vagrant, *adj.*—*Syn.* idle, wandering, roaming, traveling, roving, sauntering, strolling, ranging, prowling, straggling, perambulating, gadding, itinerant, nomadic, discursive, digressive, divergent, diverging, devious, loose, erratic, roundabout, straying, inconstant, unstable, unsteady, fluctuating, changeable, fickle, irresolute, unsettled. *Ant.* steady, staid, stable, sober, settled, fixed, stationary, immovable, restful, still, moveless, unchangeable, constant, permanent, rooted, established, untraveled, unerrant, invariable, irremovable, stuck, anchored, moored, home-loving, hermitical, eremitical, solitary, lonely, retired, secluded, alone.

vagrant, *n.—Syn.* wanderer, vagabond, beggar, tramp, rogue, gadabout, wastrel, idler, stroller, rambler, rover, ne'er-do-well, profligate, rascal, prodigal, runagate, renegade; loafer, cadger, hobo, straggler, beachcomber, larrikin (*Aus. slang*), hoodlum, hooligan, duffer, rounder, gaberlunzie (*Sc.*), tatterdemalion, sundowner (*Aus. slang*), ragamuffin, *sans-culotte* [*Fr.*], down-and-outer (*colloq.*), panhandler (*slang*), bum (*U.S. slang*), slut, wench, quean, bezonian (*Shak.*), castaway, black sheep. *Ant.* good man, noble liver, philanthropist, salt of the earth, model, pattern, exemplar, rough diamond (*colloq.*), honest person, honorable person, white (*slang*), decent man, worker, toiler, plodder, trump (*slang*), brick (*slang*), workman, artisan, craftsman, mechanic, operator, operative, doer, accomplisher, leader, guide, director, counsel, manager, governor, superintendent, supervisor, headman, chief, principal, president, adviser, captain, master, overseer, officer, judge, superior.

vague—*Syn.* uncertain, unsettled, indefinite, visionary, undetermined, unsure, casual, doubtful, dubious, indeterminate, undefined, confused, obscure, enigmatic, problematic, questionable, contingent, unreliable, provisional, dim, muddy, nebulous, indistinct, loose, ambiguous, mysterious. *Ant.* certain, sure, definite, real, undoubted, doubtless, true, authentic, authoritative, evident, unquestioned, undisputed, unquestionable, incontestable, incontrovertible, clear, unobscured, manifest, perspicuous, positive, unequivocal, unmistakable, dogmatic, absolute.

vain—*Syn.* idle, trifling, trivial, frivolous, visionary, migratory, shadowy, delusive, unavailing, valueless, ineffective, ineffectual, unreal, unprofitable, useless, futile, vapid, unsatisfying, unsatisfactory, unsubstantial, deceitful, bootless, baseless, unimportant, abortive, unserviceable, profitless, fruitless, inconstant, null, empty, worthless, inflated, proud, conceited, shallow, foppish, uppish, showy, ostentatious, upsetting, la-di-da (*slang*). *Ant.* solid, sound, substantial, valid, useful, worthy, serviceable, advantageous, beneficial, expedient, valuable, serviceable, effective, efficient, adequate, potent, competent, powerful, sufficient, profitable, real, earnest, serious, humble, modest, meek, retiring, bashful, demure, timid, coy, sheepish, unpretending, diffident, shy, unassuming, backward, unpretentious.

valiant—*Syn.* brave, bold, courageous, daring, unafraid, dauntless, undismayed, intrepid, powerful, puissant, vigorous, stout, heroic, gallant, valorous, chivalrous, spirited, high-spirited, plucky, assertive, manly, manful, lion-hearted, mettlesome, audacious, aweless, undaunted, unflinching, unshrinking, self-reliant, strong-willed, indomitable, dashing, fearless, defiant, venturous, adventurous, venturesome. *Ant.* cowardly, fearful, afraid, shy, timid, timorous, effeminate, weak, base, craven, chicken-hearted (*colloq.*), pigeon-hearted (*colloq.*), lily-livered (*colloq.*), frightened, unmanned, soft, pusillanimous, weak-minded, skulking, slinking, sneaking, dastard, dastardly, trembling, shaking, quivering, unnerved, faint-hearted, womanish, despicable, contemptible, scared, terrified, terror-stricken.

valid—*Syn.* sound, cogent, sufficient, weighty, substantial, strong, powerful, efficient, conclusive, operative, available, true, real, actual, authentic, genuine, well-founded, tested, legitimate, accurate, definite, factual, efficacious, forceful, effective, adequate. *Ant.* misleading, erroneous, erring, fal-

defective, worthless, deficient, untrue, unauthentic, spurious, counterfeit, insufficient, sham, fraudulent, fictitious.

valor—*Syn.* bravery, courage, prowess, intrepidity, boldness, gallantry, heroism, fearlessness, chivalry, defiance, pluck, derring-do, dash, manliness, spiritedness, backbone, determination, hardihood, firmness. *Ant.* fear, cowardice, poltroonery, pusillanimity, cowardliness, funk (*colloq.*), fright, consternation, dismay, alarm, white feather (*colloq.*), cold feet (*slang*), yellow streak (*slang*), timidity, effeminacy, dastardliness, faintheartedness.

value, *n.*—*Syn.* worth, price, esteem, consideration, estimate, estimation, utility, goodness, price, approbation, valuation, appreciation, consideration, advantage, remuneration, benefit, desirability, merit, quality, charge, cost, tax, toll. *Ant.* worthlessness, undesirableness, unfitness, inutility, disadvantageousness, inexpedience, inexpediency, annoyance, hoodoo (*colloq.*), jinx (*slang*), ill-wind, bad luck, misfortune, Jonah, uselessness, drawback, disapproval.

value, *v.*—*Syn.* esteem, estimate, reckon, assess, appraise, prize, treasure, appreciate, rate, figure, set store upon, compute. *Ant.* despise, condemn, discard, relinquish, disuse, repudiate, abrogate, give up, surrender, drop, forego, give away, throw away, renounce, abandon, neglect.

vanish, *v.*—*Syn.* disappear, depart, evaporate, dissolve, fade.

vanity—*Syn.* ostentation, display, show, conceit, self-esteem, self-confidence, self-laudation, self-glorification, self-applause, pretension, priggism, priggishness, vainglory, assurance, conceitedness, affectation, coxcombery, pride, swank (*Eng. dial.*), egoism, egotism. *Ant.* modesty, diffidence, bashfulness, backwardness, humility, unpreten-

tion, unobtrusiveness, timidity, demureness, humbleness, self-abasement, submission, self-distrust, self-control, reserve, coyness, shyness.

vanquish, *v.*—*Syn.* defeat, subdue, subjugate, quell, conquer, overpower, crush, beat, master, overcome, rout.

vapid, *adj.*—*Syn.* flat, insipid, bland, mild, lifeless, banal, tasteless, inane, spiritless, gentle, tame, prosaic. *Ant.* spicy, racy, pungent, piquant.

vapor, *n.*—*Syn.* mist, gas, steam, fog, cloud, smoke, spray.

variance—*Syn.* change, fluctuation, deviation, modification, vicissitude, oscillation, mutation, variety, difference, heterogeneity, diversity, incongruity, disagreement, inconsistency, dissimilarity, distinction, antithesis, inconformity, nonconformity, antitheticalness, contrariness, contrariousness, disarrangement, dissent, contrariety, contrast, disparity, unfitness, discordance, dissidence, disproportion, dissimilitude, dissension, disunion, division, split. *Ant.* union, unity, sameness, identicalness, equality, facsimile, counterpart, agreement, concord, harmony, conformity, unanimity, consistency, congruity, congruence, correspondence, concinnity, sympathy, accord, accordance, concert, concordance, uniformity, homogeneity, homogeneousness.

variation, *n.*—*Syn.* deviation, difference, aberration, alternation, modification, mutation.

variety—*Syn.* diversity, difference, medley, mixture, miscellany, change, variance, diversification, class, division, kind, sort, species, genus, race, tribe, family, assortment. *Ant.* sameness, monotony, unit, unity, individual, identity, unchangeableness, oneness, singleness, individuality, monad, cell, germ, atom, particle, molecule.

various, *adj.*—*Syn.* diverse, many, several, different, manifold, mutable.

vast—*Syn.* huge, colossal, spacious, enormous, mighty, bulky, boundless, unbounded, great, large, unlimited, ample, extensive, expansive, world-wide, far-flung, widespread, uncircumscribed. *Ant.* small, little, narrow, confined, limited, bounded, petty, insignificant, paltry, slight, inconsiderable, petty, circumscribed, trifling, trivial.

vaunt—*Syn.* boast, brag, puff, show off, swagger, blow (*slang*), trumpet, strut, bluff, bluster, exult, crow, put on side (*slang*), swank (*Eng. dial.*), jubilate, gloat, chuckle, draw the long bow. *Ant.* cringe, bow, kowtow, knuckle, bend the knee, stoop, fawn, crouch, truckle, toady, grovel, sponge, suck (*slang*), act the sycophant, lick one's boots, make a doormat of oneself.

vehicle, *n.*—*Syn.* carriage, conveyance; instrument, agency, intermediary, medium, channel.

velocity, *n.*—*Syn.* speed, impetus, pace; swiftness, rapidity, alacrity, celerity.

venerable—*Syn.* old, aged, grave, serious, sage, wise, reverend, hoary, time-worn, time-honored, superannuated, patriarchal, revered, honored, erudite, oracular, respected, esteemed, philosophical, experienced. *Ant.* young, juvenile, youthful, callow, inexperienced, immature, green, budding, modern, new, up-to-date (*colloq.*), *fin-de-siècle* [*Fr.*], newfangled, new-fashioned, novel, recent, fresh, brand-new.

venerate, *v.*—*Syn.* worship, revere, reverence, adore, cherish, respect, admire, regard, honor.

venial—*Syn.* excusable, pardonable, justifiable, allowable, trivial, exculpatory, defensible, slight, vindicatory, warrantable, extenuatory. *Ant.* mortal, deadly, serious, grave, indefensible, vicious, inexcusable, unpardonable, accusable, accusatory, unjustifiable, inexpiable, heinous, flagrant, grievous, atrocious, wicked.

venom—*Syn.* poison, virus, bane, virulence, malice, spite, malignity, malevolence, enmity, bad blood, resentment, rancor, virulence, gall, hate, hardness of heart. *Ant.* antidote, remedy, prophylactic, restorative, emetic, specific, cure, panacea, benevolence, kindness, benignity, brotherly love, charity, philanthropy, goodness, warm-heartedness, fellowship, fellow-feeling.

venture, *n.*—*Syn.* adventure, risk, hazard, peril, stake, chance, speculation, dare, experiment, trial, attempt, essay, plunge, leap in the dark, test, gamble, flyer (*slang*), potluck, flutter (*slang*), crack (*slang*), undertaking, enterprise, investment. *Ant.* intention, purpose, design, determination, decision, resolution, project, plan, resolve, predetermination, object, objective, aim, end, goal, target, reason, cause, study, proposal, judgment, deliberation, consideration, thought, thoughtfulness, looking before leaping.

venture, *v.*—*Syn.* attempt, essay, experiment, try, try out, assay, grope, feel, speculate, gamble, stake, hazard, bet, wager, play for, play the ponies (*slang*), shuffle the cards, take a hand, set the ball rolling (*colloq.*), invest. *Ant.* plan, devise, reason, scheme, think out, reflect, cogitate, consider, meditate, con over, study, mull over (*colloq.*), hammer out, weigh, ponder, dwell upon, discuss, digest, realize, take counsel, ruminate.

veracity—*Syn.* truth, truthfulness, accuracy, exactness, exactitude, credibility, reality, verity, ingenuousness, honesty, candor, frankness, openness, fidelity, probity, plain dealing, artlessness, sincerity, impartiality, fairness. *Ant.* falsehood, falsification, lying, double-dealing, trickery, artifice, chicanery, sophistry, quibble, stratagem, equivocation, double-crossing (*slang*), four-flushing (*slang*), misrepresentation, lying, falsity, falseness, mendacity, fraud, dissimulation, dissembling, fabrication, deception, deceit, delusion, imposture, guile, fiction, lie, duplicity.

verbal—*Syn.* oral, spoken, literal, vocal, unwritten, titular, nominal, lingual, phonetic, oratorical, rhetorical, elocutionary, declamatory, talkative.

verdict—*Syn.* judgment, finding, decision, answer, opinion, sentence, determination, decree, result, conclusion, upshot, deduction, adjudication, arbitrament, assessment. *Ant.* misjudgment, misconception, quirk, prejudgment, prejudice, partisanship, bias, evasion, presumption, presentiment, error, foregone conclusion, misconception, mistrial, obsession, fixed idea, *idée fixe* [*Fr.*].

vertical, *adj.*—*Syn.* erect, perpendicular, upright, plumb, straight. *Ant.* horizontal, prone, supine.

vexation—*Syn.* chagrin, mortification, uneasiness, trouble, harassment, irritation, pain, annoyance, worry, infliction, visitation, anxiety, ordeal, sorrow, distress, misery, unhappiness, desolation, infelicity, heartache, discontent, wretchedness. *Ant.* pleasure, satisfaction, contentment, peace, amusement, happiness, felicity, cheerfulness, ecstasy, enjoyment, comfort, wellbeing, delight, gladness, blessedness, rapture, enchantment, transport, delectation, joy, sunshine.

vibrate—*Syn.* swing, undulate, wave, sway, thrill, oscillate, move to and fro, quiver, fluctuate, alternate, flicker, wriggle, wabble, wobble, quaver, shake, pulsate, shuttle, rock, roll. *Ant.* stop, rest, pause, hold, close, cease, terminate, end, finish, stay, slacken, halt, tie up, discontinue, check, fasten, control.

vice—*Syn.* vileness, corruption, iniquity, depravity, immorality, guilt, crime, evil, badness, defect, fault, sin, wickedness, sinfulness, prostitution, carnality, lewdness, lust, sensuality, impropriety, scandal, profligacy, sodomy, fornication, adultery, incest, blackguardism, flagrancy, lust, Sadism, Lesbianism. *Ant.* virtue, goodness, morality, honor, decency, rectitude, integrity, merit, worth, excellence, innocence, chastity, purity, sinlessness, righteousness, clean living, honorableness, uprightness, propriety, good conduct, blamelessness, spotlessness, harmlessness, inoffensiveness, saintliness, holiness, sanctity, worthiness, godliness.

vicious—*Syn.* corrupt, bad, depraved, base, degenerate, profligate, demoralized, unruly, debased, contrary, faulty, vile, sinful, evil, harmful, obnoxious, hurtful, vitiated, foul, malignant, impure, virulent, wicked, destructive, mischievous, pernicious, evil-disposed. *Ant.* virtuous, good, gentle, harmless, innocent, upright, decent, honorable, kind, considerate, well-intentioned, helpful, high-minded, noble, charitable, philanthropic, right-minded, right, righteous, helpful, true, sterling, good-hearted, admirable, excellent, laudable, praiseworthy, exemplary.

victim—*Syn.* prey, sacrifice, dupe, come-on (*colloq.*), easy mark, Mr. Easy Mark (*colloq.*), sufferer, boob, booby, softie (*colloq.*), tool, cat's-paw, hireling, sucker, gudgeon. *Ant.* malefactor, criminal, culprit, felon, evildoer, law-breaker, jailbird, murderer, assassin, burglar, thief, con-man (*slang*), desperado, bandit, kidnapper, thug.

victor, *n.*—*Syn.* champion, conqueror, vanquisher.

victory—*Syn.* conquest, triumph, ovation, success, mastery, supremacy, ascendancy, achievement, advantage, exultation, celebration, subjugation, masterstroke, walkover (*colloq.*), lucky stroke. *Ant.* defeat, retreat, rout, disaster, destruction, overthrow, failure, frustration, disappointment, miscarriage, blunder, fiasco, breakdown, non-fulfillment, abortion, attempt, slip, stumble, oversight, botch, muddle.

view, *n.*—*Syn.* vista, survey, sight, aspect, prospect, outlook, scene, panorama.

vigilant—*Syn.* wary, watchful, wide-awake, sleepless, wakeful, circumspect, cautious, careful, alert, self-possessed, guarded, heedful, stealthy, prudent, leery (*slang*). *Ant.* careless, heedless, neglectful, negligent, thoughtless, oblivious, inattentive, incautious, inconsiderate, unwary, dull, drowsy, weary, indiscreet, impulsive, rash, foolhardy.

vigorous, *adj.*—*Syn.* energetic, lively, spirited, strong, powerful, active, robust, vital, strenuous, lusty, virile; healthy, flourishing.

vindicate, *v.*—*Syn.* extenuate, excuse, justify, advocate, exonerate, defend, acquit, support, whitewash.

vindictive, *adj.*—*Syn.* vengeful, malevolent, rancorous, resentful, unforgiving, malicious, grudgeful.

violence, *n.*—*Syn.* intensity, vehemence, passion, force, might, ferocity, fierceness, boisterousness, fury, turbulence, rage, agitation, severity.

violent—*Syn.* impetuous, furious, vehement, angry, raging, mad, frenzied, boisterous, riotous, turbulent, disorderly, uproarious, obstreperous, blustering, fuming, rampant, swearing, ravening, infuriate, outrageous, frantic, hysterical, desperate, frothing. *Ant.* gentle, mild, tender, soft, kind, kindly, humble, modest, moderate, quiet, smooth, peaceful, pacific, restful, tranquil, sober, untroubled, cool, calm, collected, tame, unruffled, peaceable, halcyon, undisturbed, composed, dispassionate, inexcitable.

virtue—*Syn.* chastity, sanctity, purity, morality, goodness, righteousness, uprightness, rec-

titude, honor, honesty, decency, right living, credibility, innocence, incorruption, guiltlessness, clean hands, clear conscience, inoffensiveness, harmlessness, sinlessness, impeccability, guilelessness, blamelessness, faultlessness. *Ant.* vice, viciousness, wickedness, badness, vileness, evil, baseness, dishonor, dishonesty, knavery, trickery, fraud, cheating, stealing, theft, misconduct, guilt, felony, sin, crime, misdemeanor, outrage, sinfulness, villainy, rascality, immorality, atrocity, depravity, corruption, impurity, Sodomy, lechery, venery, dissipation.

vision—*Syn.* phantom, apparition, image, shadow, ghost, wraith, phantasm, specter, dream, fancy, imagination, spirit, sprite, witch, warlock, fairy, banshee, manifestation, astral body, etheric body, appearance. *Ant.* reality, substance, body, solidity, actuality, matter, existence, fact, truth, thing, object, corporeity, corporality, corporeality, materiality, materialness, substantiality, substantialness, physical world, material existence.

vision—*Syn.* sight, eyesight, optics, glance, glimpse, peek, gaze, stare, view, look, survey, inspection, examination, viewpoint, ocular demonstration. *Ant.* blindness, sightlessness, darkness, ablepsia, anopsia, anopsy, dimsightedness, cataract, film, *gutta serena* [L.], "drop serene" (*Milton*), sandy blight (*Aus. slang*), teichopsia, amaurosis, cecity.

visit, *v.*—*Syn.* call, sojourn, stop, see, frequent.

vituperate, *v.*—*Syn.* vilify, berate, censure, rebuke, abuse, scold, denounce, revile, reproach, curse, upbraid, rate, condemn, calumniate.

vivid, *adj.*—*Syn.* lively, striking, fresh, quick, intense, sprightly, brilliant, strong, telling, real, bright, vibrant.

vocal, *adj.*—*Syn.* spoken, verbal, oral, articulate, eloquent, expressive, fluent.

vociferous, *adj.*—*Syn.* blatant, uproarious, strident, loud, clamorous, vehement, obstreperous, boisterous.

voice, *n.*—*Syn.* speech, utterance, sound, noise; enunciation, pronunciation, accent, articulation; expression, language, words.

void, *adj.*—*Syn.* empty, unoccupied, lacking, blank, vacuous, hollow, destitute.

volatile—*Syn.* light, airy, imponderable, subtle, buoyant, sublimated, gaseous, gasiform, vaporous, aëriferous, evaporable, vapory, vaporizable, fleeting, weak, shilly-shally, irresolute, wavering, vacillating, wabbly. *Ant.* heavy, ponderous, ponderable, serious, weighty, massive, unwieldy, cumbrous, durable, lasting, permanent, soluble, dissoluble, liquefied, liquescent, resolute, determined, steadfast, unflinching, resolved, firm, earnest, energetic, persevering.

voluntary, *adj.*—*Syn.* intentional, volitional, spontaneous, deliberate, free, uncompelled, unconstrained, gratuitous.

voluptuous—*Syn.* sensual, pleasure-loving, Sybaritic, luxurious, wanton, sensuous, hedonic, dissipated, carnal, indulgent, indulging, gratifying, satisfying, intemperate, self-indulgent, licentious, debauched, dissolute, rakish, fast, Epicurean, lustful, concupiscent, lewd, lascivious, libidinous, bestial, incestuous, salacious, erotic, ruttish, goatish, vampant, Paphian. *Ant.* ascetic, self-denying, austere, puritanical, religious, weak, starved, emaciated, hungry, consumptive, suffering, pinched, troubled, worried, tormented, harrowed, racked, harassed, dejected, melancholy, prostrated, depressed, worn-out, discouraged, faint, weary, tottering, faltering, flat, dull, cheerless, gloomy, downhearted, poverty-stricken, abstinent, abstemious, self-sacrificing, moral, pure, modest, chaste, continent.

voracious, *adj.*—*Syn.* greedy, hungry, famished, gluttonous, ravenous, rapacious, ravening.

vouch—*Syn.* assert, aver, attest, warrant, affirm, confirm, guarantee, asseverate, declare, testify, bear testimony, protest, assure, predicate, profess, put forth, maintain, contend, depose, avow, swear, take affidavit, take Bible oath, kiss the Book. *Ant.* deny, repudiate, discard, contradict, recant, rebut, confute, controvert, gainsay, negative, impugn, dispute, abjure, dismiss, ignore, disavow, contravene, reject, disclaim, disown, renounce, abnegate, forswear, deprecate, discountenance, disapprove, disprove.

vouchsafe, *v.*—*Syn.* grant, deign, award, give, allow, accord, condescend, concede, favor.

vulgar—*Syn.* common, ordinary, uncouth, rude, uncultured, unpolished, rough, ignorant, inelegant, lowborn, offensive, ill-bred, impudent, impertinent, profane, foul-mouthed, filthy, dirty, dirty-minded, obscene, nasty, boorish, clownish, plebeian, low-minded, loutish, churlish, brutish, disgusting, loathsome, odious. *Ant.* refined, polite, polished, cultured, learned, accomplished, civil, well-spoken, agreeable, attractive, fascinating, elegant, graceful, artistic, chaste, proper, tidy, trim, neat, symmetrical, pleasing, natural, charming, æsthetic, fashionable, well-bred, decorous, decent, conventional, gentlemanly, ladylike.

vulgarity, *n.*—*Syn.* indelicacy, coarseness, grossness, gaucherie, boorishness, obscenity, barbarism, inelegance, rudeness.

W

wages, *n.*—*Syn.* pay, payment, earnings, income, salary, stipend, emolument, fee, compensation, remuneration.

wait—*Syn.* tarry, linger, await, expect, look for, wait for, adjourn, prorogue, postpone, lie in wait, bide one's time, take it easy, dally, idle, trifle, lie in ambush, set a trap for, watch, watch for, keep a sharp lookout. *Ant.* forestall, anticipate, steal a march, gain time, take time by the forelock, pounce upon, spring upon, act, take action, operate, put in practice, bestow, hurry, quicken, accelerate, expedite, urge, whip, spur, goad, lose no time.

waken, *v.*—*Syn.* awake, awaken, wake, arouse, rouse, excite, stir, animate, stimulate, enkindle.

wallow, *v.*—*Syn.* flounder, grovel, revel, welter, roll, toss.

wander—*Syn.* roam, stray, range, rove, ramble, stroll, walk, move, shift, drift, glide, roll, roll on, journey, keep going, keep moving, hike, saunter, tramp, jog trot, promenade, go astray, digress, diverge, err, deviate, travel, tour, traverse, peregrinate, straggle, meander, gang awa' [*Sc.*], lose one's senses, become insane, speak foolishly, rave, blither, talk nonsensically, have bats in the belfry (*slang*), have rats in the upper story (*slang*), have a tile loose (*slang*). *Ant.* stay, heave to, lay to, pull up, pause, become sane, sober down, cool down, be sensible, keep on your shirt (*vulgar slang*), act sensibly, hew to the line, be normal, be rational, wait, remain, rest, stand firm, stand still, repose, tarry, mark time, stick, stand fast, stay at home, halt, stop, lie down, keep your ground, stay where you are.

want—*Syn.* lack, need, privation, hunger, starvation, penury, poverty, insufficiency, scarcity, dearth, exigency, emptiness, famine, depletion, pauperism, inadequacy, pittance, incompetence, stint, neediness, necessity, dearth, distress, straits, beggary, mendicity, mendicancy, indigence, impecuniosity, pennilessness, wolf at the door. *Ant.* plenty, profusion, abundance, wealth, riches, property, suffi-

ciency, competence, fullness, copiousness, full measure, enough, adequacy, affluence, luxury, cornucopia, horn of plenty, purple and fine linen, opulence, treasure, bonanza, El Dorado, Golconda, Mammon, pelf, lucre, filthy lucre, resources, capital, nest egg (*colloq.*), money, inheritance, legacy, almighty dollar (*colloq.*), spondulics or spondulix (*slang*).

warfare, *n.*—*Syn.* war, fighting, hostilities, battle, combat, struggle, conflict, operations.

warn, *v.*—*Syn.* caution, advise, summon, call, apprise, admonish, inform, forewarn, forebode, notify, counsel, threaten.

warning, *n.*—*Syn.* caution, prediction, alarm, omen, notice, advice, portent, augury, admonition, summons.

wary—*Syn.* circumspect, cautious, alert, wide-awake, heedful, prudent, thoughtful, guarded, provident, careful, vigilant, watchful, considerate, mindful, suspicious, leery (*slang*), surefooted, politic, canny [*Sc.*]. *Ant.* careless, incautious, rash, headlong, precipitate, unthinking, thoughtless, unwary, impetuous, imprudent, impulsive, heedless, reckless, wanton, devil-may-care, foolhardy, hotheaded, headstrong, giddy, light, negligent, neglectful, inconsiderate.

waste—*Syn.* squander, dissipate, destroy, throw away, lavish, scatter, spend, dwindle, wither, decay, become thin, lose flesh, lose weight, spoil, misuse, abuse, lose, be prodigal, indulge, surfeit, gourmandize, hog (*colloq.*), wallow in riches, wallow in purple and fine linen, act the spendthrift, ravage, devastate, lay waste, exhaust, consume, impoverish, deplete, empty, spill, drain, dilapidate, overrun, damage, pillage, misapply, profane, prostitute, misspend, blow lacious, false, dubious, doubtful, uncertain, ungenuine, forged, falsified, delusive, deceptive, unsound, incorrect,

in (*slang*), burn the candle at both ends, make ducks and drakes of one's money (*colloq.*). *Ant.* increase, multiply, enlarge, swell, augment, add to, double, triple, hoard, lay up, conserve, preserve, supplement, produce, accomplish, achieve, construct, erect, establish, institute, provide, supply, provision, furnish, fill, gather into, improve, mend, fatten, become stout, restore, repair, revive, render useful, use, operate, ply, utilize, absorb, acquire, recover, gain, win, procure, get, collect, raise funds, treasure up, get hold of, take possession, turn to account, bring grist to the mill, monopolize, appropriate.

wasteful—*Syn.* extravagant, profligate, dissipated, prodigal, thriftless, lavish, squandering, profuse, unthrifty, improvident, careless, devil-may-care, reckless, wild, destructive. *Ant.* saving, hoarding, miserly, petty, tight-fisted, sordid, mercenary, greedy, avaricious, close, close-fisted, chary, mean, ungenerous, shabby, penurious, stingy, parsimonious.

watchful, *adj.*—*Syn.* vigilant, alert, careful, attentive, wary, heedful, cautious, wakeful.

water, *v.*—*Syn.* wet, immerse, plunge, wash, soak, moisten, sprinkle, bathe, irrigate, dilute, deluge, drench.

wave, *n.*—*Syn.* undulation, ripple, billow, breaker, surge, roller, swell, comber.

way—*Syn.* path, track, route, highway, roadway, thoroughfare, street, avenue, driveway, road, pathway, alley, bridlepath, highroad, course, pass, lane, channel, vennel [*Sc.*], gateway, entrance, passage, approach, parkway, boulevard, railroad, tramway, trolley track, towpath, speedway, canal, mode, method, plan, design, system, means, manner, fashion, form, process, procedure, line of conduct, gait, tone, guise.

weak—*Syn.* feeble, infirm, soft, effeminate, flaccid, relaxed, unnerved, strengthless, sapless, soft, fragile, delicate, consumptive, enervated, unsubstantial, unsound, languid, shaky, broken-down, nervous, faint, worn, seedy, effete, wasted, washy, wishy-washy, shattered, sapless, unstrung, powerless, palsied, decrepit. *Ant.* strong, stout, stouthearted, vigorous, muscular, robust, sturdy, husky, able-bodied, athletic, gymnastic, manly, manful, virile, potent, powerful, puissant, sinewy, stalwart, hard, hardy, strapping, forceful, healthy, brawny, lusty, all-powerful, mighty, dynamic, peppy (*slang*), energetic, courageous.

weaken, *v.*—*Syn.* debilitate, enfeeble, reduce, enervate, devitalize, sap, attenuate, exhaust, undermine.

wealth—*Syn.* money, riches, property, assets, belongings, affluence, opulence, pelf, possessions, prosperity, abundance, competence, competency, substance, means, goods, fortune, lucre, filthy lucre, plenty, luxury, luxuriance, realty, lands, chattels, resources, estate. *Ant.* poverty, privation, want, scarcity, impecuniosity, need, pauperism, lack, indigence, beggary, mendicancy, squalor, straits, straitened circumstances, misery, wretchedness, destitution, penury, dearth, insufficiency, incompetence, inadequacy, pennilessness, distress, difficulty, wolf at the door.

weariness, *n.*—*Syn.* fatigue, tiredness, lassitude, lethargy, prostration, exhaustion, languor, faintness, ennui.

wearisome—*Syn.* tedious, tiresome, uninteresting, vapid, insipid, dull, stupid, slow, slack, tardy, sluggish, apathetic, phlegmatic, laborious, toilsome, strenuous, drooping, hard, difficult, onerous, heavy, troublesome, burdensome, fatiguing, heartbreaking, uphill, plodding, overpowering, exhausting, backbreaking, grinding, merciless. *Ant.* exhilarating, refreshing, regaling, quickening, bracing, invigorating, stimulating, restorative, recuperative, comforting, consoling, joyous, happy, bright, gay, amusing, entertaining, charming, attractive, fascinating, captivating, alluring, soothing, assuaging, delightful, sunny, genial, pleasing, gladdening, rapturous, ravishing.

weary—*Syn.* fatigue, tire, harass, annoy, jade, pain, disgust, irritate, worry, vex, anger, bother, bore, fret, chafe, grieve, distress, displease, irk, flag, exhaust, overtax, overburden, depress, discourage, dishearten, deject, lower, sink, unman, prostrate, sadden, strain, wear out, dispirit, fag, fag out. *Ant.* refresh, comfort, gladden, rejoice, regale, brace, invigorate, inspire, animate, inspirit, enthuse, brighten, strengthen, revive, please, make happy, cheer, arouse, enliven, elate, boost (*colloq.*), praise, laud, acclaim, exhilarate, delight, amuse, entertain, ease, calm, console, encourage, divert, tickle the fancy, convulse with laughter.

weight—*Syn.* gravity, heaviness, burden, load, ponderousness, ponderosity, ballast, counterpoise, mass, contents, cargo, lading, freight, shipment, influence, domination, power, control, preponderance. *Ant.* levity, lightness, buoyancy, imponderability, volatility, airiness, ethereality, nothingness, immateriality, unimportance, feebleness, powerlessness, impotence, lack of power, want of influence.

weird, *adj.*—*Syn.* eerie, uncanny, wild, supernatural, spooky, unearthly, eldritch, ghostly.

well-being—*Syn.* happiness, prosperity, welfare, fortune, blessing, godsend, luck, success, smile of fortune, fat of the land, milk and honey, loaves and fishes, right living, health, affluence, riches, wealth. *Ant.* adversity, misfortune, bad luck, evil, trouble, hardship, poverty, sickness, illness, calamity, catas-

trophe, blow, trial, infliction, sorrow, comedown, setback, drawback, persecution, tribulation, loss, bereavement.

whole—*Syn.* entire, complete, total, integral, all, aggregate, full, absolute, plenary, undivided, all-embracing, inclusive. *Ant.* part, partial, incomplete, fractional, sectional, divided, imperfect, insufficient, defective, deficient, wanting, short, mutilated, broken, reduced.

wicked—*Syn.* iniquitous, nefarious, vile, sinful, wayward, wrong, vicious, erring, dissolute, disorderly, disreputable, corrupt, immoral, impure, evil, malevolent, evil-disposed, evil-minded, shameful, base, foul, gross, atrocious, scandalous, infamous, villainous, hellish, devilish, demoniacal, fiendish. *Ant.* good, kind, loving, affectionate, innocent, spotless, stainless, white (*slang*), noble, philanthropic, sterling, right-minded, righteous, upright, fine, exemplary, pure, whole-souled, praiseworthy, laudable, meritorious, deserving, creditable, commendable, virtuous, well-intentioned, excellent, admirable.

will, *n.*—*Syn.* volition, wish, pleasure, resolution, mind, determination, desire, inclination, decision, intent, willingness.

wind, *n.*—*Syn.* breeze, air, draught, gale, blast.

winding, *adj.*—*Syn.* twisting, bending, turning, sinuous, twining, coiling, writhing, meandering, crooked, devious.

winning—*Syn.* attractive, charming, fascinating, bewitching, enchanting, dazzling, nice, captivating, alluring, pleasing, lovable, courteous, sweet, amiable, agreeable, gratifying, acceptable, inviting, delightful, appealing, winsome, seductive, entrancing, ravishing. *Ant.* repulsive, repellent, ugly, loathsome, disgusting, hateful, terrible, frightful, revolting, sickening, irritating, provoking, maleficent, malignant, unpleasing, annoying, aggravating, irksome, galling, tiresome, wearisome, unbearable, insufferable.

wisdom—*Syn.* prudence, foresight, sagacity, farsightedness, acumen, astuteness, intelligence, comprehension, acuteness, cuteness (*colloq.*), perspicacity, ability, longheadedness, discrimination, discernment, penetration, subtlety, good judgment, savvy (*slang*), head, brains, capacity, gumption (*colloq.*), horse sense (*colloq.*), profundity, sapience, inspiration, reason, clear thinking, attainment, insight, depth, prudence, understanding, discretion, reasonableness, sense, skill, judiciousness, prescience, knowledge, learning, enlightenment, information, erudition, experience, judiciousness, reasoning. *Ant.* folly, foolishness, absurdity, nonsense, flapdoodle (*dial.*), idiocy, buncombe, stupidity, silliness, misjudgment, senselessness, miscalculation, error, fatuity, vacuity, imbecility, indiscretion, imprudence, simplicity, puerility, senility, frivolity, irrationality, incapacity, ineptitude, giddiness, rashness, impetuosity, brainlessness, apartments to let (*slang*), nobody home (*slang*), shallowness, lightness, inexperience, trifling, childishness, fatuousness, driveling, dementia, incompetence, short-sightedness, tomfoolery, monkeyshine (*colloq.*), moonshine (*slang*), shallowness, drivel, piffle, rigmarole, balderdash.

wise, *adj.*—*Syn.* sagacious, discerning, profound, sensible, enlightened, intelligent, rational, sound, sage, deep, judicious, informed.

wish, *v.*—*Syn.* desire, hanker, crave, long, yearn; intend, mean.

wit—*Syn.* humor, drollery, facetiousness, jest, fun, jocularity, banter, waggery, burlesque, raillery, pleasantry, playfulness, witticism, waggishness, buffoonery, fooling, tomfoolery, repartee, badinage, persiflage, shenanigan (*slang*), wittiness, smartness, whimsicality. *Ant.* dulness or dullness, solemnity, stupidity,

sobriety, gravity, seriousness, stolidity, flatness, prosiness, heaviness, moroseness, monotony, melancholy, the blues (*colloq.*), dejection, gloom, depression, melancholia, blue devils (*slang*), doldrums, pessimism, dumps, prostration, despondency, mopishness, low spirits (*colloq.*).

wonder, *n.*—*Syn.* amazement, bewilderment, emotion, astonishment, surprise, sensation, prodigy, marvel, miracle, awe, stupor, stupefaction, admiration, wonderment, amazedness, eye-opener (*colloq.*). *Ant.* expectation, expectance, expectancy, anticipation, steadiness, commonness, imperturbableness, imperturbability, calmness, coolness, stolidity, hardheadedness, lack of imagination, *sang froid* [*Fr.*].

wonder, *v.*—*Syn.* to be surprised, to be amazed, to be dumbfounded, to be expectant, to be bewildered, to be dazed, to be curious, to feel doubt, to be in a state of uncertainty. *Ant.* expect, look for, anticipate, wait for, watch for, count upon, believe in, predict, prophesy, keep in mind, take coolly.

work—*Syn.* labor, task, toil, performance, accomplishment, achievement, deed, action, business, employment, occupation, product, production, toil, drudgery, exertion. *Ant.* idleness, ease, leisure, relaxation, vacation, rest, repose, holiday, recreation, amusement, respite, halt, stop, cessation, stoppage, lull, interruption, intermission, sloth, inactivity, laziness, indolence, remissness.

worn, *adj.*—*Syn.* used, tired, shabby, threadbare, exhausted, wasted.

worry, *v.*—*Syn.* disturb, torture, trouble, tease, harry, plague, gnaw, harass, annoy, irritate, fret, torment, pester, vex, beset.

worth, *n.*—*Syn.* value, estimation, price, excellence, virtue, merit, importance.

worthless—*Syn.* valueless, useless, unimportant, insignificant, unessential, trifling, trivial, paltry, petty, piddling, empty, unproductive, unserviceable, profitless, barren, sterile. *Ant.* valuable, precious, useful, serviceable, important, advantageous, beneficial, remunerative, profitable, gainful, productive, fertile, essential, primary, chief, choice, excellent, superior.

worthy—*Syn.* good, true, honest, honorable, reliable, trustworthy, dependable, noble, charitable, philanthropic, dutiful, virtuous, moral, pure, upright, righteous, decent, incorrupt, incorruptible, meritorious, creditable, deserving, right-minded, whole-souled, model, exemplary, sterling, sinless, stainless, blameless. *Ant.* unworthy, bad, evil, vile, reprehensible, blameworthy, untrustworthy, deceitful, treacherous, sinful, immoral, dishonest, dishonorable, blamable, vicious, wicked, iniquitous, corrupt, dissolute, profligate, recreant, disreputable, villainous, infamous, depraved, foul, coarse, gross, indecent.

write, *v.*—*Syn.* record, pen, inscribe, draw, compose, scrawl, indite, draft.

writing, *n.*—*Syn.* penmanship, calligraphy, handwriting; manuscript, document.

wrong—*Syn.* evil, injury, spite, vice, sin, bane, sinfulness, immorality, baseness, turpitude, badness, wickedness, hurtfulness, virulence, indecency, transgression, oppression, persecution, tyranny, outrage, misusage, abuse, hate, malignity, malevolence, cruelty, inhumanity, ruffianism, hatred, malice, injustice, unfairness, partiality, partisanship, iniquity, depravity, corruption, profligacy, flagrancy, wrongdoing. *Ant.* right, goodness, justice, righteousness, uprightness, honesty, honorableness, decency, morality, integrity, virtue, innocence, good behavior, good conduct, sinlessness, spotlessness, clear conscience, charity, philanthropy, benevolence, kindness, kindliness, warm-heartedness, benignity, brotherly love, sympathy, impartiality, nobleness, feeling, consideration, well-doing, loyalty, devotion, faithfulness, sincerity, truth, rectitude.

wry, *adj.*—*Syn.* twisted, warped, contorted, crooked, askew, distorted.

X

Xanthippe—*Syn.* shrew, vixen, virago, termagent, Biddy Moriarty, spitfire, she-devil, scold, porcupine, dragon, fury, fire-eater, Kate the Shrew, tigress, beldame, harridan, madcap, barracker (*Aus. dial.*), carper, defamer, detractor, calumniator, reviler, backbiter, vituperator, muckraker, ripsnorter (*slang*), blazer (*slang*). *Ant.* soother, pacifier, flatterer, courtier, sycophant, sucker (*slang*), toady, lickspittle, toadeater, booster (*colloq.*), whitewasher, puffer, tout (*colloq.*), slaverer, parasite, hanger-on, good woman, Madonna, saint, angel, helpmate, loving wife, devoted spouse.

X-rays—*Syn.* Röntgen rays, radioactivity, radium emanation, actinic rays, actinism, exradio, ultra-violet rays, refractometry, radiant energy, cathode rays.

x, y, z—*Syn.* unknown quantities, the Great Unknown, unexplored ground, prehistoric time, the Great Hereafter, the Dark Ages, virgin soil, *terra incognita* [L.].

Y

Yank, *n.*—*Syn.* Yankee, Sam, Sammy, doughboy, G.I., doughfoot.

yannigan, *n.*—*Syn.* newcomer, rookie, recruit, busher, greenhorn, tenderfoot, punk.

yard, *n.*—*Syn.* court, patio, enclosure, courtyard, close, playground.

yardstick, *n.—Syn.* rule, measure; criterion, standard, test, gauge.

yarn, *n.—Syn.* tale, story, spiel, anecdote, fabrication, fib, fairy tale.

yawn—*Syn.* gape, open wide, vent, be fatigued, droop, flag, puff, gasp, show weariness, be tired, be sleepy, be languid. *Ant.* close, close the mouth, shut the mouth, pucker the lips, be active, be energetic, be brisk, be interested.

yearn—*Syn.* desire, crave, long for, hanker after, fret, chafe, grieve, mourn, droop, pine, languish, be eager for, be desirous of, be ardent, be fervent, be importunate, be dejected, look downcast, wish, wish for, thirst for, hunger for, set one's heart upon. *Ant.* be content, be pleased, be satisfied, turn from, turn one's back upon, ignore, avoid, shun, deprecate, be merry, be cheerful, keep up one's spirits, bear up, keep a stiff upper lip (*slang*), cheer up, brighten up, look happy, take heart, drive dull care away, look on the bright side, be indifferent, have no desire for, remain passive.

yell—*Syn.* bellow, cry out, scream, shout, yelp, yap (*dial.*), bawl, roar, halloo, vociferate, whoop, howl, screech, screak, shriek, shrill, squeal, squall, ululate, yammer (*dial.*), holler (*slang*). *Ant.* be silent, be pleased, be satisfied, keep quiet, refrain, suppress, stifle, stem, keep back, repress, control, check, arrest, compose oneself, speak softly, murmur, whisper, breathe.

yellow—*Syn.* golden, saffron-like, aureate, xanthochroic, lemon, gilt, gilded, citrine, citreous, sandy, creamy, ocherous, lutescent, xanthous, xanthic, jaundiced, henna-colored, warm, sulphur-colored, amber, straw-colored;—as *slang,* cowardly, contemptible, mean, groveling, low, mean-spirited, deceitful, treacherous, false, false-hearted, cringing, slinking, sneaking, white-livered, lily-livered, craven.

yen, *n.—Syn.* desire, lust, passion, itch, urge, appetite, drive.

yes—*Syn.* assent, acquiescence, affirmation, accord, avowal, recognition, acknowledgment, confession, concurrence, unanimity. *Syn.* no, dissent, nonconformity, protest, contradiction, denial, recantation, demur, objection, difference, disagreement, refusal.

yet—*Syn.* nevertheless, notwithstanding, however, hitherto, thus far, besides, further, furthermore, now, still, but, though, although, howbeit, in spite of, in despite of, at any rate, on the other hand.

yield—*Syn.* surrender, give, give up, acquiesce, accede, relinquish, resign, abdicate, quit, forego, waive, relax, succumb, submit, cede, let go, grant, bestow, confer, allow, comply, communicate, impart, defer, capitulate, backdown (*colloq.*), humble oneself, eat crow (*slang*), cave in (*colloq.*), crouch, kneel, *kow-tow* [*China*], concede, give in to, produce, afford, bring in, return, permit, abandon, sacrifice, consent to, sanction, tolerate, suffer, bear. *Ant.* deny, protest, disallow, reject, withstand, resist, disapprove, refuse, forbid, debar, hinder, inhibit, interdict, preclude, prevent, rebuff, repulse, negative, oppose, kick against (*colloq.*), recalcitrate, stick it out (*colloq.*), counteract, clash, cross, run counter, overpower, master, overcome, antagonize, frustrate, impede, contravene, conflict with, interfere with, withdraw, withhold, retain, assert, claim, dissent, struggle, strive, strive against, endeavor, attain.

yielding—*Syn.* producing, productive, teeming, fructifying, bringing forth, accommodating, unresisting, submissive, conceding, supple, pliant, surrendering, soft, spongy, marshy, flexible, limber, resilient, ductile, plastic, malleable, tractile, mollient, tender, lithe, extensible, resigned, acquiescent, obedient, nonresistant, weak, cringing, craven, chickenhearted, timid, crouching, prostrate, unresistant, unresisting. *Ant.* unproductive, nonproductive, barren, sterile, waste, fallow, brittle, hard, tough, stubborn, adamantine, defiant, brave, courageous, lion-hearted, intrepid, fierce, ferocious, masterful, rigid, stiff, unbending, renitent, callous, bony, horny, lapidified, stony, gritty, unyielding, unbending, ossified, petrified, obdurate, intolerant, dogmatic, obstinate, opinionated, tenacious, casehardened, unchangeable, inexorable, headstrong, stiffnecked, hidebound, creed-bound, bigoted, impervious.

yoke—*Syn.* couple, link, connect, join, conjoin, harness, splice, unite, associate, bind, attach, tie, fix, strap, buckle, bracket, hitch, lay together, tack together, fasten, secure, mate. *Ant.* sever, dissever, disunite, untie, loose, liberate, free, disconnect, release, set free, disengage, detach, disjoin, cut adrift, dispart, dissociate, unloose, unbind, divide, sunder, rive, rend, separate, divorce.

yore—*Syn.* the past, past times, old times, ancient times, former times, the olden time, good old time, days gone by, langsyne [*Sc.*], auld langsyne [*Sc.*], antiquity, long ago, the days that have gone. *Ant.* the present, the future, present time, future time, recent times, yesterday, tomorrow, the days to come, the hereafter, the sweet by-and-by, futurity, the millennium.

young, *adj.*—*Syn.* youthful, immature, puerile, juvenile, adolescent; green, fresh, inexperienced.

youth—*Syn.* boy, lad, laddie, youngster, schoolboy, stripling, younker (*colloq.*), callant [*Sc.*], urchin, bantling, whippersnapper (*colloq.*), hobbledehoy, scion, hopeful, girl, lass, lassie, damsel, miss, maiden, missy (*colloq.*), schoolgirl, tomboy, hoy-

den, colleen, girleen, flapper (*slang*), minx, juvenility, boyhood, girlhood, springtime of life, heyday of youth, rising generation, school days, happy days, flower of life. *Ant.* old man (*colloq.*), pop (*slang*), graybeard, dotard, centenarian, old stager (*colloq.*), veteran, grandpa, grandfather, gaffer, oldster (*colloq.*), granny, grandma, grandmother, grandame, old woman, gammer (*dial.*), oldwife, beldame, crone, hag, witch, old age, oldness, senescence, senility, decrepitude, decline of life, seniority, sear and yellow leaf.

youthful—*Syn.* young, juvenile, boyish, girlish, puerile, budding, burgeoning, callow, juvenescent, boylike, girllike, kiddish (*colloq.*), blooming, sappy, newfledged, kittenish. *Ant.* old, aged, elderly, ripe, mellow, hoary, venerable, reverend, patriarchal, senile, gray-bearded, decrepit, withered, sere, sere and yellow, matronly, motherly, grandmotherly.

Z

zany, *n.*—*Syn.* clown, fool, jester, buffoon, comedian, comic, madcap, banana.

zeal—*Syn.* ardor, earnestness, enthusiasm, eagerness, fervor, energy, activity, hustle, hustling, bustle, bustling, intensity, inclination, willingness, snap (*colloq.*), vim, spirit, nerve, dash, pep (*slang*), promptitude, despatch, intentness, industry, assiduity, diligence, perseverance, painstaking, vigilance, fuss, flurry, haste, hurry. *Ant.* indifference, apathy, torpor, coldness, carelessness, sluggishness, laziness, reluctance, indisposition, slowness, inaction, idleness, indolence, remissness, ergophobia, languor, lethargy, drowsiness, oscitancy, otiosity, slackness, insouciance, inappetence, supineness, nonchalance, unconcern.

zealot—*Syn.* partisan, bigot, fanatic, devotee, visionary, enthusiast, dogmatist, opinionist, bitter-ender, (*colloq.*), mule, die-hard (*slang*), hustler (*colloq.*), hummer (*slang*), humdinger (*slang*), human dynamo (*colloq.*), live wire (*colloq.*). *Ant.* slacker (*colloq.*), shirker, duffer (*slang*), quitter, loafer, time-killer (*colloq.*), idler, drone, dawdler, dead one (*slang*), stiff (*slang*), bum (*slang*), bummer (*slang*), tramp, cadger (*slang*), sundowner (*Aus. slang*), lounger, lounge lizard (*slang*), hobo, Weary Willie (*colloq.*).

zealous—*Syn.* fervent, enthusiastic, eager, intense, earnest, ardent, willing, fain, inclined, desirous, alert, snappy, peppy (*slang*), hustling, bustling, brisk, animated, vivacious, spirited, diligent, assiduous, steadfast, indefatigable, sleepless, sedulous, resolute. *Ant.* lazy, idle, sluggish, inert, languid, inactive, indifferent, careless, listless, apathetic, unconcerned, devil-may-care, nonchalant, heavy, drowsy, sleepy, dormant, somnolent, lethargic, slack, otiose, supine, somniferous, phlegmatic, lumpish, dull, indolent.

zenith—*Syn.* top, pinnacle, summit, culmination, height, highest point, maximum, climax, eminence, pitch, apex, altitude, elevation, acme, tip, crest, cap, crown, culminating point. *Ant.* base, foundation, lowest point, nadir, bedrock, floor, foot, root, substratum, support, pedicle, bottom, substructure, depth, lowness, minimum.

zephyr—*Syn.* west wind, gentle breeze, mild wind, whisper, breath, breathing, whispering wind, draft, afflatus, sufflation, puff, whiff, inflation, afflation, efflation. *Ant.* storm, hurricane, tempest, squall, breeze, blast, gust, monsoon, trade wind, simoon, southerly buster [*Aus.*], gale, whirlwind, tornado, cy-clone, typhoon, mistral, sirocco, levanter.

zero—*Syn.* nothing, naught, cipher, nullity, nobody, unreality, unsubstantiality, nonentity, blank, void, phantom, shadow, dream, vision. *Ant.* something, anything, matter, material, materiality, body, substantiality, substance, stuff, corporeity, groundwork, person, object, thing, existence.

zest—*Syn.* relish, taste, pleasure, delight, desire, savor, savoriness, appetizer, gusto, sharpener, enhancement, enjoyment, flavor, twang (*dial*), sapidity, pungency, tang, sharpness, piquancy, nip, kick (*slang*). *Ant.* distaste, disgust, disrelish, detriment, sourness, insipidity, tastelessness, vapidness, flatness, staleness, unsavoriness, acerbity, acidity, acetosity, verjuice, mawkishness, jejuneness.

zigzag—*Syn.* oblique, inclined, sloping, wry, awry, crooked, thrawn [*Sc.*] sinuous, twisted, askew, transverse, diagonal, curved, loxic, bent, crinkled, serrated, falcated, furcal, furcated, jagged, straggling, meandering, devious, erratic, rambling, oscillating, fluctuating, waggling, undulatory, vibratory, indirect, spiral, tortuous. *Ant.* straight, direct, parallel, concentric, collateral, rectilineal, even, unbent, horizontal, vertical, right, true, undeviating, unswerving, regular, virgate, plumb, perpendicular, uniform, level, unvarying, invariable, unvaried, flat, plain, plane, undistorted, symmetrical, normal, conventional, inflexible, rectilinear, straight-lined.

zone—*Syn.* belt, region, district, territory, section, quarter, area, circuit, terrain, commune, precinct, ward, inclosure, ground, country, dominion, band, girdle, zodiac, meridian, latitude, sector, quarter.

KEY TO PRONUNCIATION

FOR 5,000 WORDS MOST OFTEN MISPRONOUNCED

This table of values shows at a glance the fundamentals upon which the pronunciations given in the following compilation are based.

a	short, as in hat, man, rat; also equivalent to short *o*, as in swan, wash; also to *aw*, as in halt, water.
ā	long, as in day, fade, take.
å	medial, as in ask, dance, path.
ä	open, as in arm, father, palm.
ă	as in account, sofa.
â	as in care, compare.
e	short, as in bed, den, pet.
ē	long, as in be, fear, mere.
ẽ	neutral or unaccented before final *r* of a syllable, as in baker, gather; also, represents short *i*, as in bird, fir; also short *u*, as in burn, hurt.
ê	as in event, depend.
i	short, as in fin, kid, pit.
ī	long, as in fine, kind, white.
o	short, as in bob, hot, top; often represented by short *u* (u), as in son, wagon, and in words ending in -tion.
ō	long, as in old, bone, home; represented by *oo*, as in bosom, woman; and by *ōō*, as in do, to.
ô	medial, as in horse, lord, orb.
u	short, as in cup, dumb, jump.
ū	long, as in cure, dude, mule; also represented by the wide *oo*, as in bull, bush, put; also, by the open *ōō*, as in crude, flue, jury.
æ	this ligature has the sound of long *e* (ē), as in Cæsar, pæan; also of short *e* (e), as in hæmalopia; as a digraph (*æ*) it has the sound of either long *a* (ā) or long *e* (ē); when dissyllabic, the *e* is often noted by the dieresis (¨), as in aërial, but the modern tendency is to eliminate it.
ai	this vowel digraph has the sound of long *a* (ā), as in mail, or of long *i* (ī), as in kaiser.
au	this proper diphthong has the sound of medial *o* (ô), as in fault, haul.
ea	this vowel digraph is equivalent to long *e* (ē), as in bead, each, seal; also to short *e* (e), as in bread, head, lead; also to long *a* (ā), as in break, great, pear.
eau	this vowel trigraph has the sound of long *o* (ō), as in beau; occurs only in words of French origin.
ee	this vowel digraph has the sound of long *e* (ē), as in deep, feet, sleep.
ei	this vowel digraph has the sound of long *e* (ē), as in deceive, receipt; also of long *a* (ā), as in feint, rein.
eu, ew	these digraphs have the sound of long *u* (ū), as in feud, mewl; in some words, however, *ew* is given the sound of long *o* (ō), as in sew, sewer.
oe	this improper diphthong usually has the sound of long *o* (ō), as in hoe, sloe; sometimes of *ōō*, as in doer, shoe.

339

KEY TO PRONUNCIATION
FOR 5,000 WORDS MOST OFTEN MISPRONOUNCED

oi, oy   these proper diphthongs are sounded as in boil, boy.

oo   wide digraph, sounded as in foot, hood, wool; the sound conveyed, however, is really a *u* sound between the short and the long of that letter.

o͞o   open vowel digraph, sounded as in boot, moon, root; in reality it is the long sound of *u* (ū), without the *y* element.

ou   this proper diphthong represents the sound heard in flounce, gout, house; represented by o͞o, especially in words of French origin, as in croup, ousel, soup; in some words it is equivalent to medial *o* (ŏ), as in cough, nought, trough; and in others to long *o* (ō), as in four, pour, soul; also, in a number of words, it represents short *u*, as in couple, enough, tough.

ow   this proper diphthong has the sound heard in cow, now, how; it also represents that of long *o* (ō), as in bowl, know, show.

g   hard, as in again, gay, leg.

g   soft, represented by *j*, as in edge, gin, rage; *g* is silent before final *m* and *n*, as in phlegm, sign, and when initial to *n*, as in gnaw, gnome, gnu; in some words from the French it has the sound of *zh*, as in cortege, mirage, rouge.

ph   this consonantal digraph is usually sounded as *f*, as in delph, philosophy, sophistry, though in some words it has a *v* sound, as in nephew.

q   this letter is always followed by *u*, both being sounded *kw*, as in quart, quite, quote, but in some words of French origin only the sound of *k* is heard, as in etiquette.

th   voiceless, as in birth, hearth, thing.

th   voiced, as in breathe, smooth, with; in some words only the *t* of this digraph is sounded, as in thyme.

hw   this consonant digraph is pronounced *hw*, that is, *h* with a voiceless *w*, which means that the *w* is not heard until the beginning of the vowel succeeding it, as in what, wheat, white.

û   as in unite, formulate.

x   this letter has a voiceless sound equivalent to *ks*, as in box, excite, extreme; and a voiced sound equivalent to *gs*, as in exalt, exit, exult; as an initial, it is equivalent to *z*, as in xebec, xiphoid, xylograph.

y   as a vowel, this letter has the sound of long *i* (ī), as in cry, defy, fly; also, of short *i* (i), as in city, happy, nymph; also, of *e* (short *u*), as in myrtle; sometimes it is obscure or unaccented, as in zephyr; as a consonant, that is, at the beginning of a word or syllable, it is pronounced as in yard, year, you.

z   this letter usually has the sound as heard in lazy, size, zeal; in some cases it is used to represent the pronunciation of *c*, as in sacrifice, and of *s*, as in easy; in a number of words *z* is pronounced as *zh*, the voiced correlative of *sh*, as in azure, brazier, glazier; in a few words, particularly from the French, *zh* is used to represent *g*, as in rouge, mirage.

5,000 WORDS
MOST OFTEN MISPRONOUNCED

abaft, ă-băft′
abash, ă-bash′
abattoir, a″băt-twär′
abbe, ă-bā′
abdomen, ab′dō-men
abhor, ăb-hôr′
abject, ăb′jekt
ablution, ăb-lū′shun
abnormality, ab″nôr-mal′i-ti
abolition, ab″o-lish′un
aborigines, ab-o-rij′i-nēz
abscess, ab′ses
abscond, ab-skond′
absent (adj.), ab′sent
absent (v.), ab-sent′
absolutism, ab′so-lū-tizm
absolve, ăb-solv′
absorb, ăb-sôrb′
abstemious, ab-stē′mi-us
abstinence, ab′stin-nens
abstract (v.), ab-strakt′
abstract (n.), ab′strakt
abstruse, ab-strŏŏs′
absurd, ăb-sĕrd′
absurdity, ăb-sĕrd′i-ti
abuse (v.), ă-būz′
abuse (n.), ă-būs′
abysmal, ă-biz′mal
abyss, ă-bis′
academic, ak-ă-dem′ik
academy, ă-kad′e-mi
accede, ak-sēd′
acceleration, ak-sel-er-ā′shun
accent, ak′sent
accentuate, ak-sen′tû-āt
accept, ak-sept′
acceptable, ak-sep′tă-bl
access, ak′ses
accessory, ak-ses′o-ri
acclamation, ak″klă-mā′shun
acclimate, ă-klī′māt
acclimation, ăk-kli-mā′shun
acclimatize, ă-klī′mă-tiz
accolade, ak″o-lād′
accompaniment,
  ă-kum′pă-ni-ment
accompanist, ă-kum′pă-nist
accomplice, ă-kom′plis
accost, ă-kost′
accrue, ă-krŏŏ′
accumulate, ă-kū′mû-lāt
accuracy, ak′û-ră-si
accurate, ak′û-rāt
accursed, ă-kĕr′sed
acerbity, ă-sĕr′bi-ti
acescent, ă-ses′ent
acetic, ă-sē′tik
Achilles, ă-kil′ēz
achromatic, ak-ro-mat′ik
acid, as′id
acidify, ă-sid′i-fī
acidity, ă-sid′i-ti

acme, ak′me
acoustic, ă-kous′tik
acquaint, a-kwānt′
acquiesce, ak-wi-es′
acquiescent, ak-wi-es′ent
acquisitive, a-kwiz′i-tiv
acrid, ak′rid
across, ă-krôs′
actual, ak′tu-al
acumen, ă-kū′men
adage, ad′āj
adagio, ă-dä′jō
adaptation, ad-ap-tā′shun
addict, ad′ikt
address, a-dres′
adduce, a-dūs′
adept, ă-dept′
adequate, ad′e-kwāt
adieu, ă-dū′
adjacent, a-jā′sent
adjudicate, a-joo′di-kāt
adjunct, aj′ungkt
adjust, a-just′
adjutant, aj′ŏŏ-tant
administrative, ad-min′is-trā-tiv
administrator, ad-min′is-trā″tĕr
admirable, ad′mi-ră-bl
admiral, ad′mi-ral
Admiralty, ad′mi-ral-ti
admiration, ad-mi-rā′shun
adobe, ă-dō′bă
adolescence, ad-o-les′ens
Adonis, ă-dō′nis
adoration, ad-o-rā′shun
adrenalin; adrenaline,
  ad-rē′nal-in
adroit, ă-droit′
adult, ă-dult′
advance, ad-văns′
advantage, ad-văn′tāj
advantageous, ad-văn-tā′jus
Advent, ad′vent
adventist, ad′vent-ist
adventure, ad-ven′tūr
adversary, ad′vĕr-sar-i
adverse, ad′vĕrs
advertise, ad′vĕr-tīz; ad-ver-tīz′
advertisement, ad-vĕr′tiz-ment;
  ad-vĕr-tīz′ment
advice, ad-vīs′
advise, ad-vīz′
advocacy, ad′vo-kă-si
aegis, ē′jis
Aeneid, e-nē′id
aeolian harp, ē-ō′li-an härp
aerial, ā-ē′ri-al
aeronautics, ā″ĕr-o-nô′tiks
aeroplane, ā′ĕr-o-plān
aesthetic, esthetic, es-thet′ĭk
aestheticism, es-thet′i-sizm
affiance, ăfī′ăns
affidavit, af-i-dā′vit

341

affix, ă-fiks′
affluence, af′loo-ens
afford, ă-fôrd′
afterward, âf′tĕr-wĕrd
again, ă-gen′
agape, ă-gāp′
agate, ag′ăt
aged, ā′jed; ā-jid
aggrandize, ag′răn-dīz
aggregate, ag′re-gāt
aghast, ă-găst′
agile, aj′il
agnosticism, ag-nos′ti-sizm
agrarian, ă-grā′ri-an
agriculture, ag′ri-kul-tûr
ague, ā′gū
ailment, āl′ment
aisle, īl
Alabama, al-ă-bă′mă
'a la carte, ä lä kärt′
Alamo, ä′lă-mō
a-la-mode, ä′lă-mōd′
alas, ă-lăs′
albino, al-bī′nō
albumen, al-bū′men
alcove, al′kōv
alder, awl′dĕr
alert, ă-lĕrt′
algae, al′jē
algebra, al′je-brä
algebraic, al″je-brā′ĭk
alias, ā′li-ăs
alibi, al′i-bī
alien, āl-yen
alienate, āl′yen-āt
align, ă-līn′
alimentary, al-i-men′tă-ri
alimony, al′i-mon-i
alkali, al′kă-li; al′kălī
alkaline, al′kă-lin; al′kă-līn
allege, ă-lej′
allegiance, ă-lē′jăns
allopathic, al-o-path′ik
allopathy, ă-lop′ă-thi
alloy, ă-loi′
allude, ă-lūd′
allure, ă-lūr′
allusion, ă-lū′zhun
ally, ă-lī′
Alma Mater, al′mă mā′tĕr
almanac, awl′mă-nak
almond, ä′mund; al′mund
almost, ôl′mōst
alms, ämz
alpaca, al-pak′ă
also, awl′sō
altercation, ôl″tĕr-kā′shun
alternate (v.), ôl′tĕr-nāt
alternate (adj.), ôl-tĕr′nat
alternative, ôl-tĕr′nă-tiv
alum, al′um
aluminum, ă-lū′mi-num

always, awl′wāz
amass, ă-măs′
amateur, am′ă-tûr
amatory, am′ă-to-ri
ambassador, am-bas′ă′dĕr
ambergris, am′bĕr-grēs
ambidextrous, am″bi-deks′trus
ameliorable, ă-mē′li-or-ă-bl
amen, ă-men′; ä-men′
amenable, ă-mē′nă-bl
amenity, ă-men′i-ti
amiable, ā′mi-ă-bl
amicable, am′i-kă-bl
amnesia, am-nē′si-ă
amok, ă-mok′
amorous, am′o-rus
amorphous, ă-môr′fus
amortize, ă-môr′tiz
amour, ă-moor′
ampere, am′pēr
amuck, ă-muk′
amulet, am′û-let
anaemic, ă-nē′mik
analogous, ă-nal′o-gus
analogy, ă-nal′o-ji
analysis, ă-nal′i-sis
analyst, an′ă-list
anarchism, an′är-kizm
anathema, ă-nath′e-mă
anatomy, ă-nat′o-mi
ancestor, an′ses-tĕr
anchor, ang′kĕr
anchovy, an-chō′vi
ancient, ān′shent
andirons, and′ī-ĕrnz
anemia, ă-nē′mi-ă
anesthetic, an-es-thet′ik
anew, ă-nū′
angel, ān′jel
angelic, an-jel′ik
Anglomania, ang″glo-mā′ni-ă
Anglophobe, ang′glo-fōb
angular, ang′gū-lĕr
aniline, an′i-lin; an′i-līn
anise, an′is
annex (v.), a-neks′
annex (n.), ă-neks′; an′eks
annihilate, ă-nī′hi-lāt
anonymity, an-o-nim′i-ti
anonymous, ă-non′i-mus
another, ă-nuth′er
answer, ăn′sĕr
antarctic, ant-ärk′tik
antecedent, an-te-sē′dent
antediluvian, an-te-di-lū′vi-an
antelope, an′te-lōp
antenna, an-ten′ă
anthracite, an′thră-sīt
anthropology, an-thro-pol′o-ji
antipathy, an-tip′ă-thi
antipodes, an-tip′o-dēz
antique, an-tēk′

antiquity, an-tik'wi-ti
anti-Semitism, an-ti-sem'it-izm
antiseptic, an-ti-sep'tik
antithesis, an-tith'e-sis
anxiety, ang-zī'e-ti
anxious, ang'shus
Apache, ă-pa'chê
apathetic, ap-ă-thet'ĭk
aperient, ă-pē'ri-ent
aperitif, ă-pā-rē-tēf'
aperture, ap'ēr-tûr
apex, ā'peks
Aphrodite, af-ro-dī'te
Apocalypse, ă-pok'ă-lips
apocryphal, ă-pok'ri-fal
apology, ă-pol'o-ji
apoplexy, ap'o-plek-si
apostle, ă-pos'l
apostolic, ap-os-tol'ĭk
apostrophe, ă-pos'tro-fe
apothecary, ă-poth'e-kā-ri
apotheosis, ap-o-thē'o-sis
appal; appall, a-pawl'
apparatus, ap-ă-rā'tus
apparent, ă-par'ent
appellate, ă-pel'āt
appendicitis, ă-pen-di-sī'tis
applicable, ap'li-kă-bl
apportion, ă-pōr'shun
appreciate, ă-prē'shi-āt
apprehend, ap-re-hend'
appropriate, ă-prō'pri-āt
approximate, ă-prok'si-māt
appurtenance, ă-pēr'te-năns
apricot, ā'pri-kot; ap'ri-kot
a priori, ā pri-ō'ri
apropos, ap-ro-pō'
aptitude, ap'ti-tūd
aquarium, ă-kwa'ri-um
aquatic, ă-kwat'ik
aqueduct, ak'we-dukt
Arab, ar'ăb
arabesque, ar-ă-besk'
arbitrary, är'bi-tra"ri
arboreal, är-bō're-al
arboreous, är-bō're-us
archaeology; archeology,
    är-ke-ol'o-ji
archaic, är-kā'ik
archangel, ärk'ān'jel
archduke, ärch-dūk'
archipelago, är-ki-pel'å-gō
architect, är'ki-tekt
architective, är'ki-tek-tiv
archive, är'kīv
arctic, ärk'tik
arduous, är'dū-us
arena, ă-rē'nă
argumentative, är-gû-men'tă-tiv
argyrol, är'ji-rol
aria, ä'ri-ă
arid, ar'id

aristocrat, ă-ris'to-krat;
    ar'is-to-krat
Arizona, ar-i-zō'nă
Arkansas, är'kan-saw
armada, är-mä'dă
Armageddon, är-mă-ged'on
armature, är'mă-tûr
armistice, är'mis-tis
arnica, är'ni-kă
aroma, ă-rō'mă
arraign, ă-rān'
arrant, ar'ănt
arrearage, ă-rēr'ij
arrest, ă-rest'
arsenic, är'se-nik
arterial, är-tē'ri-al
arthritis, är-thrī'tis
artichoke, är'ti-chōk
articulate, är-tik'ů-lāt
artifice, är'ti-fis
artificer, är-tif'i-sēr
artificial, är-ti-fish'al
artisan, är'ti-zan
artist, är'tist
artiste, är-tēst'
Aryan, är'yan
asbestos, as-bes'tos
ascend, ă-send'
ascendant, ă-sen'dănt
ascetic, ă-set'ik
asceticism, ă-set'i-sizm
aseptic, ă-sep'tik
asinine, as'i-nīn
asininity, as-i-nin'i-ti
askance, ă-skans'
askew, ă-skū'
asparagus, as-par'ă-gus
asperity, as-pêr'i-ti
aspersion, as-pêr'shun
asphalt, as'falt
asphyxiation, as-fik"si-ā'shun
aspiration, as-pi-rā'shun
aspirin, as'pi-rin
assault, ă-sawlt'
assent, ă-sent'
assert, ă-sērt'
assiduity, as-i-dū'i-ti
assiduous, ăsid'ū-us
assign, ă-sīn'
assimilation, ă-sim"i-lā'shun
associate, ă-sō'shi-āt
association, ă-sō"shi-ā'shun
assuage, ă-swāj'
asterisk, as'tēr-isk
asthma, as'mă
astringent, as-trin'jent
astronomer, as-tron'o-mēr
astute, as-tūt'
Atalanta, at-ă-lan'tă
atavistic, at-ă-vis'tik
ate, āt
atelier, a'te-lyā

atheism, ā'thē-izm
Athena, ă-thē'nă
athlete, ath'lēt
athletic, ath-let'ĭk
atrocious, ă-trō'shus
atrocity, ă-tros'ĭ-ti
atrophy, at'ro-fi
attache, a-tă-shā'
attitude, at'ĭ-tūd
attorney, ă-tēr'ni
attribute (v.), ă-trĭb'ŭt
attribute (n.), at'rib-būt
auburn, aw'bēru
auction, awk'shun
audacity, aw-das'ĭ-ti
audience, aw'di-ens
Augean, aw-jē'an
august, aw-gust'
aunt, ănt
auspicious, aws-pish'us
austere, aws-tēr'
austerity, aws-ter'ĭ-ti
author, aw'thēr
authoritative, aw-thor'ĭ-tā"tiv
autobiography, aw"tō-bī-og'ră-fi
autocracy, aw-tok'ră-si
autocrat, aw'tō-krat
autograph, aw'tō-grăf
autogyro, aw-tō-jī'rō
automat, aw'tō-mat
automaton, aw-tom'ă-ton
automobile, aw"tō-mō-bēl'
automobilist, aw"tō-mō'bil-ist
autonomy, aw-ton'o-mi
autopsy, aw'top-si
autumn, aw'tum
avalanche, av'ă-lănch
avaricious, av-ă-rish'us
avaunt, ă-vawnt'; ă-vänt'
avenue, av'e-nū
aver, ă-vēr'
average, av'ēr-ij
aviary, ā'vi-e-ri
aviator, ā'vi-ā-tēr
avidity, ă-vid'ĭ-ti
avoirdupois, av-ēr-du-poiz'
awakening, ă-wāk'ning
awful, aw'ful
awkward, awk'wērd
awry, ă-rī'
ay; aye (adv.), ā (always, forever)
aye; ay (adv. or interj.), ā or ī (yes)
azure, azh'ēr; ā'zhēr

B

babel, bā'bel
baboon, ba-bōōn'
bacchante, bă-kant'
bacillus, bă-sil'us

bacon, bā'kn
bacteria, bak-tēr'ĭ-ă
bade, bad
badinage, bă-dē-näzh'; bad'ĭ-nij
balalaika, bal-ă-lī'kă
balcony, bal'ko-ni
balk, bawk
ballad, bal'ăd
ballet, bal'ā
ballistics, bă-lis'tiks
balloon, bă-lōōn'
balm, bäm
balsam, bawl'săm
balustrade, bal-us-trād'
banal, ban'ăl
banality, bă-nal'ĭ-ti
banana, bă-na'nă
banquet, bang'kwet
barbarian, bär-bār'ĭ-an
barbaric, bär-bār'ĭk
barbarism, bär'bă-rizm
barbecue, bär'be-kū
bargain, bär'gen
barometer, bă-rom'e-tēr
baronet, bar'un-et
barracuda, bar'ă-kū-dă
barrel, bar'el
barrier, bar'i-ēr
basin, bā's'n
basket, băs'ket
Basque, băsk
bas-relief, bă-re-lēf'
bass, bas (one of various edible fishes allied to the perch)
bass, bās (low, deep, the lowest part in the harmony of a musical composition)
bath, băth
bathe, bā*th*
batik, bă'tēk
batiste, bă-tēst'
bauble, baw'bl
bayou, bī'ōō
bazaar; bazar, bă-zăr'
beard, bērd
beatify, bē-at'ĭ-fī
beatitude, bē-at'ĭ-tūd
beau, bō
beauteous, bū'tē-us
because, bē-kawz'
bedizen, bē-diz'n; be-dī'zn
Bedouin, bed'oo-in
been, bin; bēn
begonia, bē-gō'ni-ă
beguilement, bē-gīl'ment
behemoth, bē-hē'moth
beige, bāzh
belladonna, bel-ă-don'ă
belles-lettres, bel-let'r
belligerent, bē-lij'ēr-ent
bellows, bel'ōz
belong, bē-lông'

beloved, bê-luvd'; bê-luv'ed
beneficence, bê-nef'i-sens
beneficiary, ben-ê-fish'i-a-ri
benevolence, bê-nev'o-lens
benign, bê-nīn'
benignant, bê-nig'nant
benzine, ben-zēn'
berserk, bĕr'sĕrk
bestial, bes'chal
betroth, bê-troth'; bê-trŏth'
betrothal, bê-troth'al; bê-trŏth'al
between, bê-twēn'
bevel, bev'el
beverage, bev'ĕr-ij
bias, bī'as
Biblical, bib'li-kal
bichloride, bī-klō'rīd; bī-klō'rid
bicuspid, bī-kus'pid
bicycle, bī'si-kl
bigot, big'ot
bijou, bē-zhōō'
bilge, bilj
bilious, bil-yus
billet, bil'et
billet-doux, bĭl-ê-dōō'
billiards, bil'yerdz
billingsgate, bil'ingz-gāt
billion, bil'yun
binocular, bin-ok'û-lĕr
biogenesis, bī-o-jen'e-sis
biographer, bī-og'rā-fĕr
biologist, bī-ol'ō-jist
biped, bī'ped
biscuit, bis'kit
bismuth, bis'muth; biz'muth
bison, bī'son
bisque, bisk
bitumen, bi-tū'men
bivouac, biv'ōō-ak
bizarre, bi-zär'
blackguard, blag'ärd
blanch, blånch
blase, blä-zā'
blaspheme, blås-fēm'
blasphemy, blås'fe-mi
blatant, blā'tänt
blatherskite, blath'ĕr-skīt
blithe, blīth
blouse, blouz
bludgeon, bluj'un
boa, bō'å
boatswain, bōt'swän; bō'sn
bodice, bod'is
Boer, bōōr
boisterous, bois'tĕr-us
bolero, bō-lãr'ō
boll weevil, bōl wē'vl
Bologna sausage, bō-lō'nyä saw'sij
Bolsheviki, bol-she-vē'ki
bomb, bom; bum
bona fide, bō'nå fī'dē
bonanza, bō-nan'zä

bonbon, bôn'bôn″
bon mot, bon mō'
bonnet, bon'et
bon-ton, bôn-tôn'
bookish, book'ish
boomerang, bōōm'ĕr-ang
borough, bĕr'ō
bosom, boo'zum
botany, bot'ā-ni
boudoir, bōō'dwär
bough, bou
bouillon, bōōl'yôn
boulder, bōl'dĕr
boulevard, bōō'le-värd
boundary, boun'dă-ri
bouquet, bōō-kā'
Bourbon, bōōr'bon
bourgeois, bōōr-zhwä'
bourgeoise, bōōr-zhwå-zē'
bourse, bōōrs
boutonniere, bōō-ton-nyär'
bovine, bō'vīn
bowery, bou'ĕr-i
bowwow, bou'wou
braggadocio, brag-å-dō'shi-ō
braille, brāl
branch, brånch
brass, brås
brassiere, brä'sĕr
bravado, brå-vä'dō
bravo, brä'vō
brazier, brä'zhĕr
brethren, breth'ren
brevet, bre-vet'
breviary, brē'vi-ă-ri
bric-a-brac, brik'å-brak
brigadier, brig-å-dēr'
brigand, brig'änd
brilliant, bril'yänt
bristle, bris'l
brocade, brō-kād'
brochure, bro-shōōr'
brogue, brōg
bromide, brō'mīd; bro'mid
bronchitis, bron-kī'tis
broncho, brong'kō
brooch, brōch
brougham, brōō'um
browse, brouz
bruise, brōōz
bruit, brōōt
brunette, brōō-net'
brusque, brusk
buccaneer, buk-å-nēr'
bucolic, bû-kol'ik
budge, buj
budget, buj'et
buffet, buf'et (n. a blow with the
    hand; v. to strike with the hand)
buffet, buf'et; bōō-fā' (a cup-
    board or sideboard)
buffoon, bu-fōōn'

bulwark, bool'wẽrk
buncombe; bunkum, bung'kum
buoy, boi
bureau, bū'rō
bureaucracy, bû-rō'krä-si
burlesque, bẽr-lesk'
bury, bẽr'i
bushel, boosh'el
business, biz'nes
bustle, bus'l
busy, biz'i
butcher, booch'ẽr
button, but'n
Byzantine, biz-an'tin

C

cabal, kă-bal'
caballero, kă- bäl-yä'rō
cabaret, kab'ă-ret
cabbage, kab'ij
cacao, kă-kä'ō
cache, kash
cactus, kak'tus
cadaver, kă-dä'vẽr
cadence, kä'dens
cadet, kă-det'
Caesar, sē'zẽr
Caesarian, se-zā're-an
café, kă-fā'
cafeteria, kaf-e-tē'ri-ă
caffeine, kaf'e-in
Caiaphas, kā'yă-fas
caisson, kā'sun
cajole, kă-jōl'
calcimine, kal'si-mīn
calcium, kal'si-um
caldron, kol'drun
calendar, kal'en-dẽr
calf, kăf
calico, kal'i-kō
California, kal-i-fôr'ni-ă
caliph, calif, kā'lif
calk; caulk, kawk
calliope, ka-lī'o-pê
callus, kal'us
calm, kăm
caloric, kă-lor'ĭk
calorie; calory, kal'ō-ri
calumny, kal'um-ni
cambric, kăm'brik
Camembert cheese, kam'em-bär
   chēz
cameo, kam'e-ō
camera, kam'ẽr-ă
camisole, kam'i-sol
camouflage, ka-moo-fläzh'
campanile, kam-pă-nē'le
camphor, kam'fẽr
Canaan, kā'nan
canape, kă-nă-pā'

canard, kă-närd'
canary, kă-nā'ri
cancel, kan'sel
canine, kā-nīn'
canker, kang'kẽr
cannibalism, kan'i-bal-izm
canoe, kă-nōō'
canon, kan-un
canonic, kă-non'ik
can't, kănt
cantaloup, kan'tă-lōp
cantankerous, kan-tang'kẽr-us
cantata, kăn-tä'tă
canteen, kan-tēn'
cantilever, kan'ti-lē-yẽr
canyon, kan'yun
capias, kā'pi-as
capillary, kap'il-a-ri; kă-pil'ă-ri
capital, kap'i-tăl
capitalism, kap'i-tăl-izm
Capitol, kap'i-tul
capitulate, kă-pit'ů-lāt
capon, kā'pon
caprice, kă-prēs'
capricious, kă-prish'us
capsule, kap'sŭl
captain, kap'tin
caption, kap'shun
captious, kap'shus
capture, kap'tůr
carabineer, kar-ă-bi-nẽr'
caracul, kă-ră-kōōl'
caramel, kar'ă-mel
carat, kar'at
caravan, kar'ă-van; kar-ă-van'
carbohydrate, kär-bo-hī'drāt
carbon, kär'bon
carborundum, kär-bō-run'dum
carbuncle, kär'bung-kl
carbureter; carburetor, kär-bu-
   ret'ẽr
cardiac, kär'di-ak
caribou; cariboo, kar'i-bōō
caricature, kar'i-kă-tūr
carillon, kar'i-lon
carnivorous, kär-niv'o-rus
carol, kar'ul
carouse, kă-rouz'
carousal, kar-ou'zel
carriage, kar'ij
carton, kär'ton
cartoon, kär-tōōn'
cascade, kas-kăd'
casement, kās'ment
cashmere, kash'mẽr
cask, kăsk
casket, kăs'ket
casserole, kas'ẽr-ōl
cast, kăst
caste, kăst
castle, kăs'l; kăs'l
casual, kazh'ů-al

casualty, kazh'û-al-ti
casuist, kazh'u-ist
cataclysm, kat'ă-klizm
catalepsy, kat'ă-lep-si
catapult, kat'ă-pult
cataract, kat'ă-rakt
catastrophe, kă-tas'trō-fê
catch, kach
catchup, kach'up
catechism, kat'e-kizm
catechize, kat'i-kīz
category, kat'e-go-ri
caterpillar, kat'ĕr-pil"ĕr
catharsis, kă-thär'sis
cathartic, kă-thär'tik
cathedral, kă-thê'dral
Catholicism, kă-thol'i-sizm
Caucasian, kaw-kā'shi-an
caucus, kaw'kus
cauliflower, kaw'li-flou-ĕr
causal, kawz'al
causality, kaw-zal'i-ti
cavalcade, kav-ăl-kād'
cavalry, kav'ăl-ri
caveat, kă've-at
cavern, kav'ĕrn
caviar, kav'i-är'; caviare, kav-i-är'
cavil, kav'il
cayenne, kī-en'; kā-en'
cease, sēs
celebration, sel-e-brā'shun
celebrity, se-leb'ri-ti
celerity, sê-ler'i-ti
celery, sel'ō-ri
celestial, sê-les'chal
celibacy, sel'i-bă-si
cellar, sel'ĕr
cello, chel'ō
celluloid, sel'û-loid
cellulose, sel'û-lōs
Celt, selt; Kelt, kelt
cemetery, sem'ê-ter-i
cenotaph, sen'o-tåf
censor, sen'ser
censure, sen'shur
centenary, sen'te-na-ri
centennial, sen-ten'i-al
centipede, sen'ti-pēd
centrifugal, sen-trif'u-gal
century, sen'tu-ri
ceramic, se-ram'ik; keramic, ke-ram'ik
cereal, sē're-al
ceremony, ser'e-mo-ni
cerise, se-rēz'
certain, sĕr'tin
certificate, sĕr-tif'i-kăt
certiorari, sĕr-shi-o-rā'rī
chafe, chāf
chaff, chăf
chafing dish, chāf'ing dish
chagrin, shă-grin'; sha-grēn'

chaise, shāz
Chaldean, kal-dē'an
chalet, sha-lā'
chambray, sham'brā
chameleon, kă-mē'le-un
chamois, sham'i
champagne, sham-pān'
champion, cham'pi-un
Champs Elysees, shän zā-lē-zā'
chance, châns
chancery, chân'sĕr-i
chandelier, shan-de-lēr'
chanticleer, cant'ti-klēr
chaos, kā'os
chapeau, shå-pō'
chaperon, shap'er-ōn
charade, shå-räd'
charivari, shär-i-vä'ri
charlatan, shär'lă-tan
charlotte russe, shär'lot rūs
charmeuse, shär'mōōs
Charon, kā'ron
chartreuse, shär-truz'
Charybdis, kă-rib'dis
chasm, kazm
chassis, sha'sē
chaste, chăst
chastise, chas-tīz'
chastity, chas'ti-ti
chateau, sha-tō'
chatelaine, shat'e-län
chauffeur, shō-fēr'
chauvinism, shō'vin-izm
chef, shef
chef-d'œuvre, shā-dē'vr
chemise, she-mēz'
chemist, kem'ist
chenille, she-nēl'
cheroot, she-root'
cherub, cher'ub
Cheshire cheese, ches'ĕr chēz
chestnut, ches'nut
chevalier, shev-ă-lēr'
chevron, shev'ron
chew, chōō
chic, shēk
chicanery, shi-kän'ĕr-i
chicken, chik'en
chieftain, chēf'tin
chiffon, shif'on
chiffonier, shif-on-nēr'
children, chil'dren
chimera, kī-mē'rä
chimpanzee, chim-pan'zē
chinchilla, chin-chil'ă
chirography, kīrog'rä-fi
chiropodist, ki-rop'o-dist
chiropractic, ki-ro-prak'tik
chisel, chiz'el
chivalry, shiv'ăl-ri
chlorine, klō'rīn
chloroform, klō'ro-fôrm

chocolate, chok'o-lat
choir, kwīr
cholera, kol'ĕr-ă
chord, kôrd
chores, chōrz
chow, chou
Christianity, kris-chi-an'i-ti
chromium, krō'mi-um
chromo, krō'mō
chrysalis, kris'ă-lis
chrysanthemum, kris-an'the-mum
cigar, si-gär'
cigarette sig-ă-ret'
cinema, sin'e-mă
circassian, sĕr-kash'an
Circe, sĕr-sē
circuit, sĕr'ket
circuitous, sĕr-kū'i-tus
circumference, sĕr-kum'fĕr-ens
circumlocution, sĕr-kum-lo-
   kū'shun
circumstance, sĕr'kum-stans
citizen, sit'i-zen
Citrus, sit'rus
civil, siv'il
civilization, siv-i-li-zā'shun
clairvoyance, klăr-voi'ans
clandestine, klan-des'tin
claque, klak
clarinet, klar'i-net
clasp, klåsp
class, klås
classic, klas'ik
classicism, klas'i-sizm
cleanly, klen'li
clerk, klĕrk
client, klī'ent
clientele, klī-en-tel'
climate, klī'mat
climatic, klī-mat'ik
climber, klīm'ĕr
clinical, klin'ik-al
clique, klēk
cloth, klôth
clothes, klōthz
clue, klŏo
coagulate, ko-ag'û-lāt
coalescence, kō-ă-les'ens
coalition, kō-ă-lish'un
coarse, kōrs
cobra, kō'brå
cocaine, kō-kān'; kō'kān
cocoa, kō'kō
cocoon, ko-kŏon'
codicil, kod'i-sil
codify, kō'di-fi; kod'i-fī
co-ed, kō'ed
coerce, ko-ĕrs'
coffee, kof'ê
cogitation, coj-i-tā'shun
cognac, kō'nyăk
cognizance, kog'ni-zans

cognomen, kog-nō'men
cohesive, ko-hē'siv
coiffeur, kwå'fĕr (a hairdresser)
coiffure, koif'ûr (style of arrang-
   ing the hair)
coincidence, kō-in'si-dens
collaboration, ko-lab-ō-rā'shun
collapse, ko-laps'
collateral, ko-lat'ĕr-al
colleague, kol'ēg
collegian, ko-lē'ji-an
colloquial, ko-lō'kwi-al
cologne water, ko-lōn' wau'ter
colonel, kĕr'nel
colonization, kol"o-ni-zā'shun
colonnade, kol-o-nād'
columbine, kol'um-bīn
column, kol'um
coma, kō'mă
comatose, kom'ă-tōs
combatant, kom'bat-ant
combine, kom-bīn'
combustible, kom-bus'ti-bl
comely, kum'li
comfortable, kum'fĕr-tă-bl
comic, kom'ik
comique, ko-mēk'
comity, kom'i-ti
commandant, kom-ăn-dänt'
commandment, ko-månd'ment
commentator, kom'en-tā-tĕr
commiserate, ko-miz'ĕr-āt
commissary, kom'i-sa-ri
communism, kom'û-nizm
comparable, kom'på-ră-bl
comparison, kom-par'i-sun
competence, kom'pe-tens
complement, kom'ple-ment (n. a
   complete set; v. to supply a deficiency)
compliment, kom'pli-ment (n. delicate flattery; v. to flatter)
composite, kom'po-zit
comptroller, kon-trōl'ĕr
comrade, kom'rad
concentrate, kon'sen-trāt
concert (v.), kon-sĕrt' (to contrive together)
concert (n.), kon'sĕrt (a musical
   entertainment)
concerto, kon-cher'tō
concierge, kon-si-ärzh'
concoct, kon-kokt'
concomitant, kon-kom'i-tant
concord, kong'kord; kon'kord
concordance, kon-kôr'dans
concourse, kon'kōrs
concubine, kon'kû-bīn
condolence, kon-dōl'ens
conduct (v.), kon-dukt' (to guide)
conduct (n.), kon'dukt (personal
   behavior)

conduit, kon'dit

confectionery, kon-fek'shun-ĕr-i

conference, kon'fĕr-ens

confident, kon'fi-dent

confine (n.), kon-fīn' (a boundary or limit)

confine (v.), kon-fīn (to restrict within limits)

conflict (v.), kon-flikt' (to contend, fight)

conflict (n.), kon'flikt (a battle)

confrere, kôn-frār'

Confucianism, kon-fū'shan-izm

congeal, kon-jēl'

congenial, kon-jēn'yal

conglomerate, kon-glom'ĕr-āt

congratulate, kon-grat'ū-lāt

congressional, kon-gresh'un-al

conjecture, con-jek'tur

conjugal, kon'joo-gal

conjugation, kon-joo-gā'shun

conjure, kon-jūr' (to summon in a sacred name)

conjure, kun'jĕr (to influence by, or as if by magic)

conjurer, kun'jĕr-ĕr

connivance, ko-nī'văns

connoisseur, kon-i-sĕr'

conquer, kong'kĕr

conquest, kon'kwest

consanguinity, kon-sang-gwin'i-ti

conscience, kon'shens

conscientious, kon-shi-en'shus

conscious, kon'shus

consequential, kon-se-kwen'shal

consign, kon-sīn

consignee, kon-si-nē'

console, kon-sōl' (to give comfort to)

console, kon'sōl (an ornamental bracket supporting a cornice)

consomme, kon-so-mā'

consort (n.), kon'sôrt (a companion)

consort (v.), kon-sôrt' (to associate)

conspiracy, kon-spir'ă-si

constable, kon-stă-bl

consul, kon'sul

consummate (v.), kon'sum-āt (to complete, finish)

consummate (adj.), kon-sum'at (perfect)

contemplate, kon-tem'plat

contemporary, kon-tem'po-ra-ri

content (adj. and v.), kon-tent' (satisfied; to gratify)

content (n.), kon'tent (that which is comprised in anything)

contest (v.), kon-test' (to dispute, litigate)

contest (n.), kon'test (a struggle for superiority)

continuity, kon-ti-nū'i-ti

contour, kon-tōōr'

contract (v.), kon-trakt' (to condense, to agree upon)

contract (n.), kon'trakt (a written agreement)

contrast (v.), kon-trăst' (to compare)

contrast (n.), kon'trăst (difference of qualities made manifest by comparison)

contrite, kon'trīt

contrition, kon-trish'un

controversial, kon-tro-vĕr'shal

controversy, kon'tro-vĕr-si

contumacy, kon'tu-mă-si

contumely, kon'tū-mē-li

convalesce, kon-vă-les'

conversant, kon'vĕr-sant

converse (v.), kon-vĕrs' (to talk familiarly)

converse (n. and adj.), kon'vĕrs (reversed in order)

convert (v.), kon-vĕrt' (cause to undergo a moral change)

convert (n.), kon'vĕrt (one who has undergone a moral change)

convict (v.), kon-vikt' (to prove or pronounce guilty of a crime)

convict (n.), kon'vikt (a criminal)

convoy (v.), kon-voi' (to accompany on the way for protection)

convoy (n.), kon'voi (a protecting escort)

co-operate, kō-op'ĕr-āt

coquette, ko-ket'

cordial, kôr'jal

corduroy, kôr'du-roi

corespondent, kō-re-spond'ent (a man or woman charged with adultery in a divorce suit)

corollary, kôr'o-lă-ri; ko-rol'ă-ri

corporal, kôr'pō-ral

corporally, kôr'pō-ral-i

corps, kōr (a group of persons associated in a common work)

corpse, kôrps (a dead body)

corpuscle, kôr'pus-l

corral, ko-ral'

correspondent, kor-e-spon'dent (similar;- one with whom intercourse is maintained by letters)

cortege, kôr-tāzh'

Cortes, kôr'tes

cosmetic, koz-met'ĭk

cosmic, koz'mik

cosmopolitan, koz-mō-pol'i-tăn

cosmopolite, koz-mop'ō-līt

costume (n.), kos'tūm (dress in general; style of dress)

costume (v.), kos-tūm' (to dress in, to provide with appropriate costumes)

cougar, kōō-gēr
cough, kôf
council, koun'sil
counsel, koun'sel
countenance, koun'te-năns
coup d'etat, kōō dā'tå'
coupe, kōō-pā'
coupon, kōō'pon
courage, kur'ij
courageous, kur-ā'jus
courier, kōō'ri-ēr
courteous, kēr'te-us; kōrt'yus
courtesan; courtezan, kōr'te-zan
courtesy, kēr'te-si; kōr'te-si (politeness combined with kindness)
courtesy, kēr'te-si; kērt'si (a salutation made by bending the knees. See curtsy)
courtier, kōrt'yēr
covenant, kuv'e-nănt
covert, kuv'ērt
covetous, kuv'e-tus
covey, kuv'i
coxswain, kok'swăn; kok's'n
coyote, kī'ōt; kī-ō'te
crabbed, krab'ed
cranberry, kran'bēr-ri
cravat, krä-vat'
crayon, krā'un
creature, krē'tûr
credence, krē'dens
credulous, kred'û-lus
creek, krēk
cremate, krē'māt
crematory, krēm'ă-tō-ri
Creole, krē'ōl
creosote, krē'o-sōt
cretonne, krē-ton'
crevasse, kre-vas'
crevice, krev'is
crew, krōō
cribbage, krib'ij
critique, kri-tēk'
crochet, kro-shā'
Croesus, krē'sus
croix de guerre, krwä dē gär
crooked, krook'ed
croquet, krō-kā'
croquette, krō-ket'
cross, krôs
croup, krōōp
crucial, krōō'shal
cruller, krul'ēr
crux, kruks
cuckold, kuk'uld
cucumber, kū'kum-bēr
cudgel, kuj'el
cuisine, kwe-zēn'
cul-de-sac, kū-de-såk'
culinary, kū'li-ne-ri
culture, kul'tûr
cupboard, kub'ērd
currant, kur'ănt

current, kur'ent
cursed, kēr'sed
curtain, kēr'tin
cushion, koosh'un
cycle, sī'kl
cyclone, sī'klōn
cymbal, sim'bal
cynosure, sī'no-shōōr; sin'o-shōōr
cyst, sist
Czechoslovak, chek'ō-slō'vak

D

dahlia, dăl'yă
dairy, dā'ri
dais, dā'is
dalliance, dal'i-ăns
damage, dam'ij
damask, dam'åsk
damned, damd
dance, dåns
data, dā'tă
datum, dā'tum
daunt, dänt
dauphin, dô'fin
deaf, def
dearth, dērth
debacle, de-bä'k'l
debate, de-bāt'
debauch, de-bawch'
debauchee, deb-aw-shē'
debauchery, de-baw'chēr-i
debenture, de-ben'tûr
debonair, deb-o-nār'
debouch, de-bōōsh'
debris, dā-brē'
debt, det
debut, dā-bōō'
debutante, dā-bōō-tänt'
decade, dek'ăd
decadence, de-kā'dens
decadent, de-kā'dent
decapitate, de-kap'i-tāt
decay, de-kā
decedent, de-sē'dent
decent, dē'sent
decimate, des'i-māt
decisive, de-sī'siv
declaratory, de-klar'ă-tō-ri
declare, de-klār'
decollete, dā-kol-e-tā'
decorative, dek'o-rā-tiv
decorous, de-ko'rus; dek'ēr-us
decorum, de-kō'rum
defamatory, de-fam'ă-tō-ri
defecate, def'e-kāt
deference, def'ēr-ens
deferential, def-ēr-en'shal
deficiency, de-fish'en-si
deficit, def'i-sit
deify, dē'i-fi
deign, dān

deist, dē'ist
deity, dē'i-ti
dejeuner, dā-zhū-nā'
Delaware, del'ă-wār
delectable, de-lek'tă-b'l
deleterious, del-e-tē'ri-us
delicate, del'i-kăt
delicatessen, del-i-kă-tes'en
delight, de-līt'
delirious, de-lir'i-us
delivery, de-liv'ēr-i
deluge, del'ūj
delusion, de-lū'zhun
de luxe, de looks'
demagogue, dem'ă-gog
demand, de-mănd'
demimonde, dem'i-mond
demise, de-mīz'
demi-tasse, dem'i-tas
democracy, de-mok'ră-si
demoiselle, dem-wä-zel'
demon, dē'mon
demoniacal, de-mō-nī'ă-kăl
demonstrable, de-mon'stră-bl
demonstrate, de-mon'strāt;
   dem'on-strāt
demonstrative, dem-on'stră-tiv
demure, de-mūr'
demurrage, de-mûr'ij
demurrer, de-mur'ēr
denature, dē-nā'tûr
denizen, den'i-zen
dentifrice, den'ti-fris
deodorant, dē-ō'dēr-ănt
departure, de-pär'tûr
depilatory, de-pil'ă-to-ri
deportation, dē-por-tā'shun
depositary, de-poz'i-tă-ri
deposition, dep-ō-zish'un
depot, dē'pō; dep'ō
deprecatory, dep're-kă-tō-ri
depreciate, de-prē'shi-āt
deprivation, dep-ri-vā'shun
depute, de-pūt'
deputy, dep'û-ti
Derby, där'bi
derby, dēr'bi
derelict, der'e-likt
derisive, de-rīs'iv
derivative, de-riv'ă-tiv
derogatory, de-rog'ă-tō-ri
descend, de-send'
describe, de-skrīb'
desert, de-zert' (to forsake)
desert, dez'ort (a barren tract incapable of supporting life or
   vegetation)
desert, de-zert' (a reward or punishment deserved)
deserve, de-zērv'
design, de-zīn'
designate, des'ig-nāt
desire, de-zīr'

desist, dē-zist'
desolate, des'o-lāt
desperado, des-pēr-ā'do
despicable, des'pi-kă-bl
despise, de-spīz'
despot, des'pot
dessert, de-zērt' (a course of fruits,
   sweets, etc.)
desuetude, des'wê-tūd
desultory, des'ul-tō-ri
detail, de-tāl'
detestation, de-tes-tā'shun;
   det-es-tā'shun
detonate, det'o-nāt
detour, de-toor'
deuce, dūs
devastate, dev'ăs-tāt
deviate, dē'vi-āt
device, de-vīs'
Devil, dev'l
devious, dē'vi-us
devise, de-vīz'
devotee, dev-ō-tē'
dew, dū
dexterous, deks'tēr-us
diabetes, dī-ă-bē'tēz
diabetic, dī-ă-bet'ik
diabolic, dī-ă-bol'ik
diagnostician, di-ag-nos-tish'an
diagonal, di-ag'o-nal
diamond, dī'ă-mund
diaphanous, dī-af'ă-nus
diaphragm, dī'ă-fram
diarrhoea, dī-ă-rē'ă
diatribe, dī'ă-trib
dictionary, dik'shun-ă-ri
diet, dī'et
dietetics, dī-e-tet'iks
differential, dif-ēr-en'shal
differentiate, dif-ēr-en'shi-āt
digest (n.), dī'jest (a synopsis,
   summary)
digest (v.), di-jest' (to arrange
   methodically under proper heads
   or titles; to dissolve in the
   stomach by the action of di-
   gestive juices)
digestion, dī-jes'chun
digit, dij'it
digress, di-gres'; dī-gres'
dilapidated, di-lap'i-dāt-ed
dilate, dī-lāt'
dilatory, dil'ă-tō-ri
dilemma, di-lem'ă; dī-lem'ă
dilettante, dil-e-tan'te
dilute, di-lūt'; dī-lūt'
diminution, dim-i-nū'shun
diminutive, di-min'û-tiv
dinghy, ding'gi
diocese, dī'o-sēs
Diogenes, dī-oj'e-nēz
diphtheria, dif-thē'ri-ă;
   dip-thē'ri-ă

diplomacy, di-plŏ'mă-si; di-plom'ă-si
direct, dī-rekt'
direction, dī-rek'shun
dirigible, dir'i-ji-bl
discern, di-zěrn'
disconsolate, dis-kon'sō-let
discourse, dis-kōrs'
disease, di-zēz'
dishabille, dis-ă-bēl'
dishevel, di-shev'el
disingenuous, dis-in-jen'ū-us
disparagement, dis-par'ij-ment
dispensary, dis-pen'să-ri
dispossess, dis-po-zes'
disputable, dis'pū-tă-bl
dispute, dis'pūt'
dissect, di-sekt'
dissolute, dis'ō-lūt
dissolve, di-zolv'
dissonance, dis'ō-năns
distemper, dis-tem'pěr'
district, dis'trikt
divan, di-van'
diverge, di-věrj'
divers, dī'verz
diverse, dī-věrs'; dī'vers
diversion, di-věr'shun
divert, di-věrt'
divest, di-vest'
divide, di-vīd'
divine, di-vīn'
divorce, di-vōrs'
divorcee, di-vōr-sē'
divulge, di-vulj'
docile, dōs'il; dos'il
docility, do-sil'i-ti
doctor, dok'těr
doctrinaire, dok-tri-nār'
doeskin, dō'skin
dogged, dog'ed
doggerel, dog'ěr-el
doldrums, dol'drumz
dolorous, dol'ěr-us
domicile, dom'i-sil
dominie, dom'i-ni
donate, dō'nāt
donkey, dong'ki
Don Quixote, don ke-hō'tă
door, dōr
dossier, do-syā'
dotage, dōt'ij
dotard, dō'těrd
double, dub'l
doubt, dout
douche, dōōsh
dough, dō
doughty, dou'ti
dour, dōōr
dower, dou'er
dozen, duz'n
draft; draught, drăft

drama, drä'mă
dramatic, dră-mat'ik
dramatis personae, dram'ă-tis pěr-sō'nē
drawers, draw'ěrz
dredge, drej
drivel, driv'el
dromedary, drum'e-dā-ri
drought, drout
drudge, druj
dual, dū'al
dubious, dū'bi-us
duchess, duch'es
duchy, duch'i
due, dū
duel, dū'el
duet, dū-et'
duke, dūk
duly, dū'li
dungeon, dun'jun
dupe, dūp
duress, dū-res'; dū'res
duty, dū'ti
dynamic, dī-nam'ik
dynamite, dī'nă-mīt
dynamo, dī'nă-mō
dynasty, dī'nas-ti
dysentery, dis'en-ter-i
dyspepsia, dis-pep'si-ă

E

earl, ērl
earthy, ērth'i
easel, ē'zl
easy, ēz'i
eau de Cologne, ō dē ko-lōn'
ebony, eb'un-i
ebullience, e-bul'yens
eccentric, ek-sen'trik
ecclesiasticism, e-klē-zi-as'ti-sizm
eclair, ā-klār'
eclat, ā-klä'
eclectic, ek-lek'tik
eclipse, ē-klips'
economic, ek-o-nom'ĭk; ē-ko-nom'ĭk
economy, e-kon'o-mi
ecstasy, ek'stă-si
eczema, ek'zē-mă
Eden, ē'dn
edge, ej
edible, ed'i-bl
edict, ē'dikt
edifice, ed'i-fis
edition, e-dish'un
educate, ed'ū-kāt
education, ed-ū-kā'shun
eerie, ē'ri
effect, e-fekt'
effectual, e-fek'tu-al
effeminate, e-fem'i-nāt

effervescence, ef-ẽr-ves'ens
effete, e-fēt'
efficacy, ef'i-kǎ-si
effigy, ef'i-ji
effrontery, e-frun'tẽr-i
ego, ē'gō
egoist, ē'gō-ist
egotism, ē'go-tizm; eg'o-tizm
egotist, ē'go-tist; eg'o-tist
egregious, e-grē'jus
egress, e'gres
eight, āt
eighth, ātth
either, ē'ther; ī'ther
ejaculate, e-jak'û-lāt
eke, ēk
elan, ā-län'
elastic, e-las'tik
elate, e-lāt'
elect, e-lekt'
electricity, e-lek-tris'i-ti
electrotype, e-lek'trō-tīp
elegiac, el-e-jī'ak; e-lē'ji-ak
elegy, el'e-ji
elementary, el-e-men'tǎ-ri
elevate, el'e-vāt
eleven, e-lev'n
elf, elf
elfin, el'fin
elicit, e-lis'it
elision, e-lizh'un
elite, ā-lēt'
elixir, a-lik'sẽr
ellipsis, e-lip'sis
elm, elm
elongate, e-lông'gāt
elucidate, e-lūs'i-dāt
elude, e-lūd'
Elysium, e-lizh'i-um
emaciate, e-mā'shi-āt
emancipation, e-man-si-pā'shun
embryo, em'bri-ō
embryonic, em-bri-on'ik
emerald, em'e-rald
emeritus, e-mer'i-tus
emetic, e-met'ik
emigrant, em'i-grǎnt
emigre, ā-mē-grā'
emissary, em'i-sê-ri
emolument, e-mol'û-ment
emperor, em'pẽr-ẽr
emphasis, em'fǎ-sis
emphasize, em'fǎ-sīz
empiric, em-pir'ik
employe; employee, em-ploi-ē'
emporium, em-pō'ri-um
emu, ē'mū
emulation, em-û-lā'shun
emulsion, e-mul'shun
enceinte, än-sant'
enchant, en-chänt'
encomium, en-kō'mi-um
encore, äng-kōr'
encyclical, en-sik'li-kal

encyclopaedic, en-sī-klo-pē'dik
endeavor, en-dev'ẽr
endive, en'dīv
endocrine, en'dō-krīn
enema, en'e-mǎ
enervate, en'ẽr-vat; e-nẽr'vāt
en famille, än fǎ-mē'y
enfranchise, en-fran'chīz
engine, en'jin
English, ing'glish
engross, en-grōs'
enhance, en-häns'
enigma, e-nig'mǎ
en masse, änmas'
ennui, än-wē'
en passant, än päs-sän'
en rapport, äng rǎ-pōr'
en route, än rōōt'
ensconce, en-skons'
ensemble, än-säm'bl
ensign, en'sīn
ensilage, en-si-lij
entente, än-tänt'
entire, en-tīr'
entity, en'ti-ti
entourage, än-tōō-räzh'
entr'acte, än'träkt
entree, än-trā'
entre nous, än'tr nōō
entrepreneur, an-tre-pre-nur'
entry, en'tri
enunciate, e-nun'shi-āt
envelop (v.), en-vel'up
envelope (n.), en'vel-ōp
envisage, en-viz'ij
epaulet, ep'aw-let
ephemeral, e-fem'ẽr-al
epicure, ep'i-kūr
epidemic, ep-i-dem'ĭk
epidermis, ep-i-dẽr'mis
epilepsy, ep'i-lep-si
epileptic, ep-i-lep'tik
Epiphany, e-pif'ǎ-ni
episcopacy, e-pis'ko-pǎ-si
Episcopalian, e-pis-kō-pā'li-an
episode, ep'i-sōd
epistle, e-pis'l
epitaph, ep'i-tâf
epithet, ep'i-thet
epitome, e-pit'ō-mē
epoch, e'pok
equable, ē'kwǎ-bl
equality, ē-kwäl'i-ti
equanimity, ē-kwǎ-nim'i-ti
equation, e-kwā'shun
equerry, ek'wẽr-i
equestrian, e-kwes'tri-an
equine, ē'kwīn
equinox, e'kwi-noks
equip, e-kwip'
equitable, ek'wi-tǎ-bl
equity, ek'wi-ti
equivalent, e-kwiv'ǎ-lent
equivocal, e-kwiv'o-kal

equivocation, e-kwiv-o-kā'shun
era, ē'rä
erasure, e-rā'zhur
ere, är
Erebus, er'e-bus
ergo, ēr'gō
Erin, ē'rin
Eros, ē'ros
erotic, ē-rot'ĭk
err, ĕr
erroneous, e-rō'ne-us
erudite, ĕr'ū-dīt
erysipelas, er-i-sip'e-las
escadrille, es-kă-dril'
escalator, es'kă-lā-tēr
eschew, es-chōō'
escrow, es-krō'
escutcheon, es-kuch'un
esophagus; oesophagus,
  e-sof'ă-gus
esoteric, es-o-ter'ĭk
espionage, es'pi-o-nij
esplanade, es-plă-nād'
esprit de corps, es-prē' de kōr'
esquire, es-kwīr'
essay, es'sā
estate, es-tāt'
estuary, es'tū-ā-rĭ
ether, ē'thēr
ethical, eth'i-kal
etiquette, et'i-ket
etoile, ā-twal'
eucalyptus, ū-kă-lip'tus
Eucharist, ū'kă-rist
euchre, ū'kēr
eugenics, ū-jen'iks
eunuch, ū'nuk
euphonic, ū-fon'ĭk
European, ū-ro-pē'an
evanescent, ev-ă-nes'ent
evangelical, e-van-jel'i-kal
evangelize, e-van'jel-īz
evasive, e-vā'siv
even, ē'vn
evening, ēv'ning
event, ē-vent'
eventually, e-ven'tū-a-li
every, ev'ri; ev'ēr-i
evil, ē'vl
evolution, ev-o-lu'shun
ewe, ū
exacerbate, egs-as'ēr-bāt
exact, egz-akt'
exaggerate, egz-aj'ēr-āt
exalt, egz-awlt'
exasperate, egz-as'pēr-āt
ex cathedra, eks kă-thē'drä
excavate, eks'kă-vāt
excellent, ek'se-lent
exchequer, eks-chek'ēr
excision, ek-sizh'un
excommunicate, eks-ko-mū'ni-kāt
excruciate, eks-krōō'shi-āt

exculpate, eks-kul'pāt
excursion, eks-kēr'shun
excuse (v.), eks-kūz'
excuse (n.), eks-kūs'
execrable, ek'sē-krä-bl
execute, ek'se-kūt
executive, egs-ek'ū-tiv
executrix, egs-ek'ū-triks
exemplary, egz-em'plă-rĭ
exempt, egz-empt'
exert, egz-ērt'
exhale, eks-hāl'
exhaust, egz-awst'
exhibit, egz-ib'it; eks-hib'it
exhilarant, eg-zil'ă-rănt
exigency, ek'si-jen-si
exile, ek'sīl
exist, eg-zist'
exit, ek'sit
exodus, ek'so-dus
ex officio, eks o-fish'i-ō
exorbitant, egz-ôr'bi-tănt
ex parte, eks pär'te
expatriation, eks-pat-ri-ā'shun
expert (adj.), eks-pērt' (skilful,
  through practice or experience)
expert (n.), eks'pērt (a specialist)
expiate, eks'pi-āt
expire, ek-spīr'
explain, eks-plān'
explanatory, eks-plan'ă-to-ri
explicable, eks'pli-kă-bl
explicit, eks-plis'it
exploit (v.), eks-ploit'
exploit (n.), eks'ploit
exponent, eks-pō'nent
export (v.), eks-pōrt'
export (n.), eks'port
expose, eks-pōz'
expose, eks-pō-zā'
expository, eks-poz'i-to-ri
expostulate, eks-pos'tū-lāt
expropriation, eks-prō-pri-ā'shun
exquisite, eks'kwi-zit
extant, eks'tănt
extempore, eks-tem'po-re
exterminator, eks-tēr'mi-nā-tēr
extortionate, eks-tōr'shun-āt
extract (v.), eks-trakt'
extract (n.), eks'trakt
extraneous, eks-trā'ne-us
extraordinary, eks-trôr'di-nā-ri;
  eks-trä-ôr'di-nā-ri
extravaganza, eks-trav-ă-gan'ză
exuberance, egz-ū'bēr-äns
exult, egz-ult'

F

fabric, fab'rik
fabricator, fab'ri-kā-tēr
facade, fă-säd'

facet, fas'et
facetious, fă-sē'shus
facial, fā'shal
facile, fas'il
facility, fă-sil'i-ti
facsimile, fak-sim'i-lē
factual, fak'tû-al
failure, fāl'ûr
fairy, fār'i
fait accompli, fāt ă-kön-plē'
falcon, fal'kn; faw'kn
fallacious, fal-lā'shus
fallacy, fal'ă-si
fallen, fawl'n
falsetto, fawl-set'ō
familiar, fă-mil'yēr
familiarity, fă-mil-i-ar'i-ti
fanaticism, fă-nat'i-sizm
fancy, fan'si
fandango, fan-dang'gō
fanfare, fan'fār
farandole, fă''rän-dōl'
farcical, fär'si-kal
farewell, fār'wel
Fascism, făsh'izm
Fascisti, fä-shē'sti; făs-kēs'ti
fashion, fash'un
fast, făst
fasten, făs'n
fathom, fa*th*'um
fatigue, fă-tēg'
fatuous, fat'ū-us
faucet, faw'set
fault, fawlt
fauna, faw'nă
faux pas, fō pä'
favor, fā'vēr
fealty, fē'al-ti
feature, fē'tūr
febrile, feb'ril; fē'bril
February, feb'rŏō-ā-ri
fecund, fek'und; fē-kund'
fecundity, fe-kun'di-ti
federal, fed'ēr-al
feign, fān
feint, fānt
felicitate, fe-lis'i-tāt
felicity, fe-lis'i-ti
fellow, fel'ō
felon, fel'un
felony, fel'o-ni
feminine, fem'i-nin
Fenian, fē'ni-an
ferment (n.), fēr'ment
ferment (v.), fēr-ment'
fertility, fēr-til'i-ti
ferule, fēr'ool
festivity, fes-tiv'i-ti
fete, fāt
fetid, fet'id; fē'tid
fetish, fet'ish; fē'tish
fez, fez
fiance, fē-än-sā'

fiancee, fē-än-sā'
fiasco, fē-äs'kō
fiat, fī'at
fibril, fī'bril
fidelity, fi-del'i-ti
fidget, fij'et
fiduciary, fi-dū'shi-ā-ri
fiery, fī'ēr-i
fiesta, fyes'tä
fifth, fifth
figure, fig'ûr
filament, fil'ă-ment
filial, fil'i-al
filibuster, fil-i-bus'tēr
filigree, fil'i-grē
Filipino, fil-i-pē'nō
fillet, fil'et
film, film
finale, fe-nä'lä
finance, fi-nans'
financier, fin-än-sēr'
finis, fī'nis
finite, fī'nīt
finitesimal, fin-i-tes'i-mal
firmament, fēr'mă-ment
fissure, fish'ur
fistiana, fis-ti-ā'nă
fisticuffs, fis'ti-kufs
fistula, fis'tū-lă
fixture, fiks'tūr
flaccid, flak'sid
flagellate, flaj'e-lāt
flagrant, flā'grant
flamboyant, flam-boi'änt
flamingo, flă-ming'gō
flange, flanj
flannel, flan'el
flask, flăsk
flaunt, flänt
fledge, flej
fleur-de-lis, flōōr-de-lē'
flood, flud
floor, flōr
flora, flō'ră
florescence, flō-res'ens
florid, flor'id
florist, flō'rist
flotsam, flot'sam
fluctuate, fluk'tū-āt
flue, flū
fluid, flū'id
fluidity, flū-id'i-ti
flume, flōōm
fluorescence, flōō-o-res'ens
flute, flōōt
focus, fō'kus
foetus, fē'tus
fogy, fō'gi
foible, foi'bl
folderol, fol'de-rol
foliage, fō'li-ij
folio, fō'li-ō
folk, fōk

follicle, fol'i'kl
foment, fō-ment'
food, fōōd
foot, foot
forage, for'ij
forbear, for-bār'
forceps, fôr'seps
forbade; forbad, for-bad'
forebear, fôr'bār
forecast, fôr'kåst
forehead, for'ed
foreign, for'in
forensic, fo-ren'sik
forfend, fôr-fend'
formaldehyde, fôr-mal'de-hīd
formally, fôr'ma-li
format, for-mät'
formative, fôr'mă-tiv
formidable, fôr'mi-dă-bl
fort, fôrt
forte, fôr'tā
fortitude, fôr'ti-tūd
fortnight, fôrt'nīt
fortuitous, for-tū'i-tus
fortune, fôr'tūn
forum, fōr'um
forward, fôr'wĕrd
fossil, fos'il
foulard, fōō-lärd'
fountain, foun'tin
four, fōr
fox, foks
fracture, frak'tûr
fragile, fraj'il
franc, frangk
franchise, fran'chīz
frankincence, frangk'in-sens
frappe, frå-pā'
fraternal, frå-tĕr'nal
fraternize, frat'ĕr-nīz
frequent (adj.), frē'kwent
    (recurring often)
frequent (v.); frē-kwent' (to
    visit often)
fresco, fres'kō
Freudianism, froi'di-an-izm
fricassee, frik-å-sē'
friendship, frend'ship
frigid, frij'id
frijole, frē-hōl'
from, from
front, frunt
frontier, fron'tēr
frontispiece, fron'tis-pēs
fruition, frōō-ish'un
fugitive, fū'ji-tiv
fulcrum, ful'krum
fulgent, ful'jent
full, fool
fulminate, ful'mi-nāt
fulsome, ful'sum
fundamental, fun-då-men'tal
funeral, fū'nĕr-al
funereal, fū-nē're-al

fungus, fung'gus
fungi, fun'ji (plural of fungus)
furbelow, fĕr'be-lō
furious, fū'ri-us
furlough, fĕr'lō
furniture, fĕr'ni-tūr
furor; furore, fū'ror; foo-rō'ra
furtive, fĕr'tiv
fury, fū'ri
fuselage, fū'ze-lij
fusillade, fū-zi-lăd'
futile, fū'til
future, fū'tûr
futurity, fu-tū'ri-ti

G

gabardine, găb-är-dēn'
Gaelic, găl'ik
gage, găj
gaiety, gā'e-ti
gala, gā'lă
Galilean, gal-i-lē'an
gall, gawl
gallant (adj. and n.), gal'ant
    (brave; a person of sprightly and
    gay manners)
gallant (adj., n., and v.), gal-ant'
    (showing courtesy and respectful
    deference to women; a man who
    is attentive to women; to pay
    court to)
galleon, gal'e-on
gallery, gal'ĕr-i
Gallic, găl'ik
gallivant, gal'i-vant
gallon, gal'un
gallows, gal'ōz
galore, gă-lōr'
galosh, gă-losh'
gamete, gam'ēt
gamin, gam'in
gamut, gam'ut
gangrene, gang'grēn
gantlet, gänt'let
gaol, jāl
gape, gāp
garage, gă-räzh'; gar'äj
garbage, gär'băj
garcon, gär-sôn'
garden, gär'dn
Gargantuan, gär-gan'tū-an
gargoyle, gär'goil
garish, gar'ish
garrote, ga-rōt'
garrulity, ga-rōō'li-ti
garrulous, gar'ōō-lus
gaseous, gas'e-us
gasoline, gas'o-lēn
gasp, gåsp
gastronome, gas'tro-nōm
gauge, gāj
gaunt, gänt

gauntlet, gänt'let
gavel, gav'el
gazetteer, gaz-e-tēr'
geisha, gā'shä
gelatin; gelatine, jel'ă-tin
gelding, geld'ing
gendarme, zhän-därm'
genealogy, jē"nē-al'o-ji;
   jen"e-ăl'o-ji
general, jen'ĕr-al
generic, je-ner'ik
generous, jen'ĕr-us
genesis, jen'e-sis
genetics, je-net'iks
genial, jēn'yal
geniality, jēn-yal'i-ti
genie, jē'ni
genius, jēn'yus (a person possessed of high mental powers)
genius, jē'ni-us (a guardian spirit
   or deity)
genre, zhän'r
gentian, jen'shan
Gentile, jen'tīl
gentle, jen'tl
genuflect, jen-û-flekt'
genuine, jen'û-in
genus, jē'nus
geodetic, jē-o-det'ik
geography, je-og'rä-fi
geometry, je-om'e-tri
georgette, jôr-jet'
Georgia, jôr'ji-ă
geranium, je-rā'ni-um
germane, jĕr-mān'
germicide, jer'mi-sīd
gerund, jer'und
gestate, jes'tāt
gesticulate, jes-tik'û-lāt
gesture, jes'tûr
Gethsemane, geth-sem'ă-nē
geyser, gī'sēr
ghastly, gåst'li
ghoul, gōōl
gibberish, gib'ĕr-ish
gibbet, jib'et
gibe, jīb
giblet, jib'let
gig, gig
gigantic, jī-gan'tik
gigolo, jig'o-lō
Gila monster, hē'lä mon'stēr
gill, gil (respiratory organ of
   aquatic animals)
gill, jil (¼ of a pint, ground ivy,
   wanton girl)
gillie, gil'i
gimcrack, jim'krak
gimlet, gim'let
gin, jin
gingham, ging'am
Gipsy; Gypsy, jip'si
giraffe, ji-råf'
girl, gērl

gist, jist
glacier, glā'shi-ēr; glas'i-ēr
gladiolus, glad-i-ō'lus
glamour, glam'ēr
glance, glåns
glandular, glan'du-lēr
glass, glås
glazier, glā'zhēr
glisten, glis'n
globular, glob'û-lar
globule, glob'ûl
glossary, glos'å-ri
glucose, glōō'kōs
glue, glōō
gluten, glōō'ten
glutton, glut'n
glycerin; glycerine, glis-ēr-in
gnarl, närl
gnash, nash
gnat, nat
gnaw, naw
gnome, nōm
gnu, nōō
goal, gōl
goatee, gō-tē'
golf, golf
Golgotha, gol'go-thä
Goliath, go-lī'ath
gondola, gon'do-lä
gondolier, gon-do-lēr'
goose, gōōs
gooseberry, gōōz'ber-i
gorge, gôrj
gorgeous, gôr'jus
gormand, gôr'mand; gourmand,
   gōōr'mand
gossamer, gos'ă-mēr
gouge, gouj
goulash, gōō'läsh
gourd, gōrd
gout, gout
government, guv'ērn-ment
governor, guv'ēr-ner
gradate, grā'dāt
gradual, grad'û-al
graduate, grad'û-āt
graft, gråft
grandeur, gran'jūr
grandiose, gran'di-ōs
grand prix, gran prē'
granule, gran'ûl
grasp, gråsp
grass, grås
gratis, grā'tis
gratuity, grå-tū'i-ti
gravure, grā'vûr
grease (n.), grēs
grease (v.), grēz
greasy, grēz'i
Greenwich, grin'ij
gregarious, gre-gā'ri-us
grenade, gre-nād'
grenadine, gren-ă-dēn'
grille, gril

grimace, gri-mās'
grindstone, grīnd'stōn
gripe, grīp
grippe; grip; grip
gristle, gris'l
grocery, grō'sēr-i
gross, grōs
grotesque, grō-tesk'
group, grōōp
grouse, grous
grovel, grov'el
gruesome, grōō'sum
Gruyere, grū-yār'
guano, gwä'nō
guarantee, gar-ăn-tē'
guaranty, gar'ăn-ti
guard, gärd
guardian, gärd'i-an
guava, gwä'vä
guerilla, gē-ril'ä
Guernsey, gērn'zi
guess, ges
guile, gīl
guillotine, gil'o-tēn
guimpe, gamp
guinea, gin'i
guise, gīz
guitar, gi-tär'
gulf, gulf
gutta-percha, gut'ä-pēr'chä
guy, gī
gymnasium, jim-nä'zi-um
gymnastic, jim-nas'tik
gynecology, jin-e-kol'ō-ji
gypsum, jip'sum
gyrate, jī'rāt
gyroscope, jī'ro-skōp

H

habeas corpus, hā'be-as kôr'pus
haberdasher, hab'ēr-dash-ēr
habiliment, hă-bil'i-ment
habitable, hab'it-ä-bl
habitat, hab'i-tat
habitual, hă-bit'û-al
habitue, hă-bit'û-ā
hacienda, hä-si-en'dä
Hades, hā'dēz
halcyon, hal'si-un
half, häf
halfpenny, hā'pen-i
halitosis, hal-i-tō'sis
hallelujah, hal-e-lōō'yä
Halloween, hal-ō-ēn'
halo, hā'lō
halt, hawlt
halve, häv
handkerchief, hang'kēr-chif
handsome, han'sum
hangar, häng'gär
harangue, hă-rang'

harass, har'as
harbor, här'bēr
harem, hä'rem; hä'rem
harlequin, här'le-kwin
harmonica, här-mon'i-kä
harpsichord, härp'si-kôrd
hasten, hā'sn
haughty, haw'ti
haunt, hänt
hauteur, hō-tōōr'
Hawaiian, hä-wī'yan
hawser, haw'ser
hearth, härth
heathen, hē'thn
heather, heth'ēr
heaven, hev'n
hegemony, he-jem'ō-ni
Hegira, he-jī'rä
heifer, hef'ēr
height, hīt
heinous, hā'nus
heir, ār
heirloom, ār'lōōm
heliotrope, hē'li-o-trōp
helium, hē'li-um
Hellenic, he-len'ik
helmsman, helmz'man
hemorrhage, hem'ō-räj
Heppelwhite, hep'el-hwīt
heraldic, he-ral'dik
herb, ērb; hērb
herbarium, ēr-bā'ri-um; hēr-bā'ri-um
Herculean, hēr-kū'le-an
hereditary, he-red'i-tā-ri
heresy, her'e-si
hermaphrodite, hēr-maf'rō-dīt
hermetic, hēr-met'ik
hermitage, hēr-mi-tij
hernia, hēr'ni-ä
hero, hē'rō
heroin, her'ō-in
heroism, her'ō-izm
hesitate, hez'i-tāt
heyday, hā'dā
hiatus, hī-ā'tus
hibernate, hī'bēr-nāt
hideous, hid'e-us
hierarchy, hī'ēr-är-ki
hieroglyphic, hī-ēr-o-glif'ik
hindrance, hin'dräns
hirsute, hēr'sūt
history, his'to-ri
histrionic, his-tri-on'ik
hokum, hō'kum
holocaust, hol'o-kawst
homage, hom'ij
homeopathy, hō-me-op'ä-thi
homicide, hom'i-sīd
hominy, hom'i-ni
honest, on'est
honey, hun'i
honor, on'ēr
honorary, on'ēr-a-ri

hoof, hŏŏf
horizon, ho-rī'zun
horologe, hor'o-lōj
horoscope, hor'o-skōp
horrid, hor'id
hors-d'œuvre, ôr-dŏŏv'r
hosanna, hō-zan'ă
hosiery, hō'zhēr-i
hospitable, hos'pit-ă-bl
hospital, hos'pi-tal
hostage, hos'tij
hostile, hos'tīl
hotel, hō-tel'
hour, our
house, hous
hovel, hov'l
hover, huv'ēr
howitzer, hou'it-sēr
hue, hū
Huguenot, hū'ge-not
human, hū'man
humanitarian, hū-man-i-tā'ri-an
humble, hum'bl
humdinger, hum-ding'ēr
humidify, hū-mid'i-fi
humor, ū'mēr
humorist, ū'mēr-ist
hurrah, hoo-rä'
hurricane, hur'i-kān
hussar, huz-är'
hussy, huz'i
hustle, hus'l
hyacinth, hī'ă-sinth
hybrid, hī'brid
Hydra, hī'drä
hydrangea, hī-dran'je-ă
hydraulic, hī-draw'lik
hydrophobia, hī-dro-fō'bi-ă
hyena, hī-ē'nă
hygiene, hī'jēn
hyperbole, hī-pēr'bo-lē
hypnosis, hip-nō'sis
hypnotism, hip'no-tizm
hypochondriac, hip-o-kon'dri-ak
hypocrisy, hi-pok'ri-si
hypocrite, hip'o-krit
hypodermic, hī-po-dēr'mik
hypothecate, hī-poth'e-kāt
hypothesis, hī-poth'e-sis
hypothetically, hī-po-thet'i-kal-i
hysteria, his-tē'ri-a

I

ibex, ī'beks
icicle, ī'si-kl
iconoclast, ī-kon'o-klast
idea, ī-dē'ă
ideal, ī-dē'al
idealize, ī-dē'al-īz
identical, ī-den'ti-kal
ideology, ī-de-ol'o-ji
idiocy, id'i-o-si
idiom, id'i-um

idiosyncrasy, id-i-o-sin'krā-si
idiot, id'i-ot
idle, ī'dl
idol, ī-dol
idolatry, ī-dol'ă-tri
idyl, ī'dil
igloo, ig'lŏŏ
ignition, ig-nish'un
ignoble, ig-nō'bl
ignominious, ig-no-min'i-us
ignominy, ig'no-min-i
ignoramus, ig-no-rā'mus
Iliad, il'i-ad
illegitimate, il-le-jit'i-māt
illicit, i-lis'it
illimitable, i-lim'it-ă-bl
illiteracy, i-lit'ēr-ă-si
illuminate, i-lūm'i-nāt
illusion, il-ū'zhun
illustrate, il-us'trāt
illustrious, il-us'tri-us
image, im'ij
imagery, im'ij-ri
imagist, im'ij-ist
imbecile, im'be-sil
imbroglio, im-brō'lyō
imbue, im-bū'
imitable, im'i-tă-bl
immediate, im-mē'di-āt
immersion, im-mēr'shun
immigrant, im'i-grănt
imminence, im'i-nens
immobile, i-mō'bil
immolate, im'o-lāt
immunity, i-mūn'i-ti
immunize, i-mūn'īz
impartiality, im-pär-shi-al'i-ti
impasse, an-päs'
impeccability, im-pek-ă-bil'i-ti
impecunious, im-pe-kū'ni-us
impersonal, im-pēr'sun-al
impertinence, im-pēr'ti-nens
imperturbable, im-pēr-tēr'bă-bl
impervious, im-pēr'vi-us
impetuous, im-pet'û-us
impinge, im-pinj'
impious, im'pi-us
impolitic, im-pol'i-tik
importune, im-por-tūn'
impostor, im-pos'tēr
imposture, im-pos-tûr'
impotent, im'po-tent
imprecate, im'pre-kāt
impregnable, im-preg'nă-bl
impresario, im-prä-sä're-ō
impressionable, im-presh'un-ă-bl
impressionist, im-presh'un-ist
imprimatur, im-pri-mā'tur
impromptu, im-promp'tū
improvise, im-pro-vīz'
impugn, im-pūn'
inadmissible, in-ad-mis'i-bl
inadvisable, in-ad-vīz'ă-bl
inalienable, in-āl'yen-ă-bl

inamorata, in-am-o-rä'tă
inane, in-ān'
inanity, in-an'i-ti
inaugurate, in-aw'gû-rāt
Inca, ing'kă
incalculable, in-kal'kū-lă-bl
incandescent, in-kan-des'ent
incapacitate, in-kă-pas'i-tāt
incarnate, in-kar'nāt
incendiarism, in-sen'di-ă-rizm
incense (v.), in-sens' (to inflame with anger)
incense (n.), in'sens (any aromatic material which exhales perfume when burned)
incest, in'sest
inchoate, in'kō-āt
incident, in'si-dent
incidentally, in-si-den'tal-i
incipient, in-sip'i-ent
incisive, in-sī'siv
incisor, in-sī'sĕr
inclement, in-klem'ent
incline, in-klīn'
include, in-klōōd'
inclusive, in-klōō'siv
incognito, in-kog'ni-tō
incommunicable, in-ko-mū'ni-kă-bl
incommunicado, in-ko-mū-ni-kä'dō
incomparable, in-kom'pă-ră-bl
incompatible, in-kom-pat'i-bl
incompetent, in-kom'pe-tent
inconclusive, in-kon-klōō-siv
inconspicuous, in-kon-spik'û-us
inconvenient, in-kon-vēn'yent
incorporeal, in-kor-pō'rē-al
incorrigible, in-kor'i-ji-bl
increase, in-krēs'
incredulous, in-kred'û-lus
incubate, in'kū-bāt
incubator, in'kū-bā-tĕr
incubus, in'kū-bus
indecorous, in-de-kō'rus; in-dek'o-rus
indefatigable, in-de-fat'i-gă-bl
indefinable, in-de-fī'nă-bl
indemnification, in-dem-ni-fi-kā'-shun
indenture, in-den'tûr
indeterminate, in-de-tĕr'mi-nāt
indicative, in-dik'ă-tiv
indict, in-dīt'
indigenous, in-dij'e-nus
indigent, in'di-jent
indigestion, in-di-jes'chun
indigo, in'di-gō
indiscretion, in-dis-kresh'un
indisputable, in-dis'pū-tă-bl
indissoluble, in-dis'o-lū-bl; in-di-sol'û-bl
individual, in-di-vij'û-al; in-di-vid'-û-al

indivisible, in-di-viz'i-bl
indomitable, in-dom'i-tă-bl
indubitable, in-dū'bi-tă-bl
induct, in-dukt'
industry, in'dus-tri
inebriate, in-ē'bri-āt
inefficiency, in-e-fish'en-si
ineptitude, in-ep'ti-tūd
inertia, in-ĕr'shi-ă
inestimable, in-es'ti-mă-bl
inevitability, in-ev"i-tă-bil'i-ti
inexhaustible, in-egs-awst'i-bl
inexorable, in-eks'o-ră-bl
inexplicable, in-eks'pli-kă-bl
infamous, in'fă-mus
infantile, in'fan-til
infatuate, in-fat'û-āt
infatuation, in-fat-û-ā'shun
inference, in'fĕr-ens
infidel, in'fi-del
infinite, in'fi-nit
infinitesimal, in-fin-i-tes'i-mal
inflammation, in-flam-mā'shun
inflation, in-flā'shun
inflorescence, in-flo-res'ens
influence, in'flōō-ens
influenza, in-flōō-en'ză
influx, in'fluks
informality, in-fôr-mal'i-ti
infuriate, in-fū'ri-āt
ingenious, in-jē'ni-us
ingenue, än-zhä-nōō'
ingenuity, in-je-nū'i-ti
ingenuous, in-jen'û-us
ingot, in'got
ingrate, in'grāt
ingredient, in-grē'di-ent
inherent, in-hēr'ent
inhibit, in-hib'it
inhospitable, in-hos'pi-tă-bl
initial, in-ish'al
initiate, in-ish'i-āt
initiative, in-ish'i-ā-tiv
innate, in'nāt
innocuous, i-nok'û-us
innuendo, in-û-en'dō
inoculate, in-ok'û-lāt
inquirer, in-kwīr'ĕr
inquiry, in-kwīr'i
inquisitive, in-kwis'i-tiv
insatiable, in-sā'shi-ă-bl
inscrutability, in-skrōō"tă-bil'i-ti
insecticide, in-sek'ti-sīd
insensate, in-sen'sāt
insert (v.), in-sĕrt'
insert (n.), in'sĕrt
insidious, in-sid'i-us
insignia, in-sig'ni-ă
insipid, in-sip'id
insolubility, in-sol"û-bil'i-ti
insomnia, in-som'ni-ă
insouciance, an-sōō-si-äns'
inspiration, in-spi-rā'shun
instantaneous, ins-tan-tā'ne-us

Insufferable, in-suf'ẽr-ă-bl
insulin, in'sul-in
insult (n.), in'sult
insult (v.), in-sult'
insurgence, in-sẽr'jens
insurrectionary, in-su-rek'shun-ă-ri
integral, in'te-gral
integrate, in'te-grāt
integrity, in-teg'ri-ti
intellectual, in-te-lek'tŭ-al
intent, in-tent'
interdict, in-tẽr-dikt'
interesting, in'tẽr-est-ing
interim, in'tẽr-im
interlude, in'tẽr-lūd
intermediary, in-tẽr-mē'di-ă-ri
interment, in-tẽr'ment
intermezzo, in-tẽr-med'zō
interne, in'tẽrn
internecine, in-tẽr-nē'sin
interpolate, in-tẽr'po-lāt
interpret, in-tẽr'pret
interpretation, in-tẽr-pre-tā'shun
interpreter, in-tẽr'pret-ẽr
interregnum, in-tẽr-reg'num
interrogate, in-tẽr'o-gāt
intersection, in-tẽr-sek'shun
interurban, in-tẽr-ẽr'ban
interval, in'tẽr-val
intestate, in-tes'tāt
intimacy, in'ti-mă-si
intimate, in'ti-māt
intolerance, in-tol'ẽr-ăns
in toto, in tō'tō
intrepid, in-trep'id
intricate, in'tri-kăt
intrigue, in-trēg'
intrinsic, in-trin'sik
introspection, in-trō-spek'shun
introvert, in-trō-vẽrt'
intuitive, in-tū'i-tiv
invalid (adj.), in-val'id
invalid (n.), in'vă-lid
invariable, in-vā'ri-ă-bl
inveigle, in-vē'gl
inventory, in'ven-to-ri
invidious, in-vid'i-us
inviolate, in-vī'o-lāt
iodine, ī'o-din; ī'o-dīn
Iowa, ī'o-wă
ipso facto, ip'sō fak'tō
Iran, ī-ran'
irascible, ī-ras'i-bl
irate, ī-rāt'
iridescent, ir-i-des'ent
iris, ī'ris
iron, ī'ẽrn
ironical, ī-ron'i-kal
irony, ī'ron-i
irrefutable, ir-e-fūt'ă-b'l
irrelevant, i-rel'e-vant
irremediable, ir-e-mē'di-ă-bl
irreparable, i-rep'ă-ră-bl

irresistible, ir-e-sist'i-bl
irrevocable, i-rev'o-kă-bl
irritable, ir'i-tă-bl
isinglass, ī'zing-glás
isolate, is'o-lāt
Israelite, iz'rā-el-īt
issue, ish'ū
isthmian, ist'mi-an
isthmus, is'mus; ist'mus
Italian, i-tal'yan
italic, i-tal'ik
italicize, i-tal'i-sīz
itch, ich
itinerant, ī-tin'ẽr-ănt
itinerary, ī-tin'ẽr-e-ri

J

jackal, jack'awl
Jacobin, jak'o-bin
jaguar, jă-gwär'; jag'wär
jardiniere, zhär-dē-nyer'
jasmine, jas'min
jaundice, jän'dis
jaunt, jänt; jônt
Java, jä'vă
javelin, jav'lin
jealous, jel'us
Jehovah, je-hō'vă
jeopardize, jep'ăr-dīz
Jesuit, jez'ū-it
jetsam, jet'sam
jewel, jōō'el
Jewry, jōō'ri
jinrikisha, jin-rik'i-shă
Job, jōb
job, job
jocose, jo-kōs'
jocosity, jo-kos'i-ti
jocular, jok'ū-lẽr
jocularity, jok-ū-lar'i-ti
jocund, jok'und
jollification, jol-i-fi-kă'shun
jonquil, jon'kwil
joust, jōōst
jovial, jō'vi-al
joyance, joi'ăns
jubilation, jōō-bi-lā'shun
jubilee, jōō'bi-lē
judgment, juj'ment
judiciary, jōō-dish'i-e-ri
judicious, jōō-dish'us
Juggernaut, jug'ẽr-nawt
juggler, jug'lẽr
jugular, jōō'gū-lẽr
julienne, zhōō-li-en'
juncture, jung'tūr
junior, jōōn'yẽr
juniper, jōō'ni-pẽr
junta, jun'tă
jurisprudence, jōō-ris-prōō'dens
juror, jōō'rẽr

jury, jŏŏ'ri
justiciable, jus-tish'i-ă-bl
jute, jŏŏt
juvenile, jŏŏ've-nil
juxtaposition, juks-tă-pō-zish'un

K

Kaffir, kaf'ĕr
kaleidoscope, kă-lī'do-skōp
kangaroo, kang-gă-rŏŏ'
Kansas, kan'zas
ken, ken
Kentucky, ken-tuk'ĭ
kerchief, kĕr'chif
ketchup, kech'up
khaki, kă'ki
khedive, ke-dēv'
kiln, kil
kimono, ki-mō'nō
kindergarten, kin'dĕr-gär-ten
kindred, kin'dred
kinetic, ki-net'ik
kinkajou, king'kă-jŏŏ
kipper, kip'ĕr
kismet, kis'met; kis'mā
kitchen, kich'en
kitchenette, kich-en-et'
kleptomania, klep-tō-mā'ni-ă
knack, nak
knapsack, nap'sak
knave, nāv
knell, nel
Knickerbocker, nik'ĕr'bok-ĕr
knoll, nōl
knot, not
knout, nout
knowledge, nol'ej
kudos, kū-dos
kumquat, kum'kwot
Kurdistan, kŏŏrd-is-tan

L

labor, lā'bĕr
laboratory, lab'o-ră-to-ri
laborious, lă-bō'ri-us
labyrinth, lab'i-rinth
lacerate, las'ĕr-āt
lachrymose, lak'ri-mōs
lackadaisical, lak-ă-dā'zi-kal
lacquer, lak'ĕr
lactation, lak-tā'shun
lady, lā'di
la grippe, lă grip
laissez faire, le'sā fār'
laity, lā'i-ti
lama, lä'mă
lamb, lam
lambaste, lam-bāst'
lambskin, lam'skin

lament, lă-ment'
lamentable, lam'en-tă-bl
lance, lăns
landau, lan'daw
landlord, land'lôrd
language, lang'gwej
languid, lang'gwid
languor, lang'gwĕr
lapel, lă-pel'
lapse, laps
larceny, lär'se-ni
largess; largesse, lär'jes
lariat, lar'i-at
larkspur, lärk'spĕr
laryngitis, lar-in-jī'tis
larynx, lar'ingks
lass, lăs
lasso, lăs'ō
last, lăst
latent, lā'tent
lath, lăth
lather, lath'ĕr
latitude, lat'i-tūd
laudable, lawd'ă-bl
laugh, läf
launder, län'dĕr
laundry, län'dri
laureate, law're-āt
lava, lä'vă
lavaliere, lav"ă-lēr'
law, law
laxative, laks'ă-tiv
laxity, laks'i-ti
lead (n.), led (a soft, heavy, ductile bluish-grey metal)
lead (v.), lēd (to conduct with the hand)
leather, leth'ĕr
lectern, lek'tĕrn
lecture, lek-tur
legacy, leg'ă-si
legate, leg'āt
legend, lej'end
legged, legd; leg'ed
legion, lē'jun
legislature, lej'is-lă-tûr
legitimacy, le-jit'i-mă-si
legume, le-gūm'
Leicester, les'tĕr
leisure, lē'zhur
length, length
lenient, lē'ni-ent; lēn'yent
leonine, lē'o-nīn
leopard, lep'ĕrd
lese majesty, lēz maj'es-ti
lesion, lē'zhun
lessee, les-ē'
lessor, les'ôr
lethal, lē'thal
lethargy, leth'ăr-ji
lettuce, let'is
levee, lev'ē
lever, lev'ĕr; lē'vĕr

leviathan, le-vī'ă-than
levitation, lev-i-tā'shun
levity, lev'i-ti
liable, lī'ă-bl
liaison, lē-ā-zôn'
libation, lī-bā'shun
libertine, lib'ēr-tin
libidinous, li-bid'i-nus
library, lī'brā-ri
librettist, li-bret'ist
libretto, li-bret'ō
licentious, lī-sen'shus
lichen, lī'ken; lich'en
licorice, lik'o-ris
lien, lē'en; lī'en; lēn
lieu, lū
lieutenant, lū-ten'ant
ligament, lig'ă-ment
lilac, lī'lak
Lilliputian, lil-i-pū'shan
limousine, li-mōō-zēn'
lineage, lin'e-ij
linear, lin'e-ēr
lingerie, lan-zhe-rē'
linguist, ling'gwist
linoleum, li-nō'le-um
lionize, lī'un-īz
liquefy, lik'we-fī
liqueur, li-kūr'
liquid, lik'wid
liquor, lik'ēr
lira, lē'rā
lisle, līl
listen, lis'n
literally, lit'ēr-al-li
literary, lit'ēr-ā-ri
literati, lit-e-rā'ti
literature, lit-ēr-ă-tūr
lithography, li-thog'ră-fi
litter, lit'ēr
liturgy, lit'ēr-ji
live, liv
livelong, liv'lông
livery, liv'ēr-i
llama, lä'mä
loath, lōth
loathe, lōth
locale, lō-käl'
loco, lo'kō
locomotive, lō-kō-mō'tiv
loft, loft
loggia, loj'ă
logic, loj'ik
longevity, lon-jev'i-ti
longitude, lon'ji-tūd
loquacious, lo-kwā'shus
Lorelei, lō're-lī
lorgnette, lôr-nyet'
loss, lôs
Lothario, lo-thā'ri-ō
Louisiana, lōō-ē-ze-an'ă
Louvre, lōō'vr
lovable, luv'ă-bl

lower (v.), lō'ēr (to lessen or bring down; sink)
lower (v.), lou'ēr (to appear dark, gloomy, threatening)
lozenge, loz'enj
lubricate, lū'bri-kāt
lucidity, lū-sid'i-ti
lucrative, lū'kră-tiv
luggage, lug'ij
luncheon, lun'chun
lure, lūr
luscious, lush'us
lush, lush
lute, lūt
Lutheran, lū'ther-an
luxurious, lug-zhū'ri-us
Lyceum, lī-sē'um
lymph, limf
lynx, lingks
lyric, lir'ik

M

macabre, mă-kä'br
macadamize, mak-ad'am-īz
macerate, mas'ēr-āt
machete, mă-chā'tă
Machiavellian, mak-i-ă-vel'i-an
machination, mak-i-nā'shun
madam, mad'am
madame, mă-däm'
Madeira, mă-dē'ră
mademoiselle, mad-mwă-zel'; măm-zel'
Madonna, mă-don'ă
madrigal, mad'ri-gal
Maecenas, me-sē'nas
maelstrom, māl'strom
maestro, mă-es'trō
magdalen, mag'dă-len
Magi, mā'jī
magisterial, maj-is-tē'ri-al
Magna Charta, mag'nă kär'tă
magnanimous, mag-nan'i-mus
magneto-, mag-nē'tō
magnolia, mag-nō'li-ă
Magyar, mă'yär
maharajah, mä-hä-rä'jä
mahatma, mă-hat'mă
mah jong, mä zhong'
Mahomet, mă-hom'et
maintenance, măn'te-năns
maisonette, mă-zōng-net'
maize, māz
majolica, mă-jol'i-kă
maladroit, mal-ă-droit'
Malaga, mal'ă-gă
malaria, mă-lā'ri-ă
Malay, mă-lā'
malediction, mal-e-dik'shun
malevolence, mă-lev'o-lens
malfeasance, mal-fē'zans

malicious, mă-lish'us
malign, mă-līn'
malignant, mă-lig'nant
malignity, mă-lig'ni-ti
malinger, mă-ling'gĕr
malodorous, mal-ō'dĕr-us
Maltese, mawl'tēz
mama; mamma, mă-mä'; mä'mä
manage, man'ij
managerial, man-a-jē'ri-al
mandamus, man-dā'mus
mandarin, man-dă-rēn'
mandatory, man'dă-to-ri
manege, mă-nāzh'
maneuver; manoeuvre, mă-nōō'-vĕr
manganese, mang'gă-nēz
maniac, mā'ni-ak
manikin, man'i-kin
mantilla, man-til'ă
manufacture, man-û-fak'tûr
many, men'i
Maori, mou'ri
maraschino, mar-ă-skē'nō
marauder, mă-rawd'ĕr
marcel, mär-sel'
marchese, mär-kē'zā
marchioness, mär'shun-es
Mardi Gras, mär'de grä
margarine, mär'gă-rēn
marginalia, mär-ji-nā'li-ă
marigold, mar'i-gōld
mariticide, mă-rit'i-sīd
maritime, mar'i-tīm
marmalade, mär'mă-lād
marquis, mär'kwis
marriage, mar'ij
Marseillaise, mär-sä-yāz'
marseilles, mär-sālz'
martial, mär'shal
masculine, mas'kū-lin
masque, măsk
Massachusetts, măs-ă-chōō'sets
massage, mă-säzh'
masseur, mă-sēr'
master, măs'tĕr
mathematician, math-e-mă-tish'an
matinee, mat-i-nā'
matriarch, mā'tri-ärk
matriculate, mă-trik'ū-lāt
mature, mă-tūr'
maudlin, mawd'lin
mausoleum, maw-so-lē'um
mauve, mōv
Maya, mä'yä
mayhem, mā'hem
mayonnaise, mă-o-nāz'
mayor, mā'ĕr
meander, me-an'dĕr
measles, mē'zlz
measure, mezh'ĕr
mechanic, me-kan'ik
medicinal, me-dis'i-nal

mediocre, mē'di-ō-kĕr
mediocrity, mē-di-ok'ri-ti
meditation, med-i-tā'shun
medium, mē'di-um
megalomania, meg-ă-lō-mā'ni-ă
melancholia, mel-an-kō'li-ă
melange, mă-längzh'
melee, mā-lā'
meliorate, mēl'yo-rāt
melliferous, me-lif'ĕr-us
mellowy, mel'ō-i
melodic, me-lod'ik
melodious, me-lō'di-us
melodrama, mel-o-drä'mă
membrane, mem'brăn
memoir, mem'wär
memorabilia, mem-o-ră'bil'i-ă
menage, mă-näzh'
menagerie, me-naj'ĕr-i
mendicant, men'di-kant
meningitis, men-in-jī'tis
menopause, men'ō-paws
menstruate, men'strōō-āt
menu, men'ū
Mephistopheles, mef-is-tof'e-lēs
mercantile, mĕr'kan-til
mercurial, mĕr-kū'ri-al
meretricious, mer-e-trish'us
meridian, me-rid'i-an
meringue, mē-rang'
meritorious, mer-i-tō'ri-us
mesa, mā'să
mesmerism, mez'mĕr-izm
mesquite, mes'kēt
metabolism, me-tab'o-lizm
metamorphosis, met-ă-môr'fo-sis
metaphysics, met-ă-fiz'iks
meteor, mē'te-or
meteorology, mē-te-or-ol'o-ji
meter, mē'tĕr
Methuselah, me-thōō'se-lă
meticulous, me-tik'û-lus
metier, mā-tyā'
metric, met'rik
metropolitan, me-tro-pol'i-tan
mezzanine, mez'ă-nēn
mezzo-soprano, med'zo-so-prä'nō
miasma, mī-az'mă
micrometer, mī-krom'e-tĕr
microscope, mī'kro-skōp
microscopic, mī-kro-skop'ik
Midas, mī'dăs
mien, mēn
mignon, min-yôn'
milch, milch
millennium, mi-len'i-um
millet, mil'et
millinery, mil'i-nĕr-i
millionaire, mil-yun-ār'
mime, mīm
mimicry, mim'ik-ri
mineralogy, min-ĕr-al'o-ji
miniature, min'i-ă-tûr

minimum, min'i-mum
minnesinger, min'e-sing-ēr
minuet, min'ū-et
minute (adj.), mī-nūt' (very small)
minute (n.), min'it (1-60th part of an hour or of a degree)
minutiae, mi-nū'shi-ē
mirage, mi-räzh'
misanthrope, mis'an-thrōp
miscegenation, mis-e-je-nā'shun
miscellaneous, mis-e-lā'ne-us
mischief, mis'chif
mischievous, mis'chi-vus
misconduct (v.), mis-kon-dukt' (to mismanage)
misconduct (n.), mis-kon'dukt (bad behavior)
misconstrue, mis-kon'strōō; mis-kon-strōō'
miscreant, mis'kre-ant
misdemeanor, mis-de-mēn'ēr
Miserere, miz-e-rē're
misfeasance, mis-fē'zans
misnomer, mis-nō'mēr
misogynist, mi-soj'i-nist
Missouri, mi-zōō'ri
mistral, mis'tral
mitten, mit'n
mnemonic, ne-mon'ik
mobile, mō'bil
mobilization, mō-bil-i-zā'shun
modernism, mod'ēr-nizm
modicum, mod'i-kum
modiste, mo-dēst'
Mogul, mō-gul'
mohair, mō'hār
Mohammedanism, mo-ham'e-dan-izm
Mohican, mo-hē'kan
moire (n.), mōr (watered silk)
moiré (adj., v., and n.), mō'rā (denoting a watered or clouded appearance; to give such an appearance to a surface; a clouded or frosted appearance on textile fabrics)
moisten, mois'n
molecular, mo-lek'ū-lår
molecule, mol'e-kūl
Moloch, mō'lok
momentary, mō'men-ta-ri
Mona Lisa, mō'nå lē'zä
monarch, mon'ärk
monarchic, mo-när'kik
monasticism, mo-nas'ti-sizm
monetary, mun'e-tä-ri
money, mun'i
mongrel, mung'grel
monkey, mung'ki
monocle, mon'o-kl
monogamy, mo-nog'å-mi
monograph, mon'o-gråf

monologue, mon'o-log
monoplane, mon'o-plān
monopolist, mo-nop'o-list
monotonous, mo-not'o-nus
monseigneur, mon-sä-nyēr'
monsieur, me-syu'
monsignor, mon-sē'nyēr
monstrosity, mon-stros'i-ti
Montana, mon-tä'nä
Montessori method, mon-tes-sō're meth'od
moral, mor'al
morale, mo-rål'
moratorium, mor-å-tō'ri-um
morbidity, môr-bid'i-ti
mordant, mor'dant
morgue, môrg
moron, mō'ron
Morpheus, môr'fūs
morphine, môr'fēn
mortgage, môr'gij
mortification, môr"ti-fi-kā'shun
mortise, môr'tis
mortuary, môr'tū-a-ri
mosaic, mo-zā'ik
mosquito, mus-kē'tō
motif, mo-tēf'
motivate, mō'ti-vāt
mousse, mōōs
moustache, mus-tåsh'
mouth, mouth
mow (v.), mō (to cut down with, or as with a scythe)
mow (n.), mou (a heap of hay stowed in a barn)
Mrs., mis'is
mucilage, mū'si-lij
mucous, mū'kus
muezzin, mū-ez'in
mufti, muf'ti
mulct, mulkt
mulligatawny, mul-i-gå-taw'ni
multifarious, mul-ti-fā'ri-us
multilateral, mul-ti-lat'er-ål
multiplicity, mul-ti-plis'i-ti
multitudinous, mul-ti-tū'di-nus
mundane, mun'dān
municipal, mū-nis'i-pal
munificence, mū-nif'i-sens
muscatel, mus-kå-tel'
muscle, mus'l
Muse, mūz
museum, mū'zē'um
music, mū'zik
musicale, mū-zi-kål'
muslin, muz'lin
mustache; moustache, mus-tåsh'
mutilation, mū-ti-lā'shun
mutual, mū'tu-al
myopic, mī-op'ik
myrrh, mēr
mystery, mis'tēr-i
mysticism, mis'ti-sizm

mythology, mith-ol'o-ji

N

nabob, nä'bob
naive, nä-ēv'
naïvete, nä-ēv-tä'
nap, nap
nape, nǎp
naphtha, naf'thǎ
Napoleon, nä-pō'le-on
narcism, när'sizm
narcotic, när-kot'ik
narrate, na-rāt'
nasal, nā'zal
nascent, nas'ent
natal, nā'tal
natatorium, nā-tǎ-tō'ri-um
nation, nā'shun
national, nash'un-al
natural, nat'u-ral
nature, nā-chēr; nā'tūr
nausea, naw'she-ǎ
Navajo, nav'ǎ-hō
Nazarene, naz-ǎ-rēn'
Nazi, na'tsi
nebula, neb'û-lä
necessarily, nes'e-sā-ri-li
necromancy, nek'ro-man-si
nectarine, nek'tēr-in
nee, nā
negation, ne-gā'shun
negative, neg'ǎ-tiv
Negro, nē'grō
negroid, nē'groid
neither, nē'ther; nī'ther
nemesis, nem'e-sis
neolithic, nē-o-lith'ik
neon, nē'on
neophyte, nē'o-fīt
nephew, nev'ū
nepotism, nep'o-tizm
nether, neth'ēr
neuralgia, nū-ral'ji-ǎ
neurasthenia, nū-ras-thē'ni-ǎ
neurasthenic, nū-ras-then'ik
neurotic, nū-rot'ik
neuter, nū'tēr
neutral, nū'tral
neutrality, nū-tral'i-ti
Nevada, ne-vä'dǎ
new, nū
newsmonger, nūz'mung-gēr
niblick, nib'lik
nicety, nīs'e-ti
niche, nich
Nicodemus, nik-o-dē'mus
nihilist, nī'hil-ist
nil, nil
Nile, nīl
nisi prius, nē'si prī'us
nitric, nī'trik

nitrogen, nī'tro-jen
nobility, nō-bil'i-ti
nocturnal, nok-tēr'nal
nocturne, nok'tērn
noise, noiz
noisome, noi'sum
nomad, nom'ad; nō'mad
nomenclature, nō'men-klā-tūr
nonce, nons
nonchalance, nôn'shǎ-läns
nondescript, non'de-skript
none, nun
nonentity, non-en'ti-ti
nonpareil, non-pǎ-rel'
Norge, nôr'gā
norm, nôrm
normalcy, nôr'mal-si
nostalgia, nos-tal'ji-ǎ
nostalgic, nos-tal'jik
nostrum, nos'trum
Notre Dame, nō'tr däm
novice, nov'is
novitiate, no-vish'i-āt
noxious, nok'shus
nuisance, nū'sans
numismatic, nū-miz-mat'īk
nuncio, nun'shi-ō
nuptial, nup'shal
nutritious, nū-trish'us
nymph, nimf

O

oafish, ōf'ish
oar, ōr
oasis, ō-ǎ'sis; o-ā'sis
oath, ōth
obbligato, ob-li-gä'tō
obedience, o-bē'di-ens
obeisance, o-bā'sǎns
obesity, o-bes'i-ti
obit, ō'bit
obituary, o-bit'û-ē-ri
object (v.), ob-jekt'
object (n.), ob'jekt
objectivity, ob-jek-tiv'i-ti
obligatory, ob-lig'ǎ-to-ri; ob'li-gǎ-to-ri
oblique, ob-lēk'
oblivion, ob-liv'i-un
obloquy, ob'lo-kwi
oboe, ō'boi; ō'bo-e
obscenity, ob-sen'i-ti
obscurantism, ob-skūr'an-tizm
obsequies, ob'se-kwiz
obsequious, ob-sē'kwi-us
obsession, ob-sesh'un
obstinate, ob'sti-nat
obstreperous, ob-strep'ēr-us
obtuse, ob-tūs'
obviate, ob'vi-āt
Occidental, ok-si-den'tal

occult, o-kult'
occultism, o-kul'tizm
occupier, ok'u-pī-ẽr
ocean, ō'shăn
oceanic, ō-she-ăn'ĭk
ocelot, ō'se-lot
octave, ok'tăv
octavo, ok-tā'vō
octopus, ok'tō-pus
oculist, ok'ū-list
oddity, od'ĭ-ti
odoriferous, ō-dẽr-if'ẽr-us
odorous, ō'dẽr-us
Odyssey, od'ĭ-si
offertory, of'ẽr-to-ri
office, of'is
official, o-fish'al
officious, o-fish'us
offing, of'ing
often, of'n
ogle, ō'gl
ogre, o'gẽr
Oklahoma, ō-klă-hō'mă
oleomargarine, ō-le-ō-mär'gă-rēn
olfactory, ol-fak'to-ri
oligarchy, ol'ĭ-gär-ki
Olympiad, o-lim'pi-ad
Olympic, o-lim'pik
omelet; omelette, om'e-let
omnipotent, om-nip'o-tent
omniscient, om-nish'ent
omnivorous, om-niv'ẽr-us
onerous, on'ẽr-us
onion, un'yun
onyx, on'iks
opacity, o-pas'ĭ-ti
opening, ō'p'n-ing
operetta, op-ẽr-et'ă
opiate, ō'pi-āt
opine, o-pīn'
opinion, o-pin'yun
opium, ō'pi-um
opponent, o-pō'nent
opportunism, op-or-tū'nizm
opprobrium, o-prō'bri-um
optometry, op-tom'e-tri
opulence, op'ū-lens
oracle, or'ă-kl
oral, ō'răl
orangeade, or'enj-ād
oratorio, or-ă-tō'ri-ō
oratory, or'ă-to-ri
orchid, ôr'kid
ordinance, ôr'di-năns
ordnance, ôrd'năns
ore, ōr
organization, ôr-gan-i-zā'shun
orgy, ôr'ji
orient, ō'ri-ent
orientation, ō-ri-en-tā'shun
orifice, or'ĭ-fis
ornate, ôr-nāt'
ornithology, ôr-ni-thol'o-ji

orphanage, ôr'făn-ij
orthodox, ôr'tho-doks
orthography, ôr-thog'ră-fi
orthopedist, ôr-tho-pē'dist; ôr-thop'e-dist
oscillate, os'i-lāt
osculate, os'kū-lāt
ossify, os'i-fī
ostentation, os-ten-tā'shun
osteopath, os'te-o-path
osteopathy, os-te-op'ă-thi
ostracism, os'tră-sizm
ostracize, os'tră-sīz
ouija, wē'jă
oust, oust
overt, ō'vẽrt
overture, ō'vẽr-tūr
oxidation, ok-si-dā'shun
oxide, ok'sīd
oxygen, ok'si-jen

P

pacific, pă-sif'ik
pacificator, pă-sif'i-kā-tẽr
pacifist, pas'i-fist
paddock, pad'uk
padre, pä'drä
pagan, pā'gan
pageant, paj'ent
pagoda, pă-gō'dă
pajamas, pă-jä'măz
palace, pal'as
palate, pal'ăt
palatial, pă-lā'shal
palaver, pă-lä'vẽr
palette, pal'et
palisade, pal-i-sād'
palladium, pa-lā'di-um
palliate, pal'i-āt
Pall Mall, pel mel'; pal mal'
pallor, pal'ẽr
palm, päm
palmistry, päm'is-tri
palpitation, pal-pi-tā'shun
palsy, pawl'zi
panacea, pan-ă-sē'ă
pancreas, pang'krê-as
panegyric, pan-e-jir'ik
panegyrize, pan'e-ji-rīz
panorama, pan-o-rä'mă
pantheism, pan'the-izm
Pantheon, pan'the-on
papa, pă-pä'; pä'pä
papacy, pā'pă-si
papier-mache, pă-pyä'mă-shā'
paprika, pă'prē-kä
papyrus, pă-pī'rus
parachute, par'ă-shōōt
paradoxically, par-ă-doks'si-kal-li
parallelogram, par-ă-lel'o-gram
paralogism, pă-ral'o-jizm
paralysis, pă-ral'i-sis

paralytic, par-ă-lit'ik
paraphernalia, par-ă-fĕr-nā'li-ă
parasite, par'ă-sīt
parasitic, par-ă-sit'ik
parasol, par'ă-sol
parchesi, par-chē'si
pardonable, pär'dn-ă-bl
parent, pär'ent
paresis, pă-rē'sis
pariah, pă-rī'ă
Parliament, pär'li-ment
parlous, pär'lus
parochial, pă-rō'ki-al
parole, pă-rōl'
paroxysm, par'ok-sizm
parquet; parquette, pär-ket'
parricide, par-i-sīd
parse, pärs
parsimony, pär'si-mon-i
parsonage, pär's'n-ij
parterre, pär-tār'
Parthenon, pär'the-non
partiality, pär-shi-al'i-ti
participation, pär-tis-i-pā'shun
participle, pär'ti-si-pl
particular, pär-tik'û-lēr
particularize, pär-tik'û-lēr-īz
partridge, pär'trij
parvenu, pär've-nū
pass, pås
passage, pas'ij
passe, pă-sā'
passion, pash'un
passivity, pa-siv'i-ti
past, påst
pastel, pas-tel'
Pasteurization, păs-tēr-i-zā'shun
pastor, pås'tēr
pasture, pås'tûr
patent, pat'ent; pā'tent
paternoster, pă'tēr-nos-tēr
path, påth
pathos, pā'thos
patience, pā'shens
patriarch, pā'tri-ärk
patricide, pat'ri-sīd
patrimony, pat'ri-mo-ni
patriot, pat'ri-ot; pā'tri-ot
patron, pā'tron
patroness, păt'ron-es
paucity, paw'si-ti
pavilion, pă-vil'yun
peasantry, pez'ant-ri
pecan, pe-kan'
peccadillo, pek-ă-dil'o
peculiar, pe-kūl'yēr
peculiarity, pe-kū-li-ar'i-ti
pecuniary, pe-kū'ni-är-i
pedagogic, ped-ă-goj'ik
pedantic, pe-dan'tik
pedantry, ped'änt-ri
pedestrian, pe-des'tri-ăn
peerage, pēr'ij
Pekinese, pē-kin-ēz'

pelican, pel'i-kan
pellagra, pe-lag'ră
penal, pē'năl
penalize, pē'năl-īz
penalty, pen'ăl-ti
penance, pen'ans
penchant, pän-shän'; pen'chant
pendant, pen'dant
pendent, pen'dent
pendulum, pen'dû-lum
penetration, pen-e-trā'shun
penguin, pen'gwin
peninsula, pen-in'sū-lă
penitent, pen'i-tent
penitentiary, pen-i-ten'shă-ri
Pennsylvania, pen-sil-vā'ni-ă
pension, pen'shun
penurious, pe-nū'ri-us
peon, pē'on
peonage, pē'on-ij
peony, pē'o-ni
perambulate, pēr-am'bu-lāt
percale, pēr-kăl'
perceptible, per-sep'ti-bl
perchance, pēr-chans'
percolator, pēr'ko-lā-tēr
pere, pār
peremptory, per-emp'to-ri
perennial, per-en'i-al
perfect, pēr'fekt
perfervid, per-fēr-vid
perfidious, per-fid'i-us
perfume, per-fūm'
perfunctory, per'fungk'to-ri
perhaps, pēr-haps'
period, pē'ri-od
periodic, pē-ri-od'ik
periscope, per'i-skōp
peritonitis, per-i-to-nī'tis
permission, pēr-mish'un
permit (v.), pēr-mit' (grant
  liberty to do something)
permit (n.), pēr'mit (permission)
pernicious, pēr-nish'us
perpetrate, pēr'pe-trāt
perpetuity, pēr-pe-tū'i-ti
perquisite, pēr'kwi-zit
perseverance, pēr-se-vēr'ăns
persiflage, pēr'si-fläzh
persist, pēr-sist'
person, pēr'sn
personal, pēr'sun-ăl
personnel, pēr-so-nel'
perspective, pēr-spek'tiv
perspicacious, pēr-spi-kă'shus
perspiration, pēr-spi-rā'shun
persuasion, pēr-swā'zhun
perturb, pēr-tērb'
peruse, pe-rōoz'
perverse, pēr-vērs'
peseta, pe-sā'tä
peso, pā'sō
pestiferous, pes-tif'ēr-us
pestilential, pes-ti-len'shal

petard, pe-tärd'
petite, pe-tēt'
petrel, pet'rel
petrify, pet'ri-fī
pettifogger, pet'i-fog-ēr
petulance, pet'ū-lăns
petunia, pe-tū'ni-ă
pewter, pū'tēr
phaeton, fā'e-ton
phalanx, fā'langks
phantasy, fan'tă-si
Pharisee, far'i-sē
pharmacist, fär'mă-sist
pheasant, fez'ant
phenomenon, fe-nom'e-non
philanderer, fi-lan'dēr-ēr
philanthropic, fil-an-throp'ik
philatelist, fi-lat'e-list
philharmonic, fil-här-mon'ik
philosophically, fil-o-sof'i-kal-i
phlegm, flem
phlegmatic, fleg-mat'ik
phobia, fō'bi-ă
phoenix, fē'niks
phonetic, fo-net'ik
phonograph, fō'no-grăf
phosphorescence, fos-for-es'ens
phosphorus, fos'for-us
photographer, fo-tog'ră-fēr
photography, fo-tog'ră-fi
photogravure, fō-to-gră-vūr'
photostat, fō'tō-stat
phraseology, frāz-e-ol'o-ji
phrenology, fre-nol'o-ji
phthisic, tiz'ik
phthisis, thī'sis
physic, fiz'ik
physician, fi-zish'an
physicist, fiz'i-sist
physics, fiz'iks
physique, fi-zēk'
pianissimo, pē-ă-nis'i-mō
pianist, pi-an'ist
piano, pi-an'ō
piazza, pi-az'ă
picaresque, pik-ă-resk'
piccolo, pik'o-lō
picture, pik'tūr; pik'chur
picturesque, pik-tûr-esk';
   pik-chur-esk'
piety, pī'e-ti
pigeon, pij'un
pigmentation, pig-men-tā'shun
pilaster, pi-las'tēr
pimiento, pi-myen'tō
pinochle, pē'nuk-l
pious, pī'us
piquant, pē'kant
pique, pēk (slight anger or resentment; to wound the pride of; to
   dive down in an airplane for
   the purpose of attack)
pique, pē-kā' (French cotton material)

pirouette, pir-ōō-et'
pistachio, pis-tä'shi-ō
piteous, pit'e-us
pitiable, pit'i-ă-bl
pitiful, pit'i-fool
pittance, pit'ăns
pituitary, pi-tū'i-tă-ri
placable, plā'kă-bl
placard, plak'ärd
placidity, plă-sid'i-ti
plagiarism, plā'ji-ă-rizm
plagiarize, plā'ji-ă-rīz
plaid, plad
plait, plāt
planetarium, plan-e-tā'ri-um
plaque, plăk
plateau, plă-tō'
platinum, plat'i-num
Platonic, plă-ton'ik
plausibility, plaw-zi-bil'i-ti
plaza, plä'ză
pleasure, plezh'ûr
plebeian, ple-bē'yan
plebiscite, pleb'i-sīt
plenipotentiary, plen-i-po-ten'shi-
   ă-ri
plenitude, plen'i-tūd
plethora, pleth'o-ră
pleurisy, plōō'ri-si
plover, pluv'ēr
plumage, plōōm'ij
plural, plōō'răl
plutocracy, plōō-tok'ră-si
pneumatic, nū-mat'ik
pneumonia, nū-mō'ni-ă
poem, pō'em
poesy, pō'e-si
poet laureate, pō'et law're-āt
pogrom, pō'grŏm
poignant, poin'ant
poilu, pwä-lū'
poinsettia, poin-set'i-ă
poise, poiz
poison, poi'zn
polemic, pō-lem'ik
police, po-lēs'
politician, pol-i-tish'ăn
pollution, po-lū'shun
polyandry, pol-i-an'dri
polygamy, po-lig'ă-mi
polyglot, pol'i-glot
polytechnic, pol-i-tek'nik
pomade, po-măd'
pomegranate, pom'gran-āt
pompadour, pom'pă-dōōr
pongee, pon-jē'
pontifical, pon-tif'i-kal
poor, pōōr
popular, pop'û-lēr
porcelain, pôrs'lin
pore, pōr
pork, pōrk
porpoise, pôr'pus
porridge, por'ij

port, pōrt
portfolio, pōrt-fō'li-ō
portiere, por-tyār'
poser, pōz'ēr
poseur, po-zur'
positively, poz'i-tiv-li
posse, pos'e
posthumous, post'hū-mus
posture, pos'tūr
potable, pō'tă-bl
potassium, po-tas'i-um
potato, po-tā'tō
potentate, pō'ten-tāt
potpourri, pō-pŏō-rē'
poultice, pōl'tis
poultry, pōl'tri
pourparler, pŏōr-pär-lā'
pousse-cafe, pŏōs'kă-fā'
powwow, pou'wou
practitioner, prak-tish'un-ēr
pragmatism, prag'mă-tizm
prairie, prā'ri
prayer, prâr
preamble, prē'am-bl
precede, pre-sēd'
precedence, pre-sēd'ens
precedent (adj.), pre-sēd'ent (going before)
precedent (n.), pres'e-dent (something previously said or done, serving as an example to be followed)
preceptor, prē-sep'tēr
precinct, prē'singkt
precipitant, pre-sip'i-tant
precise, pre-sīs'
precocity, pre-kos'i-ti
precursor, pre-kēr'sēr
predatory, pred'ă-to-ri
predilection, prē-di-lek'shun
preface, pref'ăs
prefatory, pref'ă-to-ri
prefer, pre-fēr'
preferable, pref'ēr-ă-bl
preferential, pref-ēr-en'shal
prefix, prē'fiks
prejudicial, prej-û-dish'al
premeditation, pre-med-i-tā'shun
premier, prē'mi-ēr; prēm'yer
premiere, prē-mi-yēr'
premise, pre-mīz'
premonition, prē-mo-nish'un
preparatory, pre-par'ă-ti-v
preponderance, pre-pon'dēr-ans
prerequisite, pre-rek'wi-zit
prerogative, pre-rog'ă-tiv
presbytery, pres'bi-tēr-i
prescience, prē'shi-ens
present, prez'ent
presentation, prez-en-tā'shun
presentiment, pre-zen'ti-ment
presidential, prez-i-den'shal
prestidigitator, pres-ti-dij'i-tā-tēr

prestige, pres'tij; pres-tēzh'
presumptuous, pre-zump'tū-us
pretense, pre-tens'
prettily, prit'i-li
prevaricate, pre-var'i-kāt
prima donna, prē'mă don'ă
prima facie, prī'mă fā'shi-ē
primate, prī'māt
primeval, prī-mē'val
primordial, prī-môr'di-al
principal, prin'si-pal
principle, prin'si-pl
priority, prī-or'i-ti
pristine, pris'tin
privation, prī-vā'shun
privilege, priv'i-lej
probity, prob'i-ti
problematical, prob-lem-at'i-kal
proceed, pro-sēd'
process, pros'es
procrastinate, pro-kras'ti-nāt
prodigious, pro-dij'us
prodigy, prod'i-ji
produce (v.), pro-dūs' (to exhibit or bring to view)
produce (n.), prod'ūs (that which is yielded or brought forth)
professor, pro-fes'ēr
proficiency, pro-fish'en-si
profile, prō'fīl
profligate, prof'li-gāt
progeny, proj-en-i
program; programme, prō'gram
progress (n.), prog'res (advancement)
progress (v.), pro-gres' (to move forward, advance)
prohibitory, pro-hib'i-to-ri
project (n.), proj'ekt (a design or scheme)
project (v.), pro-jekt' (to throw or cast forward)
projectile, pro-jek'til
proletariat, prō-le-tā'ri-at
promenade, prom-e-näd'
promiscuous, prō-mis'kū-us
promissory, prom'i-so-ri
pronounce, pro-nouns'
pronunciation, pro-nun-si-ā'shun
propaganda, prop-ă-gan'dă
propagation, prop-ă-gā'shun
propeller, pro-pel'ēr
propensity, pro-pen'si-ti
prophecy (n.), prof'e-si
prophesy (v.), prof'e-sī
prophylactic, prof-i-lak'tik
propinquity, pro-ping'kwi-ti
propitious, pro-pish'us
proprietary, pro-prī'e-tā-ri
propriety, pro-prī'e-ti
pro rata prō rā'tă
prorate, prō'rāt
prorogue, pro-rōg'

proscenium, pro-sē'ni-um
proscription, pro-skrip'shun
prosecution, pros-e-kū'shun
proselyte, pros'e-līt
prosiness, prōz'i-ness
prospect (n.), pros'pekt (a view of something distant)
prospect (v.), prō-spekt' (to search or explore)
prospectus, pro-spek'tus
prostitution, pros-ti-tū'shun
prosy, prōz'i
protectionist, pro-tek'shun-ist
protectorate, pro-tek'tēr-āt
protégé, pro-tā-zhā'
protein, prō'te-in
protest (v.), pro-test' (remonstrate)
protest (n.), prō'test (a solemn declaration of opinion against something)
Protestant, prot'es-tănt
protuberance, prō-tū'bēr-ăns
provender, prov'en-dēr
proverbial, pro-vēr'bi-al
provincial, pro-vin'shal
provisional, pro-vizh'un-al
proviso, pro-vī'zō
provocative, pro-vok'ă-tiv
provoking, pro-vōk'ing
prowess, prou'es
proximity, prok-sim'i-ti
proxy, prok'si
prude, prōōd
prurient, prōōr'i-ent
psalm, säm
Psalter, sawl'ter
pshaw, shaw
psyche, sī'ke
psychiatry, sī-kī'ă-tri
psychoanalysis, sī-ko-ă-nal'i-sis
psychology, sī-kol'o-ji
psychosis, sī-kō'sis
ptarmigan, tär'mi-gan
Ptolemaic, tol-e-mā'ik
ptomaine, tō'mān
puberty, pū'bēr-ti
pubic, pū'bik
public, pub'lik
publicist, pub'li-sist
pueblo, pweb'lō
puerile, pū'ēr-il
pugilism, pū'ji-lizm
pugnacious, pug-nā'shus
puissant, pū'is-ănt
pulchritude, pul'kri-tūd
pullet, pool'et
pulpit, pool'pit
pulsate, pul'sāt
pumpkin, pump'kin
punctilious, pungk-til'i-us; pungk-til'yus
punctual, pungk'tū-al
punctuate, pungk'tū-āt
puncture, pungk'tûr

pungent, pun'jent
punitive, pūn'i-tiv
punt, punt
purblind, pēr'blīnd
puree, pū'rā
purgatory, pēr'gă-to-ri
purge, pērj
purist, pūr'ist
purloin, pēr-loin'
purport, pēr'pōrt
purveyance, pur-vā'ăns
pusillanimous, pū-sil-an'i-mus
pussyfoot, poss'i-foot
putrefaction, pū-tre-fak'shun
puttee, put'i
putter, put'ēr
pyorrhea, pī-o-rē'ă
pyramid, pir'ă-mid
pyramidal, pi-ram'i-dăl
pyromania, pī-ro-mā'ni-ă
Pyrrhic victory, pir'ik vik'to-ri
Python, pī'thon

Q

quack, kwak
quadrangle, kwod'rang-gl
quadrile, kwă-dril'
quadruple, kwod'roo-p'l
quaff, kwäf
quagmire, kwag'mīr
quaint, kwānt
qualitative, kwol'i-tā-tiv
qualm, kwäm
quandary, kwon'dă-ri
quantitative, kwon'ti-tā-tiv
quantum, kwon'tum
quarantine, kwor'an-tēn
quarrel, kwor'el
quartz, kwôrts
quasi, kwā'si
quay, kē
queen, kwēn
quest, kwest
querulous, kwēr'oo-lus
query, kwē'ri
question, kwes'chun
questionnaire, kwes-chun-ār'
queue, kū
quibble, kwib'l
quick, kwik
quiescent, kwī-es'ent
quiet, kwī'et
quietude, kwī'e-tūd
quietus, kwī-ē'tus
quinine, kwī'nīn
quintessence, kwin-tes'ens
quintuplet, kwin'tu-plet
Quirinal, kwi-rī'năl
quite, kwīt
quittance, kwit'ăns
quiver, kwiv'ēr
qui vive, kē vēv

quixotic, kwĭk-sot'ĭk
quizzical, kwĭz'ĭ-kăl
quoin, koin
quoit, kwoit; koit
quondam, kwon'dam
quorum, kwō'rum
quota, kwō'tă
quotation, kwō-tā'shun
quoth, kwŏth
quotient, kwō'shent
quotum, kwō'tum

R

rabbi, rab'ī
rabbinic, ra-bin'ĭk
Rabelaisian, rab-e-lā'zhi-ăn
rabies, rā'bi-ēz
racial, rā'shal
raciness, rās'i-nes
raconteur, ra-kon-tûr'
racquet, rak'et
radiant, rā'di-ănt
radiator, rā'di-ā-tēr
radio, rā'di-ō
radish, rad'ish
radium, rā'di-um
radius, rā'di-us
ragamuffin, rag'ă-muf-in
ragout, ra-gōō'
raillery, rāl'ēr-i
raiment, rā'ment
raisin, rā'zn
rajah, rā'jă
ramify, ram'i-fī
rampage, ram'pāj
rampant, ram'pant
rampart, ram'pärt
rancho, ran'chō
rancid, ran'sid
rancor, rang'kēr
random, ran'dum
ransom, ran'sum
rapacious, ră-pā'shus
rapacity, ră-pas'i-ti
rapier, rā'pi-ēr
rapine, rap'in; rap'īn
rapport, ra-pōrt'
rapprochement, ră-prōsh-män'
rapscallion, rap-skal'yun
rapture, rap'tûr
raspberry, raz'bēr-i
rathskeller, räts'kel-ēr
ratio, rā'shi-ō
ration, rā'shun
rational, rash'un-ăl
rattan, ra-tan'
raucous, raw'kus
ravage, rav'ij
ravel, rav'l
ravelings, rav'lingz
ravenous, rav'n-us
ravine, ră-vēn'

ravioli, rä-vi-ō'li
rayon, rā'on
razor, rā'zēr
react, rē-akt'
real, rē'ăl
reason, rē'zn
rebate, re'bāt
rebel (n.), reb'el (one who revolts
    from his allegiance or defies
    constituted authority)
rebel (v.), re-bel' (to rise against
    authority)
rebut, re-but'
recalcitrant, re-kal'si-trant
recapitulate, rē-kă-pit'ŭ-lāt
recede, re-sēd'
receipt, re'sēt
receive, re-sēv'
recent, rē'sent
recess, re-ses'
recipe, res'i-pē
recipient, re-sip'i-ent
reciprocal, re-sip'ro-kal
reciprocity, res-i-pros'i-ti
recitative, re-sit'ă-tiv
recluse, re-klōōs'
recognizable, rek'og-nīz-ă-bl
recognizance, re-kog'ni-zans; re-
    kon'i-zans
recognize, rek'og-nīz
recommendation, rek-o-men-dā'-
    shun
recompense, rek'om-pens
reconcile, rek'on-sīl
reconciliation, rek-on-sil-i-ā'shun
recondite, rek'on-dīt
reconnoiter, rek-o-noi'tēr
record (v.), re-kôrd' (to register
    or enroll)
record (n.), rek'ord (an authentic
    memorial)
recoup, re-kōōp'
recourse, re-kōrs'
recreant, rek're-ant
recreate, rek're-āt (to take recrea-
    tion, to reanimate, especially
    after toil)
recreate, rē-kre-āt' (to create
    anew)
recrimination, re-krim-i-nā'shun
recrudescence, rē-krōō-des'ens
recruit, rē-krōōt'
rectifier, rek'ti-fī-ēr
rector, rek'tēr
rectory, rek'to-ri
recuperate, re-kū'pēr-āt
recurrence, re-kur'ens
redolent, red'o-lent
redoubt, re-dout'
redundance, re-dun'dăns
refectory, re-fek'to-ri
referable, ref'ēr-ă-bl
referendum, ref-ēr-en'dum
reflex, re'fleks

reflorescence, rē-flo-res'ens
refractory, re-frak'to-ri
refrigerant, re-frij'ĕr-ant
refrigerator, re-frij'ĕr-ā-tĕr
refuge, ref'ūj
refugee, ref-û-jē'
refulgence, re-ful'jens
refuse (v.), re-fūz' (to deny or reject)
refuse (n.), ref'ūs (waste or worthless matter, rubbish)
refutable, re-fūt'ă-bl
regalia, re-gā'li-ă
regatta, re-gat'ă
regency, rē'jen-si
regenerate, re-jen'ĕr-āt
regent, rē'jent
regicide, rej'i-sīd
regime, rā-zhēm'
regimen, rej'i-men
regress (v.), re-gres'
regress (n.), rē'gres
rehabilitate, rē-hă-bil'i-tāt
reign, rān
rein, rān
reiterate, re-it'ĕr-āt
rejuvenate, re-jū'ven-āt
relapse, re-laps'
relaxation, rē-lak-sā'shun
relic, rel'ik
relict, rel'ikt
reluctance, re-luk'tăns
remediable, re-mē'di-ă-bl
remedial, re-mē'di-al
reminiscence, rem-i-nis'ens
remnant, rem'nănt
remonstrate, re-mon'strāt
remuneration, re-mū-ner-ā'shun
Renaissance, ren-e-säns'
renascence, re-nas'ens
rendezvous, rän'dā-vōō; ren'de-vōō
renegade, ren'e-gād
renege, re-nēg'
renunciation, re-nun-si-ā'shun
repartee, rep-är-tē'
repast, re-påst'
repertoire, rep'ĕr-twär
repertory, rep'ĕr-to-ri
repetitious, rep-e-tish'us
replenishment, re-plen'ish-ment
replevin, re-plev'in
replica, rep'li-kă
reprimand, rep'ri-månd
reprisal, re-prīz'ăl
reprobate, rep'ro-bāt
reptile, rep'til
reputable, rep'û-tă-bl
requiem, rē'kwi-em
requisite, rek'wi-zit
research, re-sĕrch'
reservoir, rez'ĕr-vwär
residuary, re-zid'u-ā-ri
residue, rez'i-dū

resiliency, re-zil'i-en-si
resin, rez'in
resonance, rez'o-năns
resource, re-sōrs'
respiration, res-pi-rā'shun
respite, res'pit
resplendent, re-splen'dent
respondent, re-spon'dent
restaurant, res'to-rant; res'to-rän
restorative, re-stōr'ă-tiv
resumé (n.), rā-zū-mā' (a summary)
resume (v.), re-zūm' (to take up again after interruption)
resuscitate, re-sus'i-tāt
retail (v.), re-tāl' (to sell in small quantities)
retail (n.), rē'tāl (sale of goods in small quantities)
retentive, re-ten'tiv
reticence, ret'i-sens
retina, ret'i-nă
retinue, ret'i-nū
retrenchment, re-trench'ment
retribution, ret-ri-bū'shun
retroactive, rē-tro-ak'tiv
reveille, rev-el-ē; re-văl'ye
revelry, rev'el-ri
revenue, rev'e-nū
reverence, rev'ĕr-ens
reverie, rev'ĕr-i
revivification, re-viv-i-fi-kā'shun
revocable, rev'o-kă-bl
revolt, re-vōlt'; re-volt'
revolutionary, rev-o-lū'shun-ā-ri
revue, rê-vū'
rhapsody, rap'so-di
rheostat, rē'o-stat
rhetoric, ret'o-rik
rheumatism, rōō'mă-tizm
rhinoceros, rī-nos'ĕr-os
rhododendron, rō-do-den'dron
rhubarb, rōō'bärb
rhythm, rithm; rithm
rhythmic, rith'mik
Rialto, re-äl'tō
ribald, rib'ald
ricochet, rik-o-shā'; rik-o-shet'
riddance, rid'ăns
righteous, rīt-yus
rigidity, ri-jid'i-ti
rigmarole, rig'mă-rōl
rind, rīnd
rinse, rins
riparian, rī-pā'ri-ån
riposte, re-pōst'
rise, rīz
risibility, riz-i-bil'i-ti
risotto, re-sot'ō
rissole, rē-sōl'
ritual, rit'û-al
rivulet, riv'û-let
roan, rōn
robust, rō-bust'

robustious, rō-bus'chus
rococo, ro-kō'kō
rodeo, rō-dā'ō
rogue, rōg
role, rōl
roll, rōl
romance, rō-mans'
Romeo, rō'me-o
Roosevelt, rō'ze-velt
root, rōōt
Roquefort, rōk'fort
rosin, roz'in
rostrum, ros'trum
rotary, rō'tă-ri
rotate, ro'tāt
rote, rōt
rotisserie, rō-tis-rē'
rotogravure, rō'to-grā-vūr
rotunda, ro-tun'dă
roue, rōō-ā'
rouge, rōōzh
rough, ruf
roulette, rōō-let'
roustabout, roust'ă-bout
rout, rout
route, rōōt
rowel, rou'el
ruction, ruk'shun
rudiment, rōō'di-ment
rue, rōō
ruffian, ruf'yan
ruinate, rōō'i-nāt
rumble, rum'bl
rumor, rōō'mēr
rupture, rup'tur
rural, rōō'ral
ruse, rōōz
Russian, rush'an
rustle, rus'l
rutabaga, rōō-tă-bā'gă

S

sabot, să-bō'
sabotage, să-bo-tåzh'
saccharine, sak'ă-rin
sacerdotal, sas-ēr-dō'tal
sachem, să'chem
sachet, să-shā'
sacrament, sak'ră-ment
sacred, să'kred
sacrifice, sak'ri-fīs
sacrificial, sak-ri-fish'al
sacrilege, sak'ri-lej
sacrilegious, sak-ri-lē'jus
sacristan, sak'ris-tan
sacrosanct, sak'ro-sangkt
safety, săf'ti
saffron, saf'run
saga, să'gă
sagacious, să-gā'shus
sagacity, să-gas'i-ti
sage, săj

sahib, să'ib
saint, sănt
St. Swithin's Day, sănt swith'inz
  dā
salaam, să-läm'
salacious, să-lā'shus
salamander, sal'ă-man-dēr
salary, sal'ă-ri
salient, să'li-ent
saline, să'līn
saliva, să-lī'vă
salivate, sal'i-vāt
sallow, sal'ō
salmon, sam'un
Salome, să-lō'me
salon, să-lôn'
saloon, să-lōōn'
salubrious, să-lū'bri-us
salutary, sal'u-tă-ri
salutatory, să-lū'tă-to-ri
salute, să-lūt'
salvage, sal'vij
salve, săv
salvo, sal'vō
samovar, sam'o-vär
sample, sam'pl
sanatorium, san-ă-tō'ri-um
sanctified, sangk'ti-fīd
sanctimonious, sang-ti-mō'ni-us
sanctuary, sangk'tu-ă-ri
sanctum, sangk'tum
sandwich, sand'wich
sangfroid, säng-frwä'
sanguinary, sang'gwi-nă-ri
sanguine, sang'gwin
sanitarium, san-i-tā'ri-um
sans souci, sän sōō-sē'
sapient, să'pi-ent
sapphire, saf'īr
Sappho, saf'ō
Saracen, sar'ă-sen
sarcasm, sär'kazm
sarcophagus, sär-kof'ă-gus
sardine, sär-dēn'
sardonic, sär-don'ik
sargasso, sär-gas'ō
sarsaparilla, sär-să-pă-ril'ă
sartorial, sär-tō'ri-al
sassafras, sas'ă-fras
Satan, să'tan
satanic, să-tan'ik
satchel, sach'el
satellite, sat'e-līt
satiate, ă'shi-āt
satiety, să-tī'e-ti
satin, sat'in
satire, sat'īr
satirist, sat'i-rist
satirize, sat'i-rīz
saturate, sat'ů-rāt
Saturday, sat'ēr-dā
saturnalia, sat-ēr-nā'li-ă
saturnine, sat'ēr-nīn
satyr, sat'ēr

sauce, saws
saucily, saw'si-li
sauerkraut, sour'krout
saunter, sän'tẽr; sawn'tẽr
sausage, saw'sij
sauterne, sō-tẽrn'
savage, sav'ij
savant, să-vän'
savoir-faire, să-vwar-fãr'
savor, sā'vẽr
savory, sā'vẽr-i
saxophone, sak'so-fōn
scabbard, skab'ärd
scalawag, skal'ă-wag
scallop, skol'op
scandalous, skan'dal-us
Scandinavian, skan-di-nā'vi-an
scant, skant
scapegoat, skāp'gōt
scarcity, skãr'si-ti
scathing, skāth'ing
scenario, shā-nä'ri-ō
scenic, sē'nik; sen'ik
scent, sent
scepter; sceptre, sep'tẽr
sceptic, skep'tik
schedule, sked'ūl
scheme, skēm
schism, sizm
schnauzer, shnou'sẽr
schnitzel, shnit'zel
scholastic, sko-las'tik
schottische, shot'ish
sciatica, sī-at'i-kă
scientific, sī-en-tif'ik
scintilla, sin-til'ă
scintillate, sin'til-āt
scion, sī'on
scissors, siz'ẽrz
scone, skōn
scourge, skẽrj
scrape, skrāp
scrapple, skrap'l
scratch, skrach
scrawny, skraw'ni
scribe, skrīb
scrip, skrip
script, skript
scripture, skrip'tûr
scrofula, skrof'û-lă
scruple, skrōō'pl
scrupulous, skrōō'pū-lus
scrutiny, skrōō'ti-ni
scullion, skul'yun
sculptor, skulp'tẽr
sculpture, skulp'tûr
scurvy, skẽr'vi
scutcheon, skuch'un
scuttle, skut'l
Scylla, sil'ă
scythe, sīth
seamstress, sēm'stres
search, sẽrch
seared, sẽrd

seascape, sē'skāp
season, sē'zn
secede, se-sēd'
secession, se-sesh'un
seclusion, se-klōō'zhun
secretarial, sek-re-tā'ri-al
secretary, sek're-te-ri
secrete, se-krēt'
secretive, se-krē'tiv
sect, sekt
sectarianism, sek-tā'ri-an-izm
section, sek'shun
sectionalism, sek'shun-al-izm
secular, sek'û-lẽr
secularism, sek'û-lẽr-izm
secure, se-kûr'
security, se-kûr'i-ti
sedan, se-dan'
sedate, se-dāt'
sedentary, sed'en-te-ri
sediment, sed'i-ment
sedition, se-dish'un
seduce, se-dūs'
seductive, se-duc'tiv
sedulous, sed'û-lus
seemliness, sēm'li-nes
seersucker, sẽr'suk-ẽr
seethe, sēth
segment, seg'ment
segregate, seg're-gāt
seignior, sēn'yẽr
seine, sān
seismic, sīs'mik
seismograph, sīs'mo-grăf
seizable, sēz'ă-bl
seize, sēz
seizure, sē'zhur
selah, sē'lă
selective, se-lek'tiv
semaphore, sem'ă-fōr
semester, se-mes'tẽr
seminary, sem'i-nā-ri
Semite, sem'īt
Semitic, se-mit'ik
Semitism, sem'i-tizm
senate, sen'āt
senile, sē'nīl
senility, sē-nil'i-ti
senior, sēn'yẽr
seniority, sēn-yor'i-ti
senor, sā-nyōr'
senora, sā-nyo'rä
senorita, sā-nyō-rē'tă
sensate, sen'sāt
sensationalism, sen-sā'shun-al-izm
sensibility, sen-si-bil'i-ti
sensitivity, sen-si-tiv'i-ti
sensitize, sen'si-tīz
sensory, sen'so-ri
sensual, sen'shū-al
sensuous, sen'shū-us
sententious, sen-ten'shus
sentient, sen'shi-ent
sentimental, sen-ti-men'tal

separate, sep'ă-rāt
separatism, sep'ă-ră-tizm
septic, sep'tik
septuagenarian, sep-tu-ă-je-nă'-ri-an
sepulcher; sepulchre, sep'ul-kĕr
sepulchral, se-pul'kral
sequence, sē'kwens
sequential, se-kwen'shal
sequester, se-kwes'tĕr
sequestration, sē-kwes-trā'shun
seraglio, se-ral'yō
seraph, ser'af
serenade, ser-ê-nād'
serene, se-rēn'
serenity, se-ren'i-ti
sergeant, sär'jent
serial, sē'ri-ăl
seriatim, sē-ri-ă'tim
series, sē'rēz
serious, sē'ri-us
sermonize, sĕr'mun-īz
serpentine, sĕr'pen-tīn
serum, sē'rum
servile, sĕr'vĭl; sĕr'vil
servitude, sĕr'vi-tūd
sesame, ses'ă-me
session, sesh'un
settee, se-tē'
setter, set'ĕr
several, sev'ĕr-al
severance, sev'ĕr-ăns
severe, se-vēr'
severity, se-ver'i-ti
sewage, sū'ij
sewer, sū'er
sewerage, sū'ĕr-ij
sextant, seks'tănt
sextet; sextette, seks-tet'
sextuple, seks'tu-pl
sexual, sek'shu-al
shaft, shăft
shagginess, shag'i-nes
shagreen, shă-grēn'
shah, shä
shears, shĕrz
sheath, shēth
sheathe, shēth
sheik, shēk; shāk
shellac, she-lak'
shepherd, shep'ĕrd
sherbet, shĕr'bet
shillalah, shi-lā'lă
shivaree, shiv-ă-rē'
shortage, shôr'tij
shortening, shôrt'n-ing
shorthorn, shôrt'hôrn'
shove, shuv
shrapnel, shrap'nel
shrinkage, shringk'ij
shrive, shrīv
shrivel, shriv'l
Shropshire, shrop'shĕr

shyster, shī'stĕr
Siamese, sī-ă-mēz'
sibilant, sib'i-lant
sibyl, sib'il
sidereal, sī-dē're-al
sidewise, sīd'wīz
sidle, sīd'l
siege, sēj
Siegfried, sēg'frēd
sierra, si-er'ă
siesta, si-es'tă
sieve, siv
sigh, sī
signalize, sig'nal-īz
signatory, sig'nă-to-ri
signature, sig'nă-tūr
signet, sig'net
significant, sig-nif'i-kant
signor, sēn'yor
signora, sēn-yō'ră
signorina, sēn-yo-rē'nă
signorino, sēn-yo-rē'nō
Sikh, sēk
silesia, si-lē'shi-ă
silhouette, sil-oo-et'
silica, sil'i-kă
silicosis, sil-i-kō'sis
simian, sim'i-an
simile, sim'i-lē
similitude, si-mil'i-tūd
simpleton, sim'pl-tun
simplicity, sim-plis'i-ti
simplification, sim-pli-fi-kă'shun
simulate, sim'ū-lāt
simulation, sim-ū-lā'shun
simultaneous, sī-mul-tā'ne-us
since, sins
sincere, sin-sēr'
sincerity, sin-ser'i-ti
sinecure, sī'ne-kûr
sine die, sī'ne dī'e
sine qua non, sī'ne kwä non
sinew, sin'ū
sinewy, sin'ū-i
sing, sing
singe, sinj
singleton, sing'gl-tun
singular, sing'gū-lĕr
sinister, sin'is-tĕr
Sinn Fein, shin fān
sinuosity, sin-ū-os'i-ti
sinuous, sin'ū-us
sinus, sī'nus
Sioux, sōō
siphon; syphon, sī'fon
sire, sīr
siren, sī'ren
sirloin, sĕr'loin
sirup, sir'up
sisal, si-säl'
Sistine, sis'tēn
situate, sit'ū-āt
situation, sit-ū-ā'shun

sizable, sīz'ā-bl
sizzle, siz'l
skein, skān
skeletal, skel'e-tal
skeleton, skel'e-tun
skeptic, skep'tik
skepticism, skep'ti-sizm
ski, skē
skilled, skild
skillet, skil'et
skirt, skĕrt
skiver, skīv'ẽr
skulk, skulk
skunk, skungk
slanderous, slan'dẽr-us
slant, slănt
slattern, slat'ẽrn
slaughter, slaw'tẽr
Slavic, slăv'ik
slavish, slăv'ish
sleigh, slā
sleight, slīt
sleuth, slooth
slicer, slīs'ẽr
slick, slik
slimy, slīm'ĭ
slipknot, slip'not
slither, sli*th*'ẽr
slitter, slit'ẽr
sloe, slō
slosh, slosh
sloth, slōth
slouch, slouch
slough, slou (a deep muddy place)
slough, sluf (the cast-off skin of
   a snake; the part that separates
   from a foul sore)
slough, sloo (a side-channel from
   a river)
Slovak, slo-vak'
sloven, sluv'en
Slovene, slo-vēn'
slovenliness, sluv'n-li-ness
slue, sloo
sluice, sloos
slur, slẽr
smilax, smī'laks
smite, smīt
smithereens, smi*th*-ẽr-ēnz'
smooth, smooth'
smoothen, smooth'n
smother, smu*th*'ẽr
smut, smut
snapdragon, snap'drag-un
snout, snout
sobriety, sō-brī'e-ti
sobriquet, sō'bri-kā; so-brē-kā'
   (Fr.)
soccer, sok'ẽr
sociable, sō'shă'bl
social, sō'shal
society, so-sī'e-ti
sociology, so-shi-ol'o-ji
sodality, so-dal'i-ti

sodium, sō'di-um
sofa, sō'fā
soften, sôf'n
soiree, swä-rā'
sojourn, sō'jẽrn; so-jẽrn'
solace, sol'ās
solarium, so-lā'ri-um
solder, saw'dẽr
soldier, sōl'jẽr
sole, sōl
solecism, sol'e-sizm
solemn, sol'em
solemnization, sol''em-ni-zā'shun
solicitation, sō''lis-i-tā'shun
solicitous, sō-lis'i-tus
soliloquy, so-lil'o-kwi
Solon, sō'lon
soluble, sol'ū-bl
solvable, sol'vā-bl
sombrero, som-brā'rō
somersault, sum'ẽr-sawlt
somnambulism, som-nam'bū-lizm
somnambulist, som-nam'bū-list
sonata, so-nä'tā
song, sông
songster, sông'stẽr
soniferous, so-nif'ẽr-us
sonnet, son'et
sonorous, so-nō'rus
sooth, sooth
soothe, sooth
soothsay, sooth'sā
sophism, sof'izm
sophist, sof'ist
sophisticate, so-fis'ti-kāt
sophistication, so''fis-ti-kā'shun
sophistry, sof'is-tri
sophomore, sof'o-mōr
soporific, sō-po-rif'ik
soprano, so-prä'nō
sorcerer, sô'sẽr-ẽr
sorcery, sôr'sẽr-i
sorghum, sôr'gum
sorrel, sor'el
sortie, sôr'tē
sotto voce, sōt'ō vō'chä
sou, soo
soubrette, soo-bret'
soubriquet, sō'bri-kā; so-brē-kā'
   (Fr.)
souffle, soo-flā'
soul, sōl
source, sōrs
souse, sous
souvenir, soo-ve-nēr'
sovereign, suv'ẽr-in
sovereignty, suv'ẽr-in-ti
Soviet, sō'vē-yet
sovietism, sō'vē-yet-izm
sow, sou (a female pig; a channel
   for running molten metal to the
   molds)
sow, sō (to scatter, as seed)
soy, soi

spa, spä

spade, späd

spaghetti, spä-get'i

spaniel, span'yel

sparse, spärs

Spartan, spär'tan

spasm, spazm

spasmodic, spaz-mod'ik

spatulate, spat'û-lāt

spavin, spav'in

specialist, spesh'al-ist

specie, spē'shi

species, spē'shēz

specification, spes''-i-fi-kā'shun

specious, spē'shus

spectacular, spek-tak'û-ler

spectrum, spek'trum

spermatozoon, spér-mä-to-zō'on

sphere, sfēr

spherical, sfer'i-kal

spheroid, sfē'roid

Sphinx, sfingks

spinach, spin'ij

spiral, spī'ral

spirit, spir'it

spiritism, spir'i-tizm

spiritual, spir'it-u-al

spiritualism, spir'it-u-al-izm

spleen, splēn

splenic, splen'ik

spoliation, spō-li-ā'shun

sponge, spunj

spongy, spun'ji

spontaneity, spon-tä-nē'i-ti

spontaneous, spon-tä'nē-us

spoon, spōōn

sporadic, spo-rad'ik

spouse, spouz

spunk, spungk

spurge, spérj

spurious, spū'ri-us

sputun, spū'tum

squalid, skwol'id

squalor, skwol'ēr; skwä'lôr

squash, skwosh

squatter, skwot'ēr

squirrel, skwēr'el

squirt, skwērt

stabilize, stab'i-līz

staccato, stäk-kä'tō

stadium, stä'di-um

staff, stäf

stagnancy, stag'nan-si

stalagmite, stä-lag'mīt

stalwart, stawl'wērt

stamina, stam'i-nä

stanch, stånch

stanchion, stan'shun

stanza, stan'zä

starred, stärd

starveling, stärv'ling

static, stat'ik

stationary, stä'shun-ā-ri

stationery, stä-shun-ēr'i

statistic, stä-tis'tik

statistician, stat-is'tish'an

statistics, stä-tis'tiks

statuary, stat'û-ā-ri

statue, stat'û

statuesque, stat-û-esk'

stature, stat'ûr

status, stä'tus

status quo, stä'tus kwō

statute, stat'ût

statutory, stat'û-to-ri

steerage, stēr'ij

stein, stīn

stenographer, ste-nog'rä-fēr

stenography, ste-nog'rä-fi

stentorian, sten-tō'ri-an

steppe, step

stereopticon, ster-e-op'ti-kon

stereotype, ster'e-o-tīp

sterile, ster'il

sterility, ste-ril'i-ti

stethoscope, steth'o-skōp

stevedore, stēv'e-dōr

steward, stū'ērd

stigma, stig'mä

stiletto, sti-let'ō

stimulus, stim'û-lus

stint, stint

stipend, stī'pend

stipulation, stip-û-lā'shun

stirrup, stir'up; stēr'up

stogy, stō'gi

stoic, stō'ik

stoicism, stō'i-sizm

stomach, stum'ak

stoniness, stōn'i-nes

stopgap, stop'gap

storage, stōr'ij

store, stōr

Stradivarius, strad-i-vā'ri-us

strait-laced, strät'lāst

strangulation, strang-gû-lā'shun

stratagem, strat'ä-jem

strategic, strä-tē'jik

strategy, strat'e-ji

stratify, strat'i-fī

stratosphere, strä'to-sfēr

stratum, strä'tum

strength, strength

strenuous, stren'û-us

Streptococcus, strep-to-kok'us

strew, strōō

stricture, strik'tûr

strident, strī'dent

stringency, strin'jen-si

structure, struk'tûr

strychnine, strik'nin

stud, stud

student, stū'dent

studio, stū'di-ō

studious, stū'di-us

stultification, stul-ti-fi-kä'shun

stupefaction, stū-pe-fak'shun

stupendous, stū-pen'dus

stupid, stū′pid
sturgeon, stēr′jun
stylist, stīl′ist
stylus, stī′lus
stymie, stī′mi
Styx, stiks
suave, swäv; swāv
subaltern, sub-awl′tĕrn
subdue, sub-dū′
subject, sub′jekt
subjectivity, sub-jek-tiv′i-ti
sublimation, sub-li-mā′shun
sublime, sub-līm′
sublimity, sub-lim′i-ti
submarine, sub-mă-rēn′
submissive, sub-mis′iv
subordination, sub-ôr-di-nā′shun
subornation, sub-ôr-na′shun
subpoena, sub-pē′nä
sub rosa, sub rō′ză
subsequent, sub′se-kwent
subservience, sub-sĕr′vi-ens
subside, sub-sīd′
subsidiary, sub-sid′i-ā-ri
subsidy, sub′si-di
subsist, sub-sist′
subsistence, sub-sis′tens
substantial, sub-stan′shal
substantiation, sub-stan-shi′ā′shun
substitute, sub′sti-tūt
subterfuge, sub′tĕr-fūj
subterranean, sub-tĕr-ā′ne-an
subtle, sut′l
subtlety, sut′l-ti
suburb, sub′ĕrb
suburban, sub-ĕr′ban
success, suk-ses′
succession, suk-se′shun
succinct, suk-singkt′
succotash, suk′o-tash
succulent, suk′ū-lent
succumb, su-kum′
suede, swād
suet, sū′et
sufferance, suf′ĕr-ăns
suffice, su-fīs′; su-fīz′
suffix, suf′iks
suffragan, suf′ră-gan
suffuse, su-fūz′
sugar, shoog′ĕr
suggest, sug-jest′
suggestion, sug-jes′chun
suicidal, sū′i-sīd-al
suicide, sū′i-sīd
sui generis, sū′i jen′e-ris
suit, sūt
suite, swēt
sulphide, sul′fīd
sulphite, sul′fīt
sulphur, sul′fur; sul′fĕr
sulphuric, sul-fū′rik
sultana, sul-tä′nä
sultry, sul′tri

sumac, sū′mak
summation, sum-ā′shun
sumptuary, sump′tu-ā-ri
sumptuous, sump′tū-us
sundry, sun′dri
superabundance, sū-pĕr-ă-bun′-
  dăns
superannuate, sū-pĕr-an′û-āt
superciliary, sū-pĕr-sil′i-ā-ri
supererogation, sū-pĕr-ĕr-o-gā′-
  shun
superficial, sū-pĕr-fish′al
superfluity, sū-pĕr-floo′i-ti
superfluous, sū-pĕr′floo-us
superinduce, sū-pĕr-in-dūs′
superintend, su-pĕr-in-tend′
superior, su-pē′ri-ĕr
superlative, sū-pĕr′lă-tiv
superstition, sū-pĕr-stish′un
supine, su-pīn′
supple, sup′l
suppliant, sup′li-ant
supremacy, su-prem′ă-si
surcease, sur-sēs′
sure, shoor
surgeon, sĕr′jun
surplice, sĕr′plis
surreptitious, sur-ep-tish′us
surveillance, sur-vāl′yäns
survey, sur-vā′
susceptible, su-sep′ti-bl
suspect (v.), sus-pekt′
suspect (n.), sus′pekt
suttee, sut-ē′
suzerain, sū′zĕ-rān
Swami, swä′mi
swan, swon
swastika, swăs′ti-kă
swath, swôth
swathe, swā*th*
swerve, swĕrv
switch, swich
swivel, swiv′l
sword, sōrd
sybarite, sib′ă-rīt
sycamore, sik′a-mor
sycophant, sik′o-fant
syllabic, si-lab′ik
syllabication, si-lab-i-kā′shun
syllable, sil′ă-bl
syllabus, sil′ă-bus
syllogism, sil′o-jizm
sylph, silf
sylvan, sil′van
symbolical, sim-bol′ik-al
symbolism, sim′bol-izm
symmetry, sim′e-tri
sympathy, sim′pă-thi
symphonic, sim-fon′ik
symposium, sim-pō′zi-um
symptomatic, simp-tum-at′ik
synagogue, sin′ă-gog
synchronism, sing′krō-nizm

synchronize, sin'krō-nīz
syncopate, sing'kō-pāt
syncopation, sing-kō-pā'shun
syndicalism, sin'di-kă-lizm
syndicate, sin'di-kāt
syndication, sin-di-kā'shun
synod, sin'od
synopsis, si-nop'sis
syntax, sin'taks
synthesis, sin'the-sis
synthetic, sin-thet'ik
syringe, sir'inj
syrup, sir'up
systematic, sis-tem-at'ik
systematically, sis-tem-at'ik-al-i

T

tabasco, tă-bas'kō
tableau, tab'lō
table d'hote, tă'bl' dōt
taboo; tabu, tă-bōō'
tacit, tas'it
taciturn, tas'i-tĕrn
tactician, tak-tish'an
tactics, tak'tiks
taffeta, taf'e-tă
Taj Mahal, täj mă-häl'
talcum, tal'kum
talisman, tal'is-man
talkative, tawk'ă-tiv
talon, tal'on
tamale, tă-mä'le
tambourine, tam-bĕr-ēn'
tangent, tan'jent
tangerine, tan-jĕr-ēn'
tango, tang'gō
Tannhauser, tän'hoi-zēr
tantamount, tan'tă-mount
tantrum, tan'trum
tapestry, tap'es-tri
tapioca, tap-i-ō'kă
tarantula, tă-ran'tu-lă
tarpaulin, tär-paw'lin
task, tăsk
tassel, tas'l
taunt, tänt
tautological, taw-to-loj'i-kal
tautology, taw-tol'o-ji
tavern, tav'ĕrn
taxidermist, tăk'si-dĕr-mist
technic, tek'nik
technique, tek-nēk'
Te Deum, tē dē'um
tedious, tē'di-us; tēd'yus
tedium, tē'di-um
teetotaler, tē-tō'tal-ēr
teetotalism, tē-tō'tal-izm
telegraph, tel'e-grăf
telegrapher, te-leg'ră-fēr
telephone, tel'e-fōn
telescope, tel'e-skōp
television, tel-e-vizh'un
temerity, te-mer'i-ti

temperament, tem'pĕr-ă-ment
temperature, tem'pĕr-ă-tûr
tempestuous, tem-pes'tū-us
temporarily, tem'po-rā-ri-li
tempus fugit, tem'pus fū'jit
tenable, ten'ă-bl
tenace, ten'ās
tenacious, te-nā'shus
tenacity, te-nas'i-ti
tenancy, ten'an-si
tenantry, ten'ant-ri
tendon, ten'dun
tenet, ten'et
tennis, ten'is
tense, tens
tension, ten'shun
tentacle, ten'tă-kl
tenuous, ten'ū-us
tepee, tē'pē
tepid, tep'id
tercentenary, tĕr-sen'te-nă-ri
terminate, tĕr'mi-nāt
termite, tĕr'mīt
Terpsichore, tĕrp-sik'o-rē
terra cotta, ter'ă kot'ă
terra firma, ter'ă fēr'mă
terrain, te-rān'
terrorist, ter'ĕr-ist
terse, tĕrs
tertiary, tĕr'shi-ā-ri
testamentary, tes-tă-men'tă-ri
testatrix, tes-tā'triks
tête-à-tête, tāt-ă-tāt
Teuton, tū'ton
texture, teks'tūr
Thais, thā'is
Thames, temz
thanksgiving, thangks-giv'ing
that, that
the, thē
theater; theatre, thē'ă-tēr
theatrical, thē-at'ri-kal
theism, thē'izm
theist, thē'ist
theocracy, thē-ok'ră-si
theologian, thē-o-lō'ji-an
theology, thē-ol'o-ji
theoretical, thē-o-ret'i-kal
theorist, thē'o-rist
theosophic, thē-o-sof'ik
theosophy, thē-os'o-fi
therapeutics, ther-ă-pū'tiks
therapy, ther'ă-pi
thereat, thār-at'
therein, thār-in'
thermostat, thēr'mo-stat
thesaurus, the-saw'rus
thesis, thē'sis
Thespian, thes'pi-an
thistle, this'l
thong, thông
thorax, thō'raks
thraldom; thralldom, thrawl'dum
thread, thred

threnody, thren'o-di
threshold, thresh'ōld
thrombosis, throm-bō'sis
throttle, throt'l
through, throo
throw, thrō
Thursday, thērz'dā
thus, *thus*
thwart, thwawrt
thyme, tīm
thyroid, thī'roid
tiara, tī-ā'rā; tī-ä'rā
tibia, tib'i-ă
tillage, til'ij
timidity, tim-id'i-ti
timorous, tim'ēr-us
timothy, tim'o-thi
tincture, tingk'tûr
tinge, tinj
tinsel, tin'sel
tiny, tī'ni
tirade, ti-rād'
tissue, tish'ū
Titan, tī'tan
tithe, tī*th*
titiliate, tit'i-lāt
titillation, tit-i-lā'shun
title, tī'tl
titular, tit'ū-lēr
tobacco, to-bak'ō
tocsin, tok'sin
toilet, toil'et
toilette, toil'et (English form)
tolerable, tol'ēr'ă-bl
tolerant, tol'ēr-ant
tomahawk, tom'ă-hawk
tomato, to-mā'tō
tongs, tôngz
tongue, tung
tonic, ton'ik
tonnage, tun'ij
tonneau, tun-ō'
tonsilitis; tonsillitis, ton-sil-ī'tis
tonsils, ton'silz
topical, top'i-kal
topographer, to-pog'ră-fēr
topography, to-pog'ră-fi
topsail, top'sāl
topsy-turvy, top'si-tēr-vi
toreador, tōr-ē-ă-dôr'
torment, tôr'ment
torpid, tôr'pid
torrential, to-ren'shal
tortilla, tôr-tēl'yä
tortoise, tôr'tis
tortuous, tôr'tū-us
torture, tôr'tûr
torturous, tôr'tûr-us
toss, tos
tote, tōt
toupee, tōō-pē'
tour, tōōr
tour de force, tōōr de fōrs'

tournament, tōōr'nă-ment
tourniquet, tōōr'ni-ket
tousle; touzle, touz'l
tout, tout
toward, tō'ērd
towel, tou'el
tower, tou'ēr
toxicity, tok-sis'i-ti
toxin, tok'sin
tractability, trak-tă'bil'i-ti
traditionist, tră-dish'un-ist
tragedian, tră-jē'di-an
tragedienne, tră-jē'di-en
tragedy, traj'e-di
trance, trāns
tranquil, trang'kwil
transact, trans-akt'
transcendental, tran-sen-den'tal
transcontinental, trans-kon-ti-nen'tal
transcription, tran-skrip'shun
transfer, trans'fēr
transferable, trans-fēr'ă-bl
transfiguration, trans-fig-û-rā'shun
transfix, trans-fiks'
transfuse, trans-fūz'
transient, tran'shent
transitory, tran'si-to-ri
translation, trans-lā'shun
transmigrate, trans'mi-grāt
transmission, trans-mish'un
transmutation, trans-mū-tā'shun
transparent, trans-pār'ent
transport, trans-pōrt'
transportation, trans-pôr-tā'shun
transverse, trans-vērs'
trapeze, tră-pēz'
travail, trav'il; trav'āl
traveler, trav'el-er
travelogue, trav'e-log
traverse, trav'ērs
treachery, trech'ēr-i
treacle, trē'kl
treason, trē'zn
treasure, trezh'ur
treatise, trēt'is
treble, treb'l
trellis, trel'is
trembler, trem-blôr'
tremendous, tre-men'dus
tremolo, trem'o-lō
tremor, trē'mor; trem'ēr
tremulous, trem'û-lus
trenchant, tren'chant
trespass, tres'pås
trestle, tres'l
triangular, tri-ang'gû-lēr
tribunal, trī-bū'nal
tribune, trib'ūn
tribute, trib'ūt
tricolor, trī'kul-ēr
trio, trē'ō
triplicate, trip'li-kăt

triumphant, tri-um'fant
trivial, triv'i-al
trombone, trom'bōn
tropical, trop'i-kal
tropism, trōp'izm
troth, trōth
troubadour, trōō'bă-dōōr
trough, trôf
trouper, trōōp'er
trousers, trou'zĕrs
trousseau, trōō-sō'
trowel, trou'el
truancy, trōō'an-si
truculent, truk'ŭ-lent
true, trōō
truism, trōō'ism
trump, trump
truncheon, trun'chun
tryst, trĭst; trist
tuba, tū'bă
tube, tūb
tubercular, tū-bĕr'kŭ-lĕr
tuberculosis, tu-bĕr-kŭ-lō'sis
Tuesday, tūz'dā
Tuileries, twĕl'er-iz
tulip, tū'lip
tulle, tōōl
tumor, tū'mĕr
tumult, tū'mult
tumultuous, tū-mul'tū-us
tundra, toon'dră
tune, tūn
tungsten, tung'sten
tunic, tū'nik
turbine, tĕr'bin
tureen, tu-rēn'
turnip, tĕr'nip
turpitude, tĕr-pi-tūd
turquoise, tĕr'kwois
tussle, tus'l
Tut-Ankh-Amen; Tutankhamen,
tōōt-angk'ă-men; tōōt-an-kă'men
tutelage, tū'te-lāj
tutor, tū'tĕr
tutti-frutti, tōōt'i-frōōt'i
tuxedo, tuk-sē'dō
twaddle, twod'l
twinkle, twing'kl
two, tōō
tycoon, tī-kōōn'
tympan, tim'pan
typhoid, tī'foid
typhoon, tī-fōōn'
typhus, tī'fus
typify, tip'i-fī
typist, tīp'ist
typographer, tī-pog'ră-fĕr
typography, tī-pog'ră-fi
tyrannical, ti-ran'i-kal
tyrannize, tir'a-nīz
tyranny, tir'a-ni
tyrant, tī'rant
tyro, tī'rō

U

ubiquitous, u-bik'wi-tus
ukase, ū-kās'
ukelele, ōō-kōō-lā'lā
ulcer, ul'sĕr
ulterior, ul-tē'ri-ĕr
ultimate, ul'ti-māt
ultimatum, ul-ti-mā'tum
ultimo, ul'ti-mō
Ulysses, ū-lis-ēz
umbilical, um-bil'i-kal
umbrage, um'brāj
umbrella, um-brel'ă
unanimous, ū-nan'i-mus
uncouth, un-kōōth'
unction, ungk'shun
unctuous, ung'tū-us
undress, un-dres'
undulant, un'dū-lănt
unenervated, un-en'ĕr-vāt-ed
unequivocal, un-e-kwiv'o-kul
unguent, ung'gwent
unilateral, ū-ni-lat'ĕr-al
unique, ū-nēk'
unison, ū'ni-sun
united, ū-nīt'ed
unlearned, un-lĕrnd'
unprecedented, un-pres'e-den-ted
urban, ĕr'ban
urbane, ĕr-bān'
urbanity, ĕr-ban'i-ti
urchin, ĕr'chin
uremia, ū-rē'mi-ă
uremic, ū-rē'mik
urethra, ū-rē'thră
urge, ĕrj
urinalysis, ū-ri-nal'i-sis
usage, ūz'ij
use (n.), ūs (application of anything to a particular purpose)
use (v.), ūz (to make use of; employ)
usher, ush'ĕr
usufruct, ū'zu-frukt
usurer, ū'zhu-rĕr
usurp, ū-zĕrp'
usury, ū'zhu-ri
utensil, ū-ten'sil
uterus, ū'tĕr-us
utilitarian, ū-til'i-tā'ri-an
Utopia, ū-tō'pi-ă
utter, ut'ĕr

V

vaccinate, vak'si-nāt
vaccine, vak'sin
vacillate, vas'i-lāt
vacuity, vă-kū'i-ti
vacuum, vak'ū-um
vagabondage, vag'ă-bon-dij

vagary, vă-gā'ri
vagrant, vā'grant
valedictorian, val"e-dik-tō'ri-an
valet, val'et; val'ā
Valhalla, val-hal'ā
valiant, val'yant
valise, vă-lēs'
vanguard, van'gärd
vanquish, vang'kwish
vantage, văn'tij
vapid, vap'id
variable, vā'ri-ă-bl
varicocele, var'i-ko-sēl
varicose, var'i-kōs
varied, vā'rid
variegate, vā'ri-e'gāt
varlet, vär'let
vase, vās; văz
vaseline, vas'e-lin; vas'e-lēn
vassal, vas'al
vast, văst
vaudeville, vōd'vil
vault, vawlt
vaunt, vänt; vawnt
Veda, vā'dă
vegetable, vej'e-tă-bl
vegetarian, vej-e-tā'ri-an
vehement, vē'he-ment
vehicle, vē'hi-kl
vehicular, ve-hik'ū-lēr
velocipede, ve-los'i-pēd
velours, ve-lōōr'
venal, vē'nal
vendee, ven-dē'
vendor, ven'dor
venire, vē-nī'rē
venison, ven'zn
ventriloquist, ven-tril'o-kwist
venture, ven'tûr
venue, ven'ū
Venus, vē'nus
veracity, ve-ras'i-ti
verbatim, vēr-bā'tim
verbiage, vēr'bi-ij
verdigris, vēr'di-grēs
verdure, vēr'dûr
verisimilitude, ver"i-si-mil'i-tūd
versatile, vēr'să-til
version, vēr'shun
vers libre, văr lē'br'
vertebra, vēr'te-brā
vertebrate, vēr'te-brāt
verve, vērv
vestibule, ves'ti-būl
vestige, ves'tij
veterinary, vet'ēr-i-nā-ri
via, vī'ă
viands, vī'andz
vibrant, vī'brant
vicar, vik'ēr
vicarage, vik'ēr-ij
vicarious, vī-kā'ri-us
vice versa, vī'se vēr'să

Vichy water, vē'shi waw'tēr
vicious, vish'us
victual, vit'l
view, vū
vignette, vin-yet'
viking, vī'king
villa, vil'ă
villain, vil'in
vin ordinaire, van ôr-dā-nār'
vinous, vī'nus
vintage, vin'tij
viola, vē-ō'lă
violin, vī-o-lin'
violoncello, vē-o-lon-chel'ō
virago, vi-rā'gō
virile, vir'il
virility, vi-ril'i-ti
virtue, vēr'tū
virtuoso, vēr'tū-ō'sō
virtuous, vēr'tū-us
virulence, vir'ū-lens
virus, vī'rus
visage, viz'ij
vis-a-vis, vē-ză-vē'
viscera, vis'ēr-ă
viscid, vis'id
viscosity, vis-kos'i-ti
viscount, vī'kount
viscountess, vī'koun-tes
vise; vice, vīs (a device with two
    jaws operated by a screw or
    lever)
vise', vē-zā' (an official indorse-
    ment on a passport)
vision, vizh'un
visor, vī'zēr
visualization, vizh-û-al-i-zā'shun
vitality, vī-tal'i-ti
vitamine, vī'tă-min; vit'a-min
vitiate, vish'i-āt
vitriol, vit'ri-ol
vituperation, vī-tū-pēr-ā'shun
vituperative, vī-tū'pēr-ā-tiv
viva, vē'vă
vivacious, vī-vā'shus
viva voce, vi'vă vō'se
vivid, viv'id
vivisect, viv-i-sekt
vixen, vik's'n
vizier, vi-zēr'
vocabulary, vō-kab'û-lā-ri
vociferate, vōsif'ēr-āt
vociferous, vō-sif'ēr-us
vodka, vod'kă
vogue, vōg
voile, voil
volatile, vol'ă-til
voluble, vol'û-bl
volume, vol'yum
voluptuous, vo-lup'tū-us
voracious, vo-rā'shus
votary, vō'tă-ri
voucher, vouch-ēr
voyage, voi'ij

vulture, vul'tûr
vying, vī'ing

W

waffle, wof'l
waft, wåft
wainscot, wān'skot
walnut, wawl'nut
walrus, wol'rus
waltz, wawltz
wampum, wom'pum
wan, won
wander, won'dĕr
wanton, won'tun
warily, wār'i-li
warrior, wawr'i-ĕr
wary, wā'ri
wassail, wos'il
wastrel, wās'trel
watch, woch
wearisome, wē'ri-sum
weary, wē'ri
Wednesday, wenz'dā
weevil, wē'vl
weight, wāt
weird, wērd
werewolf, wēr'woolf
what, hwot
wheat, hwēt
when, hwen
where, hwār
whey, hwā
whilom, hwī'lŏm
whilst, hwīlst
whimsicality, hwim-zi-kal'i-ti
Whitsunday, hwit'sun-dā
whiz, hwiz
who, hōō
whoa, hwŏ
whole, hōl
wholly, hō'li
whooping-cough, hoop'ing-kôf
whopper, hwop'ĕr
why, hwī
willy-nilly, wil'i-nil'i
wind (n.), wind (air in perceptible motion)
wind (v.), wīnd (to turn round something)
wing, wing
wistaria, wis-tā'ri-ă
witch, wich
with, with
witticism, wit'i-sizm
wizard, wiz'ărd
wonder, wun'dĕr
wont, wunt
workaday, wēr'kă-dā
worldliness, wērld'li-nes
worrisome, wur'i-sum
worsted, woos'ted
wound, wŏŏnd; wound

wraith, rāth
wrath, räth
wreath, rēth
wreathe, rēth
wrest, rest
wrestle, res'l
wrestler, res'ler
wretch, rech
wriggle, rig'l
wringer, ring'ĕr
writhe, rīth
wrong, rông
wroth, rawth
wry, rī
wryly, rī'li
Wycliff, wik'lif

X

Xanthippe, zan-tip'e
Xavier, zav'i-er
xylene, zī'lēn
xylophone, zī'lo-fōn

Y

yacht, yot
Yaqui, yä'kē
yea, yā
yeast, yēst
yellow, yel'ō
yeoman, yō'man
yew, yōō
yodel; yodle, yō'd'l
yolk, yōk
Yosemite, yo-sem'i-te
young, yung
your, yōōr
youth, yōōth
Ypres, ī'pr
Yule, yōōl
Yuletide, yōōl'tīd

Z

zeal, zēl
zealot, zel'ut
zealous, zel'us
zebra, zē'bră
zenith, zē'nith
zephyr, zef'ĕr
zeppelin, zep'e-lin
Zeus, zūs
zinc, zingk
Zion, zī'un
zither, zith'ĕr
zodiac, zō'di-ak
zodiacal, zō-dī'ă-kal
zoological, zō-o-loj'i-kal
zoology, zō-ol'o-ji
Zouave, zoo-äv'
zounds, zoundz
zwieback, tsvē'bak